POPULAR HANDBOOK OF INDIAN BIRDS

Owing to the antiquity and rarity of this book, certain pages are regrettably absent, and readability is compromised due to the blurring of the original text. If you possess any insights regarding the availability of these missing sections, kindly inform us. Your assistance is crucial in ensuring the completion of this significant work for the benefit of future generations.

POPULAR HANDBOOK OF INDIAN BIRDS

BY

HUGH WHISTLER

GYAN

Published by

Gyan Publishing House
5, Ansari Road
Daryaganj, New Delhi-110002
Phone: 011-47034999, 9811692060
E-mail: books@gyanbooks.com

Distribution Network
gyanbooks.com
India, USA, Canada, UK, Australia

ISBN: 978-93-6433-080-0 (HB)
First Published, 1935

2nd Impression 2024

Printed at: Gyan Press, Delhi.

POPULAR HANDBOOK OF INDIAN BIRDS
Author: HUGH WHISTLER

POPULAR HANDBOOK OF INDIAN BIRDS

PLATE I

1. Black and Orange Flycatcher. 2. Fairy Blue-Bird. 3. Yellow-browed Bulbul. 4. Velvet-fronted Nuthatch. ($\frac{1}{2}$ nat. size.)

[*Frontispiece*

POPULAR HANDBOOK OF INDIAN BIRDS

BY

HUGH WHISTLER, F.Z.S.

LATE INDIAN (IMPERIAL) POLICE

FOURTH EDITION
REVISED AND ENLARGED BY

NORMAN B. KINNEAR

BRITISH MUSEUM (NATURAL HISTORY) LONDON

Illustrated with twenty-four full-page plates of which seven are coloured, and one hundred and eight figures in the text, from drawings by H. Grönvold and Roland Green

OLIVER & BOYD

EDINBURGH AND LONDON

PREFACE TO THE FOURTH EDITION

THE *Popular Handbook of Indian Birds* was first published in 1928, followed by a second edition in 1935, and a third in 1941. This last edition was becoming exhausted when the author died, and Mrs Whistler asked me to prepare this new edition. Mr B. B. Osmaston, who has such a wide knowledge of Indian birds and their habits, has given very great assistance and, in addition, several ornithologists in India, Mr Salim Ali, Mr C. M. Inglis, Mr W. H. Mathews, and the Rev. F. S. Briggs, sent to Mrs Whistler their notes and suggestions which, as far as possible, have been incorporated.

In the original edition 250 birds were described, and in each succeeding issue the number was increased. In the present edition 7 more species have been added, and 12 referred to in the text. There is also one new coloured plate and five text figures all of which are the work of Mr Roland Green.

When the author of this work was preparing a new edition he was taken ill, and died on 7th July 1943. By his death, ornithology, and Indian ornithology in particular, has suffered a grievous loss. Hugh Whistler was in his prime and had become the recognised authority on everything connected with birds in India. During his seventeen years' service in the Indian Police he had made himself thoroughly acquainted with Indian birds, about which he has written so delightfully in this book. He had a happy knack of putting into words the salient characters of a species which enables them to be readily recognised in the field. Their habits too, he described in vivid word pictures, so helpful to the beginner.

Hugh Whistler was a scientific ornithologist and his name will be handed down as one of the most careful and conscientious workers. He had amassed copious notes on every aspect of Indian bird-life which were always at the disposal of other ornithologists. But the real purpose of these notes was to form a basis for a Handbook of the Birds of the Indian Empire, which he and his great friend and brother-ornithologist, the late Dr C. B. Ticehurst, had planned and, indeed, commenced to write. After the lamented death of Dr Ticehurst, Whistler had intended to carry on alone, but increasing war-work hindered this. He never let his great love of ornithology interfere with his official work, and in India those in authority did not discourage his hobby since the search for birds took him into out-of-the-way places seldom visited in the ordinary routine of duty.

At his home near Battle, Whistler had brought together a wonderful collection of bird skins, for the most part beautifully prepared by his own hands, and nothing pleased him more than to show his collection. He was ready to help others, and his many correspondents in India will miss him, since he was the authority to whom they turned for advice and guidance. Much of the recent work done there was initiated by him, and many casual observers became good ornithologists through his enthusiasm. Whatever work he undertook he did with the same thoroughness and enthusiasm with which he studied birds, and the high standard aimed at made him loved and respected by all who knew him.

N. B. KINNEAR

CONTENTS

Order PASSERES

Family CORVIDÆ

Family PARIDÆ

Family SITTIDÆ

Family TIMALIIDÆ

Family IRENIDÆ

Family ORIOLIDÆ

Family GRACULIDÆ

Family STURNIDÆ

Family PLOCEIDÆ

Family FRINGILLIDÆ

Family HIRUNDINIDÆ

Family Motacillidæ

Family Alaudidæ

Family Zosteropidæ

Family Nectariniidæ

Family Dicæidæ

Family Pittidæ

Order PICI

Family Picidæ

Family Capitonidæ

Order ANISODACTYLI

Family CORACIADÆ

Family MEROPIDÆ

Family ALCEDINIDÆ

Family BUCEROTIDÆ

Family UPUPIDÆ

Order MACROCHIRES

Family MICROPODIDÆ

Family CAPRIMULGIDÆ

Order COCCYGES

Family CUCULIDÆ

Order PSITTACI

Family PSITTACIDÆ

Order STRIGES

Family STRIGIDÆ

Order ACCIPITRES

Family GYPIDÆ

Family FALCONIDÆ

Order COLUMBÆ

Family COLUMBIDÆ

Order PTEROCLETES

Family PTEROCLIDÆ

Order GALLINÆ

Family Phasianidæ

Order HEMIPODII

Family Turnicidæ

Order GRALLÆ

Family Rallidæ

Family Gruidæ

Family Otididæ

Order LIMICOLÆ

Family Burhinidæ

Family Glareolidæ

Family Jacanidæ

Family ARDEIDÆ

Order ANSERES

Family ANATIDÆ

Order PYGOPODES

Family PODICIPIDÆ

LIST OF PLATES

 b 2

INTRODUCTION

(TO THE FIRST EDITION)

Before proceeding with the actual purpose of this book, which is to provide a popular and scientific, but not too technical, account of the Common Birds of India, there are a few general observations which I should like to make by way of introduction.

First to explain why the book has been written.

One of the commonest questions that is put by the new arrival in India is for the name of a book to teach him or her a little about the birds which intrude themselves on every one's notice. There are many excellent books on Indian ornithology, but the majority are either too advanced and scientific for the beginner or else too expensive. One search for a common bird in the volumes of the splendid *Fauna of India* series is enough to send the inquirer away frightened by the mere wealth of material and by the technical terms in the descriptions. The few popular books that have appeared of recent years have suffered from the necessity of sacrificing fullness to cheapness, and in particular the majority lack illustrations.

Pictures are what the beginner requires; a few pictures are worth pages of description. In Europe and America, where Nature-studies have made such vast strides and have now such a general appeal, the demand has made it possible to bring out numbers of cheap natural history books with excellent coloured illustrations.

In India this is not yet possible. The area is so great and the fauna and flora so rich and diverse that to describe them requires more space and wealth of illustration than in the West, while the public to purchase such books is much smaller and at present practically confined to the European population. It is, however, to be hoped that educated Indians may turn more and more to the study of the natural wonders of their land.

This book is an earnest attempt to supply a well-illustrated guide to Indian birds at a price suited to the moderate purse. That the illustrations are good is guaranteed by the name of Mr Grönvold, who stands in the front rank of living bird-artists. That the price is moderate is due to the generosity of three gentlemen, Mr F. Mitchell, Sir George Lowndes and Mr W. S. Millard, who have taken the publication outside the sphere of commercial profit; whoever buys this work should realise that their public spirit and generosity have reduced the price by a very large amount. While

Mr Millard in addition has kindly undertaken the work of arranging all the details of publication, and promised to see the book through the press.

The nomenclature follows the recognised international usage. This may be briefly explained.

Scientific nomenclature started with the Swedish naturalist Linnæus, who invented what is known as the Binomial System. In this each living creature has two Latin names, the first representing the genus, the second the species. To take an example from the first family in the book we have the Raven (*Corvus corax*) and the Common House Crow (*Corvus splendens*).

Now a species is a group in which all individuals resemble each other consistently except in such details as are due to age or sex or individual variation. Individuals of a species normally breed together and produce fertile offspring.

A genus is a wider term. It embraces one or more species which, from the possession of certain characteristics, are clearly worth separating from other groups of species. The Raven and the House Crow are obviously very nearly related to each other as compared with the Blue Magpies, though at the same time they are not one and the same species. We therefore place both birds together in the genus *Corvus*, and give them their individual specific names of *corax* and *splendens*. The Blue Magpies have each their own specific name, but their common characteristics group them together in another genus *Urocissa*.

Genera which have certain features in common are similarly linked together into families; Families are combined with other families to form Orders; while the various Orders together make up the great class Aves. It is merely a system of classification or labels, made partly for convenience and partly to express the differences and affinities that appear amongst birds. No space has been devoted in this book to a diagnosis of the Families and Orders, but their extent has been indicated in the list of species that precedes the main text.

Increased study has shown that the Binomial System alone is not sufficient to express all that is required. Abundant and widely spread species vary more or less consistently in different parts of their range, chiefly in response to climatic and geographical conditions. These geographical races or subspecies require to be recognised, and this is done by the addition of a third name after the specific name. Thus our Raven in India, which is clearly the same species as the European Raven, slightly changed by difference of habitat, is called *Corvus corax lawrencei*, to recognise the fact and to distinguish it from the typical race *Corvus corax corax* of Europe.

The selection of the Latin name is fixed by the Law of Priority, that the first name published for a species must be used for that species irrespective of any names that may have been given to it later. The various provisos to this rule need not trouble us here. If a species is divided into races the first-named race is known as the typical one, and its name gives the specific name; so that the typical race may be recognised as having its second and third names the same—*Corvus corax corax*. The surname given after the scientific name is that of the writer who originally described the species. If this surname is placed within brackets it means that he originally described the species with a different generic name to that now used.

In the heading to each species I have given the name binomially, the races, if any, being indicated under the paragraph on Distribution. Vernacular names have not been given. In my experience published lists are of little value, as few species have really established vernacular names and local names vary from district to district. My aim throughout has been to emphasise the position of our Indian birds as part of a wider scheme, and that their range in India is almost always part of a wider range.

This leads us naturally to the question of Geographical Distribution. No student of zoology can fail to observe that the fauna of the various portions of the world differ markedly in character in different areas. There have been many attempts to define the limits of these areas, though their boundaries must necessarily be vague. Six regions are now commonly accepted, the Holarctic, with its Palæarctic and Nearctic subdivisions (extending across the whole Northern Hemisphere and including Europe, a small portion of Africa, Northern and Central Asia and North America), the Ethiopian (Africa and Arabia), the Indian or Oriental (India, China, Ceylon and the Malays), the New Zealand, the Australian (including also the Pacific Islands), and the Neotropical regions (Mexico to Cape Horn).

The boundaries of the Western Palæarctic subregion of the Holarctic region march with those of the Indian region roughly along the line of the Himalayas and the Afghan and Baluchi borders; and it must be remembered that the desert areas of the Punjab, Sind and Rajputana are part of the great Palæarctic desert which starts on the Atlantic coast of North Africa and reaches the heart of China.

The Indian region of course needs to be further subdivided, as China and the Malays have characteristics that separate them off from India. India, Burma and Ceylon are usually considered as forming an Indian subregion, while the Himalayas are regarded as having closer affinities with China than with the Indian plains at their base.

The student of Indian ornithology must from the beginning realise that the avifauna of his area is not homogeneous, spread over India evenly as butter on a slice of bread. He must obtain a conception of it as divided into sections. He must realise that the most comprehensive knowledge of the birds of Simla will leave him ignorant of the species that he will meet at Ootacamund, that the avifauna of the Sind desert has hardly a common feature with the avifauna of the forests of Malabar.

The most recent endeavour to express these differences is that of Blanford in the *Philosophical Transactions of the Royal Society* (Vol. 194, 1901, pp. 335-436). He divides India, Burma and Ceylon into five primary subdivisions as follows :—

(*a*) The Indo-Gangetic plain,—This extends across the whole of Northern India from the Arabian Sea to the Bay of Bengal. Its boundaries run up the hill ranges from Karachi to Peshawar and thence along the outer spurs of the Himalayas to Bhutan and thence roughly southward to east of the Sunderbunds. The southern boundary takes a line from the Rann of Cutch to Delhi and from about Agra to Rajmahal whence it goes south to the Bay of Bengal.

(*b*) The Indian Peninsula, southwards of the above area.

(*c*) Ceylon.

(*d*) The Himalayas. This subdivision includes the whole area of the mountain ranges from their foot-hills up to the limit of tree-growth. Above forest limits the fauna becomes Palæarctic in character.

(*e*) Assam and Burma.

These five subdivisions may again be further divided largely in accordance with the influence of rainfall, while along the Himalayas there are distinct altitudinal zones which affect the fauna. Those who are interested in the subject are advised to consult Blanford's paper in the original. It is too long to be quoted here, and its conclusions may have to be modified when the geographical races of Indian birds are fully worked out.

The races of Indian birds follow some fairly defined lines. Himalayan species generally have an Eastern and Western race, meeting about Nepal, the Eastern race being generally darker and smaller. In the Peninsula the races vary to some extent in correlation with the total distribution of the species. If a bird is common and widely distributed throughout India and the neighbouring areas of the Indian subregion it will often be found to have special races in (1) the semi-desert area of the north-west; (2) the humid area of Assam and the Eastern Sub-Himalayan duars and terais; (3) the heavy rain-area of the lower Western Ghats from about North Kanara to the southern limit of the Travancore ranges; (4) Ceylon;

while a more generalised form occupies the intervening mass of the Peninsula, grading in turn into each race.

If, on the other hand, a bird has a more limited range, the influence of these areas in the formation of races appears to be less strong and the distribution of its races is harder to forecast. Humid areas produce dark birds, desert areas pale birds. North and west enlarge, south and east dwarf their birds.

Finally, one must regard the influence of migration. The avifauna of India or of any square mile of it is never stationary, but changes season by season in response to the great tide of bird-life which sweeps across it with the regularity of the tides of the sea. The fundamental principle of migration is easy to understand. With the changing of the seasons a bird which summers and nests in northern latitudes is unable to find food in those latitudes in winter. It therefore moves southwards to an area that time and circumstances have fixed as its winter quarters. In the north the bird is known as a " summer visitor " and in the south as a " winter visitor," while in the intervening countries that it travels over it is a " passage migrant." The southerly route followed in the " autumn passage " is not necessarily the same as the route by which it returns north on the " spring passage."

India lies south of the great mass of Northern and Central Asia, where winter conditions are very severe following on a short but luxuriant summer. It is not strange, therefore, that a huge wave of bird-life pours down to winter in India where insect and vegetable food is so abundant. The movement starts as early as July, and reaches its greatest height in September; it crosses the Himalayas from both ends, and gradually converges down the two sides of the Peninsula spending its strength until it ends finally in Ceylon. In spring the wave again recedes, starting at the end of February, and all the migrants have gone by the end of May.

Ceylon is one of the few countries of the world that has no summer visitors, for it lies at the end of the migration routes through India, with no land of any size to the south of it.

The Indian winter, luxuriant after the monsoons, is more suitable to the needs of bird-life than the parched Indian summer. Geographical position and physical features, therefore, combine to account for one of the chief ornithological characteristics of India, that it is practically without summer visitors from beyond its borders. The few species that fall under this category are confined to North-western India, where they are able to take a route round the head of the Arabian Gulf to winter in Africa.

The effect of migration on status is most easily shown by an example. I will take a station in the Punjab and indicate the various categories of birds to be found in it.

There are first of all the Resident species, which breed there and remain the whole year round, such as the Parrakeets and Babblers. A few Summer visitors arrive to breed, such as the Purple Honey-sucker and Yellow-throated Sparrow. These, if they are late arrivals, dependent on monsoon conditions for their food-supply, are known as Rains visitors. But both Summer and Rains visitors have this in common, for the most part, that they are species which are residents farther south in India, *i.e.*, they are summer visitors merely in the northern part of their range in India and not, as our summer visitors in England, arrivals from distant countries. A very numerous class is that of the Winter visitors which breed north of India altogether, like the Waders and Ducks. No winter visitor arrives from the south. There are two more large classes, the Spring and Autumn Passage Migrants, such as Rose-Finches and Red-breasted Flycatchers, temporarily abundant on their way to and from winter quarters farther south in the Peninsula and Ceylon.

It must be remembered, however, that Nature is seldom clear-cut in her distinctions, and a species may fall under more than one heading. The mass of Red-breasted Flycatchers, for instance, that pass through in autumn and return again in spring, will leave a few of their numbers as winter visitors. Some individuals of another species may remain as residents while the remainder migrate.

The movements indicated above come under the heading of true migration, a tide which ebbs and flows year by year in response to the annual changes of the seasons. But they are supplemented by smaller and more irregular movements known as Local migration. These are due to different causes. In India the most frequent cause is variation in the rainfall and its consequent effect on food-supply. A prolonged drought will drive away the birds from a locality, good rains will fill it with birds where previously there were none.

Along the Himalayas and the neighbouring ranges there is a marked seasonal altitudinal movement, which moves the resident birds down through the various zones in response to the lowering of the snow-line. This, particularly in severe winters, sends a wave of stragglers into the plains of Northern India in January and February. A plague of locusts or an unusual crop of seeds may temporarily upset the usual distribution of several species. And finally the rudiments of local migration may be seen in the way in which some species shift their ground in a district while breeding. This movement may be very slight, merely a matter of a few miles, yet it is of interest as showing the evolution of the great migrations from hemisphere to hemisphere.

At present we have practically no detailed knowledge on the subject of migration in India, whether true or local; records and observations on it are badly needed.

Hitherto Indian ornithology has fallen into very definite periods. The first period revolves around the pioneer work by Hodgson, Jerdon and Blyth, and found its expression in Jerdon's *Birds of India*, published in 1862.

The second period is dominated by Hume (also the founder of the Indian Congress) who directed and marshalled the labours of a number of notable workers. This period found its fitting expression not in a single comprehensive work but in the packed and miscellaneous volumes of *Stray Feathers*, a periodical which appeared in parts from 1872 to 1888.

With 1889 appeared the first volume of the *Fauna of British India, Birds*, by Blanford and Oates, followed at intervals by three other volumes. This work completely dominated Indian ornithology down to about 1922.

In 1922 Mr Stuart-Baker produced his first volume of the second edition of the *Fauna*. With this has opened the fourth period of Indian ornithology, which will be memorable for its introduction of the trinomial system. Its progress is still in the moulding, and I can only hope that this book of mine will help more than one beginner to take his share in the advancement of Indian ornithology.

The day is now over in which it was necessary to collect large series of skins and eggs in India. Enough general collecting has been done; concentration on filling in the gaps in our knowledge is now needed. Those who wish to help in the work should first familiarise themselves with what has been accomplished and learn what remains to be done. With some species the distribution of the different races still needs to be worked out and this implies careful collecting in certain areas. Of other species we still need to know the plumage changes; for this specimens collected at certain times of the year are required. In other species the down and juvenile plumages are unknown. But the greatest need of all is accurate observations on status and migration. In this all can help. Keep full notes for a year on the birds of your station, noting those that are resident and the times of arrival and departure, comparative abundance and scarcity of all the migratory kinds; and you will have made a contribution to ornithology that will in the measure of its accuracy and fullness be a help to every other worker.

The wonderful avifauna of India is still unspoilt and almost in its entirety. Let us chronicle and appreciate it while we may and endeavour in return to awake an appreciation of its value and interest so that steps to preserve it may advance *pari passu* with the destructive influences. These have already started. The irrigation of vast tracts has already made considerable changes in the fauna, the interesting desert forms giving place to less specialised and widely common birds. With the passing away of the Arms Act one of the greatest barriers to the wasteful destruction of bird-life by ignorance and greed has been broken down, at the very moment when the opening up of the country by the motor-car has lessened the number of natural sanctuaries. So in return for the interest of your study of the Indian avifauna, endeavour to protect it and awaken public opinion to the task.

In conclusion, I have to acknowledge my indebtedness on many sides in the writing of this book. While I owe something directly or indirectly to every naturalist who has worked in India, my obligations are very deep to the authors of both editions of the *Fauna* series, Messrs Blanford and Oates and Mr Stuart-Baker. Mr N. B. Kinnear of the British Museum has given me much valuable advice and encouragement. And especially I owe much to the help and enthusiasm of Dr Claud B. Ticehurst, who has kindly read through the text of the book in order to ensure its accuracy.

HUGH WHISTLER

The Common Mynah. (¼ nat. size).

POPULAR HANDBOOK OF INDIAN BIRDS

FIG. 1—Raven (⅐ nat. size)

THE RAVEN

CORVUS CORAX Linnæus

Description.—Length 24 inches. Sexes alike. Entirely black, glossed with steel-blue, purple and lilac.

Iris dark brown ; bill and legs black.

The feathers of the throat are prolonged into conspicuous hackles.

Field Identification.—Plains of North-western India. Distinguished from all other Crows by the large size, complete blackness, the throat hackles, and the distinctive call-note. Only likely to be confused with the Jungle Crow, but both species do not usually occur in the same locality.

Distribution.—The Raven is found in almost every part of the Northern Hemisphere, in Europe, Northern Africa, Asia, and North America, and is divided into several races distinguished by size and the shape of the bill. We are only concerned with one race, *C. c. subcorax*, which is the resident bird of Western Asia, Turkestan, Baluchistan, and North-western India, though it appears to some extent to be locally migratory. In India it is found in the Punjab, North-west Frontier Province, Sind, and the desert portions of Western Rajputana and occasionally in British India. No Raven occurs in the Himalayas proper until the Tibetan tracts of their northern face are reached, and there in the barren wastes above 10,000 feet is found the so-called Tibetan Raven (*C. c. tibetanus*), a huge bird, perhaps identical with the Greenland form.

Habits, etc.—In North-western India the Raven is a very abundant species in the drier and more barren portions of the plains and about the low rocky hill ranges which crop up here and there. In the irrigated and better cultivated tracts it is scarcer, as also in the more thickly wooded districts.

Although while nesting it prefers solitude, at other times it is distinctly social, and fifteen or twenty birds may often be seen together on the outskirts of villages, towns, and camps, marching sedately about the ground, turning over and examining the refuse of man. For in India the Raven is a common scavenger, bold and dissolute as any Crow; though it retains when need arises all the wariness that in England is associated with a scarce and shy bird that avoids the haunts of man. It is particularly common about cantonment stations.

The food is very varied; in addition to the scraps collected in the course of its scavenging the Raven does a certain amount of damage to crops, for instance cutting off and carrying away whole heads of millet, and a pair are generally found with the Vultures at every carcass.

The ordinary call-note is a frequently uttered deep *pruk*, *pruk*. The flight is strong and straight, and the massive head and beak project conspicuously in advance of the wings. The birds seem to pair for life, though many pairs collect together where food is plentiful. Like the other Crows the Ravens roost in companies, often fifty or sixty together, flighting to the selected spot towards the fall of dusk, flying fast and moderately low over the ground.

The breeding season lasts from December to March, though most eggs will be found in January and February.

The nest is a large, stout structure of sticks with the cup thickly lined with rags, wool, hair, and similar rubbish. It is placed either in the fork of a large tree, often close to a well or house, or on the ledges of rock and clay cliffs. The birds often exhibit a tendency to attack the climber who goes up to secure their eggs.

The clutch varies from four to six eggs.

The egg is a moderately broad oval, considerably pointed towards the smaller end; the shell is close and firm, with only a slight gloss. The ground-colour varies from greenish-blue to dingy olive or pale stone-colour. The markings are blackish-brown, sepia, olive-brown, and pale inky-purple, distributed in spots, speckles, blotches, and streaky clouds, the eggs in one clutch usually being all of one type, though there is much variety between different clutches.

In size the eggs average about 1·94 by 1·31 inches.

THE JUNGLE CROW

Corvus macrorhynchos Wagler

Description.—Length 17 inches. Sexes alike. Entire plumage black with a dark blue or purple gloss.

Iris dark brown; bill and legs black.

Field Identification.—A typical Crow, entirely black, and intermediate in size between the ordinary House Crow and the Raven; to be distinguished from the former by the absence of any grey on the hind neck and breast, and from the latter by the smaller size and the difference in call *caw caw*, that of the Raven being a hoarse bark *pruk, pruk*. Usually gregarious, except at nest.

Distribution.—India, Burma, Ceylon, extending to South-east Asia. It is divided into various races which are separated on minor points of size and coloration of the base of the feathers, and are distinguished with difficulty except in a series. Three races concern us. *C. m. intermedius* is found along the whole length of the Himalayas from Afghanistan to Bhutan and is the familiar Crow of all the Himalayan hill stations from Gulmurg to Nepal. It occurs from the foot-hills up to 13,000 feet. The smallest race, *C. m. culminatus*, occurs in Ceylon and the whole of the Indian Peninsula up to a line through Thar and Parkar, Delhi and Ambala on the west, growing gradually in size until about Calcutta it becomes the large bow-beaked *C. m. macrorhynchos* found in Assam and Burma. All these races are strictly resident and they may prove to be races of the Carrion Crow (*Corvus corone*) of Europe, which certainly has a race *C. c. orientalis* in Ladakh and Baltistan. The Rook (*Corvus frugilegus*) which occurs in North-west India in winter in vast numbers may be distinguished by its finer, more pointed beak and the bare white scabrous patch round its base in adults.

Habits, etc.—The Jungle Crow is, as its name implies, and in contradistinction to the House Crow, a bird of the forests and jungles rather than of the haunts of men throughout the Peninsula of India; though it often visits cities and villages for the sake of scavenging. It is not as bold as the House Crow in entering verandahs or in deliberately stealing food from the actual possession of man. The Himalayan race, however, is bolder in this respect than the plains bird, and in all the Himalayan sanatoria this Crow replaces the House

Crow as the common scavenger round houses, though it is never as much at home in the bazaars as is the smaller bird.

Although not actually nesting in rookeries, the Jungle Crow is found scattered throughout the extensive sal forests of the U.P. and Central India. It is usually the first bird to discover the more or less well concealed kill of a tiger or leopard, which it advertises by a peculiar loud " caw " recognised by other crows in the vicinity and of great assistance to the shikari on the look-out for tiger " Khabbar." It is a highly gregarious species, numbers feeding in company or collecting together at the scene of any object of interest, whether food to eat, a fox or bird of prey to mob, or a disturbing human element to swear at. Large numbers collect to roost in special patches of forest, though never so many together as in the case of the House Crow. In the hills this Crow is very fond of soaring and circling at a great height in the air and twenty or thirty often do this in company, exhibiting a complete mastery of all the arts of flying.

Like other Crows this species is omnivorous, scraps of human food, refuse, flying ants, fruit, berries, small mammals and birds, insects, carrion, all are welcome to it ; while it is particularly destructive to the eggs and young of all birds. I have seen it settling on the packs of mule trains crossing the high passes, travelling with them and tearing holes in the packs to get at the contained corn.

Its voice is not disagreeable, the ordinary call being a variable *caw* rather reminiscent of that of the English Rook, sometimes harsh, sometimes almost melodious in tone, and very often distinctly like the quack of a domestic duck ; a harsh *allah* or *ayah* is also uttered, and in addition as it meditates on a shady bough during the heat of the day it indulges in a succession of amusing gurgles and croaks. As I write, several are conversing in the trees outside my room, the sound recalling memories of early spring in England, with swaying elms and rooks preparing to nest.

The various races of the Jungle Crow throughout our area agree for the most part in laying their eggs from March to May, but in the plains a few nests will be found with eggs as early as the middle of December.

The nest is a large, moderately deep cup, composed of twigs and small sticks, lined with hair, dry grass, wool, coco-nut fibre and similar substances. Some nests are massive and well built ; others are somewhat sketchy affairs.

In the Himalayas they are often placed in deodars or species of pine, while in the plains mangoes and tamarinds are said to be preferred ; but with these reservations, the nest may be built in any species of tree, and it is often surprising how well so bulky a structure is concealed from a casual glance. The tree selected is occasionally in the midst of a bazaar or garden, but most pairs build away in the jungle but in easy reach of some village.

The normal clutch consists of four or five eggs, but occasionally six are laid.

The eggs are of the usual Crow type, moderately broad ovals, considerably pointed towards the smaller end; the texture is firm with scarcely any gloss. In colour they are rather variable; the ground-colour may be pale greenish-blue, pale blue, dingy olive, or pale stone-colour; the markings are blackish-brown, sepia, olive-brown, and pale inky-purple, and these take the form of speckles, spots, blotches, and streaks, thinly imposed in some eggs and in others so numerous and heavy as almost to conceal the ground-colour of the egg. There is, however, usually a marked resemblance between the eggs in one clutch.

In size they average about 1·70 by 1·18 inches.

THE COMMON HOUSE CROW

Corvus splendens Vieillot

Description.—Length 18 inches. Sexes alike. A broad collar round the neck, including the nape, upper back and breast, light ashy-brown; lower parts from the breast dull blackish-brown; remainder of plumage black, highly glossed with purple, blue and green. The feathers of the throat are shaped into hackles.

Iris dark brown; bill and legs black.

Albinistic varieties are frequently reported.

Field Identification.—A typical Crow, glossy black with a grey collar and breast. Always in company with man. It is sometimes confused with the Jackdaw (found only in Kashmir and the North Punjab), but the latter is easily distinguished by smaller size, lesser amount of grey in the plumage and by the white iris.

Distribution.—Normally from sea-level to 4000 feet throughout India, Burma, and Ceylon and extending to Siam and Cochin-China. The House Crow is divided into several races which are distinguished by slight variations in the shade of the non-black portions of the plumage. A strictly resident species.

The typical race is found throughout India, except for Sind and the North-western Punjab to Kashmir where it is replaced by a very pale race, *C. s. zugmayeri*, which also extends to the Mekran Coast and South-eastern Persia. Darker races, *C. s. insolens* and *C. s. protegatus*, are found in Burma and Ceylon respectively.

Habits, etc.—The House Crow shares with the Mynah the distinction of being the most conspicuous bird in India. The visitor to India will scarcely ever be out of sight or hearing of this ubiquitous species, from the moment of his arrival till the moment of his departure, on both of which occasions he will find the bird on the wharf by his steamer to greet or speed him. The haunts of man are the haunts of the House Crow and with him it is most numerous in cities, but the jungle and the desert suit it equally well if man is there. Miles of barren plains may be bare for weeks of

FIG. 2—Common House Crow (⅓ nat. size)

both Crows and men, but no sooner is the solitude invaded by the rough huts or tents of some wandering tribe than will appear some half-dozen Crows to keep them company. Normally it is a plains bird, but its range is steadily extending into the hills following the railway and the cart-road, until already it may be found up to 6000 or 7000 feet both in the Nilgiris and in the Himalayas. But its hold at these altitudes is precarious and would cease at once were the station abandoned. It probably is unable to withstand both the lower temperature of the Himalayas and the comparative abundance there of the stronger Jungle Crow.

This Crow is highly gregarious, and this trait is nowhere more clearly demonstrated than at the roost. Many thousands of birds sleep together in company in a selected patch of trees, often acres in extent; and the morning and evening flight from and to the roost is a most conspicuous event, as an unending stream of birds arrives or departs. In the morning the birds leave in a body, hungry and impatient for food, and the flight is soon over, but in the evening their arrival is much more protracted. An hour or two before dusk the first stragglers appear and their numbers gradually increase, until at the end an unbroken line of birds extends across the sky, till darkness falls and puts an end to the unceasing clamour that accompanies every operation of this bird's life.

During the flight small parties have the habit, so often seen amongst Rooks in England, of swirling suddenly down from a height in the sky almost to the ground. The roosting-places are always littered with the remains of dead Crows, and their mortality is heavy, partly no doubt from disease and partly from the depredations of Peregrines and Eagle-Owls. These roosting flights show no apparent diminution even during the breeding season, and this is due to the fact that this species does not breed during its first year. While not nesting in colonies after the fashion of the Rook, the House Crow is so numerous that numbers of nests may be found within a small radius.

Familiarity with man has made the House Crow bold and thievish to a degree. It sidles into rooms, alert and keen, ready to retreat at the least alarm, and with a sudden bounce and dash removes food from the table; it robs the shops in the bazaar if they are left unattended for a moment; it snatches sweetmeats off the trays of the vendors at railway stations. Yet with all this familiarity and boldness it retains the wariness and sagacity of the family and is quick to take a hint of real danger and evade it.

And not only man suffers from this impudent Crow; it mobs birds of prey, more especially the Owls and Eagles, on occasions actually buffeting them; and I have seen Vultures sitting gorged on the ground much worried by a sort of game of "Tom Tiddler's Ground" played by Crows who insisted on hopping on and off their backs. They perch on the backs of bullocks and mules pecking bits of flesh from raw saddle-galls, though at times their attentions are welcome for they also remove ticks and other vermin. They rob dogs and fowls of their food, and in general steal and bully to the utmost extent of their opportunities. Yet with all their manifold villanies there is much that is attractive about the sleek, intelligent, shameless bird that is the companion of our daily life in India. There is only one living thing that habitually gets the better of the House Crow—a claim which man certainly cannot make; the Koel's whole life-history is based on the assumption that it can at will circumvent and deceive the Crow, and this it does, substituting its own eggs for those of the Crow and making the latter bring up its young.

This bird is absolutely omnivorous; it will eat anything that man will eat, and innumerable things that he will not.

The ordinary call is a cawing note rather softer in tone than that of the larger Crows.

The breeding season is very regular in the North-west, eggs being laid from the middle of June till the middle of July. In the rest of India numbers also lay in April and May, and occasionally nests are found in November, December and January.

The nest is built in a fork of a tree, and is a shallow cup of sticks, sometimes neat and well made, sometimes sketchy and ragged; it is lined with grass roots, wool, rags, vegetable fibre, and similar miscellaneous substances. Instances are on record of nests built partly or exclusively of wire.

The normal clutch consists of four or five eggs, but six or seven are occasionally met with. The egg is a broad oval, rather pointed at the smaller end. The texture is hard and fine and there is a fair gloss. The ground-colour is any shade of blue-green, and is blotched, speckled and streaked with dull reddish-brown, pale sepia, grey and neutral tint.

In size the eggs average about 1·45 by 1·05 inches.

THE JACKDAW

Corvus monedula Linnæus

Description.—Length 13 inches. Sexes alike. The whole upper plumage, wings and tail glossy black; a broad collar from the sides of the head round the back of the neck dusky grey, becoming so pale in parts as to be almost white; chin, throat, and fore-neck black; remainder of lower plumage dull slaty-black.

Iris whitish; bill and legs black.

Field Identification.—Extreme North-western India and Kashmir. Distinguished from the House Crow by the smaller size, the fact that the grey is confined merely to a collar, the white eye, and the very musical call.

Distribution.—The Jackdaw is widely distributed in Europe, in Algeria, and in parts of Northern and Western Asia. Of its races we are only concerned with *C. m. monedula*, which apparently breeds from Scandinavia and Russia to the Yenisei and south to Persia, Afghanistan, and Kashmir. In winter numbers appear from the middle of October to the beginning of March in the North-west Frontier Province west of the Indus, and in the Punjab districts along the base of the North-western Himalayas.

The traveller to Baltistan and Ladakh will find the Magpie (*Pica pica*) common in the sparse groves in the valleys and he will be agreeably surprised at its tameness compared with the persecuted English bird. It is also found in Baluchistan.

Habits, etc.—No one who has visited the Vale of Kashmir can have failed to notice the Jackdaws, which are extremely common there all the year round, and with their cheerful, familiar calls largely contribute to the extremely English air of the European quarters of Srinagar. Great numbers live in the trees and buildings all round Srinagar, feeding in the fields and on the grassy lawns, and becoming as tame and impudent in their behaviour as the House Crow is in the plains. These birds roost in the willows of the Dal Lake, and the morning and evening flight of the Jackdaws from and to their dormitory is one of the ornithological sights of Srinagar.

In winter when it arrives in the Punjab the Jackdaw is found in flocks which associate with the immense flights of Rooks (*Corvus frugilegus*) that appear about the same time and in the same localities. The flight is strong and fairly fast, but the Jackdaw has rather quicker wing-beats than the Rook and can also be distinguished in the air by its smaller size. The call is more musical than that of most Crows, being a melodious *Jack* and *cae*, ringing with cheerfulness and well-being; these calls are responsible for the English name, the first syllable also exemplifying the English practice of personifying familiar species, as in Magpie and Jenny-Wren. The whole demeanour of the bird is pert and knowing, and it makes a delightful pet, some individuals learning to talk; though the irresistible attraction which small bright articles have for the Jackdaw often makes it a nuisance about a house when tame enough to be allowed out of its cage.

In Kashmir the breeding season is from April to June. The nest is a massive cup of dirty wool, rags, and hair on a foundation of sticks and thorny twigs, and it is placed in holes in rocks, buildings, and trees. Numbers of pairs breed in colonies wherever suitable nest-holes are available.

The clutch consists of four to six eggs.

The egg is an elongated oval, somewhat compressed towards the smaller end; the shell is fine and stout but there is only a faint gloss. The ground-colour is pale greenish-blue, speckled and spotted with deep blackish-brown, olive-brown, and pale inky-purple; these markings are sometimes fine and close, at other times bold and thinly set, but on the whole the eggs of the Jackdaw are more lightly marked than those of most of the family of Crows.

In size they average about 1·40 by 0·98 inches.

THE YELLOW-BILLED BLUE-MAGPIE

Urocissa flavirostris (Blyth)

Description.—Length 26 inches, including tail of about 18 inches. Sexes alike. Head, neck, and breast black, with a white patch on the nape; remainder of lower plumage white, faintly tinged with lilac; whole upper plumage purplish-blue, brighter on the wings and tail; flight-feathers tipped with white, the outermost edged with the same; tail long and graduated, the feathers blue, broadly tipped with white, all except the very long central pair having a band of black in front of the white.

Iris bright yellow; bill waxen yellow; legs bright orange-yellow.

Field Identification.—Purely Himalayan form; in noisy parties amongst trees. A conspicuous long tail, greatly graduated, and at the end drooping in a graceful curve. In jungle appears dull greyish-blue, with white under surface and white tips to tail-feathers.

Distribution.—The Yellow-billed Magpie is found throughout the Himalayas from Hazara to the Brahmaputra. It is divided into two races. Of these *U. f. cucullata* is the better known and is found from the Western boundary of the range to Western Nepal, being a common species about most of the hill stations of the Western Himalayas, breeding in a zone from 5000 to 10,000 feet. The typical form is found from Eastern Nepal eastwards and differs in that the under parts have a darker lilac tinge; its zone is slightly higher than that of the Western form, as it seldom occurs as low as 6000 feet. A resident species, but during the winter months it usually deserts the higher parts of its summer zone.

From Simla eastwards the closely allied Red-billed Blue-Magpie (*Urocissa melanocephala*) is often found in the same areas as the yellow-billed species; it is particularly common about Mussoorie, Tehri-Garhwal, Kumaon, and in Nepal, and may be easily distinguished by its red beak and the greater extent of the white nape-patch.

The lovely Green-Magpie (*Cissa chinensis*) is found in forest along the lower Himalayas from the Jamna eastwards and in parts of Assam, Eastern Bengal and Burma. It is brilliant green in colour (which has a tendency to fade to blue) with a black band through the eye and red bill, wings and tail.

Habits, etc.—The Blue-Magpies are, as may be judged from their handsome tails, essentially arboreal birds; though, while they are most usually to be met with in heavy jungle areas, they also venture out into the trees amongst cultivation, and at times on to bare mountain sides at high elevations. They frequently feed on the ground and then adopt a curious hopping gait, with the tail held high to prevent it coming into contact with the ground. They live in parties of seven or eight birds and are very partial to particular localities, so that once a party has taken up its abode in any particular

FIG. 3—Yellow-billed Blue-Magpie (1/6 nat. size)

nullah or patch of forest it will generally be found there. They are very active, flying incessantly from bough to bough and not hesitating to launch high into the air when flying from ridge to ridge; a party of these birds crossing a nullah out of gun-shot above one's head is a curious sight, with their long tails waving in the air and the light shining through the feathers. The flight is rather slow, laboured and undulating once the bird comes into the open. The food consists of small mammals, the eggs and young of other birds, insects, and wild fruits and berries of various kinds. This bird is very noisy; the ordinary call is harsh and grating, but it has a wide variety of notes, some of which are melodious enough.

The nest is built in a fork of a tree, usually of moderate size but with dense foliage, and is difficult to find. It is a rather large and roughly constructed cup of sticks with a lining of fine grass, roots and fibres.

The clutch consists of three or four eggs. The ground-colour varies from a pale, dingy yellowish-stone colour to a darkish rather reddish-stone colour, and there is very occasionally a faint greenish tinge. The markings consist of small specks, blotches, streaks, and mottlings of various shades of brown, sienna or purple, and they generally tend to collect in a cap or zone about the broad end of the egg.

The egg measures about 1·20 by 0·92 inches.

THE INDIAN TREE-PIE

DENDROCITTA VAGABUNDA (Latham)

Description.—Length 18 inches. Sexes alike. The whole head and neck with the breast sooty brown ; remainder of the body plumage bright rufous, darker on the back ; wing-coverts greyish-white ; wings dark brown, with a large conspicuous greyish-white patch on the sides extending almost their whole length when closed ; tail long and graduated with the central feathers elongated, ashy-grey, each feather broadly tipped with black.

Iris reddish-brown ; bill slaty horn-colour, albescent at the base ; legs dark brown, claws horn-colour.

Field Identification.—A bright rufous magpie with sooty head and neck, and impressions of grey, black and white in the wings and tail ; a strictly arboreal bird of open forest, often near gardens, usually in pairs, with a very musical call.

Distribution.—The whole of India and Burma from the Indus and the Lower Himalayas to Travancore, and from Assam to Tenasserim and Siam. A strictly resident species.

Like most widely-spread and common birds the Indian Tree-Pie is divided into several races, distinguished by size and the relative depth in colouring of the body plumage. There is much intergrading between them, and authorities in consequence differ as to their number and distribution. The typical race is found in North-east India including the outer fringe of the Himalayas from Nepal to Assam and Central India, being replaced by *D. v. pallida* in the North-western Himalayas, North-west Frontier Province, Sind, Punjab, and Rajputana. A small dark race, *D. v. parvula*, occurs in the rain area of the Western coast from South Kanara to Cape Comorin, while a small pale race, *D. v. vernayi*, occurs in the rest of Southern and Eastern India up to the Godavari River. Although essentially a bird of the plains of Continental India this Tree-Pie is found in hill country up to about 5000 feet, including the outer fringe of the Himalayas.

Two closely allied species, the Himalayan Tree-Pie (*Dendrocitta formosæ*) and the Southern Tree-Pie (*Dendrocitta leucogastra*), are common in the Lower Himalayas and from Mysore to Travancore respectively. The former is grey and brown with no rufous in the plumage except below the base of the tail. The latter has a black mask in sharp contrast to the white collar and under parts.

FIG. 4—Indian Tree-Pie (¼ nat. size)

Habits, etc.—The Tree-Pie is, as its name denotes, essentially arboreal, and it is practically never seen to visit the ground; though I have known it come into a verandah and climb about the chicks in order to catch the yellow wasp which habitually builds its nest in houses. It also climbs about trunks and branches of trees, hanging on with the claws and partly supported by the tail as it searches the crevices of the bark for insects. It is found not so much in heavy forest as in open country where large trees grow in clumps and avenues, and it is also very partial to gardens. But although it is in consequence common in the immediate vicinity of man it is a somewhat shy bird, living amidst the thicker foliage and usually only seen in glimpses as it flies from tree to tree in front of the observer. It is found in pairs or small parties. The flight is dipping, the bird alternately flapping the wings for several beats and then gliding with them stiffly outspread. The food consists of fruit, berries, insects, caterpillars, lizards, and small snakes, and this bird has the reputation of being one of the most destructive enemies in India to the eggs and young of other species.

The Tree-Pie is found throughout the sal forests of Northern and Central India and is invaluable to the initiated in pointing out the whereabouts of tiger or leopard kills. In the discovery of kills the Tree-Pie competes with the Jungle Crow.

The ordinary call is a loud and most melodious *kokli* or *googeley*, which is one of the familiar bird-notes of India. But it has a variety of other notes, some quite charming and soft, others less pleasant, particularly a raucous scolding note which is as ugly as the first is melodious.

The breeding season extends from February until the first week in August, but the majority of nests will be found in April, May, and June.

The nest is placed in trees or large bushes, in a fork usually towards the top of a tree. Mango and babool trees are most commonly favoured, though sheeshum and neem trees are also often selected, and the nest has even been found in cactus clumps. It is a shallow, open cup, sometimes large and loosely constructed, sometimes small and compact. There is a foundation of large twigs usually thorny in character, and on this is built the nest proper of finer twigs and roots, with a lining of grass roots and occasionally a little wool or straw.

The normal clutch is four or five eggs in the north, and generally two or three in the south.

The eggs are typically somewhat elongated ovals, a good deal pointed towards the small end; there is sometimes a slight gloss. In colour they are very variable, though there is always a family resemblance between the eggs composing one clutch. There are two leading types of coloration; one pale greenish in ground-colour with blotches and spots of light and dark grey brown, somewhat resembling the eggs of the Grey Shrike; the other pale reddish-white or salmon-colour with blotches of reddish and dark brown and underlying markings of lilac and neutral tint, similar in type to the eggs of the Drongos.

In size they average about 1·17 by 0·87 inches.

THE BLACK-THROATED JAY

GARRULUS LANCEOLATUS Vigors

Description.—Length 13 inches. Sexes alike. Top and sides of the head black; chin and throat black with broad white streaks, the black ending in a patch of iron-grey; body plumage vinous-grey, brighter towards the tail; wings black, closely barred with bright blue, a black patch on the coverts being bordered outwardly by a white patch; innermost flight-feathers vinous-grey with a black and

FIG. 5—Black-throated Jay (⅓ nat. size)

a white band at the end of each feather; tail black, broadly tipped with white, all but the outermost feathers closely barred with bright blue.

Iris reddish; bill steely slate, darker at tip; legs steely grey, claws darker.

The head is conspicuously crested, and the throat-feathers are long and pointed. The tail is long and slightly graduated.

Field Identification.—West Himalayan form. A noisy active bird found in parties in trees. The black crested head, with untidy white streaking on the throat, and the bright blue and black barring on the wings and tail contrast sharply with the nondescript body plumage.

Distribution.—The Suliman Hills; the Western Himalayas from Hazara and Chitral to Nepal, breeding from 5000 to 8000 feet, and occasionally higher to 10,000 feet, and in winter descending to 3500 feet. A resident species with no races.

The Himalayan Jay (*Garrulus bispecularis*), sometimes considered a race of the familiar English bird, is also resident throughout the Himalayas. It lacks the black head and crest of the Black-throated Jay, and is brighter, more rufous in colour with a squarer tail.

Loud harsh calls also draw attention to the Nutcracker (*Nucifraga caryocatactes*), another Himalayan species of Crow, which feeds largely on pine seeds. It is dark chocolate brown, spotted with white. The white of the outer tail-feathers is conspicuous in flight.

Habits.—The Black-throated Jay is a familiar species in the outer ranges of the Western Himalayas where it comes freely into the various hill stations. When in pairs in the breeding season it is quiet and secretive in habits until disturbed in the neighbourhood of the nest when it immediately becomes excited and noisy, screaming and chattering at the intruder. At other seasons it is found mostly in parties of four or five birds which in winter often combine into considerable flocks, up to twenty individuals in number, and these sometimes join forces with the Himalayan Jay and the Yellow-billed Blue-Magpie. These parties keep to trees, whether in forest or in the neighbourhood of houses and cultivation, and their whereabouts is sooner or later betrayed by the harsh *schach*, similar to the call of the English species. The food consists of grubs, caterpillars, beetles, insects, fruits, berries, seeds and the like, and some of it is taken on the ground.

From the hostility that this Jay awakens in other species in the breeding season it is obvious that they consider it a danger to their eggs and young.

The breeding season extends from the middle of April to June, most eggs being found in May.

The nest is a moderately shallow cup built of slender twigs and sticks and lined with dry roots and fibres, particularly the black horsehair-like rhizoids of fungi. It is placed in trees or thick bushes, never at any very great height from the ground. An upper fork of a small sapling affords a very favourite situation.

The clutch varies from three to six eggs, four or five being the usual number. The eggs are somewhat lengthened ovals in shape, and there is little or no gloss. The ground-colour varies from brownish-stone to pale greenish-white, and it is very minutely and feebly freckled and mottled all over with pale sepia-brown. There are usually a few dark brown hair-like lines, more or less zigzag, about the larger end.

The eggs measure about 1·12 by 0·85 inches.

THE CHOUGH

PYRRHOCORAX PYRRHOCORAX (Linnæus)

Description.—Length 17 inches. Sexes alike. The whole plumage glossy black.

Iris dark brown; bill coral-red; legs dark coral-red; claws black.

Bill slender and curved and the feathers at the base of the bill short and dense.

Field Identification.—Himalayas and Baluchistan. A very graceful black Crow with a pleasant call which is immediately identified by the coral-red bill and legs.

The slightly smaller Alpine Chough (*Pyrrhocorax graculus*) with shorter yellow bill and red legs has roughly the same distribution in our area as the Chough. The traveller in Lahul and Ladakh will find it a bold scavenger about his camp. It is commonly stated that these two Choughs are always found in separate valleys, but this is not a fact.

Distribution.—The Chough has a very wide distribution from Europe and Africa to China, mostly as a mountain bird. We are concerned with the race *P. p. himalayanus*, separated from the typical race on its slightly larger size, and this is found in North-eastern Baluchistan, Chitral and the Himalayas from Hazara to Bhutan. It is a bird of high elevations, seldom breeding below 8000 feet, most commonly in the zone from 10,000 to 12,000 feet, and sometimes up to 15,000 feet. It has been recorded up to 20,000 feet in summer, an elevation attained by very few species. In winter, stress of weather sometimes drives it down as low as 5000 feet or even 3000 feet.

Habits, etc.—Except in Baluchistan, where the Chough visits the Quetta Valley in winter, this delightful bird will only be met by the observer who leaves the ordinary Himalayan stations and travels a little further into the hills. On the outer ranges he will meet it on the Pir Panjal and the Duala Dhar, but for the most part he must enter the Main Himalayan range before he can expect to see its buoyant flight and hear its cheerful call. Once in its haunts, he will find the bird common enough in flocks and pairs and parties sometimes in the same valleys and in the same ranges as the Alpine Chough and sometimes alone. Its local distribution is a little erratic. In some places it is common; in others it is apparently absent and the reasons for this are not apparent.

The Chough usually roosts and breeds in precipitous cliffs though in the Chumbi Valley and in Tibet it also uses the numerous holes in the walls and under the flat roofs of the houses in the Tibetan villages. It feeds for the most part on the alpine pastures where it probes and digs in the soil or scatters the yak dung for the beetles and their larvæ, the wireworms, the insects and the small seeds which form its food. Further down it takes the berries of various mountain bushes such as the Ladakh thorn (*Hippophae rhamnoides*) and robs the tillage of its sparse supplies of corn. As a rule it is far from shy though it is not the shameless scavenger of the camp like its cousin the Alpine Chough. On the ground the loose thigh-feathers are conspicuous.

This Crow is an excellent flier. A party will often obviously fly for pleasure, playing and circling in the air currents in front of the cliffs where they live, or mounting high to soar in the sky till bird after bird comes plunging down again with swift slanting flight, closing the wings almost to the body.

The ordinary call is a melodious *kew* or *jack* much like that of the Jackdaw; another note is a high-pitched squeaky *chee-o-kah* and the alarm is a clear *quoick* or *kor-quick*. The voice carries far in the mountain valleys and draws attention to birds above almost out of sight.

Nidification begins in March and eggs are to be found in April and May. The nest is built in a crevice of a precipice or a hole in the roof of a hill cave and is usually quite inaccessible. In Tibetan villages it may be built in a hole in a house. The nest is made of sticks and twigs and the cup is lined with wool, though some nests consist merely of a pad of wool.

The clutch consists of three or four eggs. They are rather variable in size and shape but are typically a moderately elongated oval, slightly compressed towards the small end. The shell is tolerably fine and has a slight gloss. The ground-colour is white with a faint creamy tinge and the whole egg is profusely spotted and streaked with a pale, somewhat yellowish brown and a pale purplish grey. The markings are most dense at the broad end.

The egg measures about 1·75 by 1·20 inches.

THE INDIAN GREY TIT

PARUS MAJOR Linnæus

(Plate ii, Fig. 5, opposite page 22)

Description.—Length 5 inches. Sexes alike. Head, neck, breast and a broad line down the centre of the abdomen glossy black; a conspicuous white patch on the cheek and a fainter one on the nape; remainder of under parts white tinged with vinaceous; remainder of upper parts bluish ashy-grey, with a white bar across the wing; tail black and bluish ashy-grey, with a large amount of white on the outer feathers.

Iris dark brown ; bill black ; legs slaty plumbeous.

Field Identification.—A typical Tit ; bluish-grey above and whitish below, with black head, neck and broad abdominal stripe, and a white cheek-patch. Purely arboreal, generally single or in pairs.

Distribution.—The Great Tit (*Parus major*) is an interesting species of wide range. It extends throughout the whole of Europe, North-west Africa and the greater part of Asia to Japan and Southern China. But as is to be expected with such a wide range the species has been divided into a great number of geographical races or sub-species. These fall into two main groups ; the European group with green backs and yellow under parts (exemplified by the familiar Great Tit of England), and the Asiatic group with grey backs and whitish or buff under parts.

To this latter group belong our Indian birds, and they fall again into several races, which differ from each other in the depth and purity of their colour and in the relative amounts of black and white on the tail-feathers.

P. m. caschmirensis occupies the Western Himalayas from Kashmir to Gahrwal, visiting the Punjab plains in winter. *P. m. nipalensis* extends from Lower Nepal through Behar, Bengal, and the Duars into Assam and Western Burma. *P. m. stupæ* is found at Mount Aboo, in the Central Provinces and Orissa, and southwards to Cape Comorin, while a fourth race *P. m. ziaratensis* overlaps from Afghanistan into parts of Baluchistan and Trans-Indus Punjab. An insular race in Ceylon is the true *P. m. mahrattarum.* A resident species with slight local migrations. This species must not be confused with the White-winged Black Tit (*Parus nuchalis*) locally common in Rajputana.

Habits, etc.—The Indian Grey Tit is more properly to be considered a hill than a plains bird, and each race breeds throughout the more wooded ranges of its area from a height of about 3500 feet to their summits, even to 9000 or 10,000 feet when this is possible. But above 6000 feet it is usually rather scarce. While not strictly migratory it wanders a good deal after the breeding season, and then is found commonly in the plains area contiguous to the ranges on which it breeds. It is a bird of the more open types of forest, and while really arboreal wanders freely into bushes and scrub-jungle, and frequently visits the ground in search of food.

Although often found in small parties or included in the large mixed hunting parties of small insectivorous birds this Tit is more usually found singly and in pairs. When feeding it is very methodical, carefully examining the branches and twigs for small insects and their caterpillars and eggs, peering into every nook and cranny and bunch of leaves, and when necessary for the purpose indulging in a variety of acrobatic postures for which its sturdy build and strong legs are admirably adapted. At times it holds some article of food between its feet on a branch and hammers at it with pickaxe blows of the beak, and the noise thus made is frequently mistaken for the work of a small Woodpecker. It is a cheerful bird both in demeanour and note, and the loud whistle *tsee tsee tsee* is always a cheery welcome sound. With the spring and the approach of the breeding season this is supplemented by a number of louder and clearer calls, of which the most familiar is *zwink zwink*. When disturbed in the nest the bird endeavours to frighten away the intruder by hissing and spitting like a snake.

It is interesting to note that the young bird in the juvenile plumage is greenish in colour on the back and yellower underneath than the adult, a clear indication of the relationship between the two main types of *Parus major* and the fact that the Western birds must be considered the older and original type.

This Tit appears to be double-brooded wherever found. In the Himalayas the breeding season is from the end of March to July: while in the Peninsula the breeding season is more extended, commencing in February and lasting until November, but it varies in different localities, and the majority everywhere lay before July.

The nest is a large, shapeless mass of downy fur, cattle hair, feathers, and wool, with a foundation of grass roots and moss, the whole forming a soft pad with a saucer-like hollow for the eggs. The fur is often obtained from the droppings of carnivoræ. It is placed in a hole of some kind, whether in a wall, bank, tree or rock, and sometimes in the old nest-hole of a Woodpecker or Barbet. On one occasion I found two nests built side by side touching under the coping-stone of a wall, with one and four eggs respectively, both apparently the property of the same bird. Similar cases have been reported of the Great and Blue Tits in England. Hume has recorded two instances in which the nest was built in the open on a branch of a tree, but this is very unusual.

The normal clutch consists of four to six eggs. In shape they are a broad oval, somewhat elongated and pointed towards the small end, and have a faint gloss. In colour they are white, speckled and spotted with reddish-brown and pale purplish, these markings often tending to coalesce into a zone round the broad end.

They measure about 0·70 by 0·54 inches.

THE GREEN-BACKED TIT

Parus monticolus Vigors

Description.—Length 5 inches. Sexes alike. The whole head, neck, breast, and a broad line down the centre of the abdomen glossy black: a conspicuous white patch on the cheek and a fainter one on the nape; remainder of lower plumage deep yellow; back greenish-yellow; rump slaty-blue; wings mixed slaty-blue and black with two white bars; tail black and slaty-blue, edged and tipped with white.

Iris brown; bill black; legs plumbeous-slate.

Field Identification.—Himalayan form; the common Tit of all Himalayan hill stations. A typical Tit with white cheek-patch, black head and breast and abdominal band; distinguished from the Grey Tit by the brighter coloration, greenish back instead of grey, yellow under parts instead of greyish-white.

Distribution.—The Green-backed Tit is found throughout the Himalayas, and also further eastwards through Manipur, Chittagong and the Chin Hills to Yunnan and Formosa. Its normal breeding zone lies between 5000 and 8000 feet, but a few may be met with up to 10,000 and even 12,000 feet; during the winter numbers descend to the foot-hills below 4000 and a few even to the fringe of the plains beyond them. Apart from this seasonal altitudinal movement it is a resident species. All birds in our area belong to the typical race.

Habits, etc.—This bird resembles other Tits in being a forest-loving bird though it wanders a good deal and may be found in any type of country in the hills, cultivation or scrub-covered hill-side. While properly speaking arboreal it freely descends to undergrowth and to the ground. It is occasionally found in small flocks and parties, but is more usually found singly or in pairs, and one or more of these birds will invariably be found attached to the mixed hunting parties of small birds which are such a familiar feature of the Himalayan forests.

The food consists chiefly of insects in their various stages and also of fruits, and it is less of a seed eater and less omnivorous than the Grey Tit.

Although without a proper song, this bird has a number of not unmusical calls, which are amongst the most penetrating and familiar of the bird sounds in a Himalayan station. One note is described as a very loud four-syllable whistle which may be written *ti-ti-tee-ti*, the third syllable much prolonged. Its ordinary spring call at the commencement of the breeding season is a mewing whistle *pheeow* or *pawee*, while other calls may be syllabilised as *peeweet* or *tweentwee* and *sit-here* and *teacher*. But it must be remembered that most of the Tit family have a variety of very similar calls, hard to distinguish from one another. This species is very fond of water, bathing more regularly than most other Tits.

Nidification begins in the latter half of March and most clutches of eggs will be found in April, though fresh eggs may be still found until June ; it is possible that some birds are double-brooded.

The nest is a shapeless mass, with a hollow on top for the eggs, of soft downy fur and feathers with more or less moss by way of foundation. It is placed in a hole, either in a tree, wall, bamboo or even in a bank, though a hole in a wall is usually chosen.

The clutch consists normally of six to eight eggs, though sometimes as few as four eggs are laid.

The eggs are moderately broad ovals, some almost symmetrical, others slightly pointed at one end. In colour they are white, almost without gloss, spotted, blotched, and speckled with different shades of red and brown ; the markings vary in quantity and intensity but tend to be most numerous towards the large end. The eggs of this species in a series will be found to be rather longer and more slender and more richly marked than those of the Grey Tit.

In size they average about 0·72 by 0·52 inches.

THE YELLOW-CHEEKED TIT

Machlolophus xanthogenys (Vigors)

Description.—Length 5 inches. Sexes alike. Crown and a long pointed crest, a line through the eye and a broad band from the chin to the vent glossy black ; a line over each eye to a patch on the hind neck, the cheeks and the sides of the body canary-yellow ; upper parts yellowish-green ; wings black, the small coverts spotted with pale yellow-white, the flight-feathers edged and variegated with blue-grey and white ; tail black, washed with blue-grey, the tips of all feathers and the outer edge of the outer feather white.

Iris dark brown ; bill black ; legs dark slaty-blue.

Field Identification.—A typical greenish and yellow Tit with a pointed black crest and a heavy black band down the centre of the lower parts ; distinguished from the Green-backed Tit by the crest and the yellow cheeks. Strictly arboreal and confined to well-wooded country, particularly hills.

Distribution.—This species is confined to India and is divided into three races. The typical form occurs in the Western Himalayas from Murree to Eastern Nepal, breeding in a zone between 5000 and

PLATE II

1. Spotted Munia. 2. Red Avadavat. 3. Red-breasted Flycatcher. 4. Red-headed Tit. 5. Indian Grey Tit. 6. Himalayan Tree-Creeper. (All about ½ nat. size.)

[*Face p.* 22

7000 feet, though its distribution is somewhat capricious. *M. x. aplonotus* is found across the centre of the Peninsula from Mount Aboo and Mahabaleshwar to Parasnath Hill and the Krishna River. *M. x. travancoreensis*, a larger and duller bird, is confined to the Western Ghats and the neighbouring wooded areas from the South Konkan to the Asambo Hills. These two races are found at all elevations and differ from the typical race in having a shorter crest, the spots on the wing-coverts white instead of yellow, and the yellow parts of the plumage paler. In these two races the females have the black band on the lower plumage replaced with olive green, and in *M. x. travancoreensis* some females also have the crest olive-green.

FIG. 6—Yellow-cheeked Tit ($\frac{2}{3}$ nat. size)

Habits.—The Yellow-cheeked Tit is a very sociable bird. Except when actually breeding it is found in small parties which are apt to attach themselves to the mixed hunting parties that are commonly found in the woods which they frequent. It is arboreal in habits, spending its life in an incessant hunt in the trees for the small insects and their eggs and larvæ and the various seeds and fruits which form its food. Even the largest caterpillars are attacked and torn into pieces. Like many other birds it catches flying ants and feeds at the flowers of the cotton-tree. The call-notes are loud and joyous in tone, being very distinct from and more musical than those of other Tits. Those of the Himalayan race may be syllabilised as *tyuji tyuja* and again as *teetweenh twit-teetweenh*, while the breeding call is a loud *towit towit*. There is also a low jarring note and a chatter like that of the Grey Tit.

The Himalayan race breeds from April to June. The Continental races evidently breed a good deal later, from July to August or even September and October, though in the north of the Peninsula some pairs start in April.

The nest is built in holes in trees at any height up to about 20 feet. The hole may be a small natural cavity or one cut out by the birds themselves, a large hollow in a bough or the old nesting-hole of a Barbet or Woodpecker. The nest is the usual shapeless pad of the family, composed of a mass of wool and hair on a foundation of moss and other miscellaneous materials. It varies in size according to the circumstances of the hole.

The usual clutch consists of four or five eggs. These vary in shape from elongated to rather broad ovals and have little or no gloss. The ground is white and they are moderately thickly speckled or spotted all over. Some of the spots are large and blotchy, and in some eggs the markings tend to collect at one end.

The eggs measure about 0·70 by 0·52 inches.

THE CRESTED BLACK TIT

LOPHOPHANES MELANOLOPHUS (Vigors)

Description.—Length 4 inches. Sexes alike. The whole head including a long pointed crest, neck and breast black, except for a large white patch on the sides of the face and another on the nape; upper plumage iron-grey, the exposed parts of the wings and tail paler; two lines of rufous spots across the wing, and the inner flight-feathers slightly tipped with white; lower plumage from the breast downwards iron-grey; patches on the flanks and under the wings and tail chestnut.

Iris brown; bill black; legs dark bluish-grey.

Field Identification.—Purely West Himalayan form, common at all hill stations. A small dark Tit with an erect-pointed crest and conspicuous white patches on nape and sides of the face. Usually found in flocks and in hunting parties in forest. The two lines of rufous spots across the wing provide the readiest means of separation from another larger and darker species (*Lophophanes rufonuchalis*) which is locally common throughout the whole length of the Himalayas.

Distribution.—The Crested Black Tit is found from the Sufed Koh and Chitral along the Himalayas to Garhwal and Naini Tal. It breeds in a somewhat high zone between 6000 and 12,000 feet but in winter descends also down to about 4000 feet, and even occasionally lower, for both the above species *L. melanolophus* and *L. rufonuchalis* were found common at Rawal Pindi in January 1907. It is very common about Gulmurg, the Galis, Dharmsala, Kulu, and Simla.

Habits, etc.—This Tit is most markedly a forest bird and every variety of evergreen tree growth is frequented by it. It is always busy in the search for food, preferably high in some moss-grown oak or lordly pine, and the soft *chee-chee* note which forms a running accompaniment to all its activities will be heard long before its tiny owner is seen in the branches above one's head. Occasionally it feeds alone, but more usually two or three join together in a free-and-easy bond of companionship, while in winter these parties in turn join together in regular flocks numbering often as many as fifty birds. These flocks are frequently accompanied by Gold-crests, and in the area where this Tit occurs it is a leading spirit in all the mixed hunting parties.

Fig. 7—Head of Crested Black Tit (1½ nat. size)

It is as active and acrobatic in its movements as the Red-headed Tit, and both of these birds easily surpass the heavier Grey and Green-backed Tits in this respect. The Crested Black Tit is seldom seen at rest, but when the first stirrings of the spring turn his thoughts towards a mate, he occasionally ceases from the hunt for food and betaking himself to some lofty twig he perches there and proclaims his ardour to the world with a loud clear call, *want you, need you, want you, need you,* a sentiment that frequently finds an echo in the human heart below. There are a variety of other cheerful call-notes; a favourite song-call is *chak-cha-bink* or *kink-ka-jou* and also a loud plaintive *tyu-tyu* slowly repeated. The song is a whirring, reeling trill of the grasshopper type.

The food consists chiefly of insects.

The breeding season commences in March and the majority of eggs are laid early in April. Nests, however, may be found until June, and it is probable that there are sometimes two broods in the season.

The nest is invariably built in a hole, either of a tree, rock, or wall, whether close to the ground or 30 feet up. In the hole a substantial foundation of moss obtained from adjacent tree-trunks is first collected so as to close in the cavity to a suitable size; on this is built the nest proper which consists of a mass, large and shapeless or small and closely felted, of wool and fur, occasionally mingled with a little vegetable down and moss.

The number of eggs is very variable from four to ten, but the usual clutch consists of six to eight eggs.

The eggs are moderately broad ovals though somewhat longer in proportion than those of most Tits; the ground-colour is white with a faint gloss, blotched, spotted, and speckled with bright brownish-red, the markings often tending to form a dense confluent cap or zone about the larger end of the egg.

They measure about 0·61 by 0·47 inches.

THE RED-HEADED TIT

ÆGITHALISCUS CONCINNUS (Gould)

(Plate ii, Fig. 4, opposite page 22)

Description.—Length including tail 4 inches. Sexes alike. Whole top of the head chestnut; sides of the head and a large round patch on the throat deep black; a broad eyebrow, a broad moustachial streak, and the chin white; remainder of lower plumage ferruginous. Upper plumage and wings and tail bluish-grey, the concealed portions of the quill-feathers dark brown, and the outer tail-feathers tipped with white. The tail is long and graduated.

Iris pale yellow; bill black, gape fleshy; legs buffy-yellow.

Field Identification.—A diminutive Himalayan species invariably found in flocks in trees and bushes except when breeding; very small, with a longish tail and most conspicuous head markings of bright chestnut, black and white; no abdominal band. The flocks utter a low, harsh churring note.

Distribution.—The Red-headed Tit extends from Chitral and at Cherat all through the Himalayas across the various ranges of Assam and Northern Burma into China. There are several races in the eastern portion of its range, but in India we are only concerned with two. *Æ. c. iredalei* is found from Chitral eastwards to Sikkim, where it is replaced by the smaller and more deeply-coloured *Æ. c. rubricapillus.* The former breeds at elevations between 5000 and 8,000 feet, occurring in smaller numbers up to 12,000 feet and as low as 3000 feet in winter; the latter, however, does not go much above 7000 feet. A resident species.

The Sultan-Tit (*Melanochlora sultanea*) is found in small parties in trees at low elevations in the Eastern Himalayas, Assam and Burma. It is larger than the true Tits, heavy in build and glossy blackish save for a bright yellow abdomen and crown with a loose crest.

Habits, etc.—This Tit is purely a hill species, and in the main occupies a middle zone intermediate between the foot-hills and the higher ranges. It is more strictly sedentary than most of the other members of the family, only an occasional party descending in winter a thousand feet or so lower than the normal zone. It never visits the ground, but is equally at home in the branches of high trees in thick forest or amongst the indigo and berberis bushes of open grass-clad hill-sides.

The leading characteristic of this species is its fussy sociability. Throughout the year it is found in small flocks, and though while actually breeding individual pairs leave the company of their fellows, flocks may be met with throughout the breeding season, consisting either of late breeders who have not yet settled their domestic arrangements, or early family parties of young birds strong on the wing. As they feed they utter incessantly a soft gentle *tcheck* or a harsh *trree*, both notes alternating. And even their own society is not sufficient for these sociable little birds; the parties attach themselves to the mixed bands of Creepers, Willow-Wrens, Flycatchers, and other species of Tit which wander through the hill forests, suddenly filling with busy activity a glen or group of trees that a moment before was empty of bird-life. In these hunting parties the Red-headed Tit takes a leading and conspicuous share; it is very active and very fussy, and at the least excitement its harsh churring note of defiance and of warning is uttered and taken up by a dozen throats; while its acrobatic feats surpass those of all the other species, except perhaps the Crested Black Tit. It investigates every leaf and twig, now circling adroitly round its perch, now hanging upside down—any angle, any position, all are the same—inaction only is abhorrent to it. The parties are strangely trusting; one has only to stand still and the little gymnasts will climb and chatter in a bush a yard away, feeding with no apparent recognition of the stranger at their gates; then a sudden movement on his part or a note of warning from a bird and the flock will vanish as quickly as it came, like a little flight of arrows sped in relays by a fairy archer through the bushes. They seldom venture into the open, and then only for short flights between two clumps of trees. The flight is weak and practically never sustained for more than a few yards at a time, though when disturbed from the nest this bird can fly down-hill as fast as any Warbler for a short distance. The food consists almost entirely of insects in their various stages, but small seeds and fruits are also probably eaten.

The breeding season commences about the beginning of March and continues throughout April and May. The nest is placed in a variety of situations ranging from a tangle of matted grass near the ground to the bough of a deodar 40 feet up. But the majority will be found in stunted hill-oaks and bushes within easy reach, though seldom conspicuous. The nests are most beautiful structures, very closely resembling and recalling the familiar "bottle" nests of the Long-tailed Tit in England. They are large, upright, egg-shaped structures of moss and lichen, studded and bound together with cotton-down, cobwebs and similar substances, some 4½ inches in height and 3½ inches in diameter, with a small entrance high on one side. The walls are thick and closely woven, and there is a dense lining of feathers mixed sometimes with seed-down, the whole forming as cosy a home as it is possible to imagine.

The eggs vary in number from three to eight, but the usual clutch consists of five or six.

The tiny eggs are broad ovals, sometimes almost globular, and sometimes somewhat pointed at one end. In colour they are pinkish or creamy white, almost without gloss, and round the broad end there is a conspicuous zone of minute reddish and purple spots almost confluent and clouding into one another.

They measure about 0·56 by 0·45 inches.

THE CHESTNUT-BELLIED NUTHATCH

SITTA CASTANEA Lesson

Description.—Length 5 inches. Male: Upper plumage slaty-blue, lower plumage uniform dark chestnut-bay, except for the following markings: a black streak through the eye from the nostril to the shoulder; a white patch from the chin below the eye to the ear-coverts; middle tail-feathers ashy-blue, the next two black, with ashy-blue tips and edges, the remainder black with white markings; under tail-coverts mixed chestnut and ashy; under surface of the wings black with a white patch only visible from below.

Female: Under parts paler chestnut, and the white face markings less clearly defined.

Iris dark brown; bill black, slaty-grey at base; legs dark greenish-plumbeous.

The hind toe is greatly developed and the inner front toe dwarfed. The beak is long, stout and pointed.

Field Identification.—A small bird, slaty-blue above, chestnut-bay below, with a heavy pointed beak. Purely arboreal, running like a mouse about the bark and twigs of trees, frequently upside-down. Most Nuthatches appear very similar in the field. Of common species the Himalayan (*Sitta himalayensis*) and Kashmir (*Sitta cashmirensis*) Nuthatches are much paler, more fulvous below, the former differing from all Indian species in a white patch on the central tail-feathers. A more conspicuous species the White-cheeked Nuthatch (*Sitta leucopsis*) is found in the higher tree zone of the Sufed Koh and Western Himalayas. This is dark blue above with a black crown and creamy-white below with rich chestnut on the flanks and has a very harsh loud note rapidly repeated. Its habitat in rocky nullahs amply identifies the large Rock-Nuthatch (*S. iranica*) of Baluchistan, remarkable for its globular mud nest on a rock.

Distribution.—The Chestnut-bellied Nuthatch has a somewhat wide distribution throughout India, Assam, and Burma to Siam. It is divided into races, of which we are concerned with four. Except for the Vizagapatam Hills where *S. c. prateri* is found, the typical race inhabits the plains of India from Ferozepore, Ambala, and Khandesh on the west to Calcutta on the east. It is also found in the Wynaad and about the base of the Nilgiris. An east (*S. c. cinnamoventris*) and a West Himalayan race (*S. c. almoræ*) have

FIG. 8—Chestnut-bellied Nuthatch (½ nat. size)

heavier bills and differ in slight details of coloration. A resident species.

Habits, etc.—The habits of this species are typical of all the Nuthatches. They share with Woodpeckers and Tree - Creepers the ability to climb about the trunks and branches of trees in order to search the crevices of the bark for the insects and larvæ that live there—secure from the attentions of most insect-feeding birds; but the Nuthatches are by far the most skilful climbers of the three classes; they do not need the support of their tails against the bark, and they are infinitely more agile and lively in consequence, able to climb in any direction—upwards, downwards, upside-down or sideways, and they are also able to perch on twigs in the normal passerine manner. They are very restless and hard-working. This species is purely arboreal and is found singly or in parties, often in company with mixed hunting parties, and keeps largely to the tops of the highest or oldest trees; it is more often heard than seen, as in addition to its sharp note the sound of hammering on bark and on seeds and nuts, as it breaks into their kernels, betrays its whereabouts.

The main breeding season of the Himalayan races is in April and May, and of the typical race in February and March. All races nest in holes and hollows of trees, and the hill birds also use holes in walls. A Nuthatch's nest may always be recognised by the habit of plastering the entrance and sides of the hole with mud and clay to adapt it to the needs of the bird, such plaster-work sometimes being of considerable extent. In holes of trees the nest is usually scanty, consisting largely of flaky material like slips of bark or the seed-cases of trees, but in the case of nests built in holes in walls the nest is a much more substantial affair including a moss foundation and a lining of fur. The nest site is often close to the ground, and even when robbed is frequently repaired and used again immediately.

The clutch varies from two to six eggs. The eggs greatly resemble those of Tits; they are regular broad ovals, fragile and fine in texture with very little gloss. The ground-colour is pure white and the markings consist of small spots and speckles of brick-red and reddish-lilac.

In size they average about 0·70 by 0·55 inches.

The word Nuthatch is believed to be a corruption of an older name Nuthack.

THE VELVET-FRONTED NUTHATCH

SITTA FRONTALIS (Swainson)

(Frontispiece, fig. 4)

Description.—Length 5 inches. Male: A broad band across the forehead and a narrow streak above the eye to the nape velvet-black; the whole upper plumage and wing-coverts blue; wing black, the individual feathers more or less edged with blue; middle tail-feathers blue, the others blackish edged and tipped with blue; ear-coverts lilac; chin and throat whitish shading into the greyish-lilac of the rest of the under parts.

The female is similar to the male but lacks the narrow black eye-streak.

Iris lemon-yellow; bill coral-red, tipped above with brownish; mouth coral-red; legs brown with an orange tinge.

The hind toe is greatly developed and the bill narrow and pointed. The body has the same smell as a Woodpecker.

Field Identification.—Outer Himalayas and Peninsular India. A small bird blue above and greyish-lilac below with a heavy velvet-black band across the forehead and a coral-red bill. Arboreal in habits, running like a mouse about the trunks and branches of trees in hill forest areas.

Distribution.—The Velvet-fronted Nuthatch has two races in our area. The typical race is found in Ceylon and in the Indian Peninsula south of a line from Khandesh, the Central Provinces and Chota Nagpur, being largely confined to the forests of the Eastern and Western Ghats. It is particularly common in the Nilgiris. A slightly smaller race *S. f. corallina* is found along the submontane valleys of the Himalayas up to about 3800 feet from Dehra Dun eastwards, in the hills and plains of Assam up to about 4000 feet and throughout the whole of Burma up to about 5500 feet. This species is also found through the Malay Peninsula, Sumatra and Borneo to Java. A strictly resident species.

Habits.—The habits of this species are similar to those of other Nuthatches and like them it is often found in the mixed hunting parties. The Velvet-fronted Nuthatch is one of the most active birds imaginable, for ever on the move, nimbly running up and down and round the trunks of trees, climbing the moss-covered branches, descending head-foremost and running upside down along the lower surface of a bough. It does not, as a rule, remain long in one tree but darts quickly on from one to another, followed by its companions —for they are usually found in pairs or parties of four or five individuals —and alights with a trilling little note which although comparatively weak is audible at a considerable distance. This note which is variously described as a sharp *chick chick chick*, rapidly repeated, or a loud cheeping whistle is constantly uttered and is one of the latest diurnal bird-calls to be heard in the forest, frequently well after dusk. The male also utters a short little warble.

This Nuthatch may be found on occasion in most types of forest but is essentially a bird of the evergreen forest, though it has a decided preference for the edges of clearings and light patches. Dead trees are a favourite hunting ground. It may often be seen running along fallen logs or over small dead wood lying on the ground and sometimes it even forages in brushwood. Usually, however, it will be seen in trees and no tree is too high for it, so that the ear will often announce its presence in the head of some lofty giant where the eye has difficulty in picking up its tiny shape.

The food consists exclusively of insects.

The main breeding season of the Himalayan race is in May and June, but in South India and Ceylon the season is from the middle of February until May. The nest is built in a hole in a tree at any height from the ground up to about 40 feet but most nests will be found below 20 feet. The hole chosen is usually a small natural one, but the deserted nest-holes of Woodpeckers and Barbets are also used ; and where necessary the entrance hole is modified with plaster-work after the manner of other Nuthatches. The nest is a substantial pad of moss, green or dry, which is lined with fur and includes a good many feathers, both amongst the moss and in the lining.

The clutch consists of three to five eggs, which are very similar to those of the Tits. They are broad ovals, rather compressed towards the small end, fine and compact in texture but devoid of gloss. The ground-colour is white and the markings consist of blotches, speckles and spots of brick-dust red and somewhat pale purple, sometimes gathered in a sort of irregular zone round the broad end.

The egg measures about 0·65 by 0·50 inches.

THE WHITE-THROATED LAUGHING-THRUSH

GARRULAX ALBOGULARIS (Gould)

(Plate v, Fig. 1, opposite page 88)

Description.—Length 12 inches. Sexes alike. Upper plumage greyish olive-brown, the forehead fulvous, and a black mark in front of and below the eye; throat and upper breast pure white, sharply defined and bordered broadly with the colour of the upper parts which gradually shades off into the bright rufous of the rest of the lower plumage; four outer pairs of tail-feathers broadly tipped with white.

The tail is rounded and full.

Iris bluish-grey; bill horny-black; mouth yellow; legs slaty-plumbeous.

Field Identification.—Himalayan form. Medium-sized olive-grey bird with rufous belly, and conspicuous shining white throat patch. Found in noisy parties in heavy jungle; presence first revealed by a curious hissing note.

Distribution.—Throughout the Himalayas from Hazara to Sikkim, and in South-west China. The Himalayan birds are divided into two races. *G. a. whistleri* is the better known form and extends from the Hazara country to about Eastern Nepal, being particularly common at Mussoorie and is very numerous round Naini Tal but rather less so about Simla. The typical form is more brightly coloured with more rufous in the plumage and is slightly smaller. It is found in Nepal and Sikkim and in North Cachar. Both forms are birds of middle elevations, occurring from about 5000 to 9000 feet. A resident species.

The closely related White-crested Laughing-Thrush (*Garrulax leucolophus*) common along the Himalayas from Garhwal eastwards is easily recognised by its white-crested head and black band through the eye. In the Eastern Himalayas the Black-gorgetted Laughing-Thrush (*Garrulax pectoralis*), an olive-brown and fulvous bird with a marked black gorget band, is remarkable in having a smaller counterpart the Necklaced Laughing-Thrush (*Garrulax moniliger*). Both are common in the same localities, often joining in a mixed flock. The only member of this genus found in Southern India is the Wynaad Laughing-Thrush (*Garrulax delesserti*), which is peculiar to the hill ranges from North Kanara to Travancore.

Habits, etc.—This large Laughing-Thrush is a very sedentary species and does not move much from its chosen haunts, which consist of heavy forest in the deeper and more secluded ravines. In such places it lives in large parties which do not entirely break up even in the breeding season. They feed a good deal on the ground, turning up the dead leaves in search of insects, but they are perhaps more often seen up in the trees, searching the crevices of the bark and tearing off the lumps of moss which grow on most of the older trees in the areas that they frequent.

While thus feeding they keep up a low murmuring note, *teh. teh*, irresistibly reminiscent of a flock of Tits, though of course louder. At the least provocation this is changed into a discordant concert of noisy screaming, hissing and chattering, some of their calls being of a peculiarly eerie timbre and suited to the gloomy surroundings in which they are uttered. In fact there is something peculiarly ghostly about these birds, as a flock of them move about in the shady recesses of the forest, their white gorgets shining conspicuously as erratically moving spots of light and their weird voices breaking in upon the silence. Though not particularly shy they soon vanish if disturbed, slipping away one by one up the trees from branch to branch, and so on up the hill-side with some rapidity.

The breeding season lasts from the beginning of April to the end of June, some birds nesting until August. The nest is a large wide cup, not as a rule very deep, and is made of coarse grass, creepers, dead leaves, moss, and roots, with usually a lining of fern and moss roots. It is built in a bush or small tree, usually about 3 to 10 feet from the ground, and the usual situation is at the end of a bough or between two or three upright shoots on low, horizontal branches.

The clutch varies from two to four eggs, but the normal number is three.

The eggs are long and fairly pointed ovals with a high gloss They vary from a deep dull blue to a deep intense greenish-blue. and are darker than the eggs of all other Babblers and Laughing-Thrushes. They are without markings.

In size they average about 1·22 by 0·83 inches.

THE RED-HEADED LAUGHING-THRUSH

TROCHALOPTERON ERYTHROCEPHALUM (Vigors)

Description.—Length 11 inches. Sexes alike. Upper surface of head chestnut; sides of head and throat black, mixed below and behind the eye with chestnut; lower plumage pale fulvous, lightly scaled with black on the throat and breast; upper plumage olive-brown scaled with black about the shoulders; rump slaty-grey; wings and tail ashy, the feathers brightly edged with golden olive-yellow; a bright ferruginous bar across the wing and behind it a patch of golden-red.

Iris pale brown; bill black; legs pale brown.

The tail is rather long and full.

Field Identification.—Himalayan form. The chestnut crown, spotted neck and gilded wings and tail are not conspicuous in the forest where the bird appears nondescript in colour with a very dark head and neck. Very shy, found in thick undergrowth in parties which utter a peculiar murmuring note.

Mention may here be made of the Rufous-necked Laughing-Thrush (*Dryonastes ruficollis*), common along the base of the Eastern Himalayas, a dusky-looking bird with chestnut patches on the sides of the neck and under the tail. The Rufous-chinned Laughing-Thrush (*Ianthocincla rufogularis*), found in the lower Himalayan ranges, is rich olive-brown and grey squamated with black.

Distribution.—This fine Laughing-Thrush is widely distributed along the Himalayas and in the various mountain ranges which extend from them down to the south of Tenasserim. It is divided into a number of geographical races, which in several cases are very distinct. Two of these concern us. The typical race is common in the Western Himalayas from Chamba on the west into Nepal. It breeds from about 6000 tc 9000 feet, and in winter works down-hill to about 4000 feet. Eastwards of Nepal to the Daphla and Miri Hills in Assam it is replaced by *T. e. nigrimentum*, in which the ear-coverts are black with pinkish-white edges; this race is found at similar elevations to the other. Apart from altitudinal movements both birds are residents.

Habits, etc. — The Red - headed Laughing - Thrush is a very common bird in well-forested areas where there is plenty of undergrowth. It is, however, very shy and secretive and is therefore little known to the majority of people, though once its various notes have been learnt evidence of its abundance is surprising. In the breeding season a loud, clear, double whistle, *pheeou-pheeou*, a familiar sound in all the thicker forests, is its ordinary call. This is easily imitated and the bird readily called up. This ceases in winter, but the presence of a party in the undergrowth is revealed as one passes along a path by a soft murmur, curious but distinctly pleasant. If a nest is examined the pair that own it work backwards and forwards in the bushes a few yards away but always evading observation, and as they fuss and flirt their long tails, bowing, bobbing, jerking from side to side, now on one bough, now on another, they keep up an incessant squeaky murmuring, *chicky-cree-cree-cree-cree*, or a harsh, low chatter, *queer-que*, *queer-quee*, very difficult to describe. Rarely the birds come out into the open, but when they do so it is only to flutter and skim back into the nearest cover at the slightest excuse.

The nesting season is extended from May to August. The breeding zone is that of the Oaks, *Q. dilatata* and *Q. semicarpifolia*, or say between 8000 and 9000 feet. The nest is a large massive cup composed largely of dead leaves bound round with grass and bents, fine twigs and long strips of fibrous bark till a very solid wall has been made; moss and maidenhair enter also in the construction and the egg cavity is lined with fine grass and fine roots.

The clutch usually consists of three eggs. These are very long ovals, fine and compact in texture with a slight gloss. The ground-colour is delicate, pale greenish-blue, with a few spots, streaks, and blotches of brownish-red, mostly towards the broad end.

The eggs measure about 1·2 by 0·82 inches.

THE VARIEGATED LAUGHING-THRUSH

TROCHALOPTERON VARIEGATUM (Vigors)

(Plate iii, Fig. 1, opposite page 44)

Description.—Length 11 inches. Sexes alike. Forehead at base of beak fulvous shading into the ashy olive-brown of the whole upper plumage; sides of the face black, broken with a certain amount of white behind the eye; chin and throat fulvous with a black mark down the centre; lower plumage similar to the upper but paler and gradually changing into bright tawny-buff posteriorly. Wings brightly variegated with black, white and grey, and bright golden-yellow or red.

Tail rather long and full; the middle four pairs of tail-feathers black for three-quarters of their length, then ashy-grey or ashy-yellow and tipped with white; the other feathers ashy on the inner webs, golden or reddish yellow on the outer and tipped with white.

Iris sage green; bill black; legs pale fleshy-brown, claws dusky.

Field Identification.—Himalayan form, found in forest areas; a dull-coloured bird, chiefly conspicuous for black and white markings on the face. Shy and elusive, but rather noisy; generally in parties.

Distribution.—The Variegated Laughing-Thrush is found on the Samana and in the Himalayas from Chitral and Gilgit to Nepal. It is divided into two races. The meeting ground of these two races is about Chamba and Dharmsala. The Eastern and typical race, common in the Simla Hills, breeds mainly at higher elevations than the Red-headed Laughing-Thrush. The silver fir, birch and rhododendron forests at from 9000 to 11,000 feet constitute the breeding area, but the two species sometimes overlap in the breeding season in the zone of the high level oak. In this race the outer webs of the wing and tail-feathers are very variable in colour, ranging from bright golden-yellow to crimson. In the Western form, *T. v. simile*, which is very common in the Galis and about Murree, these outer webs are pure french-grey and do not vary. This is a forest-loving bird, of high elevations, breeding in a zone between 6000 and 11,000 feet; it is not a migrant, but in winter the majority move somewhat downhill and may then be found at any height from 4000 feet upwards.

Habits, etc.—Steep hill-sides covered with dense undergrowth are the haunts of this bird, and preferably those slopes where the undergrowth is further shaded and rendered secluded by the presence of large trees. In such situations the Variegated Laughing-Thrush is found in small parties or even in flocks numbering about twenty individuals, whose presence is betrayed by their noisy behaviour. The call-note of the species is a loud clear whistle *pitt-we-weer*, frequently repeated and ascending in scale, but in addition to this it has a variety of squeaky notes in a chattering slightly querulous tone; a curious sort of drumming note is also occasionally uttered.

The ordinary demeanour of the bird is fairly bold, but as soon as it has reason to suspect the presence of danger it becomes very shy and active, skulking in the thickest of the undergrowth, or hopping rapidly and silently up the branches of some tree, from the top of which it plunges into further cover. It appears to visit the ground but seldom, though often in the undergrowth close to it. In Lahul, where cover is scarce, the Western form *simile* which occurs there is found in the willow groves taking shelter in the thick-pollarded heads of the trees. The food consists both of fruits and berries and of insects.

The breeding season lasts from April to July, most eggs being laid in May and June. The nest is a large, massive and rather deep cup composed of coarse grass, dry stems and fibres, mixed with a few dry leaves; it is lined with fine grass, roots, or pine-needles. It is placed in bush undergrowth or more usually up in some tree, preferably a fir, often at a considerable height from the ground. Both sexes incubate the eggs.

The clutch consists normally of two or three eggs but rarely four or five are laid; in shape they are rather long ovals, with a fine texture and slight gloss. The ground-colour is a pale rather dingy greenish-blue, and the markings consist of blotches, spots, and freckles of liver-red and various shades of brown and purple; the markings are generally collected towards the larger end.

They measure about 1·11 by 0·78 inches.

THE NILGIRI LAUGHING-THRUSH

TROCHALOPTERON CACHINNANS (Jerdon)

(Plate iv, Fig. 4, opposite page 66)

Description.—Length 9 inches. Sexes alike. A broad white line over the eye, bordered above by a narrow black line and below by a black line through the eye; forehead and chin also black; whole upper plumage, wings, and tail olive-brown, the crown narrowly scaled with black, and the back of the head suffused with ashy; whole under surface bright rufous, duller on the flanks and posteriorly.

Iris red; bill and legs black.

Field Identification.—Only in Nilgiris; a dull-coloured bird, olive-brown above, rufous below, with black and white markings on the face; noisy and shy, in parties in heavy undergrowth.

Distribution.—Confined to the Nilgiris at elevations over 4500 feet. A resident species. A very similar species (*Trochalopteron jerdoni*) is represented by three hill races which are common respectively in the Brahmagherries (*T. j. jerdoni*), North Travancore (*T. j. fairbanki*) and South Travancore (*T. j. meridionale*).

Habits, etc.—This Laughing-Thrush is extremely common in the Nilgiris at all the higher elevations, as for instance at Coonoor and Kotagherry. It is found, like most of the genus, in parties which live in dense undergrowth and spend a large portion of their time on the ground searching for insects and fallen berries. It is particularly partial to the berries of the Brazil or Peruvian cherry, which has been introduced in the Nilgiris in recent times. This bird merits more than most of the family the title of Laughing-Thrush; there is something peculiarly human about the tones of its voice, and its call is certainly a laugh—a most "maniacal laugh" according to Hume. In demeanour the bird is very shy and evades observation.

The breeding season lasts from February to June.

The nest is a deep cup composed of fine twigs, moss, grass, dead leaves, and similar substances, and it is lined with moss roots, fibres, fine grass, wool, and fur. It is placed in the fork of a bush or tree at any height from the ground up to about 12 feet.

The clutch consists of two or three eggs. They are moderately broad ovals, somewhat pointed towards the small end, and of fine texture with a slight gloss. The ground-colour is a delicate pale blue which is speckled and blotched, rather sparingly, with reddish- or pinkish-brown, a few eggs having also blackish-brown spots and hair-lines, often rather cloudy at the edges.

The egg measures about 1·0 by 0·75 inches.

THE STREAKED LAUGHING-THRUSH

Trochalopteron lineatum (Vigors)

(Plate iii, Fig. 5, opposite page 44)

Description.—Length 8 inches. Sexes alike. Hoary-grey, more or less streaked throughout with reddish-brown, the shafts of the feathers being particularly conspicuous; ear-coverts, wings and tail bright reddish-brown, the tail with obsolete rayed markings, and each feather tipped with greyish-white, defined interiorly by a black line.

Iris brown; bill dusky, base of lower mandible steely-horn; feet fleshy-brown, claws livid-horny.

Field Identification.—Familiar garden bird in the Himalayas; a smallish bird with a broad floppy tail; grey and chestnut in colour, with pale streaking, appearing dark brown at any distance; skulks like a rat amongst low bush growth; movements jerky; utters a variety of squeaky notes. It must not be confused with the Striated Laughing-Thrush (*Grammoptila striata*), a bird of very similar appearance but larger and more arboreal, found throughout the Himalayas from Simla eastwards.

Distribution.—The Streaked Laughing-Thrush is found from the mountains of North Baluchistan to Chitral and Gilgit and thence along the whole of the Himalayas to Bhutan. Within this range it has been divided into five geographical races. Starting from the west, the Baluchistan bird, common at Ziarat, is known as *T. l. ziaratensis*. In Gilgit, Chitral and Northern Kashmir the race is termed *T. l. gilgit*, and this in turn gives place in Southern Kashmir to the typical race *T. l. lineatum*, which extends through the Punjab Himalayas to Garhwal and Kumaon. The Nepal and Sikkim birds are known as *T. l. setafer*, while the Bhutan bird has been separated as *T. l. imbricatum*. These races merely differ amongst themselves in degree of coloration both of the feathers and of their shafts. A resident species.

Habits, etc.—This familiar bird breeds throughout the hill ranges that it inhabits between about 5000 and 10,000 feet, occasionally ascending even a little higher. While not a migrant in any sense of the word, it tends to drift downhill during the winter months and then may be met with down to about 3000 feet and sometimes lower, as at Kohat. It may be described as a bird of the undergrowth, and provided that it has tangles of rank grass, thick bushes, or rocks combined with herbage in which to thread its secretive way, it is indifferent whether these are situated on open hill-sides or in the midst of heavy forest.

About the hill stations of the Western Himalayas, from the Galis and Kashmir across to Naini Tal and Almora, it is one of the most familiar of the station birds, living in the gardens and attracting attention by its chattering antics, and along the forest roads coming to notice by shuffling across the roads and up the bank sides in front of passers-by; in Lahul it even intrudes into the courtyards of houses. Further east it is much scarcer, and on its status there would not merit inclusion in this work.

This dull-coloured Laughing-Thrush lives both in pairs and in small parties of four or five individuals. The greater part of its life is lived within a height of 5 or 6 feet from the ground and it is practically never away from thick cover. It shuffles freely about on the ground after the manner of a large Hedge-Sparrow, working amongst the undergrowth and climbing up into the bushes; occasionally it is inspired with ambition and climbs from the bushes into thick and handy trees; but so ingrained is its parasitic devotion to Mother Earth that if it desires to proceed from one tree to another it will not fly across the open, parachuting on open wings to its foot like other Laughing-Thrushes; but it hastily drops from the first tree to the ground and thence works "in rushes, taking cover" to the base of the second tree and climbs it afresh. A party moving along or up and down the hill-side has the same tactics; one by one the individuals composing it "dribble" from cover to cover, now hopping rapidly along the ground for a yard or two, then feebly fluttering for another stretch. An extended flight must be virtually unknown to the bird. Yet with all these skulking ways and excess of caution it is in no sense shy until molested, and one may pass along a hill-path a yard or two away from an individual sitting on the hill-side and it will not bother to leave. In a bush it dips and bows, turning this way and that and incessantly flirting the heavy tail, as it utters a series of harsh squeaky notes *chit-chit-chitrr*, *chit-chit-chitrr*, *chicker-chicker* or *witti-kitti-cree*, or a soft murmuring churring note *crrer-r*.

The call-note is a loud, clear whistle *pitt-wee-are* or *titty-titty-we-are* much like that of other Laughing-Thrushes. This miscellaneous assortment of chattering squeaks together with the rustling of leaves usually indicate the presence of a party in cover where they are quite invisible; and these are amongst the most familiar bird sounds of the Western hill stations. The food is the usual mixture of insects, seeds, and small fruits common to most of the family.

The breeding season is very extended, and the bird is probably double-brooded. Eggs have been taken in every month from March to September, but most nests will be found in May and June. On the nest the bird sits very close, almost allowing itself to be caught.

The nest is a large, solid structure of dry grass, stems of herbaceous plants, fibrous shreds of bark, dead leaves, and similar materials. It is nearly circular, with a deep cup-like cavity in the centre, and this is neatly lined with fine grass roots, pine-needles or fine grass. It is always well concealed, and is placed in a thick branch of a tree, preferably perhaps a deodar, in a thick bush, or in heavy herbage on a steep bank; but it is very seldom higher than 5 or 6 feet from the ground and usually lower than that. On one occasion in Simla I found a nest owing to the strange choice of the birds in lining material. There was a coir doormat at the dining-room door leading into the verandah; and as we sat at lunch the birds kept coming and tearing fibres out of the mat in spite of the fact that the servants waiting on us were continuously passing backwards and forwards through the door.

Two to four eggs are laid, but the normal clutch consists of three eggs.

The eggs are regular and moderately broad ovals, with a slight gloss and a very smooth satiny texture. In colour they are a perfectly spotless, delicate, pale greenish-blue, of the tint usually known as "Hedge-Sparrow blue."

In size they average about 1·00 by 0·73 inches.

The nests of this species are often selected for the eggs of the Indian Cuckoo (*Cuculus micropterus*) and occasionally the Pied Crested Cuckoo (*Clamator jacobinus*).

THE JUNGLE BABBLER

TURDOIDES SOMERVILLEI (Sykes)

(Plate x, Fig. 5, opposite page 198)

Description.—Length 10 inches. Sexes alike. The whole upper plumage dull earth-brown marked with paler and darker tints of the same; tail broad and full, slightly tipped with white and faintly cross-rayed; lower plumage paler, mixed fulvous and ashy.

Iris pale yellowish white; bill flesh-coloured, gape yellowish; feet fleshy-white or yellowish-white.

Field Identification.—Found in noisy squeaking parties, usually on or close to the ground; a moderate-sized dirty-looking brown bird with a pale yellowish eye and a broad longish tail; all plumage very loose and untidy. One of the best-known birds of India.

Distribution.—The Jungle Babbler is found throughout the whole of the Peninsula of India from the Salt Range and Kohat in the north-west along the foot of the Himalayas to about the valley of the Brahmaputra in the north-east. It is divided into five races.

T. s. sindianus is a particularly pale race found in the Punjab and Sind down to Mount Aboo. *T. s. terricolor* is found throughout north and east India within a line drawn roughly through Meerut, Agra, Saugor, and Hyderabad to the Godavari delta. The typical race with a rufous tail is confined to a strip of the western coast from Bombay and Matheran to Kanara, below that grading into the dark *T. s. malabaricus* of Cochin and Travancore. A paler and greyer race, *T. s. orientalis*, occupies the rest of Southern India. A strictly resident species.

Habits, etc.—In the Jungle Babbler we have one of the few Indian birds which possesses a recognised popular name in both English and Hindustani, in both cases due to the social habits of the species. The vernacular name is "Sathbhai," the Seven Brethren, while in English for some reason (possibly their loquacity), the birds change their gender and become the "Seven Sisters." It is often wrongly assumed in consequence that the parties always consist of seven birds; but "sath" is only a reflection of the phrase "panch sath" (5 or 7), an approximate phrase like "half a dozen."

This bird is found throughout the plains and the hill ranges up to about 4000 feet in the north and higher in the south, but it is usually scarce both in thick forest and in wet marshy country. In the more desert portions of Sind and Rajputana it does not occur. With these exceptions it is found in all types of country, and apparently having a decided preference for the neighbourhood of man it is a common bird in gardens both in towns and out in the mofussil.

As indicated above, the Jungle Babbler is an eminently gregarious species, even to the extent that the parties in which it goes about do not break up in the breeding season. A sitting bird has only to be disturbed from its nest and the outcry that it invariably makes at once brings to the spot the other members of its clan. For in sorrow and in joy these Babblers are not divided; nor are they quiet. Although trees are a necessity for them, for when disturbed they immediately fly up into the branches, they feed for the most part on the ground, turning over dead leaves with incessant industry, all the while moving with a clumsy, hopping gait. As they do so they keep up a muttered concert of low remarks which at the slightest excitement break into a chorus of noisy, squeaking calls that aptly express their hysterical temperaments. Yet they are brave birds also, and at once rally to the support of any one of their number that is in difficulties, attacking his assailant. Although not in this respect quite as strong as the Large Grey Babbler (*Argya malcolmi*) they generally succeed in rescuing any of their party that falls into the clutches of the smaller hawks, who indeed treat them with respect. The captured bird grasps the assailant with its big, strong feet, and the remainder of the party fall on the latter pell-mell in a noisy, struggling mass till he is glad to let go his promised meal and decamp with the best grace possible. The flight is clumsy and ill-sustained, this species having the family habit of flying one by one for short distances from cover to cover.

The breeding season commences at the end of March and continues into September. The majority of nests, however, contain fresh eggs in the first week after the setting-in of the rains, which varies according to locality and season from 1st June to the 15th July.

The nest is built in thick bushes or small trees at almost any height from the ground, though most will be found 4 to 10 feet up. Thorn trees are commonly selected, and the nest is usually not particularly well concealed. It is a fairly deep cup, sometimes small and compact, but more usually rather loosely put together, of grass stems and roots. The lining consists of finer roots and occasionally of horse-hair.

The full clutch consists of three or four eggs.

The eggs are usually rather broad ovals, somewhat compressed at one end, of fine smooth texture with a high gloss. The colour is "Hedge-Sparrow blue," varying from a pale shade to a deep intense colour in different eggs. There are no markings.

The egg measures about 1·01 by 0·78 inches.

This bird is a favourite foster-parent for the Pied Crested Cuckoo (*Clamator jacobinus*) and the Common Hawk Cuckoo (*Hiërococcyx varius*), and it is difficult to distinguish between the eggs of host and parasite, so close is the resemblance.

THE WHITE-HEADED BABBLER

Turdoides striatus (Dumont)

Description.—Length 9 inches. Sexes alike. Upper surface of head and neck dingy greyish-white; upper plumage ashy-brown, streaked on the back with brown and white; wings and terminal half of the broad full tail dark brown; ear-coverts brown; chin, throat, and breast dark brown, the feathers edged with grey; remainder of lower plumage brown, fulvous down the centre of the abdomen.

Iris creamy-white; bill, eye-patch, and legs dead white with a yellowish tinge.

Field Identification.—Very similar in habits to the Jungle Babbler, but recognisable by its whitish head and dark brown throat and breast.

Distribution.—This species of Babbler is confined to Ceylon and Southern India, south of a line drawn through Belgaum, Hyderabad, and the lower Godavari Valley. The Indian birds are known as *T. s. affinis*, while the typical race from Ceylon differs in having the head concolorous with the back and the streaks on the back less well defined. It is a strictly resident species.

Habits, etc.—The White-headed Babbler is a plains species, and only ascends the various hill ranges up to a height of about 2000 feet. It is the Common Babbler of Madras, and in habits is very similar to the Jungle Babbler, going about in noisy, excitable parties that feed on the ground and fly up into the trees when disturbed. They hop and climb up the larger branches of the tree to the top, and then fly off to the next tree singly in extended file, with slow and laborious flight, a few rapid strokes of the short round wings alternating with gliding on outstretched pinions. The alarm forgotten, one bird drops again to the ground, followed in succession by the others of the flock, and once more they are busy turning over the leaves.

The call is a loud sibilant or whispering sort ot chatter.

The breeding season is somewhat extended and odd nests may be found almost any time in the year. The majority of eggs are, however, laid from March to July. The nest is the usual large, loosely-constructed cup of the genus, built of roots, fine twigs, and grass stems, and is built at no great height from the ground in shrubs and bushes, those of a thorny nature being preferred.

The clutch consists of three or four eggs; they are fairly regular ovals, fine and hard in texture and exceedingly glossy. In colour they are of a deep unmarked greenish-blue.

In size they average about 0·99 by 0·75 inches.

This is a favourite foster-parent for the Pied Crested Cuckoo (*Clamator jacobinus*).

THE COMMON BABBLER

ARGYA CAUDATA (Duméril)

(Plate iii, Fig. 4, opposite page 44)

Description.—Length 9 inches. Sexes alike. Whole upper plumage pale fulvous-brown, each feather streaked with dark brown; quills brown, lighter on the outer webs; tail long, graduated, and olive-brown, cross-rayed, and the shafts very dark; chin and throat fulvous-white; lower plumage pale fulvous, albescent on the abdomen, and the sides of the breast faintly striated.

Iris yellow-brown; bill light brown, base of lower mandible yellow; legs olive-yellow, claws dusky.

Field Identification.—A smallish bird, brown with dark streakings on the upper surface, and fulvous and whitish below; tail elongated and graduated. In flight looks singularly like a miniature hen Pheasant. Lives in parties in every type of open ground with bushes or grass clumps; one of the commonest birds of Northern India.

Distribution.—The Common Babbler extends from Afghanistan, Baluchistan, and South-east Persia right through India, from the outer fringe of the Himalayas east to Western Bengal and south to the Palni Hills and Rameswaram Island. With this wide range it has been divided into three races. The large and pale form from Afghanistan, Baluchistan, and South-east Persia is known as *A. c. huttoni*; a dark form with heavy streaking on the upper surface and brightly rufous under parts named by Hume *A. c. eclipes*, inhabits the plateau from Rawal Pindi and the Salt Range to Peshawar; and the rest of the range is inhabited by the typical form.

This species does not occur higher than 4000 feet in the Outer Himalayas and it avoids the higher elevations in all the continental hill ranges. In Southern India it is less common and very local. A strictly resident species.

Habits, etc.—This bird avoids swampy ground, where it is replaced throughout Northern India by a more richly-coloured and larger species, the Striated Babbler (*Argya earlii*), in which the chin and throat are rufous with dark streaks. It also dislikes heavy forest and hill areas except those low elevations within easy reach of their bases. It is essentially a bird of open country, and in Northern India is one of the most common and familiar of species found everywhere alike, in cultivation and in gardens, amongst waste rocky ravines studded with bushes, and in the desolate semi-desert areas; ground cover is the only factor that it insists upon, for it is somewhat of a skulker and prefers the neighbourhood of the ground, seldom mounting into trees or venturing right out into the open. It particularly favours those wide open plains where patches of cultivation shaded with occasional tamarisk and kikur trees alternate with stretches of waste ground on which clumps of sarpat grass and bushes of the uck and the wild caper ring their monotonous changes.

This Babbler lives in small parties of six or eight individuals and such parties may be met with throughout the year, even in the breeding season. They feed mostly on the ground, hopping rapidly about with a bouncing gait, and their long tails trailing. At the slightest alarm they take refuge in the bushes or grass near whose shelter they have been feeding. When leaving one patch of cover for another they fly off singly, one after another, with a weak parachuting flight, the wings extended, and the tail partly spread,

PLATE III

1. Variegated Laughing-Thrush. 2. Yellow-eyed Babbler. 3. Purple Sunbird. 4. Common Babbler. 5. Streaked Laughing-Thrush. (All about $\frac{4}{10}$ nat. size.)

[*Face p.* 44

looking for all the world like a number of miniature hen Pheasants breaking cover. As they fly they utter a low undertoned warbling whistle, first one bird and then another in a sort of rippling chorus.

The food consists chiefly of insects.

The breeding season is very extended, and nests have been found in every month of the year; but the majority will be found from March until May and again from July to September, as the species is double-brooded. The nest is a neat and compact cup, rather large for the size of the bird. There is usually a deep outer foundation of fine thorny twigs, coarse roots, bents, grass stems, and similar materials, while the actual cup is composed of finer grass stems and roots, often lined with a few hairs or fine mimosa leaves. It is usually built fairly close to the ground at a height of about 3 feet, in a thick bush or a clump of grass, and is generally well concealed. An occasional nest, however, may be found in higher and more open situations, as for instance 8 feet from the ground in a fork of a kikur tree.

The usual clutch consists of three or four eggs, but occasionally only two are laid.

The eggs are a moderately elongated oval, slightly compressed towards one end. They are glossy, often brilliantly so, and of a delicate pure spotless somewhat pale blue. There is very little variation in the colour of these eggs.

They measure about 0·85 by 0·63 inches.

This Babbler is frequently selected as a foster-parent by the Pied Crested Cuckoo (*Clamator jacobinus*).

THE LARGE GREY BABBLER

ARGYA MALCOLMI (Sykes)

Description.—Lengtn 11 inches. Sexes alike. Upper plumage dull brown, the feathers of the upper back with dark centres; forehead ashy-grey with fine white shaft-stripes; wings dark brown, the outer flight-feathers hoary brown on the outer webs, the others edged with the colour of the back; entire lower plumage fulvescent grey; tail full and graduated, pale brown, the central pair of feathers cross-rayed, the three outer pairs white and the next pair edged with white.

Iris bright yellow; bill dark brown, lower mandible fleshy; legs fleshy-yellow.

Field Identification.—In noisy squeaky parties in cpen cultivation; a typical sandy-brown Babbler easily recognised from the other species by its size and the broad white edge to the tail, conspicuous in flight.

Distribution.—This fine Babbler is locally common throughout the greater portion of the plains of India from a line roughly through Ludhiana, Ferozepore, and Mount Aboo in the North-west to the western boundary of Bengal, and south to the Nilgiris and Salem. It is a strictly resident species.

Habits, etc.—This Babbler does not differ in any material respect in habits from the more numerous Jungle Babbler, though it is not quite so untidy in plumage. It is particularly a bird of cultivated plains where small groves alternate with open fields and it is never found away from trees. It appears also in gardens, both in large towns and about small villages. Half of its time is spent in the trees, the other half on the ground, where it turns over dead leaves and investigates low-growing foliage in search of the insect and other small forms of life that form the major portion of its diet; seeds and fruits are also eaten.

This is one of the most gregarious species that it is possible to imagine. The birds live in small parties of six to a dozen individuals, and these parties do not break up in the breeding season, even though members of them may have nests and eggs in the vicinity. Woe to any enemy that falls foul of one of the party; the remainder fall on it tooth and nail, and in this respect the species is more valiant even than the Jungle Babbler, a fact that the smaller hawks recognise, generally not attempting to molest them. These Babblers are very noisy, with the hysterical squeaky calls typical of the family uttered on the slightest provocation.

The nest may be found in any month in the year, though the majority of the birds breed from March until August. Possibly more than one brood is reared. The nest is built at a height of some 4 to 10 feet from the ground and is usually ill-concealed, depending for its protection more on the fact that it is generally placed in some thorny tree of the mimosa type. It is a large, loosely-woven but fairly neat, cup-shaped structure, made of fine roots, small sticks, and dry grass, with generally an outer casing of thorny twigs. The cup is sometimes lined with fine grass and roots or horse-hair.

Two to five eggs are laid, but the normal clutch consists of four. The eggs are indistinguishable from those of the Jungle Babbler, rather broad ovals, compressed at one end, very glossy and smooth in texture, and an unmarked " Hedge-Sparrow blue " in colour.

They measure about 0·99 by 0·77 inches.

This Babbler is frequently selected as a foster-parent by the Pied Crested Cuckoo (*Clamator jacobinus*).

THE DECCAN SCIMITAR-BABBLER

POMATORHINUS HORSFIELDII Sykes

(Plate v, Fig. 2, opposite page 88)

Description.—Length 10 inches. Sexes alike. Upper plumage dark earthy-brown tinged with rufous and darker on the head; a white eyebrow-line edged above with black over the eye; sides of head and neck and a band bordering the breast and abdomen blackish-brown; chin, throat, breast, and abdomen white; flanks and a patch under the tail slaty-brown.

Iris brown or crimson; bill yellow, dusky at base of upper mandible; legs greenish-plumbeous.

Bill long, curved and compressed, recalling a scimitar in shape; short rounded wings; long graduated tail; shape rather ungainly.

Field Identification.—Lower India only. Scimitar-shaped bill, dark plumage with the conspicuous white eyebrow and white plastron with its dark edging are distinctive.

Distribution.—Confined to the Indian Peninsula and Ceylon. This Scimitar-Babbler is divided into a number of races distinguished by small details of coloration of the plumage and size of the bill. A greyish form *P. h. obscurus* is found in Mount Aboo, the Central Provinces and the area round Khandesh. The typical race is found from Khandala to Goa, in Mysore and in Orissa and the Upper Eastern Ghats. The rich olive-brown form *P. h. travancoreensis* occupies the Lower Western Ghats from North Kanara to Travancore, including the Nilgiris. *P. h. maderaspatensis* is confined to the Lower Eastern Ghats from the Krishna Valley southwards. *P. h. melanurus* of the low country wet zone, S.W. Ceylon, is a bright ferruginous bird, while *P. h. holdsworthi* is a more olivaceous brown and inhabits the dry zone of both low country and hills.

This species occurs both in the plains and in the hill ranges up to at least 8000 feet. It is strictly resident.

Habits, etc.—This Scimitar-Babbler is common in evergreen jungle, in bamboo thickets, in thorny scrub or in dense bush jungle on hill-sides. It is usually found in pairs or in small parties of four or five birds and sometimes double this number collect together or join the mixed hunting parties.

Individuals keep in touch with each other by a variety of mellow bubbling and whistling calls and when excited break into the torrent of loud shrieks and whistles which are used by all the Scimitar-Babblers. In the case of pairs the male acts as leader and is followed about from one bush or tree to another by the female who acknowledges every one of his musical whistles with a subdued *kroo-kroo* or *kro-kant*.

Although very shy and seldom showing themselves they readily respond to a decoy whistle and may be called long distances by such an imitation. When disturbed the birds hop along the branches with great agility as if to get under way before taking to wing.

The food consists of grubs, worms, insects and the like and in search of it the birds descend a good deal to the ground where they turn over the dead leaves in typical Babbler fashion. They cut and dig vigorously with their shapely bills in the earth, cling to the face of banks and probe the moss and bark of the trees, and when the cotton-tree is in flower they join the many species that rifle the blossoms for insects and nectar.

The breeding season extends from December to May.

The nest is a loosely-constructed globular structure, with the entrance at one side, placed on the ground in thick herbage or low in a bush. It is composed of grass or moss mixed with leaves, bracken, and roots, and is so flimsy in build that it falls to pieces on removal. There is no lining to the egg cavity.

Three to five eggs are laid.

The egg is an elongated oval, slightly compressed towards the small end. It is very fragile, smooth, and satiny in texture, with very little gloss. The colour is pure white.

The egg measures about 1·08 by 0·77 inches.

THE RUSTY-CHEEKED SCIMITAR-BABBLER

Pomatorhinus erythrogenys Vigors

Description.—Length 11 inches. Sexes alike. Upper plumage, tail, and the exposed part of the closed wings olive-brown; centre of whole lower plumage white, striped with very pale grey on the chin and throat; forehead, sides of head and neck and sides of lower plumage chestnut, washed with olive on the sides of the breast and flanks.

Iris yellowish-white; bill light horny; legs brownish-fleshy.

Bill long, curved, and compressed, recalling a scimitar in shape. Tail long and graduated; wings small and rounded; general build rather ungainly.

Field Identification.—Himalayan form. Curved bill, olive-brown upper parts and chestnut and white under parts distinctive, combined with shy habits in undergrowth and melodious call.

Distribution.—The Rusty-cheeked Scimitar-Babbler has a wide distribution, being found along the whole length of the Himalayas through Assam, Burma, and Tenasserim to Yunnan and China. It is divided into several races, of which two are found in the

Himalayas and come into our area. The Western race is the typical one and is found from the Murree Hills to about Mussoorie. The Eastern race is known as *P. e. haringtoni* and differs in its slightly smaller size and in having the whole chin, throat, and upper breast dark ashy mingled with white. It is found from Garhwal to Sikkim, but the birds from the western edge of this range are very intermediate in character.

In the Western Himalayas this Scimitar-Babbler is found most commonly between 3000 and 7000 feet, though it certainly occurs down to 2000 feet and up to 10,000 feet. The Eastern form occupies a slightly lower zone between 1000 and 7000 feet. It is a strictly resident species and appears to change its elevation very slightly with the season.

The Slaty-headed Scimitar-Babbler (*Pomatorhinus schisticeps*) is another Himalayan species found at low elevations from Kangra to Assam and into Burma. The upper parts are olive-brown with the top of the head dark-slate; a white line over the eye and the rich maroon-chestnut sides with white streaks are distinctive.

Habits, etc.—This bird is a dweller in dense undergrowth, whether in the form of thick grass and bushes on treeless hill-sides, or forests with heavy secondary growth. The greater part of its life is spent in the bushes, but it feeds a good deal on the ground under cover, shuffling amongst dead leaves, and when disturbed in this occupation it can make off at a good speed with a succession of long, bounding hops like a rat. It is a social species, usually found in small parties, whose presence would not be suspected from their skulking habits were it not for their noisiness. The call of the male consists of a pair of notes, the second rapidly following the first and being about an octave lower. If the female is within earshot, as she usually is, she replies with a single note immediately after the second note uttered by the male, so that the three notes together make a mellow whistle *kor-quee-oh*, which to the uninitiated sounds like the call of a single bird. This familiar duet, varied with a clear *quoip*, is audible some distance away. They have also a hard, scolding note reminiscent of that uttered by many of the Babblers and the Tree-Pie. A faint feeding-note *tep-tep* is only heard when the birds are close at hand. These birds respond readily to an imitation of their calls and may be decoyed in this manner. They seldom leave cover and come into the open, but when they do take to wing the flight is swift and strong, though the short wings combined with the heavy bill and tail give the bird a curious, ungainly appearance. This species is said to indulge in a habit of dancing like other members of the genus.

The food consists of grubs, beetles, earthworms, and various insects mostly obtainable on the ground, but berries are also eaten.

The breeding season lasts from April to June.

The nest is a domed structurewith a broad opening high on one side; it is loosely constructed of coarse grass, dry ferns, dead leaves, and fern roots, and there is no particular lining. It is placed on the ground in thick herbage near the edge of clumps of brushwood or scrub-jungle.

Two to four eggs are laid; they are long, narrow ovals, fine in texture with a fair gloss and pure white in colour.

In size they average about 1·11 by 0·8 inches.

THE RUFOUS-BELLIED BABBLER

Dumetia hyperythra (Franklin)

Description.—Length 5 inches. Sexes alike. Front half of crown reddish-brown; upper plumage, wing, and tail olive-brown, the tail cross-rayed; sides of the face and entire lower plumage bright fulvous.

Iris light-brown; bill livid pale horny; legs very pale fleshy.

The feathers of the forehead have stiff shafts. The tail is much graduated, the outer feather only reaching to the middle.

Field Identification.—A small olive-brown bird with bright rufous under parts; a white throat-patch in one race. Found in small parties skulking in thick cover.

Distribution.—Confined to India and Ceylon and divided into three races. The typical race is found in a wide area east of a line from the Kumaon Bhabar through Jhansi, Mhow, the Satpuras, Jalna, and Hyderabad to the Krishna River. It occurs as far east as Midnapore. To the west and south of this area, from Sambhar and Mount Aboo on the north down to the extreme south, it is replaced by *D. h. albogularis*. This race differs in its lighter coloration and in having a well-defined white patch on the chin and throat and a tinge of white on the centre of the abdomen. *D. h. phillipsi* of Ceylon is similar to the latter but has a larger bill and paler under parts.

The closely allied Red-capped Babbler (*Timalia pileata*) is common in the extensive grass plains along the terais and duars of the north-east, extending also into Assam and Burma and a considerable part of Bengal. The deep rufous crown, white streak over each eye, olive-brown upper parts, deeply-graduated tail, and the white breast with fine black streaking are distinctive.

Habits, etc.—The Rufous-bellied Babbler is a bird of thick cover. It may be found in scrub-jungle, in tall grass interspersed with thorn bushes, or in the patches and hedges of tall euphorbia plants which are a feature of many parts of Southern India. In such cover it is found in small parties of four to eight birds, which keep up a low *cheep cheep*, varied by harsh tittering notes. It is a most inveterate skulker, keeping as far as possible out of sight, one bird following another from bush to bush. On taking alarm the members of a party promptly dive into the thickest portions of the undergrowth and disperse in all directions, though they soon reassemble when the alarm is over.

The breeding season of the typical race is well defined throughout its range, being in the monsoon from June to August. Most eggs are laid in July. In the other Indian race it varies from the middle of April to the middle of October, irrespective of locality.

The nest is built on, or very close to, the ground, either amongst dead leaves, in coarse grass, or in small bushes. A favourite situation is in amongst the roots of a bamboo clump. The nest is a loosely-constructed ball of bamboo leaves or broad blades of grass, sometimes incorporating a few dead leaves. It is occasionally unlined. Usually, however, there is a slight lining of fine grass roots, fine grass stems, or a few hairs. The entrance is in the side. An unfinished nest is deserted on very slight provocation.

The usual clutch consists of four eggs, but often there are only three. The eggs vary in shape from short and broad to moderately long ovals. The texture is fine with a variable amount of gloss. The ground-colour is pure white, spotted and speckled with shades of red, brownish-red, and reddish-purple. These markings vary in character, but tend to collect in a cap or zone on the broad end.

The egg measures about 0·70 by 0·53 inches.

THE YELLOW-EYED BABBLER

Chrysomma sinensis (Gmelin)

(Plate iii, Fig. 2, opposite page 44)

Description.—Length 7 inches. Sexes alike. The whole upper plumage rufescent-brown, changing to cinnamon on the exposed portions of the wings; a patch in front above and below the eye, and the whole lower plumage white, tinged with fulvous on the flanks, abdomen, and under the tail. The tail is long and graduated, and the feathers are faintly cross-rayed.

Iris yellow, eyelids deep orange; bill black, yellowish behind nostrils; legs pale orange-yellow.

Field Identification.—A small rufous bird with white under parts and a rather long full tail; orange eyelids are conspicuous. Found in parties in undergrowth.

Distribution.—The Yellow-eyed Babbler is a bird of very wide distribution occurring throughout India, Burma, and Siam, and in China, but is rather local. As is to be expected with this wide range it has been divided into several races, of which three occur within our area. They are distinguished by depth and tint of coloration.

The typical race, originally described from China, is found through Yunnan, Siam, Burma, and Assam to Bengal, and apparently also in Madras, the Central Provinces, and Belgaum.

A dark form, *P. s. saturatior*, occurs in Nepal, Sikkim, and the Bhutan and Buxa Duars.

A pale form, *P. s. hypoleucus*, is found in Sind, Jodhpur, the North-west Frontier Province, portions of the Punjab, the United Provinces, Khandesh, and Kathiawar. While strictly speaking a plains bird, the Yellow-eyed Babbler is found along the outer Himalayas to a height of 4000 feet, and in the Nilgiris it is found up to 5000 feet. A resident species everywhere.

Habits, etc.—While occasionally met with in pairs this pretty little bird usually goes about in parties. It avoids forest and wanders about in open country frequenting tall grass, low scrub, and patches of bushes, being also a familiar garden bird. In habits it is a typical Babbler, and while rather inclined to skulk in thick cover is apt to be noisy. It appears to visit the ground very seldom. Some of its notes are quite sweet, and might almost be dignified by the name of song.

Small birds that live in parties in thick cover have all much the same habits. The individuals work from stem to stem unseen down in the thicket, picking insects, caterpillars, and their eggs from the leaves and twigs. Then one bird works to the top and suns itself for a few seconds and utters a snatch of song before plunging again into the cover below, while another bird in turn emerges for his breath of air and sunlight.

I have seen a bird at the nest feign in a most realistic manner to be wounded, swaying with wings and tail outspread on a twig, as if about to topple over and fall at any moment.

The breeding season is from June to September.

The nest is a very compact and beautiful structure, made of broad blades of grass and long strips of fine fibrous bark, coated exteriorly with cobwebs and gossamer threads and lined with fine grass stems and roots. It is generally built in gardens about 4 to 6 feet from the ground in upright forks in hedges or trees, or suspended in thick grass stems after the fashion of a Reed-Warbler's nest.

The normal clutch consists of five eggs.

The egg is a very broad oval, rather obtuse at the smaller end. The texture is fine and smooth with a slight gloss. The ground-colour is pinkish-white, and the markings are of two main types; in one the egg is so thickly and finely mottled and streaked all over with brickdust-red that the ground-colour is almost concealed; in the other the egg is sparingly and boldly blotched and streaked with the same colour, besides exhibiting a number of pale inky-purple clouds. Combinations of both types occur.

The egg measures about 0·73 by 0·59 inches.

THE SPOTTED BABBLER

PELLORNEUM RUFICEPS Swainson

(Plate xi, Fig. 4, opposite page 220)

Description.—Length 6 inches. Sexes alike. Top of the head dull rufous; a whitish line over the eye; remainder of upper plumage including wings and tail olive-brown, the tail-feathers tipped with white; sides of the head pale rufous marked with black and brown; lower plumage white somewhat tinged with fulvous and becoming olivaceous on the flanks, boldly streaked with black on the breast and sides; a patch under the tail olive-brown and white.

Iris reddish-brown; bill dark brown, lower mandible whitish; legs fleshy-white.

Field Identification.—A small olive-brown bird, whitish below, with a rufous cap and heavily streaked breast. Very shy and found skulking in thick undergrowth. Attention usually attracted to it by the loud call-note.

Distribution.—Widely distributed throughout India, Assam, and Burma, eastwards to the Malay Peninsula, Annam, and Cochin-China. It is divided into several races, of which we are concerned with four; these vary only in depth and tone of coloration and the boldness of marking on the sides of the neck. *P. r. punctatum* occurs in the Western Himalayas from Dharmsala to Garhwal. It is common in the Tea gardens and in the ravines around Dehra Dun, where it also breeds. From Nepal eastwards along the Himalayas into Assam and Burma there is *P. r. mandellii.* The species appears to be wanting across the plains of Northern India, but the typical form is found in Peninsular India south of Khandesh, Pachmarhi, and the hills of Chota Nagpur, until in Travancore it is replaced by *P. r. granti.* All the races are found at elevations from 1500 to 4000 feet, and occasionally higher, and are resident birds.

Habits, etc.—The Spotted Babbler is more often heard than seen. Except in the breeding season it is a social species, and usually goes about in small parties which keep to low brushwood and bamboo-jungle. It never ascends into trees, and spends much of its life on the ground searching for food amongst fallen leaves and tangles of grass. In such localities it is hard to approach and observe as it is very shy, and the sound of footsteps sends it hastening away through the bushes with a harsh, churring alarm note *kraa.* But feeding at their ease the parties are rather noisy, and keep up a continuous chatter, and the loud call is a familiar sound of the jungles where they live. The call is a clear mellow whistle, *wheat-eeer* or *threĕ-chēēēr*, the first syllable short, the second long and emphasised. This call may also be expressed by the words *pretty-dear*. It is easily imitated, and the bird responds freely to the imitation. There is also a sweet song in the breeding season consisting of a number of loud whistling notes rambling up and down the scale. The food consists chiefly of insects.

The breeding season is from March to May, though second broods may be found until August. The nest is placed on the ground under the shelter of a stone or bush, or occasionally 2 or 3 inches above it in the base of a clump of bamboo. It is generally amongst fallen leaves and similar rubbish, and is a large globular structure composed of leaves and grass and slightly lined with moss roots.

The clutch consists of two to four eggs. In shape they are broad regular ovals, compact and fine in texture, with a slight gloss. The ground-colour is a very pale greenish- or yellowish-white, profusely speckled and spotted all over with reddish-brown and with secondary spots of pale grey and neutral tint.

The average size is about 0·88 by 0·65 inches.

THE QUAKER-BABBLER

Alcippe poioicephala (Jerdon)

Description.—Length 6 inches. Sexes alike. Top of head ashy-grey; remainder of upper plumage olive-brown, becoming ferruginous on the wings and tail; sides of the head and neck ashy-brown; lower plumage creamy fulvous, darker on the breast and flanks and under the tail.

Iris slaty-grey; bill horny brown; legs greyish-fleshy.

Field Identification.—A small olive-brown bird with paler under parts and a greyer head. Found in small parties in undergrowth and forest chiefly in the hills of Peninsular India.

Distribution.—Widely distributed in several races through India, Assam, Burma, and Siam. The typical and most richly-coloured form is found along the Western Ghats from about Goa down to the south of Travancore, occurring at elevations from 2000 feet to 600 feet. A paler and greyer race, *A. p. brucei*, occurs irregularly in the rest of the Peninsula south of a line from Kathiawar, Pachmarhi, and Parasnath Hill at much the same elevations. A resident species.

The smaller Nepal Babbler (*Alcippe nepalensis*), common in the lower Eastern Himalayas, Assam, and Burma, is easily distinguished by a white ring round the eye and a blackish line over it.

Abbott's Babbler (*Malacocincla sepiaria*) is found in the Eastern Himalayas and Assam at low elevations. The plumage is dark brown with the under parts paler, the throat white and a rufous patch under the tail. Although a forest bird and a skulker it is confiding and tame.

Habits, etc.—There is very little to say about the habits of the Quaker-Babbler. It is an undistinguished little bird which goes about in parties of four or five individuals up to twenty or more which are confiding enough when undisturbed but shy and wary once their suspicions are aroused. They keep principally to patches of forest, but may also be found in bush-jungle, orange groves, and similar localities. They seldom or never visit the ground, and prefer as a rule to keep to undergrowth. They frequently, however, climb higher into the trees, ascending even to the topmost branches. The members of a party act independently of each other, but keep up a general communication amongst themselves by continually calling and answering as they move about. The song is of four or five quavering whistling notes of the tone-quality of the Magpie Robin's effort; it is repeated every few seconds as the bird moves about the foliage. Little seems to be recorded about their food, but the parties spend all their time searching the leaves for insects.

The breeding season seems to be very poorly defined, and nests of the typical race are said to have been found in every month of the year. The Quaker-Babbler may be double-brooded, as January to April and again July, August and September are the principal months in which nests have been recorded.

The nest is usually built in the depths of forest, and in such shady spots is built in small trees or bushes at a height of some 4 to 8 feet from the ground. It is deep and cup-shaped, composed externally of moss and dead leaves, and lined with the fine roots of mosses and ferns. The nest is usually fixed in a fork or suspended from two or three twigs, and is as a rule quite conspicuous, little effort at concealment being attempted.

The clutch consists of two or occasionally three eggs.

The egg is a moderately broad oval, somewhat compressed towards the small end. The shell is fine and somewhat glossy. The ground-colour is pale salmon marked with primary blotches and broad smudges of deep purple-brown or purple-black, with secondary markings of pale grey, inky-grey or purplish-grey. There is a good deal of variation, the markings often being reduced in size to specks and spots, while short lines and hieroglyphs are common.

The egg measures about 0·80 by 0·60 inches.

THE BLACK-HEADED BABBLER

Rhopocichla atriceps (Jerdon)

Description.—Length 5 inches. Sexes alike. The whole of the top and sides of the head black; the whole upper plumage fulvous brown; wings dark brown with the exposed parts fulvous brown; tail brown; lower plumage dull white, changing to olivaceous on the flanks and under the tail.

Iris yellow; bill dull greyish flesh-colour, the upper surface black; legs pinkish-grey to pale plumbeous.

Fig. 9—Black-headed Babbler ($\frac{4}{5}$ nat. size)

Field Identification.—Hills of South-western India. A small bird, brown above and whitish below with a more or less black cap, which is found in parties in dense forest undergrowth.

Distribution.—The typical form with a black head is found along the Western Ghats from Belgaum to the Nilgiris, being replaced in the Cochin and Travancore Hills by another race *R. a. bourdilloni* which has the black largely replaced by sooty-brown. A third race *R. a. nigrifrons* is found in Ceylon. This has the top of the head the same colour as the back and the black is confined to a broad band through each eye joining across the forehead. All three races occur from sea-level up to 6000 feet and are strictly resident.

Habits, etc.—This quaint little bird must soon be known to all who spend much time in the forests of Coorg and the Wynaad, the Nilgiris and Travancore. It is very common in the dense marshy jungles or in the heavy green thickets that border the streams, in cane-beds and in bamboo-jungle and it is also a bird of the evergreen forest. It does not as a rule ascend the trees but keeps to the undergrowth and no thicket is too dense for it, though it has something of a preference for the edges of roads and paths and clearings. In such cover the Black-headed Babbler goes about in parties of five to ten birds or even in troops of anything up to a couple of dozen individuals. The flocks are found throughout the year and their members are exceedingly active. As they move about the birds utter a continual low chattering, a harsh rather subdued *chur-r chur-r* and a characteristic habit is for a bird that has ventured too high in the vegetation to drop perpendicularly like a falling leaf into the thickets below at the slightest hint of an alarm. The food consists of insects and their larvæ.

This species is remarkable for the habit of building "cock-nests" which are apparently intended for roosting purposes. Dozens of such nests may be found at all times of the year in the jungles where the birds are common, for no effort is made to conceal them. They are very loosely and untidily constructed, thick masses of bamboo leaves with the entrance at the side and they never seem to be lined.

The true nest is much smaller and more tightly and neatly woven and it has a lining of black rootlets or fine grass. It is also much more carefully concealed, being placed in tangles of reeds and grass, in thick creepers or in bushes, usually only a foot or two from the ground. These nests also may be found in any month of the year, but the breeding season proper is said to be from May to July in the Nilgiris and a little earlier in Travancore.

The clutch consists of two eggs.

The egg is a moderately broad, very regular oval, only slightly compressed towards the smaller end. The shell is fine and satiny but has only a slight gloss. The ground-colour is white or faintly greyish-white, profusely speckled with minute dots of brownish and purplish-red, the dots being slightly more numerous towards the larger end.

It measures about 0·75 by 0·55 inches.

THE BLACK-HEADED SIBIA

Leioptila capistrata (Vigors)

(Plate v, Fig. 4, opposite page 88)

Description.—Length 9 inches. Sexes alike. Top and sides of the head black with a bushy crest; the whole of the body plumage bright rufous except the back between the wings which is greyish-brown; wings variegated bluish-grey, black and rufous with a white bar across the coverts; tail long and graduated, black with a broad sooty-grey tip, all feathers with a rufous base diminishing rapidly from the centre to the sides.

Iris reddish-brown; bill black; legs fleshy-brown.

Field Identification.—Himalayan form. A graceful rufous bird with dark crest, wings, and tail; purely arboreal and, except when breeding, in small parties; active and noisy.

Distribution.—This species is found throughout the Himalayas from the Hazara country to the Dafla Hills. It is divided into three races. The large and pale typical race is found in the western portion of this range to about Naini Tal. In Nepal it is replaced by *L. c. nigriceps* which is more rusty-red in tone and has the back reddish-brown. It is also somewhat smaller. This form grades through Sikkim and the Chumbi Valley into *L. c. baileyi* of Bhutan and Southern Tibet. This has the back sooty-brown tinged with grey. It is a strictly resident species except for some seasonal altitudinal movements. It breeds about 6000 to 9000 feet and in winter wanders down to 4000 feet.

Habits, etc.—The Sibia is a very common bird in portions of its range, as for instance at Simla and Darjeeling, where its striking appearance and ringing call attract the attention of many who are not naturalists. It is a purely arboreal species, spending most of its time at heights of 20 to 50 feet from the ground, and only rarely descending to the undergrowth. Out of the breeding season it is commonly found in parties of half a dozen birds, which usually keep to themselves but sometimes join the mixed hunting parties temporarily.

They are very active birds, running and gliding through tangles of creepers, and are also accomplished gymnasts, clinging to slender stems, head downwards, to probe the blossoms for insects. Superficially they greatly resemble the Laughing-Thrushes. They have the same habit of flitting very rapidly up a tree from branch to branch, keeping close to and partly hidden by the trunk, but they are more ready to fly from bough to bough and tree to tree and are by no means such skulkers. They come freely into the open and often launch into mid-air in open spaces amongst the trees to catch insects on the wing; but being naturally shy they disappear again into cover at the least alarm.

The plumage is not quite so loose and fluffy in appearance as that of the Laughing-Thrushes. The crest is generally held raised. The flight is heavy with a hard noisy beat of the wings, and is rather erratic and jerky as if the bird had difficulty in keeping straight. There is a characteristic habit of flying to a tree-trunk and clinging to the bark while picking some insect or larva from it.

The Sibia has a variety of notes. In winter when the birds are in parties they converse continuously with a faint *ti-te-te* note, or a little chittering sound similar to that of a Tit, uttered in concert by several of the party, some concealed in the foliage, others exposed to view on open boughs where they perch, jerking their tails suddenly up and down and occasionally flicking the wings, turning from side to side, eternally restless. A loud scolding note *tchaa-tchaa* appears to be an alarm note. During the breeding season the woods resound with their loud ringing whistle *titteree-titteree-tweeye*, which has an astonishing thrill of joy and gladness in it.

The breeding season lasts from May to August, but most birds do not nest till the rains have commenced.

The nest is a neat cup of green moss lined with black moss roots, grass, pine-needles, or fibres. It is built at heights from 10 to 50 feet from the ground in deodars, hollies, and other trees, and is often well concealed close to the trunk or in foliage; a favourate situation is also in briers and creepers overgrowing a tree.

The clutch consists of two or three eggs. They are rather broad ovals elongated at one end; the texture is fine and there is very little gloss. The ground-colour is pale greenish-white or pale bluish-green.

The markings consist of splashes, smears, and blotches of pale and dark brownish-red with a few defined spots and hair-lines of reddish-black.

In size they average about 0·98 by 0·68 inches.

THE STRIPED-THROATED SIVA

Siva strigula Hodgson

Description.—Length 7 inches. Sexes alike. Head orange-brown; upper plumage slate-green; below bright yellow, the chin pale yellow separated from the breast by a band of white feathers with narrow crescentic cross bars; moustachial streak and patch on either side of the neck black, wings black, the first primaries edged with yellow turning to orange near the base, inner feathers broadly marked with grey on outer edge and tipped with white; a black patch at base of the primaries; tail black, middle pair with chestnut-red at base, outer feathers edged and broadly tipped with yellow.

Iris reddish-brown; bill dark brown above, paler below; tip white; legs grey.

Field Identification.—A bird about the size of a Bulbul, frequenting rather open forest or woodland (not conifers) in small parties or pairs, in the spring. General colour yellowish with several narrow crescentic black cross-bars on the throat. These cross-bars are characteristic of the bird.

Distribution.—The Striped-throated Siva extends from Duala Dhar in the Kangra district of the Punjab Himalayas to Assam and Yunnan, south through Burma to Siam and the Malay Peninsula. This species has been divided into several races and, in addition to the typical *Siva s. strigula* of the Eastern Himalayas from Nepal to Assam, there is a western race, *S. s. simlænsis*, with paler head, greyer back and the chestnut on the tail more restricted. Another small babbler of similar size and habits is the Blue-winged Siva (*Siva cyanuroptera*) in which the head is bluish-grey streaked with dark blue, back, wing coverts and rump ochraceous, wings and tail appear blue and are tipped with white, throat and breast vinous grey merging into yellowish-white on belly. It is not so widely distributed, inhabiting the Himalayas, Naini Tal to the Chin Hills in Burma, breeding between 3000 and 8000 feet and moving rather lower in winter. It nests in thick evergreen forests of oak, pines and rhododendrons.

Habits, etc.—This beautiful bird breeds from 7000 to 10,000 feet and possibly even 12,000 feet and in autumn most birds are met with between 4000 and 9000 feet. They go about in small parties hunting amongst the tops of broad leaves and shrubs for insects which are their principal food. There is no song except a three-noted rather melancholy call note uttered at fairly regular intervals. In the Eastern parts of the range they are sometimes met with in the pine, as well as evergreen forests. In autumn, when the leaves of the deciduous trees change colour, the yellow plumage of this Siva blends extraordinarily well with the leaves, and their subdued call notes are reminiscent of a party of babblers.

The breeding season is May and June, and the nest is generally placed in a bush or small tree, some 4 to 12 feet from the ground. It is cup-shaped of moss roots and leaves and lined with roots.

The eggs resemble a miniature Song Thrush's.

The average size is about 0·85 by 0·63 inches.

THE RED-BILLED LEIOTHRIX

LEIOTHRIX LUTEA (Scopoli)

(Plate iv, Fig. 5, opposite page 66)

Description.—Length 6 inches. Male: The whole upper plumage dull olive-green, the throat and breast bright orange-yellow; remainder of lower plumage mixed olive-green and yellowish; a ring round the eye extending to the beak dull yellowish; the edges of the wing-feathers are brightly variegated with yellow, orange, crimson, and black; tail olive-brown, blackish at tip; the upper tail-coverts extend two-thirds of the length of the tail and terminate in a fine white line.

The female is duller in plumage and has no crimson on the wing.

Iris reddish-brown; bill orange-red, base blackish in winter; legs brown.

The tail is slightly forked with the feathers curved outwards at the tip.

Field Identification.—Himalayan species; usually in parties in undergrowth; dull olive coloration; coral-red bill, yellow eye-patch and bright shining yellow patch on throat and breast are conspicuous.

Distribution.—This species extends through the Himalayas and eastwards into China, and southwards into Southern Burma and Siam. There are several geographical races, and that inhabiting the Himalayas from Nepal to Eastern Assam, the Khasias and Chin Hills and in Arakan is *L. l. callipyga*, while it is replaced by *L. l. kumarensis* from Kumaon to Simla. This last form is a greyer tinge of green with more restricted golden colour on the crown and the red on the outer edge of the primaries reduced or absent. In the western Himalayas it is not very common, nor does it occur except at low elevations of 2000 to 5000 feet in the outer ranges; about Darjeeling it is common from 3400 to 7400 feet. It is a strictly resident bird. Of similar size and habits is the Silver-eared Mesia, *Mesia argentauris*, a striking bird with a black head, grey back, golden throat, and a dark red spot on the golden-edged wings. It occurs from Garhwal eastwards to Assam.

A common garden bird in Darjeeling is the Yellow-naped Ixulus (*Ixulus flavicollis*), a small olive-brown bird with whitish under parts, a dark brown crest and a fulvous nape. It is found throughout the Himalayas from Dharmsala eastwards, usually in parties in trees.

Habits, etc.—The Red-billed Leiothrix (or Pekin Robin of the aviculturists in England) is a bird of the hill forests, found in every type of jungle, but by preference in fir and pine forests with secondary undergrowth. It is a very lively, cheerful little bird, and except in the breeding season is eminently gregarious, going about in small parties which hunt the undergrowth for insects and occasionally move up into the trees. The ordinary call-note is *tee-tee-tee-tee-tee.* In the breeding season the cock has a delightful song of some variety and compass, which is sung from the top of a bush to the accompaniment of quivering wings and fluffed-out feathers.

The breeding season lasts from early April to September, the majority of nests being found in May and June; there are probably two broods. For breeding, the birds largely affect well-watered and jungle-clad valleys and ravines.

The nests are cups of varying depth and solidity, and as a rule they are not well hidden. They are composed of dry leaves, moss, and lichen, some nests being entirely of moss, others of bamboo leaves, so that there is a good deal of variety in their appearance; there is a lining of fine black hair-like rhizomorphs of a fungus. The site of the nest is likewise somewhat variable, though all are placed within 10 feet of the ground. Some are suspended in a horizontal fork like an Oriole's nest, others in an upright fork such as a Bulbul would choose; others again are built between several upright shoots like the nests of the Reed-Warblers.

The normal clutch consists of three eggs.

The eggs are rather broad and blunt in shape, with a hard and close texture, and a certain amount of gloss. The ground-colour varies from white to a very delicate pale green or greenish-blue. They are speckled, spotted, and blotched, often very boldly, with various shades of red-brown and purple, mingled with streaks and clouds of neutral tint and pale lilac. The markings tend to form a zone round the broad end.

The eggs average about 0·85 by 0·62 inches.

THE COMMON IORA

ÆGITHINA TIPHIA (Linnæus)

(Plate xiii, Fig. 5, opposite page 264)

Description.—Length 5 inches. Adult male in full summer plumage: whole of the upper plumage black, except the rump which is greenish-yellow, but the head and back are usually mixed with yellow to some extent; two white bars across the wing, and the quills narrowly edged with yellow; entire lower plumage deep yellow, duller and greenish below the breast. In winter the black on the body-feathers is almost all lost, and the yellow becomes paler.

Female at all seasons: greenish-yellow throughout, yellow predominating on the lower surface and green on the upper; wings dark greenish-brown with greenish-white edges to the feathers and a broad white bar across the shoulder.

Iris yellowish-white; bill slaty-blue, black along culmen; legs slaty-blue.

The feathers of the rump are remarkably soft and copious.

Field Identification.—A quiet little greenish-yellow bird, with dark wings and tail and a broad white bar across the wing, and in some cases much black on the upper parts, which creeps about in garden trees. Has a curious breeding flight.

Marshall's Iora (*Ægithina nigrolutea*), common in lower Continental India from Delhi to Khandesh, may be distinguished by the bright golden collar and large amount of white in the wings and tail.

Distribution.—The Iora is found over a very wide range of country throughout India, east of a line through the head of the Gulf of Cambay to Mount Aboo and Gurdaspur, Ceylon, Burma, Siam, and the Malay Peninsula to Borneo. It is divided into several races, of which three occur in India proper. *Æ. t. multicolor*, the darkest race with most black in the plumage, is confined to Ceylon and Rameswaram Island. *Æ. t. humei*, an intermediate race which also grades into Marshall's Iora, occupies the whole of India south of a line roughly from Mount Aboo through Central India to Orissa. The typical race occupies the rest of the Indian range merging into *Æ. t. septentrionalis* in the Punjab. In this the black on the upper parts of the male in breeding plumage is largely obsolete, diminishing in extent from east to west. All races are found in the plains and lower hills up to about 3000 feet, or locally even to 5500 feet, and are resident birds.

The lively and acrobatic Red-tailed Minla (*Minla ignotincta*) found in the Eastern Himalayas and the hills of Assam is fairly well known at Darjeeling. The black and white head, brown back and yellow under parts are well set off by brilliant scarlet in the wings and tail.

Habits, etc.—The Iora is a familiar garden bird in the greater part of India, frequenting the outskirts of villages and cultivation and the edges of forests and scrub-jungle. It is usually found in pairs, although occasionally two or three may be hunting in the same tree for the insects that form their food. It has a variety of notes, of which the most striking is a long-drawn wail *we-e-e-e-tu*, with a sudden drop of an octave on the last syllable.

In the breeding season the Iora has a striking display in which it flies up into the air and then spirals down to its perch again, with all the feathers, especially those of the rump, spread out until it looks almost like a ball; while descending it utters a strange protracted sibilant sound, recalling the note of a frog or cricket. Arrived on the perch it spreads and flirts the tail like a little Peacock, drooping its wings and still uttering the sibilant note. Then, too, the rump-feathers are arched and fluffed-out.

The breeding season is from April to July.

The nest is a very neat, delicate cup of fine, soft grasses, well plastered externally with cobwebs and spiders' cocoons. It is placed in a fork, either horizontal or vertical, of a bush or tree at heights from 3 to 30 feet from the ground.

The clutch varies from two to four eggs.

The egg is a moderately broad oval, slightly pointed towards the smaller end, fine in texture but with practically no gloss. The ground-colour is pale creamy or greyish white, with streaky longitudinal markings of grey and neutral tint, mostly at the broad end. Some eggs are erythristic in character with the ground-colour pinkish and the markings reddish.

The egg measures about 0·70 by 0·55 inches.

JERDON'S CHLOROPSIS

CHLOROPSIS JERDONI (Blyth)

(Plate v, Fig. 3, opposite page 88)

Description.—Length 7 inches. Male, entire plumage bright green except for the following markings: a black mask extending from the nostril to the eye and thence to the lower throat broken by a broad moustachial streak of bright purplish-blue; forehead and a broad band behind the black mask greenish-yellow; a patch of very bright malachite-blue by the bend of the wing.

The female resembles the male, except that the black mask is replaced by pale bluish-green with a bright greenish-blue moustachial streak.

Iris brown; bill black; legs pale blue.

Field Identification.—An active arboreal bird, particularly fond of feeding at the parasitic *Loranthus* flowers. Bright green, a black throat-patch broken by a purplish-blue moustachial streak in the male, a bluish-green throat-patch in the female. In both sexes the throat-patch is faintly bordered with yellow.

Distribution.—The genus *Chloropsis*, for which there is no English name, except the somewhat misleading one of the Green Bulbuls, contains a number of species of bright plumage, in which green predominates. They are found in India, Ceylon, Burma, Siam, the Malays, and China. Except for a large area in North-western India at least one form is found in every part of India, though no one form is predominantly familiar. To represent the genus, which is well known, I have selected Jerdon's Chloropsis. This occurs throughout the Peninsula of India from Sitapur, Fyzabad, and Basti in the north, Baroda and the Panch Mahals on the west, the Rajmahal Hills and

Midnapore on the east, down to and including Ceylon. It is a strictly resident species.

Two other species occur in India. The Gold-fronted Chloropsis (*Chloropsis aurifrons*) may be distinguished by the orange-yellow crown and by having the throat between the blue moustachial streaks also blue. It is widely distributed along the Outer Himalayas from the Jumna eastwards, in the Chota Nagpur area, and in Southern India and Ceylon. The Orange-bellied Chloropsis (*Chloropsis hardwickii*), which has orange under parts and most of the wing dark blue, occurs along the outer Central and Eastern Himalayas.

Habits.—All members of this genus have the same habits. They are arboreal birds, keeping as a rule to the tops of trees where they very often frequent the bunches of the parasitic *Loranthus*, but they also occasionally descend into low bush growth and even tall grass. Many of them prefer heavy forest, but Jerdon's Chloropsis is generally found in open country, in gardens, orchards, and groves, or in the more open patches of forest. It lives in pairs which often join the mixed hunting parties and is a very active and restless bird. It is also something of a bully and drives other birds away from the flowers of the Coral-tree at which it is a regular attendant. At the nest it is very watchful and noisy and indeed often betrays the secret of its whereabouts by over-anxiety.

A particular characteristic of Jerdon's Chloropsis, and indeed of other members of the group, is a remarkable proficiency in mimicry. It is said to have a distinct call of its own of several notes, but this is merely an item in a very varied repertory of other bird call-notes in which those of the Drongos hold a leading place.

The food consists of fruit, seeds, insects, and the nectar of various flowers.

The members of this genus are favourite cage birds in the East and have been successfully kept in aviaries in Europe.

The breeding season is from April to August.

The nest is a small, rather shallow cup composed of fine roots, grasses, and tamarisk stems without lining, but covered exteriorly with soft vegetable fibres. It is placed on a bough or in a fork of the end twigs of a branch of a tree at heights of 15 to 24 feet from the ground.

The clutch consists of three eggs.

The egg is a rather elongated oval, fine and delicate in texture with a slight gloss. The ground-colour is white or creamy-white, sparingly marked with spots, specks, blotches, and hair-lines of blackish, reddish, or purplish-brown, with a tendency for the markings to collect at the broad end.

The egg measures about 0·85 by 0·60 inches.

THE BLACK BULBUL

MICROSCELIS PSAROIDES (Vigors)

Description.—Length 10 inches. Sexes alike. Ashy-grey throughout, darker above, and albescent below the abdomen; a loose untidy crest black, with black marks at the base of the beak and encircling the ear-coverts.

Iris dark brown; bill and legs bright coral-red; claws horny-brown.

Tail bluntly forked, with the outer feathers slightly curved outwards.

FIG. 10—Black Bulbul (⅓ nat. size)

Field Identification.—A dark-looking ashy-grey bird with coral-red beak and black straggling crest; blunt forked tail creates a rough resemblance to a King-Crow: a bold, noisy bird with unpleasant squeaky calls. Purely arboreal in habits.

Distribution.—The genus *Microscelis* is of somewhat wide distribution from India to Japan, but only one species is found within the Indian Empire. This is divided into several races, of which two come within the area treated in this work. Both are mountain forms. The typical race is Himalayan, extending from Chitral and Hazara to Bhutan; the exact limits of this range are not fully known, but on the west it has been observed at Kohat in winter, and on the east it apparently extends into Assam. In Southern India south of Matheran

PLATE IV

1. Grey-headed Flycatcher-Warbler. 2. Nilgiri Blue Flycatcher. 3. Orange-headed Ground-Thrush. 4. Nilgiri Laughing-Thrush. 5. Red-billed Leiothrix. (All about ½ nat. size.)

[*Face p.* 66

the race *M. ps. ganeesa*, distinguished by the absence of the black line round the ear-coverts, breeds in the various ranges at elevations over 4000 feet. In Ceylon there is a large billed race *M. p. humii.*

In the Western Himalayas it breeds from about 4000 to 7000 feet; in the Eastern Himalayas from 2000 feet; in both areas a small number breed up to 10,000 feet. While not migratory in the true sense of the word, flocks of this Bulbul wander a good deal in the non-breeding season and may then be found in the plain areas contiguous to the mountains in which they breed, on occasion wandering even farther afield.

The Rufous-bellied Bulbul (*Ixos mcclellandii*) is found along the Himalayas from Naini Tal eastwards, and in the Assam Hills and Burma. It has the general build of a Black Bulbul with a similar crest but is bright olive green above and rufous below. The throat is untidily streaked with white. Another Bulbul which is not uncommon but rather local is the Himalayan Brown-eared *Ixos flavala.* It extends along the Himalayas from Mussoorie into Assam and North Burma. The general colour is grey, whiter below, and wings edged with yellowish-white.

Habits, etc.—The Black Bulbul is a bird of high forest trees, and except when breeding it is found in parties and large flocks, consisting sometimes of as many as a hundred individuals. These never descend to the ground, and seldom even to the undergrowth, but keep to the tops of the trees and fly from one to the other in loose, irregular order. They are very restless and seldom remain long in one place. Owing to its weak feet this Bulbul does not climb or hop about the boughs, but as compensation it is certainly one of the finest flyers in the family, being both swift and agile on the wing. In consequence this Bulbul is often mistaken for a Drongo by the inexperienced.

It is a very noisy, bold bird, and the whereabouts of a party is invariably revealed by the noise that they make; their calls are in consequence amongst the familiar bird sounds of the hills. A common note is a long-drawn nasal *weenk*, resembling the distant squeal of a pig. There is also a pretty whistle which may be syllabilised as *whew-whe* or *whee-whe*, something like the musical creaking of a rusty gate-hinge; this is often preceded by a couple of notes *squeaky-squeaky*, very similar to a call of the Drongo. Another less common note is *geagluck.*

The food consists mostly of berries of various shrubs and trees, but insects are also eaten; mulberries and bukain berries are particularly attractive to them. In the evening the birds may often be seen fly-catching from the tops of trees. They are said also to sip nectar from flowers, and certain it is that they may often be seen at the flowers of the rhododendron and other blossom-bearing trees, but it is more probable that they are taking insects from the cups.

During the breeding season, from April to the end of June, the pairs are very affectionate, feeding together, and the male remains in the vicinity while the female is on the nest.

The nest is a rather neat cup of coarse-bladed grass, dry leaves and moss, lined with fine grass stems or pine-needles and moss roots, and bound exteriorly with spiders' webs. It is placed in a fork of a tree often at a considerable height from the ground.

Three or four eggs comprise the clutch in the Himalayas, and two in the Nilgiris.

The egg is a rather long oval, a good deal pointed towards the small end, fine in texture with little gloss. The ground-colour is a delicate pinkish-white, varying in depth of colour, and it is profusely speckled, spotted, blotched, or clouded with various shades of red, brownish-red, and purple; there is a tendency for a heavy zone or cap of markings at the broad end.

The egg measures about 1·05 by 0·75 inches.

THE RED-VENTED BULBUL

MOLPASTES CAFER (Linnæus)

(Plate x, Fig. 2, opposite page 198)

Description.—Length 8 inches. Sexes alike. The whole head and throat glossy-black; the whole body and closed wings brown, the feathers of the wings, upper back, and breast edged with whitish, giving a scaled appearance, the lower abdomen and upper tail-coverts so pale as to be almost white; tail brown at base, darkening till it is almost black before the white tips of the feathers; a crimson patch under the tail.

Iris dark brown; bill and legs black.

Field Identification.—Throughout India. A common garden bird, cheerful and rather noisy in demeanour; earthy-brown in colour with a black, slightly crested head, white-tipped tail, and a bright red patch under the base of the latter.

Distribution.—The Common or Red-vented Bulbul is a very widely-spread species, occurring throughout the Indian Empire and extending to the east as far as China. With such a large and varied range it is inevitably divided up into several races which with their intermediate forms and areas are somewhat difficult to define; but the main difficulties occur in the forms that are found east of Assam. In the area covered by this work the division of the races is easily understood so long as it is recognised that the boundaries of the races about to be mentioned are not clearly defined, and in the intermediate areas between them birds will be found which cannot be clearly referred to one or other form.

Along the Himalayas together with the plains country about their base, we have an Eastern and a Western form meeting somewhere about Kumaon and Western Nepal. The Western bird is *M. c. intermedius*, found through Kashmir and the extreme North-west from Kohat down to about the Salt Range and along the Himalayas to Kumaon; its range steadily narrows as it progresses eastwards taking in less and less plains country. It is found commonly up to about 4000 feet and in smaller numbers a little higher to 5500 feet.

The East Himalayan bird from Nepal to Assam is *M. c. bengalensis*, and this, while not occurring so high in the hills, only exceptionally above 4500 feet, has a wider distribution in the plains through the Eastern United Provinces, Northern Bihar, Eastern Bengal, up to North-west Cachar and Eastern Assam. South of the area occupied by these two forms, *M. c. pallidus* extends on the west down to Ahmednagar and Khandesh, and *M. c. saturatus* on the east down to the Godavari. Southern India and Ceylon are occupied by *M. c. cafer*, which, while occurring normally up to about 2000 feet, follows the progress of man higher into the hills, even up to 8000 feet in the Nilgiris.

These races are distinguished by the amount of black in the plumage and also in some cases by size. A strictly resident species.

Habits, etc.—The Red-vented Bulbul is, in its various local forms, one of the best-known birds of India, as it is very common and very attached to the haunts of man, being essentially a garden bird. It is, however, found in all types of country, though by preference it eschews both heavy forest and barren plains. It is arboreal, the short weak legs not being adapted to progression on the ground though the bird sometimes descends to it to pick up food. The flight is quick and strong, though seldom sustained for any distance, and the beat of the wings is distinctly audible.

The Bulbul is usually met with in pairs and has a very evident affection for its mate; this fact, together with its sprightly demeanour, boldness, handsome coloration, and cheerful call-notes, contributes to make it a general favourite. It is one of the birds that everyone notices, Indian and European alike. Indians frequently tame it and carry it about the bazaars, tied with a string to the finger or to a little crutched perch, which is often made of precious metals or jade; while there are few Europeans who do not recollect Eha's immortal phrase anent the red patch in the seat of its trousers.

Occasionally small parties of this Bulbul are met with, and numbers often collect together at a spot where some particular food is plentiful or for the purpose of roosting; but normally the bird cannot be described as gregarious. At times, generally in the evenings, Bulbuls indulge in "fly-catching," sitting on the top of a bush or small tree, launching out continuously for short flights in the air, and returning again and again to the same perch.

But our friend has two vices. He is very quarrelsome and a plucky fighter, and this is part of the secret of his attraction as a pet for his Indian owners; for one of the essential ingredients of a pet in the East is that it should be a vehicle for gambling, and the owner of a good-fighting Bulbul may pocket many a small bet. Our friend is also apt to be destructive in the garden, damaging fruit and flowers and spoiling many a promising row of peas; though the unseen good that he does in the way of keeping down insect pests probably outweighs this more obvious damage.

There is something extremely cheerful and attractive about the voice of this Bulbul, though he has only one or two call-notes and no song. Yet for all time he will be credited with the reputation of a famous songster owing to the association in Persian literature between the song of the Bulbul, and the scent of roses, and the amorous delights of Persian gardens. The Bulbul of Persian literature is, however, as a matter of fact, another bird, a race of the Nightingale (*Daulias philomela africana*).

The breeding season lasts, according to locality, from February to August, but most nests will be found in May and June. Two broods are probably reared.

The nest is a neat cup composed of dry grass stems and the finest twigs and shoots of tamarisk, lined with fine roots and horse-hairs, and intermingled with dry leaves and scraps of lichen. It is placed usually in a bush or shrub between 4 and 10 feet above the ground, but is often found in a variety of unusual situations as high as 40 feet.

Two to four eggs are laid.

The egg is a rather long oval slightly compressed towards the smaller end; the texture is smooth and fragile and there is very little gloss. The ground-colour is pinkish- or reddish-white, marked with red, brownish-red, and purplish-red, with secondary markings of pale inky-purple. The markings take every conceivable form of spot, speck, blotch, and streak, and are usually so thick as practically to conceal the paler ground, but in many eggs they collect into zones and caps about the broad end.

The average measurement is about 0·90 by 0·65 inches.

THE WHITE-CHEEKED BULBUL

Molpastes leucogenys (Gray)

Description.—Length 8 inches. Sexes alike. Forehead and a long crest, curved forwards, hair brown narrowly edged with white; a patch round the eye to the beak, chin, and throat, and portions of the side of the neck black; a conspicuous white patch on the ear-coverts; the whole body and wings olive-brown, darker and greener above and paler below, becoming whitish on the lower abdomen; tail brown on the basal half, blackish on the terminal half, all feathers except the central pair broadly tipped with white; a bright sulphur-yellow patch below the base of the tail.

Iris brown; bill and legs black.

Field Identification.—A sprightly, cheerful bird found in gardens and open country; appears dull brown with a conspicuous crest, black markings about the head, and a large white patch on the face and a patch of yellow under the tail. In the typical race the crest is long and curved forwards over the beak like Punch's cap. Usually in pairs.

Fig. 11—Head of White-cheeked Bulbul ($1\frac{1}{2}$ nat. size)

Distribution.—The White-cheeked Bulbul extends throughout the Himalayas from Afghanistan to the hills of Assam, north of the Brahmaputra River, and in the north-west of the Peninsula down as far as Central India; out of India it extends west to Mesopotamia. There are three races of the bird in India. The typical form with the highly-developed "Punch cap" crest is confined to the Himalayas where it occurs from the foot-hills at about 2000 up to 6000 feet in the east and from 3000 to 9000 feet in the west. Through the plains of the Punjab south of the Salt Range, Sind, Cutch, Guzerat, Rajputana, the North-western Provinces south to Etáwah, and Central India as far east as Jhansi, Saugor, and Hoshungabad, the typical race is replaced by *M. l. leucotis* in which the crest is short and black, the under tail-coverts saffron-yellow, and the olive-brown of the upper parts is without the greenish tinge found in *M. l. leucogenys*; the bill is stouter and blunter in this form. A third race, *M. l. humii*, is found connecting these two races in the Salt Range and the elevated plateau north of it about Rawal Pindi and Campbellpur, and west of this to Bannu and Kohat. This is a truly intermediate form, the crest in colour and size and the bill in shape being intermediate between those of *M. l. leucogenys* and *M. l. leucotis*.

Habits, etc.—Throughout its range and under its different names the White-cheeked Bulbul has the same characteristics; it is a bird of open country not of forest, a dweller amongst bushes rather than a bird of the trees, a familiar and cheerful companion by the paths of man. In the Himalayas it is one of the conspicuous birds of the hill stations, coming freely into gardens and disporting itself on the open spaces that fringe the roads; it is common round the hill villages with their cultivation. But in Kashmir its sociability reaches its apex; there it comes freely into verandahs and rooms, and hops about in the house-boats with its cheery note and quaintly-cocked crest, suspecting no harm and receiving none; and many a picnic party on the shores of the Dal Lake in the historic gardens of Shalimar and Nishat Bagh have found their number added to by a pair of Bulbuls who have hopped about their table-cloth and gratefully swallowed the crumbs of cake thrown to them.

While not in any true sense a migrant, this Bulbul is subject to a certain amount of local movement. In the hills, while the majority are strictly stationary, a small proportion move down a little from their breeding zone in the winter; and in the plains *leucotis* is known to shift its quarters according to season, though usually not to any great distance.

These Bulbuls are generally met with in pairs or small parties of five or six individuals, but occasionally numbers are attracted together into a small area by the abundance of some special food-supply. They are very lively birds, incessantly bowing and posturing on the summit of a bush or flying from tree to tree; and as they do so they keep on uttering their cheery call *Quick-a drink with you*, which is a pleasant and welcome sound in a land where melodious bird-voices are scarce, and a sentiment that aptly fits the jovial roysterer that utters it. For the Bulbul is a jovial soul and companionable, ready for the fun of the day, whether it be a plentiful hatch of flying-ants to chase and devour, or a hapless sun-dazed owl to bully and torment.

It feeds chiefly on insects and fruits. It is often seen on the ground collecting ants, grubs, beetles, and the like, and in the evenings it has a habit of flying into the air like a clumsy Flycatcher in pursuit of insects. Of fruits it devours many kinds; in the hills the Berberis, in the plains the Ber and the Boquain, furnish it with a plentiful supply of berries; and a row of green peas frequently suffers badly from its attentions.

Attention must be drawn to the fact that these Yellow-vented

Bulbuls hybridise frequently in a wild state with the Red-vented Bulbuls; a fine series of these hybrids were collected by the late Major Whitehead at Kohat, and other cases have been observed at Rawal Pindi, Jhang, and Karachi.

The breeding season commences both in the hills and plains towards the end of March and continues until August, though few nests will be found after June. Apparently two or more broods are reared in the year.

The nest is a well-constructed cup, light and fragile in appearance but strong; it is composed of fine dry stems of herbaceous plants, generally rather rough in texture, mixed with dry grass stalks and shreds of vegetable fibres; there is a neat lining of some finer material, dry grass stems or grass roots for preference. The usual situation is in some thick bush at a height of 4 to 6 feet from the ground, but it is occasionally built in trees at a greater height than this.

The eggs are somewhat variable in shape, size, and colour. Typically they are a rather long oval, somewhat pointed at one end; the ground-colour is pinkish- or reddish-white with little or no gloss, thickly speckled, freckled, streaked, or blotched with red of various shades, with, in addition, tiny spots and clouds of underlying pale inky-purple.

They average about 0·88 by 0·65 inches in size, the eggs of *M. l. leucotis* being slightly smaller than those of *M. l. leucogenys*.

THE RED-WHISKERED BULBUL

Otocompsa jocosa (Linnæus)

(Plate xiv, Fig. 3, opposite page 286)

Description.—Length 8 inches. Sexes alike. A conspicuous white patch on the sides of the face, above which is a small crimson tuft springing from the lower eyelid; crest, top, and sides of the head and a narrow line below the white patch black, merging into a broad blackish-brown gorget, which is interrupted in the centre by the white of the breast; remainder of upper plumage brown, darker on the wings and tail, the latter tipped with white except on the central pair of feathers; lower plumage white, washed with brown on the sides of the body; a crimson patch under the base of the tail.

Iris brown; bill and legs black.

Field Identification.—A sprightly and common garden bird; appears dark brown above, white below, with a white patch on the cheeks, and a broken gorget across the breast; a crimson tuft below the eye, and a similar patch of colour below the tail.

Distribution.—The Red-whiskered Bulbul is another of those common species which have a wide distribution from India to China. It is, however, local and scarce in some parts of its range. Within our area there are five races. Three have white tips to the tail-feathers. These are the typical race, large and dark, which extends from outside India into the Duars and Sikkim foot-hills: *O. j. provincialis*, a paler form found in the United Provinces, the valley of Nepal and Bihar; and *O. j. emeria*, a small dark form, which extends from Lower Bengal to Madras and Gingee. The other two races lack the white tips in the tail. *O. j. abuensis*, found at Mount Aboo and in Rajputana, is extremely pale. *O. j. fuscicaudata*, a darker bird with the gorget unbroken, extends from the Tapti to Cape Comorin and Salem district, and also into the Central Provinces. This Bulbul breeds up to an elevation of 7000 feet; but on the whole the northern race is more of a plains bird, while the southern prefers the hills. Both, however, are strictly resident. The Black-crested Yellow Bulbul, *Otocompsa flaviventris*, is found along the Himalayas from the Sutlej Valley eastward into Assam and Burma, and south to the Central Provinces. It is readily distinguished by the black head and yellow breast.

Habits, etc.—The Red-whiskered Bulbuls have very much the same habits as the Red-vented Bulbuls, avoiding thick forest and preferring the haunts of men, gardens, bamboo clumps, orchards, cultivation, low scrub-jungle, and the neighbourhood of villages. They are very cheerful, lively birds with much the same calls as the Red-vented Bulbuls but louder and more musical in tone. Where they occur they are often extremely abundant. In the Nilgiris and in the hill stations of the Bombay Presidency they are amongst the commonest birds and familiar to everyone. In Port Blair, Andaman Islands, this Bulbul is common and extremely tame and takes the place to some extent of the house sparrow, a bird not found in the Andamans. The flight is strong and well sustained, but slow and jerky in character.

Their diet is both insectivorous and vegetarian; they are particularly fond of fruit, attacking the larger kinds while immature, and the smaller when ripe, and as numbers often collect to the feast they are responsible for a good deal of damage.

The breeding season is from February to May. The nest is cup-shaped, loosely but strongly built of grass bents, roots, fibres, and thin stalks, and is lined with finer grass stems and roots; a certain amount of dry leaves and ferns are worked into the bottom and are characteristic of the nests of this species. They are placed in bushes at heights below 6 feet from the ground.

Three or four eggs are usually laid in the north and two or three eggs in the south.

The egg is a broad, somewhat lengthened oval, fine in texture with a slight gloss. The ground-colour is pinkish- or reddish-white, very thickly freckled, mottled, streaked, and blotched with red of various shades, and a few secondary markings of pale inky-purple; there is a tendency for the markings to collect at the broad end.

The eggs measure about 0·85 by 0·65 inches.

THE YELLOW-BROWED BULBUL

IOLE ICTERICA (Strickland)

(Frontispiece, Fig. 3)

Description.—Length 8 inches. Sexes alike. The whole upper plumage bright yellowish-olive; wings dark brown, the outer webs olive-yellow, the inner edged with yellow; tail yellowish-olive, the shafts below and the inner edges of the feathers yellow; a line through and round the eye, the sides of the head and the whole lower plumage bright yellow, the flanks washed with olive.

Iris brownish-red or blood-red; bill horny-black; legs and feet pale blue or slate-blue.

Field Identification.—A very sprightly Bulbul, bright olive above and bright yellow below with a yellow line over the eye. Found in melodious parties in the forests of the Western Ghats.

Distribution.—The Western Ghats from Khandala to Travancore, extending inland to the Nilgiris and Palnis at all heights from the foot of the hills to 6500 feet; most numerous about 3500 feet. Also found in Ceylon.

Another yellowish bird is the White-throated Bulbul (*Criniger gularis*) which is found at low elevations in the Eastern Himalayas, Assam, and extreme South-east Bengal. The upper plumage is yellowish-olive and the lower parts bright yellow with a white throat. It is a noisy, gregarious bird found in humid forest with thick undergrowth.

Habits, etc.—The Yellow-browed Bulbul is one of the commonest forest birds of the Western Ghats where its normal habitat is the heavy evergreen forest which covers so many of the slopes of the hills. Here it keeps much to the undergrowth though it is often found about the edges of the forest and occasionally ventures into neighbouring gardens; the shade and solitude of the forest are, however, its proper home.

This species will be observed both in pairs and in noisy parties of five or seven birds which often join on to the mixed hunting parties. It is very restless in character, hopping actively about the boughs of the trees and then descending to the sapling undergrowth and then again flying on to some bare bough to give out its quiet little warble. The low-toned varying notes are difficult to describe, but the adjectives sweet and soft and mellow will at once occur to the hearer. Some of them resemble the sounds *cty, eye, te white up, te whit up* and these three modulations are continuously repeated for no small space of time. An alarm-note is somewhat harsh and jarring. In India this Bulbul is said to be largely frugivorous, feeding not only on the forest berries and fruits but on the more valuable domesticated guavas, loquats, pears, peaches and the like. In Ceylon, at any rate, it is also to some extent insectivorous.

The breeding season extends from February to May. The nest is usually built at a height of 6 to 10 feet from the ground in a small sapling or evergreen shrub in dense dark forest where the light is very poor. Occasional nests are higher, even in a branch of a large tree. The nest is not as a rule particularly well concealed. It is very distinctive in character, being a shallow cup made almost entirely of green moss or fine grasses and bents, bound with cobwebs and lined with black rootlets or fine grass and slung as a rule between two twigs in a horizontal fork. The construction is firm and compact though some are so thin that the eggs can be seen through the bottom.

The usual clutch consists of two eggs though three are sometimes found. The egg is a moderately long and rather perfect oval, almost devoid of gloss. The ground-colour is dull white or pinkish-white and sometimes even warm salmon-pink, speckled more or less thickly, and often heavily, with pale reddish-brown or pink; these markings are usually more numerous at the broad end and occasionally form a cap.

The eggs average about 0·9 by 0·65 inches.

THE WHITE-BROWED BULBUL

PYCNONOTUS LUTEOLUS (Lesson)

Description.—Length 7 inches. Sexes alike. Upper plumage dull brownish olive-green, palest on the head where it is slightly ashy and brightest on the wings; rump yellowish; two dull whitish streaks from the beak over and under the eye; chin pale clear yellow; lower parts pale ashy-whitish tinged with yellow, brightest towards the tail, the breast faintly streaked with brownish-grey.

Iris red; bill black; legs dark plumbeous.

Field Identification.—An inconspicuous but noisy bird, olive-coloured above and paler below, with a white eyebrow, which skulks in cactus and bushes in gardens and scrub-jungle.

Distribution.—Confined to Ceylon and India south of a line from Baroda on the west to Midnapur on the east. While common in Western Bengal and Orissa, in the Tributary Mahals, along the

Eastern Ghats and about Bombay, it is rare or absent on the Deccan tableland and throughout the Central Provinces. A resident species. The Ceylon race, *P. l. insulæ*, is smaller and darker.

The Striated Green Bulbul (*Alcurus leucogrammicus*) is fairly common in the Eastern Himalayas, the hills of Assam and in Burma. It is crested, olive-green above with white shaft streaks and yellow below streaked heavily with olive-brown. The pleasant song will be familiar to many at Darjeeling.

Habits, etc.—This Bulbul avoids actual forest, and prefers scrub- and bush-jungle in that netherland which is neither forest nor cultivation. It frequents the outskirts of villages, and is a great lover of the thick clumps and hedges of cactus and thorny bushes which are found round every hamlet. In such cover it is a skulker, and from the heart of its retreat it is prone to burst into a loud clear volley of whistling notes which seem to tumble over each other, so quickly are they produced. The sound is a lively, rowdy chatter with no attempt at harmony—just a burst of not unpleasing notes, ending in a frightened whistle. In Bombay and Madras it is a common garden bird. It is a plains species, and though found in the lower hills does not ascend those of any elevation. The food consists of various fruits and berries.

This bird may be found breeding according to locality in almost every month of the year, but about Bombay the main breeding season is from April to July. Apparently two broods are reared. The nest is a loose, rather untidy, and straggling cup of small twigs, lined with fine grass stems, coir, or hair. It is built in thick bushes at no great height from the ground, generally from 2 to 4 feet.

The clutch consists of two or three eggs. They are decidedly elongated ovals, fine and smooth in texture, and moderately glossy. The ground-colour is reddish-white, thickly speckled and blotched with reddish-brown, these markings mixed with clouds and spots of pale greyish-lilac. In some specimens these markings coalesce into a zone round the broad end.

The eggs average in size 0·9 by 0·6 inches.

THE HIMALAYAN TREE-CREEPER

Certhia himalayana Vigors

(Plate ii, Fig. 6, opposite page 22)

Description.—Length 6 inches. Sexes alike. Upper plumage a streaked mixture of blackish-brown and fulvous, the feathers at the base of the tail strongly tinged with ferruginous; a short streak above the eye fulvous; wings dark brown with a broad fulvous band running through all the flight-feathers except the four outermost; tail brown, regularly cross-barred with black; chin and upper throat pure white; remainder of lower plumage pale smoky-brown.

Iris dark brown; bill black, lower mandible fleshy-white; legs fleshy.

The bill is long, slender, and curved; the toes and claws are very long; the tail is graduated and composed of stiff, pointed feathers.

Field Identification.—A very small bird, mottled brown above and whitish below, with a long, curved beak and stiff tail, invariably found climbing up the bark of tree-trunks. This species is distinguished from all other Indian Tree-Creepers by the black cross-bars on the tail.

Distribution.—The Himalayan Tree-Creeper is generally distributed in the mountain ranges that encircle North-western India. The typical form is found in the Central Himalayas about Simla, Garhwal, and Kumaon. It is commonly said to occur farther east to Sikkim and Bhutan, but this is not the case. In Turkestan there is a very grey race with a long bill which is known as *C. h. tæniura.* Between the areas occupied by these two forms, in Kashmir and the North-western Himalayas and the ranges running down south along the North-west Frontier Province in Afghanistan and Baluchistan, the Tree-Creepers are intermediate in character between the above two races and have been given the name of *C. h. limes.*

The best known species in the Eastern Himalayas is the Sikkim Tree-Creeper (*Certhia discolor*) a more richly coloured species with the lower plumage earthy-brown.

Habits, etc.—During the breeding season the Himalayan Tree-Creeper is found throughout the mountain forests between 5000 and 10,000 feet. It is perhaps most numerous in the areas of the big spruce firs, but is sufficiently common wherever it is found. It is an early breeder and very hardy in spite of its delicate-looking appearance and small size, and as early as March its song is a familiar sound in the snow-bound forests of the northern slopes at a time when they are half empty of bird-life. During the winter months from November to March large numbers drift downhill and wander into the plains at the foot of the ranges, occurring at that season as far afield as Jhang, Lahore, and Saharanpur.

The Tree-Creeper cannot fail to be identified by the veriest beginner in the study of small birds. It is as much a parasite on the tree-trunks as the vegetable creepers that cover many of them. Except for an occasional scramble on a rock or the face of a steep bank the Tree-Creeper spends its entire life in a monotony of climbing, rather like a jerky brown mouse, from the bottom of a tree-trunk up to the thicker portions of the boughs, and then sweeping down through the air with a cicada-like flight to the base of a neighbouring tree where it repeats the performance. It invariably climbs upwards, neither jerking backwards and downwards like a Woodpecker may on occasion, nor running in all directions and positions like a Nuthatch, though from its habit of rather preferring the underside of a bough it is frequently moving with its back parallel to the ground. It never perches on a twig, though it sometimes climbs along the thicker ones in continuation of its progress along a bough, and it is never still longer than the interval necessary to dislodge some tightly ensconced insect. For its food is obtained entirely from the bark of the trees that it climbs, picked out from amongst the crevices and holes with the long, curved beak, and the progress of the little bird is often interrupted by a parabola of flight after a small moth which has escaped it for the moment by taking wing from its diurnal resting-place. The Creeper, while living solitary or in pairs as regards its own kind, is very social with other species, and one or two are invariably found with the mixed hunting parties of Tits and Warblers, working the trunks while they hunt the leaves and twigs, so that tree after tree undergoes a thorough scrutiny.

The ordinary call of the Tree-Creeper is a long-drawn squeak, meaningless in tone and ventriloquial in character, which comes from nowhere in particular amongst the trees, so that the bird is difficult to locate. The song is loud, but brief and monotonous, *quis-quis-quis-quis* uttered now and again in the depth of the forest, and chiefly remarkable as holding the field alone before most species in the hills have started their breeding song.

The breeding season is from March to early May.

The nest is a cup composed of fine grasses, dry leaves, moss, chips, and miscellaneous debris with a lining of feathers and fur; it is placed in a hole or crevice in a tree-trunk, and very frequently behind a loose bulging section of bark and between planks in wooden buildings. The same site is often used for many years in succession.

Four to six eggs are laid; they are regular broad ovals, fine in texture without gloss. The ground-colour is white, profusely spotted with various shades of red and brown, the markings tending in many eggs to collect in a zone about the broad end.

They measure about 0·68 by 0·50 inches.

THE WALL-CREEPER

Tichodroma muraria (Linnæus)

Description.—Length 7 inches. Sexes alike. Summer plumage: the whole of the body plumage ashy-grey, except the chin and throat which are black; a large crimson patch on the wings, including the coverts and edges of the flight-feathers; flight-feathers black, the four outer feathers each with two conspicuous white spots; tail black tipped with ashy which gradually changes to white and increases in extent towards the outer feathers.

FIG. 12—Wall-Creeper (½ nat. size)

In winter plumage the chin and throat are white and the top of the head is brownish.

The bill is long and slender, the wings rounded and the hind claws very large.

Iris dark brown; bill and legs black.

Field Identification.—Can be confused with no other species; a french-grey bird with a long slender bill and crimson patches and white spots in the wings, which spends its life climbing on banks, walls, and rocks.

Distribution.—The Wall-Creeper is found in the mountain ranges of Central and Southern Europe, and eastwards to Mongolia, Turkestan, and the Himalayas. Breeding under very similar Alpine conditions in these widely-distant areas it has not been influenced by climate towards the formation of geographical races.

In the Himalayas it breeds at great elevations between 12,000 and 16,000 feet, and also apparently in the neighbouring ranges between the North-west Frontier Province and Afghanistan. In winter it descends to the outer ranges and the foot-hills, individuals wandering well out into the plains.

The stumpy little dark brown Wren (*Troglodytes troglodytes*) with its cocked-up tail is found in the Sufed Koh, Kashmir and the Himalayas generally in the high forest zone, descending lower in winter. There are two different races but their habits are the same as those of the British bird.

Habits, etc.—This beautiful bird can scarcely escape notice where it occurs. In the Alpine fastnesses, where it breeds, it spends its life on the faces of stupendous precipices, but in winter when it comes lower down to the milder haunts of men it may be found wherever small cliffs, steep-cut banks, walls, rocks, or boulders provide the vertical surfaces on which it lives. For as the Tree-Creeper is to the tree, so is the Wall-Creeper to the stone, and it is equally rare for the one bird to invade the haunt of the other. The Wall-Creeper progresses up the vertical face of stone in a curious jerky fashion with a continual downward flick of the outermost wing-feathers; occasionally it flutters out into the air and endeavours on the wing to capture some insect disturbed by its progress, and the curious butterfly effect of this action has given the name of "Butterfly-bird" in many languages from Switzerland to Tibet. Unlike the Tree-Creeper, the Wall-Creeper has perforce to undertake long flights in the air as it passes from cliff to cliff. Then it is curiously reminiscent of a Hoopoe, the same hovering, uncertain flight as if the bird was wondering where to go, the same rounded spotted wings, the same general build, the long curved beak too, a curious case of parallelism still unexplained.

In its occasional wanderings into the plains it is often hard put to find the conditions necessary to its life and is in consequence sometimes found in curious places. Every winter one or two live on the structure of the Khalsa College at Amritsar.

The breeding season in the Himalayas is about May and June.

The nest is a pad of moss and wool, more or less mixed and lined with wool, fur, hair, and feathers, placed in some crevice in the face of a precipice, almost invariably in an inaccessible situation.

The clutch consists of four to six eggs; they are broad ovals, compressed and pointed towards the smaller end. The colour is a rather dull white sparsely freckled with deep reddish-brown, chiefly towards the broad end.

The egg measures about 0·85 by 0·55 inches.

THE BROWN DIPPER

CINCLUS PALLASII Temminck

(Plate ix Fig. 5, opposite page 176)

Description.—Length 8 inches. Sexes alike. Entire plumage dull chocolate-brown; the eyelids covered with white feathers.

Iris dark brown; bill black; legs pale brown, soles yellow.

The young bird is paler and greyer with the plumage squamated.

Field Identification.—A sombre dark-brown bird, squat in shape, with a short tail and sharp beak like a large Wren, found on running open water in the Himalayas; flies very swiftly low over the water with a shrill call.

Distribution.—This sombre species of Dipper is found throughout the greater part of Northern Asia from Siberia and Manchuria to the Himalayas and Japan; it is divided into several races, of which we are only concerned with one (*C. p. tenuirostris*). This is found in Afghanistan and Turkestan, and throughout the Himalayas to Eastern Assam north of the Brahmaputra. It is a resident species breeding mainly from the foot-hills up to about 6000 feet, but it occurs also at all heights up to 12,000 feet.

A race of the Common Dipper (*Cinclus cinclus*) of Europe is found at high elevations of the Inner Himalayas, being best known from Kashmir to Gurhwal. It is easily recognised by the pure white throat and breast.

Habits, etc.—The Brown Dipper is entirely aquatic in its habits, and is found commonly on all the open perennial streams and rivers of the Himalayas, both amongst the wooded ranges of their southern slopes and amid the arid, stony mountains of their central and inner ranges. It obtains from the water all its food, consisting mainly of aquatic insects and their larvæ, and these it captures by wading, swimming, and diving, having also the faculty of walking about on the bed of the stream under water. For these methods it is admirably adapted in structure. It is short, rotund, and stoutly built, the plumage is everywhere very dense and incapable of penetration by water, and even the eyelids are clothed with feathers; the head is narrowed in front and the feathers of the forehead are very short and lie flat.

It is a most active bird, never still and always busy. The harsh call *dzchit-dzchit* is a familiar sound along hill streams, shrill enough to be heard easily above the roar of the waters; it heralds the approach of the small plump brown bird that flies swiftly along a foot or two above the surface of the water, swaying from side to side amongst the boulders and only making a detour over land to avoid some intruder at the water's edge; the wings appear rather small for the stout body, and to make up for this they are vibrated very quickly in flight in sustained beats followed by a pause.

Settling on a stone the bird bows and jerks from side to side, or immediately starts feeding, keeping its foothold easily on slippery stones and disappearing under water either diving or walking. It swims freely on the broader pools, looking like a miniature Water-hen, now and again diving and disappearing for a while.

The breeding season is from December to May.

The nest is a large globular structure of moss and grass, stoutly constructed with massive walls, and the entrance placed at one side is comparatively large. The egg-chamber is lined with moss, roots and leaves.

The situation chosen is always close to or above the water, and the nests are wedged into hollows and clefts of rocks and boulders overgrown with mosses and ferns and damp with moisture.

The clutch consists of four or five eggs. In shape they are rather elongated ovals, very soft and satiny in texture, and almost without gloss. The colour is pure white, and the average size is about 1·00 by 0·72 inches.

THE INDIAN BLUE-CHAT

Luscinia brunnea (Hodgson)

Description.—Length 5 inches. Male: The whole upper plumage, including the exposed parts of the wings and tail, dull blue, the hidden parts of the wing- and tail-quills brownish-black; a conspicuous white line over the eye; the sides of the face and neck black; throat, breast and sides of the body bright chestnut, paler on the chin; thighs ashy-grey; remainder of lower plumage white.

Female: The whole upper plumage and the exposed parts of the wings and tail olive-brown, tinged with russet on the sides of the wings and above the tail; sides of the face russet flecked with paler; middle of chin and throat, the abdomen and a patch under the tail white; remainder of lower plumage warm fulvous-brown or olive-brown.

Iris dark brown; bill black in male, dark horny-brown in female; legs steely-brown.

Field Identification.—A spry looking bird found on or near the ground in thick undergrowth in forest in the Himalayas in summer and in South India in winter. Male looks very dark blue above and chestnut below with a conspicuous white line over the eye; female an inconspicuous olive-brown bird, more fulvous and white below. Has a characteristic song.

Distribution.—The typical race of the Blue-Chat breeds in a zone between 6500 and 11,000 feet in the Sufed Koh, through Kashmir proper and in the Himalayas to Bhutan; also in the Lichiang Range of North Yunnan. It winters mainly in the hills of South-west India between 2000 and 5000 feet from the Wynaad to South Travancore and in the central hills of Ceylon. On passage from August to October and from March to mid May it may be found here and there throughout the Peninsula except west of a line from Delhi to Agra and Baroda. A slightly smaller race *L. b. wickhami* breeds in Burma and is apparently resident.

Habits, etc.—During the breeding season the Indian Blue-Chat is a common bird in the forests of the Western Himalayas, being particularly numerous about the hill stations of Murree and the Gālis, in the ranges of Kashmir proper and at suitable elevations about Dalhousie, Dharamsala, Simla and in the Gahrwal ranges. In these forests it affects patches of undergrowth and scrub and the sheltered sides of nullahs. By the ordinary passer-by it is seldom seen, being a skulker of secretive habits; but its commonness is vouched for by the rich though quite short song, and a good way to observe the singer is to creep quietly into the centre of a patch of cover and sit there till his alarm has been forgotten. The male may then be seen at quite close quarters as he hops warbling and whistling through the cover, or sings from a perch in the undergrowth or on the lower bough of a tree. The sombre female is still more difficult to observe.

The song consists of three or four rather monotonous notes—*jerri-jerri-jerri* or *phwee-phwee-phwee*—in an ascending scale, followed by a rapidly repeated trill, *tre-tre-tre-tretre*, the last rather reminiscent of an English Robin's song. Once learnt it cannot be mistaken. The alarm-note is a harsh *tack-tack* like that of the Stonechat and in the close neighbourhood of the nest a faint, anxious squeak is uttered. A very characteristic habit is the fanning of the tail and the jerking of it slowly downwards from the level of the back, every fifth or sixth movement bringing it up again.

In its winter quarters the Blue-Chat is still a bird of shady thickets, marshy spots and banks of streams and it may also be found under coffee bushes and cardamum plants. Here it is usually found singly, flitting about the undergrowth, alighting on the ground and hopping along easily and swiftly in search of the insects that make up its food. The alarm-note and the faint squeak may be heard, but the song is not uttered in the winter quarters.

The breeding season lasts from the end of May till the end of July.

The nest is a cup of lichens and dead or skeleton leaves, lined with a little wool, pine-needles, hair or a few feathers. It is built on the ground, either in a hollow on a steep bank or between the roots and buttresses of trees, particularly large firs.

The clutch consists normally of four eggs. In shape they are true ovals, fine and close and silky in texture but without gloss. The colour is a uniform pale blue, unmarked.

They measure about 0·80 by 0·60 inches.

This species is a favourite foster parent for the Common Cuckoo (*Cuculus canorus*).

THE PIED BUSH-CHAT

Saxicola caprata (Linnæus)

Description.—Length 5 inches. Male: Deep black all over, with the exception of a large patch at the base of the tail, the lower abdomen, and a conspicuous wing-patch, which are white. In fresh autumn plumage the feathers are sometimes margined with rusty-brown.

Female: Upper plumage greyish-brown, with a rufous patch at the base of the tail; wings and tail dark brown, the feathers with pale edges; the lower plumage brownish-grey, gradually darkening on the breast and becoming more fulvous towards the tail. In fresh autumn plumage the feathers have broad grey margins which make the bird look paler in colour.

Iris dark brown; bill and legs black.

Field Identification.—Abundant in the plains and lower hills in every type of open country; the male is a conspicuous little black and white bird, the female dark brown with a rusty patch at the base of the tail. They perch on the tops of grasses and bushes and at intervals fly down to the ground to pick up insects.

Distribution.—Transcaspia, Afghanistan, Persia, India, Burma, the Philippines, and Java. The Pied Bush-Chat occurs practically throughout India, and three races are found within our limits though their detailed distribution is not very accurately known. *P. c. bicolor*, with the abdomen largely white, breeds in considerable numbers from the plains up to 5000 feet and locally higher, from the extreme North-west, Baluchistan, and Sind, along the

Outer Himalayas and the neighbouring plains. It is here largely a summer visitor, arriving in February and March and leaving in September and October. In winter it appears as far south as Hyderabad State. *P. c. caprata*, with the abdomen black, is found from Vizagapatam to Salem and across Mysore to Malabar as well as in Burma and farther afield. It grades through *S. c. nilgiriensis* (Nilgiris, Palnis and Travancore ranges) to the huge billed *S. c. atrata* which is confined to the higher ranges of central hill zone of Ceylon.

Habits, etc.—This Bush-Chat is one of the most familiar birds of the plains of India, the pied plumage of the male and its habit of perching on the tops of bushes and clumps of grass attracting the attention of all who are observant of wild creatures. It avoids heavy forest but is common about cultivation, in grasslands and in scrub-jungle, and is particularly partial to the riverain areas of Northern India where cultivation and tracts of tamarisk scrub and grass alternate.

FIG. 13—Pied Bush-Chat
(½ nat. size)

It takes practically all its food from the ground, flying down to it from some favourite vantage point which commands a view of bare ground in the vicinity, and to which it returns after the capture of each morsel with the self-satisfied spread and jerk of the tail that is common to most of the family. On occasion it launches out into the air and captures flying insects on the wing.

In the breeding season, as a display, the male drops and quivers the wings and raises the scapulars to show the white wing-patches ; there is also a very pretty love flight in which he flies up singing from the top spray of a bush with tail outspread and wings slowly beating the air above the head, and descends again to settle on another bush. In this flight, also, prominence is laid on the displaying of the wing-patches.

The ordinary note is the harsh chipping sound of two stones knocked together, common to the Chats and from which they derive their name. The song is short but very sweet and pleasing.

The food seems to consist entirely of insects.

The breeding season extends from March until August, but the majority of nests will be found from April to June.

The nest is a cup of small grass roots, bents, and the like, lined with hair, fur, and wool. It is placed in hollows in the ground, either on the level under tufts of grass and herbage or in the face of banks; occasionally holes in buildings and rocks are utilised, but the bird is normally a ground builder and the nests are always well concealed.

The clutch varies from three to five eggs.

The eggs are short, broad ovals with a fine texture and a faint gloss. The ground-colour is pale bluish-white or occasionally pale stone or pinkish-white, and the markings, which tend to collect towards the broad end, are freckles, specks, and small blotches of pale reddish-brown.

They measure about 0·67 by 0·55 inches.

THE STONECHAT

Saxicola torquata (Linnæus)

(Plate xiv, Fig. 2, opposite page 286)

Description.—Length 5 inches. Male: Upper plumage including the wings and tail brownish-black, with a conspicuous white patch of white on the wings and at the base of the tail; the sides of the head and the chin and throat black with a large patch of white bordering the sides of the neck; breast orange-rufous merging into the paler rufous of the under parts. In fresh autumn plumage the feathers are broadly edged with fulvous, which greatly obscures the above scheme of coloration, and changes the whole aspect of the bird; the edges gradually wear off revealing the true coloration.

Female: Upper plumage, wings and tail brown with smaller less conspicuous white patches on the wings, and a rufous patch at the base of the tail; line over the eye, the chin and the throat pale fulvous; remainder of the lower plumage pale orange-rufous. In fresh autumn plumage the feathers are slightly edged with fulvous, but not sufficiently for abrasion to change the plumage markedly.

Iris dark brown; bill and legs black.

Field Identification.—In open country, in both hills and plains, perching on tips of grass and bushes. Males recognised by black head, white collar, reddish breast, and white shoulder-patch. Female, a small dull brown bird similar to female of Pied Bush-Chat, but rather paler in colour with the rusty rump-patch less marked, and with traces of a white shoulder-patch.

Distribution.—The Stonechat is very widely distributed in Europe, Africa, and Asia, and is divided into a number of races, of which we are chiefly concerned with the Himalayan breeding form, known as *S. torquata indica.* This breeds in Western Siberia, Russian Turkestan to the South Urals, and throughout the Himalayas; also in the ranges that extend down the North-western Frontier to Baluchistan. In the Himalayas the majority breed between 5000 and 7000 feet, but a few nest even higher, and stragglers nest in the foot-hills, and even the plains of North-western India. In winter, from about September to April, the Stonechat migrates to the plains of India, and may then be found everywhere except in the extreme south. A resident race *S. t. leucura*, with much white in the tail, breeds in the riverain jungles and swampy areas of the terais and dunes and the Indo-Gangetic plain.

S. t. przewalskii, the dark breeding race of Tibet, and *S. t. stejnegeri*, the broad-billed race of North-eastern Asia, visit Northern and Eastern India in winter.

Habits, etc.—The Stonechat is never found in forest country. During the summer months, whilst breeding in the Himalayas, it is found on the open hill-sides, either amongst the terraced cultivation or on the bare waste slopes where rough grazing alternates with rocky screes. In winter in the plains it is largely a bird of open cultivation, being particularly partial to fields with standing crops of cotton, sugar-cane, or the various cereals. Under all circumstances its characteristics are the same. It invariably perches on some vantage-point, either a large stone or more generally the topmost twig of a bush or plant, and thence makes short flights in all directions on to the ground to capture some insect, either devouring it on the spot, or taking it back for the purpose to its perch. It is very restless and fairly shy, and is incessantly flirting its wings and tail. It does not move about on the ground, but the flight is fast and strong, and once alarmed the bird is difficult to approach. The alarm-notes, *hweet-chat, hweet-chat*, somewhat resemble the noise made by clinking two stones together, and are responsible for the bird's trivial name; they are uttered at the least provocation, as the bird is rather fussy and suspicious. The song is a short low trill, and is quite pleasant though it is audible but for a short distance.

The breeding season lasts from March to July, but most eggs will be found in April and May. Two broods are reared in a season.

The nest is a cup composed of rather coarse grass and roots, sometimes mixed with moss or dry leaves, and lined with fine grass, hair, fur, and occasionally a few feathers. It is built in holes in terrace walls, under rocks and boulders, in banks and under tufts of foliage, and is well concealed, so that it is best found by watching the parents with field glasses.

The normal clutch consists of four or five eggs.

They are rather broad ovals with little or no gloss. The ground-colour is dull pale green or greenish-white, very finely and faintly freckled with pale brownish-red; the markings are very delicate in character and tend to collect towards the broad end.

They measure about 0·70 by 0·55 inches.

PLATE V

1. White-throated Laughing-Thrush. 2. Deccan Scimitar-Babbler. 3. Jerdon's Chloropsis. 4. Black-headed Sibia. (All about $\frac{4}{10}$ nat. size.)

[Face p. 88

THE DARK-GREY BUSH-CHAT

RHODOPHILA FERREA (Gray)

(Plate xi, Fig. 2, opposite page 220)

Description.—Length 6 inches. Male: Upper plumage dark ashy-grey mixed with black; wings black edged with grey, and with a white patch on the inner coverts; tail black, the feathers increasingly margined with white outwards; a broad white streak above the eye; sides of the head black; entire lower plumage white sullied with ashy along the flanks and on the thighs. In fresh autumn plumage the upper parts have rusty margins to the feathers but these soon wear off.

Female: The whole upper plumage rufous-ashy; tail brown, broadly edged with chestnut matching the upper tail-coverts; wings brown, the feathers narrowly edged with rufous; a pale grey streak above the eye; sides of the head reddish-brown; chin and throat white; remainder of lower plumage pale rufous-ashy.

Iris brown; bill black; legs dark brown.

The tail is rather longer and more graduated than in the true Chats of the genus *Saxicola*.

Field Identification.—Common Himalayan form. Male pied black and white with the under surface white; female rufous-brown, paler below with a chestnut tail; sits conspicuously on bushes and trees on the more open hill-sides; tail comparatively long.

Distribution.—This Bush-Chat breeds throughout the Himalayas from the borders of Afghanistan and Chitral to Eastern Assam at elevations between 4000 and 10,000 feet. While not migratory in the true sense of the word, it moves to a lower zone in the winter months; at that season it is common along the waterways of Assam and Eastern Bengal, but in the west only a few straggle to the plains along the base of the Himalayas.

Habits, etc.—This is a familiar bird in Himalayan hill stations, frequenting all types of country provided that they are moderately open; it is fond of gardens and the immediate neighbourhood of man. It has the family habit of perching in conspicuous positions on the tops of bushes, but differs from the Chats of the genus *Saxicola* in its fondness for situations at the tops of trees. In such places the male sings his rather pretty but unsatisfactory little song, *Titheratu-chak-lew-titatit*—always just that length but with a few variations, and with a rising inflection that ends suddenly. It captures insects and caterpillars on the ground, and also sallies into the air to take insects on the wing. While bold and familiar in an ordinary way, it develops a very anxious demeanour during the nesting season, flirting its long tail and making a noise which has been aptly described as "geezing," recalling the winding of a watch. The nearer one approaches to the nest or fledged young the more excited become the birds, so that their very anxiety betrays the spot on the principle of the children's game of "hot and cold."

The breeding season lasts from the beginning of April to the end of July and two broods are reared, occasionally from the same nest.

The nest is the usual cup characteristic of the Chats, a structure of coarse grass, fine twigs, and moss, lined with fine roots and grass stems, horse-hair, and fur. It is placed in a hollow either on some grassy bank, beneath a stone, amongst the roots of a tree, or occasionally amongst the stones of a rough terrace wall.

The clutch consists of four or five eggs. In shape they are a broad oval, with a stout and fine texture and little gloss. The ground-colour is variable from bluish-white to bluish-green; the markings consist of faint reddish speckles which may either cover the whole egg so completely that it appears rufous rather than blue, or collect into a zone or cap about the broad end.

The egg measures about 0·72 by 0·57 inches.

This Bush-Chat is commonly victimised by the Cuckoo (*Cuculus canorus*), and a large proportion of its nests are destroyed by other enemies.

THE PIED WHEATEAR

Œnanthe picata (Blyth)

Description.—Length 7 inches. Male: Black throughout except a patch on the rump and upper tail-coverts, and the lower plumage from the breast downwards which are pure white; the tail is white except for a broad black band across the end, widening on the central pair to nearly half of the feathers.

Female: Upper plumage brown; a white patch on the rump and upper tail-coverts; wings dark brown; tail as in the male but black replaced by brown; chin, throat, and breast dark ochraceous-brown; remainder of lower plumage pale buffy-whitish.

Iris dark brown; bill and legs black.

Field Identification.—In dry open country sitting on walls, stones, and posts; male black with white rump and under parts, and a white tail banded with black which is conspicuous in flight; female brown with similar tail; flies low and fast over the ground when disturbed.

Distribution. — Breeds in South-east Persia, Baluchistan, Afghanistan, the neighbouring areas of the North-west Frontier

Province, and Baltistan. In winter migrates to India where it is abundant in Sind, Rajputana, and portions of the United Provinces, and in smaller numbers in the Punjab. Two very closely allied species, the White-capped Wheatear (*Œnanthe capistrata*) and Strickland's Wheatear (*Œnanthe opistholeuca*) winter in some numbers in North-west India, the latter breeding along the Suliman Hills. They closely resemble the Pied Wheatear, and by some writers have been erroneously considered polymorphisms of that species. The first named has the top of the head and nape greyish-white. Strickland's Wheatear has the lower parts black almost to the vent.

Habits, etc.—This handsome Wheatear is amongst the earliest of

FIG. 14—Pied Wheatear (½ nat. size)

the winter visitors to arrive in India, appearing in Sind about the middle of August; it leaves again in February and March. This, like other Wheatears, avoids forest and damp areas. It prefers open desert, thin scrub-jungle, and the drier stretches of cultivation; and in such places is particularly fond of the neighbourhood of native huts and cattle-folds, attracted no doubt by the insects that gather in their vicinity. It perches comparatively seldom in trees, but sits on low mud walls, well-posts, and similar situations where it watches for food, and thence flies down to the ground to pick up wandering beetles, ants, and other insect life. The flight is strong and fast and always low over the ground, and, perching or hopping, the carriage of the bird is very spry and upright. Each individual has its own beat with a series of observation-posts, and resents the arrival within it of intruders of the same species, chasing them away: it is however rather a shy bird, as regards man. During the midday heat it rests quietly in some shady spot, and at night it roosts in the roofs of buildings by preference. The male has a very sweet, low warbling song, which is sometimes uttered in winter. In this species, as in the allied species mentioned, there is a marked preponderance of males in India in winter, somewhat in the proportion of twenty to one female, and no explanation of the fact is known.

In Baluchistan and the Kurram it breeds from late April to June at heights from 5000 to 8000 feet and even higher. The nest is a large structure of roots, bents, and feathers, the cup being lined with wool and hair. It is placed deep in a hole in a bank, rock, or wall. The clutch consists of four or five eggs.

The egg is a blunt, broad oval, fine and close in texture, with a fair gloss. The ground-colour varies from white to pale skim-milk-blue, sparsely marked with tiny freckles and a few small blotches of reddish-brown, the markings tending to gather in a zone round the broad end.

The egg measures about 0·8 by 0·6 inches.

THE DESERT WHEATEAR

ŒNANTHE DESERTI (Temminck)

(Plate xiv, Fig. 4, opposite page 286)

Description.—Length 6 inches. Male: Upper plumage rich buff turning to a white patch at the base of the tail; wings black, the feathers margined with white or buff, and with a patch on the inner coverts white; tail black, the basal half of the feathers white; a pale buff streak over the eyes; sides of the head and neck, chin, and throat black, the feathers edged with buff; remainder of lower plumage buff, brightest on the breast.

Female: Resembles the male, but is duller and the black is replaced by brown.

Iris dark brown; bill and legs black.

Field Identification.—A typical Wheatear perching on the ground or on low bushes in arid open country; sandy in colour with dark wings, and black throat-patch in male; a white patch in the base of the tail; flies low and fast over the ground when disturbed.

Distribution.—The Desert Wheatear has a wide distribution as a breeding species in Northern Africa, Palestine, Arabia, and South-western Asia to Tibet. It is divided into several races, of which we are only concerned with two. *Œ. d. atrogularis* breeds in Western Central Asia, the Kirghiz Steppe, the South Caucasus to Eastern Persia and Afghanistan. In winter it migrates to the plains of North-western India, becoming very common in the North-west Frontier

Province, the Punjab and Sind, and reaching the latitude of Bombay to the south and Nagpur in the east. *Œ. d. oreophila*, slightly larger with more white in the wing-quills breeds in Baltistan, Ladakh and Lahul but winters south-west of our limits. This species must not be confused with the Isabelline Wheatear (*Œnanthe isabellina*), also a winter visitor to North-western India, in which both sexes closely resemble the female of the Desert Wheatear but have the black bar on the end of the tail narrower.

The Red-tailed Wheatear (*Œnanthe xathoprymna*), common about broken land in North-western India, has the tail chestnut with a black terminal band that is much as in the Blue-throat, but its habits which are like those of the Desert Wheatear distinguish it from the skulking Bluethroat.

Habits, etc.—This is a true denizen of the desert, being generally distributed and common in the wide arid plains of North-western India, where it prefers the more barren and sandy wastes, though it comes also into cultivation where this is interspersed with barren patches. It is particularly fond of broken ground, either sandy or rocky, and of old cultivation which has reverted to desert. It spends most of its time on the ground, perching on stones and little eminences or on the wild caper bushes and uck plants that are common in the localities it inhabits; from such spots it hops or flies to the ground to capture beetles and other insects, occasionally darting up into the air to take insects on the wing. It arrives in India later than most of the Wheatears, about the middle of October, and leaves again in February and early March. It flies well but keeps low above the ground and practically never perches on trees.

This species, in the race *Œ. d. oreophila*, just nests in Indian territory in farther Kashmir and Lahul on the barren hillsides and sandy plains at elevations of 10,000 to 12,000 feet.

The nest is placed in burrows, under bushes, and in holes in walls. It is a shapeless mass of grass, fine roots and twigs, wool, hair, and other materials, in which a shallow hollow is lined with hair and a few feathers.

The clutch consists of three to five eggs; these are pale bluish-green speckled and spotted with rusty-red.

In size they average about 0·80 by 0·56 inches.

THE BROWN ROCK-CHAT

CERCOMELA FUSCA (Blyth)

Description.—Length 6 inches. Sexes alike. The whole plumage dull rufous-brown, redder on the sides of the head and lower parts; tail very dark brown.

Iris dark brown; bill and legs black.

Field Identification.—Plains species, frequenting ruins, outskirts of towns, old brickyards and low rocky hills; a plain dark-brown bird familiar in demeanour, coming into occupied buildings.

Distribution.—This is purely an Indian species and is confined to a patch of country in the centre of the Peninsula, including the Southern and Eastern Punjab, the United Provinces, Chota Nagpur, the extreme North-east of the Central Provinces, and Rajputana as far east as Cutch.

Habits, etc.—The Brown Rock-Chat is a common and familiar species found both in arid stony wastes, in deep ravines and earthy cliffs, on rocky hills, and in and about villages and towns. It is a great frequenter of buildings, flitting in and out of the empty chambers and gaping windows of ancient palaces and forts, perching in the cornices of tombs and mosques, and living even in the more frequented houses and offices of the work-a-day world, the friend alike of rich and poor. It comes into rooms even when there are people moving and talking within; it is a regular Wheatear in its habits, flying from ground to roof-ridge, from window to cornice, with the strong direct flight of those birds; its food consists of insects, beetles, ants, and the like, which it captures on the ground, flying down from the elevated situations where it perches. During the breeding season it becomes rather pugnacious and readily attacks squirrels, rats, lizards, and birds in the neighbourhood of the nest.

The breeding season lasts from February to August, but most eggs will be found in March and April. Two or three broods are reared in a year, sometimes in the same nest.

The nest is a shallow, loosely-constructed cup of grass-roots, wool, hair, and similar materials, sometimes separately lined with wool and hair; occasionally it is supported by a little heap of small stones and fragments of clay. It is built in holes in rocks, buildings, and stone walls, and when in buildings may be placed on shelves and rafters without any attempt at concealment.

The normal clutch consists of three eggs, but four or five are sometimes laid.

The egg is a moderately broad oval, rather pointed towards the small end; the texture is fine with a good deal of gloss. The ground-colour is a most delicate pale pure blue; the markings consist of tiny specks and spots of reddish-brown, which tend to collect in a zone round the broad end.

The egg measures about 0·82 by 0·62 inches.

THE SPOTTED FORKTAIL

ENICURUS MACULATUS Vigors

Description.—Length 11 inches, including a long, deeply-forked tail of 6 inches. Sexes alike. A patch on the forehead and crown, a large patch on the rump, and the lower plumage from the breast downwards white; remainder of body plumage black, with round white spots on the hind neck, and lunate white spots on the back; feathers of the lower breast spotted with white; a broad white bar across the wing; the inner flight-feathers marked with white; tail black, the feathers white at the base and broadly tipped with white, and the two outer pairs entirely white.

Iris dark brown; bill black; legs white.

Field Identification.—A Himalayan bird with a peculiar loud call, found on mountain streams in forest; pied black and white, with a deeply-forked tail which droops at the end, and is incessantly swayed up and down. The markings on the upper surface form in life a white St Andrew's-Cross on a black ground.

Distribution.—The Spotted Forktail is found throughout the Himalayas, and farther eastwards through Assam and Siam to China. It is divided into several races, of which two are Himalayan. The typical race is found throughout the Western Himalayas from 3000 to 12,000 feet from the extreme North-western Frontier to Nepal. From Nepal eastwards to Sikkim and Assam, and still farther east, it is replaced by *E. m. guttatus* which has no white spots on the breast. This race is found in the Himalayas between 2000 and 8000 feet. A resident species, though it probably changes its elevation slightly at different seasons.

The Slaty-backed Forktail (*Enicurus schistaceus*), common in the Eastern Himalayas, is of the same type with a long forked tail. The crown to the lower back are slaty blue-grey. The Little Forktail (*Microcichla scouleri*), however, found throughout the Himalayas, has a very short tail, but little more than half the wing in length.

Habits, etc.—The Forktail is a water-bird, strictly confined to running streams in hill ravines, preferably those that flow under fairly thick forest. It feeds on insects which it obtains from the water and the stream-bed; it walks sedately over the stones along the margins of the water, feeding with a quick pecking motion, rather similar to that of a chicken; and as it goes the black and white plumage blends marvellously with the glint of flowing water and the dark shadows amongst the stones so that it is seldom noticed till it takes to flight. It has a habit of frequently and unexpectedly turning at right angles or from side to side, and now and again it advances with little tripping runs, the white legs passing over the slippery stones with a sure-footed celerity. Standing and moving, the beautiful forked tail is always a characteristic feature, slowly swaying upwards and downwards.

The call is a loud, rather plaintive *cheeer*, uttered both on the

FIG. 15—Spotted Forktail (⅓ nat. size)

ground and in flight, and it is usually the first intimation of the presence of the bird that flies up from the bed of a stream that one is slowly climbing and settles again by the water some fifty yards or so above; again one disturbs it and the manœuvre is repeated. Then as one reaches the limit of its territory it leaves the stream, and slipping through the neighbouring forest regains the water below one and starts to feed again; occasionally for a few minutes it perches on a bough of a tree, but this is seldom.

The breeding season lasts from April till June.

The nest is a most compact and heavy cup of green moss mixed with fine roots and a good deal of clay; the cavity is lined with skeletonised leaves. It is placed near the water, in a niche of rock or a hollow of the bank, or amongst the roots of a tree.

The clutch usually consists of three eggs, but four are sometimes laid. The egg is a rather elongated and pointed oval, fine in texture with very little gloss. The ground-colour is pale greenish or pale stone-colour, and the markings consist of fine spots and freckles of yellowish- or reddish-brown, evenly and often thinly distributed.

The egg measures about 0·68 by 0·75 inches.

THE BLACK REDSTART

PHŒNICURUS OCHRURUS (Gmelin)

(Plate viii, Fig. 1, opposite page 154)

Description.—Length 6 inches. Male in fresh autumn plumage: Body plumage black, more or less concealed by grey fringes which wear off as the winter progresses so that the bird gradually becomes blacker in appearance; the hinder parts from the rump and abdomen orange chestnut, except the central pair of tail-feathers which are brown; flight-feathers and the larger coverts brown edged with rufous.

Female: Brown tinged with fulvous, paler below and suffused with orange from the abdomen downwards; a pale ring round the eye; rump and tail chestnut, the central pair of feathers brown.

Iris dark brown; bill and legs black.

Field Identification.—Abundant winter visitor to the plains, easily distinguished from all other birds by its habit of shivering the reddish tail at short intervals.

Distribution.—The Black Redstart is a widely-spread species occurring almost throughout Europe and Asia and in portions of Africa. In this immense range it is divided into a number of races all very similar in appearance, of which two are to be found in our area. *P. o. phœnicuroides* breeds in Persia, Turkestan, and Afghanistan, and in the mountains of Baluchistan; it also breeds in the high mountain areas, over 10,000 feet, of Kashmir, Ladakh, and Western Tibet north of the Central Himalayan range, where forest country has given place to the desolate barren valleys and mountains beyond the reach of the monsoons. In the winter, from September to April, it migrates to the plains of North-western India, extending south as far as Northern Guzerat. *P. o. rufiventris* occupies a more eastern range, breeding from Tibet to China and wintering in South-western China, Burma, Assam, and North-eastern, Central, and Southern India. This form was noticed as high as 20,000 feet on migration by the Everest Expedition.

The Blue-fronted Redstart (*Phœnicurus frontalis*), easily recognisable amongst the members of its genus by the black terminal band to the chestnut tail, breeds in a high zone about 10,000 feet in the Himalayas. In winter it is common about the hill stations.

Habits, etc.—Those who are fortunate enough to travel in the high Himalayas in summer in the barren uplands of Kashmir and Ladakh, Tibet, Spiti, and Lahul, will recognise in the Black Redstart one of the most familiar of the roadside birds—all the more conspicuous because of the general scarcity of bird-life. They flit about the stones and boulders and roadside walls, now indulging in a pleasing song with wheezy jingling notes and trills, now indicating the neighbourhood of eggs or young by the low anxious alarm note; and all the time amongst their restless movements the characteristic shiver of the tail is seen. There up on the breeding grounds the bird is very shy and cautious, but in the winter when it descends to the Indian plains this trait is lost and it becomes one of the most pleasant and friendly of our garden birds; in fact its whole character appears to change and only the shiver of the tail remains to recall our friend of the barren heights. In India it is essentially a bird of open smiling cultivation and pleasant fertile gardens: it haunts the shade, not of deep groves and jungles but little patches of shade amongst the sunshine, perching on the lower branches of trees and flying down ever and anon to the ground to pick up its insect food. The call then is a curious little croak.

As in most birds that breed at high elevations the breeding season is late, eggs being laid in June. The nest is a large substantial cup of fine twigs, bents, roots, grass stems, moss, and similar materials, lined with shreds of grass, hair, and feathers. It is placed in walls (which are built of loose stones and without mortar in countries where this species breeds) or under stones on the steep hill-sides.

The clutch consists of four to six eggs. The eggs are of two types, very pale greenish-blue or almost pure white, with a slight gloss but no markings.

They measure about 0·80 by 0·60 inches.

THE WHITE-CAPPED REDSTART

Chaimarrhornis leucocephala (Vigors)

(Plate viii, Fig. 4, opposite page 154)

Description.—Length 7 inches. Sexes alike. Top of the head shining white; rest of the head, neck, back, breast, and wings black; the rump and lower plumage from the breast downwards bright chestnut; tail chestnut, a black band across the tip.

Iris dark brown; bill and legs black.

Field Identification.—A bird of the Himalayan streams and rivers where they are not closed in with trees. Quite unmistakable with shining white cap, black and chestnut plumage, and chestnut tail ending in a black bar.

Distribution.—The White-capped Redstart is found from the hills of Baluchistan and the Afghan frontier right along the Himalayas and farther east to Western China, occurring in all the higher mountain systems of this area. It breeds at elevations between 6000 and 16,000 feet, individuals wandering even higher, but the majority of nests are certainly to be found between 8000 and 13,000 feet. During the winter it descends from high altitudes and is common along all the rivers of the foot-hills to the edge of the plains.

Habits, etc.—This lovely Redstart is familiar to all who have done much travelling in the higher altitudes of the Himalayas. It is strictly a water-bird dwelling on rivers and mountain streams, whether they flow amongst the verdant slopes and wooded precipices of the Outer Himalayas or through the barren valleys of the Inner and Central Himalayas where stony scree and tortuous glaciers wind down from the snow-clad peaks. In the desolation of the latter surroundings the beautiful plumage and the cheerful ways of the bird readily attract the attention of the traveller.

It is pre-eminently a bird of the boulders amongst rushing water, and often drifts of snow, flying swiftly from bank to bank or fly-catching with little erratic flights from stone to stone, its loud plaintive squeak *t-e-e-e-e* being easily heard amongst the roar of the waters. During the breeding season different pairs have their territory defined along the torrents where they live.

As with most Redstarts, the tail is an expressive organ. Continuously the bird beats it up and down from well above the line of the back, almost to touch the stone on which it is sitting, and the action is frequently accompanied with a low bow; this is done with the feathers closed or only partly spread; but as the bird launches into flight or settles the tail is spread into a fan for a moment, a glorious glimpse of chestnut and black.

This species is stronger in flight than the Plumbeous Redstart, and profits by the fact to leave the stream-beds and pay hasty visits to wet, mossy cliffs, steep marshy hill-sides, and similar situations.

The breeding season lasts from May till August, but most nests will be found in July. The nest is a rather deep and massive cup of moss, leaves, roots, and grass, with a thick lining of wool and hair. It is placed in a hole of a wall or bank beside the water, or more rarely under a stone or amongst the roots of a tree.

The eggs vary from three to five in number, but the ordinary clutch consists of four eggs.

In shape they are broad ovals with only a slight gloss; the ground-colour is a pale blue or blue-green, sometimes tinged with pink, and the markings consist of specks and spots of reddish-brown, with underlying markings of grey and neutral tint. These markings vary in number and intensity, occasionally collecting into a cap at the broad end.

The egg measures about 0·96 by 0·65 inches.

THE PLUMBEOUS REDSTART

RHYACORNIS FULIGINOSA (Vigors)

(Plate viii, Fig. 2, opposite page 154)

Description.—Length 5 inches. Male: The whole plumage dull plumbeous-slate except the tail which is bright chestnut.

Female: The whole upper plumage dull bluish-brown, the tail white with a large triangle of brown at the end; wings brown, edged with pale rufous; lower plumage ashy-brown squamated with ashy-white.

Iris dark brown; bill black; legs dark brown.

Field Identification.—Himalayan species. Never seen away from running water, perching on the boulders and fluttering from them into the air. Male, blackish-slate with a chestnut tail; female, grey with a white tail, tipped triangularly with brown.

Distribution.—The Plumbeous Redstart is found throughout the whole length of the Himalayas, where it breeds commonly from 4000 to 9000 feet and in smaller numbers up to 13,000 feet, though it is certainly unusual to find it above 10,000 feet. During the winter it leaves the higher portion of its habitat and is then found from 6000 feet right down to the foot-hills. Apart from this altitudinal movement it is a resident species.

Habits, etc.—The Plumbeous Redstart is purely a water-bird, closely wedded to the streams and rivers of the Himalayas, eschewing their wider and more placid reaches, and preferring tumultuous waters rushing down the steeper slopes and broken by large boulders.

These graceful little birds strike the notice of even the least observant. No stretch of stream is without its pair, which spend all their time on the boulders in the middle of the rushing water, with occasional excursions to the bank or to the bough of some adjacent tree. They flit from stone to stone and continuously make erratic little fluttering darts into the air after some passing insect, or snatch some morsel from the water's brim; as they settle, the conspicuously-coloured tail, chestnut in the cock, brown and white in the hen, is slightly fanned and wagged up and down, the two movements being simultaneous and repeated at intervals until the next incursion into the air. This movement of the white tail has been aptly compared to the scintillations of light on water slightly disturbed. They are as quarrelsome as restless, and appear to have sharply-defined territories, for the male with a provocative little snatch of song is always launching attacks at the intruder from some other territory, dashing at it regardless of sex and chasing it back to its own borders. The short song is rather sweet and jingling and may be heard occasionally in winter as well as in the breeding season. It is remarkably similar to that of the White-throated Fantail Flycatcher (*L. albicollis*) and easily confused with it. It is uttered either from some rock in midstream or in the air as the little bird slowly flies with even movement but rapidly vibrating wings in a short parabola from rock to rock. This species always feeds very late into the dusk.

The breeding season lasts from April to July and two broods appear to be raised.

The nest is a neat cup of moss mixed with a few leaves and roots and lined with fine roots and fibres or wool and hair. It is placed in any sort of hole or hollow provided that it is close to running water, in ivy on a tree, in a hole in a trunk, in a hole of a rock or bank or wall, or on a small ledge. Two nests will occasionally be found a few inches apart, but these merely represent successive occupations of a favoured site.

The eggs are three to five in number, but four is the normal clutch.

They are more or less broad ovals in shape, rather pointed towards the small end, of a fine texture and with a slight gloss. The ground-colour is a pale greenish-white or sometimes a faint stone-colour, almost entirely obscured by the markings, which consist of a mottling and freckling of somewhat pale and dingy yellowish- or reddish-brown. These markings have a tendency to collect in a cap at the broad end. The eggs greatly resemble miniatures of the eggs of the White-capped Redstart.

They measure about 0·76 by 0·60 inches.

THE BLUETHROAT

Cyanosylvia svecica (Linnæus)

(Plate ix, Fig. 6, opposite page 176)

Description.—Length 6 inches. Fully adult male in breeding plumage: The whole upper plumage and wings brown; tail brown, a conspicuous chestnut patch in the base broken by the central pair of feathers; a fulvous line over the eye; chin and throat bright blue, with a chestnut spot in the centre of the blue; below the blue a blackish band and below this a broader band of chestnut; remainder of lower plumage buffish-white. The blue and chestnut of the lower plumage vary according to age, season and race and in some specimens are almost absent. Occasionally the chestnut spot is entirely absent or is replaced by a white spot.

Female: Differs from the male in having the whole lower plumage buffish-white with a gorget of brown spots across the breast.

Iris brown; bill black, fleshy at base of lower mandible; legs yellowish-brown.

Field Identification.—A brownish bird, found on the ground in herbage, preferably in damp localities; rises at one's feet with a conspicuous flash of the bright chestnut patches in the tail and dives into cover again a few yards ahead. Males have a varying amount of blue and chestnut on the throat and breast.

Distribution.—The Bluethroat is a very widely distributed Palæarctic species, occurring in different forms through the greater part of Europe, Asia, and Northern Africa. The exact number of races and their distribution has not yet been satisfactorily worked out, but the majority of birds met with in India belong to the form *C. s. pallidogularis*, which certainly breeds from West Turkestan to East Transcaspia and to the Southern Urals, and in winter migrates to almost the whole of India and Ceylon. Two other races certainly occur in India; the dark Central Siberian bird, *C. s. robusta*, is a winter visitor to the north-east, while *C. s. abbotti* migrates through the north-west; this is the form which breeds in Ladakh and is distinguished by the brilliant blue of the throat and by the fact that the chestnut throat spot is often lacking or replaced by white. In this race the female in breeding plumage is similar to the male.

The allied Rubythroat (*Calliope calliope*), with the upper plumage olive-brown and a brilliant patch of ruby-scarlet on the throat, is common in winter in North-east India down to the Godavari. It breeds in Northern Asia.

The much darker Himalayan Rubythroat (*Calliope pectoralis*) in which the ruby throat is set in a deep black breast breeds along the whole of the Himalayas at high elevations. It is common on open hill-sides in Kashmir.

Habits, etc.—From September until May the Bluethroat is a common species in India either as a passage migrant or a winter visitor, but its movements have not yet been properly worked out. It does not breed nearer than Ladakh. Although extremely common at certain times and places it escapes observation through its skulking habits. It is a bird of the ground and heavy cover, preferring dampish spots, such as reed-beds on the edge of jheels, tamarisk thickets in river-beds, heavy standing crops and similar situations. In these it feeds on the ground, only occasionally ascending to the top of the bushes to look around. Ordinarily it is only seen when one walks through cover, as it dashes up at one's feet and flies a few yards before diving headlong again into obscurity, where it runs rapidly along the ground in short bursts; at the end of each course of running the tail is elevated and slightly expanded; the dark brown tail with its bright chestnut base is very conspicuous in flight and readily leads to identification. The alarm-note and ordinary call is a harsh *tack*, but on its breeding grounds this Bluethroat is a fine songster and mimic.

C. s. abbotti breeds in Ladakh in June and July. The nest is well concealed on the ground at the base of thorny bushes, and is a cup composed of dry grass. The usual clutch consists of three or four eggs.

The egg is a rather broad oval, fine in texture with a slight gloss. In colour it is a dull, uniform sage-green, with or without pale reddish freckling, which sometimes almost obscures the ground-colour.

It measures about 0·75 by 0·55 inches.

RED-FLANKED BUSH ROBIN

IANTHIA CYANURA Pallas

Description.—Length 6 inches. Male: Head and upper parts, edges of wings, sides of head and throat down to breast dark blue; forehead and a line extending above the eye to the neck, the angle of the wings and upper tail coverts bright blue; tail black on inner webs, suffused with blue on the outer; middle of the throat and a line down to the lower breast and abdomen dusky white. A very conspicuous patch of orange chestnut on either side of the body.

Iris brown; bill dark brown, paler at base; legs brown.

The males at first are indistinguishable from the females and some breed in that dress.

Female: Dark brown above and on sides of neck, upper tail covert duller than in the male; tail brown with blue edges on outer webs of feathers; the chin, middle of throat and abdomen white, breast brownish. An orange chestnut patch on either flank as in male.

Field Identification.—The blue coloration in the male and the brown back and blue upper tail coverts of the female, together with the patches of orange chestnut on the flanks in both sexes, are characteristic of this bird.

Distribution.—This bird has a wide distribution from the Urals right across Siberia to Japan, and southward to China, the Himalayas and Indo-China. It has been divided into a number of races and two occur in the Himalayas. From Gilgit to Garhwal the form is *I. c. pallidiora*, and Nepal eastward it is replaced by a darker bird, *I. c. rufilata*.

Habits, etc.—The Red-flanked Bush Robin breeds in the higher Himalayas in open forest of Kharshu oak, birch, silver and other firs, from 6000 to 12,000 feet. In autumn most birds move down to a level from 5000 to 8000 feet, occasionally to the edge of the plains, but a few pass the winter in their breeding haunts. This is a shy bird even in the breeding season and its habits are rather similar to the Continental Robin. In the non-breeding season it delights in open spaces surrounded by trees or other cover, and scrub jungle skirting roads. It feeds chiefly on the ground. There is no song, only a monotonous three-noted call uttered at regular intervals, in which the middle note is lower than the other two.

It breeds from May to June. The nest is constructed of dry grass with finer pieces and often Musk Deer hair. It is placed in a variety of situations, among the roots of a fallen tree, on a steep slope, in a hole in a bank, or under a fallen tree. At lower levels the nests are usually in fairly thick cover, but at all times it is well concealed and protected by herbage or roots.

The clutch consists of from three to five eggs. They are broad ovals, sometimes rather pointed, pure white with a faint tinge of green and fine small specks of reddish-brown at the larger end, occasionally without any markings.

The eggs measure 0·7 by 0·55 inches.

THE INDIAN ROBIN

SAXICOLOIDES FULICATA (Linnæus)

Description.—Length 7 inches. Male: Glossy black with a blue sheen; a white patch on the shoulder; flight-feathers brown; centre of abdomen and a conspicuous patch under the tail deep chestnut.

Female: Upper plumage dark brown, the front and sides of the face paler, the tail much darker, almost black; centre of abdomen and a conspicuous patch under the tail deep chestnut.

Iris dark brown; bill and legs black.

The bill is slender and rather curved; the tail is rather long and rounded at the end.

Field Identification.—A familiar plains bird, coming freely round houses and spending most of its time on the ground. Easily identified by the habit of holding the long tail erect so as to exhibit a bright chestnut patch below its base; the male has a conspicuous white shoulder-patch and much black glossed with steely-blue in its plumage.

Distribution.—The Indian Robin is found throughout the whole of India from the Himalayas southwards to Ceylon. The typical black-backed race with a very dark, almost black female is found in Ceylon. *S. f. cambaiensis* occurs throughout Northern India from the hills of the North-west Frontier Province along the fringe of the Outer Himalayas to Eastern Bengal and southwards. In this race the male has the back brown while the female is grey and brown in colour. Between the two, races connecting them may be recognised. These are first *S. f. intermedia* which occurs in a broad belt right across the centre of the Peninsula, bounded on the north by a line from the River Tapti to Vizagapatam district and on the south by the Krishna River; and secondly *S. f. ptymatura* which occupies the rest of South India. They bridge the colour differences between the first two forms. All four races are strictly resident.

FIG. 16—Indian Robin (½ nat. size)

Habits, etc.—Those who like to dilate on the theme that the East is topsy-turvy often quote the Indian Robin amongst their numerous illustrations, pointing out that he wears his red under his tail instead of on his breast; for this bird, while in no sense a true Robin, somewhat occupies in India the place of the Robin in the West. It is a familiar bird, hanging round the haunts of men, the outskirts of villages, buildings both great and small, brick-kilns and similar situations, and it nests in a variety of curious places after the fashion of the English bird. In addition it is also partial to stony, barren hill-sides and dry ravines; in fact, the essential conditions for its presence are dryness and open country; in damp areas and in heavy forest it is wanting.

In character it exhibits the curious mixture of boldness and suspicion that is found in so many Indian birds. So long as unmolested, it hops about in the close vicinity of men and women busy at their own tasks, apparently heedless of them; but at the first hint of danger it becomes shy and unobtrusive. In the same way, though the nest may be built in a hole in a stable wall or similarly public spot, it is readily deserted if attention is paid to it.

In demeanour the bird is very sprightly, hopping about with the head held stiffly high and the tail cocked well forward over the back; in fact its normal poise is that of the English Wren, and the bird being larger with a longer tail the attitude appears more exaggerated. It feeds for the most part on the ground, and perches by preference on walls, posts, roofs, and large gnarled tree-trunks, rather than on the boughs of trees. The food consists chiefly of insects and their larvæ.

It has only an apology for a song, which is used while courting is in progress.

The breeding season is from March to August and two or three broods are reared, often in the same nest though the lining is usually replaced. The nest is placed in holes in all sorts of situations on the ground, in walls and buildings, and in plants. It is a pad of grass lined with miscellaneous soft materials, roots and fibres, wool and hair, varying in depth and neatness of construction according to the circumstances of the hole. A large proportion of nests contain a fragment of snake's slough.

Three to five eggs are laid. The egg is a rather elongated oval, more or less pointed towards the small end; the texture is fine and strong with a moderate gloss. The ground-colour is white, faintly tinged with green, pink, or brownish; the general character of the markings is a fine close speckling and mottling of different shades of reddish- or yellowish-brown, underlaid with a few secondary markings of pale inky-purple; there is a tendency for the markings to be thicker about the broad end.

The egg measures about 0·79 by 0·59 inches.

THE MAGPIE-ROBIN

Copsychus saularis (Linnæus)

Description.—Length 8 inches. Male: Head, neck, breast, and upper plumage glossy black; remainder of lower plumage white; wing black, a white patch close to the body; tail long and graduated, the two central pairs of feathers black, the remainder white.

Female: The whole upper plumage uniform dark brown, glossed with bluish; wings and tail dark brown, with white distributed as in the male. Chin, throat, breast, and sides of the neck and face dark grey, the last mottled with white; remainder of lower plumage whitish washed with fulvous on the flanks and under the tail.

Iris brown; bill black; legs dark plumbeous.

Field Identification.—Common plains species, found in gardens and familiar in habits, with a beautiful song; the male conspicuously pied black and white with a longish rounded tail, the female with a duller version of the same pattern. Carries the tail rather elevated.

Distribution.—The Magpie-Robin or Dayal-bird extends throughout India and Ceylon to China and the Malay Islands, and in this wide range is divided into a number of races.

Within our area, however (except in the extreme south, from the Nilgiris and Bangalore to Travancore, where the birds grade into the Ceylon race *C. s. ceylonensis*), all birds are referable to the typical form.

This bird is found alike in the plains and in the hills up to about 4000 and occasionally to 6000 feet. It occurs in the Outer Himalayas, but is virtually absent from Sind, Cutch, and large

FIG. 17—Magpie-Robin (½ nat. size)

portions of the Punjab and desert Rajputana. Although said to be only a winter visitor to Mount Aboo and Northern Guzerat, it is usually regarded as a strictly resident species; except that in the Himalayas it ascends a couple of thousand feet in the breeding season, and also penetrates then into some of the inner valleys.

Habits, etc.—While never particularly abundant the Magpie-Robin is very generally distributed in India, avoiding both dense forest and open bare plain. It is essentially a bird of groves, and delights to move about on the ground under the shelter of low trees; thick undergrowth it dislikes. Naturally, therefore, it is a familiar garden bird, delighting in the mixed chequer of sunshine and shade that is the characteristic of an Indian garden; it hops about under the orange and pomegranate trees, pauses for a moment to sip the water running along the irrigation channels, and then flies across amongst the trees to settle on some lower bough or on the garden wall before returning to its quest for insects on the ground. It is both confiding and unobtrusive, and as the lady of the house moves about her garden in the shade, whether she be Burra-Memsahib or some humble menial's wife, she will see the little pied bird watching her from wall or bush with friendly and attentive scrutiny. And by way of gratitude for shelter and protection (or so we like to think in spite of prosaic fact), the cock bird early in the morning and again in the evening mounts to the topmost bough of one of the garden trees and pours out his delicious song. For the Magpie-Robin is one of the best songsters in a land where singing birds are somewhat scarce.

The tail is carried very high over the back, though not usually as high as in the case of the Indian Robin ; it is frequently lowered and expanded into a fan, then closed and jerked up again over the back.

The food is obtained for the most part on the ground and consists of insects, grasshoppers, crickets, ants, beetles, and the like ; a little vegetable matter, and an occasional earthworm vary this diet.

The breeding season lasts from the end of March to the end of July, but most eggs will be found in April and May. The nest is placed in holes in tree-trunks, in banks and walls, and in the roofs of houses. It is a cup composed of roots, grasses, fibres, and feathers, with very little definite lining, and varying a good deal in depth and compactness of construction, according to the circumstances of the hole.

The clutch usually consists of five eggs.

The egg is a typical oval, hard and fine in texture with a fair amount of gloss. The ground-colour is some shade of green but is rather variable. The markings consist of streaks, blotches, and mottlings of brownish-red, usually densely laid on and with a tendency to be thicker about the broad end.

The egg measures about 0·87 by 0·66 inches.

THE SHAMA

Kittacincla malabarica (Scopoli)

Description.—Length 11 inches, including a long graduated tail of 6 inches. Male : A patch above the base of the tail white ; remainder of upper plumage, wings, and lower plumage to the lower breast glossy black ; remainder of lower plumage bright chestnut except the thighs which are whitish ; tail black, all but the two central pairs of feathers broadly white at the ends.

Female: Resembles the male, but the black is replaced by slaty-brown, and the chestnut by rufous; feathers of the wings narrowly edged with rufous.

Iris dark brown; bill black; legs pale flesh-colour.

Field Identification.—A forest bird, found in thick jungle about ravines and remarkable for its beautiful song; the male is black with chestnut belly and much white about the long graduated tail; the female plumage is a duller version of the same pattern.

Distribution.—The Shama is widely distributed in India, Ceylon, Burma, Siam, the Malays and China, and is divided into various races.

The typical race of the Shama is found along the western side of

FIG. 18—Shama (⅓ nat. size)

India, from Bombay to Travancore, and up the eastern side as far as Orissa and the Rajmehal Hills; also in the submontane tracts of the United Provinces as far west as Ramnagar below Naini Tal. The Burmese race *K. m. indica*, with a shorter tail, extends through Assam into the Duars and in the jungles of South-eastern Bengal. *K. m. leggei* in Ceylon is very different in that the female is similar to the male in colour. It is a resident species, occurring in warm well-watered jungles up to a height of 4000 feet.

Habits, etc.—The Shama is well known by repute and in story as one of the famous singing birds of India, but owing to its forest habitat and its shyness it is probably known by sight to comparatively few people. It lives in jungles and forest wherever broken ravines and low hills supply a sufficiency of the small streams and open glades to which it is partial; and the spots that it frequents generally contain a good deal of bamboo growth. It feeds mostly on the ground, searching for insects, worms and fallen fruits, but when disturbed flies up into the trees. In short, this species may be considered as taking in forest the place occupied by the Magpie-Robin in open and inhabited country.

The song is loud and beautiful with a varied range of notes, and it is chiefly uttered in the mornings and evenings, continuing late in the evening until darkness has practically fallen.

This bird has a curious habit, chiefly in the breeding season, of striking the wings together above the body as it flies across open ground.

The breeding season is from April to June. The nest is usually placed in the base of bamboo clumps amidst the mass of rubbish which collects in such situations and which forms a shelter over the nest; the nest itself is a slight cup of dead leaves and moss lined with grass.

The clutch consists of four or five eggs.

The egg is a moderately broad oval, rather pointed and compressed towards the smaller end, fine and compact in texture with a fair gloss. The ground-colour is dull greenish-stone, finely and densely freckled all over with raw sienna-brown and dull purplish, the general effect recalling the eggs of the Larks.

The egg measures about 0·85 by 0·65 inches.

THE NILGIRI BLACKBIRD

TURDUS SIMILLIMUS Jerdon

Description.—Length 10 inches. Male: Top of the head black; remainder of upper plumage dark ashy-plumbeous; wings and tail black washed with ashy; the whole lower plumage dark ashy-brown, the edges of the feathers slightly paler.

Female: The whole upper plumage dark ashy-brown; the whole lower plumage brownish-grey, streaked on the chin and throat with dark brown.

Iris brown, eye-rims yellow; bill reddish-orange; legs orange-yellow.

Field Identification.—Abundant in the Nilgiris and Palni Hills. A typical forest Blackbird but paler in colour than the English birds, so that a black cap shows up in the male.

Distribution.—Mount Aboo: Peninsular India, south of a line from Khandesh through Pachmarhi to Sambalpur: Ceylon. The well-known Nilgiri Blackbird gives its name to a group of five closely-allied sub-species, which differ chiefly in depth of coloration. *T. s. mahrattensis*, in which the pale collar is most conspicuous, is found at Mount Aboo, perhaps as a summer visitor only, and in the Western Ghats from Khandesh to Malabar, wandering in winter as far south as Travancore. The typical form is found in the Brahmagherries and Nilgiris, probably extending also to the higher ranges

PLATE VI

1. Verditer Flycatcher. 2. Grey-headed Flycatcher. 3. Ashy Wren-Warbler.
4. Tickell's Blue Flycatcher. 5. Little Minivet. (All about $\frac{3}{4}$ nat. size.)

[Face p. 110

of Western Mysore. *T. s. bourdilloni* is found in the Palnis and Travancore ranges while *T. s. kinnisii* is confined to Ceylon. The identity of the form reported in certain areas of the Central Provinces is still in doubt but a distinct race *T. s. spensei* is found along the Eastern Ghats. These Blackbirds occur up to the highest points in the various hill ranges and are mainly resident birds.

Habits, etc.—The Nilgiri Blackbird, to treat more particularly of the best-known form, is one of the commonest birds at Ootacamund and its vicinity, being found chiefly in the Sholas on the tops of the ranges, but also in other types of country. It enters orchards and gardens, and on the whole is a tame familiar species though shy when nesting. It feeds chiefly on the ground, hopping with active movements and turning over dead leaves for insects, worms and fallen fruits, but when disturbed flies up into the trees, flitting from tree to tree with powerful flight. Small berries and fruits are eaten in the trees.

The breeding season is somewhat extended, from March to August, though most nests will be found in April and May. At this period the males sing very beautifully, perching high up in the trees; they may be heard at all hours but especially in the evenings.

In the details of its breeding this bird recalls the familiar English Blackbird. The nest is a massive, well-built cup made of moss, roots, grass, and leaves largely plastered together with mud, while the egg-cavity is neatly lined with grass and roots. It is placed in a fork of a tree or shrub at any height up to about 20 feet from the ground.

The usual clutch consists of two to four eggs but five are sometimes found. The egg is a broad oval, pointed towards the smaller end; the texture is fine with a slight gloss. The ground-colour varies from bright blue-green to dull olive-green; the markings consist of spots, speckles, mottlings, and streaks of brownish-red, with secondary spots and clouds of purplish-pink or grey.

The egg measures about 1·17 by 0·86 inches.

THE GREY-WINGED BLACKBIRD

TURDUS BOULBOUL (Latham)

(Plate vii, Fig. 1, opposite page 132)

Description.—Length 11 inches. Male: Entire plumage deep glossy black, paler and duller beneath; a wide ashy-grey patch across the upper sides of the wings.

Female: Entire plumage olivaceous ashy-brown, the wing-patch being pale rufous.

Iris brown, eye-rim orange-yellow; bill coral-red to deep orange, dusky at the tip; legs brownish-yellow.

Field Identification.—Himalayan forest bird with a good song;

resembles the corresponding sexes of the English Blackbird with the addition of a broad patch on the wing, silvery in the male, rufous in the female.

Distribution.—The Grey-winged Blackbird is a common Himalayan species extending from Hazara and Kashmir on the west to the extreme east and south of Assam and Manipur. It breeds chiefly in an intermediate zone between 7000 and 8000 feet and in smaller numbers up to 10,000 and down to 4500 feet. It is in the main a resident species, but during the winter months tends to leave the higher portions of its range and drift down towards the foot-hills, stragglers at this season even venturing into the neighbouring plains districts.

The White-collared Blackbird (*Turdus albocincta*) is common in the Himalayan forests, breeding from 7500 to 10,000 feet, lower in winter. The male is black in colour with a broad white collar round the neck.

Habits, etc.—This is one of the finest and best-known songsters of the Himalayas, being frequently caged and sold under the name of *Kastura.* It is a typical Blackbird in its habits, and is more particularly a forest bird, feeding on the ground amongst the undergrowth, and turning over dead leaves and digging with its beak in places where the soil is soft. From the ground it obtains worms, grubs, insects, and fallen seeds and fruits, and it is also accustomed to eat large quantities of the various hill fruits and berries from the trees. At any time of day in the breeding season, but more particularly in the mornings and evenings, the males may be heard singing, usually from the top of a tall tree commanding a wide view around. The song is very pleasant, recalling that of the English Blackbird, but individuals vary a good deal in the merits of their performance. It is otherwise a quiet and rather shy bird, especially in the neighbourhood of the nest when it sits motionless on the bough of a tree watching the intruder.

The normal breeding season is from May to July.

The nest is a rather massive cup of roots and grasses usually stiffened with mud and liberally coated externally with green moss and similar materials, and lined with fine dry grass. The majority of nests are built in trees, some 10 or 20 feet from the ground, but others are placed on ledges of rock or on steep banks or amongst the roots of trees.

The eggs vary from two to four in number. They are of the usual Blackbird type. The ground-colour, where visible, is a pale dingy green, but it is thickly streaked, mottled and clouded with dull brownish-red sometimes so heavily as to obscure the ground-colour.

The eggs measure about 1·20 by 0·85 inches.

TICKELL'S THRUSH

TURDUS UNICOLOR Tickell

Description.—Length 9 inches. Male: The upper plumage including the wings and tail ashy-grey; lower plumage slaty-grey, paler on the chin, and becoming white towards the tail, the under wing-coverts chestnut-brown.

Female: Upper plumage olive-brown, the wings and tail darker; chin and throat white, streaked on the sides with black; breast olivaceous with a gorget of black spots across the upper part; flanks ochraceous; abdomen to the tail white; under wing-coverts chestnut-brown.

Iris brown; eye-rim greenish-yellow; bill and legs yellow.

Field Identification.—A quiet, dull-coloured Thrush which feeds on the ground and flies up into the trees when disturbed. Most familiar as the bird that feeds on the lawns at Srinagar, where it is particularly common.

Distribution.—This species is only found in the Indian Empire. It breeds commonly but locally in the Himalayas from Chitral to Eastern Nepal. It is migratory, and in winter moves down into the plains of India, being found at that season as far south as Khandala, Raipur, and Vizagapatam, travelling eastwards also to Sikkim, Cachar, and Manipur.

A rather larger species, the Black-throated Thrush (*Turdus atrogularis*), in which the male has the chin, throat and breast black, is a very common winter visitor to the Himalayas and Northern India.

Habits, etc.—This Thrush is known to everyone who has visited Kashmir, and it is one of those birds which contribute to the very English atmosphere of Srinagar.

The song may be heard from April to July and it sings at all hours of the day but more especially in the mornings and evenings, and on cloudy days with rain impending. This Thrush, in combination with the Kashmir Golden Oriole,-is responsible for the dawn chorus which is so remarkable in April and May in and around Srinagar in Kashmir. The song recalls that of the English Thrush though less full and varied, and is something as follows :—*chellya-chellya-chirrali, chellya-chellya-chellya, chellya-chellya-jalia ;* and it further recalls that familiar bird by its presence round houses and in gardens, and its habit of hopping about the lawns of the English quarter in search of worms and snails, uttering often a *juk-juk* which at other times is used as an alarm-note. Pairs are to be found in every grove round the villages, and it is a tame and familiar bird, haunting their neighbourhood in preference to the forests, where also, however, it is found in smaller numbers. At the nest, on the other hand, it is rathery shy.

It breeds in May and June. The nest is a large deep cup, sometimes neat and compact, at other times loose and untidy; it is composed of moss, either dry or green, roots, dry grass and a few leaves, and is lined with fine roots. It is placed usually at heights between 6 and 20 feet from the ground, in the heads of pollard willows or in the forks of trees or on branches close to the trunk. A few nests are found close to the ground in banks.

The number of eggs varies from three to five. They are rather variable in shape, round, elongated, or pyriform ovals. The texture is fine but there is very little gloss. The ground-colour is greenish- or reddish-white, and the whole surface is more or less thickly speckled or boldly blotched with dull reddish-brown, in some eggs the ground-colour predominating, in others the reddish tint of the markings; in all, however, the markings are thickest towards the broad end.

The eggs average about 1·06 by 0·78 inches.

THE ORANGE-HEADED GROUND-THRUSH

GEOKICHLA CITRINA (Latham)

(Plate iv, Fig. 3, opposite page 66)

Description.—Length 9 inches. The whole head, neck and lower parts as far as the vent orange-chestnut, rather darker on the crown and hind neck; the rest of the upper parts bluish-grey; wings and tail brown, washed with bluish-grey, a conspicuous white spot on the shoulder and another on the underside of the quills; vent and under the tail white.

Female: Similar to the male but the orange-chestnut is paler and the ashy-grey of the upper parts, wings and tail is replaced by brownish olive-green.

Iris dark hazel; bill very dark brown, base of lower mandible flesh-colour; legs fleshy-pink.

The tail is comparatively rather short.

Field Identification.—A typical Thrush in bearing, bright chestnut in colour with the back, wings and tail bluish-grey in the male and olive in the female. In the Southern race the sides of the face are curiously banded with brown and white and the throat is white. A forest species usually found feeding on the ground in damp and shady places.

Distribution.—The Orange-headed Ground-Thrush has a wide distribution with several races in India, Burma, the Andamans and Nicobars, the Malay States and Siam. We are concerned here with two. The typical race breeds throughout the foot-hills and lower ranges of the Himalayas from Murree to Assam and Burma, and still farther eastwards; also in Lower Bengal. In the Western Himalayas and Nepal it is a summer visitor. In the Eastern Himalayas and Assam it appears to be largely resident in the foot-hills, moving up in summer into some of the inner valleys. The north-western migrants evidently winter anywhere from the Dun to Chota Nagpore and Calcutta, stragglers wandering as far afield as Ratnagiri and Ceylon. *G. c. cyanotus* has a ring round the eye, the sides of the face and the chin and throat white; the white of the sides of the face is broken by two short oblique dark brown bands which run down from the lower border of the eye. This race is found as a resident south of a line roughly from Western Khandesh through Pachmarhi to Sirguja, occurring up to an elevation of 4000 feet.

Habits.—This Ground-Thrush is essentially a forest-loving species and it will always be found by preference in damp and shady thickets or in thick bamboo-brakes. In such places it feeds solitary on the ground under thick tangles of roots and stems of brushwood. It rummages amongst the leaves and fallen debris, tossing and turning them over in a constant search for slugs, insects, snails, caterpillars, berries, and such like, and so constant is this habit that the beak is nearly always muddy, a fact remarked by many writers. It is shy and quiet and when disturbed promptly flies up into a bough where it sits silent and motionless waiting to resume its quest for food. Living thus in the shade it is crepuscular in habits and at dusk moves out to roads and open spaces.

In the breeding season the male has a pleasant and energetic, though not very powerful, song which is uttered from a perch well up in a tree. This is only heard in the early mornings and late evenings and the bird is something of a mimic, introducing the calls of other species into its song. It has also a peculiar note or loud whistle, something like the noise of a screeching slate-pencil, which is used apparently as an alarm-note.

The breeding season in the Himalayas is from the end of April until nearly the end of June. In Peninsular India it is later, from June to August and even September.

The nest is a rather broad solid cup of moss, grass, stalks, bents and similar materials. Inside it is lined with fine roots and the black hair-like roots of moss and ferns. A good deal of mud and clay is usually built into the foundations. The nest is placed in a fork of a moderately sized tree, usually at no great height from the ground.

The clutch consists of three or four eggs, and five have been recorded. The egg is a moderately broad oval, a good deal pointed towards the small end. The shell is fine and fairly glossy, some eggs having a really fine gloss. The ground-colour is a pale bluish- or greenish-white and it is thickly freckled, blotched and streaked with brownish- or purplish-red. Some eggs have the markings fine and very thickly spread over the whole surface. Others have them thick, bold and blotchy all over the larger half with only a few small spots scattered over the rest of the egg. Intermediate varieties also occur.

The egg measures about 1·00 by 0·75 inches.

THE BLUE-HEADED ROCK-THRUSH

MONTICOLA CINCLORHYNCHA (Vigors)

(Plate ix, Fig. 4, opposite page 176)

Description.—Length 7 inches. Male: Whole head bright cobalt-blue, divided by a broad black line from the beak through the eye to the back and shoulders, which are also black; rump and the lower plumage chestnut; wings black washed with blue, and with a conspicuous white patch on the inner quills; tail black washed with blue.

Female: Upper plumage, wings and tail olive-brown tinged with ochraceous; chin and throat whitish; lower plumage whitish, tinged with ochraceous on the breast and largely barred with dark brown.

Iris dark brown; bill black, gape yellow; legs dusky brown.

Field Identification.—Familiar song bird in summer along the lower Himalayas in light open forest, perching on trees and railings; male easily recognised by the blue head and throat, chestnut rump and lower plumage and white patch in the wings; female brown with a scaled appearance, and a rather conspicuous dark eye.

It must not be confused with the larger Chestnut-bellied Rock-Thrush (*Monticola rufiventris*), also found throughout the Himalayas, whose male lacks the chestnut rump and white wing-patch.

Distribution.—This bird breeds in the hills along the boundary of the North-western Frontier Province and throughout the Himalayas to East and Southern Assam and the Chin and Kachin Hills. The majority breed between 3500 and 6000 feet, but a few range up to 9000 feet.

It is a migratory species, passing down from about October to April into the plains and continental ranges of India and portions of Burma. It avoids Sind and the plains of the Punjab and becomes most common in winter in the hill ranges of the Western Ghats from Khandala to South Travancore.

Habits, etc.—The Blue-headed Rock-Thrush is in the breeding season a bird of the more open hill forests, being especially typical of the areas in the lower Himalayas which are clothed with the Cheel pine (*Pinus longifolia*). Here the song of the male is a very familiar and pleasant feature; it is a pretty three-note warbling song of *tew-ti-di, tew-ti-di, tew-ti-di, tew* (the *tew* descending in the scale and getting louder at each repetition), and it is commonly sung in the mornings and evenings. The bird itself is by nature secretive and not often seen until one is familiar with the alarm-note *ee-tut-tut*, a low, pleasant sound which soon gives away its whereabouts on a tree bough; then the bird is found to be confiding and to allow a near approach. It feeds both on insects and on berries, and in pursuit of the former sometimes flies out from a tree into mid-air, hovering with wings outstretched, after the capture gliding down again to its post amongst the branches. Similarly, it often floats with wings outstretched, singing as it goes, from the top of a tall tree down to a lower one. In winter it is a solitary species.

The breeding season proper is from April to June, but occasional nests may be met with until August. The nest is a neat shallow cup of moss, grass, fir-needles and dead leaves, and is lined with fine roots or a little hair. The favourite situation for it is in a hollow in a bank by the side of a road or path, but it is also placed in hollows amongst the roots of trees.

The clutch consists of four eggs. The egg is a rather long oval, very blunt at the small end, of slightly coarse texture with a little gloss. The ground-colour is pinkish-white, very closely and minutely freckled and mottled all over, but most densely at the large end, with pale dingy salmon-colour.

The eggs measure about 0·92 by 0·72 inches.

THE BLUE ROCK-THRUSH

Monticola solitaria (Linnæus)

Description.—Length 9 inches. Male: Whole plumage dull dark blue, rather brighter over the eye, on the sides of the head and on the throat, the feathers of the upper parts with brown fringes and the feathers of the lower plumage more or less barred with blackish and fringed with white; wings and tail dark brown washed with dark blue, most of the wing-feathers tipped with creamy white.

In summer the wearing off of the fringes on the body makes the plumage a brighter, more uniform blue with the wings dark in contrast.

Female: Whole upper plumage, wings and tail similar to the male but the colour is much duller, almost ashy-brown in tint; chin, throat and upper breast creamy-buff the feathers margined with sooty-black, giving a scaled appearance; remainder of lower plumage creamy-buff barred with sooty-black.

Iris hazel; bill blackish-horn, mouth yellow; feet black, claws dark horn.

Field Identification.—A dark looking bird, the male bluish, the female speckled with buff and brown, invariably found perching solitary on rocks, brick-kilns or buildings and rather shy if approached.

Distribution.—A widely distributed species found in South Europe, Africa and the greater part of Asia. It is divided into many races. Of these we are chiefly concerned with the Central Asian and Himalayan race *M. s. pandoo* which breeds in our area from Chitral and Gilgit along the Himalayas to Sikkim at all elevations from 4500 to 15,000 feet. From September and early October until April it spreads over the greater part of India and Burma, stragglers also reaching Ceylon. It also winters in Siam, Indo-China, the Malay States and Sumatra. A greyer race *M. s. longirostris* breeds along the North-west Frontier of India from the Samana to North Baluchistan and winters in Africa. Another form *M. s. affinis* with faint traces of chestnut on the lower plumage of the male is a winter visitor to the Eastern Himalayas and Assam.

Habits, etc.—The Blue Rock-Thrush is one of those birds that is strongly attached to a particular type of terrain. In the breeding season in the hills it is very much a bird of the rocks, frequenting boulder-clad hill-sides, open rocky ground or if it is breeding down in the tree zone, rocky screes, gorges or cliffs in open ground between the forests. With this insistence on the letter of its needs it is able to occupy a very much wider altitudinal range for breeding than most species.

In winter, too, its special propensity is to the fore. Rocks it must have to live on and if they are not available in the shape of hills and boulders it finds a substitute in quarries, ruined forts and unoccupied buildings, rocks on the sea-shore or even at the worst it takes refuge on brick-kilns and piles of stone. In all these places the habits and demeanour of the bird are the same. It perches up on a point of vantage—be this boulder or cornice—sitting very erect and solitary, reminding the observer that it is the Sparrow that sitteth alone on the house-top as Canon Tristram pointed out long ago in his studies of the Holy Land. Always shy and wary, if approached it bows and flirts the tail nervously before flitting to another vantage point some distance away. In winter it frequently roosts under the roof of a house.

The male has a fine song, a soft melodious but rather short whistle reminiscent of that of an English Blackbird, which is uttered both from a perch and on the wing and this may be heard occasionally also in the winter. When courting the male indulges in slow vol-planing flights which show off his blue plumage to advantage in the sunlight.

As to food the bird is fairly omnivorous. Insects are taken from the ground and on the wing; larvæ, worms, snails, lizards, berries and seeds all are grist for its mill.

The breeding season is from April to July.

The nest is placed in a hole or cleft of the rocks on steep precipitous ground and is usually partly screened from view, difficult to reach and often inaccessible. It is a shallow cup of roots and dry grass, lined with fine roots.

The clutch consists of four or five eggs. The egg is a regular oval very smooth in texture with a fine gloss. The ground-colour is an excessively pale, slightly greenish-blue, sometimes unmarked, at other times speckled mostly at the large end with very minute brownish-red spots.

It measures about 1·10 by 0·75 inches.

THE WHISTLING-THRUSH

MYOPHONUS CÆRULEUS (Scopoli)

(Plate vii, Fig. 2, opposite page 132)

Description.—Length 12 inches. Sexes alike. Entire plumage deep blue-black, becoming brighter and bluer on the wings and tail, and duller and browner on the abdomen; a velvety black patch in front of the eye; all the body-feathers more or less tipped with deep shining blue; some of the wing-coverts tipped with white.

Iris dark brown; bill yellow, blackish along top; legs black.

Field Identification.—A large, strong "Blackbird," bright prussian-blue in favourable lights, found near water in the Himalayas; noisy with harsh whistling calls; bold and conspicuous; black legs and black eye-rim at once distinguish it from the true Blackbirds, which have those parts yellow.

Distribution.—This Whistling-Thrush, found in Turkestan, China and southwards, is represented in our area by the race *M. c. temminckii*, which extends throughout the Himalayas from the hills of Baluchistan and the Afghan Frontier to the extreme east of Assam and to the neighbouring hill tracts, being replaced by another (*M. c. eugenei*) from Eastern Burma to Cochin-China. It breeds from the foot-hills at about 2000 feet up to 12,000 feet, though the majority of nests will be found between 5000 and 9000 feet. Although strictly speaking a resident species, its fine powers of flight tend to make it wander a good deal, and in the winter months numbers move down into the foot-hills while stragglers even appear in the plains far out of sight of the hills. There are records from as far south as Jhang and Rhotak.

An allied species, the Malabar Whistling-Thrush (*Myophonus horsfieldii*), which has a bright blue forehead and a brilliant patch of cobalt-blue on the wing, is common in the vicinity of Pachmarhi in Central India and in South-western India, especially in the Nilgiris, and it is known as the "Whistling-Schoolboy."

Habits, etc.—This very common and typical Himalayan bird may be considered in some senses as a water-bird, a bird of rivers and mountain streams. True it is that it may be found anywhere in the mountains, dashing across the face of some precipitous crag, flitting through the trees of the gloomiest pine forest or feeding on an open hill-side, but a little observation will invariably show that its head-quarters are in some gorge watered by purling stream or rushing torrent. And further proof may be found in its song and calls; the call is a loud, melodious whistle, and the song is loud and well sustained, of the type of most of the Thrush family; but in both call and song there is something of harshness and unpleasantness, a squeaky, eerie timbre, which prevents either from being beautiful, but which are clearly intended to carry them above the roar of rushing waters; in this they succeed, and the voice of this bird heard in some deep nullah where the water's roar stills all lesser sounds is appropriate in the extreme, and matching its surroundings attains to beauty.

There is something very tight-trussed and neat about the Whistling-Thrush as it hops and flies from boulder to ledge, from wall to branch; its hard, shiny feathers are pressed close to the body, and as the long tail sways slowly upwards above the long legs the bird seems the living embodiment of all the qualities of vitality and fitness that one associates with nature and the hills.

The bird lays commonly from the end of April to June, but nests may be found until August, as apparently two broods are often reared.

The nest is a very massive and heavy cup of moss dragged up by the roots with mud still adhering to them; there is a thick lining of fine grass roots and moss.

It is placed in the near vicinity of water, and is generally well protected, either by concealment or by difficulty of access; for the bird is very cunning in its arrangements. Sometimes it builds in a mossy bank or in some rocky crevice where the structure of the nest and overhanging foliage protect the site from wandering eyes; at other times the nest stands out patent to view, conspicuous in the extreme, on the face of some precipitous cliff, or in a hollow on a giant boulder encircled by rushing water or otherwise inaccessible. An occasional nest may be found in a tree.

The clutch consists of three to five eggs.

The eggs are typically very long and pointed, fragile, and rather rough in texture. The ground-colour is french-grey, greyish-white or pale greenish, speckled and freckled with minute pink, pale purplish-pink or pinkish-brown markings. These markings are generally rather thin, and there is a curious faded appearance about these eggs which is most unusual.

They measure about 1·40 by 1·00 inches.

THE RED-BREASTED FLYCATCHER

SIPHIA PARVA (Bechstein)

(Plate ii, Fig. 3, opposite page 22)

Description.—Length 5 inches. Adult male: Upper plumage brown, ashy on the head; sides of the head bluish-ashy with a white ring round the eye; wings dark brown; tail blackish-brown, the basal two-thirds of the feathers white, except of the central pair; chin, throat and breast reddish-buff; remainder of lower plumage white washed with buff on the sides.

Female and immature male: The whole upper plumage brown, the wings and tail darker brown, the basal portions of all the tail-feathers except the central pair white as in the adult male; a whitish ring round the eye; whole lower plumage dull white, washed with buff on the sides.

Iris dark brown; bill brown; legs blackish-brown.

Field Identification.—A small brown bird with whitish under parts, and in some individuals with the throat and breast red, which fly-catches in trees; easily recognised by the habit of jerking the tail upwards at intervals, thus exhibiting the white patches in its base; quiet in demeanour.

Distribution.—The Red-breasted Flycatcher is widely spread as a breeding species throughout Europe, Siberia, and Northern and Central Asia generally, and is divided into two races which migrate southwards in winter. Both races are winter visitors to India and differ merely in slight details of coloration. The typical race breeds in Europe and Western Siberia, and is a most abundant winter visitor to India from October until May. It arrives in India, *via* the north-west corner, and extends down to Malabar and the Nilgiris in the south, and east as far as Behar and Assansole in Bengal. The breeding bird of North-eastern Asia (*S. p. albicilla*) winters mostly in North-eastern India, Burma, and China, but has occurred also as far as Belgaum, the Nallamallais, and Travancore.

The Kashmir Red-breasted Flycatcher (*Siphia hyperythra*) of very similar coloration, but with a more chestnut-red breast bordered with black, breeds commonly in Kashmir between 6000 and 8000 feet and winters in Ceylon.

Another Flycatcher with white in the tail is the Orange-gorgeted Flycatcher (*Siphia strophiata*). It has the throat and breast sooty with a central orange patch. Common in the Sikkim area from 9000 to 1000 feet.

Habits, etc.—The main requisite of the Red-breasted Flycatcher is trees, and provided that there is a sufficiency of such cover it is a matter of indifference to it whether it is in forest, in open cultivation, or in the neighbourhood of towns and villages. Although often descending to the ground to capture an insect it is an arboreal species and a true flycatcher in its habits, frequenting chiefly the shady places within the boughs of large trees in which it sedately hawks and flits from bough to bough. It is rather shy and secretive, and is jerky and restless in its movements, constantly flirting the tail over its back so that the white patch in the base of the feathers catches the eye sooner even than the red breast of the adult male. There is a very distinctive, harsh, jarring note which is commonly uttered, while a plaintive piping call, *phwee-phwee-phwee*, repeated at short intervals, is used to express anger or alarm. It has a sweet and rather varied song in the breeding season, but this is not heard in India. For its size this is a very pugnacious little bird, and fights freely with others of its own species.

The Red-breasted Flycatcher does not breed in our limits, but the breeding season in Kashmir of the allied species, *S. hyperythra*, is in May and June. The latter nests in holes in trees at any height from 6 to 40 feet from the ground. The nest is a neat little cup of moss and dead leaves mixed with grass, chips and hair and lined with hair and feathers. The clutch consists of four or five eggs. These are rather broad ovals, pale sea-green or pale pinkish-stone in colour, freckled closely with rusty-brown.

They measure about 0·65 by 0·50 inches.

TICKELL'S BLUE FLYCATCHER

MUSCICAPULA TICKELLIÆ (Blyth)

(Plate vi, Fig. 4, opposite page 119)

Description.—Length 6 inches. Male: The whole upper plumage dark blue, still darker on the sides of the face, and brighter in a line from the nostril over each eye; wings and tail black, washed with blue; throat, breast and upper abdomen bright ferruginous; remainder of lower plumage pure white.

Female: A duller replica of the male.

Iris brown; bill black; legs greyish-brown.

The bill is wide and flattened at the base and fringed with long hairs.

Field Identification.—Peninsular India. A dark blue bird with the throat and breast reddish and the rest of the lower parts white. No white line over the eye. Flits about the inner side of trees and bushes in shady woods and groves and continually sings a merry little song.

Distribution.—Widely distributed through India, Ceylon, Burma,

Malay Peninsula, Siam, and Annam. The typical race is found practically throughout India at all elevations except north-west of a line through Mussoorie, Sambhar, Mount Aboo, and Kathiawar. It extends eastwards into Assam and Burma. In Ceylon it is replaced by *M. t. nesea* which is decidedly darker above. A resident species except for short local migrations.

This species may very easily be confused with the Blue-throated Flycatcher (*Muscicapula rubeculoides*) which breeds throughout the Himalayas and wanders into many parts of the Peninsula and to Ceylon in winter. The male has the chin and throat dark blue, whereas in Tickell's Blue Flycatcher the ferruginous of the breast comes up to those parts, leaving only a tiny patch on the chin at the base of the beak blue. Another and very common Himalayan species breeding from 7000 to 9000 feet, which also winters down in India as far south as the Deccan, is the White-eyebrowed Blue Flycatcher (*Muscicapula superciliaris*). The male has the whole of the upper parts and an interrupted collar across the breast blue, and in the West Himalayan race there is a conspicuous white line above the eye and a white patch in the side of the tail. Lower parts white.

At a higher level—9000 to 10,000 feet—is yet another common Himalayan species, best known in Kashmir, the Slaty-blue Flycatcher (*Muscicapula tricolor*). The upper parts are slaty-blue, lower parts whitish and there is a white patch in each side of the tail.

Habits, etc.—Tickell's Blue Flycatcher is another forest-loving species which is found in thick cover and shade, and particularly haunts the banks of wooded streams. In such localities it flits about amongst the boughs and hunts for insects, particularly in the network of aerial roots and creepers which are a feature of some of the southern jungles. It is a wary bird and not always easily observed. When one is walking quietly through the jungle this Flycatcher will usually, when first met, come up close within a few yards and give vent to its short song as if challenging the intruder. Then it disappears and is not easily approached again.

The short metallic song is quite pleasing. It consists of a couple of sharp "clicks," followed by a little tune of five or six notes, which recall the song of the White-browed Fantail-Flycatcher, but are harsher and not so loud. The song is incessantly repeated.

The breeding season lasts from March to August, but the majority of nests are to be found in June and July.

The nest is a small cup of moss or dry leaves lined with fine roots and a little hair placed in a small hole or hollow in a variety of situations—in banks or rocks, in brickwork, on the window-ledges of ruined houses. A very favourite situation is one of the numerous hollows formed by the roots of a wild fig-tree, banyan, or peepul, where they have anastomosed with the trunk of some enclosed tree.

The usual clutch consists of three or four eggs. The egg is a moderately elongated oval, somewhat blunt at the small end. The texture is fine with a slight gloss. The ground-colour is dingy greyish-white, freckled with dingy olive-brown. The freckling is so excessively fine that the egg appears a dull olive-brown, rarely tinged with rufous or reddish, more especially towards the broad end.

In size the egg measures about 0·75 by 0·56 inches.

THE VERDITER FLYCATCHER

EUMYIAS THALASSINA (Swainson)

(Plate vi, Fig. 1, opposite page 110)

Description.—Length 6 inches. Male : A black patch in front of the eye ; the whole plumage bright verditer-blue, concealed portions of the wings and tail blackish-brown ; under tail-coverts broadly fringed with white.

Female : Resembles the male, but is duller in colour throughout, and the chin and sides of the throat are mottled with white.

Iris brown ; bill and legs black.

The bill, which is flat, and viewed from above almost forms an equilateral triangle, is fringed with hairs.

Field Identification.—Familiar summer bird about houses and gardens in the Himalayas ; a conspicuous verditer-blue in colour, perching on exposed situations and hawking insects in the air with active flight.

Distribution.—The Verditer Flycatcher breeds throughout the Himalayas, in Assam, the Burmese Hills, Yunnan, Shan States, Siam, Annam, and Western China. It is divided into races, of which only the typical one concerns us. This breeds in the Himalayas from 4000 to 10,000 feet, and during the winter migrates down into Peninsular India, missing out most of the Punjab, Sind, and desert Rajputana, and extending as far as Travancore.

The small and very dark looking Sooty Flycatcher (*Hemichelidon sibirica*) is common throughout the length of the Himalayas. It perches higher than most species, often at the tops of the largest trees.

Habits, etc.—The Verditer Flycatcher in summer is one of the few birds of the Himalayan hill stations which attract the notice of even the least observant. It is a bold and confiding bird, frequenting jungle and garden alike, and perching in open exposed positions, where its brilliant colouring catches the sunlight and renders it conspicuous. Like other Flycatchers, it swoops into the air from its perch to take insects on the wing ; but while other species often return to the same perch with the captured insect, the Verditer

Flycatcher continues its flight and perches in a new place, thus continually changing its ground and bringing itself more to notice. The flight is very strong and swift. During the breeding season it affects forest areas rather than the more open hill-sides; during the winter it appears in any type of country where there are large trees. Its usual perch is a bare twig at the top of a tree, but it is also partial to telegraph wires; it does not as a rule perch on buildings, though it enters verandahs and porches in search of a nesting site. Normally it is found solitary or in pairs, but small parties collect on migration.

There appears to be no call-note, but the male has a loud and fairly good song.

It breeds from April till the middle of July, and probably two broods are reared.

The nests are remarkably true to type, fairly solid cups of green moss, lined with fine black moss roots. The majority are built under the overhanging crests of banks where the action of water and the binding qualities of tree-roots combine to form a gloomy hollow, in the side of which the nest placed in a hole is distinguished with difficulty. Banks by the side of roads and paths are especially affected. Other sites are under the small hill bridges, amongst the timber-work, or in the rafters and eaves of buildings. As the bird is very shy at the nest and always dashes out of it at the approach of passers-by and in front of them, it continually brings itself and its nest to notice.

The normal clutch consists of four eggs, though three or five may occasionally be found. The eggs closely resemble those of the English Robin. In shape they are a moderately broad oval, somewhat compressed towards the smaller end. The shell is fragile and with little gloss. The ground-colour is pinky-white, in some entirely devoid of markings, in others with a more or less conspicuous reddish-pink zone or cap of mottled or clouded markings, not defined specks or spots, which are generally nearly confluent.

In size the egg averages about 0·78 by 0·57 inches.

THE NILGIRI BLUE FLYCATCHER

EUMYIAS ALBICAUDATA (Jerdon)

(Plate iv, Fig. 2, opposite page 66)

Description.—Length 6 inches. Male: The whole plumage dull indigo-blue, becoming ultramarine-blue on the forehead and above the eye and duller and whiter towards the vent; a black spot in front of the eye; wings and tail dark brown, all feathers edged with blue, and the tail-feathers, excepting the central pair, pure white at the base.

Female: The whole upper plumage dull greyish-olivaceous with a dull blue patch above the base of the tail; wings dark brown, all feathers edged with rufescent; tail blackish edged with blue, all feathers, except the central pair, pure white at the base; lower plumage dull bluish-grey, tinged with olivaceous on the throat and with white about the vent.

Iris dark brown; bill horny-black; legs blackish-brown.

The bill is rather wide at the base and slightly flattened and fringed with hairs.

Field Identification.—A rather sombre-coloured Flycatcher with white patches in the base of the tail, found commonly in forest in the hills of extreme South-west India. The male has a good song and is dull dark blue in colour, rather brighter on the crown.

Distribution.—A resident species, confined to the hills of extreme South-west India where it is common in the Nilgiris, Biligirirangams, Nelliampathies, Palnis and Travancore ranges. It is most common at an elevation of 4000 to 7000 feet but may be found somewhat lower.

Habits, etc.—The Nilgiri Blue Flycatcher is essentially a forest-haunting species and is abundant enough in those hills where it is found. It frequents overgrown hill streams and nullahs, the undergrowth which flanks paths and tracks through the sholas and cardamum plantations and the edges of forest clearings. It also often visits gardens.

This species ordinarily perches in a somewhat upright position on a twig and utters the typical Flycatcher *click click* as it twitches its tail up and down. The song is very sweet, somewhat feebler than but very similar in character to that of the Pied Bush-Chat. Heard in a shola it has a somewhat penetrating quality. It lasts from five to ten seconds and is constantly uttered from some exposed twig on the top of a tree and it may be heard in most months of the year. The female also sings on occasion. The food consists almost entirely of insects but a certain amount of small fruit is also apparently eaten.

The breeding season lasts from March till June but most eggs will be found about April. The nest is usually built in a cavity in a bank, more particularly on the inner sides of the paths which intersect the hill-jungles and sholas; but it may also be found in holes in rocks and walls and trees, under the eaves of houses and in the wood-work of bridges. The nest itself is a soft mass of fine moss on a slight foundation of coarse moss and lichen or a few twigs. The egg-cavity can hardly be said to be lined, but a greater proportion of very fine black moss-roots enter into the composition of the nest here than elsewhere. One or two feathers are occasionally added.

The clutch consists of two or three eggs. These vary a good deal in shape, size and colour, but are normally an elongated oval in shape with little or no gloss. The ground-colour varies from creamy-white to a pretty, warm *cafe-au-lait* colour. In some eggs there are no discernible markings ; only the tint grows deeper and brighter towards the large end, becoming pale reddish-brown, brownish-red or red as the case may be. In other eggs there is a regular zone of minute spots, or very rarely blotches, round the broad end. Taken, however, as a series the eggs of this species average a rather deeper, warmer salmon-pink colour than those of the Verditer Flycatcher.

In size they measure about 0·8 by 0·6 inches.

THE BLACK AND ORANGE FLYCATCHER

OCHROMELA NIGRORUFA (Jerdon)

(Frontispiece, Fig. 1)

Description.—Length 5 inches. Male : Top and sides of the head and hind-neck black ; wings black ; remainder of plumage rich orange-chestnut, somewhat paler on the throat and abdomen.

Female : Similar to the male but the black of the head and neck is replaced by greenish-brown, mottled with rufous in front of the eye.

Iris brown ; bill blackish-brown ; legs greyish-brown.

The coarse broad bill is fringed with long hairs.

Field Identification.—Hills of South-west India. A small orange-coloured bird with blackish head-cap and wings but tail also orange. Found flitting about near the ground in the undergrowth of shady woods where its presence is revealed by an incessant chirruping note, easily mistaken for that of an insect.

Distribution.—Confined to the hill ranges of South-west India and resident at elevations from 2500 to 7000 feet and probably most common about 5000 feet. It is recorded from the Wynaad (scarce), the Nilgiris and Biligirirangams, the Palnis and the Travancore ranges, but is curiously local and patchy in its distribution.

Habits, etc.—The Black and Orange Flycatcher must very soon become well known to all observers at Ootacamund and Kodaikanal. It is a bird of dense woods and thickets, preferring the most retired, shady and damp, swampy patches in the breeding season though at other times it ventures into the lighter woods and sholas. In such places it flits about the undergrowth singly or in pairs, reminding the English observer of a Robin in its ways. At one moment it is seated motionless on the low branch of a tree or a fallen stump or some thick tangle of dead branches. The next it makes a short swoop at an insect in the air or descends to the ground for a second to pick one up ; but whatever it does or wherever it goes you will notice that it seldom leaves the neighbourhood of the ground, usually keeping within a foot or two of it. In spite of its preference for dark woods and secluded spots this Flycatcher is by no means a shy bird and it does not resent observation from close quarters provided that one keeps motionless.

There is no true song, but the male is far from silent, uttering a somewhat metallic high-pitched chirrup *chiki-riki-chiki* or *chee-r-ri-ri* every few seconds which gives away its whereabouts, though the chirrup might easily be mistaken for that of an insect.

The breeding season proper is from March to May and a few eggs may still be found in June. The nest is a very remarkable structure for a Flycatcher, a large and regular ball of dry sedge and coarse grass, with a small entrance hole at one side near the top. It is entirely devoid of lining but is placed on a foundation of dead leaves. These are usually wedged into the centre of a small bush or clump of foliage, but the bird is also fond of building in the cluster of new shoots that rise from the stump of a tree that has been felled. The nest is normally built at a height of two to three feet from the ground and occasionally lower.

The clutch consists of two eggs.

The egg is a long oval in shape and the shell is very fine and delicate with little or no gloss. The ground-colour is pale greyish-white or buffy-white, faintly but profusely freckled all over with pale pinky-grey or reddish and these markings sometimes form indistinct caps or zones on the large end of the egg.

The egg measures about 0·70 by 0·52 inches.

THE GREY-HEADED FLYCATCHER

CULICICAPA CEYLONENSIS (Swainson)

(Plate vi, Fig. 2, opposite page 110)

Description.—Length 5 inches. Sexes alike. Head, neck and breast ashy, darker on the crown; remainder of plumage greenish-yellow, duller and greener above and brighter and yellower below; concealed portions of wings and tail dark brown.

Iris dark brown; bill brown; legs yellowish-brown.

The bill, viewed from above, is triangular in shape and thickly fringed with long hairs.

Field Identification.—A forest bird; very small, greenish-yellow, with an ashy head and neck; very active and erratic in its movements amongst shady trees and rather noisy.

Distribution.—Generally distributed throughout India, Ceylon, and Burma, extending also eastwards to Siam, Cochin-China, Java, and Borneo, this common Flycatcher is divided into several races. We are concerned only with two of these, which breed in the Himalayas and other hill ranges from 3000 to 8000 feet and are locally migratory, moving down into the plains after the breeding season. *C. c. pallidior* breeds along the Himalayas from Hazara to

Bhutan, and is found in winter in the North-west Frontier Province, Punjab, United Provinces, Central Provinces, and the Bombay Presidency as far as Northern Kanara. It is only a straggler in the dry and more open plains of the North-west. In the Nilgiris and Travancore ranges it is replaced by the more richly-coloured typical race, also found in Ceylon.

The Brown Flycatcher (*Muscicapa latirostris*), a small brown and white species with a spotted breast, will catch the eye of anyone who knows the English Spotted Flycatcher, which it much resembles in habits and appearance. It is found throughout the whole of India except the Punjab plains, North-west Frontier Province, Sind, and Rajputana, being known to breed at low elevations in the Himalayas, in the Vindhyan Hills, and North Kanara.

Habits, etc.—On its breeding grounds this Flycatcher is a bird of heavy forest, preferring those ravines and hill-sides where the age and the size of the trees provide wide shady arcades chequered with occasional patches of sunlight; in such places as it hawks insects in the air it flits incessantly from bough to bough, now catching the gleams of sunlight, now hidden in the gloom, eternally restless, eternally cheerful. Its call or song is a long, loud, clear trill, *che-tut-tut-teee* or *wit-tweet-chitat-chitat*, which sounds through the glades, occasionally becoming harsher and louder with something in it of the "stone on ice" note of the common Indian Nightjar, though rather hurried and different in tone; or it might be described as *tyu-jit* followed by a prolonged twittering note. Except when in family parties after breeding it is solitary in disposition, though one or two individuals invariably accompany the mixed hunting parties of small birds which are such a feature of the hill jungles.

The breeding season lasts from April to June. The nest is a most charming little structure of bright green mosses, lichens, and cobwebs, in shape half a cone or quarter of a sphere, and it is applied to the perpendicular side of a tree-trunk or rock on which there is plenty of moss with which it assimilates. The cavity is usually unlined, but occasionally moss roots are used. It is placed at all heights from the ground.

The clutch consists of three or four eggs.

The egg is a moderately broad oval, very blunt in shape with very little gloss. The ground-colour is white or dingy yellowish-white, and the markings consist of spots and blotches of grey and yellowish-grey, the majority being collected in a zone round the larger end.

In size the eggs average about 0·60 by 0·48 inches.

THE RUFOUS-BELLIED NILTAVA

NILTAVA SUNDARA Hodgson

Description.—Length 6·5 inches. Male: Head, rump, patch on either side of the neck and in the angle of wing shining blue; rest of upper parts very dark blue; throat black, and the remainder of the lower surface chestnut. Wings dark brown edged with purplish blue; tail black edged blue. Female: Olive brown with an ochraceous tint; tail and under tail coverts rufous; foreneck white with a small patch of brilliant blue on either side.

Iris dark brown; bill black; legs brown.

Field Identification.—A rather unobtrusive bird, the size of a robin, frequenting moderate dense jungle. The male is easily recognised by the beautiful bright blue of the upper plumage and chestnut under parts. The glistening blue spots on either side of the neck in both sexes make it impossible to confuse it with Tickell's Blue Flycatcher or the Blue-throated Flycatcher.

Distribution.—From the Murree Hills in North-west Himalayas, east to Szechuan and south through Yunnan and Burma to South China and Siam. In the Himalayas there is an eastern and western race. The former, *N. s. sundara*, ranges from Nepal to Assam, ascending the hills as high as 8000 feet, while in the Outer Himalayas between 5000 and 9000 feet. From Kumaon to Murree it is replaced by a paler form, *N. s. whistleri.* Both these forms move lower down in the autumn to the foothills and in some localities to the adjoining plains. Closely allied, but two inches larger, is the Large Niltava, *Niltava grandis*, in which the male lacks the chestnut on the breast and the back is a dull bluish ashy, while the female is a reddish olivaceous brown with the usual brilliant blue neck spots. It inhabits the Himalayas from Nepal to Burma and Yunnan at altitudes from 3000 to 7000 feet.

Habits, etc.—Although this Flycatcher is by no means uncommon, it is apt to be overlooked in spite of the gay plumage, since it keeps to a great extent to thick evergreen undergrowth and, as a rule, rather damp spots. It does, however, frequent in some parts of its range pine forests, but only where there are damp nullahs with plenty of undergrowth on the banks of streams running through them.

The breeding season is from April to July. The nest is usually in a crevice in rocks or the trunk of a tree, sometimes amongst the roots; and occasionally in the long grass on the rocky banks of streams. It is well concealed, constructed of grass and lined with fern stems, and closely resembles that of the common Robin.

The eggs are blunt ovals varying from three to four, and they too are similar to those of the Robin, but often more densely mottled with pale pinkish-brown.

They measure 0·85 by 0·63 inches.

THE PARADISE FLYCATCHER

TCHITREA PARADISI (Linnæus)

(Plate ix, Fig. 2, opposite page 176)

Description.—Length 9 inches, exclusive of the sharply-graduated tail; in older males the central pair of feathers form ribbon-like streamers up to 10 inches in length.

Adult male: Pure white; the head, neck and crest glossy bluish-black; the upper parts faintly streaked with black, the wing- and tail-feathers heavily lined with black.

Female and young male: Head, neck and crest glossy bluish-black; a collar round the neck, chin, throat and upper breast dark ashy merging into white on the abdomen; remainder of upper parts, wings and tail bright chestnut.

The plumages of the male are not yet fully understood and individuals will be found in various stages intermediate to the extremes above described. A phase in which the long streamers and the upper parts are chestnut instead of white may be dimorphic to the fully white adult.

Iris dark brown; bill and rim round the eye bright cobalt-blue; legs plumbeous-blue.

The bill is flattened and swollen and fringed with coarse hairs.

Field Identification.—Older males cannot be confused with any other species owing to the central pair of tail-feathers being elongated into ribbon-like streamers 10 inches long, white or chestnut in colour. These droop gracefully in rest or stream out behind the bird in flight. Females and younger males have a crested, glossy black head and bright chestnut upper parts, wings and tail, and ashy or white under parts. Purely arboreal, active and lively.

Distribution.—The Paradise Flycatcher occurs from Turkestan, Afghanistan and Baluchistan, through India and Burma, and still farther eastwards. It is divided into several races, of which we are concerned with three. The typical race occurs throughout the Peninsula from the Western United Provinces to the Brahmaputra, southwards to Cape Comorin and visiting Ceylon in winter. In that island there is a resident race as well, *T. p. ceylonensis*, which has always had the adult male chestnut instead of white. The paler race, inhabiting Afghanistan, Turkestan, Kashmir, and the Himalayas to Eastern Nepal is known as *T. p. leucogaster.* A third race *nicobarica*, with the head, neck and breast ashy-grey and the cap and a short crest only black, is found in the Duars and Upper Assam, migrating in winter to the Nicobars and Andamans.

Very little is definitely known about the status and movements of this common and widely-spread bird, but it is undoubtedly migratory to a large extent. In the North-western Himalayas and Salt Range it is a summer visitor, only arriving about March and April and departing about September; in most of the Punjab it is purely a passage migrant in those months. To Sind it is a scarce winter visitor; in many other localities it is undoubtedly a resident.

Habits, etc.—The Paradise Flycatcher has been aptly named; the long waving tail plumes recall the ornaments of the true Birds of Paradise, and for sheer beauty of contrast and purity of coloration and for grace of form and movement, the adult male must be without a rival in India. If Paradise is the home of perfection, there indeed must this bird find a place. In nature its beauty is enhanced by its surroundings; for it is a bird of pleasant groves and well-watered shady nullahs, where stray gleams of sunshine strike through the boughs, bringing into colour sprays of foliage and illuminating patches of the ground and throwing them into relief by contrast with mysterious shadows. In such a spot the Paradise Flycatcher delights to dwell, perching on the sprays, and disappearing into the shady depths, now hidden from sight, now caught in the rays of sunshine as he flies across the intervening spaces. The long streamers give a curious effect to the flight; the bird appears to float softly along without particular volition or ability to direct its course, moving in a series of dreamy impulses; though the younger birds with short tails show themselves possessed of strong and decided flight. All food is taken on the wing, and that the bird is capable of speed and skill in the air is proved by the fact that dragon-flies are sometimes captured.

This species is purely arboreal, its feet being too short and weak for progress on the ground. It is a very lively and cheerful bird, incessantly on the move; males often flirt their tails about, opening and closing the feathers and making play with the long streamers. When sitting on a twig the carriage is very upright.

The ordinary call-note is harsh and disappointing, a sharp grating note; but the song is a low pleasant warble of distinct merit, though it is not very often heard.

The breeding season differs according to locality. In Northern India it lasts from April to June; in the south it is earlier, commencing about February. Probably more than one brood is raised.

The nest depends for protection on its position rather than on concealment; though at first sight it escapes notice by its ridiculous conspicuousness; it is too easy to see, the eye and brain are looking for something more difficult to find. It is a very neat and compactly-built cup, either shallow and rounded or a deep inverted cone; it is built of soft grass, scraps of leaf and moss, all very firmly plastered together with spiders' webs and studded with small cocoons and pieces of lichen; there is a neat lining of fine grass and hair, the

PLATE VII

1. Grey-winged Blackbird ($\frac{1}{3}$ nat. size.)

2. Himalayan Whistling-Thrush ($\frac{1}{4}$ nat. size.)

[Face p. 132

whole forming a structure worthy in its beauty of the architect. It is placed on a twig or stem, growing at any angle or at any height from the ground from 5 to 40 feet. The branch of a tall mango tree in the plains, and a thick brier stem in the hills are favourite situations. Both sexes incubate, and the male may be seen on the nest with the long streamers drooping over the side. In different pairs the males may be found in every stage of plumage, as they commence to breed when a year old.

The eggs are in shape a rather long oval, somewhat pointed towards the small end, and they are usually dull and glossless. The ground-colour varies from pale pinkish-white to a warm salmon-pink and is more or less thickly spotted with rather bright brownish-red spots which tend to form an irregular cap or zone at the broad end. A few tiny, pale, inky-purple blotches occur also about the broad end. The eggs resemble in miniature one of the types of egg laid by the Common King-Crow.

They measure about 0·80 by 0·60 inches.

THE BLACK-NAPED FLYCATCHER

Hypothymis azurea (Boddaert)

(Plate xi, Fig. 1, opposite page 220)

Description.—Length 6 inches. Male: Head, neck and breast brilliant lilac-blue, a minute patch about the base of the bill, a large patch on the back of the head and a crescentic bar on the throat deep velvet-black; remainder of upper parts dark blue; wings and tail sooty-black, washed with dark blue; remainder of lower parts white.

Female and immature birds: Head, neck and breast dull ashy-blue; remainder of upper parts, wings and tail dark ashy-brown; remainder of lower parts white.

Iris dark brown; bill dark blue, edges and tip black; leg plumbeous, claws horny.

The bill is broad and flattened at the base and fringed with long hairs; legs weak.

Field Identification.—A slender, rather elongated bird of which the male is blue throughout except for the white abdomen. The blue of the head and neck is very brilliant and emphasised by the black velvet skull-cap, set well back, and the black crescent on the throat. The female lacks these velvet patches and is much browner, with only a wash of blue about the head and neck. Usually solitary, catching flies about trees.

Distribution.—A widely-distributed species, occurring in India, Ceylon, Assam, Burma, Yunnan, Siam, and Indo-China across to the Philippines. There are several races. The Indian race, *H. a. styani*, which also extends eastward to Hainan, occurs throughout the whole country except north-west of a line from Lucknow, Sehore, and Western Khandesh. *H. a. ceylonensis*, restricted to Ceylon, lacks the black on the throat. It is largely confined to the various hill ranges, but apparently does not occur much over 4000 feet. A resident species with slight local movements.

Habits, etc.—This beautiful Flycatcher is found in well-wooded parts of the country where it frequents patches of thick jungle and is particularly fond of shady nullahs overhung by lofty trees. It is also fond of bamboo jungle and may be found in open country in clumps of trees or in single trees near villages. It is usually solitary, flying from tree to tree, remaining a short time in each, capturing insects on the wing. Now and again it flits actively amongst the branches, spreading its tail after the fashion of a Fantail-Flycatcher. It never descends to the ground. The food consists of a variety of small insects and as it captures these it utters a sharp little call which resembles one of the calls of the Grey Tit. At times several individuals join the mixed hunting parties and travel with them through the trees.

The breeding season lasts from the latter half of April until August, most nests being found in June and early July. The season is somewhat earlier in the north than in the south.

The nest is a deep little cup composed internally of fine grass stems well woven together. Externally it consists of rather coarser grass and vegetable fibres and it is practically coated with cobwebs by which numerous small white cocoons and tiny pieces of dry leaves and lichen are attached to the nest. Sometimes some green moss is mingled with the cocoons. It is very neat and rather massive in construction. The nest is usually placed in a slender fork of an outer branch of a tree at no great height from the ground or fastened to some pendant bamboo spray.

The clutch consists of two to four eggs, three being the usual number. The egg is a miniature of that of the Paradise Flycatcher. It is a moderately broad and very regular oval, slightly compressed towards the smaller end. The shell is very fine and smooth, with little or no gloss. The ground-colour varies from almost pure white to pale salmon-pink; the markings consist of minute specks or small spots of red or reddish-pink, varying much in intensity and mingled with a few small pale purple spots. As a rule the markings are most plentiful towards the larger end of the egg, tending to form a zone or cap.

The egg measures about 0·69 by 0·53 inches.

THE WHITE-BROWED FANTAIL-FLYCATCHER

LEUCOCIRCA AUREOLA (Lesson)

Description.—Length 7 inches. Sexes alike, except that the female is rather browner above. Forehead and a very broad stripe above the eye white; remainder of head black, the feathers of the cheeks, chin and throat edged with white; remainder of upper plumage, wings and tail brown, the wing-coverts tipped with white, and all but the central pair of tail-feathers tipped with white, progressing more broadly outwards, till the outermost feather is almost entirely white; sides of the breast black; remainder of lower plumage white.

Iris brown; bill and legs black.

The bill is large and flat and fringed with long hairs. The tail is very ample and rounded, spreading into a fan.

Field Identification.—Common throughout the plains. A small black and white bird, with a charming bar of song, which pirouettes about the shady branches of trees incessantly fanning its tail.

Distribution.—This Fantail-Flycatcher is found practically throughout India, Ceylon, Assam, Burma and South-west Siam. In India it is found from the plains up to about 4000 feet in the Outer Himalayas. It is divided into races, of which we are concerned with two. The typical race is found throughout Northern India though it does not occur in Kashmir, the North-west Frontier Province or Baluchistan. The southern boundary is not well-defined but all birds from the Madras Presidency belong to the darker Cingalese race (*L. a. compressirostris*) in which the white tips to the tail-feathers are shorter and two central pairs are without white tips.

Mention must be made of two closely-allied species which are locally common. The White-throated Fantail (*Leucocirca albicollis*), which frequents shady ravines and may be easily distinguished by the sooty-brown colour of the lower parts, is found along the Outer Himalayas up to about 7000 feet from Murree on the west (and with a wide distribution east of our area). The White-spotted Fantail (*Leucocirca pectoralis*) is resident in Central and Southern India from Mount Aboo and Goona to the Palnis, being particularly well known in the Nilgiris. It is somewhat similar to the White-browed Fantail in appearance but may be distinguished by having a brown pectoral band across the white under parts. All are resident species though slight local movements may be detected.

Habits, etc.—The various Fantail-Flycatchers are all very much alike in their habits and characteristics. The White-browed Fantail is a bird of open country, frequenting groves of trees in cultivation, gardens and roadside trees, being strictly arboreal, and only descending to the ground for occasional momentary visits. For liveliness and grace it is not to be surpassed. It is never still, and the whole livelong day it dances and pirouettes, filled with an inimitable *joie-de-vivre.* It flits amongst the leafy boughs of some giant mango tree with a short jerky flight, and where it settles there it postures; it turns from side to side with restive, jerky movements; like a ballet-dancer before her mirror it tries new steps and attitudes; down drop the wings, up jerks the head, and all the time the dainty round fan of the tail is opened and closed and flirted with all the coquetry and grace of a beauty of Andalusia. Never was bird better named; watch it for the first time and within the first few seconds the name of Fantail rises unbidden to the mind. Now and again the bird leaves the shelter of the branches and launches into the air, seeming to tumble, bent on suicide; a rapid snap at some tiny insect invisible to human

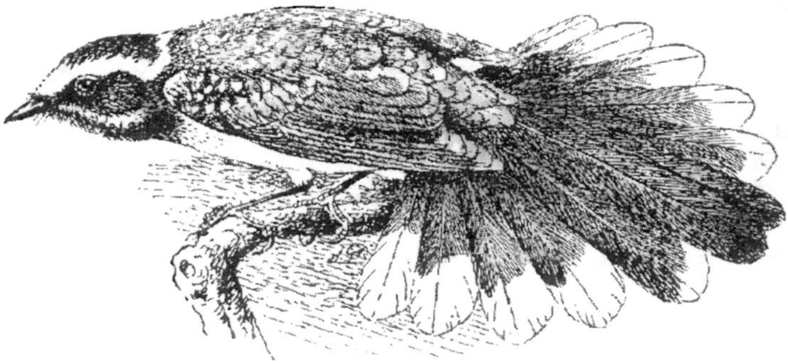

FIG. 19—White-browed Fantail-Flycatcher (½ nat. size)

eye, a swift recovery, and it has returned to the cool shelter of the leaves, and is once more bowing and dancing. Now and again the happy little dancer breaks into song, a few notes in a regular scale, which seem more a human melody than the song of a bird, and break off just as groping memory has almost remembered their source. The song stops suddenly in the middle of the scale (it is always the same and always stops in the same place), and with a sharp twittering note the bird is off to another tree where the minuet begins afresh.

Amongst the other attractions of this dainty bird is its boldness; song and dance go on in spite of human presence, and I have seen one fly down and snap an insect off the shoulder of a servant who was talking to me. The food consists entirely of insects, mostly of the minutest size, and throughout the whole of the bird's movements can be heard the snapping of its beak as it feeds.

Eggs may be found from the end of February to the early part of August; though the majority will be found in March and July. Two broods are reared, and this often from the same nest.

The nest is a most beautiful structure. It is a tiny cup, small, even for the size of the bird, and is attached to the upper surface of a twig or small branch, often at the junction of a fork. Viewed from the ground it has much the appearance of a small hornet's nest.

It is made of fine fibres and grasses closely welded and bound with cobwebs and sometimes studded with small cocoons or spiders' egg-bags. There is a neat lining of fine grass stems. It is built at any height from 4 to 40 feet from the ground. Even in the nest the bird is restless, often turning about, spreading her tail, or flying off for a minute or two. The male remains very faithfully in the vicinity, and without the least hesitation launches out to attack passing Crows or other possible enemies.

The eggs vary from two to four in number, while three is the usual clutch. They are moderately broad ovals compressed towards the small end. The ground-colour varies from pure white to very pale yellowish-brown or dingy cream colour; and the markings are generally largely confined to a broad irregular zone near the large end of greyish-brown specks and spots, with secondary markings of neutral tint and pale grey or faint inky-purple. They are rather like miniature Shrikes' eggs.

They measure about 0·66 by 0·51 inches.

THE GREAT GREY SHRIKE

Lanius excubitor Linnæus

Description.—Length 10 inches. Sexes alike. A very broad band from the beak through the eye black; upper plumage bluish-grey, merging into white over the wings; wings black, variegated with grey and white; tail black, the feathers growing increasingly white outwards; the whole lower plumage white.

Iris dark brown; bill and legs black.

Beak strong and hooked, with a deep notch at the tip of the upper mandible; tail rather long and graduated.

Field Identification.—Plains of Continental India. A grey and white bird with a heavy head marked with a conspicuous black band through the eye and with much black in the wings and tail; solitary or in pairs, in open country sitting on the tops of large bushes.

Distribution.—The Great Grey Shrike in various races has a very wide distribution through Europe, Africa, Asia, and Northern America. In Northern India it is represented by a resident form named *L. e. lahtora*, which is common and generally distributed. It is found from roughly the line of the Indus and from the foot of the Himalayas to the Rajmahal Hills, Manbhum and Lohardaga in Bihar, southwards to Belgaum and Chanda. It is not found in the hill ranges.

Habits, etc.—This Shrike is a familiar species in open country, preferring the more barren stretches of semi-desert country or wide open plains to cultivation, though it is found also in the latter. Forest areas it avoids. It is found solitary or in pairs and is very conspicuous from its white, black and grey plumage and its habit of perching on the tops of bushes and small trees. It captures most of its food on the ground, leaving its vantage-point from time to time to fly down after a toothsome morsel and in returning to the perch it flies low over the ground and then turns sharply up to settle; the flight is undulating but strong. Each bird or pair have their own beat and resent the intrusion of other species. The alarm-note is a harsh grating call, but the bird is capable of considerable powers of mimicry which serve it as a song. The food consists largely

FIG. 20—Great Grey Shrike (⅓ nat. size)

of beetles, crickets, lizards, and ants, and like other Shrikes this species has the habit of impaling surplus food on thorns to form a larder.

The breeding season extends from January to October, but the majority of eggs are laid in March or April. Two broods are sometimes reared.

The nest is a large bulky cup, solid and well constructed, and placed at moderate heights from 4 to 12 feet up in a thick bush or small tree, preferably thorny in character. It is composed of thorny twigs, coarse grass roots and the like, thickly lined with wool, fibres, cotton and other miscellaneous materials soft in character.

The eggs vary in number from three to six. In shape they are a broad oval, somewhat pointed towards the smaller end. The texture is fine and close and there is a slight gloss. The ground-colour is delicate greenish-white, moderately blotched and spotted with various shades of brown and purple, the markings in nearly every case collecting into a wide zone round the broader end.

The eggs measure about 1·05 by 0·80 inches.

THE BAY-BACKED SHRIKE

LANIUS VITTATUS Valenciennes

(Plate ix, Fig. 1, opposite page 176)

Description.—Length 7 inches. Sexes alike. A broad band through the eye joined by a broad band across the base of the beak black; crown and upper neck grey, divided from the black by a whitish area; back and shoulders deep chestnut-maroon; rump white; wings black, with a white patch at the base of the outer flight-feathers; tail black with much white on the outer feathers; lower parts white except for the breast and flanks which are fulvous.

Iris dark brown; bill and legs black.

The bill has a notch at the tip of the upper mandible; tail rather long and graduated.

Field Identification.—Common in cultivation; a small bird with a longish tail, broad grey and white head with heavy black marking, maroon back and black and white tail, the markings sharply defined and conspicuous; perches in exposed positions.

Distribution.—This Shrike is a purely Asiatic species, occurring from the west in Afghanistan and Baluchistan right across the whole Peninsula of India to Darbhanga, the Rajmahal Hills and Midnapur. It occurs in the Himalayas, but sparingly at heights up to 6000 feet, extending often far into the valleys as in Chitral. In the south it reaches Cape Comorin but it avoids the rain areas of the south-west. In portions of its range it is migratory, but for the most part it is a resident species.

Habits, etc.—This charming little Shrike is a bird of open country and cultivation with groves of trees, and it avoids both desert country and thick jungle. It perches on telegraph-wires and the lower boughs of trees, and on large bushes some 6 to 10 feet from the ground, and watches thence for insect life to stir in the vicinity; a desirable morsel spied, it flies down to secure it, and after a meal upon the ground returns to its perch. It has a fixed territory, and seldom stirs far from its established perch. The food consists of insects, caterpillars, beetles, and the like.

The ordinary call is a harsh churring note, but the bird has a pleasant little warbling song and is something of a mimic, imitating the notes of other birds.

The breeding season lasts from March to September, and it is possible that two broods are often reared. The nest is a rather massive, compactly woven and very beautiful cup composed of fine grass, rags, feathers, soft twine, and a few fine twigs, the exterior being neatly plastered with cobwebs; it is lined, as a rule, with fine grass. The situation chosen for the nest is in the fork of a small tree, at heights usually about 6 to 10 feet from the ground. The nest is seldom well concealed, and though the bird generally comes close to an intruder and feigns readiness to attack, its attention is easily distracted by the sight of a caterpillar or other succulent morsel.

The clutch consists normally of four eggs, but as many as six may be found. The eggs are very typical of the genus, broad rather blunt ovals, fine in texture with a slight gloss. The ground-colour is dull white tinged with stone, greenish or grey; near the middle of the egg towards the broad end is a wide, conspicuous but broken and irregular zone of feeble spots and blotches of pale yellowish-brown and pale lilac, a few of these specks and frecklings being also dotted about the rest of the surface of the egg.

The eggs measure about 0·83 by 0·66 inches.

THE BROWN SHRIKE

LANIUS CRISTATUS Linnæus

Description.—Length 7 inches. Sexes alike. Upper plumage reddish-brown, brighter on the crown and nape; a faint white line over and a broad blackish line through the eye ending with the ear-coverts; wings dark brown, the feathers margined with rufous; tail reddish-brown with pale tips to the feathers; lower plumage fulvous, whiter on the throat and belly and usually with the breast and flanks barred finely with black.

Iris brown; bill horny-brown, paler at gape and base of lower mandible; legs bluish-grey, claws brown.

The bill has a notch at the tip of the upper mandible; tail fairly long and graduated.

Field Identification.—A typical Shrike, reddish-brown above with a dark line through the eye and fulvous white below. Found sitting on bushes and fences in open country and the possessor of a very harsh voice.

Distribution.—This Shrike breeds over a great part of Central Asia and Siberia and Northern China and in winter migrates south to North-east Africa and southern Asia generally. We are concerned with two races. The typical race winters in India east of a line from Cawnpore to Mhow and also in Ceylon and Burma. The Turkestan race *L. c. phoenicuroides* which is more brightly coloured and has a small white patch in the wing breeds in Baluchistan and passes on passage through the North-west Frontier Province, the Punjab and Sind to its winter quarters in North-east Africa.

A very similar species is the Pale-brown Shrike (*Lunius isabellinus*) which is a common winter visitor to the more barren areas of North-west India. The upper parts are sandy-brown and there is a small white patch at the base of the wing-quills.

Habits, etc.—This Shrike may be found in the cold weather in every type of country ranging from cultivation and dry scrub or mixed bamboo jungle to the fringes of forest and often for considerable distances within forest where cart-tracks and clearings encourage it to enter. In such terrain the bird is found singly, sitting on a telegraph-wire or a fence or a bush or small tree from which it keeps a keen lookout for its insect prey, launching out to capture it either in the air or on the ground. It is apt to be shy and difficult to approach and is always an active bird except when sheltering from the heat of the day.

The voice is singularly harsh, *chr-r-r-ri*, comparable with but easily distinguished from the call of the Rufous-backed Shrike.

This species is one of the earliest to arrive and one of the latest to depart of the winter visitors to India. The first arrivals may be noted at the end of August, even as far south as Ceylon, and some birds wait into May. A few non-breeding birds also seem to linger in the plains throughout the hot weather.

In Baluchistan the race *L. c. phoenicuroides* breeds in May and June in a zone between 5000 and 7000 feet. The nest is a massive cup of the usual Shrike type built of grass and bents and lined with seed-down, wool and scraps of cloth. They are placed in trees or more usually in low thorn bushes.

The clutch consists of four to six eggs.

The eggs are rather variable in shape, some being long ovals and others more broad. The ground-colour varies from pale cream to warm salmon-pink or less commonly pale stone-colour or various shades of pale greenish. The markings are spots and blotches, mostly in a zone round the broad end, and they vary also according to the ground-colour from chestnut red to grey-brown and olive-brown with secondary markings of lavender and grey.

The egg measures about 0·75 by 0·65 inches.

THE RUFOUS-BACKED SHRIKE

LANIUS SCHACH Linnæus

Description.—Length 10 inches. Sexes alike. Forehead and a broad band through the eye black; crown to the centre of the back clear pale grey merging on the shoulders and rump into bright rufous; wings black with often a small white patch at the base of the outer flight-feathers; tail black and brown, the feathers tipped with rufous;

the whole of the lower plumage white, washed with rufous on the flanks and vent.

Iris dark brown; bill and legs black.

A notch at the tip of the upper mandible; tail rather long and graduated.

Field Identification.—Perches conspicuously in open country; slender build with heavy head and long tail, conspicuous black mark through eye, grey back with rufous edging, dark wings and tail and pale under parts very distinctive; distinguish from Bay-backed Shrike by larger size, less black on face, and grey not maroon back.

Distribution.—*Lanius schach* is a common and widely-distributed form of Shrike which occurs throughout India to China, and is divided into several races. Four of these occur within our area. The best known is *L. s. erythronotus*, with pale grey upper parts and much rufous on the lower back and scapulars, which breeds in Turkestan, Gilgit, Kashmir, the Outer Western Himalayas, North-west Frontier Province, Baluchistan, Sind and the Punjab, and winters in Peninsular India. *L. s. nepalensis*, with the upper parts dark bluish-slate and the rufous confined to the rump, breeds in Tibet, and is a common winter visitor to the Nepal Valley and the Outer Eastern Himalayas. *L. s. tephronotus*, breeding in Suru and Lahul, and visiting Upper India in winter, is intermediate between those two races. *L. s. caniceps*, very similar to *erythronotus* but with less rufous on the upper parts, is resident in Central and Southern India and Ceylon, breeding abundantly in the hill ranges of the south-west. The Tibetan and Lahul races breed up to 10,000 to 12,000 feet, and the other races up to 7000 to 8000 feet.

FIG. 21—Head of Rufous-backed Shrike ($\frac{1}{1\frac{1}{2}}$ nat. size)

A species of similar type, but at once recognised by the black head, is the Black-headed Shrike (*Lanius nasutus*) which is found in some numbers throughout the north-eastern quarter of India from Kumaon down to Nagpur and Vizagapatam district, breeding locally in parts of this area.

Habits, etc.—This bird is a typical Shrike, avoiding both forest areas and desert, and preferring fairly open ground about cultivation where a conspicuous perch on top of a bush or tree gives it a view all around. The southern form, *caniceps*, is apparently strictly resident, but the northern races are largely migrants, and their movements remain to be worked out, the situation being obscured by the fact that in some areas a proportion of individuals are resident and winter where they breed. This Shrike has the ferocity and boldness which is a characteristic of the larger members of the genus. It sits up on its perch motionless, its sharp eyes watching the ground intently for moving life, cricket or mouse, grasshopper or newly-fledged bird, and all alike succumb to the sudden dash and the strong-hooked beak. And its hunting never stops, for even if its voracious appetite is satisfied it has the family habit of maintaining a "larder" in which the surplus prey is stuck on to thorns. It is this habit which has given to Shrikes the popular name of "Butcher-bird." Small birds and mammals, bumble-bees, grasshoppers, dragon-flies, beetles, butterflies, and the like may all be found firmly lodged in a favourite tree, often eight or ten of them together. On occasions, when feeding, the Shrike holds its food up in one foot after the fashion of a Parrot.

The ordinary call-note is harsh and scolding, *gerlek-gerlek* or *julek-julek*, followed by a yapping *yaon-yaon*. The song is short and pleasant but not often heard, while the bird is an excellent mimic, often reeling off a regular repertory of other birds' notes.

The breeding season is somewhat irregular. Nests may be found in different areas from February to August, and probably more than one brood is raised; but most nests will be found from April to July whatever the locality.

The nest is a large, massive cup, sometimes neat and well built, at other times a most disreputable structure. It is composed of a medley of materials, twigs, roots, bents, grass, rags, and lumps of wool, and the lining consists of fine grass or wool and hair. It is placed in a tree or bush, preferably a thorny one, at heights varying from 4 to 20 feet from the ground. The nest of the Tibetan race may, however, be found in small bushes, only a foot from the ground, but often there is not much choice of site in the barren hill-sides where it breeds.

The clutch consists of three to six eggs.

In appearance they are typical of the genus, broad heavy eggs, with very little gloss. The ground-colour is a delicate greenish-white, in some eggs pale stone-colour or creamy; the markings consist of small specks and larger blotches of brown or reddish-brown, with secondary markings of neutral tint and dark grey. They are never very thickly distributed and generally tend to form a zone about the broad end.

They measure about 0·92 by 0·70 inches.

THE PIED-SHRIKE

Hemipus picatus (Sykes)

Description.—Length 5 inches. Male: Top and sides of the head and neck and the back glossy black, the feathers of the rump broadly tipped with white; wings black, a white line running through the centre of the closed wing; tail black, all but the middle feathers broadly tipped with white, the whole outer edge of the outer feather white; cheeks and sides of the neck white, produced to form an indistinct half-collar; lower plumage pale vinaceous-grey shading into white on the chin and under the tail.

Female: Similar to the male but the black is replaced by sooty-brown.

Iris yellowish-brown; bill black; legs blackish-brown.

The bill is broad and flattened like that of a Flycatcher.

Field Identification.—A small black and white or brown, black and white bird found in parties in trees, hopping about the branches like Woodshrikes or flying into the air to catch insects like Flycatchers. Largely confined to hill jungles.

Distribution.—The typical race as described above is found in Saugor district; along the west coast of Peninsular India from the Satpuras to the Travancore Hills; in parts of the Eastern Ghats; in Lower Bengal and Lower Assam and into Lower Burma and Tenasserim. It extends also further east to Sumatra and Borneo. It occurs from 500 to about 6000 feet.

In the Sub-Himalayan ranges up to 5000 feet from Simla (very rare) eastwards, in Upper Assam and Upper Burma to Northern Yunnan and North Siam it is replaced by *H. p. capitalis* in which the male differs in having the back and rump smoky-brown instead of glossy black. The females are indistinguishable. There is also an island race, *H. p. leggei*, in Ceylon. In this the male and female are exactly alike and indistinguishable from the male of the typical race. The racial differences in this species thus form a most interesting evolutionary sequence. A resident species.

Habits, etc.—The Pied-Shrike is a strictly arboreal bird. It is found in many types of tree-growth, in lofty trees, in the fringe of evergreen jungle, in the foliage of secondary growth in thin jungle and even on occasion in roadside bushes and mere scrub. Except in the breeding season it is found in small parties of about half a dozen individuals and these often join the mixed hunting parties. In habits these birds resemble both the Flycatchers and the Wood-shrikes and between the latter and the true Shrikes they form a very definite connecting link. Like the Woodshrikes the members of a party follow each other from tree to tree, searching the twigs and leaves for the insect life which forms their food. Like the Flycatchers they capture winged prey by launching graceful sallies after it into the air, turning and twisting in mid-air with great agility. The notes, frequently uttered, are a little trill—*whi-ri-ri, whi-ri-ri, whi-ri-ri-ri,* etc.—very reminiscent of a cheap squeaky cracker whistle.

The breeding season of the typical form is from March to May in Western India, but that of the brown-backed race *capitalis* is apparently somewhat later, about May and June. The nest is a very beautiful structure; it is composed of grass and fine roots covered externally with cobwebs and pieces of grey lichen and moss, taken apparently from the tree on which it is built, so that it corresponds almost exactly with the branch or fork in which it is placed. This is usually at a considerable height from the ground and the branch chosen is often a bare one. In shape the nest is a shallow cup with a cavity 1½ inches across and ½ inch deep, and it is so small for the size of the bird that when the latter is sitting the whole of the tail and the body down to the lower part of the breast is visible to the observer below. The bird, in fact, merely appears to be sitting on a small lump of moss and lichen.

The nestlings have a remarkable habit of sitting motionless with their eyes shut and their heads raised together in the centre of the nest, so that they and the nest together appear to form a dead spur of the branch on which the nest is built.

The clutch consists of two or three eggs.

The eggs are very Shrike-like in appearance, rather elongated ovals somewhat obtuse at both ends and entirely devoid of gloss. The ground-colour is a pale greenish or greyish-white, profusely blotched, spotted and streaked with darker and lighter shades of umber-brown and dull inky-purple. These markings are usually in a zone at one end. In some specimens the markings are sparse and small.

In size the eggs average about 0·65 by 0·5 inches.

THE COMMON WOOD-SHRIKE

TEPHRODORNIS PONDICERIANUS (Gmelin)

(Plate ix, Fig. 3, opposite page 176)

Description.—Length 6 inches. Sexes alike. The whole upper plumage ashy-brown, the feathers of the wings edged paler; tail dark brown, the central pair of feathers tinged with ashy, the two outer pairs almost entirely white; a broad whitish streak over the eye, and a broad dark band below it; lower plumage ashy, paler down the centre.

Iris yellowish-brown; bill dark horn; legs dark plumbeous-brown.

Field Identification.—Common plains species; arboreal, in parties; a quiet grey bird with a pale eyebrow and a dark band through the eye, and white outer feathers in the tail.

Distribution.—The Wood-Shrike is found almost throughout India, Burma, Ceylon, Siam, and Annam, and is divided into races. The typical race is found from the base of the Himalayas to Cape Comorin, and on the east to Burma; on the west it is replaced by *T. p. pallidus*, a paler bird, which is found from the line of the River Indus through the Punjab and Sind to about Kalka, Ambala, the Western United Provinces and Khandesh. The race found in Ceylon, *T. p. affinis*, which is darker below. It is a resident species.

A very similar but larger species, the Nepal Wood-Shrike (*Tephrodornis gularis*), is found in the Eastern Himalayas and has another race on the Western Ghats from Belgaum southwards. In the latter the adult has the upper parts a bluish-ash colour.

Habits, etc.—The Wood-Shrike is a very quiet, unobtrusive little bird which is almost entirely arboreal, hopping about the branches of trees and searching the stems and leaves for insects and their larvæ. Occasionally it descends to the undergrowth and even to the ground in its search for food, but this is unusual and it normally moves from tree to tree, never leaving their cover. Forest is avoided, the trees preferred being those of gardens, hedgerows and cultivation, wayside trees and small groves. It is generally met with in pairs, but in winter small parties collect and hunt in company.

The males have a very sweet and distinctive call of several whistling notes, *wheet wheet*, followed by a quick repeated interrogative *whi-whi-whi-whi*, besides which some low trills are uttered in the breeding season.

The breeding season lasts from February to June, but most eggs will be found in March and April. The nest is a very beautiful structure, and rather small for the size of the bird. It is a broad, shallow cup, composed of fine bents, fragments of bark and grass stems, bound together with silky fibres and smeared exteriorly with cobwebs, the whole being very compact and neat. The interior is lined with wool and hair. The nest is built in a small horizontal fork of a tree from 5 to 30 feet from the ground and is difficult to see until the bird betrays it.

The clutch consists of two or three eggs. They resemble the eggs of the true Shrikes and are broad, regular ovals, of fine texture, with very little gloss. The ground-colour is cream, stone, or pale greenish-white, spotted and blotched with yellowish- and reddish-brown; many of these markings are gathered into a conspicuous but ill-defined zone round the broad end, in which are intermingled clouds of pale and dingy purple.

The eggs measure about 0·75 by 0·61 inches.

THE SCARLET MINIVET

PERICROCOTUS SPECIOSUS (Latham)

Description.—Length 9 inches. Male: Upper plumage to the middle back, chin and throat glossy black; remainder of body plumage scarlet; wing black with a very broad band of scarlet running through it, and with large round scarlet spots on the later secondaries; tail scarlet, the central pair of feathers black.

Female: Forehead yellow, fading on to the crown; upper plumage deep grey; rump and upper tail-coverts olive-yellow; lower plumage yellow; wings blackish-brown, with a broad band of yellow running through them, and with round yellow spots on the later secondaries; central pair of tail-feathers black; the next pair black with the end of the outer web yellow; remaining tail-feathers yellow with a black patch at their bases.

Iris brown; bill and legs black.

The tail is long and very deeply graduated.

Field Identification.—Hill species; purely arboreal; found in flocks which immediately attract attention by the scarlet and black plumage of the males and the yellow and dark plumage of the females. The larger size and oval spots on the secondaries distinguish it from the Short-billed Minivet.

Distribution.—The Scarlet Minivet has a wide distribution through the Himalayas, part of Peninsular India, Assam, and Burma to China and Hainan, as a resident species, though it appears to move altitudinally according to season. It is divided into several races, of which two concern us. The typical race is found throughout the Lower Himalayas, below about 6000 feet from the Sutlej Valley eastwards. *P. s. semiruber*, with the central tail-feathers largely red, is found in Lower Bengal, Orissa, the Central Provinces, and the Vizagapatan Ghats.

Another similar species, the Orange Minivet (*Pericrocotus flammeus*), is common and resident along the forests of the Western Ghats from Khandesh to Cape Comorin, occurring also in the Shevaroy Hills and Ceylon. It is found up to 6000 feet. In this the male has the lower parts orange-red.

Habits, etc.—This Minivet keeps to well-wooded country, and is a purely arboreal species, never descending to the ground. Out of the breeding season it is found in small flocks which travel through the tops of the trees searching for insects, usually alone, but sometimes in company with other species of insectivorous birds. Like other Minivets, these birds flit from tree to tree in follow-my-leader fashion, the red and yellow of the two sexes glinting in the sunlight, while their cheery pleasant calls still further enhance the pleasure of meeting with a flock.

The breeding season of the Himalayan race is from the end of April to early June.

The nest is a shallow, massive little cup composed of fine twigs, roots and grass-stems, bound together exteriorly with spiders' webs, and studded with lichens, mosses and scraps of bark. It is placed on a bough of a tree, and is well concealed, appearing to be merely an excrescence of the wood.

The clutch consists of two or three eggs. These are moderately broad ovals, fine in texture and with practically no gloss. The ground-colour is pale sea-green, and the markings consist of spots and blotches of dark brown and lavender.

They measure about 0·90 by 0·67 inches.

THE SHORT-BILLED MINIVET

PERICROCOTUS BREVIROSTRIS (Vigors) [1]

(Plate xiii, Fig. 3, opposite page 264)

Description.—Length 7 inches. Male: Upper plumage to the middle back, chin and throat glossy black; remainder of body plumage scarlet; wing black with a broad band of scarlet running through it; central tail-feathers black; the next pair black with the greater portion of the outer web scarlet; the others all scarlet with a black patch at their bases.

Female: Forehead greenish-yellow, fading on to the crown; upper plumage light grey tinged with olive; rump and upper tail-coverts olive-yellow; lower surface yellow; wing blackish-brown with a broad band of yellow running through it; central tail-feathers black; the next pair yellow with some black on the inner webs; the others all yellow with a black patch at their bases.

Iris dark brown; bill and legs black.

The tail is long and very deeply graduated.

Field Identification.—Purely arboreal; found in flocks which attract attention by the scarlet and black plumage of the males and the yellow and dark plumage of the females. Distinguished from the Scarlet Minivet by the smaller size, by the greater amount of black in the tail, and by the absence of the scarlet (in female yellow) round spots on the secondaries.

Distribution.—The Short-billed Minivet has a wide distribution through Northern India, Assam, and Burma to Eastern China. It is divided into races, of which we are concerned with two. The typical

[1] Some years ago it was pointed out that two distinct species were included under the name *brevirostris*, but as the question of the correct name has not been definitely decided it is considered advisable to leave the scientific name as it appeared in the previous editions.

race breeds between about 3000 and 10,000 feet on the Sufed Koh and all along the Western Himalayas from Gilgit and Murree to Nepal, moving in winter, from about November to the end of March, into the plains of the Punjab, Rajputana, United Provinces, Central Provinces, and Lower Bengal. From Sikkim eastwards to Assam and Northern Burma it is replaced by *P. b. affinis*, which is a more darkly-coloured bird in both sexes.

The Rosy Minivet (*Pericrocotus roseus*) in which the colours of the male are rose-pink and brown is found throughout the Lower Himalayas, as far west as Hazara, and also locally in the Peninsula.

Habits, etc.—Except when actually breeding the Short-billed Minivet is an essentially gregarious bird, living in family parties which join with others to form flocks that sometimes number as many as thirty or forty individuals. These are strictly arboreal, frequenting the tops of trees and not descending even to the undergrowth. They are, however, by no means shy, and feeding in the trees or flitting one by one across a patch of open the scarlet and black of the males and the yellow of the females is so conspicuous and so attractive in the sunlight that the Short-billed Minivet is one of the best-known birds of the Himalayas and Northern India. There is something particularly cheerful, too, about the pleasant call, a Tit-like chatter, *swit-swit-switi-tatit*, or *swisweet-sweet-sweet*, though the bird has no proper song. The food consists chiefly of insects and their larvæ.

The breeding season lasts from April to July. The nest is a shallow but massive little cup of fine twigs, bents and roots, matted with cobwebs, and studded with lichens to resemble the twig on which it is placed. It is placed on a bough of a tree usually at a great height from the ground.

The clutch consists of two to four eggs. They are moderately broad ovals of fine texture; the ground-colour is white tinged with cream or greenish, and the markings consist of blotches and spots of brownish-red, with secondary markings of grey and neutral tint.

The egg measures about 0·75 by 0·60 inches.

THE LITTLE MINIVET

PERICROCOTUS PEREGRINUS (Linnæus)

(Plate vi, Fig. 5, opposite page 110)

Description.—Length 6 inches. Male: Entire upper surface grey except the rump which is flame-coloured; wings blackish-brown with a slight central patch of flame-colour; tail long and deeply graduated, blackish-brown, all but the central pair of feathers broadly tipped with flame-colour; sides of the head, chin and throat blackish-grey; breast flame-colour, gradually paling into the white of the vent.

Female: Paler throughout; the whole lower plumage is white tinged with yellow.

Iris brown; bill and legs black.

Field Identification.—Plains bird; common in small parties, fluttering about trees; small with long tails, dull coloured with a conspicuous flame-coloured patch on the rump and wing, and in the males also on the breast.

Distribution.—The Little Minivet is found throughout India, Ceylon and Burma, extending on the east to Siam and Cochin-China; it is divided into several races. This species is unusually susceptible to climatic and geographical influences. In Sind and the South-west Punjab it is a pale desert bird, *P. p. pallidus.* On the humid west coast from North Kanara to Travancore, *P. p. malabaricus* (with a black throat in the male) is as richly coloured as any tropical species. In Ceylon an island race, *P. p. ceylonensis,* approximates to another richly coloured race, *P. p. vividus* (with a grey throat) in the Duars, Assam, and Burma. Whilst in the greater part of India the typical form, itself strictly speaking an intermediate, connects these variations, remaining unchanged through the immense area of the Peninsula from the Cauvery to the Sutlej, and on the edges of their ranges grading into them. A strictly resident species.

Another small species, the White-bellied Minivet (*Pericrocotus erythropygius*), is found practically throughout India, except the extreme north-west. The male is glossy black and white with a red rump and a beautiful rosy flush on the breast.

Habits, etc.—This Minivet is a plains bird, and only ascends those lesser ranges whose elevation and character cause them scarcely to differ from the plains. It is, like other Minivets, a purely arboreal species, frequenting trees in open but well-timbered country, particularly in the neighbourhood of cultivation; forests it avoids. Except in the breeding season it goes about in parties which flit gracefully amongst the branches, uttering a low, pleasant note and occasionally fluttering and hovering to reach those insects or their eggs and larvæ which cannot be picked with ease from a perch on the twigs.

The breeding season of this species is very extended, lasting, according to locality, from March to September, earlier in the north than in Central India and the south. The nest is a very beautiful little structure which is almost impossible to find, except by watching the birds, owing to its situation, size and character. It is a tiny shallow cup, about two inches in diameter and one inch in depth, and is built in a horizontal fork or on a small bough of a tree usually at a considerable height from the ground. It is composed of very fine twigs or grass stems, with sometimes also a few feathers, carefully bound together with cobwebs and coated with scraps of bark, lichens and dead leaves, so that viewed from the ground it is virtually impossible to distinguish from an excrescence of the branch on which it is built; the cavity is sometimes lined with fine down and cobwebs.

The normal clutch consists of three eggs.

In shape the egg is a rather blunt, broad oval, fine in texture and without gloss. The ground-colour is a pale delicate greenish-white or creamy-buff, and the markings consist of brownish-red specks, spots and blotches, always more numerous towards the large end where there is a tendency to form an irregular cap.

They measure about 0·67 by 0·53 inches.

THE BLACK-HEADED CUCKOO-SHRIKE

Lalage sykesi Strickland

Description.—Length 7 inches. Male: Entire head, neck, and upper breast deep black; upper plumage dark grey; wings black, the smaller coverts and inner flight-feathers grey or margined with grey and white; tail black, the outer feathers broadly tipped with white, the central pair entirely ash-grey; lower breast ashy-grey fading into the white of the rest of the lower plumage.

Female: Upper plumage ashy-grey, most of the feathers faintly barred with paler and darker grey; wings dark sooty-brown, the smaller coverts and inner flight-feathers grey or margined with grey and white; tail as in male; lower plumage white, finely barred with black fringes to the feathers except towards the tail.

Iris brownish-red; bill and legs black.

The feathers are very stiff, downy and loosely attached, recalling the plumage of Cuckoos and Doves. Tail graduated.

Field Identification.—Male: Grey above, white below with black head and neck and largely black wings and tail. Female: Ashy-grey with the lower parts barred black and white. An arboreal species found in small parties. In the breeding season remarkable for the whistling call.

Distribution.—Confined to India, Assam, and Ceylon. Distributed very generally throughout India except north-west of a line through Kangra, Sambhar and Mount Aboo. Occurs at all elevations up to rarely 7000 feet. Birds from Kangra have been separated as *L. s. eximia* on their darker colour. Evidently a local migrant, but the movements have not yet been worked out.

Another species, the Large Cuckoo-Shrike (*Graucalus javensis*), length 10 to 12 inches, is found throughout India, with the exception of the Punjab plains, Sind and desert Rajputana. The plumage is largely grey with more or less grey barring on the white lower parts. It keeps to the tops of trees and attracts attention by its loud, querulous and rather Parrot-like cry. A rather larger bird is the Dark-grey Cuckoo-Shrike, *Lalage melaschista,* found from Murree to Eastern Assam and extending into the peninsula. It is a uniform dark grey with black wings and tail, the latter tipped with white.

FIG. 22—Black-Headed Cuckoo-Shrike ($\frac{3}{5}$ nat. size)

Habits, etc.—The Black-headed Cuckoo-Shrike is found in well-timbered open country rather than in heavy forest, and is very partial to large trees surrounding villages or the avenues of large trees which line so many of the roads of India. It also enters gardens and orchards and feeds along hedgerows. It never descends to the ground. Except in the breeding season this species is usually found in small parties which fly from tree to tree, slowly and carefully examining the foliage for the insects and larvæ which form its food. The search is continued from bough to bough until the tree has been thoroughly inspected when the flock flies off to another tree. It is usually a silent bird, but during the earlier part of the breeding season the male may frequently be heard repeating for minutes together three loud and clear whistling notes in a descending scale. Each time that he flies from tree to tree the song is repeated. The flight is easy and somewhat undulating and the strokes of the wing fairly rapid.

The breeding season in the greater part of the bird's range is from June to August, but in the extreme south it is said to be somewhat earlier, in April and May.

The nest is a very shallow rather broad cup of slight construction. It is made of thin twigs and roots and the exterior is lightly covered with spiders' webs. The situation chosen is on a branch of a tree, either in a fork or at the junction of the branch with the trunk, usually at a height of 10 to 20 feet from the ground.

The clutch consists of two or three eggs. The egg is a moderately broad oval, rather blunt at both ends. The shell is fine in texture and slightly glossy. The ground-colour is pale greenish-white, thickly blotched and streaked throughout with rather pale brown. The markings tend to be most numerous towards the broad end.

The egg measures about 0·85 by 0·65 inches.

THE ASHY SWALLOW-SHRIKE

ARTAMUS FUSCUS Vieillot

Description.—Length 7 inches. Sexes alike. Entire body plumage dull ashy, greyer on the head and paler from the breast downwards, a blackish mark in front of the eye. Wings and tail deep blue-grey, the latter tipped with white; the longer upper tail-coverts white; the lower tail-coverts whitish, finely barred with ashy.

Iris dark brown; bill clear pale blue, brownish at tip; legs slate.

Bill curved, conical and pointed; tail short and square and the long wings when closed reach to its end.

Field Identification.—Social, found in flocks; a dull grey bird that looks like a large heavy Swallow, soaring continuously into the air from a perch and incessantly uttering a harsh cry.

Distribution.—This interesting bird is found in the whole of India east of a line drawn from about Simla to Godra in the Panch Mahals. It is a resident in the plains and foot-hills up to about 2000 feet, and in summer ascends the Himalayas up to about 5000 feet. It is also found in Ceylon and eastwards through Burma towards Siam and Western China. There are no races.

Habits, etc.—The Swallow-Shrike is a gregarious bird, breeding in colonies and spending its time in large flocks which feed and rest together. It is specialised for the purpose of feeding on the wing, and in the air looks like a large grey Swallow, though easily distinguished by the constantly uttered harsh cry and by the slow-sailing flight. The flocks settle in rows on some lofty bough or the top of a tall bamboo and thence sally into the air in pursuit of passing insects; they fly round in a wide circle, though seldom for more than a minute or two at a time, and then return to the perch where they huddle closely together. During the heat of the day they are quiescent, and they feed mostly in the early mornings and late evenings, being partly crepuscular in their habits. They are very bold when breeding, and attack passing Crows and Hawks, and at times even swoop at the climber who essays to take their nest. They never visit the ground.

FIG. 23—Ashy Swallow-Shrike (½ nat. size)

The breeding season is in April, May and June. The nest is usually placed on the top of broken projecting stumps of branches or occasionally in holes; a favourite site is in palm trees, on the bases of the leaves or the rough projections whence leaves have fallen. The site is usually 30 to 40 feet from the ground.

The nest is a shallow, loose cup of fine grass, roots, fibres, feathers and similar miscellaneous materials, with, as a rule, no definite lining. The clutch consists of two to four eggs, which rather resemble those of the Shrikes. In shape the egg is a rather narrow oval, a good deal pointed towards one end, fine in texture and with a slight gloss. The ground-colour varies from white to buffy-cream colour. The markings which tend to collect in a zone round the broad end consist of spots and clouds of reddish-brown and deep purple-brown, with secondary markings of lavender and purplish-grey.

In size the eggs average about 0·95 by 0·65 inches.

PLATE VIII

1. Black Redstart. 2. Plumbeous Redstart. 3. Starling. 4. White-capped Redstart. 5. Brahminy Mynah. (All about $\frac{1}{2}$ nat. size.)

[*Face p.* 154

THE KING-CROW

DICRURUS MACROCERCUS Vieillot

Description.—Length 13 inches, including the tail 6 inches long. Sexes alike. The whole plumage black, glossed with blue; a small white spot sometimes present at the base of the bill.

Iris red; bill and legs black.

The tail is long and deeply forked, the outer feathers curling slightly upwards at the ends.

Field Identification.—One of the commonest birds throughout India, perching on trees and telegraph-wires; noisy and pugnacious; deep black with a long, gracefully-forked tail.

Distribution.—The common Black Drongo or King-Crow is a widely-spread species occurring throughout India and Ceylon and eastwards to China and Java. In this wide range it is divided into several sub-species, based entirely on the variations in size and relative lengths of wings and tails, so that individual specimens are not easily identified. In India there is a progressive diminution in size as one travels southwards. The longest-winged and largest-tailed race, *D. m. albirictus*, is found throughout northern India from the Lower Himalayas roughly to the southern fringe of the Indo-Gangetic plain. All birds south of that area to Cape Comorin may be treated as one form, *D. m. peninsularis*, whilst the smallest race from Ceylon is known as *D. m. minor*. A resident species with some local migrations. Found from sea-level up to about 5000 feet.

The much smaller and more highly burnished Bronzed Drongo (*Chaptia ænea*), and the heavily-built Hair-crested Drongo (*Chibia hottentotta*), with an almost square tail and a tuft of long hairs springing from the forehead, share a somewhat similar distribution along the Outer Himalayas, near the eastern border of the Central Provinces and in South-west India.

Habits, etc.—In the King-Crow we have another of the most familiar birds of India, attracting attention by its graceful shape, its fearlessness and pugnacity, its abundance, and the wideness of its distribution. This bird has no connection with the family of Crows; it belongs to a very highly-specialised and distinct family, the *Dicruridæ*, which appears to occupy a position between the Shrikes and the Birds of Paradise. The familiar name is due partly to the colour "as black as a Crow" and partly to its pugnacity and fearlessness in defence of the nest, which leads it to attack all predaceous enemies. It is a common sight to see a pair of these birds chasing a Crow through the air, stooping at and around it with a mastery of flight and power, like that of a Falcon, accompanying the performance with a series of angry calls that attract the attention of the least observant; verily it is King of the Crows, who, otherwise, are a match for bird and mammal, even including the arch-mammal man. And if necessity arises it does not hesitate to attack Eagle, Falcon or Hawk with the same courage.

But the King-Crow is not a mere bully: harmless species it does not molest, and it has long been noticed that a tree containing a King-Crow's nest usually also contains the nest of a Golden Oriole, a Red Turtle-Dove, or some other equally gentle bird, and

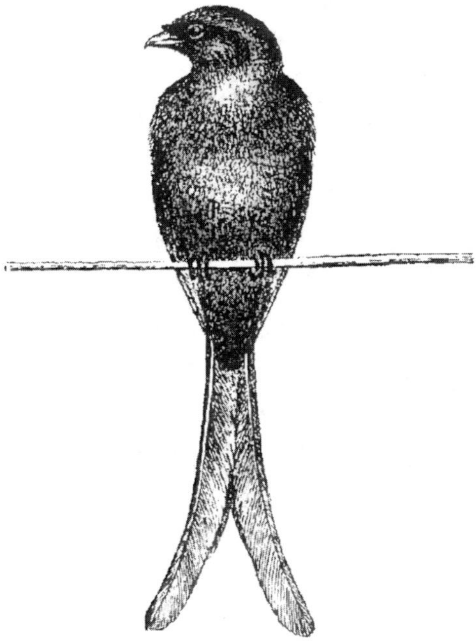

FIG. 24—King-Crow (½ nat. size)

it is difficult to resist the conclusion that these species recognise the fact that the presence of the King-Crow's nest above their heads is a guarantee of protection from all ordinary marauders.

The King-Crow is found in every type of country, though it certainly prefers the neighbourhood of open cultivation. Its chief need is a vantage-point on which to perch, swaying and flicking its long tail, and watching ceaselessly for every insect that stirs in the air or on the ground. It seldom perches on buildings, but prefers a bare dead bough at the summit of a tree or a telegraph-wire. One may travel for days on an Indian railway and the King-Crows dotted along the wires will be one of the unchanging sights of the journey. And from the chosen perch they are incessantly flying either to capture an insect on the wing, returning to eat it on the perch, or down to the ground to settle there and eat some more sluggish quarry. Their whole build, however, precludes any progression on the ground or about the branches of a tree and their movements are entirely aerial. Herds of grazing cattle are generally accompanied by one or more of these birds which travel with them, perching on the back of one of the animals and hawking the grasshoppers disturbed by the progress of the herd through the grass. The bird also attends ploughing operations, perching on small bushes and clods of earth in the vicinity and watching for larvæ exposed in the furrows. At times the King-Crow is somewhat of a pirate, robbing Mynahs and Hoopoes as they search industriously for tasty morsels on the ground. The food consists entirely of insects, dragon-flies, crickets, grasshoppers, moths, bugs, etc., and their larvæ.

The call-notes are loud and cheerful though somewhat metallic in tone. The Punjabi names of *Kalcheet* and *Kalkalichi* are onomatopœic and fairly represent the more common calls, but it is impossible to represent the evident fury imported into the bird's tones when it is driving an intruder from the vicinity of the nest. The song is short but not pleasing.

While undoubtedly in the main a resident species, the King-Crow is certainly migratory to some extent; but, as is almost inevitable, with so abundant a species in which a large proportion of individuals are sedentary, the extent and meaning of these movements is difficult to observe and has not yet been worked out.

The breeding season extends from April to August. The nest is a broad, shallow cup of tiny twigs and fine grass stems and roots neatly and strongly woven together and exteriorly bound round with a good deal of cobweb; some nests are lined with fine grass, horse-hair or roots. The side of the nest is thicker than the bottom through which the eggs are often visible against the sky. It is suspended in a horizontal fork of a tree, for the most part at a considerable height from the ground and a little way in from the extremity of the chosen bough. A second clutch of eggs is often laid in a nest that has been robbed.

Three to five eggs are laid, but the usual clutch consists of four. The egg is a rather long oval, somewhat pointed towards the smaller end; the shell is fine and rather fragile and usually without gloss. The coloration is very variable. Some eggs are pure white and spotless; others are white with fine black spots; while a third type is pale salmon-colour spotted with rich brownish-red, blackish- and purplish-brown; there are infinite variations on these types, but the markings are never very large or densely distributed.

The egg measures about 1·05 by 0·75 inches.

THE INDIAN GREY DRONGO

DICRURUS LONGICAUDATUS Jerdon

Description.—Length 12 inches, including tail 6 inches. Sexes alike. The whole upper plumage indigo with a high gloss; the lower plumage dark grey; a blackish patch in front of the eye.

Iris red; bill and legs black.

Tail long, slender and widely forked at the end, the outer feathers curling upwards.

Field Identification.—In the field appears black with a long, slender forked tail, and is only distinguished from the King-Crow with difficulty, by the more slender build, unless close enough for the lighter duller colour of the under parts to be recognisable.

Distribution.—The Grey Drongo is a very widely-spread species in India, Burma, Ceylon, and still farther east, and has been divided into a number of races based on differences of measurements and the comparative darkness or lightness of the plumage, but several of these are probably unnecessary. *D. l. longicaudatus* is found, as a summer visitor from March to September, in the Himalayas from Hazara to somewhere in Assam, being replaced in Lower Burma and the Malay Peninsula by *D. l. intermedius*. *D. l. longicaudatus* is found also as a winter visitor throughout the greater part of Continental and Peninsular India, avoiding Sind, Punjab, Guzerat and portions of Rajputana. It also reaches Ceylon in winter.

The Grey Drongo is particularly a hill species, for the most part breeding at altitudes between 4000 and 7000 feet, but also lower and up to 10,000 feet.

The White-bellied Drongo (*Dicrurus cærulescens*) is widely distributed and locally common throughout the greater part of India, except in the Punjab, Sind, and Rajputana. The brownish-grey throat and breast and white belly distinguish it easily from all other species, though it must be remembered that the young of the King-Crow have the lower abdomen largely marked with white. The song of this King-Crow is almost meruline in character, and is superior to the songs of all other species of Drongo.

Habits, etc.—The Grey Drongo is typically a resident of well-wooded hills, preferring those of more open character to the neighbourhood of dense forest. It has the same habits as the Black Drongo, perching on high trees and hawking insects in their vicinity. But as its favourite tree is usually on the side of some afforested mountain-slope it normally flies at greater heights from the ground than its Black cousin, and seldom descends actually to the ground. It is a magnificent flier, turning and twisting with extreme speed and skill, and it has the pugnacity of the family, hunting larger birds from the vicinity of its nest with great courage. It is usually found singly or in pairs, but the pairs do not object to the vicinity of others of their own species, and several birds often collect together to mob a common foe or to work some desirable feeding ground. During migration small parties travel together.

The Grey Drongo has much the same range of musical calls as the Black Drongo, some harsh and scolding, others sweet and cheerful; a common call may be given as *drangh-gip* or *gip-gip-drangh*. There is a short but pleasant song, and in addition the bird is something of a mimic.

The food consists entirely of insects, the majority of which are taken on the wing. A bird has been seen to settle by a bee-hive and deliberately pick up and eat the bees.

The breeding season is in May and June.

The nest is a strong shallow cup, placed in a horizontal fork of a tree at any height from 12 feet upwards, and often quite inaccessible. It is built of fine grass stems, slender twigs and roots, plastered with cobwebs and lichens and lined with finer grasses and hairs. The bottom of the nest is usually thin enough for the eggs to be visible through it against the sky.

The egg is a moderately broad oval, fine in texture and without gloss. There are two main types of coloration. The first is pinkish-salmon colour, streaked, blotched, and clouded with reddish-pink of a darker shade. In the other the ground-colour is pale pinkish-white boldly blotched and spotted, mostly in a zone round the broad end, with brownish-red and faint inky-purple.

The egg measures about 0·95 by 0·74 inches.

THE LARGE RACKET-TAILED DRONGO

DISSEMURUS PARADISEUS (Linnæus)

Description.—Length to end of central tail-feathers 14 inches; outer tail-feathers up to 13 inches extra. Sexes alike. Entire plumage black, glossed with blue except on the inner webs of the wing-quills, throat and lower abdomen; some white spots under the wing.

Iris crimson; bill and legs black.

An erect crest of long hackle-like plumes on the forehead falling backwards over the nape; the outer pair of tail-feathers greatly elongated, the middle portion of the shaft webless, the terminal four inches having the outer web very narrow and the inner web broad and twisted upwards; a twist in the shaft reverses the apparent position of these webs.

Field Identification.—A glossy black bird, immediately identified by the plumed crest and the extraordinary development of the outer tail-feathers into rackets on the end of the wire-like shafts.

Distribution.—Throughout the greater part of India, Burma, and Ceylon to Siam and the Malay Peninsula. It has been divided into a number of races differing in the size and quality of the crest and tail. *D. p. grandis* breeds along the Himalayas from Kumaon to Eastern Assam and through to Yunnan, from the plains up to 3000 and occasionally 4000 feet; it extends east of a line roughly from Kumaon to Mount Aboo southwards to Sambalpur, Raipur and the northern reaches of the Godavari River. *D. p. malabaricus*, an altogether smaller bird, occupies the rest of India south of the above range. In Ceylon there are two races, both still smaller, one *D. p. ceylonensis* confined to the dry zone, and the other with different outer tail feathers, *D. p. tophorhinus*, restricted to the wet zone. It is a resident species.

FIG. 25—Large Racket-tailed Drongo ($\frac{1}{5}$ nat. size)

This species must not be confused with the Lesser Racket-tailed Drongo (*Bhringa remifer*) of the Eastern Himalayas, Assam and Burma which has the rackets fully webbed on both sides, lacks the crest and has the feathers of the forehead produced in a curious flat pad over the base of the beak.

Habits, etc.—This wonderful Drongo, known familiarly as the Bhimraj, is a forest species, inhabiting by preference the densest and dampest of the Indian forests, though it is also found in any well-wooded country and even comes into gardens. It appears to have a special partiality for bamboo jungle and is entirely arboreal in its habits. It is more sociable than other Drongos, often going about in parties of four and five. These parties appear to wander a good deal in search of food, flying from tree to tree, swooping at insects on the wing or capturing them from the branches. The bird also hunts from a fixed station, returning again and again to the same tree. Its food consists of a variety of insects, wasps, beetles, butterflies, locusts and their larvæ, and it is accustomed to devour quantities of bees.

The call is very striking, beginning with a harsh chuckle and ending in a peculiar metallic creaking cry, expressed by the syllables *tse-rung, tse-rung*. It has in addition a number of musical calls and whistles and is justly celebrated as a very fine mimic, imitating all the birds of the locality. It makes a delightful pet, fearless and most amusing with its imitations of noises about the house and garden.

The breeding season is from March to May, and, when nesting, the bird is accustomed to harry passing birds of prey. The nest is the usual cup-cradle of the Drongos, slung in the fork of a small outside branch of a tree, usually at a great height from the ground. It is composed of fine twigs and grass stems well interlaced and firmly attached to the fork and strengthened with cobwebs; the outside is usually decorated with lichen, moss and scraps of bark.

The clutch consists of three or four eggs. They are rather long and pointed, fine in texture and with little gloss. The ground-colour varies from white to rich cream, marked with blotches, spots and specks of reddish-brown or purple and secondary markings of lavender and pale neutral tint. The markings tend to collect towards the broad end.

The egg measures about 1·15 by 0·82 inches.

THE INDIAN GREAT REED-WARBLER

Acrocephalus stentoreus (Hempr. and Ehrn.)

Description.—Length 7 inches. Sexes alike. Upper plumage olive-brown; an indistinct fulvous buff line over the eye; wings and tail dark brown, washed with olive-brown; chin and throat creamy-white; remainder of lower plumage fulvous buff, paler about the vent.

In worn plumage the upper parts become much greyer and the lower parts whiter.

Iris yellow-brown; bill blackish-brown, base of lower mandible fleshy-livid; legs steely plumbeous. Inside of mouth salmon-red.

The tail is somewhat graduated.

Field Identification.—One of the largest of the Warblers. A dull olive-brown bird with fulvous under parts, chiefly remarkable in the hand for the rich salmon-red mouth. Normally found in dense reed-beds where it is very noisy.

Distribution.—This species is widely distributed from Egypt and Palestine through Western and Central Asia to India, Ceylon and Burma. It is divided into races. Indian birds belong to the race *A. s. brunnescens* which also breeds in Transcaspia, Persia and Turkestan. In our area it is known to breed in suitable jheels in

Sind, Baluchistan, North-west Frontier Province, Kashmir, the Punjab and the United Provinces, and possibly also in Khandesh and Bombay. It is largely migratory and is found in winter or on passage throughout India. A smaller and more richly coloured race, *A. s. meridionalis*, is resident in Ceylon.

Habits, etc.—The Great Reed-Warbler is normally a bird of dense reed-beds though it may also be found in any other thick cover over water, such as the mangrove swamps along the tidal creeks of the Bombay and Sind coasts. In such places it is more often heard than seen. The call and alarm note is a harsh *chack chack*, while the song is very distinctive, never forgotten when once heard. It is very loud and variable, hard and metallic for the most part, but also interspersed with pleasant bars. But the essential burden of the refrain, constantly recurring, is the loud *karra karra karreet karreet karreet* or *prit prit pritik* which suddenly bursts out of a reed-bed with astonishing vehemence. It is to be heard everywhere in the lakes of the Kashmir Vale even amongst the house-boats by the Dal Darwaza in Srinagar. The singer himself usually keeps out of sight, climbing about the reed stems and the heaps of debris a few inches above the surface of the water. Although such a skulker the bird is not particularly shy and allows a close approach, while at intervals it climbs to the tops of the reeds or even into neighbouring trees, singing a few bars of the song from such a vantage-point before returning to the shady depths of the reed-bed. The food consists of the various aquatic larvæ and insects, small snails and slugs and aquatic seeds to be found in such situations.

On migration the Great Reed-Warbler may be found almost anywhere, skulking in garden bushes, hopping about in the boughs of trees. It is then silent, save for the call-note.

The breeding season, which is of course dependent on the growth of reeds, is from late May to August, most eggs being found in June and July.

The nest is a very deep massive cup, which is woven round the stems of four or five reeds usually at a height of about 2 feet above the water. The nest is built of coarse water grass, shreds of leaves and bark of the reeds, the fibrous roots of water-plants and similar materials, and it is lined with finer materials of the same sort.

The clutch varies from three to six eggs, but four is certainly the normal number. The egg is a moderately elongated oval with a fine shell but no gloss. The ground-colour varies from greenish- or bluish-white to creamy stone-colour. The markings consist of very fine stippling overlaid with fairly bold and well-marked spots and blotches of greyish-black, inky-purple, olive-brown, yellowish-olive, and reddish-umber-brown, with here and there pale underlying clouds of pale inky colour. The markings are usually most dense towards the broad end, and there is a great deal of variation, not all the above markings and colours always appearing in one specimen.

The egg measures about 0·90 by 0·60 inches.

BLYTH'S REED-WARBLER

Acrocephalus dumetorum Blyth

Description.—Length 5 inches. Sexes alike. An indistinct fulvous streak over the eye; the remainder of the upper plumage and the sides of the face and neck brown distinctly tinged with olivaceous; wings and tail brown, the feathers edged with olivaceous; the whole lower plumage pale buff, paler on the chin, throat and abdomen.

Iris light brown; bill brown above, flesh-coloured below; gape and mouth yellow; legs brown, soles yellowish.

Tail somewhat graduated.

Field Identification.—A miniature edition of the Great Reed-Warbler with the mouth yellow instead of salmon-red; much less of a marsh bird, being found in any sort of cover except in heavy forest.

Blyth's Reed-Warbler is usually confused with two other Warblers of similar size and appearance. The differences from the Booted Warbler will be found under that species (p. 164). The Paddy-Field Warbler (*Acrocephalus agricola*) has the upper plumage russet in tint instead of olivaceous and is normally found near water in reed-beds or similar cover.

Distribution.—Blyth's Reed-Warbler breeds in Russia and Western Siberia from Esthonia to Irkutsk and southwards to Northern Persia and Turkestan. It is a very common passage migrant from August to October and again from March to May through the Himalayas and in the plains north-west of a line from the Rann of Cutch to Lucknow and a more or less common winter visitor to the rest of India and Ceylon. It also occurs in Assam and parts of Burma.

Habits, etc.—The observer in India must not be deceived by the name of Blyth's Reed-Warbler, for on passage and in winter quarters the neighbourhood of water has no special attraction for this species. In winter it is a bird of thick cover, found in any type of country other than thick forest. All that is essential to it is concealment, and whether this be found in the hedgerows of village cultivation or the scrub of the barren plains on the Deccan plateau, in the tamarisk of a river-bed in the plains or the dense bracken thickets or water-logged patches of the South Indian hills, it is content. It hops about the hidden stems in search of insects, solitary by habit though numerically abundant; and the observer is lucky who learns much more of it than the single harsh note ***tschuk*** uttered at intervals of a few seconds, varied occasionally by ***churr-r-r*** or ***chr-chr***.

On passage in Northern India this Warbler may be found anywhere, in the trees of shady gardens and orchards, in isolated bushes on barren hill-sides and of course in any patch of thick cover. On spring passage the song is freely uttered. It is a vigorous and rather pretty song of a rambling character and would remind an English naturalist rather of a Linnet than of the Reed-Warblers of his own reed-beds.

The food consists chiefly of insects and their larvæ.

Blyth's Reed-Warbler does not nest within our limits.

The breeding season in the northern part of its range is about June. The nest is built both in marshy and dry localities—reed-beds are rarely chosen—in varied types of undergrowth and is a deep cup of bents and grasses, lined with hair, slung by the sides to the supporting vegetation.

The clutch usually consists of four or five eggs. They are said to be very variable. The ground-colour is bluish- or greenish-white or suffused brownish-grey, scantily but rather boldly spotted and blotched with olive-brown and ashy-grey.

The average size is about 0·7 by 0·5 inches.

THE BOOTED WARBLER

Hippolais caligata (Lichtenstein)

Description.—Length 5 inches. Sexes alike. A pale buffy-white line over the eye; upper plumage brown with a pale olivaceous tinge; wings and tail dark brown, the feathers edged with olive-brown, the outer tail-feathers faintly tipped and the outermost feather also edged with whitish; whole lower plumage very pale buff, the throat and middle of the abdomen whitish.

Iris brown; bill blackish-brown above, yellowish-brown below; gape and mouth yellow; legs steely blue-grey.

Tail slightly graduated.

Field Identification.—A very indefinitely coloured little Warbler, brown above and pale buffy-white below with a pale streak over the eye. Usually found creeping about in bushes uttering a clicking note.

Distribution.—This species is divided into two forms which were formerly ranked as two separate species. The typical race (or Booted Warbler of literature generally) breeds in Central and Eastern Russia and Western Siberia, occurs on passage (March-May and August-September) in Persia, Afghanistan, Baluchistan and North-west India and winters from Central India to Ceylon. It does not occur east of the Duars and the Lower Brahmaputra. The other race *H. c. rama* (or Sykes' Tree-Warbler of literature) breeds in Persia, Turkestan, Afghanistan, Baluchistan, the Punjab and Sind and winters in India and Ceylon. It has not been recorded east of Moghulserai and Assensole.

In fresh autumn plumage *caligata* is a darker and more fulvous brown and *rama* is more of a uniform mouse-grey brown in tint, but these differences are soon obscured by wear and bleaching and the two races are most easily separated by the length of tail measured from the base between the two central feathers. This is below 50 millimetres (2 inches) in *caligata* and above that figure in *rama* In other details, more particularly the bill, *rama* is correspondingly larger. The two forms cannot be separated in the field. Both these races require to be distinguished from Blyth's Reed-Warbler (*Acrocephalus dumetorum*). In the first place, their general coloration is much greyer.[1] In both the minute first primary or flight-feather of the wing is 3·5 to 10 millimetres longer than the primary coverts, whereas in Blyth's Reed-Warbler and the allied Paddy-field Warbler (*Acrocephalus agricola*) this feather is usually shorter than or equal to the primary coverts and never exceeds them by more than 3 millimetres. In the Booted Warbler the bristles that line the base of the beak are small and weak; and finally the tail is much less deeply graduated and the white edge to the outer tail-feather is distinctive.

Habits, etc.—In the cold weather the Booted Warbler is a bird of any kind of dry country where bushes abound, save actual forest. It frequents gardens, scrub-jungle and babool trees in open fields and in such places it will be found skulking in the undergrowth or creeping about the branches of the babool trees. In the latter case its movements are very reminiscent of those of the Willow-Warblers and like the Siberian Chiff-Chaff it often flies out from the extremity of a bough to take insects on the wing. In general, it is very unobtrusive and seldom shows itself, but a subdued *chuck* or *chick* or *chur-r*, incessantly uttered at intervals of a second or two, records its gradual progress. Although solitary by nature, these Warblers are often numerically so abundant, especially on passage, that numbers will be found in suitable localities.

The song is said to be sweet and powerful and uttered both by night and day. It is not heard, however, on passage or in winter quarters and is confined to the breeding ground. In Baluchistan this species breeds in every orchard and garden of the Quetta Valley and particularly in the thick rose-hedges which surround the lucerne fields. In the Punjab and Sind it is a bird of the grass-jungles and

[1] This species differs in tint according to wear and race. If I have appeared inconsistent in describing the exact shades of brown, it is due to that fact and also the necessity of emphasising the varied contrasts of colour.

tamarisk-beds of the riverain tracts. In some areas it is so numerous that the breeding appears to be almost colonial.

The breeding season lasts from the second half of March to the beginning of July. The nest is a neat, compact little cup of grass, bits of rotten bark, hair, string and other soft material, built on a framework of grass and lined with fine grass stems, feathers and cotton. At Quetta it is usually placed in the heart of a rose-bush. In the Punjab and Sind it is built either in a tamarisk or in a thick tuft of grass and in the latter situation it is usually a foot or less from the ground.

The clutch varies from three to five eggs. The egg is a broad blunt oval, of fine and close texture without gloss. There is much variety, but the ground-colour is generally a very pale grey-white tinged with greenish or pinkish and marked with spots and speckles, blotches and fine hair-lines and scrawls of black, purple, red-brown or pinkish-grey.

In size the egg measures about 0·6 by 0·5 inches.

THE TAILOR-BIRD

Orthotomus sutorius (Pennant)

(Plate xiii, Fig. 6, opposite page 264)

Description.—Length 5 inches. Sexes alike. A rufous cap on the forehead; remainder of top and sides of head ashy-brownish, shading off into the shining but sullied white of the entire lower surface; there is a concealed dark spot on each side of the neck, and the thighs are rufous; remainder of upper plumage yellowish-green, the concealed parts of the wings and tail brown.

Iris reddish-yellow; bill dark horny, lower mandible pale flesh colour; legs straw colour to pale fleshy-red.

Bill rather long and sharp; in the breeding season the male acquires very long and pointed central tail-feathers, two inches longer than in winter.

Field Identification.—A familiar small garden bird of the plains, green above, white below with a rufous cap; carries the tail (which is long and pointed in summer, short and rounded in winter) erect over the back like a Wren; has a loud, strident call.

Distribution.—In the Tailor-bird we again have a common bird, of wide distribution from India to China, which is divided into several races. The typical race, small, with a large bill and no difference between the summer and winter plumage, is confined to the low-country in Ceylon, and in the hill zone a darker race, *O. s. fernandonis.* The Indian race, *O. s. guzerata,* is larger, and in the breeding season develops the long tail-feathers. It is found throughout the country except in the more extreme desert areas, and from about Eastern Bengal and the Duars it is replaced by a more richly coloured bird, *O. s. patia.* The Indian form occurs in the Outer Himalayas up to 4000 feet, stragglers even ascending to 7000 feet, and in the southern ranges it also is found up to 4000 feet. The Tailor-bird is a most strictly resident species, neither migrating nor moving about locally.

Habits, etc.—By name and repute the Tailor-bird is certainly one of the best-known birds of India, yet the number of people who can identify it by sight or sound or give any idea of its appearance is probably very small indeed. Like many other famous persons, the Tailor-bird is insignificant in appearance, a small, rather gawky, green bird, with a pointed tail and a rufous crown, which climbs about in undergrowth and is mostly hidden from sight. It is a bird of gardens and even verandahs, of the outskirts of villages, of patches of low evergreen undergrowth. Forest and bare desert areas are alike abhorrent to it. Where man has settled and made his home there will the Tailor-bird be found. Although seldom seen by the unobservant it is not shy, but with endless activity hops about the bushes and creepers round a house, investigating the flower-pots in the verandah and willingly feeding within a few feet of people, provided that they are not moving about. And as it goes it constantly utters the loud, discordant, strident call, loud for so small a bird and unmistakable when known, which is a familiar sound in every garden though known to few as the note of this species. When the note is uttered the throat swells and reveals the concealed black spots on the sides of the neck. The head and tail are held stiffly over the back after the manner of the English Wren. The flight is very curious; it seldom lasts for more than a yard or two from cover to cover, and the bird flies with obvious effort, the long tail flicking upwards over the back in a manner that can only seem a hindrance. The food consists entirely of insects.

But all the fame of the Tailor-bird is of course centred in its nest, and with the unfairness of the world it undoubtedly receives alone in popular estimation the credit as an architect which should be distributed amongst several species. For certain of the Wren-Warblers build nests on exactly the same principles as the Tailor-bird, and in addition build other beautiful types of nest, which it does not.

The nest itself is a deep, soft cup of cotton-wool and down, with a slight lining of a few horse-hairs, and occasionally a few fine grass stems. For it the bird prepares an aerial cradle by sewing two or more leaves together, the nest being placed within the cavity so formed. There is a good deal of variety in the method of sewing the leaves together; two large ones may be joined down their edges, several smaller leaves may be sewn together, or the nest may be slung between two or three leaves which are sewn to it and not to each other. The sewing is done with threads of cobweb, silk from cocoons, wool or cottons; the bird pierces a hole in the leaf with its sharp beak and draws the thread through, contriving in some manner to make a knot on the outside sufficient to prevent the thread slipping back; except that each stitch is made separately it would pass well for the work of human hands. It is frequently stated that dead leaves are picked up and sewn to the side of the nest, but this is an error, and the explanation is simple. These leaves were green and fresh when the work began, but they are injured and die from the effect of the stitches, and curling in the heat break loose from their parent stem.

The nest is placed at all elevations, either in low bushes, in the hanging boughs of loquat and similar trees, or high up in some lordly mango tree. The only essential condition is a tough large type of leaf; but most nests will be found within 6 feet of the ground.

The principal breeding season is in May, June, and July, but occasional nests may be found in other months. The bird is very suspicious of interference, and readily deserts a half-built nest which has been found and looked at.

Three to six eggs may be found, but the normal clutch is certainly three or four. They are rather long and pointed in shape, very thin and delicate, and with but little gloss. They fall into two types of coloration, with the ground-colour either reddish-white or pale bluish-green; the former is more common. The markings consist of bold blotches or sometimes ill-defined clouds, mixed with speckles, spots, and dashes of red, reddish-brown, brown, black, or purplish-black. These are seldom dense in character and there is a tendency for the larger markings to collect towards the broad end of the egg.

The eggs measure about 0·64 by 0·46 inches.

THE FANTAIL-WARBLER

Cisticola juncidis (Rafinesque)

Description.—Length 4 inches. Sexes alike. Winter plumage: The whole upper plumage, including the wings, dark blackish-brown, the feathers broadly edged with fulvous; rump plain rufous; a broad eyebrow, the sides of the face, except for the brownish ear-coverts, and the whole lower plumage buffy-white, becoming buff on the breast and flanks; tail dark brown, central feathers edged with fulvous and remainder with white tips and a black subterminal bar.

The male in summer has the top of the head and neck plain brown and the tail a quarter of an inch shorter with rufous patches above the black bar.

Iris yellow-brown ; bill fleshy, darker along the top ; legs fleshy. The tail is rounded and expands into a perfect fan.

Field Identification.—Plains species ; a minute, streaked black and brown bird, with pale under parts, found in thick herbage ; skulks until disturbed, then has a curious mounting flight in the air, accompanied by a loud clicking note.

Distribution.—The Fantail-Warbler has an immense range in Southern Europe, Africa, and Asia, and is divided into several races. Of these, *C. j. cursitans* occurs throughout practically the whole of India from the North-west Frontier Province and Sind, but not Baluchistan, to Assam, Burma, Siam, and Yunnan. It occurs here

FIG. 26—Fantail-Warbler (⅞ nat. size)

and there in the various hill ranges up to about 6000 feet, but is, properly speaking, a plains bird. In the main resident, it is also locally migratory. A darker bird, *C. j. salimalii*, is resident in Travancore, and replaced in Ceylon by the larger-billed *C. j. omalura*.

Habits, etc.—The Fantail-Warbler is typically a bird of low, thick cover in wide open spaces, and it is found therefore in stretches of grassland, in patches of reeds and tamarisk thickets, or the raised grassy bunds of rice cultivation. In such cover it skulks and is very retiring, seldom climbing above the stems, and would not come to notice save for its curious habits of flight. When disturbed the bird jerks itself high into the air, and after flying some distance falls headlong again into cover. During the breeding season the male soars in the air in a most erratic fashion, rising and falling in jerks but keeping roughly above the area of which the centre is the nest site, and towards this he falls very quickly at intervals as if intending to settle ; just, however, as he nears the ground he shoots up into the air again and resumes his soaring jerks. All the time he utters a creaking, clicking note which rises to its climax as each aerial jerk reaches its highest point, coinciding with it. When feeding young the parent approaches the nest in somewhat similar fashion, flying well up in the air though not to the height of the male's display; as it comes it utters a note which is softer and more level in tone than the display song, but the whole approach rather resembles the above display and may easily be mistaken for it. The young in the nest when disturbed utter a menacing, hissing note.

The breeding season lasts from April to October, but is connected with the rains, the birds never breeding when the weather is dry.

The nest is built in a tuft of green grass near to the ground, and is a very delicate and beautiful affair, being composed of white cobwebs with a lining of vegetable-down, the green blades of growing grass being incorporated in the sides of the structure. In shape it may be oval with the entrance near the top, a long deep purse narrowing towards the top, or a cup with a canopy woven over it.

The clutch varies from three to seven eggs, but five is the usual number.

The eggs are rather short ovals in shape, fine and delicate in texture with a fair amount of gloss. They are pure white, faintly tinged with blue, or even very occasionally a definite pale blue, finely spotted and speckled with reddish-brown; there is a tendency for these markings to collect into a cap or zone.

In size the egg averages about 0·59 by 0·46 inches.

THE RUFOUS-FRONTED WREN-WARBLER

Franklinia buchanani (Blyth)

(Plate xii, Fig. 1, opposite page 242)

Description.—Length 5 inches. Sexes alike. Upper plumage including the wings reddish-brown, brighter on the head; a mark over the eye and the whole lower plumage white, sullied with fulvous on the sides of the head and towards the tail. Tail brown, rather long and graduated, all except the central pair of feathers tipped with white preceded by a dark spot.

In winter the tail is half an inch longer.

Iris reddish-yellow; bill brown, lower mandible pale fleshy; legs pale fleshy-brown.

The Wren-Warblers of the genus *Franklinia* have twelve tail-feathers, which readily distinguishes them from the genus *Prinia* with ten tail-feathers.

Field Identification.—A small plains bird found in scrubby bushes in open arid country; brown above with a reddish crown and whitish below, a long full tail edged with white. Wren-Warblers of the genus

Franklinia are found in parties, while those of the genus *Prinia* are found usually singly or in pairs.

Distribution.—A purely Indian form. It occurs in the plains of the whole of the north-west corner of India, from the North-west Frontier Province and the Upper Punjab through the United Provinces, Sind, and Rajputana down to the Central Provinces, the Deccan, and Western Bengal and Behar as far as Ranchi and Hazaribagh. A purely resident species.

Habits, etc.—This quaint little bird avoids damp and well-timbered localities, and is by preference a bird of semi-desert localities. It is in its element in the bare sandy plains of the Lower Punjab, Sind, and Rajputana, where the most conspicuous vegetation is the wild caper, whose tight thorny bushes rise in little mounds all over miles of open country. Here this Warbler is abundant, and one of the most noticeable birds, living in energetic little troops which are always on the move, creeping in and out of the bushes and running like mice on the ground at their base. It is also addicted to dry, stony hills with low bush-jungle, and ventures into the lighter crops such as cotton and mustard. During the breeding season its very cheerful little song is a marked feature of the plains that it inhabits.

The breeding season extends from March to September, and probably two broods are reared.

The nest is usually an oval domed structure, with the entrance near the top at one side. It is built of fine grass stems and tow-like vegetable fibres, and the egg cavity is softly lined with vegetable-down and a felt-like substance formed of dry portions of the ber bush. A few nests are cup-shaped or purse-like and suspended. The site chosen is generally very close to the ground, a matter of inches, but it may be occasionally 3 or 4 feet above it. It is built in bushes, a favourite situation being either a low close caper bush, or in a heap of dead thorn loppings overgrown with grass. The clutch varies from three to six eggs, but the usual number is five.

The egg is a moderately broad oval, the shell very delicate and fine with a fair gloss. The ground-colour is white, slightly tinged with greyish or greenish; it is thickly and finely speckled all over with somewhat dingy- or purplish-red, and there is a slight tendency for the markings to collect towards the broad end.

The average measurement is 0·62 by 0·48 inches.

FRANKLIN'S WREN-WARBLER

FRANKLINIA GRACILIS (Franklin)

Description.—Length 4 inches. Sexes alike. Summer plumage: Upper plumage dark ashy-grey, the wings and tail washed with brown; lower plumage white, a broad ashy band across the breast and the flanks washed with ashy.

Winter plumage: An indistinct white streak over the eye; upper plumage brown, the wings and upper tail-coverts washed with chestnut-brown, the tail washed with grey; whole lower plumage white, washed with grey and fulvous. In winter plumage the tail is half an inch longer and the indistinct spots towards the ends of the tail-feathers are more pronounced.

Iris brownish-yellow; eye-rims orange; bill dark brownish-black; legs yellowish-orange, claws dark horny.

Tail sharply graduated, of twelve feathers.

Field Identification.—A small bird with a longish tail found in parties in low open scrub. Summer plumage ashy-grey above, white below with a broad ashy band across the breast. Winter plumage warm brown above, sullied white below with no breast band, the two plumages so different that they would never be taken for the same bird.

Distribution.—Ceylon, India, Assam, Burma to Tenasserim, Siam, Annam, and Laos. Found throughout India except the Punjab Plains, North-west Frontier Province, Sind, and desert Rajputana. Occurs up to about 4000 feet, both in the Himalayas and in the ranges of the Peninsula. A strictly resident species with the following races:—

The typical race has sharply defined summer and winter plumages as already described. It is found in Rajputana, the United and Central Provinces, the Bombay Presidency and in North Hyderabad as well as in Arakan. *F. g. hodgsoni* is found along the Outer Himalayas from Murree and Kashmir to the Duars, in Assam and in the Kachin Hills in Burma. This race has a more rusty tint in winter plumage. *F. g. albogularis* of South India has the upper parts darker in summer plumage and is whiter on the lower parts in winter plumage. *F. g. pectoralis* in Ceylon is also a dark bird but is more remarkable for having summer and winter plumage alike, both of the summer type. In this it agrees with the three species of Wren-Warblers of the genus *Prinia* found in Ceylon.

Habits, etc.—Franklin's Wren-Warbler is a bird of all the more open types of country. By preference it is found in open scrub-jungle where low bushes grow amidst coarse grass and scattered small trees, but it is also met with in hedgerows, fairly light forest, in cultivation broken by patches of cover and even in reed-beds and mangrove swamps. In such localities it is met with in small parties which lead a life of great activity, hunting incessantly for insects in the grass and bushes or running on the ground at their base. It seldom ventures into trees at any height above the ground. It is a very poor flier, proceeding by curious little jerky flights, the tail jerking awkwardly as it goes. There is a feeble little twittering song.

The main breeding season is in the rains from July to September, but in the hills the birds are said to breed earlier from about April to June.

The nest is a small cup of fine dry grass and vegetable fibres, felted here and there on the outside with small lumps of woolly vegetable-down. It is carefully sewn with cobwebs, silk from cocoons or wool into one or two leaves which often completely envelop it, leaving no part visible. It thus closely resembles the nest of the Tailor-bird, but as compared with that species the situation chosen is normally closer to the ground at a height of 2 or 3 feet, and more nests are sewn to a single leaf only.

The clutch consists of three or four eggs, the latter being usual. The eggs vary considerably. They are typically rather slender ovals, a good deal compressed towards one end; the shell is exquisitely fine and glossy. The colour varies from pure white or pure bright blue, unspotted, to almost any shade of pinky-white, pale grey-green or greenish-blue, speckled all over or in a zone or cap at the broader end with reddish-brown.

The egg measures about 0·58 by 0·42 inches.

THE LESSER WHITETHROAT

Sylvia curruca (Linnæus)

(Plate xii, Fig. 2, opposite page 242)

Description.—Length 6 inches. Sexes alike. Upper plumage earthy-brown, the whole top of the head contrasting brownish-grey; a broad band through the eye dark brown; wings dark brown, edged paler; tail dark brown, a large portion of the outer feathers white; the whole lower plumage greyish-white.

Iris yellow-brown; bill dusky, lower base slaty horn; legs plumbeous.

Field Identification.—Brown above, dirty white below, with a darkish cap and a white edge to the tail; a very quiet, shy bird, which creeps about in trees and is particularly partial to acacias.

Distribution.—The Lesser Whitethroat is a widely-distributed breeding species in Europe and Northern Asia, migrating southwards to Africa and Southern Asia in winter. There are several races, of which we are concerned with two. *S. c. blythi* differs from the typical European form in having the second primary always shorter than the sixth, usually between it and the seventh in length. It breeds in Siberia and Manchuria, and is a very abundant winter visitor to the plains of India, extending on the south to Ceylon, and on the east to Behar and Western Bengal. *S. c. minula* differs from *S. c. blythi* in its smaller size and considerably paler upper parts. It breeds in Transcaspia and Eastern Turkestan, and in winter appears in North-western India in the North-west Frontier Province, Punjab, Sind, and Rajputana. Both races, therefore, are to be found on the same ground in North-western India, and the identification of some individuals is a matter of difficulty. Both races commence to arrive about September and leave about April, though *blythi* stays a little later than *minula*. The typical race does not occur in India. A darker allied species with a larger bill, Hume's Whitethroat (*Sylvia althœa*), which breeds in Kashmir and winters in Southern India, is easily confused with these two races.

The Orphean Warbler (*Sylvia hortensis*) is a winter visitor to the greater part of India except the extreme north-east. It breeds in Baluchistan and the North-west Frontier Province. Of the habits and general appearance of the Whitethroats it is larger with a marked cap, grey in females and black in males.

Habits, etc.—Both the races of Lesser Whitethroat that arrive in India are very similar in their habits in winter; they spend their time creeping about in small bushes and trees looking for insects and caterpillars, and are very silent except for an occasional *tack* note. While *blythi*, however, living in any type of country except deep forest, prefers trees, and more especially the various species of acacia, with whose pollen its head is often stained yellow, *minula* is usually found in the low-stunted bushes and scanty tree growth of semi-desert country.

The breeding habits of both races are very similar in their respective ranges, where they lay about May and June. The nests are neat but rather fragile cups of grass and roots, lined with horse-hair or fine grass stems; they are built in bushes within a few feet of the ground.

The clutch consists of four to six eggs; these are rather broad ovals, creamy-white in colour, rather boldly but sparingly marked with sepia-brown and grey.

They measure about 0·66 by 0·5 inches.

THE CHIFFCHAFF

Phylloscopus collybita (Vieillot)

(Plate xii, Fig. 3, opposite page 242)

Description.—Length 5 inches. Sexes alike. Upper plumage brown, faintly tinged with green; a distinct buff line over the eye, with a darker line through the eye; wings and tail dark brown, finely edged with olive-yellow; lower plumage buff, darker on the breast and flanks; wing-lining primrose-yellow.

Iris dark brown; bill dusky brown; legs brownish-black.

Field Identification.—A very small brown bird, with pale buff under parts and a buff line over the eye, which creeps about in trees and in herbage near water, often in small parties, uttering a plaintive note.

Distribution.—The Chiffchaff is very widely distributed throughout Europe, Africa, and Asia in a number of races. The typical form does not occur in our area, but two others are found as winter visitors. *P. c. sindianus* breeds in Kashmir territories and Central Asia and is a somewhat local winter visitor to the North-west Frontier Province, Punjab, Sind, United Provinces, and Rajputana. The Siberian Chiffchaff, *P. c. tristis*, which breeds in Northern Asia, is found from about September to the end of April in India, over the whole of the northern and central plains as far south as Bombay and Orissa, often in great numbers. In freshly moulted plumage it can be distinguished from *P. c. sindianus* by the tinge of green in the upper plumage, and from the typical English Chiffchaff by the absence of yellow in the lower plumage.

Habits, etc.—There are in the Indian Empire about thirty forms of the genus *Phylloscopus*, which includes the well-known English Chiffchaff and Willow-Wren. Their distribution is very variable, but as far as India is concerned, it may be stated that none breed anywhere in the country except in the Himalayas and on the higher ranges on the frontiers of Afghanistan and Baluchistan, and there is no part of India where several forms may not be met with either as passage migrants or as winter visitors. Their identification is a matter of great difficulty, based on minor points of size and wing formula and slight differences of plumage, which in practically every case ring the changes on greens, browns, and yellows; though in the field this is assisted by slight differences in habits and voice.

The Siberian Chiffchaff is a very common winter visitor to Northern India wherever trees in leaf or cultivation exist. It is met with both singly and in small parties, which search for insects up in the trees, in hedges, or in various crops, and it often flies out from the extremity of a bough to take an insect on the wing. It is particularly fond of cotton fields, lucerne, tamarisk, and acacias, and it has a characteristic habit, seldom shared by others of the genus, of hunting in reed-beds and other vegetation low over water. The call-note is a very plaintive *tweet.* Passage migrants in March on their way north freely sing a typical song, *chiff-chaff, chiff-chaff,* like that so well known in England.

P. c. sindianus breeds in Gilgit, Baltistan, Ladakh and Lahul from May to July.

The nest is a large structure of dry grass and bents, domed with the entrance at one side; it is profusely lined with feathers on a layer of fine vegetable-down. The situation chosen is on or close to the ground in herbage, low bushes or thorny hedges.

The usual clutch consists of four eggs. They are rather broad ovals, very fragile with a slight gloss; the colour is white, spotted with chestnut-red, chiefly towards the broad end.

The average size is 0·65 by 0·48 inches.

THE YELLOW-BROWED WARBLER

Phylloscopus inornatus (Blyth)

Description.—Length 4 inches. Sexes alike. Upper plumage dull olive-green, with obscure traces of a pale streak down the crown; a broad buffy-white line over the eye; sides of the face mottled with buffy-white; wings and tail dark brown edged with greenish, two buffy-white wing-bars, the upper rather obscure; entire lower plumage sullied white.

Iris dark brown; bill dark brown, base of lower mandible yellowish; legs greyish-brown.

Field Identification.—This is another of the minute green or brown birds which hunt for insects in the foliage of trees, and are only to be discriminated with much practice and knowledge both in the field and in the cabinet. The greenish colour, dirty white below, the double wing-bar and the call-note *tiss-yip* are guides to the identity of this particular species.

Distribution.—Breeds throughout a large portion of Siberia and Central Asia, migrating southwards in winter. It is divided into three races. The typical form breeds in Siberia, migrates through the greater part of Asia and winters in Bengal, Assam, Burma, and eastwards to Southern China. *P. i. humii,* differing in the brighter olive-green of the upper parts, breeds in the Western Himalayas between 7000 and 12,000 feet, and in Turkestan, Tian-Shan, and Afghanistan. Starting at the end of August it spreads in winter through India southwards to Travancore and eastwards to Bengal

PLATE IX

1. Bay-backed Shrike. 2. Paradise Flycatcher. 3. Common Wood-Shrike. 4. Blue-headed Rock-Thrush. 5. Brown Dipper. 6. Bluethroat. (All about ½ nat. size.)

[*Face p.* 176

and Orissa, but curiously enough avoids Sind. The return migration takes place about April. *P. i. mandelii*, which breeds in Kansu and Szechwan and is found in Bengal and Lower Assam in winter, has the head darker than in the other races.

Habits, etc.—In India the Yellow-browed Warbler is always solitary and spends its time in the boughs of trees searching for insects and uttering as it goes a note which is best described by the syllables *te-we-ut* or *tiss-yip*, rather sibilant and plaintive. In the breeding season the only song is a loud, double chirp uttered by the male, really only an elaboration of the above note.

It has a trick of nervously flirting its wings as it feeds and moves about the boughs. This species in winter seldom comes down low near the ground, nor is it found in bushes by water like the Siberian Chiffchaff.

The breeding season in the Western Himalayas is in May and June. The nest is built on the ground on some sloping bank or ravine-side, either in open ground or at the edge of forest. It is a rather large globular structure, with the entrance at one side. The materials consist of rather coarse grass, with an inner lining of fine grass roots or hair; feathers are not used.

Three to five eggs are laid, but the usual clutch is four. The egg is a broad oval slightly compressed towards one end, fine in texture with very little gloss. In colour it is pure white, speckled and spotted with reddish-brown or purple, the markings tending to form a cap or zone round the broad end.

The egg measures about 0·56 by 0·44 inches.

THE GREENISH WILLOW-WREN

Phylloscopus trochiloides Sundevall

Description.—Length 5 inches. Sexes alike. Upper plumage dull olive-green, the concealed portions of the wings and tail dark brown; a pale yellow bar across the greater wing-coverts; a broad pale yellow streak above the eye with a darker line below it; lower plumage dull white washed with primrose-yellow.

Iris dark brown; bill brown, lower mandible horny yellow; legs greyish-brown.

Field Identification.—Olive-green above, yellowish-white below, with one pale wing-bar, and a pale eye-streak; a quiet, undemonstrative species creeping about in the foliage of trees.

Distribution.—Breeds from Eastern Europe to Eastern Siberia southwards to Persia and the Himalayas being divided into several races of which the following concern us. *P. t. viridanus* (as described above) breeds from Pomerania and the Baltic Provinces to Western Siberia, Altair, North-western Mongolia and Dzungaria to Gilgit and Kashmir. It winters in India below lines from Meerut to Bombay and from the Sikkim Tera to Calcutta. On passage it is very common in parts of the Himalayas, Punjab and North-west Frontier Province. A greyer race, *P. t. ludlowi*, breeds in Baltistan and winters in the upper Eastern Ghats. This race intergrades through Gahrwal and Kumaon into the much darker *P. t. trochiloides* which breeds in the Eastern Himalayas and South-western China and winters in North-eastern India.

P. t. nitidus breeds in the Caucasus, Transcaspia and Persia, passes in considerable numbers through North-western India on passage and winters in South-western India and Ceylon. It is a much brighter green above, bright primrose-yellow below and has two pale yellow wing-bars.

Habits, etc.—This Willow-Wren spends its whole time in the winter in creeping about the foliage of trees collecting insects and their larvæ and eggs; it is more silent than most of the other common species, but has as call-note a penetrating *chi-wee*. During the spring and autumn passage it often swarms in North-western India, every tree containing one or more individuals.

In the Himalayas it breeds from May to July. The nest is a large, untidy ball of grass and moss, mixed sometimes with a few roots and dead leaves, the cavity being lined with wool and hair. The entrance is on one side. It is always placed on steep ground, either in the open or amongst scrub and herbage.

Four eggs are laid, pure white, very fragile and soft in texture with practically no gloss.

They measure about 0·6 by 0·45 inches.

THE LARGE CROWNED WILLOW-WREN

PHYLLOSCOPUS OCCIPITALIS (Blyth)

(Plate xii, Fig. 4, opposite page 242)

Description.—Length 5 inches. Sexes alike. Upper plumage olive-green, the crown of the head darker and with a broad irregular streak down the centre; a well-defined yellowish line above the eye and a dark line through it; concealed portions of the wings and tail dark brown; two yellowish wing-bars, the upper less distinct, and both tending to disappear in worn plumage; lower plumage white suffused with pale yellow.

Iris dark brown; bill brown, lower mandible yellow; legs greyish-brown.

Field Identification.—The common breeding Willow-Wren of the Western Himalayan stations; green above, white below, with a marked eye-streak and a pale streak on the top of the head; rather bold and noisy in demeanour.

Distribution.—A purely Asiatic Willow-Wren, which breeds very commonly in Turkestan, Afghanistan, and the Western Himalayas as far east as Nepal. In the Western Himalayas it breeds at elevations between 6500 and 9000 feet, being the common breeding Willow-Wren of all the hill stations. In winter it migrates through or winters in the whole of India (except Sind), extending to Travancore, Orissa and Bengal.

Habits, etc.—This Willow-Wren spends most of its time in trees when in the plains, but in the hills it feeds a good deal in bushes where it wanders with the mixed hunting parties of small insectivorous birds. Its call-note is a loud sharp *tit-wheet* or *chip-chip, chip-chip.* When breeding it has a loud song, the most monotonous repetition of a rather shrill whistling note seven times repeated, and at that season is much addicted to flirting its wings; then, too, the males become combative and quarrelsome.

In the Himalayas the breeding season is in May, June, and July. The nest is placed in holes, either amongst the roots of trees, in banks and walls, or even under the eaves of houses. It varies in shape according to the circumstances of the hole, being either a well-made domed structure or a mere pad, and is composed chiefly of moss; grass, hair and wool are sometimes added as a lining.

Four to six eggs are laid; they are rather elongated ovals, often sharply pointed at the smaller end, fine in texture and pure white with a slight gloss.

They measure about 0·65 by 0·50 inches.

THE GREY-HEADED FLYCATCHER-WARBLER

SEICERCUS XANTHOSCHISTOS (Gray)

(Plate iv, Fig. 1, opposite page 66)

Description.—Length 4 inches. Sexes alike. Top and sides of the head and neck and the upper back pale ashy-brown; a paler streak down the centre of the crown and another above the eye; remainder of upper plumage yellowish-green, the concealed portions of the wings and tail brown, the two outer pairs of tail-feathers white on the inner webs; the whole lower plumage bright yellow.

Iris dark brown; bill dark brown, lower mandible yellow; legs olive-brown; soles yellow.

Field Identification.—Abundant Himalayan form, of the Willow-

Wren type in appearance; upper parts grey and green, with pale stripes on the head, lower parts bright yellow; white outer tail-feathers conspicuous. Noisy and bold in trees and undergrowth.

Distribution.—A Himalayan species, extending from the hills of the North-west Frontier Province on the west into Assam and the Chin Hills in the east. It is divided into Eastern and Western races which meet about Nepal. The Eastern race is the typical one, while the Western race, *S. x. albosuperciliaris*, is considerably paler throughout, especially about the head. It breeds between 3500 and 7000 feet, and while some birds winter in this zone the majority move lower, and numbers of the Western race penetrate into the plains in portions of the Punjab and United Provinces.

Another common species in this genus is the Black-browed Flycatcher-Warbler (*Seicercus burkii*) in which the lateral bands on the head are blackish. A marked yellow ring round the eye. It is found throughout the Himalayas as far west as Dharmsala.

Habits, etc.—This pretty little Warbler is a very familiar species about the Himalayan hill stations. It is found in all types of wooded hills, coming freely also into cultivation and gardens. Except when nesting it is purely arboreal and it hunts incessantly for insects through the leaves and twigs of trees and bushes, both singly and in the mixed hunting parties. Its song is a loud and rather monotonous, though not unpleasing, trill of several notes, which is one of the most familiar sounds of the Lower Himalayas. The call-note is a rather plaintive *pritt-pritt* or *tyee-tyee.*

The breeding season lasts from March to June in the Western Himalayas and from April to August in the east.

The nest is a large, globular-domed structure, with a rather large entrance high on one side. It is composed chiefly of moss with which are mixed dry leaves and grasses and other miscellaneous rubbish. The cavity is thickly lined with hair and wool in the Western race, and more sparingly with vegetable downs and roots in the Eastern race. The nest is usually placed on a grassy bank at the foot of a bush and is well concealed and difficult to find unless the bird is watched to it.

Three to five eggs are laid, but the normal clutch consists of four eggs. The egg is a moderately broad oval, of fine texture, with a fair amount of gloss. The colour is pure white.

The egg measures about 0·60 by 0·5 inches.

THE BROWN HILL-WARBLER

SUYA CRINIGERA Hodgson

(Plate xii, Fig. 6, opposite page 242)

Description.—Length 7 inches, including tail of 4 inches. Sexes alike. Winter plumage: Upper surface fulvous-brown, streaked with black except on the rump; wings brown, edged with rufous; tail long and graduated, brown, obsoletely cross-rayed, the feathers with indistinct pale tips preceded by a darker spot; lower plumage fulvous, slightly flecked with blackish on the throat and breast, and whitish on the middle of the abdomen.

Summer plumage: Upper surface dark brown, the feathers edged with olivaceous; lower plumage uniform pale fulvous, the feathers of the breast showing their dark bases; wings and tail as in winter except that the tail is shorter.

Iris yellow-brown; bill, summer black, in winter brown, lower mandible fleshy; legs fleshy-pink.

Field Identification.—Northern hill form; a small brown bird, paler below and usually streaked above, with a very long graduated tail; usually skulks in grass and bushes, but sits in elevated and exposed positions to utter a loud, reeling song.

Distribution.—The Brown Hill-Warbler has a wide distribution in the hills that bound the whole of Continental India, through Assam and Burma, reaching on the east as far as China. It is divided into several races, of which two concern us. The typical race is found from the North-west Frontier Province, along the whole of the Himalayas, as far as North-western Assam, at elevations from 2500 to 7500 feet and sometimes higher. *S. c. striatula,* which is much colder and greyer in coloration, is found from plains level up to about 3000 feet in the Punjab Salt Range and the hills running from the western limit of the typical form along the North-western Frontier down to Baluchistan. It is a resident species.

Habits, etc.—This hill bird avoids forest and keeps either to grassland and the neighbourhood of cultivation, or else to scrub-jungle on bare stony hill-sides, often in the most barren and desolate hills. It is capable of bearing great extremes of temperature. It is rather a skulker and spends most of its time clambering about like a mouse in the interior of bushes and tangles of vegetation, threading its way deftly amongst the stems and often descending to the ground. The flight is rather weak and jerky, and the bird seldom flies far at a stretch. The long tail is an expressive feature, freely jerked in response to the bird's emotions. The bird is, however, best known to people through the medium of its song, a wheezy, scraping series of notes repeated to monotony like the sound of a saw; this song is very commonly heard on open hill-sides round the hill stations of the Himalayas, and the little bird utters it from the top of a bush or tall plant, or from a telegraph-wire often high above a nullah.

The breeding season lasts from May to July, but the majority of birds lay in May.

The nest is a flimsy, oval-domed structure, with the entrance towards the top at one side; it is composed of grass-blades felted with grass down, the bottom of the interior being lined with fine grass-stems. It is built within 4 or 5 feet of the ground, in small thorny bushes, in herbage or in the grass.

The normal clutch consists of four eggs. The egg is in shape a regular but somewhat elongated oval with a fair amount of gloss. The ground-colour varies from white to pale salmon-pink; the markings consist of fine speckles, spots and blotches of reddish-brown, sometimes scattered over the whole surface but more usually tending to collect in a marked zone or cap round the broad end.

In size the eggs average about 0·70 by 0·50 inches.

THE STREAKED WREN-WARBLER

PRINIA GRACILIS (Lichtenstein)

Description.—Length 5 inches, half of which is tail. Sexes alike. Upper plumage fulvous-brown streaked with dark brown; sides of face mottled brown and white; wings brown edged with fulvous; tail, long and graduated, brown, distinctly cross-rayed, the feathers tipped with white preceded by a dark spot; the whole lower plumage very pale fulvous.

Iris yellow; bill black in summer, in winter brown, the lower mandible horny-yellowish; legs fleshy-white, claws brown.

This and the following species of the genus *Prinia* have ten tail-feathers as opposed to twelve in *Franklinia.*

Field Identification.—A minute bird with a long graduated tail, streaked light and dark brown above and pale below; chiefly found in coarse sarpat grass in riverain tracts. A miniature of the Brown Hill-Warbler. Distinguished from the other Wren-Warblers by the streaks on the upper plumage.

Distribution.—This Wren-Warbler has a wide distribution through Northern Africa, Palestine, Southern Arabia, Persia, and Northern India generally. It is divided into several races, of which we are concerned with two. *P. g. lepida* is found in Afghanistan, North-west Frontier Province, Punjab, Sind, the United Provinces, and Rajputana.

A rather darker race, *P. g. stevensi*, is found in Assam and Eastern Bengal and in the Ganges delta. A strictly resident species.

Habits, etc.—This, the smallest of the Wren-Warblers of the genus *Prinia*, is essentially a bird of riverain areas, frequenting the low sandy-ground, studded with clumps of sarpat grass and thickets of tamarisk, which is found in the wide and partly dry beds of the great rivers of Northern India. Where similar conditions are reproduced along the sides of canals and in the neighbourhood of jheels there also will the bird be found. In such localities it creeps about the stems of the grass and tamarisk, at a height of two or three feet from the ground, venturing into the open occasionally to fly from clump to clump, no light task to so clumsily-balanced and weak a flier. It constantly makes a curious snapping noise with its bill.

When nesting the cock bird chooses a high stem of grass in the vicinity of the nest, and from it untiringly pours out a feeble monotonous song, which betrays the site to those who know his habits.

The breeding season lasts from March to August, and it is probable that two broods are reared. The nest is a tiny oval-domed structure with the entrance hole high on one side; it is built of fine grasses and shreds of grass-blades, the inside being softly lined with the pappus of grass seeds. It is placed about 2 feet from the ground in the centre of the thick clumps of sarpat grass, which by then have usually been cut off about 3 feet from the ground for village purposes.

The clutch consists of three or four eggs.

The egg is a broad oval, rather pointed towards the smaller end, and fine in texture with a decided gloss. The ground-colour is greyish-, greenish- or pinkish-white, and the markings consist of a fine and thickly distributed freckling of brownish-red and purplish-grey, with a tendency to form a cap or zone at the broad end.

In size it averages about 0·53 by 0·44 inches.

THE ASHY WREN-WARBLER

Prinia socialis Sykes

(Plate vi, Fig. 3, opposite page 110)

Description.—Length 5 inches, of which half is tail. Sexes alike. Summer plumage: Whole upper plumage dark ashy, sometimes with a white line over the eye; lower plumage including sides of face pale buff; wings rufous; tail long and graduated, rufous, the feathers tipped with white preceded by dark spots.

Winter plumage: Top of head ashy with a rufous tinge; a short white line over the eye; remainder of upper plumage including wings and tail rufous-brown, the tail having the same markings as in the summer plumage, but being one inch longer; lower plumage buff, except the chin, throat and central abdomen which are white.

Iris yellow-brown; bill black; legs fleshy.

Field Identification.—A very small bird with a long tail; upper parts dark ashy, lower parts warm buff. Found singly or in pairs in rank herbage, particularly in gardens, attracting attention by its sharp call-note.

Distribution.—The Ashy Wren-Warbler is one of the commonest birds of India and is widely distributed throughout the whole continent from the Outer Himalayas to Ceylon, though it is not found in Kashmir, the North-west Frontier Province, Baluchistan, or Sind. On the east it reaches Eastern Assam. There are four races: *P. s. brevicauda* of Ceylon and the typical race, found throughout the Peninsula south of a line between Mhow and Lohardugga, have their winter plumage similar to the summer plumage. The former is, however, smaller with a shorter tail. *P. s. stewarti* of Northern India assumes the very distinct winter plumage described above. In the Duars and Upper Assam it is replaced by *P. s. inglisi*, a darker bird with a fine short beak. All races are strictly sedentary.

Habits, etc.—This little bird is found both in the hills and the plains. But while in the north it is only found up to about 4000 feet in the hills, in the warmer south it occurs up to about 7000 feet, literally swarming in suitable places in the Nilgiris. It is a bird of open country, avoiding forest, and preferring cultivation, whether in the shape of gardens or arable land. It is perfectly at home in the close vicinity of houses and villages, and may equally be found in open, rolling grassland. In all these localities it requires cover in the shape of bushes, tangles of weeds and other herbage or crops and it is very fond of fields of sugar-cane. As in the case of the Indian Wren-Warbler, therefore, this species is compelled to move its ground slightly according to the state of the crops in which it lives. Its habits are the same as those of that species, but it is perhaps more excitable and noisy during the breeding season, its very anxiety often betraying the nest which it is anxious to preserve from marauders. The call-note is very loud and sharp, and the song is less of a jingle than that of the Indian Wren-Warbler.

This bird appears often to be double-brooded and nests may be found from March till September; but the majority are undoubtedly built with the commencement of the rains in June or July and the growth of the bush vegetation in which the little bird delights to have his being.

The nest is very variable and falls into three types. The first type closely recalls the nest of the Tailor-bird, sewing entering largely into its composition. Either the nest is placed within the orifice formed by sewing together the edges of two or three leaves, or else it is attached to a single large leaf whose edges are drawn about it, and partly enclose it; large soft leaves, such as those of the sunflower, fig and bindweed, are preferred for the purpose. The actual nest in this type is a deep cup of fine dry grass stems and roots, mixed and lined with a few horse-hairs, all visible portions of the outside and the corners of the cavity between the stitches being plastered and stuffed with a rough felting of vegetable cotton and fibre and similar materials. The sewing is either a genuine in-and-out stitch used to draw the edges of leaves together, or else the mere pushing of rough knots of cotton through punctured holes in the leaf.

The second type of nest is an oval-domed structure of varied shape and size, with the entrance on one side. It is composed of fine shreds and stems of grass, fibres and threads, the result being a drab-coloured ball; it is built in thick bushes and occasionally is steadied by the sewing of a leaf or two to the outside.

The third type of nest is a rough shapeless ball of roots or grass thrown together between the stems of a plant and hardly attached to them.

The clutch consists of three or four eggs, and occasionally as many as six. The eggs are very handsome. They are a rather perfect oval with a tendency to vary to a globular shape; there is a high gloss. In colour they are a rich brick-red, sometimes paler and yellower, sometimes deeper and of a mahogany tint. There is occasionally a clouded zone of deeper coloration about the broad end.

They average about 0·64 by 0·47 inches in size.

In the Deccan this bird is a common foster-parent for the Indian Plaintive Cuckoo (*Cacomantis merulinus*).

THE JUNGLE WREN-WARBLER

Prinia sylvatica Jerdon

Description.—Length 6 inches, female rather smaller. Sexes alike. Summer plumage: The whole upper parts greyish-brown, a pale buff line over the eye; wings dark brown, the edges of the feathers washed with fulvous; central tail-feathers greyish-brown, the others growing progressively paler and whiter until the outer pair is almost entirely white; lower plumage pale whitish-buff.

Winter plumage: Upper plumage warm ruddy fulvous, a pale buff line over the eye; wings dark brown, the edges of the feathers washed with ruddy fulvous; tail dark brown, all but the central pair of feathers with pale fulvous tips, preceded by dusky subterminal spots; lower plumage white washed with ochraceous on the breast and flanks.

Iris and eye-rim orange; bill black in summer, in winter horny-brown, lower mandible fleshy; mouth black in summer, brownish-pink in winter; legs pale fleshy brown, claws darker.

Field Identification.—A small brown Warbler with a fairly long graduated tail, in summer showing white in the outer feathers; it chiefly comes to notice from its habit of sitting on the top of a bush and persistently uttering a triple note.

Distribution.—Throughout India from the Himalayas to Ceylon. It is divided into two races in India and a third in Ceylon.

The northern race, *P. s. gangetica*, is found across Northern India from Gurdaspur and Jodhpur to the Duars and Midnapur. In this race there are distinct summer and winter plumages as described above. The Ceylon race, *P. s. valida*, on the other hand, has the summer and winter plumage alike, a darker brown above and a more yellowish fulvous below without white on the lateral tail-feathers. This is correlated with a breeding season that lasts the year round in the island. The typical race (Hyderabad, Mysore, Madras Presidency) lies between the two both in coloration and in the degree of difference between the two plumages. All these races are strictly resident.

Habits, etc.—This Wren-Warbler is more particularly a bird of broken boulder covered hills dotted with sparse and stunted vegetation of the cactus and thorn-bush type. It is also found in bush and scrub-jungle, in light forest interspersed with grass or in grass on the edge of heavier forest. In such terrain it comes to notice from its habit of perching on a large boulder, on a dead bough, or on the top of an isolated bush or tree and there uttering a soft melodious but ventriloquistic call for some minutes at a stretch, repeating it again after a pause of two or three seconds. This call is a warbling *pretty* or *tissip*, reminiscent of a Tailor-bird's call but louder and easily distinguished from it. Each *pretty* is preceded by a curious subdued ventriloquistic *pit*, uttered in a different key so that the song is really formed by a succession of triple notes. As soon as the bird has finished its song it descends hurriedly into the cover below with a quick jerky flight. It also has a peculiar habit of rising into the air for a short distance and making a noise (with the wings or beak I am not certain which) like a diminutive cracker, returning afterwards often to the same perch, sometimes to a fresh one. This habit is shared by *Prinia inornata* and *socialis*. The alarm-note at the nest is a loud *pit pit pit pit pit*. This species is wary and difficult to approach and the nest is readily deserted.

The breeding season in India is from July to the end of August. The nest is comparatively large and is placed in the centre of a thorn bush, usually on rocky ground, or in the middle of a tussock of coarse grass. It is a dome-shaped ball of grass with the entrance on one side and is often fairly conspicuous, as the outside is smeared over with white vegetable-downs and fibres or with cobwebs.

The clutch consists of four or five eggs. They are somewhat elongated ovals, of hard and fine texture with a fair amount of gloss. The ground-colour is a greenish or greyish stone-colour finely and often rather sparsely freckled with faint reddish-brown. In some eggs these markings are almost invisible. They are, however, usually gathered into a conspicuous zone round the broad end.

The egg measures about 0·75 by 0·50 inches.

THE INDIAN WREN-WARBLER

PRINIA INORNATA Sykes

(Plate xii, Fig. 5, opposite page 242)

Description.—Length 5 inches, including tail 2 inches. Sexes alike. Summer plumage: Upper plumage dull earthy-brown, the wings and tail edged with pale fulvous; the tail long, graduated and cross-rayed; dark subterminal spots on the feathers are hardly visible except from below. A ring round the eye, and a line above it dull whitish; the whole lower plumage pale buff.

In winter plumage the whole of the upper parts, wings and tail are more rufous in tint, and the tail is an inch longer.

Iris yellow-brown; bill black in summer, in winter brown with the base of the lower mandible fleshy; legs flesh colour.

Field Identification.—A plains bird, common in cultivation; very small, with a long tail; dark brown above, buff below, appearing rather dingy in the field; black beak noticeable in summer; makes a curious snapping noise in flight. To be distinguished from the Ashy Wren-Warbler by its dingier plumage and by having the crown brown instead of bluish-ashy.

Distribution.—The Indian Wren-Warbler is found throughout the Indian Empire south of the Himalayas, in the outer fringe of which it occurs up to about 4000 feet, and it also extends farther to the east. It is divided into several races: *P. i. franklinii*, in the Nilgiris, Palnis and probably also the Travancore range, and *P. i. insularis*, Ceylon, are very dark in colour, the latter having a very large beak, and showing no difference between the summer and winter plumages. In the typical race, found in Central and Western India, the summer and winter plumages differ as described above. This race grades on the one hand into the paler and more brightly coloured *P. i. terricolor* of the North-west Frontier Province, Punjab, Sind, and the United Provinces, which has also a much longer tail in winter. *P. i. fusca* of the Nepal and Sikkim Terai, the Duars and Upper Assam, is more saturated in colour with a more pronounced fulvous wash on the lower parts.

The Pale Bush-Warbler (*Homochlamys pallidus* Brooks).—Is here mentioned on account of its very remarkable song which attracts attention in spring, and although common the bird itself is difficult to see as it is a great skulker in low dense bush jungle. The song, which is loud and clear for such a small bird, consists of two phrases, the first of five notes and the second of three only, the two phrases separated by an interval of about five seconds. The second part is, moreover, in a different and higher key than the first. Each phrase begins with a long-drawn note and the whole song may be syllabised as follows: "You . . . mixed-it-so-quick," then an interval of five seconds, followed by: "He'll . . . beat you."

This little bird is similar to many of the other small Warblers, is of an olive-brown with pale yellow supercilium and the lower plumage dull greyish. It is found in the breeding season from Kashmir and Hazara to Garhwal and Kumaon at from 7000 to 9000 feet, but its winter quarters are unknown, though some pass through Dehra Dun on passage in spring and autumn. A nearly allied species, but rather smaller and with the upper plumage tinged rufous, is the Strong-footed Bush-Warbler, *Homochlamys fortipes*, found from Nepal to the Burmese Hills. It has the same striking song as the Pale Bush-Warbler but with a very slight difference.

Habits, etc.—This quaint little bird is one of the commonest of Indian resident birds, though from its small size and skulking habits it does not attract much attention. It is particularly a bird of standing crops, sugar-cane, wheat, millet, and the like, and it is also partial to long grass; in bushes and other low cover it is sometimes found but not so commonly. Bare ground and forest are abhorrent to it. Like others of the Wren-Warblers, it is a poor flier, its top-heavy labouring flight being almost laughable. As is indicated by the large strong legs, its chief mode of progression is on foot, and it spends its life climbing about the stems of the cover in which it lives, threading its way about with dexterity; when disturbed in the crops it rapidly progresses from stem to stem, then takes to flight over the top of the seed-heads, flies heavily for a yard or two, and finally plunges back into the midst of the cover, where it again commences to climb and hop rapidly along. As it flies it makes a snapping noise almost like the crackle of an electric spark.

While in no sense a migrant, its dependence on crops for cover necessitates a certain amount of local movement according to season. Its skulking habits render it indifferent to the presence of man, and it occurs commonly in the vicinity of houses and villages and in gardens. The food consists of insects.

The song of this bird is a familiar sound in the cultivation, where it lives. It makes up in vigour for what it lacks in beauty, consisting merely of a series of loud jingling wheezy trills, that rather suggest the shaking of a bunch of keys.

The breeding season lasts from March to September.

The nest is a very elegant and distinctive structure, globular or a long purse-shape, domed, with the entrance high on one side; it is semi-transparent, being made of a regular lace-work of fine strips torn from the blades of green grass, woven in and out, and anchored here and there with similar grass-work to the surrounding stems and leaves. There is no lining. It is placed from 3 to 6 feet from the ground in standing crops or clumps of sarpat grass or thorny bushes.

The eggs, too, are very distinctive and beautiful. They are a moderately long oval, with a strong shell, fine in texture and highly glossy. The ground-colour is pale greenish-blue (or rarely pinkish-white) marked boldly with blotches, clouds and fine hair-lines of deep chocolate and reddish-brown.

The egg measures about 0·61 by 0·45 inches.

This bird is a favourite foster-parent for the Indian Plaintive Cuckoo (*Cacomantis merulinus*).

THE FAIRY BLUE-BIRD

IRENA PUELLA (Latham)

(Frontispiece, Fig. 2)

Description.—Length 10 inches. Male: Deep velvet-black except for the top of the head and neck, the whole upper plumage, the lesser wing-coverts and a faint bar on the wing and a patch under the tail shining ultramarine blue with lilac reflections.

Female: Dull peacock-blue, the feathers with dark shafts; wings and tail blackish-brown washed with peacock-blue.

Iris crimson; eye-rims pinkish; bill and legs black.

Field Identification.—Eastern Himalayas and the hills of Assam and South India. Male quite unmistakable, deep black with shining blue upper parts. Female dull peacock-blue throughout. Found in parties in high trees. Has a very characteristic call.

Distribution.—The species is found in Ceylon, India, Burma, the Andamans and Nicobars, the Malay Peninsula and Siam, Annam and Cochin-China. In India we are concerned with two races. The typical race is found in Ceylon and in the Western Ghats from Travancore to Belgaum and in the Chitteri Hills of the Eastern Ghats.

In these hills it is found from their bases up to about 5000 feet. A slightly larger form, *I. p. sikkimensis*, is found at the edge of the plains in the lower ranges of the Himalayas from Sikkim to the Miri Hills and in the Khasia Hills, Cachar and Manipur in Assam.

Habits, etc.—The Fairy Blue-Bird is a forest-haunting species and it is more particularly a bird of the evergreen forest. Except in the breeding season it collects into small parties of five or six individuals and more rarely into flocks of anything up to thirty or forty birds. These frequent the tops of high trees though they occasionally come down into the undergrowth and in the middle of the day habitually descend to the banks of streams and small rivers in order to drink and bathe. They are very bright and lively birds always on the move, hopping from branch to branch and flying from tree to tree, uttering a very distinctive call as they go. This is variously described as a pretty bubbling whistle, a pleasant musical *weet-weet* or a rich mellow percussive *whats-it* repeated every few seconds.

This lovely bird is by no means as conspicuous as one would imagine from looking at a stuffed specimen. Indeed in shady forest the male generally looks as black as a Drongo or from its movements might be mistaken for a Thrush and its satin-blue back is only conspicuous for a few moments as the bird flutters across some sunlit piece of open jungle. Females and the similarly coloured young males compose many of the parties and these are tame enough, allowing a close approach as they feed quietly on berries regardless of the observer. Adult males are rather shyer.

The food is said to consist almost exclusively of wild fruits and berries. When the various fig-trees are in fruit numbers of Blue-Birds congregate to feed there in company with Hornbills and Pigeons and other fruit-eating birds. The nectar is also sipped from *Erythrina* trees and the pollen from the flowers will often be seen on the faces of the birds.

The breeding season ranges from January to May, but most eggs will be found in March and April.

The nest is usually built in a sapling between 10 and 20 feet from the ground and the sapling chosen is in the depth of damp forest where tall trees exclude the sun. The nest is a shallow saucer of roots, twigs and bents, usually intermixed with green moss and with an outer cover of the same.

The normal clutch consists of two eggs. The shape is a blunt oval and the texture is close-grained and fine with a moderate gloss. The ground-colour is greenish-white, streaked, spotted and blotched with reddish-brown and inky-grey and underlying paler shades of the same. The blotches are usually heavy and often are almost entirely confluent over the larger end.

The egg measures about 1·10 by 0·75 inches.

THE GOLDEN ORIOLE

Oriolus oriolus (Linnæus)

(Plate x, Fig. 3, opposite page 198)

Description.—Length 9 inches. Male: Rich golden-yellow except a broad line through the eye, practically the whole of the wings and the central portions of the tail, which are black.

Female: Upper parts yellowish-green; wings brown, the feathers tipped and edged with greenish; tail brownish-black tipped with yellow; under parts whitish, washed with yellow and streaked with dark brown.

Iris dark crimson; bill dark pink; legs dark slate.

The tail is slightly rounded.

Field Identification.—Shy and purely arboreal species, concealing itself in thick foliaged trees, its presence revealed by the liquid whistle *wiel-a-wo.* Male, a glorious golden-yellow, with black wings and tail; female greenish with dark wings and tail.

Distribution.—The Golden Oriole is widely spread over Europe, Africa and Asia. The typical race just skirts Sind and Baluchistan on passage, but within our area we are really concerned with only one form, *O. o. kundoo*, which differs chiefly from the typical race in the fact that in the adult male the black of the lores, *i.e.*, the eye-stripe, extends behind the eye. This form breeds in Turkestan and Gilgit, in Southern and Eastern Afghanistan, in the hill areas of Baluchistan, throughout Kashmir and the Western and Central Himalayas, and in the plains from Rajputana to Western Bengal and south to Mysore. It winters also as far south as Cape Comorin.

In the mountain areas and in the northern part of the plains of India the Golden Oriole is merely a summer visitor, moving farther south in August and September and returning to its breeding grounds in April and May.

In the Himalayas it is found up to 10,000 feet, though in the outer ranges it is scarce at over 6000 feet.

Habits, etc.—With the ripening of the mangoes in spring the Golden Oriole arrives in Northern India. To that circumstance, combined with the resemblance of the greens and yellows of the two sexes to the fruit and leaves of their favourite tree, is due the popular Anglo-Indian name of Mango-bird. Orioles are strictly arboreal, descending, as a rule, neither to undergrowth nor to the ground, and by nature they are very shy and secretive, keeping to the thickest portions of the boughs and being better known as disembodied voices than as birds; for the loud mellow whistle *pee-ou-a* or *wiel-a-wo* is one of the pleasantest and most familiar of Indian bird sounds, being heard alike in garden and forest, greeting the dawn and saluting the parting day. There is, in addition, a faint but very sweet and plaintive song, though from its very faintness it is little known. The flight is strong and dipping, though seldom long sustained, as the bird prefers to travel from tree to tree.

The food consists of insects, caterpillars, berries and fruit.

The breeding season ranges from May to August, but the great majority of eggs are laid in June and July.

The nest is built in some large tree, usually at a height of over 20 feet from the ground. It is a moderately deep cup, suspended invariably within a slender fork towards the extremity of one of the boughs, and often in a situation where no climber can reach. From below it looks like a round ball of grass wedged into the fork, and the sitting bird within is completely hidden; but in the hand it proves to be a most beautifully woven cup, hung from the fork of two twigs and secured to them, much as a prawn net is to its wooden framework. The cup is deep and rounded to prevent the eggs rolling out in a high wind. It is composed of fine grass and slender strips of tenacious bark fibres, and the ends of these are wound round and round the supporting twigs. Some nests contain no extraneous matter, but others have all sorts of odds and ends woven into the fabric, scraps of newspaper, rags, shavings, snake-sloughs, thread, and the like. There is always a neat lining of fine grass stems. There is some variation in the thickness and size of the nests.

The clutch consists of two to four eggs. These vary a good deal in shape and size, some being pyriform, and others long and cylindrical; the texture is fine and with a high gloss. In colour they are a pure china-white; the markings consist of well-defined black spots and specks more or less thinly sprinkled over the surface of the egg, chiefly at the large end. In some cases the spots are pale yellowish-brown or deep reddish-brown, often surrounded with a nimbus of the same colour.

The eggs measure about 1·10 by 0·80 inches.

THE BLACK-HEADED ORIOLE

ORIOLUS XANTHORNUS (Linnæus)

Description.—Length 9 inches. Sexes alike. Bright golden-yellow except the following parts which are black, the head, chin and throat, the greater portion of the wings, the shafts of the tail-feathers and a patch on the tail formed by the ends of the two (or three) central pairs of tail-feathers.

In immature plumage both sexes have the black of the chin and throat replaced by black and white striping.

Iris crimson ; bill deep pink ; legs plumbeous.

Field Identification.—Arboreal ; abundant in well-wooded plains. A bright golden bird with black head, wings and tail, which is very active and noisy in the trees.

Distribution.—The Black-headed Oriole extends through the greater part of India, Ceylon, and Burma eastwards to Cambodia and Siam. We are concerned with three races which differ in size and the amount of yellow edging to the wings and to the feathers of the forehead and crown of immature birds. The typical race inhabits the sub-Himalayan ranges from Kangra to Upper Assam, as well as the Gangetic plain. *O. x. maderaspatanus* inhabits India south of the Gangetic plain with a western limit of Mount Aboo and Kathiawar. *O. x. ceylonensis* is confined to Ceylon. Resident everywhere.

Along the Himalayas from Kulu eastwards is found another handsome species, the Maroon Oriole (*Oriolus traillii*), the colours of which are sufficiently suggested by its name.

Habits, etc.—This Oriole is a common bird in fairly well-timbered but open country, being specially partial to groves, avenues and gardens. It is an arboreal species, though occasionally it descends to the ground to capture insects, on which it feeds freely, though its chief food must be considered the fruits of the various species of wild figs. It is found solitary or in pairs, though the family parties keep together for a short time after the young are fledged.

These Orioles are very active creatures, full of the joy of life, and they delight to indulge in aerial games, following each other from tree to tree, darting through the foliage with their bright plumage flashing in the sun. They have a range of melodious notes, freely uttered on such occasions, and the pairs call to each other incessantly *yū-hū-a-yu*, answered by *tū-hu-ēē* or *te-hēē*. In addition to their varied range of melodious calls they sometimes utter harsh cawing notes, and the newly-fledged young have a churring cry rather like that of a young Starling.

The breeding season lasts from April to the end of August. The nest is a deep cup, carefully suspended between two twigs, and is composed chiefly of tow-like vegetable fibres, thin slips of bark and similar materials ; externally it is decorated with scraps of lichen and bark, and there is a lining of fine grass or fine twigs of tamarisk. It is suspended near the end of a bough at heights of 20 to 35 feet above the ground.

The normal clutch consists of three eggs, but two to four are found. The egg is a somewhat elongated oval, fine in texture and moderately glossy. The ground-colour varies from creamy- or pinkish-white to pale salmon-colour. The markings consist of spots and streaks of dark brown and inky-purple, sparingly distributed, and generally towards the broad end; some of the spots are surrounded by a reddish-pink cloud.

The average size of the egg is about 1·14 by 0·82 inches.

THE INDIAN GRACKLE

GRACULA RELIGIOSA Linnæus

Description.—Length 10 inches. Sexes alike. The whole plumage black glossed with green and purple, a patch of white in the base of the wing-quills.

Iris brown; bill orange-red with a yellow tip; wattles and facial skin bright yellow; legs orange-yellow, claws blackish-brown.

The sides of the face and the nape are ornamented with bare fleshy wattles which differ in shape in the various races.

Field Identification.—A large black Mynah with yellow bill and legs, yellow wattles behind the eyes and a white patch in the wing. Noisy and tree-haunting, usually seen in parties in large trees.

Distribution.—A resident species with some local movements. This Grackle is widely distributed in India, Ceylon, Burma, the Malay Peninsula, Sumatra, Java and Borneo. It is divided into several races of which we are concerned with the following. *G. r. intermedia* is found at low elevations, 1000 to 2000 feet, along the Himalayas from Kumaon eastwards, as well as in Eastern Bengal and Assam. In this form the wattle ends on the nape in a broad pendant lobe; the patch of feathers in the middle of the wattle below the eye is small and narrow and does not reach to the lower edge of the wattle. *G. r. indica* is found along the Western Ghats from North Kanara to the extreme south at all heights up to 5000 feet and also in Ceylon in the low country. This is a smaller bird with a weaker bill. The wattle ends in a small inconspicuous lobe and then turns upwards on to the nape in a tongue about a quarter of an inch long; the patch of feathers in the middle of the wattle is rather larger than in *intermedia* and reaches the bottom edge of the wattle. *G. r. peninsularis* is a connecting link found in Sambalpur and in the Northern Circars from Gumsoor to Bastar. From *indica* it is immediately distinguished by the absence of the tongue of wattle from the nape to the crown. It is smaller than *intermedia* with a finer and shorter bill. *G. r. andamanensis* which is common in the Andamans and Nicobars used to be exported to Calcutta in large numbers as cage birds.

G. r. ptilogenys, which has no wattle on the side of the face, only a long pendant lobe on either side of the neck, is an inhabitant of the hill zone in Ceylon. Owing to the destruction of forests it is now also in the low country alongside *G. t. indica*.

Habits, etc.—This Grackle is a tree-haunting species found in all types of forest, whether evergreen or deciduous, in the shade trees of coffee and other plantations and in trees near cultivation. Out of the breeding season it is found in small parties and flocks which keep very largely to the tops of the trees unless curiosity brings them to the lower boughs to investigate some local movement or phenomenon.

FIG. 27—Indian Grackle ($\frac{9}{10}$ nat. size)

They do also occasionally visit the ground and there they progress not by walking like other Mynahs and Starlings but by Sparrow-like hops. The flight is straight and powerful. The chief characteristic of these Grackles is, however, their voices; they are very noisy, using a great variety of notes, some melodious, some wheezing and some harsh and shrieking. They are first-rate mimics, too, and in captivity can be easily taught to talk, so that, with their tame and confident demeanour, they make favourite cage-birds and are to be found in all the good bird markets.

The food consists of insects, fruits and berries collected upon the trees, but termites are captured on the wing. This species is very partial to the nectar obtainable from the flowers of trees like *Bombax*, *Erythrina* and *Grevillia* and in such trees will be found in loose association with Hornbills, Barbets and Green Pigeons.

The breeding season is mainly from February to May but a few nests may be found later until October. The nest is a miscellaneous collection, sometimes very small, of grass, feathers, dirt and touchwood in the bottom of a hole in a tree from 10 to 40 feet from the ground. The tree chosen is by preference a dead one, too rotten and unsafe for a man to climb, and it is usually in open ground either in a clearing in a forest or in cultivation. The nest hole is generally in the trunk and may be excavated by the Grackle itself.

The clutch consists of two or three eggs. In shape these are very regular ovals, the shell being very close and fine but with little gloss. The ground-colour is a delicate pale sea-green or greenish-blue, more or less profusely spotted and splashed with pale purple, purplish-brown and chocolate-brown.

The size of the egg is rather variable, but it averages about 1·30 by 0·90 inches.

THE ROSY PASTOR

Pastor roseus (Linnæus)

Description.—Length 9 inches. Sexes alike, except that the female is duller and with a shorter crest. The whole head, long bushy crest, throat, upper breast, wings, and tail glossy black, the feathers lightly tipped with buff; thighs, a patch on each flank and under the tail black tipped with white; remainder of the plumage rose-colour.

Iris brown; bill pink with the basal half of the lower mandible black; legs pink.

Field Identification.—A handsome crested bird, rose-pink with black head, wings and tail; found in flocks which behave like and in the distance look like flocks of Common Starlings; very abundant; the flocks feed on the ground and perch in trees.

Distribution.—The Rosy Pastor breeds through a wide area in South-eastern Europe, occasionally as far west as Italy and Hungary; and in Asia from Asia Minor to Turkestan. It winters in India, and wanders also irregularly through the greater part of Europe. In India it is found as a winter visitor through the whole of the plains to as far east as Manbhoom in Bihar, being especially abundant in the north-west. It arrives early in July and leaves about May, being absent as a species, therefore, for a very short time, though doubtless the latest birds to depart are far from being the earliest to return.

The Spotted-wing Stare (*Psaroglossa spiloptera*) found along the base of the Himalayas is common in Assam. The silvery upper parts with brown scale marking, dark chestnut throat, bright rufous under parts and white spot in the wing are distinctive.

Habits, etc.—The Rosy Pastor greatly resembles the Common Starling in its habits while in winter quarters in India. It collects in flocks which feed on fruit and berries, grubs, insects, grasshoppers, and locusts (being particularly useful in the destruction of the last) in every type of open country, though cultivation and grassy lands are chiefly preferred. These flocks associate with the flocks of Common Starlings and Mynahs, roosting and feeding in company with them, though as a rule the three species do not join into a common flock; and these flocks may be seen flighting between the roosting places and feeding grounds in the morning and evening very regularly. When light and distance do not allow of the distinguishing of colour it is impossible to recognise apart the flocks of Starlings and Pastors, the build, size and flight of the two species being identical. Pastors feed largely on the ground, and when a field of

FIG. 28—Rosy Pastor (⅓ nat. size)

grass is being irrigated a pink and black cloud of these birds will often be seen in pursuit of the flooded-out insect life, quarrelling and chattering and jumping into the air as they move along.

On their first arrival numbers of the birds are in the brown juvenile plumage, and at all seasons the flocks contain not fully adult birds, whose plumage is sullied and dull in tint.

From March onwards the birds are affected by the approach of the breeding season (as the state of their internal organs testifies), and the flocks spend much of their time in tall trees, enjoying the sun and singing a typical Starling song, a jumble of discordant grating noises mixed with some melodious warbling notes. At this season they become very fat in preparation for migrating and are eagerly pursued by native sportsmen, whose aim is to secure as many as possible with a single shot.

The breeding season in Europe and Asia is in May and June. The birds breed in huge colonies on rocky ground or in old ruins, wherever they can find a sufficiency of holes in which to place the untidy masses of grass, twigs and straw which form the nests; the egg cavity is lined with roots and feathers. Such breeding colonies move about in the most capricious manner, occupying a suitable locality one year and abandoning it the next, their movements being probably dependent on the food-supply.

The clutch consists usually of five or six eggs. These are very pale bluish-white, unmarked, similar to but paler and more glossy than those of the Common Starling. In shape they are rather pointed ovals, hard in texture with minute pores.

They measure about 1·10 by 0·80 inches.

THE STARLING

STURNUS VULGARIS Linnæus

(Plate viii, Fig. 3, opposite page 154)

Description.—Length 9 inches. Sexes alike, except that the female is generally duller and more spotted. Winter plumage: Black, the feathers lightly tipped with buff; wings and tail brown, edged with velvety black. The whole plumage is irridescent, with a high gloss of red, purple, green, and blue. The feathers of the head, neck and breast are developed into hackles. In summer the buff tips wear off, leaving the plumage more completely black.

Iris: male dark brown, female pale yellow; bill brown, base of lower mandible steely or yellowish-horn, in breeding plumage lemon-yellow; legs reddish-brown, claws darker.

Field Identification.—Gregarious, and collecting in large flocks in winter, which feed on the ground in cultivation and perch in trees. A glossy black bird, looking rather as if oiled, and more or less spotted finely with buff.

Distribution.—The Starling is a bird of very wide distribution in Europe, Asia and Africa, the typical race being one of the best known of English birds. It is divided into a number of closely allied forms, whose differences lie in the distribution of the colours of the brilliant gloss which gives the bird a curious highly-oiled appearance. The distinctions are small, but must be recognised as they are correlated with distinct breeding areas. The winter ranges of several forms, however, overlap, with the result, as the birds are highly gregarious, that several forms may then often be found in one flock, a fact which causes the uninitiated to believe that the

1. Green Bee-Eater. 2. Red-vented Bulbul. 3. Golden Oriole. 4. Coppersmith. 5. Jungle Babbler. (All about $\frac{1}{3}$ nat. size.)

[*Face p.* 198

differences exhibited by different specimens are purely due to individual variation.

The identification of Starlings is normally a matter for the expert, and many intermediate specimens occur which cannot be definitely attributed to any particular form; while no two authorities agree on the number of forms to be recognised. But for general purposes the majority of Starlings met with in India belong to four races. They may be distinguished as follows (the colours refer to the gloss; the wing is measured in millimetres closed from the bend of the shoulder to the tip of the feathers):

S. v. minor.—Small form, wing 110-118 mm.; head, throat and ear-coverts green; mantle and rump reddish-purple.

S. v. humii.—Medium form, wing 119-125 mm.; head deep purplish-blue; reddish-purple on the throat, chin and hind neck; ear-coverts deep metallic green; mantle coppery-red to bronze; rump bronze-green.

S. v. poltaratskyi.—Large form, wing 124-135 mm.; head, throat and ear-coverts purple; mantle and rump green.

S. v. porphyronotus.—Large form, wing 125-137 mm.; head and throat green, ear-coverts more or less purple; mantle and rump red-purple.

S. v. minor is a local and resident form in Sind. *S. v. humii* is the breeding bird of the Valley of Kashmir; in winter it appears in the bordering districts of the Punjab. *S. v. porphyronotus* breeds at Yarkand and neighbouring areas, and in winter visits Afghanistan, Kashmir, Punjab, Sind, and the United Provinces. *S. v. poltaratskyi* breeds in Siberia, and in winter extends through the plains of India from the north-west to Bengal and south to Baroda, being the commonest of the Indian Starlings.

In the plains of India these Starlings may be looked for from October to March, but occasional parties occur a little earlier and later.

Habits, etc.—Apart from the fact that the little Sind Starling may be recognised by its smaller size, and both it and *S. v. humii* can be recognised by inference on their breeding grounds, it is quite impossible to distinguish the various forms of Starling in India in winter until they have been shot. They are highly gregarious, and collect into common flocks which feed in cultivation on the open plains, sometimes also in company with Mynahs and Rosy Pastors. The chief characteristic of the flocks is hurry; they feed on the ground, digging their bills into the crevices of the soil and extracting the various harmful grubs and insects on which they feed; and all the time the flock advances with a bustle and hurry, not hopping but with a quick purposeful step, the birds in the rear frequently flying over to settle in front of the leaders. Fruit, berries and grain are also eaten.

When disturbed the flock flies up and settles on the tops of trees, where, if no danger threatens, the birds at once commence to warble in the sunlight and preen their feathers, soon flying down again to continue their progress on the ground. The flight is swift and strong, short, sharp beats of the wings alternating with periods of gliding, the flocks flying in close order as if drilled, the mass wheeling and turning with remarkable precision. Some of the flocks are very large and by their flight and density can be identified from a considerable distance.

The breeding season of *S. v. humii* in Kashmir is in April and May. The males then indulge in the peculiar wheezy, squeaky song, sitting on a roof or top of a tree in an exposed position, flirting the wings uneasily at intervals as they sing.

The Starling builds in holes of trees (particularly affecting pollarded willows), in river-banks and in buildings, constructing a loose nest of grass roots with a few feathers. The clutch consists of five or six eggs. These are somewhat elongated in shape, a good deal compressed towards the short end. The shells are strong and glossy, with the surface a good deal pitted. In colour they are a very uniform pale sea-green-blue.

The average measurement is 1·13 by 0·83 inches.

THE GREY-HEADED MYNAH

Sturnia malabarica (Gmelin)

Description.—Length 8 inches. Sexes alike. The whole upper plumage dark grey, the feathers of the head and neck long and pointed with whitish shafts giving a hoary appearance; wing blackish, all but the flight-feathers, which are merely so tipped, edged with silvery-grey; tail blackish tipped broadly with ferruginous, the central pair of feathers silvery-grey; entire lower plumage rufous, palest towards the chin and throat which are streaked with whitish-grey and deepest towards the tail.

Iris light blue; bill blue at base, green in the middle, and yellow at the tip; legs brownish-yellow.

Field Identification.—A rather silvery-looking bird with finely-hackled head and neck, rufous under parts, and dark wings and tail. In chattering flocks on the tops of trees.

Distribution.—A widely-distributed species in the plains of India, extending eastwards to Siam, the Malay Peninsula, and the islands of the Bay of Bengal. It is divided into several races, of which we are concerned with two. The typical form is found east of a line drawn approximately from Mount Aboo to Dehra Dun, ascending the Himalayas to a height of about 5000 feet. *S. m. blythii*, which has the whole head white, is found down the west coast of India from Belgaum to Travancore. This species appears to be locally migratory and at Ranchi and in South-west Bengal is a common winter visitor, but there is not much information regarding other parts of the country.

Habits, etc.—This little Mynah is more purely arboreal than most species of Mynah and Starling, and is shyer and more difficult to observe. It is usually found in parties and small flocks which frequent the tops of trees and indulge in a good deal of squabbling and chasing about from branch to branch especially when the attraction is the flowers of the coral-tree or the silk-cotton tree. From these they extract the nectar and they are also fond of the figs of the banyan and peepul trees, the berries of lantana scrub and a number of other fruits as well as insects. At times the flocks descend and feed on the ground. The usual note is a sort of chatter, but there is also quite a pleasant song.

The breeding season lasts from April to June.

The nest is built in a hole of a tree, either dead or living, at any height from 20 to 50 feet from the ground, and there is rather a preference for trees growing in open patches cleared in the midst of forest. Natural hollows and old Barbet's nest holes are used, but in some instances the birds enlarge holes for themselves by pecking away decayed wood round an existing small hole. The nest is a small pad of grass or green leaves.

The clutch consists of three to five eggs.

The egg is a moderately elongated oval, rather pointed towards the small end. The shell is fine and delicate with a distinct gloss. In colour it is a very delicate pale sea-green without markings.

The average size is about 0·95 by 0·70 inches.

THE BRAHMINY MYNAH

TEMENUCHUS PAGODARUM (Gmelin)

(Plate viii, Fig. 5, opposite page 154)

Description.—Length 8 inches. Sexes alike. Top of the head, including a long bushy crest, black; the sides of the head, the whole of the neck and the entire lower plumage rich buff, except the thighs and a patch under the tail which are white; the feathers of the neck, throat and breast are elongated into hackles. The remainder of the upper plumage grey except the outer flight-feathers which are black; tail rounded, brown, all but the central pair of feathers broadly tipped with white.

Iris greenish-white ; bill blue at the base, greenish in the middle, yellow at the tip ; legs bright yellow.

Field Identification.—Common plains species. A rather small, sprightly bird, grey above, warm buff below, with the top of the head black and crested ; the rounded tail is conspicuously edged with white in flight.

Distribution.—This is a familiar bird throughout India and Ceylon, extending on the west to the Valley of the Indus and on the east to the longitude of Calcutta. It is locally common everywhere except in the more arid and barren portions of the Punjab, Sind, and North-west Frontier Province, and in the more humid and overgrown localities of Lower Bengal. In the Outer Himalayas it extends ordinarily as a summer visitor up to 4500 feet, but in Gilgit and Chitral it is common even to higher elevations. In the main a resident species, but also locally migratory.

Habits, etc.—The Brahminy Mynah is partial to open, well-cultivated localities with plenty of trees, and is tame and familiar in its habits, neither avoiding nor seeking the neighbourhood of man, but rather being indifferent to his existence. It feeds for the most part on the ground, often in company with other species of Mynahs and Starlings, retiring when sated to the trees in which it normally lives. It is found singly, in pairs and in small parties. It is quite a good songster, with a pleasant warbling song and makes a charming pet ; it is also a good mimic, learning the songs of other birds with ease.

Under the name of " Pawi " or " Papaya " it is familiar to Indians and comes a good deal into their folk-lore.

The breeding season lasts from May to August, but in Upper India the majority of eggs are laid in June.

The nest is placed in holes in trees at heights of from 15 to 30 feet above the ground, and also in Southern India in holes in the roofs of buildings. The cavity is roughly lined with feathers and dry grass, or dead leaves and similar soft materials. Nest-boxes affixed to trees are much favoured by this species.

The clutch consists of three to five eggs.

The egg is a rather elongated oval, fine and hard in texture, and rather glossy ; in colour it varies from very pale bluish-white to pale blue or greenish-blue. There are no markings.

In size the eggs average about 0·97 by 0·75 inches.

THE COMMON MYNAH

Acridotheres tristis (Linnæus)

(Introduction, p. xxviii)

Description.—Length 8 inches. Sexes alike. Whole head, neck, and upper breast black; remainder of body plumage rich vinous-brown, darker above and paling into whitish on the lower abdomen. Outer flight-feathers dark brown, with a large white patch at their base; tail strongly rounded, blackish, all but the central pair of feathers broadly tipped with white.

Iris reddish-brown, flecked with white; bill and a fleshy wattle below and behind the eye bright yellow; legs yellow, claws horny.

Field Identification.—One of the most general and abundant birds of India; to be seen walking about in pairs on the ground everywhere in the plains. Rich vinous-brown in colour, with a conspicuous yellow face-wattle; in flight the rounded white-edged tail and a large white patch in the wings are conspicuous.

Distribution.—The whole of the Indian Empire except Northern Kashmir, Baluchistan and Tenasserim, south of Mergui. A darker form found in Ceylon is separated under the name of *A. t. melanosternus.* The Mynah occurs in the Himalayas up to 8000 feet and is a strictly resident species.

Of late years this species has been introduced into South Africa, Mauritius, New Zealand, and other countries, but not with happy results, as it has proved destructive to more interesting indigenous species.

Habits, etc.—The Mynah shares with the House-Crow the distinction of being the commonest and best-known bird in India, being found wherever man is found, in populous city or in lonely jungle village. But the House-Crow, with all his audacity, has an uneasy conscience and is ever in expectation of the moment when his sins will find him out. The Mynah, on the other hand, has no such feelings. He is always perky and self-confident, secure in his occupation of some particular beat and ready to wage war on all who dispute it with him; and the appearance of a snake, mongoose or bird of prey is sufficient to collect all the Mynahs of the neighbourhood, whose harsh scolding reveals the presence of the intruder and is always worth investigation; many a dangerous snake has lost its life through the information given to man by the Mynahs.

Normally these birds live in pairs and there is a very obvious affection between them. They feed together on the ground, striding along with rapid, determined paces, stopping occasionally to preen each other's feathers or to indulge in a few quaint remarks or gesticulations expressive of extreme self-satisfaction. The voice is a strange mixture of harsh gurglings and liquid notes, *keeky - keeky - keeky, churr - churr, kok - kok - kok*, and the last notes are invariably accompanied by a quaint, stiff bobbing of the head, generally close in front of the mate. If disturbed when feeding on the ground the birds rise with a querulous note of alarm.

Several often collect into small parties, and at the roost these parties collect into large flocks which sleep in groves of trees after the most noisy and quarrelsome proceedings as they take up their places for the night. At intervals during darkness short bursts of chattering are to be heard. Such favourite roosting places are shared with House-Crows and Green Parrakeets, often, too, with Bank Mynahs and Starlings.

The Mynah is very omnivorous in its tastes; I have known them carry away the carcasses of small birds that I had skinned; house scraps, fruit, grain, earthworms, insects of all kinds, grasshoppers, crickets, caterpillars, and grubs are all eagerly devoured. Flocks of grazing cattle and the various agricultural operations are invariably attended by a pair of these birds; and their services in the destruction of locusts and grasshoppers must be very valuable to the Zamindar.

The normal breeding season lasts from June to August, and the nests being usually in a very hot position the birds leave much of the incubation of the eggs to the temperature of the air. They themselves feel the heat a good deal and may constantly be seen walking about, with their beaks gaping.

The nest is built in roofs of houses, and in holes in walls, trees and wells; and the birds readily adopt nest-boxes or chatties which may be hung up for their use. Occasionally the old nest of a Kite or Crow or squirrel is adopted and relined, and instances are on record of their building nests in a creeper or on the bough of a tree.

The nest is a shapeless and often large mass of miscellaneous material, straw, feathers, fine twigs, bits of cotton, strips of rag, pieces of rope and string, snakes' sloughs, and the like.

Three to six eggs are laid, but the normal clutch consists of four or five. They are rather long, oval, pear-shaped eggs, hard and glossy in texture, varying in colour from pale blue to pure sky-blue or greenish-blue, without markings. The small black spots that are sometimes found on these eggs are the work of parasites.

They measure about 1·20 by 0·86 inches.

THE BANK MYNAH

ACRIDOTHERES GINGINIANUS (Latham)

Description.—Length 9 inches. Sexes alike. The top and sides of the head black; the whole body plumage slaty-grey except the centre of the abdomen which is pinkish-buff; wing black, a patch of pinkish-buff at the base of the outer flight-feathers; tail strongly rounded, black tipped with buff.

Iris deep maroon-red; bill gamboge; a naked wattle beneath and behind the eye brick-red; legs yellow.

Field Identification.—Plains of Northern and Central India; gregarious; strongly resembles the Common Mynah in demeanour and general effect, but the wattle is red instead of yellow, the body plumage slaty-grey instead of vinous-brown, and the wing-patch and tips of the tail-feathers pinkish-buff instead of white.

Distribution.—A purely Indian species, found throughout the whole of the northern half of India from the Himalayas southwards to a line between Bombay and Orissa, and from the North-west Frontier Province and Sind to Eastern Bengal. Normally a plains species it ascends the Outer Himalayas locally, venturing into the sheltered valleys. A resident species, but wandering locally in obedience to the food-supply.

Habits, etc.—The Bank Mynah is often found in company with the Common Mynah and is very similar to it in habits, but differs in one or two important particulars. Although sometimes found in crowded market-places, scavenging on the ground amongst cattle and people, or wandering about busy station platforms, it is more a bird of cultivation and the open country-side, and is in particular addicted to the neighbourhood of water, feeding about the banks of rivers, in old water-logged brick-kilns and borrow-pits. It is also much more social in its habits, not merely flying, feeding and roosting in flocks, but also breeding in very definite colonies with a breeding economy quite different to that of the common species.

The breeding season lasts from the middle of April to the middle of July, but most eggs will be found in May.

It builds almost exclusively in earthen banks and cliffs, in holes which it excavates for itself, always in the vicinity of water and generally over running water. A few small colonies also breed below the surface of the ground in the sides of wells, in holes in the brickwork or in tunnels driven into the sandy soil. The nest chamber is situated at the end of a tunnel some three inches in diameter and anything up to seven feet in length, and these tunnels usually twist about in all directions and also communicate with each other, so that a large colony may be a regular warren. In the nest chamber a loose nest of feathers, roots and grass is constructed, and it also often contains pieces of snake's slough.

The normal clutch consists of four eggs, but five are often laid.

The eggs are short and broad ovals, hard in texture with a high gloss. They are unmarked, of various shades of very pale sky-blue or greenish-blue, generally slightly darker in tint than the eggs of the Common Mynah.

In size they average about 1·05 by 0·82 inches.

THE JUNGLE MYNAH

ÆTHIOPSAR FUSCUS (Wagler)

Description.—Length 9 inches. Sexes alike. Top and sides of the head black; remainder of upper plumage ruddy cinerous-brown; wings black with a large white patch at the base of the outer flight-feathers; tail broadly rounded, the feathers tipped with white; lower plumage dark ashy-brown, whitish under the tail.

Iris bright yellow or blue; bill basal half bluish-black, remainder orange-yellow; legs orange-yellow.

There is a curious erect tuft of feathers above the nostrils.

Field Identification.—A shy forest Mynah, chiefly found in hill ranges; to be recognised from the Common and Bank Mynahs by the darker plumage, the absence of a bare face wattle and by the tuft of erect feathers above the nostrils.

Distribution.—The Jungle Mynah is widely spread in the Himalayas, in portions of India and through Assam and Burma to Siam and the Malay Peninsula. It is divided into races, of which we are only concerned with two.

The typical race, slate-coloured above with a yellow iris, breeds throughout the Himalayas, from Hazara eastwards, from the foot-hills up to about 7000 feet. It is also found in Lower Bengal and the Chota Nagpur area to Bundelkund and Raipur.

A browner race, *Æ. f. mahrattensis*, in which the iris is grey, bluish-white or pale blue, occurs in the Shevaroys and down the Western Coast, chiefly on the Ghats, from Ahmedabad to Cape Comorin. Though abundant in many localities it is rather a local species. A resident bird in the main, but also a local migrant.

Habits, etc.—As its name denotes, this Mynah is properly a bird of the forest, though it often associates with the Common Mynah, and frequents the neighbourhood of houses. Except when actually paired for breeding it is found in parties and flocks that feed mostly on the ground, taking to the trees when disturbed. In flight, habits, gait, and behaviour it greatly resembles the Common Mynah, except that it is neither so bold nor such a scavenger, and it is probably mistaken by most people for that species.

The breeding season lasts from March to July, but most eggs will be found in April.

The vast majority of the nests of this species are built in holes in trees, generally in large trees at a considerable height from the ground ; but nests may be found in holes in other situations, in walls and ruins, in chimneys, and in the thatch of old houses. The nest is

FIG. 29—Head of Jungle Mynah (1½ nat. size)

merely a lining to the hole selected, and varies in size and materials, being a collection of fine twigs, dry grass, feathers, moss, wool, and the like.

There is a distinct tendency for the birds to nest in colonies.

The clutch varies from three to four eggs, but the majority of nests contain five eggs.

The egg is in shape rather a long oval, usually somewhat pointed towards the small end ; the texture is hard and glossy. It varies in colour from that of skim milk to pale blue or greenish-blue, and there are no markings.

The average measurement is about 1·20 by 0·83 inches.

THE PIED MYNAH

STURNOPASTOR CONTRA (Linnæus)

Description.—Length 9 inches. Sexes alike. The entire head and neck black, except for an elongated white patch from the base of the beak through the eye backwards ; upper plumage, wings and tail black or blackish-brown, except for the lower rump and a broad line along the shoulders white ; remainder of lower plumage pale vinaceous-grey.

Iris yellowish-white, eyelids and a bare patch in front of the eye orange; bill basal half deep orange, remainder white; legs yellowish-white, claws horny.

Field Identification.—Common plains species in cultivation. A conspicuously pied black and white bird found in parties feeding on the ground and flying up into a tree when disturbed; an obvious Mynah in habits and bearing.

Distribution.—The Pied Mynah is common and widely distributed in India and the Burmese countries to Java, being divided into several races, of which two are found within our area. The typical race is found in Eastern Bengal and Assam. A paler bird, *S. c. dehræ*, is found in continental India east of a line through Ludhiana, Hissar and Sehore, extending down to Hyderabad in the Deccan and eastwards to Western Bengal, Bihar and Orissa. It is a resident species, though there are signs of small local migrations.

FIG. 30—Pied Mynah (⅓ nat. size)

Habits, etc.—The Pied Mynah differs from the Common Mynah in the fact that it is a bird of open cultivation, never entering in or perching on houses, though it may frequently be found in gardens. Wherever found it is common, living generally in small parties that spend their time hunting over grassland where the pied plumage renders them conspicuous. Like the Common Mynah, this species is a frequent attendant on cattle, and on the grazing grounds of the Northern Circars vast flocks of several hundreds collect together.

In diet it is undoubtedly chiefly insectivorous, catching grasshoppers, crickets, and beetles on the ground, and extracting caterpillars, ants, worms, and other insects from amongst the roots of grass. But it feeds, too, on fruits and berries, being very partial to the fruits of the genus *Ficus*, and it also does a certain amount of damage to crops. Like the Common Mynahs, and indeed often in company with them, the Pied Mynahs roost in huge vociferous mobs in groves of trees.

The breeding season lasts from May to August, but the majority of eggs are laid in June and July.

This species builds in trees, generally out in open fields, at heights of 10 to 30 feet from the ground; sometimes the nests are in colonies, numbers being placed in one large tree. The nest is a large clumsy lump of material, variable in shape, but usually domed, depending for safety not on concealment but on its position in the midst of thorns or towards the extremity of a bough; it is built of straw, grass and twigs, and roots and rags, the last often trailing in streamers below the nest. The egg cavity is thickly lined with feathers. Very rarely the nest is placed in a hole in a tree.

The eggs are four to six in number, but most clutches consist of five eggs. They are moderately broad ovals, a good deal pointed towards the small end, and there is a high gloss. In colour they vary from a delicate bluish-white to a pure though somewhat pale sky-blue, the blue being often tinged with green. There are no markings.

They measure about 1·10 by 0·82 inches.

THE BAYA WEAVER-BIRD

Ploceus philippinus (Linnæus)

(Plate xiii, Fig. 2, opposite page 264)

Description.—Length 6 inches. Male in breeding plumage: A mask, including the sides of the head, chin and throat dark blackish-brown; remainder of the head and the breast bright yellow; upper plumage brownish-black, the feathers broadly margined with bright yellow; rump and remainder of lower plumage fulvous; wings and tail dark brown, edged with fulvous.

Male in winter plumage, and female: The whole upper plumage is fulvous, streaked with blackish-brown, the streaks dying away on the rump; wings and tail dark brown edged with fulvous; a clear fulvous line over the eye; remainder of plumage clear fulvous, darker on the sides of the head, breast and flanks.

Iris brown; bill yellowish-horn, becoming in the breeding male dark horny-brown, yellowish about the base; legs flesh-colour.

Bill rather heavy and conical.

Field Identification.—Abundant plains bird, found in flocks; majority are fulvous birds streaked heavily with blackish on the upper parts, but males in the breeding season have a conspicuous dark brown mask emphasised by surrounding yellow; yellow on the breast distinguishes this from other species of breeding Weavers. Will usually be noticed in connection with long woven grass nests hanging in colonies from boughs of trees.

Distribution.—This Weaver is found in India, Ceylon, and Burma, extending eastwards to Siam, the Malay Peninsula, Java, and Sumatra. It is divided into several races.

O

The typical race is found throughout Ceylon and the greater part of India, extending in the north-west to about the line of the Sutlej. In the Eastern sub-Himalayas and Bengal it is replaced by *P. p. burmanicus*, which differs in the smaller extent of yellow on the throat and breast and in Travancore by the darker *P. p. travancoreensis*. While largely a resident this Weaver is also locally migratory.

Habits, etc.—As in the case of the Tailor-bird, our common Indian Weaver-bird is known by its nest to thousands who would never recognise the owner thereof. Out of colour the parties of Weavers would pass with most people as parties of Sparrows, and never be given a second thought, but when the male dons his yellow breeding plumage and dark mask he is a handsome bird and easily recognised. This species avoids heavy forest and is really a bird of open cultivation where babool trees and palms stand in the midst of grasslands and arable fields, damp and well-watered localities being rather preferred. It feeds on seeds of various kinds, and does a good deal of damage in certain crops, though, like the Sparrow, it largely compensates for this by the caterpillars, grasshoppers, and various insects on which the young are fed. A colony of Weavers' nests is one of the most familiar and typical of Indian country scenes. The nests are long, graceful structures of woven grass, retort shaped, with the mouth of the retort pointing downwards to the ground. These nests hang in groups of ten or a dozen on a tree, suspended by short plaited ropes from the ends of the outer boughs, or in vacant spaces in the centre of the tree, and the soft greens and browns of the nests, the rounded swelling lines of their construction, contrasting with the hard yet feathery foliage of an acacia, form a picture of nature hard to beat. Large colonies may consist of fifty to a hundred nests, occupying several adjacent trees; while many colonies are built in lofty palm trees, hanging like tassels from the crown of leaves.

The nests are built of strips of sarpat grass, rice-grass, plantain leaf, coir, jowar leaf or coco-nut fronds. These strips the bird prepares for itself by cutting a notch in the side of a blade of grass and tearing off the strip above it, a foot or two long. They are cut when green, and new nests may be recognised from old by their colour, and the same difference of colour betrays old nests which have been repaired and used again.

The construction of the nest has often been described, but Mr Salim Ali appears to be the first observer who has correctly unravelled the economy of a breeding colony. According to his account, the colony is founded by a number of fully adult males in breeding condition but still unmated. Each bird selects a suitable twig and winds a number of strands about it until a firm support for the intended nest is secured. From this depends a mass of strips which are worked up into a pendant loop to form the skeleton of the structure. Porches are built over the upper part on each side, one developing and broadening out later into the egg-chamber, the other which is not so bulgy being produced into the entrance tube. About the time that the egg-chambers are complete hen-birds begin to arrive in the colony and though the various cocks press their attentions on them it appears that each hen deliberately makes choice amongst the nests, accepting later the cock whose nest has pleased her fancy. Henceforth the female occupies herself with making the interior of the nest to her liking whilst the male completes the entrance tunnel. The egg-chamber is left unlined, but small pellets of mud are often worked into the walls, a habit of which the original significance if any appears to be lost. As soon as the nest is completed, the eggs laid and incubation started by the hen, the cock proceeds to build a second nest which in due course is chosen by another prospecting female and the whole process is repeated till she too is safely on her eggs. If circumstances are favourable a third hen may be similarly provided for.

It will be seen that this account explains the fact, often recorded, that males are apparently considerably in excess of females in the colonies, and also accounts for the unfinished "cock-nests," second or third nests abandoned by males in which the reproductive fervour is waning.

When entering the nest the bird flies straight up the tunnel without perching at the entrance.

The breeding season is rather extended, from April to November, but most colonies are occupied during the rains.

Two is the normal clutch of eggs, but three or four are sometimes laid. The egg is a rather long oval, somewhat pointed towards the small end; the texture is fine, and the colour is a dead glossless white, unmarked.

It measures about 0·82 by 0·59 inches.

THE STRIATED WEAVER-BIRD

Ploceus manyar (Horsfield)

Description.—Length 6 inches. Sexes alike. Winter plumage: Upper plumage blackish-brown, the feathers edged with fulvous; a yellow line over the eye and a short transverse yellow line on each side of the neck; wings and tail blackish-brown the feathers edged with fulvous becoming greenish on the edges of the quill-feathers; chin and throat white washed with pale yellow, the bases of the feathers blackish-brown; remainder of lower plumage pale fulvous white, the feathers of the breast and flanks with broad blackish-brown shaft-streaks and the breast washed with buff.

Summer plumage: In both sexes wear removes the fulvous edges of the feathers so that the upper plumage and sides of the head become dark brown, the chin and throat brown and the breast and flanks more harshly streaked; the yellow transverse line on each side of the neck disappears. In the male the crown becomes bright shining golden yellow by moult.

Iris brown; bill brownish-horn, blackish in summer; legs pale fleshy-brown, claws dusky.

Bill rather heavy and conical.

Field Identification.—Plains of India. A streaked brown Sparrow-like bird with a yellow line over the eye and another behind the ear. In breeding plumage the male has a golden crown. Found in flocks usually in reed-beds.

Distribution.—India, Ceylon and Burma south to about Moulmein in Tenasserim: also in Java. The typical race is found in Java. Birds from India and Ceylon all belong to the race *P. m. flaviceps* which gives place in Burma to the dark richly coloured *P. m. peguensis.* In India this Weaver is found throughout the whole area south of the Himalayas, but owing to its dependence on water and reed-beds the distribution is very local and the bird will not be found at all through considerable tracts of country.

An even more locally distributed species is the Black-throated Weaver-bird (*Ploceus bengalensis*) which is found here and there throughout Northern India down to Bombay and Bastar. It is very similar in plumage to the Striated Weaver-bird, but lacks the dark streaks on the lower plumage and has a black band across the breast.

Habits, etc.—There is little to say of the habits of the Striated Weaver-bird in distinction from those of the Common Baya except to emphasise that it is much more of a water-haunting species. As a rule, it only breeds where large stretches of water are choked with reed-beds or where rivers and canals exist whose banks are fringed with reed and rush or bordered with thickets of high grass. In such places it is often very numerous indeed, living and nesting in the reeds and feeding in flocks on the grass seeds or on insects found in the grass. Each individual colony is, however, small, consisting of some half dozen nests, and the colonies, though sometimes near to colonies of the other two species, are separate from them.

The breeding season is from July to September.

The nest is very similar in shape, materials and construction to that of the Baya. It differs from it, however, in one important particular. The nest of the Baya tapers above to a point and is suspended by that point alone from one twig or other support. The nest of the Striated Weaver is, on the other hand, suspended from some forty or fifty ends of the grass or rushes which are bent over by the birds and incorporated in the top of the nest, giving it a cluster of supports and a clumsier and more massive appearance as regards the upper part. The tubular entrance is usually shorter in this species. Some nests have acacia flowers cemented to the nest with cow-dung.

The usual clutch is of two eggs, but three, four and rarely five may be found. The egg is a moderately broad oval, a good deal pointed at the small end and of a perfectly pure, almost glossless white. The texture is fine and compact and the shell though thin is firm and strong.

The egg measures about 0·80 by 0·58 inches.

THE WHITE-THROATED MUNIA

UROLONCHA MALABARICA (Linnæus)

(Plate xi, Fig. 3, opposite page 220)

Description.—Length 5 inches. Sexes alike. Upper plumage and wings dull earthy-brown, except the outer flight-feathers which are black; upper tail-coverts white; tail dark brown, margined with rusty; remainder of plumage pale buffy-white, flanks faintly cross-barred with rusty.

Iris dark brown; bill plumbeous-horn, tinged with lavender below; legs pale purplish-pink.

Bill heavy and conical. Tail rather long, graduated and pointed.

Field Identification.—A small, rather elongated brown bird, whitish below and on the base of the tail; found in cheeping parties in thorn scrub or feeding on the ground; rather tame and stupid; several together are often disturbed out of big grass nests.

Distribution.—The White-throated Munia is found in Afghanistan and Baluchistan, and it extends from the Himalayas (in Hazara and Gilgit) across to Eastern Bengal and south to Cape Comorin and Ceylon. It ascends the Himalayas up to 4000 or 5000 feet, and is a sedentary species.

Several other Munias are locally common. The best known is perhaps the White-backed Munia (*Uroloncha striata*) which is found along the Western Ghats, parts of the Madras Presidency, the Chota Nagpur area and much of the Outer Himalayas. This is blackish in colour with the rump and the lower parts from the breast white.

The Rufous-bellied Munia (*Uroloncha kelaarti*) is a familiar bird in the Nilgiris.

Habits, etc.—The White-throated Munia has always seemed to me one of the dullest of our Indian birds; it has no migrations, no changes of plumage, no habits of interest, and in its breeding arrangements it has some of the failings that one generally expects to find amongst domesticated birds.

It is a bird of open country, rather preferring arid spots and the neighbourhood of thorny scrub. It is found in small parties which are tame and dull, taking to flight in close order when disturbed and uttering a small *cheet-cheet-cheet* or *tee-tee* note. The bird lives on small seeds which it gathers often from the ground, though it is very partial to feeding on the heads of pampas grass and various crops like millet and dari. Some of these birds are generally to be found in a Weaver colony, showing a disposition to trespass in the nests and affording a hint as to the origin of the parasitic habits of other members of this family in Africa.

The nest is a large globular structure, composed entirely of grasses of various sorts, particularly their flowering heads. A small circular entrance, moderately well concealed and rather difficult to find, leads into the egg chamber, which is lined with finer grasses and vegetable downs. It is usually built in thorn bushes, about 5 to 10 feet from the ground, but occasional nests are placed in creepers or about the walls of houses.

The ownership of these nests seems somewhat loosely defined, as it is no uncommon thing for more than one hen to lay in the same nest. I have myself found twenty-two eggs in one nest, ranging from fresh to hard set, and twenty-five have been recorded; while four to eight eggs appears to be the normal clutch. Even when the structure is not being used for its proper purpose it is often tenanted as a dormitory, and six or eight of these small birds may be disturbed from it in the evenings. Both birds of the pair frequently brood the eggs together.

The main breeding season apparently commences with the rains and continues till the end of the year, but nests may be found in every month, and the species probably is very irregular in its breeding habits; young birds on occasion breed before they are a year old.

The eggs are pure white, spotless, and devoid of gloss; typically they are rather broad and perfect ovals, but there is a good deal of variation in their shape.

They average about 0·60 by 0·47 inches in size.

THE SPOTTED MUNIA

UROLONCHA PUNCTULATA (Linnæus)

(Plate ii, Fig. 1, opposite page 22)

Description.—Length 5 inches. Sexes alike. Wings and upper plumage dull chocolate, barred on the rump with brown and yellowish and giving place to glistening yellow on the upper tail-coverts; tail fulvous yellow; sides of the head, chin and throat rich chestnut; lower plumage white, all the feathers except on the abdomen banded with fulvous brown, giving a scaled appearance.

Iris deep reddish-brown; bill bluish-black, paler below; legs plumbeous.

Bill heavy and conical. The tail is rather long, graduated and pointed.

Field Identification.—A small bird, easily identified by the white under plumage with dark scale markings, the chocolate upper plumage with yellow above the tail and the chestnut of the face and throat. Found in pairs and flocks perching in bushes and hedges.

Distribution.—This Munia is found throughout the greater part of India, Ceylon, and Burma, extending eastwards to China. It is divided into two races, of which we are only concerned with *U. p. lineoventer.* This is found throughout the Himalayas as far west as Dalhousie up to a height of about 6000 feet and in the continental ranges and the Nilgiris to their summits. It is found also throughout the plains except in the North-west Frontier Province, the Punjab, Sind, and portions of Rajputana. This race also extends to Western Assam. It is a local migrant.

Two species of Munia have black heads and chestnut upper parts and a black patch in the middle of the belly. The Chestnut-bellied Munia (*Munia atricapilla*) has the lower parts chestnut and is found along the base of the Himalayas, in Bihar and Orissa, South-east Bengal, and in Assam. The Black-headed Munia (*Munia malacca*) has the lower parts white. It is found locally in South India up to the Central Provinces.

Habits, etc.—The Spotted Munia avoids heavy forest and the more barren plains, and is most numerous in open country where scrub-jungle alternates with cultivation, and the vegetation is luxuriant. In such places it is found in flocks which feed largely in low-seeding herbage and settle in the bushes, flying when disturbed in close order like a swarm of bees, with a curious petulant little note of *kitty-kitty-kitty.* They are fairly tame and familiar and come freely into gardens.

The breeding season is usually during the rains in July and August, but in the Nilgiris it is more extended from February to September.

The nest is a big clumsy structure, shaped liked a melon, and very large for the size of the bird. The entrance hole is placed on one side and is often difficult to find, so untidy are the walls of the nest. It is wedged into the fork of a tree or bush at heights from 5 to 7 feet from the ground and occasionally higher, and the site is often prepared with a rough platform of the same materials as those of which the nest is constructed. These consist of coarse blades and stems of grass, rice, and barley straw, and leaves of bajera and jowar. The egg cavity is lined with fine grasses and roots.

The situation chosen is generally a thick thorny tree or bush, but creepers on houses and trellis-work in gardens are also favoured.

The clutch varies from four to ten eggs.

The egg is pure white, a somewhat elongated oval, fine in texture and without gloss.

It measures about 0·65 by 0·46 inches.

THE RED AVADAVAT

AMANDAVA AMANDAVA (Linnæus)

(Plate ii, Fig. 2, opposite page 22)

Description.—Length 4 inches. Male in breeding plumage: The whole body plumage, except a black patch from the abdomen to under the tail, crimson more or less mottled with the ashy-brown bases of the feathers showing through; a patch above the base of the tail, and the sides of the neck, breast and body spotted with white; wings brown, the feathers nearest the body tipped with white; tail blackish, the outer feathers tipped with white.

In winter plumage the male resembles the female, but has a greyer throat and upper breast.

Female: Upper plumage brown; upper tail-coverts dull crimson with minute white tips; wings and tail as in the male; a blackish mark in front of the eye; chin and throat whitish; sides of the head and neck and the breast ashy-brown; remainder of lower plumage dull saffron, flanks washed with ashy.

Iris orange-red; bill red, dusky about nostrils; legs brownish-flesh.

Bill short and conical.

Field Identification.—A tiny bird found in flocks in damp areas with reeds or in pampas grass; males are reddish, females brown and yellow, both sexes much spotted with white. Well known under the name of "Lal" as a cage and aviary bird, netted in numbers for sale.

Distribution.—The Red Avadavat is found from India, through Burma to Siam, Cochin-China, Singapore, and Java. It is divided into two races, but only the typical form occurs within our limits. In India it is found practically throughout the country from the foot of the Himalayas, which it ascends to about 2000 feet, down to Cape Comorin, and from Baluchistan and the North-west Frontier Province eastwards. It is, however, wanting in the more dry and barren plains of the North-west. In the Nilgiris it ascends to 6000 feet. A resident species.

A closely allied species is the Green Munia (*Sticospiza formosa*), in which green and yellow are the dominant colours, whilst the flanks are strongly barred. Widely distributed in a broad belt across the centre of the Peninsula.

Habits, etc.—This Avadavat is chiefly found in well-watered and well-wooded localities, and it is very partial to heavy grass jungles and patches of reeds and grass on the outskirts of jheels. In such localities it is found in flocks which perch on the heads of the tall flowering grasses, whence they fly in a cloud with their shrill little call-note when disturbed. They are very bright and lively in their demeanour, and being tame and confiding are easily captured in numbers, and make delightful pets. They are to be seen in dozens in the cages of the bird-catchers, and are exported in large numbers to Europe for sale to aviculturists.

The breeding season is very irregular and varies according to locality, so that nests may be found in every month of the year. The greater number, however, nest in the rains and early winter. Two broods a year appear to be raised.

The nest is a large melon-shaped structure with the entrance at one side; it is built of grasses of various types and the cock bird often continues to add material to it after the eggs are laid and the female is sitting. The cavity is lined with fine grass, downs, and sometimes with feathers. It is well concealed as a rule, being built in the bases of thick bushes or clumps of grass or reeds, never higher than 3 feet from the ground and often practically on it.

The normal clutch consists of five or six eggs, but various numbers up to fourteen have been recorded, and probably sometimes two females lay in one nest.

The eggs are very fine and delicate in texture, without gloss, a regular oval in shape, often rather pointed at one or both ends. The colour is pure white.

In size they average about 0·55 by 0·43 inches.

THE BLACK AND YELLOW GROSBEAK

PERISSOSPIZA ICTEROIDES (Vigors)

(Plate xv, Fig. 1, opposite page 308)

Description.—Length 9 inches. Male: The whole head, chin and throat, the wings and tail and the thighs dull black; remainder of plumage bright yellow, tinged with orange on the hind neck.

Female: The whole head and neck and the upper parts dull ashy-grey, becoming more fulvous above the tail; quills of the wing and tail black, the inner wing-quills and the central tail-feathers washed with ashy-grey; breast ashy-brown; remainder of lower plumage bright tawny fulvous.

The bill is very heavy and conical in shape.

Iris brown; bill olive-green in male, horny-green in female; legs fleshy-pink, claws dusky.

Field Identification.—West Himalayan form. A large heavily built Finch with a heavy conical greenish beak. The male is bright yellow with black head, wings and tail, the female dull ashy-colour with fulvous under parts. Conspicuous when feeding on the ground but difficult to see in trees and usually found through its distinctive call-note *tre-ter tre-ter*.

Distribution.—A resident species in the Western Himalayas from Naini Tal to Hazara and Chitral; also in the Sufed Koh. It breeds in the spruce and silver fir forests between 7500 and 9000 feet, and in winter some drift lower to about 4000 feet.

It must not be confounded with the very similar Allied Grosbeak (*Perissospiza affinis*) which is found in the Himalayas from Hazara to Bhutan. This species frequents the high level silver fir and birch forests between 10,000 and 11,000 feet. Its call notes are quite distinct from those of *P. icteroides*. In this the male has the thighs yellow and the yellow of the upper parts more orange. The female is a greener bird.

Both these Grosbeaks are easily distinguished by the bill from the Black-headed Oriole (*Oriolus xanthornus*) which many people confuse with them in spite of the different distribution (see p. 193).

Habits, etc.—This Grosbeak is a bird of the Himalayan forests where it is found in all types of forest both deciduous and evergreen, but more particularly in stretches of silver firs and deodars. It feeds a good deal in the undergrowth and on the ground, often venturing on to the roads, but otherwise keeps mostly to the highest trees so that it is more often seen than heard. For the call-note, *tre-ter tre-ter* or *trekatree trekatree, trekup trekup*, uttered by both sexes, isone of thefamiliar sounds of a Himalayan forest or a Himalayan sanatorium. The song note of the male is a pretty whistle, *tre-trui, tre-trui* or *tra trui-tree*. The feeding note is *chuck chuck*.

The food consists of the fresh shoots of conifers and the seeds from their cones as well as the fruits of shrubs and plants in the undergrowth.

Out of the breeding season the birds collect into parties and small flocks.

The breeding season begins in April and continues until July and perhaps even until September, but most eggs are certainly to be found in June.

The nest may be built at any height from 18 to 60 feet from the ground and the usual situation is against the main trunk of a conifer, preferably a spruce, deodar or silver fir. It is, however, on occasion built on a horizontal bough and also in a non-coniferous tree such as a yew, lime or wild cherry. The materials of the nest, which is a wide cup, are fine twigs, lichens and silvery plant-stems with often a certain amount of moss. The cup is lined with dry grass and rootlets.

The clutch consists of two or three eggs.

The egg is broad in shape and rather pointed towards the small end; the texture is smooth and hard with a slight gloss. The ground-colour is pale greenish-grey marked with numerous blackish-brown tangled lines, some thick and bold, some very fine twisted and intertwined, in a zone round the broad end and more or less underlaid by faint inky-purple clouds. A few blackish-brown spots and odd streaks are also found on the rest of the egg's surface.

The egg measures about 1·00 by 0·08 inches.

THE RED-HEADED BULLFINCH

Pyrrhula erythrocephala Vigors

Description.—Length 5·5 inches. Male: A broad band of black round the base of the bill and extending round the eye; head and neck rich reddish-brown, paler on the throat and breast; back ash-grey; rump white margined in front by a black band. The upper tail coverts and tail glossy black; wings black with a band of greyish-brown; abdomen greyish-white. In worn plumage the red of the head is tinged with yellow. Female: Similar to male, but the head and neck are yellowish-green and the lower parts brown or drab.

Iris light brown; bill black; legs pale fleshy-brown.

Field Identification.—A low monosyllabic call note. The black wings and tail and white rump are characteristic of all bullfinches. The white rump especially catches the eye at once when the birds are in flight. The red head in the male and yellowish-green of the female are characteristic of this species.

Distribution.—Himalayas from Kishtwar to Bhutan. In the breeding season this Bullfinch is found in silver fir, spruce, and deodar forests from 9000 to 12,000 feet where some birds remain throughout the year, while others in the autumn wander down to the valleys to about 6000 feet and occasionally as low as 3500 feet. It is common in winter in the vicinity of Simla, Naini Tal, Mussoorie and Darjeeling. Another species is the slightly larger Brown Bullfinch (*P. nipalensis*) ranging from Kangra to Bhutan at an elevation of from 6500 to 11,000 feet in summer; at other seasons between 5000 and 7000 feet. The general colour is ashy-brown with black wings, tail and rump; this last has a white cross-band. The sexes are alike, except that in the male the outer edge of the innermost feather of the wing is crimson, while in the female it is yellow.

Habits, etc.—In the non-breeding season this Bullfinch is found in small parties, not infrequently of one sex. Its food consists of seeds and fruits of trees, shrubs and herbaceous plants. Small parties may sometimes be seen feeding on the seeds of rank nettles on the hillsides. At the end of April or May the birds pair and at this season frequent willows, attracted by the catkins. It is very tame and utters a low musical whistle similar to the British bird.

The Red-headed Bullfinch is a late breeder and the eggs are laid as a rule in August. The nest is built on a branch of a tree some distance from the ground, and is the usual Bullfinch type; thin twigs and moss, lined with fine roots.

The eggs vary from three to four in number, and resemble those of a Greenfinch more than the common Bullfinch. They are a dull grey-white with a faint tinge of green, marked with small specks and blotches of brown or red-brown, some almost dark grey.

The egg measures about 0·8 by 0·6 inches.

THE COMMON ROSEFINCH

CARPODACUS ERYTHRINUS (Pallas)

Description.—Length 6 inches. Adult male: Entire body-plumage dull crimson, largely mixed with brown on the back and sides, and brightest on the rump, chin, throat, and breast; the lower parts grow paler posteriorly till under the tail they are whitish; wings and tail brown, edged with rufous.

In breeding plumage the margins wear off the feathers and so leave the bird a brighter crimson.

Female and immature male: The whole plumage olive-brown streaked with brown, wings and tail margined with ochraceous; a double whitish bar across the wing-coverts.

Iris dark brown; bill horny-brown; legs dusky brown.

Bill rather heavy and conical.

Field Identification.—Found in flocks in trees and crops; a dull brown bird, the size of a Sparrow, streaked with dark brown and with

1. Black-naped Flycatcher. 2. Dark-grey Bush-Chat. 3. White-throated Munia. 4. Spotted Babbler. 5. Red-winged Bush-Lark. ($\frac{3}{5}$ nat. size.)

[*Face p.* 220

a pale double wing-bar ; a small proportion of individuals consist of adult males in a dull scarlet dress.

Distribution.—Widely distributed over Eastern Europe and Asia, the Common Rosefinch is divided into several races differing in the extent and brightness of the red colour of the males : opinions differ as to the validity of some of these races, but the majority of Indian birds certainly belong to the form *C. e. roseatus.* This breeds throughout the higher Himalayas and the mountains of Central Asia generally at heights of 10,000 feet and upwards. It is migratory, and after breeding spreads over almost the whole of India and Northern Burma, going as far south as the High Range in Travancore ; it is most abundant in the central and western half of the Peninsula, while the South-eastern Punjab and Sind lie out of the main line of migration and only stragglers reach those parts. More data is required about the movements of this species, which arrives in the northern plains about September, and reaches Southern India at the end of November, and moves north again from March to May.

Habits, etc.—During migration and in the winter months in India the Common Rosefinch is generally met with in flocks which are quiet and unobtrusive in behaviour, feeding as a rule in undergrowth or in millet and similar crops. They avoid heavy forest and are found in any type of open country, visiting gardens and the neighbourhood of villages. The flocks are sometimes of some size and they feed very largely on the ground, flying up into trees when disturbed. The full-plumaged males are always in a minority, as first-year males breed in the female dress.

The food consists of wild cherries, mulberries, and a variety of other seeds and fruits ; buds and shoots are also eaten. The bird is very fond of the watery nectar contained in the flower of the coral-tree, and particularly frequents that tree when in blossom.

Ordinarily in India the bird is very quiet, but on the spring migration the males commence their loud pleasant song, which, albeit somewhat monotonous, is such a feature of the barren wastes of Gilgit, Ladakh, Spiti, and other Tibetan areas. There, during the summer months the birds frequent and breed in the scanty patches of scrub usually in the vicinity of water.

The breeding season is from June to August. The nest is a cup-shaped structure of grass lined with finer roots and stems and occasionally hair. It is placed in low bushes and the bird is a very close sitter, allowing itself almost to be caught rather than leave the nest.

The clutch consists of three or four eggs. They are rather broad ovals, pointed towards the smaller end, and fine and smooth in texture. In colour they are a beautiful deep blue, with a few scrawls and spots of chocolate colour, some pale, some almost black.

They measure about 0·80 by 0·60 inches.

THE HIMALAYAN GREENFINCH

Hypacanthis spinoides (Vigors)

Description.—Length 5 inches. Male: A broad line over the eye, some markings on the sides of the face, an indistinct collar round the neck, the rump and the whole lower plumage bright yellow; remainder of upper plumage greenish-brown mixed with black and darkest on the head; wings dark brown, variegated with yellow, black and a little white; tail dark brown, all but the two central pairs of feathers largely mixed with yellow increasing externally.

The female resembles the male, but is slightly duller with less yellow in the wing-coverts.

Fig. 31—Himalayan Greenfinch (½ nat. size)

Iris brown; bill fleshy-horn, tipped dusky; legs brownish-flesh.

The beak is conical, sharp and pointed.

Field Identification.—Himalayan species; usually gregarious when breeding and gathering into flocks in winter; recognisable in the field by the pleasant twittering note, the habit of flying high in the air, and the yellow under parts, eye-streak and wing-markings.

Distribution.—A Himalayan species, found throughout the whole of that range. It breeds commonly but locally at heights from 4000 to 9000 feet, and occasionally higher to 11,000 feet, and in winter it wanders down into the foot-hills and the plains at their base. On the west it is common in winter in the Peshawar Valley, and even appears in the Afghan Hills down to the Samana. On the east it has been found in Manipur, and is replaced by a darker race in the Shan States and Yunnan.

The well-known Goldfinch, conspicuous with its crimson face and golden wing-bar, is common in the Western Himalayas, Kashmir, and Baluchistan, coming down to the North-west Frontier Province and Northern Punjab in winter. It lacks the black head marking of the English species and belongs to the Asiatic species *Carduelis caniceps.*

Habits, etc.—The Himalayan Greenfinch avoids heavy deciduous forest, and while breeding prefers to frequent patches of open deodar forest on hill-sides in the neighbourhood of cultivation. Several pairs breed more or less together in such suitable localities. Out of the breeding season the birds collect into flocks, often of some size, and these flocks wander about the lower hills in a very erratic manner, so that no regular calendar of their movements can be worked out. When in flocks they very definitely prefer open cultivation studded with trees, and their favourite food is the seed of the wild hemp which grows in large patches where buffaloes have been kept. They are easily attracted to gardens by planting sunflowers, as they are very fond of the seeds of that plant.

The ordinary call-note is a cheerful twitter, *twit-it-it* or *teh-teh-tah*, rather reminiscent of the call of the English Goldfinch; it has also a very sweet-toned note, *twee-ah.* The song, on the other hand, is more like that of the English Greenfinch, a very amorous sounding *screeee* or *treeee-tertrah.* The love flight also resembles that of the latter bird. I have seen a bird flying past suddenly descend in a circle to a tree, with the wings spread and extended high above the head and the tail partly open.

The breeding season is late, compared with most Himalayan birds, from July to early October, and this is correlated with curious features in the moults of plumage.

The nest is a neatly-constructed cup of the familiar Linnet type, composed of fine grass roots, with a good deal of hair interwoven in the interior as lining, and the exterior is often blended with moss to assimilate it to its surroundings. It is usually placed in a deodar or spruce fir at a considerable height from the ground, and may be in a fork or clump of foliage close to the trunk or on the top of a vertical bough near its extremity.

The clutch consists of three or four eggs.

The eggs are regular ovals, slightly pointed towards the smaller end; the texture is fine and delicate without gloss. The ground-colour is a very delicate pale sea-green, and the only markings are a number of fine black spots and specks, usually most numerous towards the broad end.

The eggs measure about 0·70 by 0·52 inches.

THE YELLOW-THROATED SPARROW

GYMNORHIS XANTHOCOLLIS (Burton)

Description.—Length 6 inches. Male: The whole upper plumage ashy-brown; wings brown, darker on the quills, with two wing-bars, the upper whitish the lower buff, a chestnut patch above the upper bar; tail brown, narrowly edged with paler; chin dull white; a conspicuous yellow patch on the throat; remainder of lower plumage pale ashy, becoming whitish on the abdomen.

FIG. 32—Yellow-throated Sparrow (⅗ nat. size)

The female has a less conspicuous yellow patch on the throat, and the chestnut patch on the wings is replaced with rufous-brown.

Iris dark brown; bill black or brown; legs greyish-plumbeous. The beak is rather long, conical and pointed.

Field Identification.—Plains and lower hills. A slim bird, dull in plumage, with a chestnut patch on the wing and a bright yellow patch on the throat; arboreal and rather noisy in the summer; in winter collects into flocks which feed on the ground, flying into trees when disturbed.

Distribution.—The Yellow-throated Sparrow extends from Iraq, Persia and Afghanistan almost throughout India. It is divided into two races. The Persian and Afghan race, *G. x. transfuga*, distinguished by its pale coloration, extends into Sind and the South-western Punjab, while the birds of the remainder of the Punjab are somewhat intermediate in character. The typical race is found throughout the rest of India down to Travancore, and on the east to about Midnapur in Bengal. In the Himalayas and other ranges it ascends to about 4500 feet. While resident in the main it is also partly migratory.

Habits, etc.—The Yellow-throated Sparrow is a common and generally distributed species in all open country, cultivation and barren land alike, but it avoids heavy forest, and is not a house bird, though it will nest in trees in gardens, and readily use nest-boxes placed for the use of birds. It is essentially a Tree-Sparrow, and spends most of its time in the upper branches of trees, where its monotonous chirping note recalls, but is different from, the chirp of the Common House-Sparrow. Out of the breeding season it collects into large flocks, and these feed on the ground, searching under trees for their fallen seeds and for the seeds of grasses and weeds. It is very fond of the flowers of the wild caper, and its forehead is often stained with their pollen.

It breeds from April to July and is probably double-brooded.

The nest is usually a mere pad of dry grass thickly lined with feathers, but, as with many species that breed in holes, it varies a good deal according to its site, and is sometimes quite a pretentious structure built neatly of a variety of materials. It is placed in holes and hollows of trees, usually at a height of 15 to 20 feet from the ground, but sometimes much lower. The old nest-holes of Woodpeckers and Parrots are often appropriated.

The clutch consists of three or four eggs. They are moderately elongated ovals, rather dull and glossless in texture. The ground-colour is greenish-white, very thickly streaked, smudged and blotched all over with very dingy brown of a tint between sepia and chocolate.

In size they average about 0·74 by 0·55 inches.

THE HOUSE-SPARROW

Passer domesticus (Linnæus)

Description.—Length 6 inches. Male: Top of head ashy-grey, bordered from above the eye with chestnut which gradually encroaches until the whole hind neck, back and shoulders are chestnut streaked with black; rump ashy-grey; wings variegated chestnut and dark brown with two conspicuous pale bars; tail dark brown edged paler; a patch from the beak to the eye and a broad patch from the chin to the upper breast black; cheeks and remainder of the lower plumage white, tinged with ashy on the flanks.

In fresh autumn plumage the colours are somewhat obscured by ashy fringes to the feathers, but these gradually wear off.

Female: A pale rufous-white streak over the eye; upper plumage pale earthy-brown, streaked with black and rufous on the upper back; wings dark brown, variegated with rufous and with two whitish bars; tail dark brown edged paler; whole lower plumage ashy-white.

Iris brown; bill brown, black in the male in summer; legs brown.

The bill is short and stout.

Field Identification.—Well known to everyone and almost universal, but it may be noted that the Indian bird differs from the European in the white cheeks of the male.

Distribution.—As is well known, the House-Sparrow is very widely spread through Europe, Northern Africa and the greater part of Asia; it has also been introduced into America and Australia, and many other places.

It is divided into a number of sub-species, of which we are concerned with two: *P. d. griseigularis* is the large, brightly-coloured breeding bird of the Inner Himalayas and Tibetan areas from 5000 to 15,000 feet. It is partly migratory, and large numbers visit the plains of North-western India in winter. *P. d. indicus* is smaller and from its haunts often a dirty looking bird. This race is found throughout India to Ceylon, Assam, and Burma. The birds of the Outer Himalayas are intermediate between the two races.

In the stations of Quetta and Darjeeling the Tree-Sparrow (*Passer montanus*) is common about houses. It is distinguished by the black spot in the middle of the white cheeks and the fact that the female does not differ from the male.

Habits, etc.—There can be no bird that is more universally known and recognised than the House-Sparrow. It avoids heavy forest, but is otherwise found everywhere, sometimes scarce but more usually abundant, dependent only on food-supply: and its food-supply is generally connected in some way with man, on whom it has virtually become a parasite. The larger and more prosperous a city or village the more the Sparrow flourishes, and in the open shops and houses of the East it is only considered less of a pest than rats and mice, because it is less offensive to eye and nose. In the food shops it pilfers every variety of grain and cake, pattering over the floors, delving into the dishes and sacks, ejected one moment and returning again the next with undiminished ardour. In private houses it comes in more for shelter than for food, searching for nesting places in the rafters and on the walls, littering the whole place with a selection of the varied assortment of rubbish that in its eyes is the most suitable nesting material possible. And in private houses, having more leisure and inclination for song, it makes a further nuisance of itself with the noisy and incessant chirruping which serves it for that purpose. For the breeding note is a rather shrill *chissick*, differing but little from the ordinary *tchirp* of daily life.

But, like all true townsmen, the Sparrow likes an occasional holiday in the country, and it times its holidays to coincide with the opportunities of visiting ripening corn or fruit in huge flocks which often do a considerable amount of damage. But in fairness credit must also be given for the considerable number of insect pests which are certainly destroyed by the Sparrow, who feeds its callow chicks to a large extent on insects and caterpillars.

Nests may be found in any month in India, and more than one brood is certainly reared in the year; but the main breeding season is apparently from April to June.

The nest is a large, shapeless structure, based on an oval and domed plan with an entrance on one side, stuffed into any sort of hole or cavity available, provided that it has some connection with the works of man. Trees are on the whole seldom used in India. Grass, straw, rags, wool, and any other materials available are used in the construction of the nest, and the egg chamber is thickly lined with feathers.

The clutch usually consists of four or five eggs. They are rather elongated ovals, fine in texture with a slight gloss. The colour is very variable, and the eggs in one clutch often vary amongst themselves, one egg usually being much lighter than the rest. The ground-colour is greyish- or greenish-white, generally finely and uniformly spotted with dark and light shades of ashy-grey and brown. In some eggs these markings are replaced by big blotches and spots.

In size they average about 0·80 by 0·50 inches.

THE CINNAMON SPARROW

PASSER RUTILANS (Temminck)

Description.—Length 5 inches. Male: Upper plumage and lesser wing-coverts bright cinnamon-rufous, streaked with black on the back; wings black edged with rufous and fulvous and with a white wing-bar; tail brown with narrow greenish margins; a small black patch from the bill to the eye; a patch behind the eye pale yellowish-white; chin and throat black, with a bright yellow patch on each side of the throat; lower plumage greyish-yellow, growing yellower towards the tail.

Female: Whole upper plumage ruddy-brown, streaked on the back with black and fulvous and reddish on the rump; wings and tail dark brown edged with fulvous, a white bar across the wing; a broad conspicuous fulvous line above the eye, with a broad dusky band through the eye; lower plumage pale ashy-yellow.

Iris reddish-brown; bill brown, black in male in summer; legs dark reddish-brown.

Field Identification.—Himalayan species, common about hill stations; smaller than the House-Sparrow; male easily distinguished by cinnamon-red upper plumage and yellow lower plumage, female by the broad conspicuous pale band above the eye.

Distribution.—The Cinnamon Sparrow is a widely-spread species occurring throughout the Himalayas and farther eastwards to China, Japan and Formosa. It is divided into races, of which *P. r. cinnamomeus* breeds along the Himalayas from Chitral and Hazara to Kumaon and is replaced in the Eastern Himalayas by the larger *P. r. schaferi* and in Assam, Burma and Yunnan by the darker *P. r. intensior.* In the Himalayas it breeds at elevations between 4000 and 8000 feet, and in winter collects into a lower zone along the foot-hills, on the east coming right down into the Duars.

Immense flocks of dark Sparrow-like birds are often found swinging along the open hill-sides of the Inner Himalayas, both east and west, and feeding on the ground. These are usually Stoliczka's Mountain-Finch (*Fringillauda nemoricola*).

Habits, etc.—The pretty little Cinnamon Sparrow is really a forest Sparrow, though it lives mostly in oak and rhododendron forest in the near vicinity of houses and often frequents gardens. In winter it collects into large flocks which move down into the cultivation in the foot-hills and feed on the ground, picking up stray grains of rice and corn in the deserted fields, and flying up when disturbed into neighbouring trees. These flocks are often of considerable size. The call-note and pretence of a song are very similar to those of the House-Sparrow, but they are distinguishable in tone and slightly more melodious.

The breeding season is from April to August, and probably two broods are reared. The nest is a large, loose structure of dry grass, lined warmly with feathers, and it is usually built in holes in trees at no very great elevation from the ground. Some nests are built under the eaves of houses and in verandahs and old Swallows' nests.

The clutch consists usually of four eggs, but five and six are sometimes laid.

The egg is a moderately elongated oval, fine in texture and with a slight gloss. The ground-colour is white, with a greyish or greenish tinge, speckled, spotted, streaked, and blotched with various shades of brown, sometimes thinly with a tendency for the markings to collect at the broad end, at other times closely and thickly over the whole surface of the egg, almost concealing the ground-colour.

The egg measures about 0·75 by 0·55 inches.

THE WHITE-CAPPED BUNTING

EMBERIZA STEWARTI Blyth

Description.—Length 6 inches. Male: The top of the head and the ear-coverts pale grey; a broad black line over the eye; chin and upper throat black, produced down the sides of the lower throat which with the fore-neck is white; sides of the head streaked with fulvous and rufous; upper plumage chestnut, the concealed portions of the wings dark brown; tail brown margined with rufous, the two outer pairs of feathers white; a broad gorget over the breast chestnut; remainder of lower plumage pale fulvous.

In fresh autumn plumage the colours are obscured with dull fringes to the feathers but these gradually wear off revealing the colours.

Female: Upper plumage ashy-brown streaked with blackish except on the sides of the face; a patch above the base of the tail chestnut with blackish feather-shafts; wings brown, the feathers edged with fulvous; tail brown margined with rufous, the two outer pairs of feathers almost entirely white; lower plumage pale fulvous streaked with brown.

Iris brown; bill brown, paler below; legs pinkish-fleshy.

Bill conical and sharply pointed, the edges of the two mandibles not completely in contact.

Field Identification.—Western Himalayas, extending to North-west India in winter; a quiet, unobtrusive little bird, often in parties in bushes and trees; male, chestnut above with a chestnut band across the breast, greyish-white top to the head and blackish face markings; female, dull-brown streaked darker; in both sexes the flash of white feathers at the edge of the tail is conspicuous.

Distribution.—Breeds in Turkestan, Afghanistan, Baluchistan, Kashmir, and the Western Himalayas as far as West Nepal, at heights from 4000 to 10,000 feet. From September to April it moves down into the foot-hills and extends into the plains of the Punjab and Western United Provinces, Rajputana and Central India.

A smaller and duller species resident in the Peninsula is the Striolated Bunting (*Emberiza striolata*), which is found, usually in dry stony hills, in North-west India as far as Etawah, Saugor, and Cutch. It is a brownish-looking bird with a grey head, streaked with black.

Habits, etc.—This Bunting is somewhat local in its distribution, but when and where it occurs it is usually very numerous, avoiding thick forest and barren plains and preferring scrub-jungle on the edges of cultivation. It feeds mostly on the ground, collecting minute seeds, and except in the breeding season is generally found in loose scattered flocks, which when disturbed fly up and take refuge in the trees. When not feeding the flocks sit stolidly in trees and bushes. The call-note is a twitter, rather like that of a Linnet, and the breeding song is of the usual dull, reeling note of the genus.

The breeding season in our area is from May to July.

The nest is a cup composed of roots, dry grass, and fibres, and is situated in a hollow in the face of a bank or rock, generally fairly well screened with hanging grass. The clutch varies from three to five eggs.

The egg is a short, broad, regular oval, fine in texture but with only a slight gloss. The ground-colour is white, mottled and clouded all over with pale purple-grey or slaty-grey, and superimposed are a few small dark brown spots.

The egg measures about 0·78 by 0·59 inches.

THE MEADOW-BUNTING

Emberiza cia Linnæus

Description.—Length 7 inches. Sexes alike. Head, throat and upper breast pale bluish-grey, marked with two broad black lines along the crown, a black line through the eye, and one passing from the base of the beak below the ear-coverts and circling behind them up to the crown; remainder of body plumage chestnut-brown, on the back darker and streaked with black; wings blackish-brown, the feathers edged with rufous and chestnut; tail blackish-brown, the central feathers edged with chestnut, the three outer pairs with conspicuous white tips.

In fresh autumn plumage the colours are obscured by pale fringes to the feathers which gradually wear off.

FIG. 33—Head of Meadow-Bunting (nat. size)

Iris dark brown; bill plumbeous-slate darker above; legs fleshy-yellow.

Beak conical and sharply pointed, the edges of the two mandibles not completely in contact.

Field Identification.—North-western India. A chestnut-brown bird with a pale head, conspicuously lined with black, which shows a white flicker in the tail as it moves; usually feeding on the ground, and abundant in open country round all hill stations of the Western Himalayas.

Distribution.—The Meadow-Bunting has a wide range through Southern Europe, North-western Africa, Transcaspia, the Himalayas, Northern China, and Eastern Siberia, and has in consequence been divided into a number of geographical races. *E. c. stracheyi* breeds throughout the Western Himalayas from 4000 to 11,000 feet from the Hazara country and Gilgit to about Kumaon. It is a resident species, though it undergoes a certain amount of seasonal elevational movement. Numbers of Meadow-Buntings appear in winter on the northern and western parts of the Punjab; they, however, belong to a paler race, *E. c. par*, which breeds from Transcaspia to Chitral.

Habits, etc.—In the Western Himalayas this strikingly-marked little Bunting is one of the commonest birds. It avoids thick forest and is found on all the more open hill-sides in cultivation and grass-land alike, searching the ground and herbage for seeds and insects, or creeping about the roads and paths, where its tameness contrives to bring it into universal notice. It is very partial to the more open patches of deodar forest, isolated on otherwise bare hill-sides. Although almost entirely a ground-feeder, it flies up into the trees when disturbed, and its note, a slow, melancholy squeak, is one of the most familiar sounds of the Western Himalayas. The song is very poor, a mere jangle of odd notes and squeaks, uttered either from a tree or on the ground.

The breeding season is very extended, lasting from April to September, and two or three broods are probably reared.

The nest is a rather large but loosely built cup of dry grass, bents, roots, and similar materials, lined with fine roots and hair. It is usually placed on the ground under a large stone or in herbage at the foot of a bush or bank or between the rough stone blocks of the terrace walls of hill cultivation; but occasionally it is built in the thick foliage of a tree, 2 or 3 feet from the ground.

The clutch consists of three to five eggs, but the normal number is probably three. The egg is a moderately elongated oval, close and delicate in texture with very little gloss. The ground-colour is pale greenish-white, grey, or pale stone-colour. The markings consist of the most delicate and intricate tracery of blackish-brown lines drawn over faint and pale inky-purple streaks and marbling. These markings tend to be confined as a cap or zone to the broad end of the egg. Here and there a dark spot, like a fly caught in a spider's web, is seen amongst the network of lines, which are so characteristic of the eggs of the Bunting family, and are familiar to all through the English Yellow-hammer.

The egg measures about 0·83 by 0·63 inches.

THE BLACK-HEADED BUNTING

EMBERIZA MELANOCEPHALA Scopoli

Description.—Length 7 inches. Male: Top and sides of the head black; a yellowish collar on the hind neck connected with the deep yellow of the entire lower plumage; remainder of upper plumage and lesser wing-coverts deep orange-chestnut; the upper tail-coverts brown; wings and tail dark brown edged with ashy-fulvous.

In fresh autumn plumage the colours are much obscured with dark fringes to the feathers which gradually wear off.

Female: Upper plumage fulvous-brown streaked with dark brown; wings and tail dark brown edged with fulvous; entire lower plumage delicate fulvous, washed with ochraceous on the breast and becoming yellow towards the tail.

Iris dark brown; bill pale greenish-horn, browner above; legs fleshy-brown.

The bill is conical and pointed and the edges of the mandibles do not entirely meet.

Field Identification.—Winter visitor to the plains in flocks, often particularly abundant. Females are streaked brown birds; males are chestnut above, yellow below, with black heads; yellow is the dominant impression given by the flocks which are usually found in crops, flying up into trees when disturbed.

Distribution.—This bird breeds in South-eastern Europe, Asia Minor, Palestine, Syria, Upper Mesopotamia, and Persia, but not within our limits, where it is only a winter visitor. It crosses to and from India by a route over the western boundary of Sind, passing through Sind in August and September and again in March and April; thence it spreads into the plains generally as far east as Delhi, Nagpur and Chanda, and as far south as Belgaum.

The Red-headed Bunting (*Emberiza bruniceps*) is another species with much yellow in the plumage, the males being distinguished by a chestnut head. It is also found in flocks as a winter visitor to the greater part of India. The wide breeding range includes Baluchistan.

Habits, etc.—As we know it in India, this Bunting appears in very large flocks, sometimes in company with the allied Red-headed Bunting. It affects cultivation and scrub-jungle and feeds chiefly on grain and seeds.

On the spring passage vast clouds of these birds may be seen in the ripening crops; on being flushed they fly into the nearest tree, making it appear a yellow mass, and it is noteworthy that these flocks then consist almost entirely of males. These flocks are very bold and are only driven with difficulty from a field where they have decided to feed, and owing to their numbers they can be responsible for a good deal of damage. In the autumn they also do a certain amount of damage to jowar and similar crops, but on that passage they are not usually so noticeable.

The breeding season is about May in Western Asia and South-eastern Europe. The nest is a cup of straw and grass lined with hair and roots and it is usually placed in a vine, a bush or a small tree. The clutch consists of four to six eggs, and these are pale greenish-blue, spotted throughout with ashy-brown and grey, but mostly towards the broad end.

They measure about 0·87 by 0·62 inches.

THE CRESTED BUNTING

MELOPHUS LATHAMI (Gray)

Description.—Length 6 inches. Male: Entire plumage including a pointed crest black, except the wing, tail and thighs which are chestnut, some of the feathers being tipped with black.

In fresh autumn plumage the feathers have ashy fringes which gradually wear off.

Female: Crest less conspicuous; upper plumage dark brown, the feathers edged paler; wings and tail dark brown much marked with cinnamon; lower plumage dull buff streaked and mottled on the throat and breast with dark brown and growing more rufous under the tail.

Iris dark brown; bill blackish, fleshy at lower base; legs fleshy-brown, toes darker.

Field Identification.—A solitary bird, found about bushes on rocky hill-sides; conspicuous pointed crest; male black with chestnut wings and tail; female much paler, brownish with cinnamon-tinged wings and tail.

FIG. 34—Head of Crested Bunting ($\frac{1}{1\frac{1}{2}}$ nat. size)

Distribution.—The Crested Bunting is found along the Outer Himalayas from Hazara to Bhutan, at elevations up to 5000 or 6000 feet. In the plains it is found from the Koochawan Hills and Mount Aboo across to Bengal and as far south as Mahableshwar and Satara. Farther east it extends to Assam, portions of Burma and to China. It is, however, very local and capricious in its distribution, and is locally migratory. Indian birds all belong to the race *E. l. subcristata*.

Habits, etc.—The Crested Bunting is in the main a solitary bird, though occasionally it collects into small parties of four or five individuals. It avoids both bare plains and forests and is essentially a bird of rocky hills or of open cultivation on the hill-sides, where stony ground and low scrub-jungle provide fairly undisturbed resorts for it. It feeds on the ground at all times of the day collecting small grass seeds, but perches and sings on the tops of bushes. When old buildings and walls are found in the locality it is very partial to them, perching on them and seldom moving far away.

In demeanour the Crested Bunting is a vivacious, lively, bold little bird, usually carrying the crest erect. On the ground and walking its attitude is very Peacock-like. The head and breast are held very upright, while the tail, which seems to trail behind, is rather expanded. It has a pretty, little simple call, but the song of the male is rather monotonous, one or two notes only, constantly repeated.

The nests are rather variable; some are loosely constructed, shallow saucers made of grass roots without lining; others are neat cups of grass and moss, lined with fine grass, fibres, and the roots of moss and ferns or horse-hair. They are placed in holes in banks, in walls, under rocks, or in heavy herbage on the ground.

The clutch consists of three or four eggs.

The egg is a rather broad oval, usually blunter towards the small end; there is very little gloss. The ground-colour varies from pale greenish-white to pale stone-colour; the markings consist of spots, freckles and blotches of red, brown and purple, usually most dense about the broad end. These eggs entirely lack the fine hair-lines and scroll-like writing so characteristic of the eggs of the true Buntings.

The egg measures about 0·79 by 0·63 inches.

THE INDIAN SAND-MARTIN

Riparia paludicola (Vieillot)

Description.—Length 4 inches. Sexes alike. The whole upper plumage greyish-brown, most of the feathers margined paler; wings and tail darker brown; lower plumage pale grey, growing whitish towards the tail.

Iris brown; bill black; legs dark brown.

The bill is very weak and flat, with a broad gape, the wings long and pointed and the tail slightly forked.

Field Identification.—Common plains Swallow, incessantly flying about sandy banks of water-channels in which its nest-tunnels are excavated. Highly gregarious, small and plain, dull brownish, paler below.

Distribution.—India, Assam and Burma and eastwards to Southern China, Formosa and the Philippines. It is found throughout the greater part of India from about the Central Punjab and the Indus valley in Sind on the west, and the Himalayan foot-hills on the north, down to the Bombay Presidency, the Deccan and Cuttack. While not strictly migratory it moves about a good deal locally. The Indian race is *R. p. brevicaudata.* It must be carefully distinguished from the Common Sand-Martin (*Riparia riparia*), which has the under parts white with a well-defined brown collar across the breast and a small tuft of feathers on the back of the tarsus above the hind toe. This has two races in India. *R. r. indica* breeds in the North-west Frontier Province and the North-western Punjab, while *R. r. diluta,* which breeds in Western Siberia, visits North-western India down to Sind in winter.

Habits, etc.—The Sand-Martin is extremely gregarious in its habits, spending its whole life in flocks whether in or out of the breeding season. It is amongst the earliest of breeding birds in India, nesting generally from November to February, though in some localities birds will be found at the nest-holes as late as May. The colonies nest in sandy cliffs and banks, generally choosing those in the vicinity of running water, though occasionally they occupy banks over ponds or in dry nullahs. They feed almost invariably in the vicinity of water and spend the greater part of their lives hawking insects, high or low in the air according to circumstances, over the surface of swiftly-flowing rivers or the placid waters of jheels and tanks. When not at the breeding colonies they roost in reed-beds and are early astir in the mists of dawn, flitting hither and thither like phantom moths and welcoming the day with their loud hard squeaks. They have no objection to the presence of man, and hawk freely over and about the houses of water-side villages; while a forest fire with its wholesale dispersal of insect life is sufficient to draw them from their usual haunts, in company with other insectivorous birds to share the feast. The alarm-note is a harsh *ret* and the song is a chattering twitter, not so agreeable as that of most other Martins and Swallows.

The nest is a slight pad of grass lined with feathers. It is placed in a chamber at the end of a narrow tunnel, a foot or two long, which is excavated by the bird itself in a sandy bank, numbers of nest-holes being situated together in colonies. The clutch varies from three to five eggs.

The egg is a slightly elongated oval, rather pointed towards the smaller end; the texture is fine and delicate and there is no gloss. The colour is pure white, without markings.

In size the egg averages about 0·68 by 0·48 inches.

THE DUSKY CRAG-MARTIN

Riparia concolor (Sykes)

Description.—Length 5 inches. Sexes alike. Upper plumage, wings and tail dark sooty-brown, a white spot on the inner web of all the tail-feathers except the central and outermost pairs; cheeks, chin, throat and fore-neck rufescent streaked with brown, remainder of lower plumage rufescent grading into sooty-brown.

Iris dark brown; bill and legs brown.

The bill is very weak and flat, with a broad gape, the wings long and pointed, and the tail slightly forked.

Field Identification.—Plains species, generally in twos and threes about houses. Distinguish from Sand-Martin by larger size, much darker colour, and by the row of white spots on the tail; also by the difference in nesting habits.

Distribution.—This is a purely Indian and Burmese species, the typical race extending from the foot of the Himalayas down to the Nilgiris. On the west it is found very locally about Kohat and Bannu and in the South-eastern Punjab, and it occurs in Rajputana though not in Sind. On the east it extends to Behar and Chanda. It is a resident species.

This species may be easily confused with the larger Crag-Martin (*Riparia rupestris*) which breeds in the Himalayas and is fairly common in winter in the hills of Western India from Mount Aboo to the Palnis.

Habits, etc.—Although generally distributed and familiar enough from its habit of breeding in towns, this little Martin is never very abundant and does not gather into the immense flocks in which others of the family may at times be found. A few may be seen wherever a range of cliffs or the ancient ruins of forts or mosques provide a shady lee in which they sail backwards and forwards in a very leisurely manner. Usually two or three will be found together, and as they hawk about they call to each other a soft, melodious *chit-chit-chit*, uttered rapidly. In some of the older towns they nest on the houses and then may be seen in the streets hawking above the heads of passers-by, though usually they prefer places that are not much frequented by mankind.

The breeding season is extended, lasting from January to October according to locality; two broods are reared.

The nest is a semicircular cup composed of pellets of mud, and coming down into a well-defined point beneath. It is applied by the side to a perpendicular surface of wall or rock, but usually in sheltered positions in a niche or under a ledge in a cliff, or under balconies and eaves of houses. The nest is lined first with soft flowering grasses and fragments of straw and then with feathers. The nests are never built in colonies, though chance may cause two or three pairs to occupy any suitable site.

The eggs are rather elongated ovals, sometimes rather pointed towards the small end. The texture is fine and fragile with a slight gloss. The ground-colour is white, and they are all more or less thickly speckled and spotted, and sometimes blotched, with different shades of yellowish- and reddish-brown. These markings tend to collect towards the broad end.

In size the eggs average about 0·72 by 0·52 inches.

THE WIRE-TAILED SWALLOW

Hirundo smithii Leach

Description.—Length 5 inches, with a lengthened wire-like shaft to the outer pair of tail-feathers 7 inches extra. Sexes alike, except that the wire is shorter in the female. Top of the head bright chestnut; sides of the head and neck and the whole upper plumage glossy steel-blue, concealed portions of the wings and tail dark brown; all the tail-feathers except the two central pairs with a white spot on the inner web ; lower plumage white.

Iris dark brown ; bill and legs black.

Bill weak with a broad gape ; wings long and pointed.

Field Identification.—Plains and lower hills ; invariably near water. A dark steel-blue swallow, with chestnut cap and white under parts. At a close range the wires in the tail afford easy identification, but at a distance it may be recognised from any other swallow by the pure shining white of the lower surface and wing lining.

Distribution.—The Wire-tailed Swallow is divided into two races ; one is purely African and is found in various parts of that continent. ***H. s. filifera***, the Indian race, is widely spread, ranging from the Himalayas where it is found up to 5000 feet south to Mysore and the Nilgiris. On the west it ranges to the North-west Frontier Province

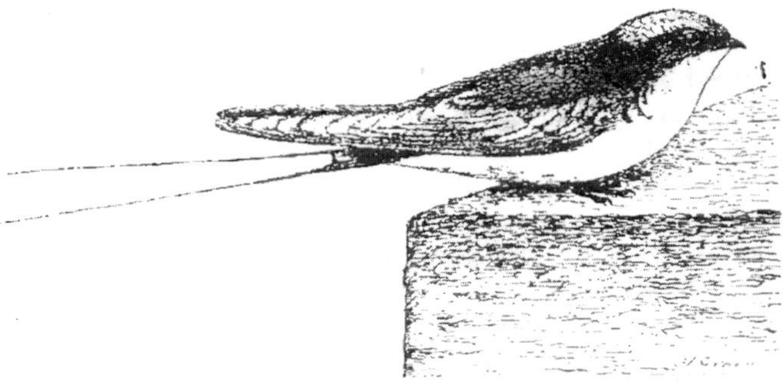

FIG. 35—Wire-tailed Swallow ($\frac{2}{3}$ nat. size)

and Sind. On the east it is found as far as Bengal, reappearing again in Pegu and Tenasserim. In the main a resident bird, it is also migratory in many areas.

The familiar Swallow of Europe (*Hirundo rustica*) breeds along the Himalayas, in very great numbers in Kashmir, and occurs throughout India in winter. The combination of the long forked tail, absence of a pale rump band, the red throat patch and dark gorget and the warm creamy flush to the white under parts allow of easy identification.

Habits, etc.—The Wire-tailed Swallow is essentially a bird of the neighbourhood of water. In particular it is fond of the great canals of Northern India, skimming over their surface with its long tail-wires conspicuous and its bright colours flashing in the sun. Where canals are not available it frequents the neighbourhood of rivers, streams and jheels, and also is partial to rice fields ; but in heavy forest, in desert areas, and over wide cultivated plains it will not be found.

This species never collects or breeds in colonies, though family parties are seen in the breeding season, and on migration a few join the flocks of other migrating Swallows and Martins. The twittering note and short sweet song are very similar to those of other Swallows. This species perches very freely on telegraph-wires and the parapets of bridges and wells, but it does not as a rule perch on trees, and only descends to the ground to gather mud for its nest.

Long after they are able to fly the young are fed in the air by the old birds, parent and youngster circling round and round, and then with a complacent twitter clinging together for an instant during which the mouthful of insects is transferred.

The breeding season is very prolonged and two broods are reared; most eggs will be found from March to August, the time varying with the locality, but eggs have been found in every month of the year except December.

The nest is a rather shallow cup composed of mud pellets, fastened at one side to a slanting or perpendicular surface of wall or rock. It is lined with feathers. The situation chosen may be under a bridge or culvert, under shelves of rock, or in the arches and under the roofs of buildings. If not immediately over water, where it is very often within a foot or two of the surface, it is always in its near vicinity, and nests have been recorded even down inside wells. Most of the building is done by the female, the male accompanying her but not as a rule carrying any mud.

The clutch consists of three or four eggs. In shape they are a long narrow oval, rather pointed at the smaller end. The texture is fine and delicate with a slight gloss. The ground-colour is white and the markings consist of speckles, spots and blotches of reddish-brown and brownish-red; there is the usual tendency for the markings to collect towards the broad end.

The eggs measure about 0·72 by 0·53 inches.

THE CLIFF-SWALLOW

Hirundo fluvicola Jerdon

Description.—Length 5 inches. Sexes alike. Top of the head dull chestnut with black shaft-streaks; a broad line through the eye dull brown; back and shoulders glossy steel-blue; wings, tail and rump dull brown; entire lower plumage white, more or less tinged with fulvous and streaked with brown, except on the abdomen.

Iris brown; bill black; legs dark brown.

The tail is very slightly forked; bill weak with a broad gape; wings long and pointed.

Field Identification.—Plains species, highly gregarious, nesting in colonies near water and building immense clusters of mud nests. Very similar in size, shape and demeanour to Sand-Martins (with which it often flies), but distinguished by the chestnut cap and blue-black back.

Distribution.—A purely Indian species. It is found through a considerable portion of India, from Rawal Pindi and the foot-hills of the Himalayas (up to 2500 feet) in the north to Coimbatore in the south. On the west its boundary is not accurately known, but it is not found in Sind or the South-western Punjab ; it extends to the east as far as Gonda, Mirzapur and the Wardha Valley. A local migrant.

Another small species, the Nilgiri Swallow (*Hirundo javanica*), with steel-blue upper parts, chestnut throat and grey below, is a common resident in the higher hill ranges of South-western India. It is very familiar about dwellings and builds the ordinary cup type of mud nest.

Habits, etc.—This is one of the purely social Swallows, spending all its life both in and out of the breeding season in big flocks which never separate. It is somewhat local and erratic in its distribution, but within its range it abounds wherever there is water, in combination with cliffs or masonry against which it can plaster its huge nest colonies.

The flocks usually hawk about in the near vicinity of water, often in company with Sand-Martins, which in flight they somewhat resemble. On the wing the birds sing very often, the feeble twittering song typical of the family. They drink a good deal, sweeping down and taking mouthfuls from the surface of the water, and the newly-fledged young are fed on the wing.

This species is double-brooded, nesting from February to April, and again in July and August. The nest is made of tiny pellets of clay which the birds collect from the ground with their beaks, and it consists of a small circular chamber entered through a short tubular mouth. This entrance tube is not applied to the surface against which the nest is constructed, after the fashion of the Striated Swallows, but it sticks out from the side of the nest into the air free of attachment. Numbers of nests are built together in a cluster, and with their tubular mouths they present rather a peculiar appearance, somewhat like a honeycomb in which each cell is a separate nest. A colony may consist of any number of nests, from twenty to about six hundred, so that in the areas which it inhabits this Swallow is often very abundant. The nests are lined with dry grass and feathers.

The favourite site for one of the colonies is on the face of overhanging cliffs or beneath the arches of masonry bridges ; but perpendicular sites, like the walls of buildings, are not despised, and the bird appears to be indifferent whether the colony is in a secluded lonely spot or in a busy thoroughfare ; but the close vicinity of water is essential.

The clutch consists normally of three eggs, but four are sometimes found.

The egg is variable in shape but is normally a long oval, pointed towards the smaller end. The texture is fine and delicate, with a slight gloss. The ground-colour is pure white, some eggs being unmarked, others being slightly mottled, speckled or clouded with pale yellowish- or reddish-brown. These markings tend to congregate at the broad end.

The eggs measure about 0·76 by 0·53 inches.

THE RED-RUMPED SWALLOW

HIRUNDO DAURICA Linnæus

Description.—Length 6 inches. Sexes alike. Upper plumage glossy steel-blue, except the rump which is chestnut; concealed portions of wings and tail dark brown, an indistinct white patch on the inner web of the outermost tail-feather; sides of the head mixed rufous and brown, the ear-coverts and a more or less distinct collar round the neck chestnut; the whole lower plumage pale rufous finely streaked with brown.

Iris brown; bill and legs black.

The bill is weak and small with a wide gape; wings long and pointed; tail deeply forked.

Field Identification.—Rather more deliberate in flight than the other true Swallows, and the tail appears differently shaped owing to the different angle of the fork; seen from above the chestnut rump is unmistakable, and from below the uniformly striated under parts.

Distribution.—The Red-rumped, Striated or Mosque Swallows are a widely-spread group which occur from Southern Europe and Africa to China, and in this great range are divided into a number of races. Within our area we are concerned with four: *H. d. erythropygia* breeds throughout the plains of India from about 4000 feet along the Outer Himalayas down into the Nilgiris; on the west it extends to Cutch, the Punjab and the North-west Frontier Province (though not apparently to Sind); and on the east to about Calcutta. In the Himalayas it is replaced by *H. d. nipalensis* as a breeding bird; to the west this form breeds in a higher zone from 4000 to about 9000 feet; to the east it replaces *H. d. erythropygia* even in the foot-hills. This race is rather larger, with a more deeply-forked tail, the rump patch is paler in colour, and the under parts are more heavily striated. A third form, *H. d. scullii*, like the last in colour but smaller, comes into our area as a breeding bird in Kashmir, Gilgit and the Afghan and Baluchistan borders. *H. d. japonica*, breeding in Manchuria, China and Japan, appears in India as a winter visitor. All races are to some extent migratory, and in winter all will be found in similar localities in the plains, but their movements require working out.

Habits, etc.—Like other members of the family these Swallows are chiefly remarkable for their nesting habits. During the breeding season they are found in pairs which frequent the neighbourhood of buildings and therefore of man, and from their tameness attract his attention. On migration and during the winter they collect into small parties or into flocks numbering up to 200 or 300 individuals. They spend the greater part of the hours of daylight on the wing, flying backwards and forwards over a self-appointed beat, hawking insects on the wing, occasionally resting on telegraph-wires and more

FIG. 36—Red-rumped Swallow (½ nat. size)

rarely on trees and buildings. The flight is slower and more deliberate than that of the English Swallow and the note is rather different, a plaintive *pin*. The nest is a remarkable structure of fine mud pellets collected by the birds, a mouthful at a time, from the edges of puddles, and it takes several weeks to build; it is usually described as "retort-shaped," and is always built under rocks or culverts or bridges or under the ceilings of houses and verandahs; a narrow tubular passage, like a white ant gallery on a large scale, some 2 inches in diameter and from 4 to 10 inches in length, runs along the under surface of the rock or roof and enters a round hemispherical chamber also applied to the under surface of the site and with no other entrance than the passage. The whole affair is rather large for the size of the birds, and the egg-chamber is sparingly lined with pieces of dry grass and feathers. The same site is used year after year, though the actual nest is usually destroyed by the elements.

1. Rufous-fronted Wren-Warbler. 2. Lesser Whitethroat. 3. Chiffchaft.
4. Large Crowned Willow-Wren. 5. Indian Wren-Warbler.
6. Brown Hill-Warbler. (All about $\frac{3}{5}$ nat. size.)

[*Face p.* 242

The breeding season lasts from April to August, but July is the month in which most eggs will be found; probably because a structure of dry mud would be more likely to give way under the influence of the dry heat before the rains commence.

The normal clutch consists of three eggs though four may be found. They are long, oval in shape, slightly compressed towards one end, with shells of exquisite fineness and with a very slight gloss. The colour is pure unmarked white.

They average about 0·78 by 0·55 inches.

THE WHITE WAGTAIL

Motacilla alba Linnæus

(Plate xiv, Fig. 6, opposite page 286)

Description.—Length 8 inches. Male in winter plumage: A patch on the back of the head roughly connected with a crescentic gorget on the breast black; remainder of head and lower plumage white, tinged with ashy on the flanks; upper plumage ashy-grey; wings black, the feathers broadly margined with grey and white; tail black, the two outer pairs of feathers largely white.

In summer plumage from the chin to the breast is black.

The female is duller and less distinctly marked.

The above description applies to the adult winter male of *M. a. dukhunensis*, but the species is very variable in its plumage according to age and season, as are the other races, and the identification of these Wagtails is a matter of much study. A rough guide to Indian birds is given below.

Iris dark brown; bill and legs black.

Field Identification.—The White Wagtails are small, dainty birds of black, white and grey plumage, which walk about on the ground, usually in parties, incessantly wagging their long tails up and down; partial to the neighbourhood of water, wading in shallow portions of it.

Distribution.—The White Wagtail is a very widely-spread species, breeding in various forms almost throughout Europe, North-western Africa and Northern Asia. The dark resident form of the British Isles is known under the familiar name of the Pied Wagtail. Four of these races are found commonly in various parts of India. The only one of these four that breeds with us is *M. a. alboides*, which is the common breeding Wagtail of Kashmir, parts of the higher Himalayas and Southern Tibet. In the winter it moves down into the foot-hills from Kashmir to Assam and also Burma. *M. a. personata* breeds in Turkestan, Gilgit, Afghanistan and Eastern Persia, and is common in the plains of India in winter, extending to Belgaum in the south and

Calcutta in the east. It commences to arrive in August and September and departs in April and May.

M. a. dukhunensis is the West Siberian breeding race whose range extends west to the Caucasus, Volga and Urals. It arrives about September and October and leaves again in April and May, having spread meanwhile throughout the whole of the plains down to Travancore.

M. a. leucopsis breeds in Eastern Siberia and China, and in winter visits the eastern side of India to about Nepal and Mirzapur on the west and also Assam and Burma.

The four races of White Wagtail that occur in India afford a curious case of parallelism; they may be divided into two sections by the colour of the ear-coverts and sides of the neck, and in each of these sections in full breeding plumage one form has the back grey and the other black. All four races of White Wagtail can easily be distinguished from the Large Pied Wagtail by their white foreheads, the black on the head extending to the base of the beak in the latter species, which also has a different series of moults and plumages.

M. a. dukhunensis and *M. a. leucopsis* both have the ear-coverts and sides of the neck white. In the former bird the back is grey and in the latter black in breeding plumage.

M. a. personata and *M. a. alboides* have the ear-coverts and sides of the neck black. In breeding plumage here also the first form is grey on the back and the latter black.

In all four races the back normally becomes grey in winter plumage, though usually a few black feathers remain in the black-backed forms to indicate the type of summer plumage. *M. a. leucopsis* and *M. a. dukhunensis* may then, however, be separated by the greater wing-coverts, which have their outer webs entirely white in the former and merely margined with white in the latter. *M. a. personata* and *M. a. alboides* have no distinguishing mark in the absence of black feathers on the back. There is, however, a great deal of variation in the plumage of Wagtails in India in winter, and considerable study is required before individuals can be correctly identified.

Habits, etc.—In winter the habits of all four races of White Wagtail are very similar, and indeed two or three races may often be found associating together. The White Wagtail is a sociable bird, usually occurring in parties which collect together into large flocks about the migration periods and often associate with other species. They occasionally perch in trees or on buildings, but most of their time is spent feeding on the ground, preferably in damp places or actually about the margins of water, into which they wade freely. Forest country is avoided, and in very dry localities they are comparatively scarce. Where possible they roost in reed beds and at suitable places very large numbers of White Wagtails, Yellow Wagtails, and Yellow-headed

Wagtails collect together at night. The most marked characteristic is indicated by the name ; as the bird runs about—for it never hops—the long tail is incessantly wagged up and down. The flight also is very characteristic in long, dipping curves, and on the wing the call-note *chiz-zit* is constantly uttered. The song is a pleasant but poor performance.

Our only breeding race builds in Kashmir from May to July, a cup-nest on or near the ground, in hollows under stones or in heaps of drift wood. The nest is composed of dry grasses, roots, bents, and similar rubbish, and the cup is lined with hair. The clutch consists of four or five eggs.

The egg is a rather broad oval, pointed towards the small end, fine in texture with a slight gloss. The ground-colour is greyish-white, speckled and spotted finely and closely, with pale brown and brownish-grey. There is a tendency for the markings to be thicker at the broad end.

The egg measures about 0·78 to 0·62 inches.

THE LARGE PIED WAGTAIL

Motacilla maderaspatensis Gmelin

Description.—Length 9 inches. Adult male : A broad white streak over the eye from the nostril to behind the ear ; head, upper breast and entire upper plumage black ; wings black, the quills finely edged with white, and a broad tapering white patch running the whole length of the folded wing ; tail black, the two outer pairs of feathers largely white ; remainder of lower plumage white, tinged with ashy on the flanks. The female resembles the male, but the black is not so pure in tone being usually mixed with ashy-brown.

Iris dark brown ; bill and legs black.

Field Identification.—Found singly or in small family parties by water, walking about on the ground and wagging the long tail. Rather larger and darker than the White Wagtails, and has the black of the forehead extending to the beak and enclosing a white eye streak. The only species of Wagtail that breeds in India south of the Himalayas.

Distribution.—Confined to India and Ceylon. This Wagtail occurs throughout India from the North-west Frontier Province and Sind (where it is rare) to the Duars and Western Bengal, and from the Outer Himalayas, which it ascends to 5000 feet, to Cape Comorin ; in the Nilgiris it is found at all elevations in the neighbourhood of water. It avoids the low country of Bengal proper. A purely resident species.

Habits, etc.—This Wagtail is found solitary, in pairs or in family parties, in the neighbourhood of water, provided that it be running water or ponds or tanks. In ordinary marshy ground, beloved of the Yellow Wagtails, it is not usually found. It feeds along the edges of the water, searching for insects, the long tail incessantly wagging up and down as the bird trips along. It perches freely on rocks and buildings, but practically never settles on trees. It is curiously partial to the clumsy ferry-boats that ply on the larger Indian rivers, and not only perches and voyages on them, but on occasion even nests in them. The flight of this and other Wagtails is rather distinctive, jerky, with an incessant rise and fall in the air in a series of undulating curves; and they share with the Larks and Pipits the distinction of being the smallest birds that walk and run on the ground as opposed to hopping like Robins and Sparrows. The call-note is a loud *chiz-zit*, chiefly uttered in flight, and there is a short musical song.

The breeding season is from March to May, but eggs have been found in December and January on the Cauvery.

The nesting habits of this species are very variable; it will nest in any sort of hole provided that it is close to water, though it occasionally stretches this definition to include the drainage holes on roofs. In such places it either lays its eggs on bare earth in the bottom of the hole, or makes the very scantiest of nests consisting of a few blades of grass, or a tolerably well-made cup of all sorts of varied materials, grass, hair, wool, tow, roots, fibres, string and the like. In fact, Hume's description of it as an irregularly-minded bird is the only just way of describing its nesting habits.

The normal clutch consists of four eggs, though three or five are sometimes laid. The eggs, too, are variable, either long or broad ovals in shape, rather pointed towards the smaller end. The ground-colour varies from pale brownish to greenish-white. The markings are clouds, smudges, streaks, spots and specks of brown of various shades in every possible combination.

In size the egg measures about 0·9 by 0·65 inches.

THE GREY WAGTAIL

MOTACILLA CINEREA Tunstall

Description.—Length 8 inches. Male and female in winter plumage: The upper plumage bluish-grey tinged with green; a patch at the base of the tail yellowish-green; a dull whitish line over the eye; wings dark brown, edged with yellowish-white; tail black, margined with greenish, the three outer pairs of feathers almost entirely white; chin, throat and fore-neck white; remainder of lower plumage yellow, growing brighter towards the tail.

In summer plumage in the male the chin, throat and fore-neck become black, bordered with a broad white moustachial streak, and with white tips to the black feathers.

In the summer plumage of the female the yellow is less brilliant than in the male, and a variable mixture of black, white and dull yellow take the place of the black patch of the male.

Iris brown ; bill horn-colour, paler at the lower base ; legs fleshy-brown.

Field Identification.—A solitary bird, generally about water. Differs from all the other Wagtails in the comparatively longer and more slender tail and in the blue-grey colour of the upper parts. In flight the long tail and sulphur-yellow belly and under tail-coverts are conspicuous.

Distribution.—The Grey Wagtail is widely distributed, chiefly about mountain streams, in Europe and Northern Asia, migrating southwards to Africa and Southern Asia in winter. It is divided into races, of which only one concerns us.

This Eastern race (*M. c. melanope*) breeds from the Yenesei across Siberia to the Pacific and south to the Himalayas. In winter it spreads throughout the plains of India to Ceylon, and eastwards to Malaysia.

Habits, etc.—During the breeding season in the Himalayas the Grey Wagtail is essentially a bird of the mountain streams and rivers where they flow with considerable strength through boulder-strewn beds. In winter when it appears in India from August until April, it is seldom able to discover these conditions, and then has to be content with tripping about the margins of a variety of tamer waters, and even with feeding on roads and other waterless places. It is a solitary species, and does not gather into flocks like the other Wagtails. The call-note is a rather shrill *tzit-zee*, which is chiefly uttered on the wing as the bird takes to flight and flies swiftly away low over the ground, rising and falling in buoyant curves and exhibiting conspicuous glimpses of the sulphur-yellow of the lower plumage. The tail-wagging of the genus is most pronounced in this species owing to the comparatively greater length of tail.

The breeding season in the Himalayas is in May and June.

The nest is a neat cup of grasses, bents and various roots and fibres, thickly lined with hair. It is built on the ground under boulders in river-beds, or amongst stones and herbage at the edge of streams.

The clutch consists of four or five eggs.

The egg is a broad oval, rather compressed and pointed towards the smaller end, with a fine hard texture but little gloss. The ground-colour is yellowish or brownish-white, closely mottled and clouded all over with pale yellowish-brown and brownish-yellow, with a very uniform effect. A black twisted hair-line or two is generally present about the broad end.

The egg measures about 0·70 by 0·54 inches.

THE YELLOW WAGTAIL

MOTACILLA FLAVA Linnæus

Description.—Length 7 inches. Male in fresh winter plumage: Top of the head bluish-grey, the feathers tipped with olive; upper plumage dull olive-brownish, wings dark brown, edged with fulvous; tail black, narrowly edged with olivaceous, the two outer pairs of feathers white; a broad band on the sides of the head dark slaty-blackish; the whole lower plumage yellow sullied about the breast. In a few individuals there are traces of a white line over the eye.

Male in fresh summer plumage: Top of the head dark slaty-grey; upper plumage yellowish-green; wings and tail as in winter but with the feather edges of the wings decidedly yellowish; a broad band on the sides of the head black; the whole lower plumage bright yellow. Traces of a narrow white line over the eye are sometimes visible.

Female: Resembles the male, but has the head green and upper parts dark olive-brown, greenish-olive on the rump, the yellow of the lower plumage paler and more sullied on the breast, and the band on the sides of the head duller and browner; a fulvous line over the eye is generally present.

This description applies to typical specimens of the race *M. f. thunbergi.* Race, age and sex cause great variation in the plumages of this species which needs expert study.

Iris brown; bill blackish-brown, paler at base of lower mandible; legs dark horn.

Field Identification.—Plains except in the summer; typical Wagtails found in mixed flocks containing two or three forms, of which a small proportion are in bright adult plumage, greenish above yellow below, while the majority are in dull nondescript plumages; always feeding on the ground in damp grassy spots, active and wagging their tails.

Distribution.—In the Yellow Wagtails we have a most difficult group of birds; the adult males may be distinguished with a certain amount of ease, but females and young birds are exceedingly hard to discriminate, and the whole group needs a great deal of study before one can claim to know even a little about them. Here it is possible only to indicate the outlines of the subject.

Formerly it was the custom to treat the various forms of Yellow Wagtail as separate species. More recently various groupings have been adopted, but here I prefer to treat them as geographical races of one widely-distributed species which breeds throughout the greater part of Europe and the Mediterranean countries and Northern Asia, and migrates southward in winter.

No race breeds in India, but we are concerned with the following three forms as common winter visitors :—

Syke's Yellow Wagtail (*M. f. beema*) breeds in West Siberia. Winters in India, south to Belgaum and the Cumbum Valley and east to Calcutta.

The Grey-headed Yellow Wagtail (*M. f. thunbergi*) breeds in North Scandinavia, Russia and Siberia ; migrates through Europe to Africa and to every portion of India, Ceylon and Burma.

The Eastern Black-headed Wagtail (*M. f. melanogrisea*) breeds in Turkestan and winters in India south to Belgaum and east to Benares.

The following key will serve to indicate the salient differences in the adult males of the three races in summer plumage :—

M. f. beema.—Crown paler grey ; cheeks white ; a broad and distinct white superciliary streak over the eye.

M. f. thunbergi.—Crown dark slaty-grey ; cheeks blackish ; superciliary streak very indistinct or absent.

M. f. melanogrisea.—Crown black ; cheeks and ear-coverts deep black ; superciliary streak very indistinct or absent.

Care must, however, be taken not to confuse the Yellow Wagtails with the three races of the Yellow-headed Wagtail (*Motacilla citreola*) that also appear in India in winter, and of which one race breeds commonly in the Himalayas. The adult males of this species have the entire head bright yellow, and at all ages and seasons the Yellow-headed Wagtails may be distinguished from the Yellow Wagtails by a broad yellow superciliary streak and by a certain amount of yellow on the forehead.

An olive-brown Wagtail with two black bands across the breast, which wags its tail from side to side, not up and down, is the Forest Wagtail (*Dendronanthus indicus*), found chiefly in North-east India, Assam, Burma, and Southern India.

Habits, etc.—The Yellow Wagtails, as we know them in winter, are birds of marked and typical habit. They commence to arrive in Northern India at the end of August and pass through on passage until about October ; they start to return to Northern India about February and have left again by the end of April. Farther south of course their status varies proportionately.

They are found in flocks mingled irrespective of race, and spend their days feeding on the ground in open grassy places, preferably damp in character, or about the edges of jheels or in the pastures that surround the larger rivers. They are very partial to the neighbourhood of droves of cattle, feeding all round the legs of the grazing animals, no doubt finding that their presence attracts or disturbs a varied insect life. In suitable places very large numbers collect, and morning and evening they flight in a most conspicuous manner, travelling at a moderate height above the ground with the dipping flight and shrill *chiz-zit* calls which are common to all Wagtails. They roost at night in reed-beds, and suitable places are used by immense congregations of the various forms of Yellow Wagtails, Yellow-headed Wagtails and White Wagtails.

In their northern quarters the Yellow Wagtails breed about June, building a well-concealed nest of grasses and bents with a thick lining of hair. It is placed on the ground in thick vegetation in low-lying, damp ground or cultivation.

The eggs vary from four to seven in number, and are rather broad ovals, pointed towards the small end, with a fine texture and little gloss. They are ochraceous-grey or brown in colour, so finely speckled as to be almost uniform, and generally exhibit one or two black hair streaks.

In size the eggs average about 0·75 by 0·55 inches.

THE INDIAN TREE-PIPIT

Anthus hodgsoni Richmond

Description.—Length 6 inches. Sexes alike. The whole upper plumage brown with a greenish tinge, the feathers streaked or centred with blackish except on the rump; wing dark brown, margined with fulvous; tail dark brown, the two outer pairs of feathers tipped diagonally with white; a broad streak over the eye fulvous, growing white posteriorly; lower plumage pale fulvous, the whole breast and sides of the throat boldly streaked with black; flanks washed with olivaceous and faintly streaked.

Iris dark brown; bill dark brown, base of lower mandible fleshy; legs flesh-colour.

In summer the greenish tinge wears off, and the eye streak becomes white.

Field Identification.—A small brown bird, whitish below, streaked with blackish above and about the breast; found in parties feeding on the ground in shady spots and flying up into the trees when disturbed; has a faint plaintive note and wags the shortish tail after the fashion of a Wagtail, only more slowly.

Distribution.—This Pipit breeds in Siberia, Northern China, and Japan, and on the higher Himalayas about 7000 to 12,000 feet. In winter it migrates southwards to Southern Japan, Southern China, Cochin-China, and India. At that season it is found in India throughout the greater portion of the plains, occurring as far west as Rajputana and Guzerat, and in the foot-hills of the Himalayas to Dharamsala.

Southwards it extends to the Palni Hills. Himalayan breeding birds are heavily streaked and belong to the race *A. h. berezowskii*. Most birds found in winter in the Peninsula belong to the lightly streaked typical form.

The closely-allied Tree-Pipit (*Anthus trivialis*) which lacks the greenish tinge on the upper parts and has a less conspicuous eye-stripe fulvous throughout, is a winter visitor practically throughout India. It breeds in Europe and Northern Asia, including the higher ranges of the Western Himalayas.

Hodgson's Pipit (*Anthus roseatus*) which breeds at high elevations in the Himalayas and winters in Northern India and Assam, is rather similar to these two Pipits but may be recognised from them and all other Indian forms by the primrose-yellow under wing-coverts. In breeding plumage the throat and breast become vinaceous.

Habits, etc.—In winter this Pipit is found in small parties which frequent fairly open country with plenty of shady trees; they are partial to gardens, groves of mango trees and similar situations, and feed quietly on the ground in sparse herbage, collecting small insects and the seeds of grass and weeds. When disturbed they fly up into the nearest tree with a short plaintive call and wait quietly there until the coast is clear for them to resume their feeding. When in trees they walk about on the boughs in a manner unusual amongst small passerine birds, and have a habit of swaying their tails up and down, after the fashion of a Wagtail. The flight is rather slow and dipping, similar to that of the latter bird. In the breeding seasoh the male has a fine song, Lark-like in character, rather than the usual wheezy Pipit song. It is uttered as the bird flies into the air and then volplanes with wings and tail outspread down to the ground or to the topmost twig of a tree.

The breeding season in the Himalayas is from May to July. The nest is a shallow cup composed of moss and dry grass, lined with fine dry grass-stems and a few hairs, and it is placed in a hollow in the ground, in the shelter of a tuft of foliage or a creeping plant, such as *Cotoneaster*. It is built either on an Alpine pasture above the limits of tree-level, or in open grassy glades in the midst of the higher mountain forests. The bird is very shy at the nest and is then observed with difficulty, either disappearing into the forests or rising into the air in a series of jerky flights. When flushed off the nest it sometimes flutters down the hill-side as if wounded.

The clutch consists of four eggs. The egg is a slightly elongated oval, rather pointed towards the small end; the texture is fine with a slight gloss. In colour the eggs are closely speckled with dingy rather purplish-brown, so closely and evenly marked that no ground-colour is visible.

They measure about 0·90 by 0·65 inches.

THE INDIAN PIPIT

ANTHUS RUFULUS Vieillot

(Plate XIV, Fig. 1, opposite page 286)

Description.—Length 6 inches. Sexes alike. Upper plumage fulvous-brown, the feathers centred with blackish-brown; a fulvous streak over the eye; wings dark brown margined with fulvous; tail dark brown, the outermost feather almost entirely white, the next to it with an oblique white tip; lower plumage pale fulvous, darker on the flanks, the sides of the throat and fore-neck and the whole breast streaked with dark brown.

Iris brown; bill brown, base of lower mandible yellow; legs flesh-colour.

The claw of the hind toe is long and slender, longer than the toe itself.

Field Identification.—A small brown bird, pale fulvous below and streaked on the breast, which runs about on the ground, rising with a plaintive note and a flash of white in the tail, to settle again but a short distance away. Distinguished from the Tree-Pipits by the long hind claw and the fact that it does not settle in trees. It must, however, be remembered that several species of Pipit are locally common in India, and their identification is a matter of considerable knowledge and experience.

Distribution.—This Pipit occurs throughout practically the whole of India, Burma and Ceylon, breeding in the plains and also in suitable places in the Himalayas and other ranges up to about 5000 feet. Farther east it extends to Siam, Lombok and Timor. In the main it is a resident species though it performs certain local migrations. There are several races. The typical race is found throughout the greater part of India, being replaced in the Punjab and Sind by the pale *A. r. waitei* and in the south-west and Ceylon by the darker *A. r. malayensis.*

Practice is required to tell this species from the Tawny Pipit (*Anthus campestris*), a winter visitor to most of India except the extreme south. It is slightly larger, more sandy in colour, and when adult unspotted on the breast.

There are two very large Pipits (length 8 inches) in India, easily separated by the length of the hind claw. The Brown Rock Pipit (*Anthus similis*) breeds in the Western Himalayas, Baluchistan, the Salt Range, the Western Ghats and the Nilgiris. It has a short hind claw. Richard's Pipit (*Anthus richardi*) with a long hind claw is a winter visitor to India, most common in Bengal and the Madras Presidency.

Habits, etc.—This Pipit is essentially a bird of cultivation with low crops and of grass-land; it is particularly partial to the stretches of sandy soil with closely-grazed grass which are found about the margins of jheels and in the dry beds of the larger rivers. Here it runs and feeds on the turf, rising when disturbed with the slightly plaintive note which is typical of the genus. It is usually found in pairs, which are jealous of their respective territories, driving away birds of the same species and possible enemies such as Shrikes.

This Pipit perches freely on bushes and tufts of grass, but usually only when breeding; it does not settle on trees. In the breeding display the male rises in the air in one ascending succession of dipping curves, uttering all the time a jangling, rather Bunting-like song; arrived at the highest point in the air he then falls to earth again, in an abrupt curve, with stiff, partly extended wings. When disturbed suddenly from the nest the female flutters along the ground as if wounded, a habit common to most of the Pipits.

The breeding season extends from March to July and two broods are apparently raised. The nest is placed on the ground under or in the midst of tufts of grass; it is usually cup-shaped, but in some examples there is a slight dome. It is composed of dry shreds and blades of coarse grass, or fine dry roots, with a slight lining of fine pieces of root and grass with a few hairs.

Three or four eggs are laid, but the former number is more common.

The eggs are moderately broad and rather perfect ovals, scarcely pointed at all towards the small end; they are hard in texture with a slight gloss. In colour they are brownish- or greenish-stone colour, thickly streaked, clouded, and spotted with dull brownish- or purplish-red, with brown of different shades and pale purplish-grey. These markings often tend to form a cap at the broad end, and altogether there is a good deal of variation in shape and colour between different clutches.

They measure about 0·8 by 0·6 inches in size.

THE LITTLE SKYLARK

Alauda gulgula Franklin

(Plate xv, Fig. 5, opposite page 286)

Description.—Length 6 inches. Sexes alike. Upper plumage, including a short indistinct crest, brown with darker centres and tawny margins to the feathers; a pale fulvous streak over the eye; wings dark brown, the feathers margined with rufous; tail dark brown, margined with rufous, the two outer pairs of feathers largely pale buff; lower plumage pale buff, washed with fulvous on the sides and breast, the throat spotted and the chest streaked with brown.

Iris dark brown; bill and legs yellowish-brown.

The hind claw is very long and straight.

Field Identification.—A streaked brown bird, buffish-white below and with pale buff edges to the tail which become conspicuous in flight. Feeds and settles on the ground in open country, but sings in a characteristic soaring flight. Distinguished from the Pipits by the heavier build, short crest, the more crouching gait, and the fact that when approached it squats instead of running.

Distribution.—The Little Skylark is found throughout a large area of Southern Asia from Turkestan eastwards to Siam and Cochin-China and southwards to Ceylon and Tenasserim. It is divided into several races distinguished by size and depth of coloration, and these are sometimes treated as races of the well-known Skylark of Europe (*Alauda arvensis*), of which one race, *A. a. intermedia*, arrives in North-western India in winter in large numbers. It appears, however, better to keep the two species separate. We are concerned with several races of the smaller bird which vary in small details of size and tint. The Turkestan race, *A. g. inconspicua*, just comes into our area in Baluchistan. *A. g. lhamarum* is the breeding bird of the higher Himalayas from Kashmir to Sikkim, at heights from 5000 to 14,000 feet, wandering in winter in flocks down to the foot-hills. *A. g. weigoldi* breeds at high elevations in Bhutan and S. Tibet. *A. g. punjaubi* is the pale bird of the Punjab and the United Provinces as far east as Moghulserai and Dinapur. *A. g. australis* is the large and dark bird of the Nilgiris, Cochin and Travancore, whilst the typical race occupies the rest of Eastern, Central and Southern India and also Ceylon.

The flocks of Skylarks (*A. a. intermedia*) which arrive in winter may be distinguished by the larger size and more pointed wing, the 5th primary falling short of the tip of the wing by over 5 millimetres.

Habits, etc.—The Skylark is a bird of open country, dwelling almost exclusively in cultivation or on grazing lands contiguous to it. In such localities it lives and feeds on the ground, picking up seeds and insects and fallen grains of all the cultivated cereals. On the ground it is quite inconspicuous, both owing to its protectively coloured plumage and to its habit of preferring to squat instead of running when approached. It squats as long as possible; then suddenly springs into life with a liquid bubbling *chirrup*, and flies low over the ground with a fluttering undulating flight, only mounting high into the air if it proposes to travel far.

In spring the males have a well-sustained though rather monotonous song, into which the imitations of other birds' calls are introduced. When singing the bird mounts to a great height in the air, almost vertically, with the head to the wind and the wings fanning rapidly; having attained its pitch it remains there for a long time, keeping roughly in the same place; it starts to descend in the same fashion as it rose, but when it is some 25 yards or so from the ground the song ceases, and the bird falls rapidly with the wings held stiffly open. The song is also occasionally uttered on the ground.

The breeding season is from March to July, and even later till November in the Southern Indian race. Two broods are reared.

The nest is placed on the ground in a shallow depression scratched by the birds themselves, sheltered by a clod of earth, a tuft of grass or a small stunted bush. It is a shallow cup of dry grass, usually lined with finer grasses. Three to five eggs are laid.

The egg is a moderately broad oval, rather pointed towards the smaller end, with a fine silky texture and a slight gloss. The ground-colour is greyish- or yellowish-white, concealed almost entirely by the markings which are fine spots and frecklings of pale yellowish-brown, purplish-brown or very pale inky-purple.

In size the eggs measure about 0·83 by 0·62 inches.

THE SHORT-TOED LARK

CALANDRELLA BRACHYDACTYLA (Leisler)

Description.—Length 6 inches. Sexes alike. Upper plumage pale greyish mealy-buff, the feathers streaked with blackish-brown; wings dark brown edged with fulvous; tail dark brown edged with fulvous, the two outer pairs of feathers partly very pale buff; a buff streak over the eye; lower plumage dull whitish, washed with brown on the breast which is sometimes streaked; a half-concealed blackish spot on each side of the breast.

Iris brown; bill dark horny-brown, fleshy below; legs brownish-flesh-colour.

Field Identification.—Winter visitor in large flocks to the plains of India, feeding in stubbles and open barren country; a small sandy-coloured Lark with a dull semi-concealed dark spot on each side of its breast in place of the usual streakings.

Distribution.—The Short-toed Lark is a widely distributed bird in Europe, Northern Africa and Asia, and is divided into a number of races, the identification and distribution of which are a matter of considerable difficulty. The differences are based on small details of colour, tint and measurement. Two forms are found amongst the hordes which appear as winter visitors in India. *C. b. longipennis*, the grey-tinted breeding bird of Eastern Central Asia, is found in the north-west of India down to a line roughly between Bombay and

Kumaon ; while to the south-east of that line down to about Belgaum and into Assam a more rufous bird (*C. b. dukhunensis*) appears.

A very closely allied species (*Calandrella acutirostris*) also appears locally in India in winter. This may be distinguished without difficulty from the forms of *C. brachydactyla* by an examination of the tip of the wing, as it has the first four long primaries equal, whereas in *C. brachydactyla* the fourth long primary is considerably shorter than the first three which are equal.

A third and smaller species of Short-toed Lark, the Sand-Lark (*Calandrella raytal*), with two races is found as a resident in India. This is most easily distinguished by the fact that it spends its whole life about the sand-banks of the larger rivers, running about near the edge of the water.

Habits, etc.—The Short-toed Lark is only a winter visitor to India, arriving about September and leaving in April. Numerically it must be very abundant, as it is found in flocks often of large size, and these flocks are common in open country, feeding both in stubbles and on waste ground generally, even on that of the most strictly desert character. The food consists of small seeds, but insects are also eaten. These birds never perch except on the ground, where owing to their small size and protective coloration they are practically invisible ; when approached the birds of a flock rise irregularly, a dozen or two at a time, and when all are in the air they join into a compact flock which flies with a peculiarly free and swinging motion. The call-note is low and rather harsh. This is one of the birds that is eaten in India under the name of Ortolan, a species which itself is never found amongst the great numbers of birds that figure on the table in India under its name.

The breeding habits of the Short-toed Lark in its more northern home are similar to those of other Larks ; a small cup of dry grass lined with wool and hair is placed in a slight depression of the ground. The eggs vary from three to five ; the ground-colour is yellowish- or brownish-white, finely freckled and spotted with brownish- and ashy-grey spots.

The egg measures about 0·75 by 0·55 inches.

THE BENGAL BUSH-LARK

MIRAFRA ASSAMICA McClelland

Description.—Length 6 inches. Sexes alike. Upper plumage dark ashy-brown streaked with blackish except on the rump ; wings dark brown, the coverts margined with pale ashy and the quills with much chestnut on both webs ; tail brown margined with ashy rufous, the two outer pairs of feathers largely edged with pale rufous; sides of the head mixed fulvous and brown; chin and throat pale fulvous-white; remainder of lower plumage darker fulvous, the breast coarsely streaked with triangular brown marks.

Iris yellowish-brown; bill dusky, fleshy-white below; legs fleshy-white.

Field Identification.—Plains bird, found in open country feeding on the ground and perching often on bushes. Dark ashy-brown above, fulvous below with much chestnut in the flight-feathers. Distinguish from the Red-winged Bush-Lark by its rather heavier build and darker, more ashy upper parts.

Distribution.—This species of Bush-Lark is found throughout the north-eastern part of the Indian Peninsula north and east of a line drawn roughly from Ambala district to Cuttack, extending through Bengal into Assam and thence into parts of Burma. A permanent resident with no races.

The Singing Bush-Lark (*Mirafra javanica*) may be recognised from all other Indian Bush-Larks by having the inner web of the outer tail-feather largely white. It is a curiously local bird, restricted in places even to particular fields, but its general distribution includes almost the whole of India, except the Lower Punjab, Sind, Western Rajputana and parts of the Madras Presidency.

Habits, etc.—This Lark is found in the better watered and fairly well-wooded tracts of its range, frequenting open plains and cultivated fields and often being seen on the roads. It feeds on the ground, collecting small seeds and insects, but perches freely on bushes and small trees, and like the rest of its genus has a breeding flight in which the rather weak song is uttered.

The breeding season is in May and June.

The nest is a loose, flimsy pad of grass and roots, as a rule too loosely constructed to be removed undamaged; it is placed on the ground in a depression overhung by tufts of grass and is usually surmounted by a sketchy dome of grass and roots, with the entrance hole at one side or at the top.

The number of eggs varies from two to five. The egg is a moderately broad oval, fine and delicate in texture with a slight gloss. The ground-colour is white, faintly tinged with grey or stone-colour. The markings consist of fine freckles and spots of yellowish- or pale purplish-brown, with a tendency to collect in a cap or zone about the broad end.

In size they average about 0·83 by 0·61 inches.

R

THE RED-WINGED BUSH-LARK

MIRAFRA ERYTHROPTERA Blyth

(Plate xi, Fig. 5, opposite page 220)

Description.—Length 6 inches. Sexes alike. Upper plumage fulvous-brown, streaked with blackish-brown; wings brown, the coverts edged with fulvous, and both webs of the quills largely chestnut; tail blackish-brown, the central pair of feathers pale brown margined with fulvous, and the two outer pairs of feathers partly pale fulvous; a pale fulvous streak over the eye; chin and throat whitish; remainder of lower plumage pale fulvous, with triangular spots of blackish-brown on the breast.

Iris brown; bill horny-brown, fleshy below; legs flesh-colour.

Field Identification.—A small unobtrusive Lark found in parties on the ground in sandy scrub-covered country broken with cultivation; brown and fulvous in colour with much chestnut in the flight-feathers.

Distribution.—Confined to India. Found throughout the whole of India from the outer foot-hills of the Himalayas to about the latitude of Nellore and east to the longitude of Calcutta. It is divided into two races. A pale race, named *M. e. sindianus*, is found in Lower Sind, in portions of the Punjab, in Jodhpur, and eastwards to Etawah. The rest of the range of the species is occupied by the typical race. A purely resident bird.

There is some doubt as to whether the well-known Madras Bush-Lark (*Mirafra affinis*) is not really a race of this species. It is larger and darker with less chestnut in the wings. It is found south of a line from Orissa through Hyderabad to Belgaum and also in Ceylon and in general is extremely common.

Habits, etc.—This, like other species of Bush-Lark, is somewhat patchily distributed, being common in some localities and absent in others that appear equally suitable. It is typically a bird of sparse desert scrub-jungle, where thorn bushes, light grass and euphorbia grow on a sandy soil mixed with outcrops of rock, though it may also be found in cultivation. It is usually collected in small parties, which feed unobtrusively on the ground, squatting at the approach of an intruder and then suddenly springing into flight; they fly fairly fast but with an erratic rather hesitating course, as if unable to decide in which direction to proceed, and soon settle again after being disturbed. In the breeding season the male has a singing flight in the air, parachuting down to settle either on the ground or on the top of a euphorbia or other bush. This species often perches on telegraph-wires.

The breeding season is rather irregular, and extends from March to October. The nest is a mere pad of grass mixed with a little vegetable fibre in the form of a very shallow saucer. It is built on the ground in various situations, in depressions on open ground or in cover at the base of bushes, and is difficult to find.

The number of eggs varies from three to five, but the normal clutch is four. The egg is of a very perfect oval shape, fine in texture with a slight gloss. The ground-colour is white tinged with greenish or brownish, finely speckled and dotted all over with reddish, brownish or purple; the exact tint and density of the markings is very variable but their distribution is usually uniform.

The egg measures about 0·76 by 0·59 inches.

THE CRESTED LARK

Galerida cristata (Linnæus)

Description.—Length 7 inches. Sexes alike. Upper plumage, including a sharp-pointed crest, earthy-brown, streaked with blackish; wings brown, the feathers with sandy margins, and the quills with a large rufous patch on the inner webs; tail brown, the feathers edged with sandy, the outer pair of feathers largely pale rufous; a pale fulvous streak over the eye; lower plumage pale fulvous streaked with brown on the breast and less distinctly on the flanks.

Iris light brown; bill and legs horn-colour.

Field Identification.—A typical sandy-brown Lark found in open country in Northern India and easily distinguished by the erect tuft of pointed feathers on the head.

Distribution.—A widely-distributed species found throughout the greater part of Europe and South-western Russia, in Northern Africa and a large extent of Asia. It is divided into over twenty races which to some degree are correlated with types of soil. Of these we are concerned with two only. *G. c. chendoola* is the resident bird of India. It is found throughout the north-west parts of Continental India, from the foot-hills of the Himalayas at about 4000 feet down to the Central Provinces and the boundary of Bengal.

G. c. magna, the breeding race of Central Asia, East Persia, Afghanistan and Baluchistan, is a winter visitor in considerable numbers to Sind, and probably other areas of the extreme north-west. It is recognisable by its larger size and more sandy colour. Two allied species, smaller and more rufous in colour, Sykes' Crested Lark (*Galerida deva*) and the Malabar Crested Lark (*Galerida malabarica*) are residents in Peninsular India. The former is widely distributed from Sambhar and Etawah southwards through Central India, the Central Provinces, Bombay Presidency and Hyderabad to Mysore. The latter is confined to the west coast from Ahmedabad to Travancore and Mysore state. The Malabar Crested Lark is the larger and darker of these two species, with the breast more heavily streaked and the light parts of the tail much deeper rufous.

Habits, etc.—The Crested Lark is very common in the sandy open plains of North-western India, both in and about cultivation and in the more desert areas. It lives and feeds on the ground, and likes, in particular, the neighbourhood of rough country tracks and roads where it finds corn and insects about the droppings of passing animals. The resident race is usually found in twos and threes, but the large Central Asiatic race in winter may be found in large flocks of up to a hundred individuals. The bird is far from shy, and on the ground allows a very near approach, walking about with its crest erected and merely flying for a short distance when it does rise. The call-note is a rather sweet *tee-ur*. The song is short and pleasant, and is uttered both on the ground, from the top of a bush or during a soaring flight. This Lark is frequently seen sitting on telegraph-wires.

FIG. 37—Head of Crested Lark ($1\frac{1}{2}$ nat. size)

The breeding season lasts from March to June. The nest is placed on the ground in a depression in the shelter of a small plant or by a stone or clod of earth. It is a shallow, open cup, composed of dry grass with a lining of wool, vegetable fibres or fine grass, and occasionally a few feathers.

The normal clutch consists of three eggs, though four and five are occasionally found. The egg is a broad oval, rather pointed towards the small end, with a fine texture and slight gloss. The ground-colour is greenish- or yellowish-white, speckled, spotted and blotched, with various shades of brown and purple ; the markings are usually regularly distributed, but they sometimes tend to collect in a zone at the broad end.

They measure about 0·87 by 0·65 inches.

THE RUFOUS-TAILED LARK

AMMOMANES PHŒNICURA (Franklin)

Description.—Length 6 inches. Sexes alike. Upper plumage dark brown; wings brown, margined with sandy-brown, much rufous on the inner concealed webs of the quills; tail with its coverts deep rufous, a broad black bar across the end; sides of the head mixed rufous and brown with a pale rufous streak over the eye; entire lower plumage rufous, the chin, throat and breast streaked with brown.

Iris brown; bill horny-brown, base of lower mandible fleshy; legs fleshy. The bill is thick and slightly curved.

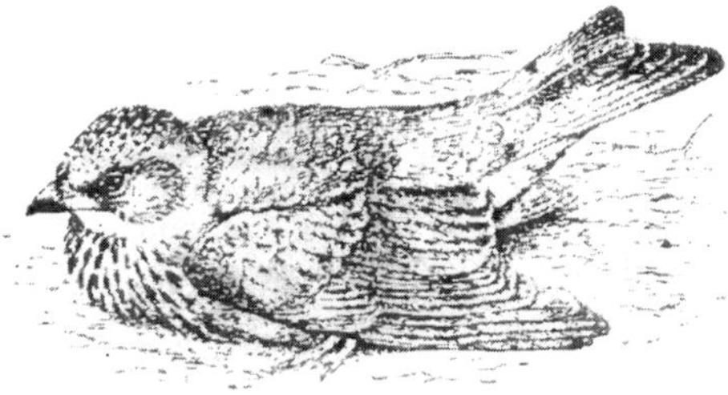

FIG. 38—Rufous-tailed Lark (½ nat. size)

Field Identification.—Plains species; found in parties on open plains; a brown Lark, rufous below, and easily distinguished from all other Larks by the bright rufous tail with a black bar at the end.

Distribution.—This handsome Lark is found in North-western Africa, the Cape Verde Islands, East Persia, West Baluchistan, and India, being divided into several races. Only the typical race is found in India. Its western limit is roughly a line drawn from the Rann of Cutch up to Hissar and thence to the Ganges. The northern boundary is the Ganges itself to about Dinapur, and south of this the bird is found over the whole of the Peninsula down to about Coimbatore. It is a resident species but moves about locally.

The sandy-coloured Desert-Lark (*Ammomanes deserti*), found in other races as far as North-western Africa, is resident in the low desert hills of the North-west. It is chiefly remarkable for the habit of building a little wall of stones round its nest.

Habits, etc.—The Rufous-tailed Lark finds its favourite haunts in open plains, stubbles and ploughed fields, and out of the breeding season is usually found in small parties. It normally keeps to the ground, where it feeds on seeds and insects, but in the breeding season it often perches on a low bush and thence utters its short twirling melodious note. It also perches on telegraph-wires.

The breeding season lasts from February to April. The nest is placed in open fields or plains in a slight depression on the ground, either natural or scratched out by the birds themselves, and is sheltered generally by a clod, or stone or tuft of foliage.

The clutch consists of three or four eggs. The egg is a moderately elongated oval, slightly pointed towards the smaller end; the texture is fine and there is a slight gloss. The ground-colour is creamy or white tinged with yellowish, freckled and speckled all over with yellowish- or reddish-brown and a few secondary markings of pale inky-purple; the markings tend to be most dense at the broad end.

The eggs measure about 0·85 by 0·62 inches.

THE ASHY-CROWNED FINCH-LARK

EREMOPTERYX GRISEA (Scopoli)

Description.—Length 5 inches. Male: Upper plumage pale ashy-brown, concealed portions of the wings dark brown; tail dark brown, central pair of feathers light brown, the outermost pair largely white; a large patch over the ears, and the sides of the breast whitish; remainder of the sides of the face and the lower plumage dark chocolate-brown.

Female: Upper plumage and wings and tail dark brown tinged with grey and rufous; the outer pair of tail-feathers largely white; sides of the face and a line over the eye rufous; lower plumage pale rufous.

Iris brown; bill bluish-flesh, darker above; legs brownish-flesh.

The bill is very short and deep, and curved on the upper surface.

Field Identification.—A small lark, sandy grey-brown in colour, with the lower surface dark chocolate-brown in the male. Found in flocks in open plains country and often very numerous. To be distinguished from the allied species, the Black-crowned Finch-Lark (*Eremopteryx frontalis*) of North-western India, which in the male has a black crown and white forehead.

Distribution.—This Lark is a purely Indian species, except that it occurs also in Ceylon, being found from the foot of the Himalayas to Cape Comorin and from the western borders of Sind and the North-west Frontier Province to the longitude of Calcutta. The birds of the North-west (Sind, Cutch, Punjab, Rajputana and the Western United Provinces), where the annual rainfall is less than 25 inches, are paler in coloration and have been separated as a race, *E. g. siccata*. The Ceylon race (*E. g. ceylonensis*) has a heavy bill. Throughout its habitat the species appears to be resident.

Habits, etc.—This quaint little aberrant Lark is one of the most generally distributed birds of India : it is only found in open country away from trees, and though it occurs up to nearly 3000 feet in the Salt Range it is, strictly speaking, only a species of the plains. It prefers waste ground, fallow fields and semi-desert areas, feeding on the minute seeds that litter the ground. Found in pairs with a strictly defined territory while breeding, it collects, often, into large flocks at other times. On the ground their coloration renders these Larks very inconspicuous, and an observer walking along is often astonished at the number which rise one by one around him and then fly away in a dense flock from ground which was seemingly empty of life.

FIG. 39—Ashy-crowned Finch-Lark ($\frac{2}{3}$ nat. size)

The breeding season lasts from January to September, and apparently two broods are raised. While breeding the males are indefatigable songsters, singing both on the ground and in the air, in the latter case while the bird is rising and falling in a series of deep stoops, keeping over and about the same patch of ground; reaching its highest pitch it closes its wings and falls steeply, to recover and mount again while still some height above the ground. Near the end of its fall, if the observer is close at hand, a whirr can be heard, due to the pressure of the air in the wing-feathers. The song is a sweet but monotonous trill, *trrreeee*, without variation.

The nest is a slight pad of threads and soft vegetable fibres with a few feathers and pieces of fine grass. It is invariably placed on the ground either in a slight depression in the open or in the shelter of a clod of earth, stone or tuft of grass.

The clutch consists of two eggs, but three are sometimes found. The eggs are moderately elongated ovals, slightly pointed at one end, with a slight gloss. The ground-colour is yellowish-, greenish- or greyish-white, marked fairly thickly and in a variety of ways with various shades of yellowish-brown, earth-brown and grey.

In size they average about 0·70 by 0·50 inches.

THE WHITE-EYE

Zosterops palpebrosa (Temminck)

(Plate xiii, Fig. 1, opposite page 264)

Description.—Length 4 inches. Sexes alike. The whole upper plumage greenish golden-yellow, the concealed portions of the wings and tail dark brown; a white ring round the eye, emphasised in front and below by a black mark; chin and throat bright yellow; lower plumage greyish-white; under tail-coverts yellow.

Iris yellow-brown; bill black, bluish-grey on base of lower mandible; legs plumbeous.

The bill is slender, curved and pointed.

Field Identification.—Plains and hills; purely arboreal; very abundant. A small, bright yellow bird with greyish-white breast and abdomen, liable to be mistaken for a Willow-Wren, but easily distinguished by the sharp little curved black beak and the white ring round the eye. The constant *tseer-tseer* note is also distinctive.

Distribution.—The White-Eyes or Zosteropidæ are a large family of small birds spread over Africa, Southern Asia and Australia. The present species has a wide distribution in Asia and is divided into a number of races, of which we are concerned with four only, which differ only in small details of size and tint of coloration. The typical form is found from Sikkim and Bhutan eastwards to Assam and Yunnan, and southwards to Bengal and probably Orissa and the Eastern Central Provinces. *Z. p. occidentis* is found along the Himalayas from the extreme north-west to Nepal, breeding normally up to 8000 feet and even higher. In the plains it is found as far west as Kohat, and from there it extends through the whole of North-western India south to Mysore. In Sind it is unknown except for a small isolated colony in the mangrove swamps of Karachi. *Z. p. nilgiriensis* is the race found in the Nilgiri and Travancore ranges, while *Z. p. salimalii* is confined to the Eastern Ghats as far north as the Godavari. In the main a resident species the White-Eye is also locally migratory.

Habits, etc.—The White-Eye is a purely arboreal species which practically never descends to the ground. It is found indiscriminately

PLATE XIII

1. White-Eye. 2. Baya Weaver-bird. 3. Short-billed Minivet. 4. Purple-rumped Sunbird. 5. Common Iora. 6. Tailor-bird. (All about ½ nat. size.)

[Face p. 264

in all types of country where there is sufficient tree growth, though it, perhaps above all, prefers gardens and hill jungles close to cultivation where there is a mixture of trees and flowering shrubs, and in consequence a variety of food; for it feeds both on insects, weevils, ants, and their eggs and larvæ, and on vegetable matter, such as small buds, seeds and wild fruits.

Except when separated up into pairs for breeding the White-Eye is found in small parties and in flocks, which do not as a rule associate with other birds but hunt busily through the foliage, invariably coming to notice through a rather monotonous querulous *chee-chee-chee* or *tseer-tseer* note which is uttered all the time; they are very active and busy little birds, and when disturbed fly off still uttering their note to start operations afresh in another tree.

In the breeding season the males sing freely; the song is short and rather pretty. It begins so low as to be almost inaudible and becomes louder and louder until at the end it is almost harsh, and this is repeated over and again without variation.

Most nests will be found about April, but there appear to be at least two broods, and the breeding season extends according to locality from January to September.

The nest is a delightful little cup slung like a miniature Oriole's nest between two twigs, though very rarely it may be placed in an upright fork. It is usually composed of very fine grass-stems, coated exteriorly with cobwebs and studded with small cocoons and pieces of vegetable down, but in shape, depth and materials it is somewhat variable. In site, too, there is no uniformity. Many nests are placed in undergrowth and bushes not higher than 6 feet from the ground; while as many are built in large trees, mangoes being perhaps the favourite, at any height up to 60 feet.

The clutch varies from two to four eggs.

In shape the egg is a somewhat lengthened oval, a good deal pointed toward the smaller end; the texture is very fine, practically without gloss. The colour is a very delicate and pure pale blue or greenish-blue, without markings.

The average size is 0·62 by 0·47 inches.

THE YELLOW-BACKED SUNBIRD

ÆTHOPYGA SIPARAJA (Raffles)

Description.—Length 6 inches, including elongated central pair of tail-feathers 1 inch. Male: Front of crown metallic-green; nape brownish-green; sides of head and neck, back and smaller wing-coverts dull crimson; rump bright yellow; larger wing-coverts and quills dark brown, the feathers edged with brownish-olive; tail violet-black, the central pair of feathers and the edges of the others metallic-green; chin, throat and breast bright crimson, a conspicuous moustachial streak metallic-violet; a pale yellowish-white patch under the wing; abdomen dull greyish-olive.

Female: Upper plumage, including the sides of the head and neck dull olive-green; wings and tail dark brown, the feathers edged with golden olive and the outer tail-feathers tipped with whitish; the whole lower plumage dull olive-yellow; a pale yellow patch under the wing.

The immature male resembles the female but has the chin and throat pinkish-red.

Iris dark brown; bill blackish-brown, lower mandible horny-brown; legs chocolate-brown.

FIG. 40—Yellow-Backed Sunbird (½ nat. size)

The bill is long, slender, curved and sharply-pointed with minute serrations along the cutting edge of both mandibles towards the tip. In the male the tail is graduated, the central pair of feathers exceeding the rest by 1 inch and being sharply pointed.

Field Identification.—Male, scarlet with a yellow rump and olive-grey abdomen and long pointed tail; Female, short-tailed and nondescript olive colour, darker above. Bill sharp, thin and curved. A shy and active forest bird, found feeding at flowers.

Distribution.—The typical race of the Yellow-backed Sunbird is found in Sumatra. In our area we are concerned with four other races. The West Himalayan race (*Æ. s. mussooriensis*) and the East Himalayan race (*Æ. s. seheriæ*) agree with each other in plumage as described above but the western bird is slightly larger. This is apparently a summer visitor to the outer ranges up to 7000 feet, but is not known to occur west of Dharmsala. *Æ. s. seheriæ* is found in the Eastern Himalayas at similar elevations and extends also through the greater part of Assam, both in the plains and in the hills up to 7000 feet. It is also found in the Chota Nagpur area. A third race (*Æ. s. miles*) with dull grey under parts is said to be found in Nepal. A fourth race (*Æ. s. vigorsi*) is found along the western coast of India from the valley of the Tapti to the foot of the Nilgiris. It is a rather darker race than the others and is more particularly distinguished by having a patch of metallic-violet behind the ear in addition to the moustachial streak and by having the crimson of the under parts finely streaked with yellow. Other races are found in Burma and eastwards.

There are several other Sunbirds of the long-tailed genus *Æthopyga* which are locally common. The best known are the Nepal Yellow-backed Sunbird (*Æ. nipalensis*) with the whole head and hind neck metallic green and the lower parts yellow flecked with red, and the Black-breasted Yellow-backed Sunbird (*Æ. saturata*), a very blackish-looking species with violet and blue metallic feathers. Both are common in the Eastern Himalayas and parts of Assam.

Habits, etc.—Little seems to have been recorded about the habits of the various races of the Yellow-backed Sunbird. It is very largely a bird of heavy moist forest, more especially evergreen forest, and it is said to be particularly partial to ravines for breeding purposes. At Dharmsala a few used to come into my garden to visit the blossoms of a large orange-bush, covered with jasmine, at the side of the house, and they also fed from the flowers of a red gladiolus, a yellow iris and a weed with a small red flower. The iris flowers were pierced by the bird with a tiny hole at the base, the mouth of the flower being disregarded. The flight was swift and the birds were very active and shy. The call-note is a loud and distinct *tszip* which is very like the noise of scissor-blades opening and shutting.

The breeding season in the Himalayas is from April to July but the Western Ghats race (*vigorsi*) apparently nests somewhat later, from May to October. The nest is pear-shaped with the entrance at one side and this is sometimes shaded by a little porch.

The nest is usually slung from the roots of plants and bushes which are exposed by the rain washing away the sides of banks, but odd nests may be found attached to small bushes and even bamboo sprays. The materials vary a good deal. Some nests look like a mass of fine black rootlets loosely felted with grass ; others appear to be a tangle of wind-blown cobwebs which have caught in a branch. Oddments of all kinds are added as external decorations. The interior is lined with fine grass stems and the bottom of the cavity is thickly filled with fine silky seed-down.

The clutch consists of two or three eggs. In shape they are broad blunt ovals, fine and very fragile in texture with no gloss. The ground colour is white or creamy, flecked, speckled and even blotched with brick-red, reddish-brown or brown, the markings tending to form indistinct caps or zones at the larger end of the egg.

The egg measures about 0·6 by 0·45 inches.

THE PURPLE SUNBIRD

CINNYRIS ASIATICUS (Latham)

(Plate iii, Fig. 3, opposite page 44)

Description.—Length 4 inches. Male in summer plumage: The whole head, neck, upper plumage, throat and breast metallic-black with greenish-purple reflections; flight-feathers dull brownish-black; tail bluish-black; a narrow band across the breast coppery-brown, of varying extent and sometimes absent; remainder of lower plumage dull purplish-black; a brilliant tuft of crimson and yellow feathers under each wing.

Male in winter plumage, assumed only from about September to December, resembles the female with the addition of a broad stripe of dark metallic-violet from the chin to the abdomen. It retains the dark wings.

Female: Upper plumage, wings and sides of the head and neck greenish-brown; tail dark brown, the outer feathers narrowly tipped with white; lower plumage rather bright yellow.

Iris brown; bill and legs black.

Bill long, curved and sharply pointed, with minute serrations along the cutting edges of both mandibles towards the tip.

Field Identification.—Abundant garden bird in the plains; a minute bird with a long curved beak; male metallic-black, female brown and yellow. Active and feeds about flowers.

Distribution.—This Sunbird has a wide range in Southern Asia from Persia on the west to Cochin-China on the east, and is divided into races. The typical race is found in Ceylon and from about 5000 feet along the Outer Himalayas throughout the whole of India except in the north-west. There in Sind and Baluchistan it is replaced by the Persian form, *C. a. brevirostris*, with a shorter bill, while birds from the Punjab are mostly intermediate in character between the two races. In the main a resident species, it is also locally migratory, being found in North-western India only from March to September. In the ranges of Southern India it is found up to 7500 feet.

The very similar Loten's Sunbird (*Cinnyris lotenia*) with a much larger beak is common in South India up to Bombay on the west and the Nallamallais on the east. In some areas it replaces the Purple Sunbird; in others it is found with it.

Habits, etc.—From their small size and brilliant metallic plumage and occasional habit of hovering in front of a flower this and other Indian members of the numerous family of the *Nectariniidæ* are responsible for the frequently found belief that Humming-birds occur in India. The true Humming-birds are, however, confined to America and its islands, and they belong to a totally different Order of birds allied to the Swifts and Nightjars.

The Sunbird resembles the Humming-bird in being largely dependent on flowers for its food. It feeds at the blossoms of the various flowering shrubs and trees, taking from them not only their nectar but also the various small insects, caterpillars, spiders and flies that they attract, and in return assists to pollinate many species. The case of the flower of *Loranthus longiflorus* may be quoted as an instance. In this species the bud remains closed and therefore unfertilised until extraneous pressure is exerted. This is supplied by the Sunbird which hops about the plant gently squeezing the tops of mature buds in its mandibles. The pressure causes the bud to open. The bird thrusts its bill into the flower, sucks up the nectar with its specially adapted tongue and passes on to a second bud. In the process the anthers of one flower deposit their pollen on the forehead of the bird, only to be brushed off against the mature stigma of the next flower. The long tongue is almost tubular in structure and is capable of extrusion beyond the beak.

The Sunbird usually perches on the twigs and stems of the plant, flitting actively from flower to flower and indulging in a variety of gymnastics to reach the desired food ; but when need arises it can hover with rapidly vibrating wings though only for a short time. By this dependence on flowers it is emancipated from preference for any particular type of country. In the dry desert areas of the north-west it flits and perches about the low-growing ankh and wild caper ; in the tropical forests of the south it feeds high from the ground about the blossoms of some lofty tree ; and throughout its range it is a familiar garden bird attracting notice by the boldness of its visits to the flowers that line verandahs or grow over porches. Its swift darting flight and shrill chirping note also call attention to its presence, and it has the rare merit in India of being a good songster. For the male perches on the topmost twig of a tree with a good many repetitions of the sharp chirp and then breaks into a loud full song which seems surprisingly good for so small a bird and recalls the notes of a Canary or Willow-Wren.

The breeding season varies a good deal according to locality, and in different parts of India eggs may be found from January to August ; most nests will, however, be found in April and May. There are at least two broods, and these are reared in rapid succession, sometimes even from the same nest.

The nest is a pear-shaped or oval structure with a small round or oval entrance at one side, often sheltered by a little projecting cornice. It is built of a most miscellaneous assortment of materials, hair, fine grass, twigs, dead leaves, chips of bark and fragments of decayed wood, seed cases, scraps of rag or paper, and especially caterpillar droppings, all neatly plastered together with silky fibres and cobwebs. The whole structure is suspended from a twig by a short rope of these materials, and a pendant irregular tassel of the same generally hangs from the bottom of the nest.

The nest is generally placed some 3 or 4 feet from the ground, hanging under a bough or a bush, at times suspended from the spines of a prickly pear bush, but occasionally it is attached to a hook or pendant piece of rope in the ceiling of a verandah. The interior of the nest is neatly and softly lined with seed-down.

The clutch consists of two or three eggs.

The egg is typically a moderately broad oval, somewhat pointed towards the small end, but the shape is rather variable. The texture is fine and fragile with very little gloss. The ground-colour is dull whitish with a tinge of green, grey or brown, and the markings consist of minute and ill-defined spots and freckles of grey, brown and dull purple of various shades. In some eggs these markings are regular and thickly disposed over the whole surface; in others they chiefly collect in a zone or cap about the broad end.

In size the eggs average about 0·64 by 0·46 inches.

THE PURPLE-RUMPED SUNBIRD

CINNYRIS ZEYLONICUS (Linnæus)

(Plate xiii, Fig. 4, opposite page 264)

Description.—Length 4 inches. Male: Top of the head metallic-lilac; rump metallic-purple; remainder of upper plumage dull crimson; wings brown edged with rufous, metallic-lilac and dull crimson on the smaller coverts; tail black with pale tips to the outer feathers; sides of the head coppery-brown; chin and throat metallic-purple; a collar below the throat maroon; remainder of lower plumage bright yellow, white under the wings.

There is no separate winter plumage as in the last species.

Female: Upper plumage ashy-brown; wings brown margined with rufous; tail black with pale tips to the outer feathers; an indistinct white line above the eye, with a dark line below it through the eye; cheeks, chin and throat pale ashy-white; remainder of lower plumage yellow, white under the wings.

Iris dull red; bill and legs black.

The bill is long, slender, curved and pointed, with minute serrations along the cutting edge of both mandibles towards the tip.

Field Identification.—Central and Southern India. A minute bird of brilliantly variegated, partly metallic, plumage in the male, lilac on the head, crimson on the back, purple on the throat, and yellow below. The female is dull in colour with a white throat contrasting with the yellow under parts. Active in trees about blossoms.

Distribution.—A purely Indian species. It is found throughout India south of a line passing through Khandesh, Raipur and Sambalpur in the Central Provinces, and Lohardaga, Burdwan and Dacca in Bengal; also in Ceylon. In the Nilgiris it is found up to 2500 feet. This is the Common Sunbird of Bombay, Madras and Lower Bengal. A resident species.

The Small Sunbird (*Cinnyris minima*) is common along the Western Ghats from Bombay to Travancore. It is the smallest of the group in India, and the male is very brilliant with a green cap, deep crimson breast and upper parts, lilac rump and purple throat.

Habits, etc.—This beautiful Sunbird is very common over large areas of India, preferring if anything well-watered tracts and extensive forests, though it also comes freely into gardens and about houses. It is found singly or in pairs, and is very active, incessantly flitting about from tree to tree and flower to flower in search of the insects and caterpillars on which it feeds, and is purely arboreal, never descending to the ground. The call is a feeble shrill sort of chirp, easily distinguishable from the louder call of the Purple Sunbird.

The breeding season is very extended, nests having been found in almost every month of the year, but normally the bird appears to be double-brooded, nesting about February and August.

The nest is a most lovely structure, similar to that of the Purple Sunbird, a hanging purse with the entrance near the top on one side surmounted by a little portico.

The body of the nest is chiefly composed of very fine grass or vegetable fibres, and it is thickly studded exteriorly with scraps of lichens, spiders' webs, fragments of bark, dried petals, and a variety of similar materials. The egg cavity is thickly lined with vegetable down or feathers. The nest is suspended from a fine twig, over which the top of the nest is firmly worked with fibres and down, and a tassel of the same material as the outside covering of the nest often hangs below it.

The clutch consists of two eggs. The egg is a moderately broad oval, rather elongated and pointed, with a delicate close-grained shell almost devoid of gloss. The ground-colour is a dingy greenish- or brownish-white; it is freckled, clouded and streaked with minute greyish-brown markings, which tend to collect in a zone or cap about the broad end.

In size the eggs average 0·65 by 0·47 inches.

TICKELL'S FLOWER-PECKER

DICÆUM ERYTHRORHYNCHOS (Latham)

Description.—Length 3 inches. Sexes alike. Upper plumage ashy-olive, the feathers of the crown with dark centres, and the concealed portions of the wings brown; tail dark brown; lower plumage buffy-white.

Iris brown; bill pale fleshy-livid, darker above; legs bluish-plumbeous.

Bill curved, sharply pointed and finely serrated along the cutting edges.

Field Identification.—A tiny olive bird with paler under parts, and a curved beak, which rather resembles a female Sunbird. Has a sharp note and is purely arboreal, frequenting parasitic plants on trees. It is easily confused with the Nilgiri Flower-Pecker (*Dicæum minullum*), common along the Western Ghats, which is darker with a darker bill.

Distribution.—Confined to India, Ceylon (separated as *D. e. ceylonense*) and Southern and Western Burma. It occurs along the Himalayan foot-hills, up to elevations of 4000 feet, from Kangra to Assam. South of the foot-hills it is found virtually throughout India except in the dry regions of the North-west, *i.e.*, North-west Frontier Province, Baluchistan, the Punjab, Sind, and Rajputana. It is a resident species, and in places like Bombay and Poona very abundant.

Habits, etc.—Tickell's Flower-Pecker is a bird of far more importance than would seem to be warranted by its small size and inconspicuous plumage; for its distribution appears to be entirely dependent on the presence or absence of the harmful parasitic plants of the genus *Loranthus*, and the spreading of these parasites appears in turn to be largely the work of the Flower-Pecker.

In Western India, for example, *Loranthus longiflorus* is found on over a hundred species of trees and in particular it is a serious scourge to the mango. Its beautiful clumps of flowers will be noticed up on the trees in every month in the year and a little observation will show that this Flower-Pecker, which is entirely arboreal, seems to have regular feeding territories in which it flits about the *Loranthus* at all hours of the day. The bird is very restless. It flies from tree to tree, often high in the air; it flies from clump to clump and on the clumps it hops from bunch to bunch of flowers; and all the time it utters a loud, almost incessant squeak *chik-chik-chik*, which is occasionally varied by a series of twittering notes which might be called its song. Each berry is tested with the mandibles. If ripe it is plucked and swallowed, broad end first. After finding and bolting down three or four ripe berries, one after another, the bird retires to the extremity of some bare bough and sits quiet for a few minutes with the feathers partly puffed out. It is during this interval that the mischief is done; for hardly has the bird been there a couple of minutes than you see him becoming uneasy and presently one of the seeds is extruded, evidently with some effort. The seed is invariably extruded broad-end first and by a final jerky and dipping motion of the posterior part of the body, during which the bird often pivots round from its normal crosswise position on the branch to one nearly along it. The extruded seed which is copiously covered with viscous matter and has a viscid thread-like process at each end promptly adheres to the perch. Digestion is extremely rapid and each seed appears to pass out some three or four minutes after the berry was eaten. Immediately it has got rid of the unnecessary ballast the Flower-Pecker flies off to another clump uttering its lively note, and the process starts afresh. In this manner the parasitic seed is conveyed not only to other branches of the same tree but to other trees in the neighbourhood.

FIG. 40a—Tickell's Flower-pecker (½ nat. size)

The breeding season is from February to May.

The nest is very similar to that of the Purple Sunbird, being a small pear-shaped structure, suspended by the stalk from a twig with the entrance high on one side. It is placed in a tree at heights of 10 to 20 feet from the ground. It is constructed of fine vegetable fibres, externally covered with cobwebs, small chips of bark, splinters of rotten wood and the excreta of caterpillars, while the interior is lined with the softest, silkiest downs and fibres. The female sits looking out through the entrance.

One to three eggs are laid. These are rather elongated ovals, pure white and glossless.

In size they average about 0·58 by 0·41 inches.

THE THICK-BILLED FLOWER-PECKER

PIPRISOMA AGILE (Swainson)

Description.—Length 5 inches. Sexes alike. Upper plumage ashy-brown, washed with olive-green above the tail; wings dark brown, edged with olive-green; tail dark brown, edged with olive-green, the feathers tipped slightly with white, growing broader on the outermost feathers; sides of the head and neck ashy-brown; chin and throat white; remainder of lower plumage creamy-grey streaked on the breast and flanks with ashy-brown.

Iris orange-brown; bill bluish-slate, darker above; legs dull bluish-slate.

The bill is short and coarse with the lower mandible unusually deep and swollen.

Field Identification.—A tiny dull-looking bird, ashy-brown above and dull creamy-grey below, with the breast faintly streaked. Has a sharp note and is purely arboreal, frequenting parasitic plants on trees. May easily be distinguished from other Flower-Peckers by the swollen-looking bill.

Distribution.—The typical race is found throughout India from the foot-hills of the Himalayas, which it ascends locally to 5000 feet, down to Ceylon. Ceylon birds are separated at *P. a. zeylonicum.* It is not found west of a line from Kangra to Sirsa and Baroda or east of Sikkim and Midnapur. In Assam and Burma to Siam it is replaced by *P. a. modestum* which is greener above and has the lower mandible less swollen.

Habits, etc.—At first sight there is not very much to distinguish the habits of the Thick-billed Flower-Pecker from those of Tickell's Flower-Pecker. It is generally distributed and fairly common in well-wooded country and it has the same habit of flying about singly from clump to clump of the parasitic *Loranthus* that grows on the branches of trees; its feeding circuits are also well defined. Its voice and notes are similar to those of the other species though they are perhaps distinguishable as being somewhat shriller and more metallic. It twists its little tail from side to side as it feeds amongst the clumps. There is, however, a difference in the feeding habits of the two species and this is evidently correlated with the different types of beak. As has been related above, Tickell's Flower-Pecker swallows the ripe fruit of the *Loranthus* whole and voids the viscous seeds on to the bough where it sits for digestion. The Thick-billed Flower-Pecker, on the other hand, does not swallow the fruit entire. It plucks it off the clump and with its finch-like beak separates the fleshy epicarp from the sticky seed, swallowing the former and getting rid of the latter by scraping it off on a neighbouring twig with a sweeping side-to-side motion of the head.

In this way three or four berries are eaten before the bird flies off again on its endless round. It will be noted that in this way the deposition of the seeds is confined to the neighbourhood of the parent clump and they are not dispersed so widely as by Tickell's species.

In addition to *Loranthus* berries this species feeds on a variety of other fruits, particularly those of the Lantana scrub and the figs of Peepul and Gulair trees. It also eats the soft juicy parts of Mhowa flowers and small spiders.

The breeding season is from February to June. The nest is a most remarkable structure, a small, rather full-bottomed, purse-like bag, hung from a small twig as nearly horizontal as possible, the entrance hole being immediately below the twig. It is composed of a felt-like fabric, so soft and pliable that it may be rolled and unrolled in the hand; this is made from fibres, spiders' webs and the down taken from the young shoots and flower-buds of various plants. The down of *Loranthus* is commonly used. The nest is hung in trees at all heights up to 30 feet from the ground. Mango-trees are particularly favoured.

The clutch consists of two or three eggs, but four may be found. These vary a good deal in shape and colour but are typically rather elongated ovals, somewhat coarse in texture and without gloss. The ground-colour varies from rosy-white to a decided pink and it is speckled, spotted and even blotched with markings that vary from brownish-pink to claret colour. They are most numerous towards the broad end, often forming a zone or cap.

In size the egg measures about 0·65 by 0·45 inches.

THE INDIAN PITTA

Pitta brachyura (Linnæus)

(Plate xvi, Fig. 4, opposite page 330)

Description.—Length 7 inches. Sexes alike. Top of head pale fulvous, with a broad black band down the centre, which is joined by a very broad black band from below the eye; a narrow white line over the eye; back and shoulders green; lower rump shining pale blue; tail black, tipped with dull blue; wing black with a conspicuous white patch in the flight-feathers, and with the coverts green and blue; chin and throat white; remainder of lower plumage fulvous, a patch of bright scarlet under the tail.

Iris dark brown; bill black; legs pale purplish-flesh.

Field Identification.—A coarsely-built bird with a short tail and strong legs, adapted for life in heavy jungle; plumage variegated with blue, green, black, white, fulvous and crimson, but not conspicuously bright in the shade though the lines on the head are distinct. Shape and upright carriage are distinctive.

Distribution.—This Pitta is found throughout almost the whole of India from Dharamsala in the Himalayan foot-hills to Sikkim, and Eastern Rajputana in the plains to Calcutta. Southwards it extends down to Ceylon. It breeds in the Himalayan foot-hills and in Central and Western India and in the former area is a summer visitor only, wintering in Southern India and Ceylon. Exhausted birds on passage sometimes take refuge in outhouses and other unexpected places.

These lovely birds invade the sal forests of the submontane tracts of the United Provinces about the middle of May. The forests soon ring with their loud four-noted musical calls (they have no song). They start breeding at once and continue throughout the rains after which in September they begin to migrate south. As these forests are very malarious in the rains they are scarcely ever visited at the breeding season of the Pittas so that few Europeans, or even Indians, have seen these beautiful birds in their forest home.

Habits, etc.—The Indian Pitta belongs to a family of birds which has no equivalent in Europe. All its members are compact, stoutly-built birds with a short stumpy tail, broad rounded wings and long stout legs, and, as this structure suggests, they are essentially ground-living birds, hopping and running with great facility and spending only a small portion of their time either on the wing or in trees. All are of great beauty, and the distribution of the various members of the family is very sporadic and curious. Most of them occur to the east of our area but the Blue-naped Pitta (*Pitta nipalensis*), a large brown species with a blue hind-neck, is common in the lower ranges of the Eastern Himalayas and in Assam.

The nearly allied Long-tailed Broadbill (*Psarisomus dalhousiæ*) is found along the lower Himalayas from Mussoorie eastwards. It is a gaudy-looking bird, green with blue in the wings and tail, a black head and a yellow throat and is remarkable for the flat broad bill and the tail of narrow graduated feathers.

The Indian Pitta, by preference, lives in deciduous forest or scrub-jungle, but it may also be found in gardens and comparatively open country, especially if there are small ravines overgrown with bushes and trees to afford it the cover that it requires. It is not shy and may easily be approached. It has a sweet call *whēēt pe-u* or *pea-to-yew*, a loud, clear and far-reaching note which is uttered again and again. When calling, the head and shoulders are thrown right back, the chest out and the bill points upwards after the manner of a cock crowing. The food consists largely of beetles, ants and other insects.

The breeding season is from June to August.

The nest is a huge globular structure with a circular entrance at one side. It is composed of dry leaves and grasses wound round with strips of fibre or held together with twigs and roots, and is lined with green leaves or fine twigs and roots. Some nests are found on the ground or near it in low branches, but the majority are built in the forks of trees at heights from 10 to 30 feet from the ground.

The clutch consists of four or five eggs. In shape they are broad and regular ovals, so broad as to be almost spherical. The texture is very fine and hard with a high gloss.

The ground-colour is china-white, and the markings consist of spots, speckles and sometimes hair-lines of deep maroon, dark purple and brownish-purple, with secondary markings of pale inky-purple. These rich colours, together with the spherical shape and high polish, give the eggs of this species a very distinctive appearance.

In size the eggs measure about 1·00 by 0·86 inches.

The word Pitta is due to the latinisation of a Telugu word, meaning "small bird."

THE SCALY-BELLIED GREEN WOODPECKER

PICUS SQUAMATUS Gould

Description.—Length 14 inches. Male: Top of the head and crest crimson; upper plumage green, strongly tinged with yellow at the base of the tail; wings brownish-black washed with green, all the quills conspicuously spotted and banded with yellowish-white and white; tail brownish with narrow white bars, the lower surface washed with yellow; a broad yellowish-white line over the eye, bordered above and below with blackish lines; another broad yellowish-white line below the eye from the base of the beak; throat and breast pale greyish; remainder of lower plumage greenish-white, with scale-like markings of black.

Female: Has the crimson of the head replaced by black, marked with leaden and greenish-grey.

Iris dark pinkish-red, with an outer ring of pale pink; bill yellow, horn-coloured about nostrils; legs greenish-plumbeous.

This and the following Woodpeckers have these peculiarities of external structure. The bill is long and stout and modified into a cutting weapon with the end of the upper mandible vertical and chisel-shaped. The tongue is excessively long, worm-like and capable of great protrusion; it is supplied with viscid mucus from the large salivary glands and the point is horny and barbed. The toes are arranged in two pairs, the 2nd and 3rd toes pointing forwards, the 4th toe being directed backwards with the 1st toe or hallux. The tail is graduated, with very stiff-pointed feathers.

Field Identification.—Himalayan forest form: a medium-sized greenish bird with pale under parts scaled with black which climbs up the trunks of trees in a series of jerks, and moves from tree to tree with noisy undulating flight. Distinguish from a similar species, the Black-naped Green Woodpecker (*Picus canus*), which is found in the same area and farther eastwards into Assam and Burma; this has the lower plumage unscaled and only the front half of the top of the head crimson in the male.

Distribution.—This Woodpecker is distributed through Transcaspia, Baluchistan, Afghanistan, and the Western Himalayas; it is divided into two races, of which the typical race is found in the Western Himalayas from the Valley of Nepal to Chitral and Gilgit, from about 5000 to 11,000 feet. A resident species with little, if any, altitudinal seasonal movement.

FIG. 41—Scaly-bellied Green Woodpecker (¼ nat. size)

A very similar but smaller species the Little Scaly-bellied Green Woodpecker (*Picus xanthopygæus*) is locally distributed throughout India, but not west of a line from Ambala to Mount Aboo.

Habits, etc.—This fine Woodpecker is a common resident in the Western Himalayas and is found in all types of forest, also occasionally wandering out into trees in the open cultivated country. It is not very shy, and is easily observed as it works its way up the trunk of a tree, now stopping to dislodge a piece of bark and then hammering lustily with its chisel-like beak at a piece of grub-infested wood. Occasionally it feeds on the ground, searching there for ants and termites. When not feeding it sometimes rests in a commanding position on an upright bare stump of a bough at the top of a tree, whence a clear view can be obtained. In such a situation it sits for a considerable time, moving the head, neck and upper part of the body from side to side with a swaying motion, varying the proceedings by occasionally drumming rapidly with its bill on the wood. The ordinary spring call is a loud, clear, wild-sounding melodious *klee-gu* or *pea-cock*, or simply the syllable *peer*, which echoes through a nullah and is audible a long way off. While hunting for food a constant *tjupk-tjupk-tjupk-tjupk* note is kept up, and this repeated loudly is also the alarm cry. The flight is strong, fast and undulating, the hard coarse wing-feathers making a distinct noise.

The breeding season extends from March to May, but most eggs will be found in April. The nest hole is excavated in the trunk or bough of a tree and consists of a passage running down from 20 to 30 inches into the nest chamber which is often a natural decayed hollow inside the wood. In this the eggs, five or six in number, are laid on chips and debris.

The egg is a rather elongated oval, somewhat compressed towards the smaller end. The texture is very fine and delicate, with a brilliant gloss; the colour is pure china-white.

The eggs measure about 1·28 by 0·93 inches.

THE BROWN-FRONTED PIED WOODPECKER

DRYOBATES AURICEPS (Vigors)

(Plate xvi, Fig. 3, opposite page 330)

Description.—Length 8 inches. Male: Forehead and crown umber-brown; crest golden-yellow in front, crimson behind; sides of the head and neck and the chin white finely mixed with black; ear-coverts very pale brown; upper parts black, broadly barred with white across the upper back and shoulders; wings black, conspicuously spotted with white; tail black, the outer feathers barred with buffy-white; lower parts fulvescent-white, tinged with yellow in the centre of the abdomen, streaked with black, and bordered on the sides of the cheeks by a brown band which becomes black and breaks up into spots on the sides of the neck; a patch of pale crimson under the base of the tail.

The female lacks the gold and crimson on the crest which is merely yellower than the forehead and crown.

Iris crimson; eye-patch plumbeous; bill horny-plumbeous; legs dull plumbeous-green.

Field Identification.—Common West Himalayan form. A dull-coloured Woodpecker, black barred with white above, whitish with dark streaks below, a reddish patch under the tail and a yellow and brown top to the head, crested in the male with crimson. Quiet and familiar in its habits.

The complete red crown of the male and the black crown of the female easily distinguish the very similar Fulvous-breasted Pied Woodpecker (*Dryobates macei*) which is common at low elevations throughout the whole length of the Himalayas from about Murree eastwards. It is also found in Lower Bengal and towards Vizagapatam.

Another common species, confined to the Western Himalayas and particularly noticeable in Kashmir, is the Himalayan Pied Woodpecker (*Dryobates himalayensis*). This is black and white with the crown crimson in the male, but the back is black with a white patch on each shoulder, not barred.

In appearance the Sind Pied Woodpecker (*Dryobates scindianus*) of the more barren areas of North-west India is very similar.

Distribution.—Found throughout the Western Himalayas from Chitral and Hazara to Nepal at elevations between 2000 and 7500 feet and in smaller numbers up to 9000 feet. Here it is a resident species, but it is also found in Afghanistan, and from there wanders in winter into the Samana and Kohat.

Habits, etc.—This is the ordinary common Woodpecker of the hill stations of the Western Himalayas from Murree to Mussoorie. It is found chiefly in the forests of oak and cheel pine, but wanders into cultivation and gardens, and is a familiar species, very indifferent to the near neighbourhood of man. I have known a pair roost nightly on the top of the pillars supporting a verandah roof of a forest rest-house, and one winter a single bird slept regularly in a nest-box affixed to a tree near my house.

The call-note is a rather loud plaintive *peek*, repeated at regular and monotonous intervals. It is traced to its source with difficulty, as the sound at times can be very ventriloquial, and then at last the bird will be found sitting at the extremity of some dead bough at the top of an oak, continually jerking its body and twisting its head and neck from side to side as it surveys the world below, glancing here, there and everywhere on the alert for possible danger. When the bird is down on a tree trunk busy feeding the sound is easier to locate, and as this Woodpecker is far from shy and very common it is easy to observe and procure if required.

The breeding season is in April and May. The nest hole is the usual cleanly excavated tunnel and nest chamber in the trunk or large bough of a tree, and no nest is made, the eggs being laid on chips and debris at the bottom of the hole; very occasionally a natural hollow in a tree is used. The site of the nest may be at any height from 5 to 40 feet from the ground.

The clutch varies from three to five eggs.

The egg is a rather lengthened and pointed oval, fine and glossy in texture, and pure unmarked white in colour.

In size it averages about 0·92 by 0·68 inches.

THE MAHRATTA WOODPECKER

Dryobates mahrattensis (Latham)

Description.—Length 7 inches. Male: Forehead and crown brownish-yellow, a small crest scarlet; back of neck smoky-brown; back and shoulders brownish-black and white irregularly mixed; wings blackish-brown heavily spotted with white; tail blackish-brown, spotted with white, which from below appears fulvescent;

chin and throat and the front and sides of the neck whitish, with a brown stripe on the sides of the neck which breaks up into longitudinal streaks on the sides of the breast; remainder of lower plumage streaked with brown, a bright scarlet patch in the middle of the lower abdomen.

The female lacks the scarlet on the crest.

FIG. 42—Mahratta Woodpecker (½ nat. size)

Iris deep red; eye-patch plumbeous; bill clear plumbeous; legs bright plumbeous.

Field Identification.—Abundant plains species. A small dingy Woodpecker, spotted sooty-brown and white on the upper parts with a brownish-yellow top to the head, and in the male a scarlet crest.

Distribution.—This Woodpecker is found in India, Northern Ceylon, Upper Burma, and Cochin-China. In India it is found from the foot of the Himalayas, which it ascends to about 2500 feet, or more, down to the extreme south. In the north-west it is found at Peshawar and Rawal Pindi, but it is scarce to the west of the Indus and in Sind and Rajputana, nor is it found in South-eastern Bengal. It is a strictly resident species. The typical race belongs to Southern India, and northern birds may be separated as *L. m. aurocristatus*, but the line of demarcation is not very marked.

The Indian Pygmy Woodpecker (*Dryobates hardwickii*) is well distributed throughout India south of the Himalayas, except in Sind and the greater part of the Punjab and Rajputana. Its dull plumage and small size—for it is only as big as a Sparrow—readily distinguish it from the rest of the family.

Another species, the Himalayan Pygmy Woodpecker (*Dryobates nanus*) is found along the foot-hills of the Himalayas.

Habits, etc.—This little Woodpecker, though common, is somewhat locally distributed, and it avoids both the drier, more open plains and heavy forest. It is a bird of cultivation and groves, roadside avenues, low scrub-jungle and gardens, and in such localities it feeds quietly on the tree-trunks and branches, paying little or no attention to passers-by. Owing to its small size it is rather apt to get into trouble with other small birds and squirrels, but it is a courageous bird and resists with spirit their endeavours to trespass in its laboriously constructed nest hole. It is always found solitary, except when paired for the breeding season. Like many other Woodpeckers, this species drums with its beak on a dead bough, apparently as an outlet for sexual emotion.

The ordinary call-note is a rather weak *peek*, uttered at short intervals.

The breeding season lasts from February to April, but most eggs will be found in March. The nest hole is excavated in a bough of a tree, usually one leaning out of the perpendicular, and the entrance hole is made on the underside of the bough. It is small, about 1½ inches in diameter, and the entrance tunnel is about 15 inches long. No nest is made, the eggs being laid merely on chips of wood at the bottom of the irregular chamber to which the tunnel leads.

The clutch consists of three eggs. These in shape are a rather lengthened oval, fine and glossy in texture, and pure white in colour.

In size they average about 0·87 by 0·68 inches.

THE RUFOUS WOODPECKER

Micropternus brachyurus (Vieillot)

Description.—Length 10 inches. Sexes alike. The whole plumage chestnut-brown, duller and darker on the lower parts and with the following markings; top of the head washed with dusky brown, the feathers slightly paler at the edges; upper parts from the mantle and the wing- and tail-feathers with black transverse bars; a patch of feathers under the eye tipped with crimson ; feathers of the chin and throat broadly edged with fulvous.

The plumage is very variable. The colour varies from dull to bright chestnut or bay and the head from chestnut to dark brown while the barring on the upper parts may be fairly general or virtually absent.

The female is said to lack the patch of crimson under the eye, but there seems to be some doubt about this and I have had no opportunity of verifying the fact by dissection.

Iris brownish-red ; bill blackish-brown, base of lower mandible plumbeous ; legs and feet greyish-brown.

The first toe is very poorly developed.

Field Identification.—A chestnut-coloured Woodpecker with a certain amount of black barring on the back, wings and tail and a squamated throat. Found in open country and largely dependent on the Tree-ants for its economy.

Distribution.—There are three races of the Rufous Woodpecker in our area. *Micropternus b. phaioceps*, as described above, is found along the Eastern Himalayas from Nepal to Upper Assam, in Assam, Bengal and Bihar, in the Chota Nagpur area and rarely in the Central Provinces (Balaghat and Chanda). It is also found in Burma and Tennasserim. *M. b. humei* from the Western Himalayas (Garhwal and Kumaon) is slightly larger and paler. *M. b. jerdonii*, a smaller bird with the throat squamation dark chocolate and white in colour, is found along the western coast from the neighbourhood of Bombay to the South Travancore hills, in the Sheveroy Hills and in Ceylon. All races are birds of low elevations from sea-level to about 4000 feet or occasionally 5000 feet.

Habits, etc.—The Rufous Woodpecker is not a bird of heavy forest. It prefers tea-gardens with light shade trees, open cultivated country with bamboo clumps or fairly open deciduous forest. On occasion it enters banana cultivation and clinging to the smooth trunks of the banana trees bores into the soft tissues near the base of the leaves and sucks the sap. It is not as a rule very numerous and will generally be found singly, feeding at no great height from the ground and sometimes even on it. The call is a high-pitched *ke-ke-ke-ke* somewhat of the timbre of the Common Mynah's call and the bird is much addicted to drumming.

It is, however, in connection with the Tree-ants of the genus *Cremastogaster* that one usually thinks of this Woodpecker. In the first place the plumage of the bird is always smeared with some gummy substance, particularly on the head and breast and on the tail. It has also a strong peculiar smell and one presumes that both of these features are due to the formic acid of the ants and their larvæ. These form a large part of the bird's food, but they also affect the plumage more directly. The ants are particularly ferocious ; they are instant to attack and once they get hold of anything they never let go. As the

Woodpecker climbs a tree it is always meeting with the wandering ants and the plumage, particularly the tail, rubs against them. They seize the feathers and are rubbed to pieces but the heads remain, sometimes in scores, adhering to the feathers.

FIG. 43—Rufous Woodpecker ($\frac{1}{3}$ nat. size)

The connection of ant and woodpecker is, however, still more intimate, for the woodpecker is dependent on the ant for its nesting-places.

The nests of the tree-ants of the genus *Crematogaster* must be well known to all who wander in Indian jungles. They look like large cellular balls of black papier-maché and measure anything from

8 inches to 2 feet in diameter and are built in trees and bamboos at any height from the ground between 7 and 70 feet, but most often between 10 and 30 feet. They are usually built round the fork of a sapling and the material of the nest is exceedingly hard.

In these ant-nests the woodpecker excavates its own nest hole, not when they are abandoned but whilst they are in active use and tenanted by their own makers. The entrance tunnel is made at one side and the cavity is some 5 or 6 inches in diameter. The ants do not interfere with the sitting bird or the eggs and young, and the woodpeckers do not apparently interfere with the owners of the occupied nest. This remarkable situation is emphasised by the character of the eggs.

They are slightly elongated ovals, fine in texture and very strong and hard, and of course pure white. Their peculiarity is that the surface is mat instead of highly polished like most woodpeckers' eggs, and the shell is so translucent that the yolk does not give a pink tinge to the whole egg but shows through as a yellow ball.

The normal clutch consists of three eggs. The breeding season of all Indian races is from February to June.

The egg measures about 1·00 by 0·75 inches.

THE GOLDEN-BACKED WOODPECKER

Brachypternus benghalensis (Linnæus)

(Plate xvii, Fig. 4, opposite page 352)

Description.—Length 11 inches. Male: Top of the head and a crest bright crimson, the feathers partly marked with black or white; sides of the head and neck white, streaked with black along a narrow line at the edge of the crimson and in a broader band through the eye from the nostril to the nape; hind neck, lower back and tail black; upper back and shoulders rich golden-yellow, sometimes tinged with orange-red; wing-coverts black at the shoulder, gradually changing to golden olive-yellow, the smaller feathers spotted with fulvescent white; flight-feathers brownish-black boldly spotted with white, and all but the outer feathers with the outer webs washed with golden olive-yellow; chin, throat and fore-neck black with numerous short white stripes, this pattern gradually merging into that of the breast where the feathers are buffy-white with broad black borders; these black borders become cross bands on the flanks and below the tail and gradually die away on the lower abdomen which is practically white.

Female: Differs from the male in having the front half of the crown black, each feather being tipped with white.

Iris red-brown, eyelids greenish-plumbeous; bill slaty-plumbeous; legs dark greenish-plumbeous, claws dusky.

Field Identification.—Common plains bird. Found climbing up the bark of trees or flying from tree to tree with heavy undulating flight; black and white plumage with vivid crimson crest and brilliant golden back immediately catch the eye, while the loud call is a well-known sound.

Distribution.—Found almost throughout India and Ceylon as a resident species divided into races. A pale and much spotted form, *B. b. dilutus,* is found in Sind, Baluchistan and the neighbouring portions of the Punjab, grading on the edges of its range into the typical race which extends throughout Northern India from the foot-hills of the Himalayas to Eastern Bengal and Assam. It is found in the Central Provinces, but in Hyderabad State grades into *B. b. puncticollis,* with much more black on the throat; this is found throughout Southern India with the exception of the rain area from Cannanore to Cape Comorin where the richly-coloured *B. b. tehminæ* is found. *B. b. intermedius* of Ceylon is smaller and paler.

This Woodpecker must be distinguished from the larger Tickell's Golden-backed Woodpecker (*Chrysocolaptes guttacristatus*) and the two smaller Golden-backed Three-toed Woodpeckers (*Dinopium javanense* and *D. shorei*). All four are very similar in appearance but the Golden-backed Woodpecker may be separated by the black rump (as opposed to red), by the presence of white spots on the shoulder and by having the chin and throat spotted black and white (as opposed to white with certain defined black lines). Also the female has a red crest, absent in the others. Tickell's Woodpecker is found along the base of the Himalayas as far west as the Jumna, the west coast from Khandesh southwards and locally from Chanda to Calcutta. *D. javanense* is found along the west coast from Goa southwards. *D. shorei* has the same distribution in the Himalayas as Tickell's Woodpecker. Both species lack the small first toe.

The well-known Wryneck (*Jynx torquilla*) breeds in Kashmir and is a winter visitor to most parts of India. It is grey and brown like lichen-covered bark with the lower parts finely barred.

Habits, etc.—The Golden-backed Woodpecker is one of the best-known of our Indian species, both from its brilliant coloration and from the fact that it is a bolder bird than most of its family. It avoids forest areas, and is found, by preference, in open, cultivated districts and gardens where avenues of ancient trees provide it with a happy hunting ground. In such places it lives singly or in pairs, climbing busily about the trunks and branches of the trees; it progresses in a series of jerks and always rests with the body in a perpendicular position with the head upwards; it virtually never perches on a twig or branch crossways, and when it wishes to descend a foot or two to search some special crevice in the bark it moves down backward with the same awkward jerks with which it ascends. The wonderful adapta-

PLATE XIV

1. Indian Pipit. 2. Stonechat. 3. Red-whiskered Bulbul. 4. Desert Wheatear. 5. Little Skylark. 6. White Wagtail.
(All about $\frac{1}{2}$ nat. size.)

[*Face p.* 286

tion of the structure of a Woodpecker to its needs is easily apparent. The strong claws grasp the crevices of the bark and from their position automatically tilt the cone-shaped body backwards on to the stiff graduated tail which presses into the bark so that the bird's own weight increases the firmness of its stance. In this position the long neck affords a swing for the blows of the pickaxe beak which chip off the bark and rotten wood revealing the lurking places of insects and their larvæ. Then the long-barbed tongue, with its sticky salivr, is extruded, collecting food from the borings and crevices. At the same time it is curious to note that although this and other Woodpeckers do feed on the wood-boring larvæ of beetles and on tree-living termites, the major portion of their food undoubtedly consists of ants which might easily be obtained without any special adaptation of structure. These are mostly obtained on tree-trunks, though occasionally the bird descends to the ground to procure them.

The flight is heavy and undulating, with rapid noisy beats of the wings: and one bird often follows another from tree to tree.

The call is a loud harsh scream, of several syllables, which is uttered both from a tree and on the wing.

The breeding season varies according to locality, from February to July. The nest hole is bored by the birds themselves in the branch or trunk of a tree, at any height from 4 to 40 feet from the ground. Normally the entrance, which is about 3 inches in diameter, runs in for a few inches horizontally and then turns downwards into a large oval chamber some 6 inches in diameter in which the eggs rest on chips and debris. But when tunnelling, the birds often hit upon a natural cavity in the wood which is then utilised, however deep or large it may be.

The normal clutch consists of three eggs. The egg is a long oval rather pointed at the smaller end; the texture is fine and hard with a high gloss, and the colour is pure unmarked milk-white.

It measures about 1·10 by 0·80 inches.

THE GREAT HIMALAYAN BARBET

Megalæma virens (Boddaert)

(Plate xv, Fig. 2, opposite page 308)

Description.—Length 13 inches. Sexes alike. Head and neck black with deep violet-blue edges to the feathers; back and shoulders brownish-olive, the upper back streaked with greenish-yellow; a broad patch above the base of the tail grass-green; wings blackish-brown, washed with blue-green and olive-brown; tail green above, below blackish, washed with pale blue; upper breast dark olive-brown; remainder of lower parts blue down the centre, striped yellow and brown on the sides with a scarlet patch under the tail.

Iris brown; bill yellow; legs greenish-horny.

In this and the following species of Barbet the bill is large and somewhat flattened and swollen, with a wide gape fringed with hairs; the feet have the 1st and 4th toes directed backwards and the 2nd and 3rd toes directed forwards as in the Woodpeckers, but the claws are weaker, as the Barbets perch like ordinary birds and do not climb on perpendicular trunks and boughs.

Field Identification.—Himalayan form, best known by the call, a loud melancholy *mee-ou* which resounds through a whole nullah. In spite of the gaudy plumage when closely examined, in the forest it appears a dark dully-coloured bird, chiefly conspicuous for the large yellow bill and the red patch under the tail. Purely arboreal.

Distribution.—This handsome Barbet extends from the Salt Range throughout the Himalayas into Assam and Burma and eastwards to China. It is divided into two races, of which we are concerned with only one. This race, *M. v. marshallorum*, is found throughout the whole of the Himalayas from Hazara on the west to Bhutan and Assam on the east. It breeds at elevations from 4000 to 8000 feet, and in winter moves down to a lower zone, even extending into the foot-hills and the plains that border thereon.

Habits, etc.—During the breeding season this Barbet is an inhabitant of shady wooded nullahs, preferably those clothed with deciduous trees, and though seldom seen, except when it ventures into roadside bushes after fruit, is well known about the hill stations as a disembodied voice. The bird sits high up in some shady tree, uttering monotonously time and again its mournful cry, a weird melancholy *peeee-oh* or *mee-ou* or *pyillo*, which is audible half a mile away as it resounds through the nullah, and being partly ventriloquial, as the bird turns its head from side to side, is traced to its origin with difficulty. Another characteristic note is *gyok-gyok-gyok*, and occasionally a harsh *karr-r* uttered with reiteration. Often two or three of the birds answer each other from different trees, each appearing as if it were trying to outdo the others with the loudness of its voice.

The hillmen have a legend that the bird is the reincarnation of the soul of a suitor, who died of grief at the unjust termination of his lawsuit, and that eternally his plaint rises to heaven *un-nee-ow, un-nee-ow*—injustice, injustice.

In winter these birds collect into small parties and then move down into the lower and more open hill jungles, where they feed on various fruits and are then very tame.

The flight is strong and vigorous, with great undulations like the flight of a Woodpecker, the beat of the wings producing a similar noise.

This bird breeds in May and June and excavates its own nest hole in the trunks and boughs of the larger trees, usually at a great height from the ground, but occasionally within easy reach. The entrance passage is usually short and leads into a rounded chamber in which the eggs rest on chips and debris; sometimes the passage leads straight into a natural hollow, which saves the birds the trouble of excavating an egg chamber.

The normal clutch consists of four eggs. They are variable in shape but are normally rather lengthened ovals, regular and somewhat obtuse at both ends. They are very fragile, fine in texture, and pure white with little gloss.

They measure about 1·37 by 0·98 inches.

THE GREEN BARBET

THEREICERYX ZEYLANICUS (Gmelin)

(Plate xvi, Fig. 1, opposite page 330)

Description.—Length 10 inches. Sexes alike. Head, neck and breast brown, with narrow pale shaft-streaks; upper plumage bright green, in places with narrow pale shaft-streaks terminating in whitish spots; flight-feathers brown, edged paler; tail bright green, washed below with pale verditer-blue.

Iris reddish-brown; a large naked space round the eye to the base of the beak orange; bill dead fleshy-pink; legs light yellowish-brown.

Field Identification.—Common arboreal plains bird, best known from its loud resounding call, *kotur-kotur-kotur*. In appearance a coarse green bird, with brownish head and a swollen conspicuous beak. Needs to be distinguished from the closely allied Lineated Barbet (*Thereiceryx lineatus*) of the Lower Himalayas, in which the pale stripes are much broader and the naked eye-patch does not extend to the base of the beak.

A third species of very similar appearance, but smaller, the Small Green Barbet (*Thereiceryx viridis*) is extremely common in the Shevaroys and along the west coast from Khandala to Cape Comorin.

Distribution.—This Barbet is confined to India and Ceylon; it is divided into three races. The typical form, small and dark, is found in Travancore and Ceylon. *T. z. caniceps*, the largest and palest race, is found in Northern India. Its distribution is rather irregular; it is found in the North-west Provinces, and along the foot of the Himalayas up to about 2500 feet as far west as Kangra and Gurdaspur, in Eastern Guzerat, the Central Provinces and South-western Bengal, the forest tracts between the Ganges and Godavari, and in portions of the Madras Presidency; also about Mount Aboo. An intermediate race, *T. z. inornatus*, is found along the west coast from Bombay to Coorg. It is a strictly resident species.

Habits, etc.—Like several other birds in India, this Barbet is exceedingly well known by sound to many people who do not know it by sight. It is purely arboreal, affecting richly-wooded and well-watered localities, especially in the neighbourhood of hills which it ascends to an altitude of about 3000 feet. It feeds chiefly on the fruit of wild fig trees, such as the banyan and peepul, and living high from the ground amongst their heavy foliage, is hard to see; for the green plumage blends with the leaves, and the curious flesh-coloured beak and yellow eye-patch simulate the berries; as if aware of this protective coloration it relies on it for concealment and is still and silent in the presence of danger. The flight is strong but rather heavy and undulating.

The presence of the bird is, however, revealed by the call, which is one of the familiar sounds of India. It may be heard throughout the year, though it is most persistent from January to June, when the breeding season urges the bird to its greatest efforts. It occasionally calls at night. The call is loud and monotonous and starts with a harsh sort of laugh, followed by a disyllabic call, which may be written *tur-r-r-r kutur-kotur-kotur*; another method of expressing it is by a repetition several times of the word *Pakrao.*

The eggs are laid in March and April. The nest hole is a chamber excavated in one of the larger branches of a soft-wooded tree with a short entrance tunnel which is neatly cut and rounded. It is excavated by the birds themselves, and they work very hard and continuously until it is finished. The hole is at any height from 6 to 50 feet from the ground. There is no nest, the eggs being merely laid on chips at the bottom of the hole.

The clutch consists of two to four eggs, which are laid rather irregularly, so that eggs in different stages of incubation may be found in the same clutch. The eggs are somewhat elongated very regular ovals, dull white, slightly glossy and unusually fragile for their size.

They measure about 1·20 by 0·87 inches.

THE BLUE-THROATED BARBET

Cyanops asiatica (Latham)

Description.—Length 9 inches. Sexes alike. Top of the head crimson, broken by a transverse black band above the eyes which turns backwards and borders the red over the ears; the transverse band has a yellow border in front; remainder of upper plumage grass-green, the flight-feathers blackish-brown, and the under surface of the tail washed with pale blue; sides of the head, chin, throat and fore-neck pale verditer-blue, with a crimson speck on each side at the lower base of the beak, and with a large crimson spot on each side of the neck; remainder of lower plumage yellowish-green.

Iris brown; eyelids orange; bill greenish-yellow, blackish above; legs dingy green, claws blackish.

Field Identification.—Sub-Himalayan species with a conspicuous call, ***kuttooruk***; a bright green bird with a gaudy mixture of black, crimson and blue about the head. Purely arboreal.

Distribution.—This rather gaudy species is found from the Himalayas to Assam, Burma and Siam, and is divided into several races. We are merely concerned with the typical form, which is a resident species throughout the Lower Himalayas and the Sub-Himalayan forests from Chamba eastwards, extending also into Lower Bengal, Assam and Burma. It is found from the level of the plains up to about 6000 feet.

Habits, etc.—The Blue-throated Barbet is found not so much in thick forest as in the more open hill jungles, where villages and cultivation have let in the sun and caused the growth of that rich and varied tree flora which is a great feature of the lower hills. In such places wild fruits of various kinds are extremely common, and on these the Barbet lives, wandering freely from tree to tree without fear of man, even nesting in the middle of the villages. It is purely arboreal and never descends to the ground, the variegated green plumage rendering it almost invisible in the thickly foliaged trees. Invisible it may be but inaudible it is not, especially in the spring; Bussant Bairi—the old woman of the spring—has a loud hard voice which echoes through the villages with its incessant call of ***kuruwak-kuruwak-kuruwak*** or ***kuttooruk***. By some hill tribes this bird is killed for food.

The breeding season lasts from April to July.

The nest hole is excavated in the trunk or bough of a tree generally at a height of 10 or 15 feet from the ground, a small or medium-sized tree being usually chosen. The entrance hole is only about a foot long, and in the nest chamber the eggs are laid merely on debris, though occasionally a pad of fibres, grass and other materials is found beneath the eggs.

The clutch consists of three eggs. These are pure white in colour, fine and compact in texture, sometimes with a slight gloss. The shape is a rather broad or elongated oval, somewhat pointed towards the small end.

The egg measures about 1·09 by 0·83 inches.

THE COPPERSMITH

XANTHOLÆMA HÆMACEPHALA (P. L. S. Müller)

(Plate x, Fig. 4, opposite page 198)

Description.—Length 6 inches. Sexes alike. A broad patch across the forehead and a broad gorget across the fore-neck bright glistening crimson; a streak above the eye and a broader patch below it and the chin and throat bright yellow; a golden-yellow band round the lower edge of the crimson gorget; a black band through the eye from the nostril and another from the gape below the cheeks, both merging into a broader black band which passes behind the ears and over the top of the head; remainder of the upper plumage olivaceous-green tinged with greyish on the back and sides of the neck, and slightly streaked with yellowish on the back: concealed portions of the flight-feathers blackish; lower plumage yellowish-white, streaked broadly with olivaceous-green especially on the flanks; tail faintly washed below with verditer-blue.

Iris brown; eyelids dull crimson; bill black; legs coral-red, claws black.

Field Identification.—Plains species, purely arboreal, and most familiar from its monotonous call; a small heavily-built greenish bird with gaudy yellow, crimson and black markings about the head.

Distribution.—Widely distributed through the greater part of the Indian Empire and Ceylon, and farther eastwards to the Malay Peninsula, Sumatra, and the Philippines. In India we are concerned only with one race, *X. h. indica*. This is not found in Baluchistan, the North-west Frontier Province or the South-western Punjab. With these exceptions it is found throughout India from the outer foot-hills of the Himalayas below 3000 feet, right down to the south. It is, however, rare in Sind and Cutch and in Southern Malabar. A strictly resident species.

A very similar bird, the Crimson-throated Barbet (*Xantholæma rubricapilla*), with the chin and throat crimson and the lower parts pale green unstreaked, is common along the west coast from above Goa to the extreme south. It is represented in Ceylon by a yellow-throated race.

Habits, etc.—The Coppersmith or Crimson-breasted Barbet is another of those Indian birds whose voice is more familiar to most people than its form. It is found in every type of open country where large trees abound and is purely arboreal, sitting and feeding amongst the green leaves with which its plumage assimilates, and never descending either to bushes or the ground. The flight is fairly strong and straight, with quick regular beats of the short wings, and the bird has no hesitation in flying high from tree to tree, often for a considerable distance.

The outstanding characteristic of the bird is its voice; the note is a loud but mellow *took*, in which is the unmistakable ring of metal, like the tap of a small hammer on metal; and this is repeated indefinitely at regular intervals as if a veritable coppersmith were at work; its monotony can be most exasperating as the sound never changes or varies except that it is somewhat ventriloquial; when the bird turns its head from side to side the call appears to come from different directions, as if two smiths were smiting alternately the same anvil. As the thermometer rises so does the persistence of the bird grow, and then its note may be definitely included amongst the hot weather worries of India. It usually calls from near the top of a tree, sometimes indeed clinging to the side of an upright twig. The call may be heard throughout the day, but not after dark.

The food consists almost entirely of the fruit of the various species of wild fig.

The breeding season is from February to May.

The eggs are laid in a hole in the bough of a tree, which is used and lengthened year by year until it may attain the length of 4 or 5 feet. The entrance is invariably a neat round hole cut by the birds themselves, usually on the under surface of the bough; but though the gallery and nest chamber may both be the work of the birds themselves, the gallery often cuts into a natural decayed hollow which is then smoothed and used. When the passage of several years has lengthened the hollow unduly a new entrance is frequently cut nearer to the egg chamber. There is no nest, the eggs merely lying on chips and debris. The nest hole is at any height from 7 to 40 feet from the ground.

The clutch consists of three or four eggs. They are long, narrow and nearly cylindrical in shape, very fragile and smooth in texture, with little or no gloss. The colour is pure unmarked white.

In size the egg averages about 0·99 by 0·69 inches.

THE BLUE-JAY

CORACIAS BENGHALENSIS (Linnæus)

(Plate xvii, Fig. 2, opposite page 352)

Description.—Length 13 inches. Sexes alike. Top of the head bluish-green; back and sides of the neck deep vinous; upper plumage dull greenish-brown, a patch of blue above the base of the tail; wings mixed blues and greens, the quills being deep purplish-blue marked conspicuously with a broad band of pale blue; tail deep blue, with a broad subterminal band of pale blue, interrupted by the central pair of feathers which are dull greenish; sides of head and throat purplish-lilac, streaked with whitish; breast vinous, also faintly streaked with whitish; remainder of lower plumage pale blue.

Iris greyish-brown; naked skin round the eye gamboge; bill blackish-brown; legs brownish-yellow.

The three front toes are more or less united at the base.

Field Identification.—One of the best-known birds of India; a heavy lumpy-looking nondescript-coloured bird which, as it takes to flight, reveals glorious Oxford-blue wings and tail, banded with Cambridge-blue.

Distribution.—The Blue-Jay or Indian Roller is widely spread throughout India, Burma and Ceylon, occurring also to the west as far as Amara, and to the east to Siam and Cochin-China. Several races have been distinguished. The typical race extends from the Persian Gulf throughout Northern India to Eastern Bengal. In the southern half of the Peninsula and Ceylon it is replaced by *C. b. indica*, while the darker and more mauve Burmese bird is known as *C. b. affinis*. The Common Roller of Kashmir, however, which may be easily distinguished by having the lower parts pale blue throughout and by lacking the wing and tail-bars, is *C. garrula semenovi*, a race of the European bird. This species is very plentiful on migration in the plains of North-western India. It should be emphasised that these birds are in no way related to the true Jays which belong to the Crow family.

The Indian Roller is a plains bird, and does not ascend the Himalayas over about 4000 feet; while in the main a resident species, it is locally migratory.

Very similar in appearance is the Broad-billed Roller *Eurystomus orientalis*, not rare in the foothills of the Himalayas, from Kumaon eastwards. It also occurs in South-west India and Ceylon but is far from common. It is a dull blue colour with a very distinct pale blue wing bar noticeable in flight.

Habits, etc.—Under the familiar name of Blue-Jay this Roller is one of the best-known of our Indian birds. It is a bird of open country, avoiding heavy jungle and preferring cultivation. There is very little variation in its habits; except in the breeding season it is found singly, but is so common that single birds will be met all over the countryside every quarter mile or so. It chooses an elevated open perch on which to sit, a dead bough of an ancient tree, the woodwork over a well, a ruined building, a telegraph post or wire, or in default of something better, a thorn bush or stone heap. On such a spot it sits motionless, the bright colours concealed or blending with the variegated tints of an Indian landscape; but all the while the large dark eyes are watching the ground in every direction; and a grasshopper has only to walk along a blade of grass, or a cricket or mouse to emerge from its burrow, and the Roller has launched itself straight at the spot to capture the toothsome morsel, settling on the ground beside it, and then flying back to its perch. To my last day in India I shall never lose the thrill that comes to me every time that I see the sudden transformation, as the dark lumpy bird reveals the banded glory of its wings and tail.

In early February the Roller betrays the secret of its name; its sedateness is exchanged for the love flights in which it rises and falls in the air with wildly flapping wings and harsh grating screams, advertising to all and sundry that Spring is in the air. The ordinary flight is strong and buoyant with slow but continuous flapping of the wings; occasionally it pursues insects on the wing, but this is not usual.

This bird is sacred to Shiva, who is said to have assumed its form.

The breeding season lasts from the end of March until July. The nest is invariably built in a hole, either in a tree or a building. It is a formless pad of tow, vegetable fibres, grass, old rags and similar materials, but it varies in size according to the circumstances of the hole adopted, and occasionally the eggs are merely laid on debris and chips in the bottom of the hole without any real nest being constructed.

The eggs are four or five in number. They are very broad ovals, sometimes almost spherical, highly glossy and hard in texture, of an unmarked pure china-white.

In size they average about 1·30 by 1·05 inches.

THE GREEN BEE-EATER

Merops orientalis Latham

(Plate x, Fig. 1, opposite page 198)

Description.—Length 9 inches, including 2 inches for the elongated central pair of tail-feathers. Sexes alike. Entire plumage bright green, in places tinged with blue, markedly so on the chin and throat; the crown to the upper back tinged with golden-ferruginous; flight-feathers rufous, washed exteriorly with green and finely tipped with blackish; a mark in front and below the eye and a fine gorget-line black.

Iris blood-red; bill black; legs dark plumbeous.

The bill is long, slender and curved; the feet are feeble with the three anterior toes united at the base, and the two central tail-feathers are long and pointed.

Field Identification.—Abundant plains species, easily identified by its long slender shape, with long beak and elongated central tail-feathers, and by the green plumage, with a coppery sheen from the wings in flight. Smaller than all other Indian Bee-Eaters. Hawks from trees and telegraph-wires.

Distribution.—This little Bee-Eater has an extensive range from Egypt through India, Ceylon and Burma to Siam and Cochin-China.

In this wide area it has, of course, been divided into several races, of which we are concerned with two. The typical race is found throughout India and Ceylon, with the exception of Sind, the Punjab, North-west Frontier Province and Baluchistan where it is replaced by *M. o. beludschicus*, a rather paler bird with a bluer throat. While ordinarily a plains bird, this Bee-Eater ascends the Outer Himalayas and other hill ranges occasionally to a height of 5000 to 6000 feet and even higher. It is locally migratory, though the movements still require to be worked out.

Habits, etc.—The Green Bee-Eater avoids heavy forest and the wetter tracts of India, and is most abundant wherever the country is open, frequenting both cultivation and desert areas. It is certainly one of the commonest birds of India, and attracts attention from its beautiful coloration and from its favourite perch being on the telegraph-wires. It also settles on trees, low bushes and walls, but only visits the ground for nesting purposes, the small and weak feet rendering the bird incapable of progression by walking or hopping; like other Bee-Eaters it spends its life hawking insects from a perch to which it returns after every flight, usually carrying a captured insect of some size which is battered to death and eaten there. The flight is free and graceful, and when the bird is travelling it is somewhat undulating. The note is a pleasant, cheerful but rather monotonous trill, *tree-tree-tree-tree*, which is usually uttered on the wing.

These birds are fond of living in small parties and they are very social at the roost, two or three hundred often collecting to sleep in a clump of trees.

The breeding season lasts from the middle of March until the beginning of June.

The eggs are laid in a circular chamber reached by a tunnel excavated in the ground, usually in the face of a perpendicular bank or cutting; the entrance tunnel may be anything up to 5 feet in length, and the opening is circular and very neatly cut, all the work being done by the birds themselves. No nest is built, the eggs being merely laid on the bare floor of the cavity.

The clutch varies from three to five eggs. They are nearly spherical in shape, pure white in colour without markings, and the texture is hard and brilliantly glossy.

They average 0·75 by 0·7 inches in size.

THE BLUE-TAILED BEE-EATER

Merops superciliosus Linnæus

(Plate xvi, Fig. 2, opposite page 330)

Description.—Length 12 inches, including elongated central pair of tail-feathers 2 inches. Sexes alike. A broad black streak from the beak through the eye, bordered narrowly above and broadly below by blue; upper plumage green tinged with rufous passing on the rump into verditer-blue; the wings more rufous-green than the back and tipped with blackish; tail verditer-blue, dark brown below, the long central pair of feathers tipped with black; throat chestnut passing into green on the breast, and this in turn into blue under the tail.

Iris crimson; bill black; legs dusky-plumbeous.

The bill is long and curved, the three exterior toes are united about their bases, and the central pair of tail-feathers are elongated and pointed, projecting 2 inches beyond the others.

Field Identification.—Common plains species, partial to the neighbourhood of water. Easily identified by long slender shape, with long sharp bill and central tail-feathers; distinguish from Green Bee-Eater by large size, chestnut throat and greenish under parts and generally duller coloration.

Distribution.—Throughout the greater part of the Oriental region. We are concerned with only two races. *M. s. javanicus*, as described above, occurs from India, Ceylon and Burma to Java. It is generally but locally distributed almost throughout India, except in Sind. It occurs along the foothills of the Himalayas up to about 3000 feet. *M. s. persicus* is more of a desert bird and is confined in India to parts of the North-west. It is a bluer, less bronzy-green below; there is more blue on the sides of the head and the upper surface of the tail is green.

The European Bee-Eater (*Merops apiaster*) breeds very abundantly in Kashmir. The brilliant yellow throat and blue under parts immediately identify it, whilst the brown and yellow upper parts are conspicuous in the field.

Habits, etc.—This fine Bee-Eater is common in well-cultivated and open country, provided it is not too dry. It is particularly partial to the neighbourhood of water, and may be found in large flights on the banks of rivers and about jheels and tanks. These birds perch on open elevated situations, such as tall half-withered trees standing in water or on telegraph-wires, and continually dart into the air to take a passing insect which they take back and eat on their perch: but it is a familiar sight, especially in the evenings, to see a flock drifting along through the air, flying fast with beating wings for a few yards and then soaring with stiff open pinions, catching insects as they go. The call-note is freely uttered on the wing and is a rather mellow and characteristic sound, a rolling whistle or chirp *teerp*. The food consists entirely of insects, chiefly dragon-flies and bees.

The breeding season is from March to June. The birds nest in colonies, excavating their nest holes in the face of natural banks or in mounds like those that mark the site of old brick-kilns. The eggs are laid on the soil in a rounded chamber which is reached by a tunnel some 4 to 7 feet long. This tunnel is usually not quite straight.

The clutch normally consists of four or five eggs.

The egg is pure white with a very high gloss and fine hard texture. In shape it is a spherical oval.

The average size is about 0·88 by 0·75 inches.

THE CHESTNUT-HEADED BEE-EATER

MEROPS LESCHENAULTI (Vieillot)

Description.—Length 8·5 inches. The sexes are alike. A line under the eye and through the ear-coverts black; head, neck and lower back chestnut; upper tail coverts pale blue; wings and tail green tinged with black; throat very pale yellow separated from the breast by a dark chestnut band, bordered on the posterior margin with black; breast, abdomen and under tail coverts grass-green varying in shade.

Iris crimson; bill black; legs dusky black.

Field Identification.—From other Bee-eaters described above this species is distinguished by the square tail, the two middle tail feathers not prolonged, and the chestnut back.

Distribution.—The Himalayan Terai from the Kumaon foothills eastward through Assam and Burma to the Malay Peninsula and the Andaman Islands. The species is very rare on the east side of the Peninsula, but on the Malabar coast it is not uncommon though local, and is found from Belgaum to Travancore and Ceylon. In the thicker forests in Kanara, both above and below Ghats, it is generally distributed, and in the Nilgiri and Pulney Hills is common up to 5000 and 3000 feet respectively, while in the Travancor Hills it is not rare. It occurs in Mysore and Hyderabad but is local. In the Himalayas it is not found above 4000 feet. Another striking species is the Blue-bearded Bee-eater (*Alcemerops athertoni*) grass-green in colour except the forehead, throat and upper breast which are blue. It is a forest bird found from Kuman along the lower Himalayas to Assam and south to Tenasserim, also on the Malabar coast from Belgaum to Travancore, and has occurred in south-west Behar and Orissa.

Habits, etc.—In some parts of its range in South India, this

Bee-eater is locally migratory. No birds are found in the western slopes of the Nilgiri Hills between June and November, and in Coorg large flocks seen in June disappeared by the end of the month. In the non-breeding season the species is met with in small parties of from four to eight birds, or in flocks of a hundred or more. As a rule it is restricted to forested country or maidans interspaced with trees, and occasionally frequents the vicinity of cultivated areas surrounded by forests. The birds roost in company in trees or in tall reeds on river banks, and towards sunset collect in flocks preparatory to settling down for the night. At this time they behave like flocks of starlings and there is much calling and flying about. The note is not to be distinguished from that of the Blue-tailed Bee-eater.

The eggs are laid from February to May, according to the latitude. The nest is at the end of a tunnel, excavated by the birds themselves, and is an enlarged chamber some six by eight inches without any nesting material. The tunnel is about two inches in diameter and varies very much in length according to the material in which it is excavated. It is usually from three to eight feet, at times as much as ten feet when in soft sand, but if in hard earth or clay it may not be more than a foot or so. The nests are generally near water, in a bank of a river or stream, and sometimes even in a sandbank in a river. Not infrequently the birds are flooded out and betake themselves to nearby nullahs where they make a new tunnel. The birds sit very close and both remain in the nesting chamber at night. Sometimes they breed in colonies, but more often several pairs breed within a short distance of one another.

The eggs are four to eight in number, pure glossy white.

They measure 0·87 by 0·76 inches.

THE PIED KINGFISHER

Ceryle rudis (Linnæus)

Description.—Length 12 inches. Male: Top of the head with a small crest black streaked with white; a conspicuous white line over the eye; a black line from the beak through the eye connecting with a narrow black line to the black gorget; an indistinct white collar on the hind neck; upper plumage mixed black and white; flight-feathers white with irregular black bars; tail white, with a broad black terminal band; lower plumage silvery-white with two black gorgets across the breast, the upper being the broader; some black spots on the sides of the throat and flanks.

The female lacks the hinder gorget and has the other broken in the centre.

Iris brown; bill and legs black.

The bill is long, heavy and pointed; the feet are weak, the outer toe being largely united to the centre toe.

Field Identification.—Common plains bird, always found by water, and conspicuous for its habit of hovering and plunging for fish. Pied black and white plumage, with a big sharp bill.

Distribution.—This Kingfisher has a wide distribution from Egypt to China, but in India we are concerned only with the race *C. rudis leucomelanura*, which is found practically throughout India, Burma and Ceylon in the plains. It does not ascend higher than about 2500 feet in the hill ranges, being replaced above that height in the Himalayas by the larger Himalayan Pied Kingfisher (*Ceryle lugubris*) of rather similar coloration. It is a strictly resident species.

FIG. 44—Pied Kingfisher (½ nat. size)

Habits, etc.—The Pied Kingfisher is to be found in the plains wherever there is water, except in the midst of forest. As a breeding species it is largely confined to the banks of rivers, but having a voracious appetite and strong flight it wanders far afield and appears at every jheel and tank, also to some extent visiting tidal creeks and backwaters where the water is brackish; in places it may even be found on the seashore.

In such situations this bird may readily be watched at its fishing, for it is very common and its diet consists entirely of small fish. It flies over the water at a height of some 10 to 20 feet above the surface, and suddenly catching sight of a shoal of fish below checks itself dead in mid-air and hovers with the wings vibrating rapidly and the bill pointing perpendicularly downwards, as if taking aim. From this position it plunges headlong into the water, and if the aim has been true it emerges with a small fish in the bill and flies away with it, uttering cries of satisfaction; but often the plunge is unsuccessful, or the bird checks itself in mid-dive and hovers again, or goes off finally without diving at all. In flight a sharp querulous twittering cry is freely uttered. When not fishing the bird rests on a high bank or post, and these favourite perches are often marked by the pellets of indigestible fish-scales which the bird disgorges, like the castings of the birds of prey. When resting the bird at intervals gives its tail a sharp upward flick.

The breeding season is very early, commencing about December and lasting until April. The eggs are laid in a circular chamber at the end of a tunnel, 1 to 5 feet long, which is invariably excavated in a perpendicular bank face over running water. There is no nest, but the floor of the egg-chamber is partly covered with fish-scales and similar debris from broken-up pellets.

The clutch consists of four to six eggs. They are very broad ovals, often almost spherical, of a hard texture with a high gloss. The colour is pure china-white.

They average about 1·20 by 0·95 inches in size.

THE COMMON KINGFISHER

ALCEDO ATTHIS (Linnæus)

(Plate xvii, Fig. 5, opposite page 352)

Description.—Length 7 inches. Sexes alike. Top of the head finely banded with black and blue; a band from the beak below the eye to the side of the neck bright ferruginous ending in a conspicuous white patch; a black mark in front of the eye; a broad moustachial stripe bright blue; upper plumage bright blue becoming greenish on the sides and wings; hidden portions of wings and underside of tail brown; chin and throat white; remainder of lower plumage ferruginous.

Iris dark brown; bill black, sometimes orange-red at lower base; legs coral-red, claws dusky.

The bill is long, heavy and sharply pointed; the feet are weak, the 3rd and 4th toes being partly united.

Field Identification.—Generally common by water over which when disturbed it flies low and fast, uttering a hard sharp squeak; a small stout bird with disproportionately large beak and brilliant plumage, green and blue above and chestnut below.

Distribution.—The Common Kingfisher is a widely-spread species in Europe, Northern Africa and Asia, and has in consequence been divided into a number of races; of these we are concerned with three. *A. a. pallasii* of Western Siberia and Persia is the bird which is so common in summer about the waterways and lakes of Kashmir, appearing in winter in Baluchistan and as far as Sind in the plains. *A. a. bengalensis* is a smaller resident species throughout the plains of India, except in the extreme south, occasionally ascending the mountain ranges up to a height of about 6000 feet. These races differ only in size but *A. c. taprobanus* of Ceylon and the lower part of Southern India is a much bluer bird.

A much larger species (length 15 inches) with a very heavy beak the Stork-billed Kingfisher (*Ramphalcyon capensis*) is locally distributed through the wetter parts of India, Ceylon, Assam and Burma. The top of the head is brown, a collar and the lower parts buffy yellow and the back, wings and tail greenish-blue.

Habits, etc.—The Common Kingfisher is, as is well known, purely a water-bird, frequenting fresh water of every description, and occasionally also wandering to the confines of tidal creeks and the seashore. Its food consists of tiny fishes and various aquatic insects, larvæ and other organisms.

This Kingfisher usually captures its food by plunging obliquely into the water from an overhanging bough, stump or clump of reeds or similar vantage point on which it sits motionless waiting for something to come within its reach; but at times it hovers over open water with the body erect at right angles to the surface, and some 10 to 15 feet above it, and from this position dives perpendicularly into the water.

The flight is very swift and straight, generally low above the surface of the water, and as the bird goes it utters a loud call *ch'kee* which draws attention to the short shuttle-shaped form and brilliant colours of the passing bird. It is a very pugnacious species, and once a pair have established their right to a stretch of water they are very intolerant of the presence of others of their kind.

The breeding season is rather irregular, but the majority of eggs will be found from March to June.

The nest is excavated in the face of a perpendicular bank, generally at the edge of water, but occasionally at a considerable distance from it. The entrance tunnel is anything up to 3 feet in length, and is very narrow, about 2 inches in diameter; it terminates in a circular chamber some 5 inches in diameter and 3 or 4 inches in height. The chamber and passage always contain minute fish bones disgorged by the birds, but no nest is constructed, the eggs lying merely on the floor of the chamber.

The clutch consists of five to seven eggs. These are almost spherical in shape, pure unmarked china-white in colour, of hard texture with a high gloss.

In size they average about 0·8 by 0·7 inches.

THE WHITE-BREASTED KINGFISHER

HALCYON SMYRNENSIS (Linnæus)

(Plate xvii, Fig. 3, opposite page 352)

Description.—Length 11 inches. Sexes alike. Head, neck and lower plumage deep chestnut-brown, with a conspicuous white patch extending over the chin, throat and central breast; remainder of upper plumage blue, tinged with greenish, a blackish band along the side of the wing; flight-feathers black with a conspicuous white patch towards their base.

Iris brown; bill dark dull red; legs coral-red, claws dusky.

The bill is long, very heavy and pointed; the feet are weak, the 2nd and 3rd toes being partly joined together.

Field Identification.—Found over water or land indifferently, and one of the most characteristic birds of the plains. Noisy, and conspicuous with the heavy red beak, the white breast-patch set in deep chestnut and the greenish-blue upper parts; in flight the white wing-patch is very noticeable, as is the large beak.

Distribution.—This handsome bird has an immense range from Asia Minor through Persia, India, Ceylon, Burma, and the Malay Peninsula to Southern China. Of the races into which it is divided we are concerned with two. The typical form, *H. s. smyrnensis*, is found throughout India except in Travancore where it is replaced by *H. s. fusca* of Ceylon which is a darker chocolate-brown and a bluer green in colour. This species wanders occasionally into the Himalayas and other ranges up to a height of 6000 feet. It is strictly resident.

Habits, etc.—While the other Kingfishers described in this work are purely water-birds, living chiefly on fish, this very typical Kingfisher is mainly a land bird and feeds largely on insects, lizards, frogs and such small fry, which it captures after the manner of a Roller, flying down to them on the ground from an elevated perch. It is said very occasionally both to plunge into water after fish and has been observed diving after fresh-water crabs which it beats to pulp before swallowing, also to take insects on the wing. The flight is strong and direct, and on the wing a loud screaming cry is uttered which is one of the familiar sounds of India. This species avoids heavy forest and actual desert areas, but is found in every other type of country, either wet or dry.

The breeding season lasts from March to July. The eggs are laid in the usual chamber at the end of a tunnel, which, as in the case of the other species, is excavated in the faces of banks and borrow-pits, usually, but by no means always, in the vicinity of water. The shafts of unbricked wells are sometimes selected as a nesting site.

The eggs are four to seven in number. They are almost spherical in shape, pure unmarked china-white in colour, with a hard texture and high gloss. As incubation proceeds they lose their gloss and become stained, and are sometimes covered with small black spots apparently the excreta of parasites.

In size they average 1·15 by 1·05 inches.

THE GREAT HORNBILL

DICHOCEROS BICORNIS (Linnæus)

Description.—Length 52 inches. Sexes alike. Head black; neck fulvescent white; upper plumage and wings black, a broad white bar across the wing and all the quills with their bases and ends white; tail and its upper and under coverts white, a broad black band near the end of the tail; breast black; abdomen white.

Iris, male blood-red, female pearly white; bill and casque yellow, tinged with red at the tip and with orange in the middle. In the male the front and back of the casque are black, together with the ridge of the bill just in front of the casque. In the female the back of the casque is red. Bare skin round the eye fleshy pink, eyelids black; legs greenish plumbeous.

Bill large, stout and much curved. A broad casque covering the head and the base of the bill, broad, flattened and rounded behind rising at the sides and projecting in two points in front. Conspicuous eyelashes. Tail long and rounded. Toes joined at their base.

Field Identification.—Western Ghats and Lower Himalayas only. A large ungainly forest bird of black and white plumage, unmistakable from the heavy double casque over the huge curved beak. Very noisy and in flight recognisable by the noise made by the wings. The white neck suffices to distinguish this species from the smaller black and white Hornbills of the genus *Hydrocissa* found in the Western Ghats, Peninsular India and the Himalayas which have the neck black and the casque single.

Distribution.—Widely distributed from India, Assam and Burma through the Malay Peninsula to Sumatra. All but Sumatran birds belong to the typical race. In India this is confined to the Western Ghats from near Bombay to Cape Comorin and to the lower Himalayan ranges up to 5000 feet from Kumaon eastwards.

Habits, etc.—The Great Hornbill is a forest bird and generally keeps to the largest trees where it may be found in parties of half a dozen birds or upwards. It is difficult to overlook the presence of this species. In flight it may be heard a mile away by the loud droning noise of the air rushing through the base of the outer wing-quills which are not fully covered by their under-covert feathers in the usual manner. In a tree they are noisy, apt to indulge in the most extraordinary rattling roars, cacklings and bellows.

The flight is an alternation of a series of flapping of the wings and of sailing with the wings motionless, but the flapping predominates and the flight is less undulating than in some of the other species of Hornbill.

FIG. 45—Great Hornbill ($\frac{1}{0}$ nat. size)

The food mainly consists of fruit and this is picked with the tip of the bill, jerked into the air and caught in the throat and swallowed. These Hornbills are, however, omnivorous feeders and readily take insects, lizards, grain and other food, all of which is jerked into the air and caught in the manner described.

Nothing is known about the purpose of the curious casque, which is not solid but cellular and partly hollow in structure. Captive birds are said to be very destructive, using the bill as a pickaxe—if this habit is general in the wild state it is possible that the casque is in the nature of a shock-absorber.

The breeding season is from January to April. The breeding habits do not appear to differ in any important detail from those described at length under the Grey Hornbill. The same nest hole is used year after year for long periods.

The eggs vary in shape from very broad ovals, obtuse at both ends to moderately elongated ovals, distinctly pointed at the small end. The shell is tolerably hard and compact but is very commonly covered with tiny pimples and roughnesses and in most specimens the entire surface is somewhat conspicuously pitted with pores. The colour is pure white with a certain amount of gloss, but as the interior of the nest is intolerably dirty the eggs become dirty and stained to a uniform chocolate-brown.

They measure about 2·60 by 1·88 inches.

THE GREY HORNBILL

Tockus birostris (Scopoli)

Description.—Length 24 inches. Sexes alike. Upper plumage light brownish-grey, with pale whitish streaks over the eyes; the cheek and ear-coverts blackish-grey; flight-feathers dark brown, fringed and tipped with grey or white; tail long and graduated, brown, each feather with a broad sub-terminal darker band glossed with green and a white tip; chin to the breast grey merging into white on the abdomen.

Iris red-brown; bill black, whitish about tip; feet dark plumbeous.

Bill large, curved and laterally compressed, with a small pointed spur above, known as a casque; eyelids furnished with lashes.

Field Identification.—A large ungainly grey bird with a long graduated tail and a small pointed casque on the top of the narrow curved beak. Arboreal plains species, with a peculiar squealing cry.

Distribution.—A purely Indian species. It is found from the base of the Himalayas at about 2000 feet throughout the better wooded parts of India, except from Bombay to Travancore along the Malabar Coast where it is replaced by an allied species, the Malabar Grey Hornbill (*Tockus griseus*), which lacks the casque on the beak. It is absent from the North-west Frontier Province, the Northern and Western Punjab, Sind, and portions of Eastern Rajputana. It is rare in the Gangetic delta of Lower Bengal which forms its eastern boundary. A resident species.

Habits, etc.—The Grey Hornbill is an entirely arboreal species, which is found about old trees in well-timbered, fairly open country, coming into gardens and avenues, and avoiding thick forest. It is found in small parties which fly about from bough to bough, eating the various species of wild figs and other fruits and seeds, green leaves, and a certain quantity of insects, such as hornets. When flying from tree to tree across the open the flight is heavy and undulating with alternating flappings and glidings, and all the movements of the bird are clumsy and ungainly. The cry is a harsh squeal, distinctly reminiscent of that of the Common Kite.

The breeding season is from April to June, and, like other Hornbills, this species is chiefly remarkable for its curious nesting arrangements.

The eggs are laid without the construction of any nest in a large hole in the trunk of a tree, at any height from 10 feet upwards. The

FIG. 46—Grey Hornbill ($\frac{1}{5}$ nat. size)

cotton tree or the peepul is usually selected. When ready to lay the female enters the nest-hole and remains therein until the young are about a week old. She spends the first two or three days in plastering up the entrance to the hole with her own ordure, which is very viscid and strong and hardens into a clay-like substance. For this work she uses the flattened sides of her beak as a trowel.

When the work is completed only a narrow vertical slit is left, about the width of a man's finger and two or three inches deep. After this the droppings are thrown out daily through the slit. The female is now completely a prisoner and is dependent on the male for all her food. This he brings held in his beak; he perches on a neighbouring bough and then flies to the entrance of the nest hollow, where he clings with his claws to the bark and feeds the female who extrudes the point of her beak through the slit to receive the food. This habit is perhaps responsible for the curious fact, observed in captivity with reference to some species of Hornbill, and perhaps connected with all, that at intervals the epithelial layer of the gizzard is cast in the form of a closed sack containing the seeds of fruit on which the bird has been feeding.

During the period spent incubating in the nest the female becomes very fat and dirty, and on first emergence is so stiff that she can hardly fly. In some species of Hornbill the moult apparently takes place during the period of imprisonment.

The clutch varies from one to five eggs.

The eggs are broad rather perfect ovals, very fine and smooth in texture and without gloss. They are a dull uniform white with a creamy tinge, and naturally become somewhat discoloured as incubation progresses.

In size they average about 1·7 by 1·22 inches.

THE HOOPOE

UPUPA EPOPS Linnæus

Description.—Length 12 inches. Sexes alike. Head and a long fan-shaped crest, the feathers increasing in length from front to back, rufous-fawn, the feathers of the crest broadly tipped with white and black; back and sides of the neck and a broad patch across the shoulders to the bend of the wing dull ashy-fawn colour; remainder of the back broadly banded with black and fawny-white, the bands continuing across the wing-coverts; quills of the wing and tail black, the primaries with a white band across their tips, the secondaries with three or four white bands evenly distributed throughout their length, and the tail with a single white chevron-shaped band near the centre; chin whitish; throat and breast pale rufous-fawn, ashy on the sides of the breast; remainder of the lower plumage white, largely streaked with black and ashy-grey.

Iris red-brown; bill horny-black, fleshy at lower base; legs plumbeous-slate.

The bill is long, slender and curved, with a very short tongue; wing rounded.

Field Identification.—The fawn-coloured plumage and the black wings and tail, banded with white, the long curved bill, and the broad fan-shaped crest, freely lowered and raised, put the identity of this species beyond all doubt at the first glance.

Distribution.—Widely distributed in Europe, Africa and Asia, the Hoopoe is divided into a number of sub-species, of which we

PLATE XV

2. Great Himalayan Barbet ($\frac{1}{4}$ nat. size)

1. Allied Grosbeak ($\frac{1}{3}$ nat. size)

[*Face p.* 308

are concerned with three; these are not very easily recognised, and vary in small details of size and coloration. *U. e. orientalis* is the resident species of Northern India, and southwards it shades about the Bombay Presidency into *U. e. ceylonensis* which extends to Ceylon, and is also a resident bird. The typical form *U. e. epops* breeds in the Himalayas and in winter migrates southwards into the plains; at that season it is common in Sind, the Punjab and the United Provinces. The typical race has a patch of white in the longer feathers of the crown between the fawn and the black, this colour being either absent or only represented by a slight trace in the two resident races,

FIG. 47—Hoopoe (⅓ nat. size)

which are also slightly smaller. The southern bird is also more richly coloured.

Mention must be made of two curious birds—the Red-headed Trogon (*Harpactes erythrocephalus*) of the Eastern Himalayas and Assam and the Malabar Trogon (*Harpactes fasciatus*) from the Malabar Coast and the Chota Nagpur area. The male of the former is rose-pink and chestnut; the male of the latter is chestnut with a black head and red belly. They are arboreal birds with soft mewing calls and remarkable for soft dense plumage and long square-ended tails.

Habits, etc.—The Hoopoe avoids areas of thick forest and is found very commonly in open country, more especially in the neighbourhood of groves of trees, thin scrub-forest, and the outskirts of villages where it frequents mud-walls and deserted or ruined buildings It feeds almost entirely on the ground and is very partial to grassy lawns, the neighbourhood of avenues and other similar localities favourable to the various ground-feeding larvæ which form the greater portion of its food. It walks and runs with great ease and methodically quarters the ground, probing the roots of grass and the interstices of the soil or turning over leaves and rubbish for the insects, caterpillars and grubs that shelter there. When disturbed it flies up into trees or on to buildings, but does not usually feed anywhere except on the ground.

While feeding the crest is depressed and closed, but it invariably erects it for a moment on settling after flight. Ordinarily the flight is slow and hesitating with a good deal of undulation as if the bird were uncertain of its destination; but its extended migrations and wanderings show that this weakness is only apparent, and the bird has no difficulty in avoiding capture by trained falcons, mounting easily into the air away from them.

The call is a loud rather mellow *hoot* or *hud* repeated two or three times, which has given rise to the names current in various languages, all onomatopœic in origin. There is also a harsh grating note which is generally used at the nest.

The presence of definite names for this species in numerous languages indicates the hold that the Hoopoe has obtained on the imagination and interest of man from the earliest ages; nor is this strange in view of its tame disposition and striking appearance.

Realistic portraits of the Hoopoe have been found in mural paintings both of ancient Egypt and of Crete, and from that time onwards mention of the bird runs through literature and legend to the present day. In Western legend the bird is most familiar as the form assumed by Jereus, King of Crete, for his punishment; while Mohammedan countries regard the bird as the favourite and confidante of Solomon whose magnificence dowered its crown. The Hoopoe is the Lapwing of the Bible. The most prominent attribute of the bird, however, in literature, is its use in magical or medical prescriptions; use of its different parts is recommended by various authors, most frequently in connection with visions or the power of memory, from Egyptian days down to the *Pharmacopœia Universalis* of Dr R. James (1752).

The breeding season extends from February to July, but the majority of nests will be found in April and May.

The nest is a very poor affair, being merely a slight collection of grass, hair, leaves or feathers, placed roughly on the floor of the hole selected. For the site the chief requisite is darkness, and the bird nests in holes of every sort, in trees, walls and roofs, or even on the floor in closed and deserted huts.

When breeding the female develops an unpleasant smell, and as she seldom leaves the nest, being largely fed therein by the male, and never cleans it out when the young are hatched, the nest becomes very offensive and smelly; this fact was well known to the classical authors, and doubtless accounts for the Hoopoe being "unclean" in the Jewish law. It is, however, freely eaten by Christian populations in Southern Europe.

The clutch varies from three to ten eggs, and as incubation commences with the laying of the first eggs, there is generally a good deal of variation in the size of the young in a nest.

The egg is a rather lengthened oval, often somewhat pointed at the smaller end, and sometimes also at the broader end as well. The texture is smooth and hard and without gloss. There are no markings, and the colour, when fresh, varies from pale greenish-blue to pale olive-brown, though as incubation progresses the eggs become stained a dirty brown.

The egg averages about 1·00 by 0·66 inches in size.

THE INDIAN SWIFT

MICROPUS AFFINIS (Gray)

Description.—Length 6 inches. Sexes alike. A broad white band across the rump, and the chin and throat white, the feathers more or less dark-shafted; remainder of the plumage dark blackish-brown, somewhat glossy, paler on the top of the head and under the tail, and with a deep black spot in front of the eye.

Iris dark brown; bill black; legs vinous-brown.

Bill short and hooked with an excessively broad gape; wings stiff and sickle-shaped, specialised for great speed; tail short and rather deeply forked; feet weak and adapted to clinging to perpendicular surfaces, the four toes being directed forwards, though the first is more or less reversible.

Field Identification.—A small black bird with a white rump, entirely aerial and gregarious in its habits, the narrow sickle-shaped wings indicating the extreme specialisation of its structure. Abundant over towns and villages.

Distribution.—From North-western Africa through South-eastern Asia, India, Ceylon and Burma to the Malay Peninsula. It is divided into races, of which we are concerned merely with the typical race. This is found throughout India and Ceylon, very common in some places and wanting in others, with no apparent reason for its capricious distribution. In the Himalayas it is not common, but may be found up to a height of 6000 feet. It is locally migratory, but information on this point is sadly defective.

A similar but larger species, the White-rumped Swift (*Micropus pacificus*) is found along the Himalayas and in Assam, and with it in the Western Himalayas one meets also the Common Swift (*Micropus apus*) which lacks the white rump.

The Alpine Swift (*Micropus melba*) will be found locally and seasonally common throughout the Himalayas and India. It is twice the size of the Indian Swift and can be easily recognised by having the under surface of the body white, with a dark band across the breast. The still larger Needle-tailed Swifts of the genus *Hirundapus* (Himalayas and South-western India) are probably the fastest flying birds in the world. They owe their name to the stiff and pointed ends of the shafts of the tail-feathers which extend beyond the vanes like needles.

FIG. 48—Indian Swift (¼ nat. size)

Habits, etc. — The Common Indian Swift is highly gregarious, being usually found in flocks of fifty or more individuals, which breed together in colonies, and spend the hours of daylight in company hawking insects including small beetles, often at an immense height from the ground. The nest colonies are perhaps most frequently found about buildings, whether these be the ordinary dwelling-houses of an Indian village or town, or ruined temples, shrines and forts. They also nest under bridges and rocks on steep hill-sides or in precipitous nullahs.

The birds occupy these nest colonies continuously. Not only do individuals breed somewhat irregularly so that a large colony will be found at any time to have eggs or young in some of the nests, but the nests are also used for sleeping and resting. Otherwise the whole of their life is spent in the air, rushing with swift curving flight, several rapid beats of the wings and then a glide, and at times uttering the curious squealing call which so aptly seems to express the fierce joy of an aerial creature in its element. The flocks usually feed in loose open order, but at times, especially in the evenings, they collect together into a " ball," mounting high into the air as a squealing, careering mass.

Owing to its highly specialised structure this Swift is quite unable to perch on a tree or to visit the ground. Should it tumble accidentally to the ground, the short curious legs and feet are of no assistance in helping it to rise, but a stroke or two of the wings will generally lift the bird off the ground.

The nest colonies are very conspicuous; they consist of a number of large globular nests composed of feathers, grass and straws cemented together with saliva so as to form a tough material. These nests are constructed on the under surfaces of rocks or roofs singly, or in a mass with one nest built against another; while in some instances the nests are built inside a hole with merely a little material plastered around the entrance. These birds feel cold greatly, and wet weather or a cold snap may send them half torpid to their nests.

The eggs are very long and narrow ovals, much pointed towards the small end; the texture is rather frail and almost without gloss. In colour they are a pure and spotless white.

They average in size about 0·85 by 0·55 inches.

THE PALM-SWIFT

Cypsiurus batassiensis (Gray)

Description.—Length 5 inches. Sexes alike. Dull brown above, head slightly darker, wing and tail feathers much darker; beneath pale greyish-brown, chin and throat palest.

Iris reddish; bill black; legs dusky-brown.

Bill short with a wide gape; toes arranged in two pairs, the 1st and 2nd inwards, the 3rd and 4th outwards; tail deeply forked; wing narrow and sickle-shaped.

Field Identification.—Aerial in its habits, hawking in company round palm-trees; distinguish from the Indian Swift by its smaller size, slower flight, longer tail, and absence of the white rump band.

Distribution.—This Swift is found throughout Ceylon and the whole of India except in the Punjab and Sind. In Rajputana it is only found about Mount Aboo. It is represented by another race, *T. b. infumatus*, in Assam and Burma and the farther East.

Habits, etc.—This quaint little Swift may be said to be parasitic on the toddy-tree or fan-palm (*Borassus flabelliformis*), and it is only found in the areas where that tree grows, though very occasionally it breeds in some other species of palm. The nest is built in the palm and the birds spend their lives hawking for insects including small beetles in the vicinity, flying round and about with a rather irregular flight which is somewhat slower than that of most species of Swift. They sometimes cluster together on the leaves of the palms between the ribs of the fronds, and move up and down the leaf with a shuffling mode of progression owing to the shortness of their legs; colonies of bats are found in similar situations and a single tree may contain a colony of both bird and mammal.

Although the birds live in colonies, not more than two or three pairs usually nest in the one tree. It is interesting to note that in the Garo and Naga Hills where the people thatch their houses with palm-leaves the allied race, *T. b. infumatus*, nests in the leaves on the roofs as well as on the trees.

The breeding season lasts almost the year round according to locality, and at least two broods appear to be reared.

The great fan-leaves of the palm get bent by the wind and hang down so that the points of the leaves turn somewhat inwards, and it is to the under surface of that portion of the leaf which is bent inwards that the nest is attached. The bent portion of the leaf stands at an angle of from 40 to 70 degrees, so that the under surface becomes in fact an upper surface, and presents a sloping furrowed bank to which the nest is attached. In one of these furrows formed by the large pleats of the leaf, and always about the centre of this latter is firmly glued a tiny nest, shaped like a watch-pocket, composed of fine vegetable down or fine feathers cemented together by the bird's own saliva. The main body of the nest is fairly soft, but the rim of the front is matted into a sort of cord to withstand the pressure of the bird's weight.

The usual clutch consists of three eggs, but four or five are sometimes laid.

The egg is a long oval, slightly compressed towards one end; the texture is fine, the colour white, and there is usually no gloss.

In size the egg measures about 0·70 by 0·45 inches.

THE INDIAN CRESTED SWIFT

Hemiprocne coronata (Tickell)

Description.—Length, 9 inches. Male: Crest dark ashy-blue; upper plumage dull ashy-blue, including the innermost flight-feathers; remainder of wings and tail black, glossed with greenish-blue; a velvet-black patch in front of the eye with a very narrow white line above it; a streak below the beak and a large patch behind and below the eye chestnut; chin paler chestnut; lower plumage ashy-grey becoming white under the tail.

Female: Similar to the male but the chestnut streak below the beak is replaced by white and the chestnut patch behind the eye by the colour of the upper parts; chin ashy-grey.

Iris dark brown; bill black; legs pinkish-brown.

Bill short with a very wide gape; a distinct crest on the forehead;

wings and tail long, the latter deeply forked ; a patch of silky down feathers on each flank.

Field Identification.—An ashy-grey bird with wings and tail glossy blackish. The male has a bright chestnut patch on the ear. Resembles a Swallow rather than a Swift with its long pointed wings and deeply forked tail. Found in parties hawking insects and settling on trees. A loud call.

Distribution.—Confined to India, Ceylon, Assam, Burma and Siam. No races. In India it is found locally throughout the whole country from the sub-Himalayan area southwards, except in the Punjab, Sind and parts of Rajputana. A resident species which occurs at all elevations up to 4000 feet and possibly higher.

FIG. 49—Indian Crested Swift (⅜ nat. size)

Habits.—The Crested Swift is a bird of forests and well-wooded country where it is found in small parties and sometimes even in flocks that hawk about for insects with a wheeling graceful flight which in character and pace recalls that of a Swallow rather than a Swift. It constantly perches in trees, usually preferring the topmost branches and those which are dead or bare of leaves. It sits upright and erects the crest. The call is loud and Parrot-like, *teé-chee*, and this is uttered frequently, both on the wing and from a branch, whilst the bird is particularly noisy in the evenings when preparing to roost. Should there be a tank or pool of water or river near its haunts this Swift is fond of descending rapidly from the air to the surface of the water, touching it and mounting again in one graceful curve.

The breeding season in India is from March to June.

The nest is a most remarkable structure. It is a very shallow half-saucer, composed of thin flakes of bark and a few small feathers gummed together with inspissated saliva on the side of a horizontal branch. The nest is nowhere more than an eighth of an inch in thickness, and is at most half an inch deep in the deepest part. The largest outside measurement is 2 inches, which is to say that the nest can be covered by a crown-piece. The branch chosen is usually a dead one often at the top of a high tree, but many nests are built much lower on small trees growing in open scrub-jungle. Viewed from below the nest has all the appearance of a knot and would seldom be detected were it not for the fact that the female returns at frequent intervals to it. The single egg completely fills the nest. The parent bird sits across the nest and the branch to which it is attached so that the latter takes her weight.

The egg is a very elongated oval, obtuse at both ends and with little or no gloss. It is white with a slight greyish-blue tinge.

It measures about 0·94 by 0·61 inches.

THE INDIAN NIGHTJAR

Caprimulgus asiaticus Latham

Description.—Length 10 inches. Sexes alike. Upper parts yellowish-grey, with black elongated spots down the centre of the crown, and very narrow black shaft stripes on the back; on the hind neck a broad buff collar broken with dusky markings; a series of large black spots and bright buff markings on the sides of the back; some buff patches on the wing-coverts; the first four flight-feathers with a conspicuous white or pale buff spot; central pair of tail-feathers like the upper plumage but with narrow broken black cross-bars, the two outer pairs tipped with patches of white; lower plumage buff faintly barred and mottled with brown; a white spot on each side of the throat.

Iris dark brown; bill dark brown; legs pinkish-brown.

This and other species of Nightjar have the following peculiarities of structure: Eye large and lustrous; bill short, weak and hooked, but when opened displaying an enormously wide gape fringed with long stiff hairs; three toes in front, one behind, the long central toe having the claw pectinated inside probably to clean insect scales from the gape bristles; the plumage is very soft and loose in character.

Field Identification.—A Nightjar is a large softly-plumaged, dully-mottled brown and grey bird, with an erratic flight like a moth, which hawks about open spaces near trees as dusk turns into darkness. Travellers by motor-car at night often find Nightjars sitting in the roads, their eyes gleaming uncannily in the light of the lamps. This is the smallest of the Indian species, and size and the call described afford the only chance of identifying it from the others in the field.

There are several Nightjars in India which are difficult to identify without close study, their call-notes and the arrangement of spots on the wing and tail being the chief guides. Franklin's Nightjar (*Caprimulgus monticolus*) utters a loud grating chirp *choo-ee* which when close at hand sounds exactly like a whip-lash cutting the air. Horsfield's Nightjar (*Caprimulgus macrurus*) has a very loud resonant *chaunk* like the blows of an adze on a plank, with a surprising volume of sound when close. The Jungle Nightjar (*Caprimulgus indicus*) gives a monosyllabic *chuck chuck chuck* repeated some half a dozen times at the rate of five *chucks* in two seconds. The European Nightjar (*Caprimulgus europeus*) whirs like a gigantic grasshopper. All these calls can be heard at night for a considerable distance.

Distribution.—Practically throughout India and Ceylon and in Burma down to about Moulmein. On the West it reaches portions

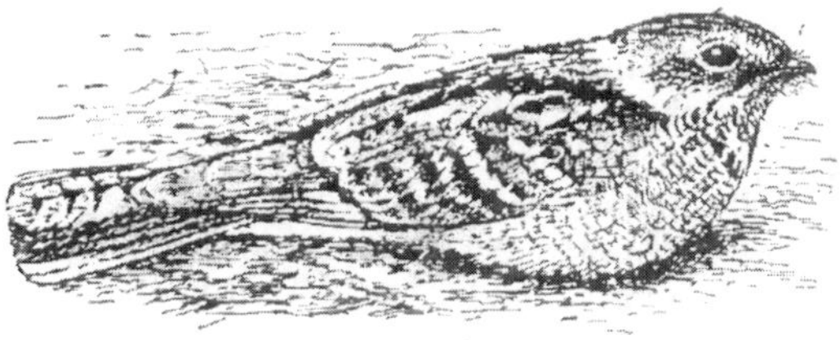

FIG. 50—Indian Nightjar (½ nat. size)

of the Eastern and Southern Punjab and Sind, but is scarce and local in these two provinces, being replaced there by other species. Status uncertain, but probably locally migratory.

Habits, etc.—This is a bird of the plains and of open and cultivated country, where it is found in gardens and groves, often in the near vicinity of houses. It spends the day upon the ground sleeping in some secluded spot under a bush or tree, and only awakes to activity at dusk, being entirely nocturnal in its habits. With the dark it takes to wing and then hawks for insects, moths and beetles. The flight is very characteristic, a long-tailed, long-winged bird, flying like a moth. It is very erratic in direction, the bird wheeling hither and thither, now diving, now shooting straight upwards, with rapid flappings of the wings combined with gliding movements in which the wings and tail are widely extended. The whole performance takes place in absolute silence, owing to the soft texture of the feathers, except sometimes for an audible smack when the wing-tips meet above the head, and for a slight chuckling note which is occasionally uttered. The long central toe prevents progression on the ground.

The breeding-call is very characteristic. It is best described as *chak-chak-chak-char-r-r-r* or *tuk tuk tuk tukaroo* resembling the sound of a stone skimming over the surface of a frozen pond, the note being repeated slowly at first and then more quickly; it is audible for a considerable distance. When perching on a tree the Nightjar sits lengthwise on a bough, not crossways after the fashion of most birds.

The plumage of this and other Nightjars, of which many forms occur in India, provide the most perfect example possible of protective coloration. During the long hours that the bird spends by day sitting motionless on the ground it is absolutely invisible, and it is unconsciously aware of that fact, only springing into life when the intruder comes within a yard or two.

To the huge mouth is due the name and the legend widely spread in many countries and languages that the "Goatsucker" feeds from the udders of cows and goats. It is considered of evil omen.

The breeding season varies, according to locality, from March to September. No nest is made, the eggs being simply deposited on the ground in some undisturbed spot, often under the shelter of a tree or bush. The clutch consists of two eggs.

The egg is a long cylindrical oval with very little difference in the two ends; the texture is fine and there is a slight gloss. The ground-colour varies from pinkish stone-colour to deep salmon-pink, blotched, clouded, spotted and streaked with different shades of pale reddish- and purplish-brown, with faint secondary markings of inky-purple.

The egg measures about 1·04 by 0·77 inches.

THE CUCKOO

CUCULUS CANORUS Linnæus

Description.—Length 13 inches. Adult male: The whole upper plumage dark ashy, a patch at the base of the tail rather paler; wings browner and rather glossy, the quills being barred on their inner webs with white; tail long and slightly graduated, blackish-brown tipped with white, the concealed inner webs notched with white and with white spots along the shafts; chin, throat, sides of the neck and upper breast pale ashy; remainder of lower plumage white, narrowly barred with blackish.

The adult female is rather browner in tint, and has an ill-defined and variable buffy-brown breast band. The female is dimorphic, having a rather scarce reddish "hepatic" phase.

Iris yellow; bill dark brown, lower mandible greenish; mouth rich reddish-orange; legs yellow.

Nostrils round; wing long and pointed; the tarsus is partly feathered in front; the feathers of the rump are long and thick and somewhat stiff, forming a sort of pad. Toes arranged in pairs, the 1st and 4th pointing backwards.

Field Identification.—Very Hawk-like in shape and swift flight; an ashy-grey bird with whitish under parts, barred with black from the breast downwards; presence in a breeding locality heralded by the well-known call long before the bird is seen, as it is shy and keeps largely to leafy trees.

Distribution.—The Cuckoo has been succinctly described as a migratory bird found at one season or other throughout the greater part of the Old World and even in Australia. Of the various races into which it has been divided we are concerned with two. *C. c. telephonus* breeds in Northern Asia eastwards to Japan and southwards to the Himalayas, but it is replaced in the North-west by the typical race, *C. c. canorus*, which is more broadly barred on the under parts. This breeds in the Himalayas and also apparently in some of the ranges of Central India, at least as far east as Ranchi. Both races in winter migrate to the plains of India, some birds even reaching Ceylon.

Cuckoos also breed very numerously in the hills of Assam south of the Brahmaputra, and these may be separable as a third race under the name *C. c. bakeri*.

Three other species of the genus *Cuculus* are locally common in India and the Himalayas. In plumage they nearly resemble the Common Cuckoo, but their calls are very distinctive. The Himalayan Cuckoo (*Cuculus optatus*) has a dull booming note, *hud-hud-hud-hud*, rather similar to that of a Hoopoe. The Indian Cuckoo (*Cuculus micropterus*) has a call of four syllables, variously described as *bouko-tako*, *kyphul-pakka*, *orange-pekoe* or *kithe-toppan*. The Little Cuckoo (*Cuculus poliocephalus*) is smaller than the others and has a wild screaming note, resembling the words "that's your smoky paper."

Habits, etc.—The familiar call of the Common Cuckoo, with all its treasured memories of the woods and meadows of an English Spring, is a welcome sound about the Himalayan stations, recognised with pleasure by all the European population. It is curious, however, and indicative of the Indian attitude towards nature that the hillmen appear to have no knowledge of the breeding habits of the Cuckoo or interest in the bird; for in Europe, literature and legend have combined to make this one of the best known of birds, whilst its habits of imposing its domestic duties on other birds are familiar to everyone.

In the Himalayas the Cuckoo arrives about the end of March or beginning of April, and is noisy until about June. The calls of the male *cuck-oo* or *cuck-cuck-oo* sometimes preceded by a harsh *know-wow-wow* are easily recognised, but the equally loud "water bubbling" call of the female is not so universally known. In India the bird is found in every type of wooded country, but rather prefers open cultivation to heavy forest. The food consists chiefly of injurious insects, large hairy caterpillars being particularly favoured. The resemblance of a Cuckoo on the wing to a Hawk is most marked.

In its breeding habits the Cuckoo is a parasite, the eggs being laid in the nests of other species to whom the duty of hatching them and of rearing the chicks is entirely left. A great variety of foster-parents are chosen, the favourites in India being perhaps various Pipits and Chats. In the majority of instances the Cuckoo settles on the chosen nest and lays its egg in the ordinary way. In some cases, however, this is clearly impossible from the site or size of the nest, and then the Cuckoo apparently clings to the outer surface of the nest or its containing site and ejects the egg from the vent into the nest cavity, sometimes with unfortunate results.

When the young Cuckoo is hatched, a curious provision of nature comes into play. It proceeds to eject the rightful eggs or young of the nest by getting them on to its back and gradually pushing them over the side, to die unnoticed below the nest. A hollow formation of the back in the early days of the Cuckoo's life is obviously adapted to this purpose and the reason for it is evident. The great bulk of the Cuckoo, compared with the size of the foster-parents, requires all the food that the latter can bring. So great is this disproportion in size that the foster-parents frequently have to perch on the back of the young Cuckoo, after it has left the nest, in order to place food in its mouth.

In the Himalayas the Cuckoo lays in May and June.

Estimates vary as to the number of eggs that a hen Cuckoo lays, but it is believed that the number may reach twenty in a single season. No hen normally lays twice in the same nest, though she frequents one particular locality, and as far as possible prefers to lay in the nests of one particular species of bird. If two or three Cuckoos' eggs are found in one nest they are usually the produce of as many hens. The species probably does not pair, mating taking place promiscuously.

The eggs are broad ovals, very blunt in shape, with the shell thick and heavy in texture and with only a slight gloss. They vary greatly in colour, the ground-colour being white, pink or stone-colour, spotted, streaked and mottled with brownish or yellowish-red and pale purple. Small black spots are nearly always present. Occasionally blue eggs may be found.

The egg measures about 0·97 by 0·72 inches.

THE COMMON HAWK-CUCKOO

Hierococcyx varius (Vahl)

(Plate xvi, Fig. 5, opposite page 330)

Description.—Length 13 inches. Sexes alike. Upper plumage ashy-grey, the flight-feathers browner and broadly barred with white on their inner webs ; tail grey tipped with rufescent, and with four or five rufescent bars, the terminal bar broadest ; chin and throat white tinged with ashy ; fore-neck and breast rufous mixed with pale ashy, the lower breast with bars ; abdomen white tinged anteriorly with rufous and partly barred with grey.

Iris yellow ; eye-rim yellow ; bill greenish, black along top ; legs yellow.

Structure as in the Common Cuckoo. In this genus the remarkable resemblance of adult Cuckoos to Hawks is carried a stage further, in that the immature plumage also resembles the immature plumage of Hawks.

Field Identification.—Common plains bird, Hawk-like in appearance and arboreal in habits, and in the field not easily to be recognised from the Common Cuckoo except by its remarkable call of *brain-fever* ; in the hand the bands on the tail are distinctive.

Distribution.—This species is confined to India and Ceylon. In India it is very generally distributed from the base of the Himalayas southwards. Its western boundary is roughly a line through Ambala, Jodhpur and Cutch, and on the east it has been recorded in North Cachar in Assam and Dacca in Eastern Bengal. While generally speaking a resident species it is also locally migratory.

Habits, etc.—The Common Hawk-Cuckoo is a bird of well-wooded country, and it is almost entirely arboreal. Like most of the Cuckoos, it is remarkable for its voice, on account of which it is usually called the Brain-fever bird, a name which is given erroneously to the Koel in areas where the Hawk-Cuckoo does not occur ; but the name rightly belongs to the Hawk-Cuckoo, both because its call is infinitely the more wearisome of the two and because it resembles the words, *brain-fever, brain-fever*, uttered again and again in loud crescendo tones, each repetition higher in the scale ; this cry may also be written *pipeeha-pipeeha-pipeeha*, and a third rendering which includes the overture that precedes the triple note is *Oh, lor, oh, lor, how very hot it's getting —we feel it, we feel it, WE FEEL IT*. There is also a call which I can only describe as a whirring ascending trill. The *brain-fever* call is exceedingly loud and shrill and can be heard for a considerable distance, uttered as it is from the top of a tree, and as the bird repeats it at intervals for an hour or more at a stretch, either by day or night, it often becomes a very real nuisance. The call is uttered at any time of the year, but the bird is most vociferous from early spring into the rains, when it is breeding. The food consists of berries and fruits as well as insects, and like other Cuckoos it is very partial to those hairy caterpillars which most birds will not eat.

The breeding season lasts from April to June and the bird is parasitic, laying its eggs in the nests of various Babblers; the egg is distinguishable from those of its hosts with difficulty; in colour it is a similar deep blue, but it is somewhat larger as a rule, with a softer, more satiny surface, a less glossy and thicker shell, and a more spherical shape. It is almost impossible to distinguish between the eggs of the Hawk-Cuckoo and the Pied Crested Cuckoo. When hatched the young Hawk-Cuckoo ejects the young of the rightful owners of the nest.

The egg measures about 1·00 by 0·8 inches.

THE INDIAN PLAINTIVE CUCKOO

Cacomantis merulinus (Vahl)

Description.—Length 9 inches. Male: Entire upper plumage dark ashy; wings dark brown, washed with greenish-bronze, the edge and a patch on the underside of the flight-feathers white; tail nearly black, the outer feathers banded obliquely on the inner webs with white; lower parts ashy, paling to white under the tail.

Female: Whole upper plumage bright chestnut, the back and wings barred with black, the head, neck and rump irregularly spotted with black; tail chestnut, a few black marks on the shafts of the feathers, a black bar and a white tip at the end of each feather; lower parts white, lightly barred with black, the chin, throat and upper breast suffused with chestnut.

The plumages and plumage-stages of this Cuckoo are very variable, but the above are descriptions of normal adults.

Iris reddish-brown; bill dark brown; legs dingy yellow or brownish-grey.

The bill is slightly curved; wing pointed; tail graduated. The toes are arranged in pairs, the 1st and 4th pointing backwards.

Field Identification.—A small active Hawk-like bird with pointed wings and graduated tail which, in the rains, attracts attention by its loud plaintive whistle. The male is dark ashy-grey; the female chestnut above and on the throat and white below, largely barred with black.

Distribution.—Very widely distributed throughout India, Ceylon,

Assam, and Burma eastwards to the Malay States, South China and Hainan. We are concerned with two races. *C. m. passerinus* is the ordinary Indian form which is found practically throughout the Peninsula down to Ceylon from the Outer Himalayas as far west as Abbottabad and as far east as the Brahmaputra. It is not, however, found in the Punjab Plains, Sind, Cutch, Kathiawar or most of Rajputana. In the Himalayas it is most common in a zone between 1500 and 3000 feet, rarely occurring above 6000 feet. In the Peninsula it is found at all elevations. The Burmese race, *C. m. querulus*, is found in Assam, Eastern Bengal and occasionally farther west as far as Nepal, Behar, Raipur and the Cumbum Valley. In this form the male has the white of the lower parts replaced by rufous. Both races are to some extent migratory, but their movements have not yet been worked out.

The Banded Bay Cuckoo (*Penthoceryx sonneratii*) may easily be confused with the females of the Plaintive Cuckoos, as its upper plumage is banded with dark brown and bay and the lower parts are white, finely barred with brown. The heavier bill is distinctive. It is widely distributed in India, but is most common along the Western Ghats.

Habits, etc.—Like many others of the family this Cuckoo is best known to many by its call which well justifies the popular name. The ordinary call is a clear loud plaintive whistle *ca-weer* which is somewhat difficult to locate as the bird turns its head about, producing a ventriloquial effect. There are also more complicated calls, an ascending whistle of four notes and another which may be syllabised as *yeh chelte rahi*. Like other species this Cuckoo not only calls by day; it calls freely in the gathering dusk and on moonlight nights may be heard at midnight. The bird is found in all types of lightly wooded country, in scrub, open forest, gardens, groves, tea gardens and similar places and may be known by its small size and swift flight. It calls often from the tops of bushes and trees but also from inside them, and in general is very restless and active. The food consists largely of caterpillars.

The breeding season is in the rains from July to October. The bird is parasitic and is believed to lay chiefly in the nests of the Indian Wren-Warbler, the Fantail-Warbler and the Tailor-bird. The eggs are long narrow ovals with one end appreciably smaller than the other. The shell is stout and heavy but fine in texture and there is a slight gloss. The ground-colour is white or pale blue marked with light reddish blotches. The egg, therefore, agrees fairly well with those of the foster-parents. The degree of selective specialisation thus attained is further emphasised in the Deccan where a bright pink egg is commonly laid in the nest of the Ashy Wren-Warbler, whose own egg is a bright brick red.

The egg measures about 0·75 by 0·55 inches.

THE PIED CRESTED CUCKOO

Clamator jacobinus (Boddaert)

Description.—Length 13 inches. Sexes alike. Upper plumage including the crest black, glossed with green; flight-feathers dark brown with a broad white band running through them; tail long and graduated, the feathers tipped with white, most broadly on the outer feathers; lower plumage white, sometimes sullied by the dark bases of the feathers.

Iris red-brown; bill black; legs leaden-blue.

Upper portion of the tarsus feathered; toes arranged in pairs, the 1st and 4th pointing backwards.

Field Identification.—A conspicuous bird black above, white below, with a white band through the wing visible in flight and white

Fig. 51—Pied Crested Cuckoo (¼ nat. size)

tips to the long tail-feathers; a rather noticeable crest. Arboreal, and attracts attention by the loud call.

Distribution.—This Cuckoo is found in a wide area in Africa (Abyssinia and the Sudan to British East Africa; also West Africa) and throughout India, Ceylon and part of Burma. In India it is found throughout the plains and hills alike, and in the Outer Himalayas extends up to about 8000 feet.

The typical race is a resident in Ceylon and part of the Madras Presidency. The rest of India and Ceylon is inhabited by a larger form, *C. j. pica*, which is migratory. Its movements have not been fully worked out, but there is good reason to believe that it winters in Africa.

The larger Red-winged Crested Cuckoo (*Clamator coromandus*), common in Assam and Burma, is found in smaller numbers in the Himalayan foot-hills from Garhwal eastwards and in Ceylon. It is a straggler in the Peninsula.

The Drongo-Cuckoo (*Surniculus lugubris*) is found in the Outer Himalayas, Peninsular India and Ceylon. It is remarkable for its close resemblance to a King Crow (*Dicrurus macrocercus*) which must cause it often to be overlooked. The song consists of three notes in a rising scale.

Habits, etc.—The Pied Crested Cuckoo is a bird of open, well-wooded country, and as it is partial to damp, well-watered localities it is a rains visitor only from June to August or September to a large portion of the Continent. Although mostly arboreal, it is more ready than most Cuckoos to perch in low bushes near the ground, and some of its food is actually taken from the ground. The food consists chiefly of caterpillars, but ants, spiders, beetles, mealy-bugs, red-cotton bugs and terrestrial molluscs are also eaten; a few green leaves are also eaten, possibly for digestive reasons. It is neither shy nor retiring, and one bird may often be seen chasing another. It is as noisy as the other Cuckoos, and has a variety of shrill metallic calls, faintly reminiscent of the Koel's wildest shrieks, but the common call-note may perhaps be best expressed by the syllables *ple-ue*.

In the north the breeding season is during the rains from June to August, but down in the Nilgiris the birds are said to lay from January to March, the period being determined in both cases by the habits of the local foster-parents.

The Pied Crested Cuckoo is parasitic, and lays its eggs in the nests of Babblers and Laughing-Thrushes. The Babblers (*Turdoides somervillei*, *Argya caudata*, *A. earlii*, and *A. malcolmi*) are the common fosterers in the plains, the Streaked Laughing-Thrush (*Trochalopteron lineatum*) in the Himalayas, and the Nilgiri Laughing-Thrush (*T. cachinnans*) in the Nilgiris. The young Cuckoo ejects the rightful offspring from the nest.

The egg is a very perfect oval, blunt at both ends, thick shelled, fine in texture and with a high gloss; in colour it is a very delicate full sky-blue, varying somewhat in depth of tint.

It measures about 0·94 by 0·73 inches.

THE KOEL

EUDYNAMIS SCOLOPACEUS (Linnæus)

Description.—Length 17 inches. Male: Black throughout with a bluish-green gloss.

Female: Brown with an olive gloss, spotted throughout with white, except on the wings, tail, breast and abdomen which are barred with white.

Iris bright crimson; bill dull green; legs plumbeous.

The tail is long and graduated. Tarsus strongly scutellated in front. The toes are arranged in pairs, the 1st and 4th pointing backwards.

Field Identification.—Purely arboreal, male black, female brown and white in spots and bars, and from its noisy cries of *ko-el ko-el* one of the best-known birds of the Indian plains.

Distribution.—The Koel is found throughout India and Ceylon, though in the North-west Frontier Province and in Sind it is only

FIG. 52—Koel (male above, female below) (½ nat. size)

locally common. It is not found in the Himalayas and is scarce in the foot-hills at their base. East of the Bay of Bengal it extends as far as China and the Malay Peninsula, but these birds have been separated as another race. It is locally migratory, but its movements have not yet been worked out.

Habits, etc.—This bird holds amongst Indians a position analogous to the position of the Common Cuckoo in Europe, in that they are all familiar with its call and welcome its arrival, and to some extent are acquainted with its appearance, but on the other hand they mostly appear to be ignorant of its parasitic breeding habits.

It is a bird of groves and gardens, haunting patches of large trees in whose shady boughs it finds concealment and whose fruits it eats. It never descends to the ground. The usual diet consists of fruit, especially of the banyan, peepul and other figs, but snails are also eaten.

The call is known to everyone in India. It consists of two syllables *ko-el* repeated several times, increasing in intensity and ascending in the scale, with an indefinable sound of excitement in it. This call appears to be uttered by both sexes and it is often heard at night—an unmistakable token of the hot weather. Another call *ho-y-o* is apparently the property of the male alone. A third call of the "water-bubbling" type is probably common to both sexes. These are all breeding notes and the bird is silent out of that season. In places where the Hawk-Cuckoos are little known the Koel is sometimes called the Brain-fever bird, but that name rightly belongs to the bird which calls "brain-fever."

The Koel is parasitic on the Common House Crow (*Corvus splendens*) in whose nests it lays, destroying one or two of the rightful owner's eggs; the birds are numerous and it is not unusual to find two or three of their eggs in one Crow's nest, while as many as eight have been recorded. The breeding habits of this Cuckoo have not been sufficiently studied, but the young probably eject the eggs or young of the Crows, and it is said that the female Koel often feeds her own offspring after they are fledged. Great enmity exists between the adult Koels and House Crows, and the latter are often to be seen chasing the former; but considerable respect is due to the Koel as the one living creature that persistently gets the better of that clever scoundrel the Crow.

The male nestling Koel is black like the adult. The female provides an exception to the ordinary rules of plumage inheritance and is much blacker than the adult, evidently in order to deceive the foster-parents.

The majority of Koel's eggs are laid in June, but they are dependent on the local breeding season of the Crows. The eggs roughly resemble Crows' eggs but are considerably smaller. They are a moderately broad oval, somewhat compressed towards the smaller end; the texture is compact and fine and there is no gloss. In colour they are variable; the ground-colour may be of various shades of green or stone-brown. They are marked with specks, spots, streaks, and clouds of olive-brown, reddish-brown, and dull purple, these markings being predominantly streaky in character, and often tending to coalesce towards the large end.

The eggs average about 1·20 by 0·9 inches in size.

THE SMALL GREEN-BILLED MALKOHA

Rhopodytes viridirostris (Jerdon)

Description.—Length 15 inches. Upper parts dark ashy with a green gloss which becomes much stronger and more metallic on the wings and tail; feathers of the tail broadly tipped with white; under parts dark ashy, the throat and breast streaked with greyish-white and the belly washed with fulvous yellow.

Iris claret, a fine outer ring white; loose crinkled bare skin round the eye sky-blue; bill apple-green; legs olive-slate; claws dusky.

Fig. 53—Small Green-billed Malkoha (⅓ nat. size)

Bill deep with the top of the upper mandible sharply curved; feathers of the throat and breast forked, there being no web to the end of the shaft so that the feathers look as if damp and partly stuck together; tail long and graduated.

Field Identification.—A clumsy-looking ashy-coloured bird with green beak and sky-blue eyepatch and a long graduated tail tipped with white; found skulking in bushes and hedges.

Distribution.—Confined to India and Ceylon. It is a strictly resident species found in Orissa and in Peninsula India from Hyderabad State southwards.

The larger but very similar Green-billed Malkoha (*Rhopodytes tristis*) of the Central and Eastern Himalayas, Assam, Burma and further east is usually treated as a separate species. It has the eye-patch crimson.

Habits, etc.—This quaint Cuckoo is a very sedentary species and individuals appear much attached to particular localities, being usually to be found within a radius of a few hundred yards. They are met with singly or in pairs in lightly wooded and scrub country of the deciduous type, in bush jungle on hill-sides, in bamboo forest or in large hedges of prickly *Euphorbia*. They are skulkers with much the same habits as the Crow-Pheasant, but unlike that bird are seldom seen on the ground, keeping more in the cover of low bushes and trees and making their way through the branches with great adroitness. If a bird is caught in the open it will often " freeze," sometimes in the most grotesque attitude, hoping thereby to escape detection. The flight is feeble and it unwillingly takes wing and that for no distance.

The food consists of large insects, grasshoppers, mantides, caterpillars and the like.

The breeding season is from March to August.

The nest is a slight structure of sticks, a mere shallow saucer, little better than that of a Dove, and it is lined with a few leaves which are fresh and green when plucked but of course soon fade. It is placed in the centre of a thorn bush or cactus some 5 or 6 feet from the ground.

The clutch consists of two eggs. In shape they are almost spherical being very blunt and rounded at both ends. The texture is fine, but very chalky and quite without gloss and the colour is dull white.

The egg measures about 1·12 by 0·90 inches.

THE SIRKEER

TACCOCUA LESCHENAULTII Lesson

Description.—Length 17 inches. Sexes alike. Upper surface, wings and central tail-feathers dark olive-brown, the wing and tail-feathers slightly glossed with satiny olive-green ; outer tail-feathers black with broad white tips ; chin, throat and breast and a patch under the tail olive-brown, very pale almost buff on the chin ; abdomen dark rufous ; the shafts of nearly all the feathers are dark glistening brown, which is especially noticeable on the breast.

Iris reddish-brown ; bill cherry-red, yellow at the tip ; legs plumbeous.

The bill is curved and sharply hooked ; a curious grille of stiff black curved eyelashes with white bases protects the eye. Tail long, broad and deeply graduated ; two toes in front and two behind.

Field Identification.—A large dull olive-brown bird with a heavy tail and a striking red and yellow beak. Usually found walking about on the ground amongst bushes or thick cover.

Distribution.—Confined to Ceylon, India and Assam. In India it is very generally distributed and resident, but is absent or very rare north-west of a line from Simla to Jodhpur and Cutch. Divided into three races. The typical race is found in Ceylon and Southern India, certainly as far north as Hyderabad. *T. l. sirkee* from the Northern Punjab, Mount Aboo, Northern Guzerat, Cutch and Sind is a paler bird with a yellowish throat and breast. A darker and larger race, *T. l. infuscata*, is found in the Eastern Himalayas. These races all intergrade. Occurs at all elevations up to 6000 feet and even occasionally higher.

Habits, etc.—The Sirkeer is by preference a bird of scrub-jungle, secondary growth, large gardens and other places where comparative quiet and freedom from disturbance are combined with patches of dense cover in which it can take refuge. It is largely terrestrial in its habits, stalking about the ground in search of a very mixed diet of fruits, seeds and berries, grasshoppers, beetles and other small fry. It is a poor flier and as a rule is very loath to take to wing, preferring to thread its way into the centre of a thicket. It runs well, keeping the body in a horizontal position and stopping at intervals to raise itself and have a good look round.

The display savours of the grotesque, both birds taking part in it, opening their beaks and bowing low to each other, meanwhile expanding the tail to make the most of the black and white markings of the outer feathers. During the display curious clicking sounds are uttered, but the Sirkeer is normally a very silent bird.

The normal breeding season is not well known, but nests have been found from March to August.

The nest is a broad saucer-shaped structure of twigs lined with green leaves, usually those of the tree in which it is built. It is placed in some foliage-shrouded fork in a low or thick tree or even a bush and is seldom at any great height from the ground.

The clutch consists of two or three eggs. The egg is a broad, very perfect oval with a rather coarse and chalky texture. The colour is pure white. Many eggs are covered with a pale yellowish-brown glaze of uncertain origin which is readily removed by washing or scraping.

The egg measures about 1·40 by 1·05 inches.

PLATE XVI

1. Green Barbet. 2. Blue-tailed Bee-Eater. 3. Brown-fronted Pied Woodpecker.
4. Indian Pitta. 5. Common Hawk-Cuckoo. (All about $\frac{1}{3}$ nat. size.)

[*Face p.* 330

THE CROW-PHEASANT

CENTROPUS SINENSIS (Stephen)

Description.—Length 19 inches. Sexes alike. Wings chestnut, the quills tipped with dusky; the remainder of the plumage black, glossed with green, steel-blue and purple.

Iris crimson; bill and legs black.

The bill is deep and rather curved; the wings are short and rounded; the tail long, broad and graduated; the feathers of the head, neck and breast are harsh and coarse; the hind toe has a long straight claw, recalling that of the Skylark.

Field Identification.—A big black bird with chestnut wings, which

FIG. 54—Crow-Pheasant ($\frac{1}{5}$ nat. size)

from its size and voluminous tail is often mistaken for a game bird. Common about hedgerows and gardens and feeds much on the ground.

Distribution.—The typical race of the Crow-Pheasant is a bird of wide distribution, extending across from China to North Assam, the Himalayas to Kashmir, and the plains of Northern India down to Sind. South of Bombay and from the Ganges to Ceylon it is replaced by a smaller form *C. s. parroti.* It is an entirely resident species.

A much smaller species, the Lesser Coucal (*Centropus bengalensis*), is found in the Himalayan terai, in Orissa and Bengal and South-western India. Whilst the adult resembles the Crow-Pheasant in coloration, the immature plumage with brown and white streaking is very different.

Habits, etc.—The Crow-Pheasant is one of the common birds of India, and owes this name, as well as the familiar sobriquet of the Griffin's Pheasant, to the fact that its heavy build and slow gait and its habit of feeding on the ground leads it to be mistaken by new arrivals in India for a game bird. It avoids forest, and is found in cultivation, bush-jungle, or waste land, and is pre-eminently a bird of the broad strips of bush and tree growth mixed with pampas grass which grow along the sides of village roads or the banks of rivers and canals. It is found also in gardens and about villages. In such situations it walks about sedately on the ground, picking up wasps, beetles, caterpillars, locusts and grasshoppers and catching small lizards, snakes, and other similar food, and when disturbed it flies or runs into the heavy masses of bush and grass. The call is a peculiar dull-booming sound, *hood-hood-hood*.

Although a member of the family of the Cuculidæ, the Crow-Pheasant belongs to the big group of the non-parasitic Cuckoos. It is one of those birds that breeds in the rains, and eggs may be found from June to September.

The nest is normally a large globular domed affair, with the entrance at one side from which the tail of the sitting bird projects. Occasionally, however, a rough saucer nest is made. The nests may be placed at any height from the ground, either in the centre of a dense thorny bush or clump of pampas grass, or in exposed positions in the forks of trees. They are either fairly neat structures of dry twigs lined with green leaves, or loosely built balls of dry reeds and coarse grass.

The eggs vary from three to five in number.

They are broad, regular ovals, symmetrical at both ends; in texture they are rather coarse and chalky and dull pure white in colour; but the surface is frequently covered with a sort of epidermis of pale yellow-brown glaze which gives a certain amount of gloss and can readily be removed.

In size they average about 1·4 by 1·2 inches.

THE LARGE INDIAN PARRAKEET

Psittacula eupatria (Linnæus)

Description.—Length, including long pointed tail, 19 inches. Male: Upper plumage grass-green, rather darker on the wings and brighter on the forehead and rump; a large deep red patch near the bend of the wing; median tail-feathers passing from green at the base into verditer-blue and then into yellowish at the tip; lower surface of tail yellow; a dark line from the nostril to the eye; a rose-pink collar round the sides and back of the neck, with a bluish-grey tinge to the nape above it; chin and a stripe from the lower base of the beak to the rose-collar black; lower plumage dull pale green growing brighter towards the tail.

The female lacks the rose-collar and the black stripe that joins it.

Iris pale yellow with a bluish-grey inner circle; bill deep red; feet plumbeous.

In this and the following Parrakeets the bill is thick and deeper than long, the upper mandible is movable, sharply pointed and curved, coming down over the short square lower mandible; a fleshy cere * at the base of the bill; tongue short, swollen and fleshy. The tail is very long and graduated, the central feathers narrow, pointed, and exceeding the others in length. The foot has two toes in front and two behind.

Field Identification.—Green plumage, massive head and hooked red beak, long pointed tail, swift flight and screaming cries easily identify a bird as a Parrakeet. Entirely green head (except for black chin and stripe and rose-pink collar) separate this from all other Indian Parrakeets except the Green Parrakeet, which is at once recognised by the smaller size and absence of red shoulder-patches.

Distribution.—The Large Indian Parrakeet is found practically throughout India, Ceylon, and Burma. It is divided into four races which are separated on size and comparative details of coloration.

The typical race is South Indian, found in Hyderabad, Mysore, Travancore, and Ceylon. *P. e. nipalensis* is found in Northern and Central India from the valley of the Indus (though not indigenous to Sind), and the Himalayan foot-hills (up to 4000 feet), and Assam down to Kamptee, Raipur, Sambalpur, and the Northern Circars; also to the Satpura Range in Khandesh. *P. e. indoburmanicus* is found in Burma and *P. e. magnirostris* in the Andaman Islands. A resident species.

Habits, etc.—This fine Parrakeet is found in practically any type of country in which large trees are numerous. It lives in parties and flocks, which may be observed at all times of the year, though individual pairs often separate while breeding; but as many pairs usually breed together in suitable spots, the birds when off the nest are social and fly about together.

The flocks collect to roost in large avenues and groves of trees, and in the evenings they have a very regular flight to such roosting places, travelling for miles to them at a great height with a swift direct straight flight. While flying they frequently utter the loud shrill call.

The food consists of various grains, seeds and fruits, both wild and cultivated, and as the birds are numerous, large and greedy, they do a considerable amount of damage in cultivation. This species is a common cage-bird in Northern India and becomes very tame though it seldom learns to talk.

The breeding season is from February to April. No nest is made,

* Cere (from *cera,* wax) is a term applied to the soft, generally rather swollen skin which covers the base of the upper bill, especially well defined in parrots and birds of prey.

but the eggs are laid in holes in buildings and trees, usually at a considerable height from the ground. The hole used in a tree is generally a deep natural hollow, but a certain amount of shaping and excavating is done by the birds themselves.

The eggs vary from two to five in number. They are broad and regular ovals in shape, stout and rather coarse in texture, with a slight gloss. The colour is pure unmarked white.

They measure about 1·32 by 1·00 inches.

THE GREEN PARRAKEET

PSITTACULA KRAMERI (Scopoli)

(Plate xvii, Fig. 1, opposite page 352)

Description.—Length 16 inches. Male: Upper plumage bright green, washed with pale bluish-grey about the back and sides of the head and paler about the bend of the wing; median tail-feathers green at the base then bluish-grey, other tail-feathers green with yellow inner webs, tipped with yellow and yellow underneath; a fine blackish line from the nostril to the eye; a rose-collar round the neck except in front; chin and a band from the lower base of the beak to the rose-collar black; lower plumage yellowish-green.

The female has the rose-collar and black band replaced by an indistinct emerald-green ring.

Iris pale yellow; bill cherry-red, lower mandible blackish; feet dusky slate or greenish.

Field Identification.—Most abundant and well-known plains species, usually in parties; easily distinguished by the green plumage, massive hooked red bill, long pointed tail, swift arrow-like flight, and the harsh screaming notes. There is no red wing-patch in this species.

The Blue-winged Parrakeet (*Psittacula columboides*) of the Western Ghats and Nilgiris has the head and breast grey with a complete black ring (followed in the male by an emerald-green ring) round the neck. The green and blue wings are scale-marked with yellow.

Distribution.—The typical form is African. We are concerned with two races. The northern form, *P. k. borealis*, with the lower mandible either red or black is found from Baluchistan across to Assam and Burma. It intergrades gradually—and an arbitrary boundary may be fixed at the 20° of latitude—into *P. k. manillensis* of Southern India and Ceylon which is slightly smaller and darker and has the lower mandible black. This bird does not ascend the Himalayas above 4000 feet and it avoids most hill-ranges and tracts of unbroken forest. A resident species.

Habits, etc.—The Green Parrakeet is one of those species in India which everyone knows. It is excessively abundant, living in pairs in the breeding season, and gathering into parties and flocks at other times, which from their universality, the damage that they do in gardens and fields, their noisiness, and their brilliant coloration, are known to all and sundry.

Normally this Parrakeet is arboreal and it is a wonderful climber, being equally at home in every position, but it flies down to feed on crops and garden plants, and occasionally settles on the ground to pick up food-stuffs, and there its awkward sidling gait, due to the long tail and the short zygodactyle feet, is very quaint. But specially adapted for climbing and for holding food these feet amply compensate for their awkwardness on the ground. There is something especially sedate and knowing about the demeanour of the Parrakeets, which is further heightened when they sit on one foot and with the other hold up a piece of food to be eaten bite by bite. The flight is very swift and straight and these birds have the habit of an evening roosting flight, flock after flock hurrying in succession along the same line to some patch of trees where they roost in company with flocks of Crows and Mynahs. The ordinary call is a harsh, rather shrill, inarticulate scream, but when courting the male has a pleasant murmuring warble which he utters as he scratches the head of the hen with the point of his bill, and joins his beak to hers in a loving kiss. The hens are very accomplished flirts and their behaviour in the presence of the favoured male is most amusing. This species of Parrakeet is one of the universal cage-birds of India and it becomes delightfully tame; individuals may be taught to say a few words, but the best of them never talk as well as the African Grey Parrots.

The breeding season extends from February to May, though most eggs will be found in March.

No nest is made, but the eggs are laid on debris in holes in walls and buildings or more commonly in trees. The hole may be a natural one, but often the bird excavates a tunnel and chamber very similar to those of the Woodpeckers.

Four to six eggs are laid. The egg is a moderately broad oval, slightly pointed towards one end; the texture is hard and compact with a slight gloss, and the colour is pure unmarked white.

The average size is 1·20 by 0·95 inches.

THE BLOSSOM-HEADED PARRAKEET

PSITTACULA CYANOCEPHALA (Linnæus)

Description.—Length 14 inches. Male: Head red, washed with blue, giving the effect of the bloom on a plum, sharply defined with a narrow black collar from the chin round the neck; behind the black collar extends an area of verdigris-green; upper plumage yellowish-green, becoming verdigris on the wings and rump; the quills are green with pale edges, and there is a deep red patch near the bend of the wing; the median tail-feathers pass from green at the base into blue with conspicuous white tips; the remaining tail-feathers are largely yellow with the greater portion of the outer webs green; lower plumage bright yellowish-green.

The female has the red head replaced by dull bluish-grey (plum-blue) and a yellow ring replaces the collars of black and verdigris.

Iris yellowish-white; bill orange-yellow, lower mandible blackish; legs dull green.

Field Identification.—Distinguish from the other species by the smaller and more slender build, the more pleasing call, the plum-coloured head (red-plum in male, blue-plum in female), the orange beak and the conspicuous yellow tips to the tail-feathers.

Care must be taken not to confuse the female with the slightly larger Slaty-headed Parrakeet (*Psittacula himalayana*) of the Himalayas in which both sexes have a slate-grey head. It is useful to remember that the tip of the tail, usually very conspicuous in flight, is whitish in the Blossom-headed Parrakeet and bright yellow in the Slaty-headed Parrakeet.

Distribution.—The Blossom-headed Parrakeet is found almost throughout India, Ceylon and Burma, extending still farther eastwards to Cochin-China, Siam, and Southern China. It is divided into two races, of which we are only concerned with the Western and typical race. This is found in India throughout the plains to Mount Aboo, Sambhar and the Eastern Punjab, extending still farther west along the Himalayan foot-hills to the neighbourhood of Murree. It extends eastward to about Sikkim where it joins on to the range of the paler eastern form *P. c. bengalensis*. In the Western Himalayas it ascends to about 5000 feet. Locally migratory.

Habits, etc.—This beautiful Parrakeet is, to a large extent, a forest bird, though it is found anywhere also in well-wooded but cultivated districts. Like other Parrakeets, it is a social species, being found in parties, which feed on seeds and fruits in forest trees; but this species very seldom descends to the ground. The flight is very strong and swift, faster than that of the other two species dealt with in this work, and of the three kinds it has much the most musical call. It is not usually kept in captivity by the natives of India.

The ordinary breeding season is from February to May, though in the South it also breeds in December.

Four to six eggs are laid in the nest hole which is usually excavated by the birds themselves, being a tunnel and nest-chamber like those of a Woodpecker in the branch of a tree, usually at some height from the ground. Occasionally a natural hole in a tree is utilised. In either case no nest is built, the eggs lying on chips and debris in the bottom of the chamber.

The egg is a broad oval, rather pointed towards the small end. The texture is fine though without gloss. The colour is pure white, but it loses its freshness as incubation progresses.

The egg measures about 1·0 by 0·80 inches.

INDIAN LORIKEET

CORYLLIS VERNALIS Sparrman

Description.—Length 5·5 inches. Grass green above, wings and tail darker, rump and upper tail coverts crimson, lower parts yellowish green. The male has a small patch of blue on the throat which is absent in the female.

Iris yellowish white; bill coral red, tip yellow; cere darker red; legs and feet yellowish or pale orange.

Field Identification.—A very diminutive parrot, about the size of a sparrow, bright green with crimson rump.

Distribution.—The Indian Lorikeet ranges from the Nepal Terai eastward through Eastern Bengal and Assam to Burma and Siam. In the peninsula of India it is only known on the east coast from the vicinity of Vazagapatam; on the west side it is by no means uncommon in many areas between Bombay and Cape Comarin, ascending the Nilgiris to some 6000 feet and extending east as far as the Pulney Hills.

Habits, etc.—This little parrot is a bird of open deciduous and evergreen forests and small tree and bamboo jungle, as well as orchards and plantations. In the Himalayan foothills it is found up to about 3000 feet. To some extent it is migratory depending on the blossoming of certain trees and the ripening of fruits. The food consists of various kinds of fruits and berries as well as the seeds of bamboos and, at certain times of the year, it feeds to a great extent on the nectar of flowers, especially those of the Coral tree (*Erythrina*). Curiously enough, that of the Silk Cotton tree (*Bombax malabaricus*) so much sought after by many birds—is not much patronised. The small figs of the Peepal and Banyan trees are a great attraction, and a flock of Lorikeets feeding in one of these trees is very difficult to see owing to their small size and green plumage blending with the leaves. When feeding they warble and utter a twittering note, but there is no clamour as when parrakeets are present. The flight is swift with rapid wing beats and on the wing they utter a *chee-chu-*

FIG. 54*a*—Little Lorikeet.

chu. Small parties have a curious habit of collecting on the top of a tree, then a single bird will suddenly dash off and fly around, wheeling in circles, whistling loudly and dash back again to the tree, settle down, and another will fly off. Lorikeets have been known to raid jars attached to Toddy Palms and afterwards picked up, intoxicated, from having indulged too freely in the liquor. They roost at night suspended by their feet with the head downwards.

The eggs are laid from February to April, according to the locality.

The nest is a small natural hole in a tree, from ground level to about fifteen feet up, and at times the nesting chamber is actually below the level of the ground.

The clutch is from three to four in number, broad, blunt ovals, white in colour, but often stained with the rotten wood in the nesting chamber.

They measure 0·75 by 0·6 inches.

THE MOTTLED WOOD-OWL

STRIX OCELLATUM (Lesson)

Description.—Length 18 inches. Sexes alike. Top of the head and neck tawny ferruginous, the feathers tipped with black containing white spots; remainder of the upper parts finely mottled with black and white and barred and streaked with black, the partly concealed bases of the feathers tawny ferruginous; an irregular white stripe, crossed by fine black bars, down each side of the back; wings similar to the back, the outer flight-feathers being dark brown crossed with paler mottled bars, the base of the inner webs largely tawny ferruginous; tail tawny at the base, mottled black and white towards the end, the feathers crossed with pale mottled bands and black bars, the outer feathers tipped with white; face mottled and barred with black and white; a large white patch on the throat; lower plumage white barred with fine black lines, the bases of the feathers pale tawny ferruginous.

Iris dark brown; eyelid orange; bill black; claws dusky.

This and other Owls are remarkable for the following features. The head is large, and the eyes are directed forwards in a facial disc, composed of feathers radiating from each eye, the outer margin being surrounded by a conspicuous ruff of close-textured feathers; bill short and hooked, with the nostrils set in a cere almost concealed by a mass of bristly feathers; the orifice of the ear very large though concealed with feathers; plumage soft and very copious; outer toe reversible; claws sharp and curved.

Field Identification.—A large Owl with a typical Owl "face" but no ear-tufts. Most beautifully barred and mottled in brownish-black and white with tawny patches wherever the feathers are ruffled. Nocturnal but may be seen by day sleeping in large trees.

Distribution.—Peculiar to India. Generally distributed throughout the country up to the base of the Himalayas except in Sind, the North-western Frontier Province and most of the Punjab. A strictly resident species. In the Himalayas it is replaced by races of the European Brown Owl (*Strix aluco*), a mottled grey or brown bird of similar aspect, which is found at all elevations from 4000 feet up to the limits of tree level, occurring in all the hill stations.

In Southern India and Ceylon another representative of this group is the Brown Wood-Owl (*Strix indranee*), a very dark brown bird, also found sparingly in the Himalayas.

Habits, etc.—Very little has been recorded about the habits of the Mottled Wood-Owl which lives the secluded life of its genus. It is not a bird of dense forests but is found in well-wooded country where large mango-topes or roadside avenues of ancient trees provide it with holes to nest in and cover to spend the day. In such localities it sleeps away the day in some shady refuge, emerging at nightfall to hunt the surrounding country. It lives entirely on squirrels, rats and mice and must be one of the birds most beneficial to Indian agriculture. The call is said to be a loud harsh hoot.

The breeding season extends according to locality, for it is said to be somewhat earlier in the southern half of India than in the north, from November until April. There is little or no nest, the eggs being laid on a little dry touch-wood, a few dry leaves or the miscellaneous rubbish that collects in some large cavity in the trunk or a bough of an ancient tree or in the depression at the fork of two or more large branches. Such a site may be chosen at heights from 8 to 25 feet from the ground.

The clutch varies from one to three eggs, but two is the normal number. The egg is rather large for the size of the bird, a very round oval of fine texture and little gloss. The colour is white with often a very delicate creamy tinge.

The size is about 1·99 by 1·67 inches.

THE BROWN FISH-OWL

KETUPA ZEYLONENSIS (Gmelin)

(Plate xviii, Fig. 2, opposite page 374)

Description.—Length 22 inches. Sexes alike. Upper plumage rufescent-brown with broad black shaft-streaks, the upper back and wing-coverts much mottled with brown and fulvous; there are some buff and white spots along the shoulders; flight- and tail-feathers dark brown with paler mottled whitish-brown bands and tips; throat white; lower plumage whitish, streaked and narrowly and closely barred with wavy brownish-rufous markings.

Iris bright yellow; bill dusky greenish-horn; legs dusky yellow.

In this species there is an aigrette of long and pointed feathers over each eye; the tarsus is bare of feathers and granular, with prickly scales on the soles.

Field Identification.—A massive, solemn, brown bird with yellow eyes surmounted by ear-tufts (the head recalling that of a cat); plumage grey and brown with pronounced streaks. Sleeps by day in trees and on the ground. Immediately distinguished from the Eagle-Owls by the bare tarsus.

Distribution.—This fine Owl is a widely-distributed species, ranging from Palestine on the west through India, Burma and Ceylon to China in the east. It is divided into several races, but all Indian birds belong to the race *K. z. leschenaulti*. In India it is found throughout the Continent from the foot-hills of the Himalayas on the north, and Sind and the North-west Frontier Province on the west. In Southern India it is found up to the summits of the hill-ranges. The typical race from Ceylon is smaller and darker. A resident species.

Habits, etc.—This large Owl is always found in the vicinity of water, and its food, though including birds and small mammals, consists very largely of fish and crabs which it catches at the edge of rivers and streams. In view of this diet its feet and claws are unlike that of most other Owls. The tarsus is almost entirely free of feathers which are replaced by granular scales, and the soles of the feet are thickly covered with prickly scales particularly adapted for holding slippery prey, while the large well-curved claws have sharp cutting edges as well as highly-sharpened points. In fact the whole foot very strongly resembles that of the Osprey, the well-known Fish-Hawk.

The Fish-Owl sleeps by day in some large heavy-foliaged tree or in the face of some rocky cliff, and with the fall of dusk wings its way to the neighbouring water, uttering a strange screaming call which resembles that of an Eagle or Norfolk Plover rather than that of an Owl.

Another call is described as a loud dismal cry *haw-haw-haw-ha*, or a deep triple note *hu-who-hu*.

The breeding season is from December to March, but most eggs will be found in February. This Owl nests in clefts and ledges of rocky banks or mud cliffs, in holes and hollows of ancient trees, or in the deserted nests of Fishing-Eagles and Vultures. These varied sites are lined with a few sticks and feathers or dry leaves and grass.

The clutch consists of two eggs. These are very perfect broad ovals, close-grained and compact in texture, with a slight gloss, though the whole surface is freely pitted. The colour is white with a faint creamy tinge.

In size they average about 2·38 by 1·88 inches.

THE ROCK EAGLE-OWL

BUBO BENGALENSIS (Franklin)

Description.—Length 22 inches. Sexes alike. Head and neck bright tawny-buff, heavily streaked with rich dark brown; above the whitish facial disc edged with a blackish ruff two conspicuous "horns" or "aigrettes" of feathers deep blackish-brown edged with fulvous; upper plumage deep rich brown, mottled and spotted buff and white, most conspicuously on the sides of the wings and above the tail; flight-feathers rich deep tawny with brown bars, dusky at the tip; tail barred buff and brown, the central pair of feathers mottled with those colours; chin and throat whitish; remainder of lower plumage buff, broadly dashed with dark blackish-brown on the breast and streaked and cross-barred with the same on the abdomen and flanks, the markings dying away again under the tail and on the legs.

Iris orange-yellow; bill horny-black; claws dusky.

The tarsus is thickly feathered.

Field Identification.—A large solemn bird, mottled tawny-buff and blackish-brown, with conspicuous tufts above large orange eyes, which sits motionless by day amongst rocks and ravines and occasionally in trees. This bird and the Brown Fish-Owl are difficult to distinguish in the field when the legs are not visible. The Fish-Owl carries the ear-tufts lower and is reddish-brown in general colour while the Eagle-Owl is yellowish-tawny with more black on the head.

Distribution.—The Rock Eagle-Owl is virtually confined to India, though it is found rarely in Burma. It is found in the Western Himalayas and Kashmir up to about 5000 feet. In the plains it occurs from the North-west Frontier Province and Sind across to Upper Bengal and southwards generally, though it is not found in Ceylon. A resident species.

The Long-eared (*Asio otus*) and Short-eared (*Asio flammeus*) Owls are medium-sized species of very similar type to the Eagle-Owls. They appear as winter visitors to the plains, the former confined to North-western India. The latter is widely distributed and is usually flushed from ground cover, often in parties.

Habits, etc.—This is the commonest of the larger Owls of India, being very abundant in Northern and Central India. It lives by preference in hollows and clefts of rocky cliffs or ruined buildings, in broken rain-worn ravines, and in brushwood on stony hill-sides, and when these are wanting takes refuge in clumps of trees. Though mainly nocturnal, it sometimes moves by day and long after sunrise may be seen perched on the summit of a rocky scree, looming large in view against the clearness of the new-born sky. It feeds on frogs, lizards, snakes, mammals, birds and insects. The call is a loud *dur-goon* or *to-whoot*, solemn and deep in tone, but when disturbed by day it will sit on a rock bowing and squawking at the intruder, and hissing and snapping with its bill.

The breeding season extends from December to May, but most nests will be found from February to April.

No nest is made, the eggs merely lying in a hollow scraped in the soil, generally in a ledge or recess of a cliff or bank-face,

FIG. 55—Rock Eagle-Owl (½ nat. size)

but some eggs are laid on the ground at the foot of a tree or under a bush.

The normal clutch consists of four eggs, but two or three are sometimes laid.

The egg is a very perfect broad oval, white with a faint creamy tinge. The texture is close and fine, with a distinct gloss.

The egg measures about 2·10 by 1·73 inches.

THE DUSKY EAGLE-OWL

Bubo coromandus (Latham)

Description.—Length 23 inches. Sexes alike. The whole plumage including aigrettes on the head greyish-brown with dark shaft-stripes, the feathers finely mottled and vermiculated with whitish especially on the lower surface ; a few buff and white spots about the shoulders ; flight- and tail-feathers brown with pale mottled cross-bands and tips.

Iris deep yellow ; bill horny-whitish ; claws black.

The tarsus is thickly feathered.

Field Identification.—Very similar in the field to the Rock Horned-Owl, but it is a grey, not a tawny bird, and it is always found sitting in trees ; the eyes are paler.

Distribution.—This fine Owl is found throughout the greater part of the Indian Peninsula extending from the Indus Valley right away to Eastern Bengal, and south to the Carnatic and Mysore, though it is absent from various areas such as the Bombay Deccan, the Western Ghats and the Malabar coast. It is strictly resident.

Habits, etc.—This Owl avoids the most heavily afforested tracts and lives in woods and groves in open country in well-watered areas. It is particularly partial to the avenues of large trees which grow along the great canal systems of Northern India. By day it sleeps in the trees, sitting in a thickly foliaged bough or close up to the trunk, and wakes to activity about dusk, though it begins to call an hour or two before sunset. The call-note is very characteristic, *wo-wo-wo, wo-o, o-o*, a deep solemn hoot which almost resembles the distant sound of a train puffing its way along. The eared head of this bird with its great yellow eyes is particularly cat-like, especially when it is seen looking over the edge of a nest.

The food consists chiefly of Jungle and House Crows which often roost in great numbers in the groves that it inhabits ; it also takes various small mammals, birds, lizards and frogs, and also robs nests of their eggs and young.

It breeds very early in the year, from December to March. The nest is a large rough cup of sticks placed in a fork of a large tree some 30 or 40 feet from the ground. It is generally lined with green leaves or dry grass, and is sometimes a large structure added to and used year after year. While the female is sitting the male sleeps nearby in an adjacent tree, the spot being marked by the remains of meals that strew the ground below. It is comparatively common for this Owl to appropriate the old nests of Eagles and Vultures, and occasionally also it lays in the hollows of trees or in depressions at the junctions of branches, depositing a few leaves in the place by way of lining.

The normal clutch consists of two eggs, but one, three or four eggs are also rarely found. Incubation commences with the laying of the first egg.

The egg is typically a broad oval, but variations in shape and size are common; the texture is rather coarse with more or less gloss; the colour is dead white with a rather creamy tinge.

In size the eggs average about 2·33 by 1·39 inches.

THE COLLARED SCOPS-OWL

Otus bakkamœna Pennant

Description.—Length 10 inches. Sexes alike. Facial disc light brown, faintly banded darker; broad streaks over the eyes merging into aigrettes buffy-white, mottled with blackish; ruff buffy-white with dark brown edges; upper plumage buff, closely vermiculated, streaked and speckled with blackish except for a conspicuously paler collar round the back of the neck and a buff and black-spotted band down the shoulders; flight-feathers brown with paler mottled bands and tips; tail brown with pale cross-bands, the feathers more or less mottled; lower plumage buffy-white, irregularly black shafted, and except towards the chin, tarsus and tail much stippled with fine broken wavy cross-bars.

Iris brown; bill greenish- or yellowish-horny; feet greenish-yellow.

The tarsus is thickly feathered.

Field Identification.—A small Owl with conspicuous ear-tufts and dark eyes, the general effect of the plumage being buff, rather richly marked with dark brown, especially about the head. Presence seldom detected until the call is heard.

Distribution.—This handsome little Owl is found throughout the Oriental region generally, from Muscat on the west to Japan on the east. It is divided into a number of races, of which the following occur in our area as resident birds. They differ merely in details of colour, tint and size, and in the amount of feathering on the toes. The typical race is found in Ceylon and Southern India up to Madras and the Southern Konkan. *O. b. marathæ* is found in the Central Provinces to Sambalpur and Manbhum in Southern Bengal. *O. b. gangeticus* is found in the United Provinces east to Allahabad and at Mount Aboo. *O. b. deserticolor* is the pale bird of Sind and Baluchistan. In the Lower Himalayan ranges up to 6000 feet there are two forms: *O. b. plumipes* is found from Hazara to

Garhwal, while the bird of Nepal, Sikkim and Burma is known as *O. b. lettia.*

The Scops-Owls are a large and difficult group; this species may be distinguished from the others by the wing formula: the first primary is shorter than the eighth, while the second primary is in length between the sixth and seventh or the seventh and eighth.

FIG. 56—Collared Scops-Owl (⅛ nat. size)

Habits, etc. — The Collared Scops-Owl is thoroughly nocturnal, only awaking to activity just as the dusk has almost merged into night; at this hour its low mournful call *whaat* uttered slowly and sedately at long intervals may be heard in the depth of a well-foliaged tree, and thus it may be heard again and again until dawn brings the first flush of light. That is all that is generally known of this Owl unless by chance it is noticed fast alseep in a tree in the daytime; though this is seldom, as it hides itself carefully away.

The food consists chiefly of insects.

Two other very nocturnal species are only known to most people by their calls in the Himalayan hills stations. A very regular and rhythmic *wuck-chug-chug*, which goes on endlessly like the working of a pump-engine, is the call of the Indian Scops-Owl (*Otus sunia*). A plaintive double whistle with a slight interval between the two notes *phew-phew*, with the tone of a hammer on an anvil, is uttered by the Himalayan Scops-Owl (*Otus spilocephalus*). A single clear four-noted whistle, often repeated—also a familiar night sound of the hill stations—indicates the presence of the Pygmy Owlet (*Glaucidium brodiei*), which is little larger than a Sparrow.

The breeding season extends from January until April. The eggs are laid in a natural hole in a tree which is slightly lined with leaves and grass. A pair once deposited their eggs in a large nest-box placed in a tree in my garden. The clutch varies from two to five eggs. These are almost spherical in shape, pure white, fine in texture and fairly glossy.

They measure about 1·25 by 1·05 inches.

THE SPOTTED OWLET

ATHENE BRAMA (Temminck)

(Plate xix, Fig. 4, opposite page 396)

Description.—Length 8 inches. Sexes alike. Forehead and a streak above the eye whitish; upper parts, wings and tail greyish- or earthy-brown, the top of the head with small white spots, the rest of the upper plumage more or less boldly spotted and in places almost barred with white; an indistinct whitish half-collar on the hind neck; the quills with pale broken cross-bars; the tail with four to six white cross-bars; chin, throat and sides of the neck white; a broad brown band, somewhat broken in the centre, across the throat; lower plumage white with brown bands and spots on the feathers, dying away towards the tail.

Iris pale golden-yellow; bill and feet greenish-yellow.

The facial disc and ruff are very indistinct in this Owl.

Field Identification.—One of the most familiar birds of the plains. A small spotted brown and white Owl with bright yellow eyes, which is very wide awake by day and makes most extraordinary noises about dusk; found everywhere, especially in gardens about houses, in twos and threes.

The eerie long-drawn shriek also heard round houses is the cry of the Barn Owl (*Tyto alba*), unmistakable with its queer pinched face and figure and buffy yellow and white plumage.

Distribution.—Throughout the Peninsula of India from the North-west Frontier Province, Baluchistan and Sind to Assam and Cachar, and from the foot-hills of the Himalayas (up to 3000 feet) to Cape Comorin. It also occurs in parts of Burma and Siam. It is divided into races, distinguished by slight differences in coloration. The typical race occurs in Southern India up to about Bombay; while north of that all Indian birds, including those of Baluchistan, belong to the race *A. b. indica.* A strictly resident species.

Habits, etc.—In the Spotted Owlet we have the most common and familiar Owl of India, known to everyone who spends even the shortest time in the country. It affects desert, cultivation and forest alike, living equally at home in rocks and ruins, in trees and houses. It is particularly partial to gardens. This quaint little bird is, of course, nocturnal in its habits, and towards dusk emerges from the hole in which it has spent the day, and signalises its emergence by the most varied assortment of squeaks and squeals and chatterings, uttered in short bursts as if moved by the spirit to sudden vituperation. It then flies off to commence its hunting, flying with a characteristic undulating flight with quick flappings of the wings, though seldom going far at a stretch. It hovers occasionally some 15 or 20 feet above the ground, much after the fashion of a Kestrel, though not so gracefully and skilfully. About houses and streets it perches often in the glare of lamps to profit by the insects attracted to them, and where people dine out in their gardens it hunts round the table with a perfect disdain for their presence.

But though truly nocturnal, it is less sleepy by day and intolerant of the light than most Owls. It sits out in the sunlight near the entrance to its hole, and is then wide awake enough, promptly bowing and nodding and glaring if looked at, finally taking to wing or popping back into its hole to avoid the annoyance; occasionally it calls and chatters by day, but not very often. Three or four often live together. The food consists almost entirely of insects, and the nest holes and resting places will be found littered with pellets containing the indigestible portions of beetles and crickets, proving the amount of good done by these little birds. Small mammals and birds and lizards are, however, occasionally taken.

The breeding season is from February to May, most nests being found in March and April. No very definite nest is made, but the eggs generally rest on a few feathers, dry grass and other rubbish which is usually already present in the hole, though perhaps sometimes gathered by the Owlet itself. The favourite nesting site is a natural hole in a tree, but holes in buildings and clefts in rocks are often used.

The number of eggs varies from three to six. They are pure white in colour, moderately broad ovals of a close uniform satiny texture.

They average in size about 1·25 by 1·04 inches.

THE JUNGLE OWLET

Glaucidium radiatum (Tickell)

Description.—Length 8 inches. Sexes alike. Whole upper plumage dark blackish-brown finely barred with pale rufous on the head and neck and with white on the remainder, some white and rufous blotches on the wing-coverts; wing-quills blackish-brown barred with pale chestnut, the bars becoming more distinct towards the body; tail sooty blackish with narrow white cross-bars; lower plumage banded blackish-brown and white or pale rufous, the dark bands gradually disappearing towards the tail and on the thighs; chin, a line below the cheeks, a large patch on the upper breast and the centre of the abdomen pure white.

Iris yellow; bill greenish-horny, cere greenish; feet dirty greenish-yellow, tips of claws blackish.

The facial disc and ruff are indistinct. Legs feathered and toes covered with coarse hairs.

Field Identification.—A small dark-looking Owl, finely barred with blackish-brown, white and chestnut, which is partly diurnal in its habits. Lives in trees and has an easily recognisable call.

Distribution.—A sedentary species confined to India and Ceylon. The typical race is fairly generally distributed, except in the Eastern Ghats, throughout India from Saharunpur, Gwalior and Mount Aboo to North Cachar and Hylakandy in Assam. In the Himalayas it is

FIG. 57—Jungle Owlet (½ nat. size)

found only in the outer and warmer valleys. In Peninsular India it is found both in the plains and in the hills up to about 5000 feet. It is confined to the dry zone in Ceylon.

This species must not be confused with the very similar Large Barred Owlet (*Glaucidium cuculoides*) which is very common throughout the Lower Himalayan ranges where its rising crescendo of squawks, supplemented by a long quavering whistle in the breeding season, is a familiar sound by day.

Habits, etc.—The Jungle Owlet is usually confined to the more jungly and forest-clad tracts of both the plains and the lower hills though in the cultivated plains of the United Provinces a pair or two may be found in almost every mango tope.

As a rule, it is an inveterate skulker, remaining in its hole in spite of any noise. When disturbed it settles on a branch and remains perfectly still, sitting bolt upright and staring intently at the intruder until it senses that it is discovered, instantly taking wing to a fresh place of concealment, and if pursued it repeats the performance. Sitting thus it looks exactly like the stump of a dead bough. It sees well by day and Vidal records how one dashed out of a tree to capture a *Phylloscopus* he had shot which was fluttering slowly to the ground in the full blaze of the sun.

The Jungle Owlet makes its appearance in the evening a little later than the Spotted Owlet and retires as a rule a little earlier in the morning, its principal feeding hours being apparently the hour after sunrise and the hour before sunset. If undisturbed the pairs sit together and sun themselves before retiring to their hole, sometimes remaining thus up till midday. Like the Spotted Owlet it often perches on telegraph-wires.

This Owlet calls both by day and night. The call is peculiar but rather pleasing, something of a chirp in several different keys very different to the discordant noise of the Spotted Owlet. It is described as *too-to-to-too*, drawn out to a considerable length and sometimes terminating in double or treble notes.

The flight is both rapid and strong, the wings being often partially closed. It kills and devours all kinds of small birds as well as locusts, lizards, crickets, ants and even butterflies.

The breeding season is from March till June.

No nest is constructed, but the eggs are laid in holes in small trees, usually some 10 or 20 feet from the ground.

The clutch consists of three or four eggs. They are normally very broad ovals, smooth and satiny to the touch but with scarcely any gloss. The colour is pure white.

The egg measures about 1·25 by 1·05 inches.

THE KING VULTURE

SARCOGYPS CALVUS (Scopoli)

Description.—Length 32 inches. Sexes alike. Glossy black, brownish on the shoulders and lower back and rump; the crop is dark brown almost surrounded with white down; a large white and downy patch on each flank by the thighs.

Iris reddish-brown or yellow; bill dark brown; cere dull red; legs dull red.

The head and neck are bare, deep beefsteak-red in colour with a flat pendent wattle behind each ear; there are conspicuous bare red patches on each side of the crop and in front of each thigh.

Field Identification.—Black plumage and the bare red head and neck wattles are distinctive both on the ground and in flight; in flight also the white thigh-patches are conspicuous at all distances, and place the identification beyond all doubt; the wings appear rather pointed in flight, and a whitish line generally seems to run through them.

Distribution.—This fine Vulture is found throughout India and Burma, though not in Ceylon, extending on the south-east into the Malay Peninsula, Siam and Cochin - China. In the Outer Himalayas it breeds up to a height of 5800 feet and ranges in search of food up to about 8000 feet. It is a strictly resident species.

FIG. 58—King Vulture ($\frac{1}{10}$ nat. size)

Habits, etc.—Although generally distributed and common throughout India, this species is never abundant, as it is not colonial like most of the large Vultures but lives solitary or in pairs; only one or two will ever be found at a carcass with scores of the other species, which mostly hold this bird in wholesome respect and give way before its superior spirit and demeanour; hence the name of King Vulture, though it is also frequently known as the Black or Pondicherry Vulture. It is not partial to very heavy forest or pure desert, and is most common in open cultivated plains where it rests upon the trees; it never settles on cliffs. In flight the wings are held well above the line of the back.

The breeding season lasts from the latter end of January until the middle of April, but most eggs are probably laid in March. The nest is a large flat structure of sticks, lined towards the centre with leaves and dry grass, and it is probably repaired and used for several years in succession. The nest is placed as a rule on the extreme top of large trees, 30 to 40 feet from the ground, but in localities where large trees are scarce it has no hesitation in building on cactus, on low thorny trees and even on low bushes close to the ground; but under no circumstances does it ever breed on rocks or buildings. Occasionally it utilises the old nests of Eagles.

Only a solitary egg is laid. The normal shape is a round oval; the shell is very strong with a moderately fine texture, usually without gloss. When freshly laid the colour is a nearly unsullied pale greenish-white, but as incubation advances the shell becomes discoloured.

In size the eggs average about 3·35 by 2·50 inches.

THE HIMALAYAN GRIFFON

GYPS HIMALAYENSIS Hume

Description.—Length 4 feet. Sexes alike. Head and neck naked save for some yellowish-white hair-like feathers on the head and yellowish-white down on the neck; a ruff of loose-textured pointed feathers round the neck whitish and pale brown; back whity-brown, unevenly coloured, with traces of pale shaft-stripes; lower back whitish merging into buff; wings dark brown with pale tips to the coverts, the quills and tail-feathers blackish-brown; lower plumage light buff-brown, darker on the crop, with broad whitish shaft-streaks.

Iris brownish-yellow; bill pale horny-green; cere pale brown; legs dingy greenish-white.

Build squat and heavy, accentuated by the bare head and neck with the loose ruff. The beak is deep and laterally compressed with the upper mandible strongly hooked.

Field Identification.—The huge pale-coloured Vulture found commonly throughout the Himalayas. Seen from below it is pale khaki with the hinder margins of the open wings and the tail black, and it flies high in the sky with the appearance of an aeroplane. Khaki-colour, down-covered head and neck and white neck ruff are distinctive when the bird is sitting still.

Distribution.—A resident mountain species found throughout the whole length of the Himalayas from Kabul to Bhutan; also in the Pamirs, Turkestan and Tibet.

The exact relationship between this species and the Griffon Vulture (*Gyps fulvus*) is not very clear nor are they ordinarily separable in the field. The Griffon is apparently common over the greater part of North-western India, occurring in diminishing numbers southwards to the Deccan and eastwards to Assam.

The smaller Vulture of similar coloration but remarkable for its dark head and neck bare of down is the Long-billed Vulture (*Gyps indicus*). This is common throughout India generally except in the alluvial plains of the North-west.

Habits, etc.—This Vulture is familiar to all who have visited the

1. Green Parrakeet. 2. Blue-Jay. 3. White-breasted Kingfisher. 4. Golden-backed Woodpecker. 5. Common Kingfisher. (All about $\frac{1}{5}$ nat. size.)

[*Face p.* 352

hill stations of the Himalayas, as it is the great khaki-coloured bird which may be seen at all hours wheeling and soaring in the sky often at immense heights, or flying fairly low over the hill-side, travelling straight and fast with a tearing noise. The wings are held stiff and straight in a line with the back and the whole bird irresistibly recalls the passage of an aeroplane. Seen at a distance, the wings appear very broad and square ended, and at short ranges it can be seen that the pressure of the air causes the feathers at the ends of the wings to splay out and turn upwards like the fingers of a hand. Like other Vultures, this species has its fixed resting places, which are usually on the rocky face of some magnificent cliff or mountain spur; here the birds congregate to digest a recent meal, sitting motionless, hunched up in the traditional Vulture attitude, or squatting and sunning on the ledges like gigantic chickens. These favourite spots have doubtless been used for hundreds of years, and the white stains about them are often visible two or three miles away. Immediately after a heavy gorge at a carcass the Griffons congregate on trees in the immediate vicinity until digestion has started and they feel able to face the flight to the resting place. The food consists entirely of carrion from carcasses and the bird never kills a prey for itself.

The breeding season is from December to March. The birds nest in small colonies, seldom of more than four to six pairs, on the rocky ledges of precipices and crags. Sometimes the solitary egg lies on the bare ledge, at other times it is supported merely by a few twigs and roots or a little dry grass, but generally there is a huge nest of sticks.

The egg is somewhat variable in shape, but is typically a rather long and pointed oval. The texture is rather coarse and there is practically no gloss. In colour it is greenish- or greyish-white; some eggs are unmarked, but the majority are more or less blotched and streaked with various shades of brown, some quite heavily.

In size they average about 3·75 by 2·75 inches.

THE WHITE-BACKED VULTURE

Pseudogyps bengalensis (Gmelin)

Description.—Length 35 inches. Sexes alike. Sparse brownish hairs cover the bare head and neck and at the back of the neck white downy tufts introduce a ruff of short pure white down; upper plumage blackish-brown with a large white patch above the base of the tail; crop black, bordered on each side by white down; breast and abdomen brownish-black with narrow whitish shaft-streaks. The under wing-coverts, upper flanks and thigh-coverts white.

Iris brown; skin of the head and neck dusky-plumbeous; bill dark plumbeous, whitish along the top, the cere polished horny-black; legs blackish.

Field Identification.—A huge humped-up square-looking bird which broods on the trees with the naked head and neck shrunk into the shoulders. Dark leaden colour with conspicuous white rump-patch prevent adults being confused with any other Vulture.

FIG. 59—White-backed Vulture (⅛ nat. size)

In flight if the white rump-patch is invisible the rather pointed wings with their white lining and the white sides combined with the general blackish colour render identification easy.

Distribution.—Found throughout India and Burma (but not Ceylon) to the Malay Peninsula and Annam. It is not found in Baluchistan, but is otherwise very generally spread throughout our area, working even up to 8000 feet in the Western Himalayas, where, however, it does not breed above 3600 feet. It is a resident species, but wanders a good deal according to food-supply, and our campaigns on the North-west Frontier usually lead to a temporary extension of its distribution in areas where it is not normally found. This is the commonest of all the Vultures of India, and must be familiar to those who have visited the Towers of Silence in Bombay.

Habits.—The White-backed Vulture breeds in colonies in large trees on the outskirts of populous towns, near villages, and in the avenues of huge trees that line roads or canals. Here they settle to the work of preparing the nests often as early as September and will be found at them until well into March; but the majority of eggs will be found in November, December and January. In addition to these colonies there are favourite roosting and resting sites where the birds may be found all the year round though their numbers sensibly diminish in the nesting season. When not sitting sluggishly at either nest-colony or roosting site, the White-backed Vulture spends its life on the wing, usually at an immense height from the ground, soaring in wide circles with almost motionless wings held level with the body or slightly backwards; when travelling to fresh ground it flies with a direct but somewhat laboured flight with regularly beating wings.

For years scientific controversy raged over the method by which Vultures found their food, and there were two schools of thought that pressed respectively the claims of sight or smell. The explanation is so simple that it is difficult to realise that there was ever any doubt about it.

An animal dies somewhere, whether in the open or under cover; if it has not been watched before death by the crows and pariah dogs, it is soon found by one or other of them; a single crow or a single dog pulling at a carcass is immediately noticed by others of the tribe and a number collect; the carcass is fresh, the skin unbroken, so in the first stages of the feast there is more confusion and skirmishing than actual feeding. This attracts the kites, which wheel round backwards and forwards over the scene looking for detached morsels, which they snatch with a dashing swoop. One or two of the carrion-feeding eagles sitting heavily on the tops of trees within a mile or so of the spot observe the kites and join the mêlée, the others yielding them place of honour at the feast. By this time it is inevitable that the concourse has caught the eye of one of the Vultures which are patrolling the sky far overhead; it descends lower to verify the existence of a carcass and finally descends to the ground nearby with the peculiar tearing rush that unmistakably indicates food. Vulture follows Vulture, as they patrol with a lively interest in each other's movements, the circle of interest widening like the ripples of a stone thrown into water. Settled on the ground the Vultures run in clumsily on foot, bickerings ensue, and the weaker scavengers give place to the jostling, striving mass of Vultures which cover the carcass and gradually devour everything but the largest bones. Gorged, they sit around on the ground, or with difficulty rise into surrounding trees, till digestion allows them to wing a heavy way to the resting place ; and there they sit and meditate until returning hunger again sends them on patrol.

This species never nests upon rocks or buildings, but invariably on trees. The nest is a large irregular structure of sticks, either wedged in the fork of a tree or right on top of it ; it is repaired and reoccupied year after year until it often attains great dimensions. A slight hollow on the top is lined with green leaves to receive the single egg. While pairing these birds indulge in a loud roaring noise. They pair on the nest.

The eggs are fairly regular ovals in shape, the shell very thick and strong, and generally without gloss. The majority are greyish- or greenish-white in colour, unmarked, but some eggs are slightly speckled, spotted and blotched with pale reddish-brown.

They average about 3·25 by 2·40 inches in size.

THE NEOPHRON

NEOPHRON PERCNOPTERUS (Linnæus)

Description.—Length 24 inches. Sexes alike. The whole plumage is white except the flight-feathers which are black and brown.

Iris dark brown ; bill horny, cere yellow ; legs fleshy-white.

The head and upper neck are naked with the skin deep yellow ; the bill is slender and lengthened, straight at the base and deeply hooked at the end ; the neck is surrounded by a ruff of hackle-like feathers ; wings long and pointed ; tail wedge-shaped.

Field Identification.—Exceedingly abundant about the haunts of man. A large white bird with dark wing-quills and a bare bright yellow head, accompanied by dark chocolate-brown birds which are the immature of the species. The bird might easily be mistaken for a very large hen, except for something peculiarly repulsive about its appearance.

Distribution.—The Neophron or Egyptian Vulture has a wide range in Southern Europe, in Africa and in Asia. The typical or Western race extends to the North-western corner of India, being found in Sind, Baluchistan, North-west Frontier Province, Upper Punjab, and the Western Himalayas. In the remainder of India it is replaced by *N. p. ginginianus*, which is a rather smaller bird with a yellow bill, the typical race having the bill dark brownish-horn with a dark tip. Intermediate birds are found about Delhi. It is a resident species, but there are indications of slight local migration.

Habits, etc.—This Vulture is only to a slight extent social, and is usually found singly or in pairs, though a number may often collect in the neighbourhood of food. It haunts towns and villages, and while ready to eat any form of garbage or carrion appears mainly to live on human excrement; hence the detestation in which this species is commonly held by all classes. It has no fear of man, and perches on buildings and trees in the most crowded bazaars, or stalks sedately about open spaces, graveyards and camping grounds, looking in gait and appearance much like a large, disreputable old hen; hence the name of "Pharaoh's Chicken," which is often applied to the Western race in Egypt.

The breeding season lasts from the end of February to the end of May, but most eggs will be found in March and April. The nest is placed on rocky precipices, earthy cliffs, buildings and trees, often in very exposed and frequented situations.

FIG. 60—Neophron ($\frac{1}{8}$ nat. size)

The nests are the most filthy, disreputable structures, a foundation of sticks, lined with old rags, wool, earth, and anything else soft that comes to hand, the dirtier the better apparently. The eggs are laid in a shallow hollow on top of the mass. One to three eggs are laid, but the usual clutch consists of two.

The eggs are variable in shape, size and colour, and are often very handsome; the normal shape is rather a broad oval, somewhat compressed towards one end; the texture is coarse and generally rather chalky, but in some specimens there is a fine surface glaze. The colour is dirty white overlaid with a wash of varying shades of deep rich brown-red, sometimes so dark as to be deep purplish-red, and sometimes fading to light yellowish-red with much of the ground-colour visible. Other eggs are spotted and blotched with purplish-red and ashy shell-marks.

In size they average 2·6 by 1·98 inches.

THE LÄMMERGEIER

Gypaëtus barbatus (Linnæus)

Description.—Length 4 feet. Sexes alike. A marked patch from above the eye to and including the stiff bristles over the nostrils and a beard of bristles under the chin black; remainder of head and throat white speckled with black; neck and lower plumage white, tinged often very richly with bright ferruginous, and usually with an imperfect black gorget across the breast; upper back and lesser wing-coverts black with narrow white shaft-stripes; the remainder of the upper plumage, wings and tail deep silvery-grey, the shafts of the feathers white and the edges blackish.

Iris pale orange, the sclerotic membrane blood-red; bill horny, darker at tip; legs plumbeous-grey.

The bill is high, compressed, and much hooked at the end; wings long and pointed, with an expanse of 8 to 10 feet; tail long, pointed and graduated.

Field Identification.—Almost always seen in flight, a huge bird with long pointed wings and wedge-shaped tail; this last feature is distinctive from every large bird in India except the Neophron. The beard is distinct up to some distance and shows black against the pale head and bright rufous neck and breast of the adult; upper plumage silvery and black. Immature birds, however, are dull blackish all over, but can be identified by the same shape and beard as in the adult.

Distribution.—The Lämmergeier or Bearded Vulture is widely distributed as a mountain bird in Southern Europe, Africa and Central Asia, being divided into several races. It is a common bird along the Himalayas and tributary ranges down the North-western border of India, and birds from this area, although sometimes considered identical with European birds, are described as forming a separate race *G. b. hemachalanus*. A resident species.

Habits, etc.—Like other species that have fired the imagination of mankind from the earliest days of his civilisation, the Lämmergeier has several well-known names in different languages. Lämmergeier or the Lamb-Eagle is a relic of the days before this grand bird had become extinct in the Alps, when confusion with the more courageous Golden Eagle and the innate propensity of the multitude to exaggeration combined to credit the bird with all manner of depredations amongst sheep, goats and chamois, and even children. Another well-known name, Ossifrage or Bone-breaker, being based on a real observation, is found in several languages. For the Lämmergeier prefers, above all things, to feed on bones, swallowing the smaller whole and carrying the larger high up into the air and dropping them to shatter in pieces on the rocks below, where at its leisure it collects and devours the fragments. From this habit, applied also to tortoises in the Levant, is due the legend of the death of Æschylus, who is said to have been killed by the dropping of a tortoise on his head.

The bird is purely a mountain species, and it spends its days beating along the hill-sides, following the major contours or soaring high over the ravines; living things it seldom kills, but it descends to offal of every description, picking trifles on foot even from a rubbish dump at a hill station. Carcasses it does not dispute with the Vultures. It waits till they have finished and then descends to the feast of its desires, the blood-stained bones that lie drying in the sun.

In flight the wings are held in a line with the body, but from their shape and the pressure of the air they slope downwards and up again at the tips, so that in horizontal section the bird has the shape of an unstrung bow; like this it travels and soars indefinitely without flapping, merely banking slightly from side to side, though now and again it rings the changes on majestic flapping and gliding. By way of courtship it indulges with its mate in aerial gymnastics which reveal its perfect mastery of the science of flight. Normally it is silent, but when courting it indulges in loud squealing.

The breeding season commences in November and lasts until March, and most eggs will be found about January.

The nest is placed in some almost inaccessible situation in the face of a cliff, usually on a ledge under a projecting rock. It is a huge, shapeless heap of sticks strewn about and mixed with rags, large bones, feathers and droppings.

The clutch consists of two or three eggs. These are typically rather broad ovals, pointed towards the smaller end. The texture is rather coarse and glossless, the colour of the shell appearing pale dingy yellow when held up against the light.

The colour is rather variable, from pale uniform salmon-buff to reddish- or orange-brown, clouded, blotched and mottled with deeper markings of the same tint; or the egg may be dull white with spots, streaks, and blotches of pale washed-out reddish-brown and purple.

In size the egg measures about 3·25 by 2·65 inches.

THE TAWNY EAGLE

AQUILA RAPAX (Temminck)

(Plate xviii, Fig. 1, opposite page 374)

Description.—Length: Male 25 inches, female 28 inches. Sexes alike. The coloration is very variable, but is generally uniform brown, varying from a dirty buffish-brown to deep rich umber-brown; the quills are dark blackish-brown, mottled and barred with whitish about the base, and the tail is dark greyish-brown with more or less distinct cross-bands. In some specimens there is a very distinct dark mask on the front of the head and face, and parts of the plumage are often spotted with light brown.

Iris hazel-brown; bill pale bluish-grey, blackish at tip; cere dull yellow; feet yellow, claws black.

The nostril is ear-shaped; bill strong, curved and sharply hooked; top of the head very flat; legs feathered down to the toes. The plumage is coarse in texture.

Field Identification.—A large brown or blackish-brown bird of rather fierce appearance with its flat head, sharply-hooked beak, and feathered legs armed with sharp claws, which sits heavily on the tops of trees or soars in great circles above the Kites, from which it is easily distinguished by the rounded tail. There are, however, several other common species of Eagle, and it requires some knowledge and practice to distinguish them from it. Of these the most easily recognisable is the very large Steppe-Eagle (*Aquila nipalensis*), which in flight exhibits two pale wing-bars. A winter visitor to India as far south as Seoni and Raipur.

A very black-looking Eagle, seen above tree-level in Baluchistan and the Himalayas, is usually the Golden Eagle (*Aquila chrysaëtus*). A longish tail and often light patches in the wing and tail-quills assist recognition.

Distribution.—*A. rapax vindhiana*, the common Eagle of India, is the Oriental race of *A. rapax*, which is found throughout the greater part of Africa. It is found throughout most of India from Baluchistan and the North-west Frontier Province to Lower Bengal and Upper Burma; but it is wanting on the Malabar coast and in Ceylon. In the Himalayas it occurs and breeds up to about 4000 feet. It is a resident species.

Habits, etc.—This Eagle avoids heavy forest and the damper portions of the country-side, being particularly a bird of those dry sandy plains with a moderate amount of tree growth which are such a feature of Northern India. It divides its time between soaring high in the air like the Vultures, and with them keeping watch for carcasses, or sitting lumpily on the summit of a tall tree watching the surrounding country-side. Although in being partial to carrion it offends against the traditional idea of an Eagle, it is a fine lordly-looking bird and has plenty of courage, taking hares and large birds, and in particular chasing and robbing falcons and hawks of their booty. This habit causes it to be a great nuisance to the falconer as it chases trained falcons mistaking their jesses for prey. At other times no quarry is too small for it. I have seen it robbing a Babbler's nest of young and a Plover's nest of eggs, and when locusts or termites swarm it always joins the feast; while frogs, lizards and snakes are readily devoured.

Eggs are laid from the middle of November until June, but the majority will be found in January.

The nest is a large flat structure of sticks and thorny twigs, lined as a rule with straw and coarse grass and often with green leaves. It is built not in a fork but on the extreme tops of trees so that the Eagle may settle in the nest without brushing its wings against the branches. The favourite tree is the dense thorny kikar or babool tree.

The clutch consists of one to three eggs.

The egg is normally a somewhat broad oval, slightly pointed at one end; the texture of the shell is hard and fine, usually with a slight gloss. The ground-colour is dull greyish-white; many eggs are unmarked; others are marked, though generally sparingly, with streaks, spots and blotches of brown, red and purple of varying tints.

The eggs average about 2·60 by 2·10 inches.

THE CRESTED HAWK-EAGLE

SPIZAËTUS CIRRHATUS (Gmelin)

Description.—Length: Male 26 inches, female 29 inches. Sexes alike. There are two main colour phases, of which the dark phase is usually considered adult and the pale phase immature.

Dark phase: Crest black lightly tipped with white; top and sides of the head and neck brown streaked with blackish-brown; upper plumage umber-brown, the depth of colour in individual feathers variable; wing-quills brown above, whitish below, barred and tipped with black, inner webs white towards the base; tail brown above, whitish below with four or five broad umber-brown cross-bars and the tips of the feathers paler; lower plumage white, heavily streaked with umber-brown, darkest on the breast; thighs and a patch under the tail brown, partly barred with white; feathers of the tarsus mottled rufous brown and white.

Pale phase: Crest as above; top and sides of the head and neck white overlaid with creamy brown, many of the feathers with dark brown shaft-streaks; remainder of upper plumage dark umber-brown, some feathers paler and many broadly edged with white; wing-quills and tail as above but dark bands are narrower and more in number. The whole lower plumage white, some of the feathers with dark

FIG. 61—Crested Hawk-Eagle (⅛ nat. size)

brown shafts and rufous-brown spots, the thighs and feathers under the tail heavily mottled with brownish-rufous.

Iris leaden-grey, pale straw-colour or golden yellow; bill plumbeous-black, cere plumbeous in dark phase, yellow in pale phase; feet yellow, claws black.

Nostril ear-shaped; bill strong, curved and sharply hooked; a tuft of long feathers springing from the back of the crown; legs feathered to the base of the toes.

Field Identification.—A lightly-built, slender Eagle with a proportionately long narrow tail, upper parts dark brown; lower parts either pure white becoming rufous towards the tail, or white heavily streaked with blackish-brown. Underside of the wings in flight is white barred and spotted with blackish-brown. A curious tuft of long black feathers springs from the crown. Found amongst trees and rather noisy.

Distribution.—The typical race is very generally distributed in India south of the Indo-Gangetic plain and a smaller race, *S. c. ceylanensis*, occurs in Ceylon. A rather paler race, *S. c. limnaëtus*, with little or no crest, which is also found in a melanistic phase practically black throughout, is found in the sub-Himalayan terai from Garhwal to Eastern Bengal, Assam and still farther eastwards. The very similar Hodgson's Hawk-Eagle (*Spizaëtus nipalensis*) of the Himalayas and Western Ghats and Ceylon has the lower parts much more definitely barred. The correct classification and distribution of the various Hawk-Eagles is not yet satisfactorily known.

The curious crest of these Hawk-Eagles, whilst very distinctive, may lead to confusion with the Crested Honey-Buzzard (*Pernis ptilorhynchus*) found throughout India and the rarer and more local Crested Hawks of the genus *Baza*. None of these, however, have the legs feathered more than half-way down the tarsus. The Honey-Buzzard, moreover, has very distinctive scale-like feathering on the face, whilst the Bazas have the lower parts transversely banded and are much smaller.

Another very courageous bird of similar size and appearance is Bonelli's Eagle (*Hieraëtus fasciatus*) which is found sparingly throughout India. It has, however, no crest.

Habits, etc.—The Crested Hawk-Eagle is a bird of forests and also of well-timbered country in the neighbourhood of cultivation. In habits it resembles the Hawks far more than the Eagles, and it soars far less than the true Eagles, being more often seen flying through the trees than above them. It spends much of its time sitting on the tops of high trees watching the surrounding ground for prey to appear. A covey of partridges or a young pea-fowl has only to feed out into the open, a hare to move from its form, and the Hawk-Eagle dashes down and pounces on it. It also feeds on jungle-fowl and other ground-feeding species as well as squirrels, rats, lizards, and the like. The call is a prolonged shrill scream and the bird is very vociferous, while the young bird in the nest is extremely noisy when it is being fed.

The breeding season lasts from December to April, most eggs being found in January. The nest is a large and comparatively deep structure of sticks, loosely put together with the twigs hanging down untidily. It is always profusely lined with green leaves, preferably those of the mango. It is built, very high up as a rule, in the fork of a large tree and, though the favourite tree appears to be a mango, any kind of tree may be selected.

The clutch invariably consists of a single egg. The eggs are rather variable in shape and appearance, but the majority are rather broad and regular ovals, appreciably pointed at the small end. The shell is very strong and glossless, but by no means coarse. Held up against the light it is pale green. The colour is dull greenish-white, never quite unmarked but seldom well marked. The markings vary from an almost imperceptible stippling to a couple of dozen moderate-sized spots and lines, the latter thin and inconspicuous but occasionally arabesque in character. The markings are confined to the large end and vary in colour from reddish-brown to brownish-yellow.

In size the egg measures about 2·60 to 2·0 inches.

THE CRESTED SERPENT-EAGLE

Hæmatornis cheela (Latham)

Description.—Length 28 inches. Sexes alike. A short full crest black, the basal half of the feathers white; upper plumage dark brown with a dull purplish gloss, some feathers tipped with white; flight-feathers blackish with three bars brown above whitish below; tail brown and black with the tip pale and a broad conspicuous whitish band; lower parts brown, spotted with numerous white ocelli and barred finely with dark brown, there being great variation in the tints of the colour.

Iris intense yellow; bill plumbeous, blackish above and at tip; cere, conspicuous bare skin in front of the eyes, and the gape yellow; legs dingy yellow.

The bill is rather long and deeply hooked; wings short and rounded; tail rather long; legs strong, the tarsus bare of feathers.

Field Identification.—The full crest mixed with white, the peculiar purplish-brown coloration with the white ocelli beneath, the broad white bar in the tail and the barred wings are most distinctive; these points combined with the noisy whistling calls render this Eagle easier than most to identify.

Distribution.—The Crested Serpent-Eagle is widely distributed in the Oriental Region from the Western Himalayas to Southern China, and is divided into a number of well-marked races; those in India illustrate to a remarkable degree the tendency of Indian birds to decrease in size from north to south.

The typical race is found in Northern India from Hazara to Sikkim along the Outer Himalayas (which it ascends to about 7000 feet) and in the plains from Rajputana to Bengal and Assam. In Peninsular and Southern India it is replaced by the smaller *H. c. melanotis* in which the breast is usually unbarred and the tail-bands are grey, not white. A still smaller form, *H. c. spilogaster*, is found in Ceylon.

This Eagle is a resident species, though individuals apparently wander to some extent. In Sind and the Punjab it is very scarce.

Another striking Eagle, found in open country throughout India, is the Short-toed Eagle (*Circaëtus ferox*), which is noteworthy for

FIG. 62—Crested Serpent-Eagle (1/6 nat. size)

its ability to hover stationary in the air like a Kestrel. It is brown above and white below, the crop-region being streaked and the flanks crescent-spotted with brown. The head appears larger than in most Eagles.

Habits, etc.—This handsome Eagle is found in well-wooded and well-watered country, being particularly partial to the pleasant sub-Himalayan valleys where mountain streams run down through the rice-fields and amongst big groves of mango trees. Its food consists chiefly of snakes, lizards and frogs, but insects are also taken. It is rather a noisy bird, frequently uttering on the wing a plaintive whistling call of several notes, *kuk-kuk, queeear-queeear-queeear*, the first two short notes being only audible at close range, the others carrying a great distance. It is very bold, and I have ridden up within a yard or two of one which was standing on the ground holding a snake in its talons. The claws are usually dirty with mud, indicating how large a portion of the food is procured about paddy fields and jheels. In flight the wings appear very broad and rounded, and they are held sloping backwards, while the long tail is only partly spread. This Eagle generally soars over forests and well-wooded ravines in preference to barren and open ground, and it often rises to an immense height, travelling fast or soaring in great circles.

The breeding season lasts from March to May.

The nest is always placed in trees, not on the topmost branches as in the case of the Tawny Eagle, but in a fork within the branches of the tree. It is small for the size of the bird, a cup loosely made of sticks and twigs and lined with fresh leaves, fine twigs and grass roots.

The single egg is a broad oval, usually rather pointed at the smaller end; the texture is rough and glossless and the shell strong.

The ground-colour is bluish- or greenish-white, with specklings, spottings and clouds of pale purple or purplish-brown or brownish-red; some eggs are very heavily marked and handsome.

In size they average about 2·75 by 2·2 inches.

THE WHITE-EYED BUZZARD

BUTASTUR TEESA (Franklin)

(Plate xix, Fig. 2, opposite page 396)

Description.—Length 17 inches. Sexes alike. Upper plumage brown, sometimes with a rufescent tinge, the feathers with dark shafts; the white bases of the feathers below the back of the head show through and form a conspicuous patch; sides of the wing mottled or barred with white; quills brown above, whitish below, pure white at their bases and barred towards the tips, the tip of the wing black; tail rufous-brown above, whity-brown below, with indistinct blackish bands; chin and throat white with a dark brown stripe down the centre and a dark stripe down each side; sides of the head and neck and the breast brown, with dark shafts on the breast and white spots and bands on the lower breast and abdomen; thighs and a patch below the tail white with pale rufous bars.

Iris pale yellowish-white; cere, gape and base of bill orange, the tip black; legs dingy orange-yellow; claws black.

The bill is compressed and sharply curved; wing long and pointed; tarsus bare with short toes, the scales forming a network instead of transverse shields on the front.

Field Identification.—A medium-sized brown Hawk, heavy in build with pointed black-tipped wings; easily identified by the whitish eyes and the three dark stripes on the white throat.

Distribution.—Common throughout the greater part of India from the foot-hills of the Himalayas, which it occasionally ascends to about 4000 feet down to Central India; south of this it becomes rare, though it is found throughout the Peninsula. On the west it extends to Baluchistan and the North-west Frontier Province, and to the east it is found throughout Northern Burma. While generally a resident species it is locally migratory.

Habits, etc.—The White-eyed Buzzard avoids both hills and forest and prefers open country with low scrub and cultivation. It is a dull, sluggish creature, unusually tame for a bird of prey, and spends most of its time sitting on a telegraph post, tree or low bush, from which it makes occasional journeys to the ground to capture the grasshoppers and other insects which form its food. It also sits on the ground or on the mounds of earth that mark field boundaries and skims along low over the ground from one mound to another. Sometimes it even walks about on foot. The flight is quick and strong with rapid beats of the wings. At the commencement of the breeding season it is fond of soaring and is very noisy, freely uttering its plaintive, mewing cry, ***pit-weer, pit-weer***.

The breeding season lasts from March to May, but most eggs will be found in April. The birds are very leisurely over the preparation of their nests, which are shallow cups composed loosely of twigs and sticks without lining. They are built in the forks of trees about 20 feet from the ground; there is a tendency to prefer a thickly-foliaged tree like a mango, often one of a clump.

The eggs vary in number from two to four, but the usual clutch is three. In shape they are broad ovals, of fine texture with a slight gloss, greyish-white or pale bluish-white in colour. They are usually unmarked, but occasional specimens will be found marked with reddish-brown, though this is very rare.

In size they average about 1·85 by 1·50 inches.

PALLAS' FISHING-EAGLE

Haliaëtus leucoryphus (Pallas)

Description.—Length 33 inches. Sexes alike. Forehead whitish; top of head and neck fulvous passing into dark brown on the rest of the upper plumage, wings and tail; a broad white band across the tail towards the end; sides of head and neck with the chin and throat whitish; remainder of lower plumage brown, darker on the flanks and lower abdomen.

Iris greyish-yellow; bill dark plumbeous, cere and gape light plumbeous; legs dull white, claws black.

Bill strong, curved and sharply hooked; top of the head very flat; feathers on neck long and pointed; upper third of the tarsus feathered; plumage rather coarse in texture.

Field Identification.—Northern India. A large Eagle, common along the great rivers and the larger jheels, which is easily recognised

FIG. 63—Pallas' Fishing-Eagle (⅛ nat. size)

by the combination of dark brown plumage with a whitish-looking head and a conspicuous white band near the end of the tail. Attracts attention by the loud call.

Distribution.—Southern Russia, through Central Asia to Trans-baikalia and south to the Persian Gulf, Northern India and Northern Burma. In India it is not found on the coast, but is well distributed in the alluvial Indo-Gangetic plains. Its southern limit is not accurately recorded, but it certainly occurs as far south as the Indravarti River. A resident species with no sub-species.

This species is only likely to be confused with the large Grey-headed Fishing-Eagle (*Icthyophaga ichthyaëtus*) which is found throughout most of Northern and Central India. In this the tail is white except for a broad dark brown band at the end.

The Osprey *Pandion haliætus* is frequently seen in the cold weather in the vicinity of salt or fresh water, perched on a dead bough or sailing round in search of fish. It is of medium size, dark brown above, white below, and the head whitish with a dark streak along the side.

Habits, etc.—Pallas' Fishing-Eagle is a familiar species to all whom duty or pleasure takes about the great rivers of Northern India or the large jheels found in that alluvial plain. Sooner or later attention is attracted by the loud raucous call, which some compare to the shrieking of an ungreased cart-wheel, a sound which carries great distances in the flat open plains. The author of the call may be seen perched on the top of some gigantic cotton-tree or on a low mud-cliff or else beating up and down the river with somewhat hurried flight. It soars well and attains tremendous heights in the air where it still can be identified by the white band in the tail.

The staple food of this Eagle is undoubtedly fish. It does not plunge for them like the Osprey but takes those which have ventured into the shallows or become stranded in drying pools. Its great strength allows it to capture quite large fish, the case of a thirteen-pounder taken being actually on record. When fishermen are dragging a river with nets they are often attended by one or more of these Eagles, which try to steal any fish left unattended on the bank. Mud-turtles, frogs and reptiles are taken and any wounded duck or goose on a river soon falls a prey to Pallas' Eagle, though it is hardly fast enough to take them when uninjured. It is also a pirate, trying to rob Cormorants and Terns of their fish or Harriers and Eagles of their varied booty. Water-side carrion is not too mean for its attention, and on the Ganges it habitually feeds on human corpses. But all things considered it is a fine bird and comes much nearer to the popular conception of an Eagle than many other of the Indian species of that group. It belongs to the same genus as the Bald Eagle, which is the national symbol of America.

The breeding season is from the beginning of November until February, the majority of eggs being laid in December.

The nest is a huge platform of sticks, some of which are often as thick as a man's arm, with a superstructure of thinner sticks and twigs. The slight depression made to hold the eggs is lined with fine twigs and green leaves and sometimes rushes and straw. The whole structure is rough and rugged and takes a long time to build as much of the material brought to it is rejected or dropped. It may be repaired and used again from year to year, having often been borrowed in the meantime by an Owl or Lugger Falcon or even a Vulture.

The nest is placed right at the top of a large tree, generally an isolated one within easy distance of a jheel or river. The solitary cotton-trees which stand as landmarks in an Indian river-bed afford favourite eyries.

The clutch consists of two or three eggs. If the first egg is taken this species will still lay the remaining eggs of the clutch in the nest. The egg is normally a broad oval in shape and the texture is rather fine and smooth. The colour is greyish-white, but the shell appears intensely dark green if held to the light.

The egg measures about 2·77 by 2·17 inches.

THE BRAHMINY KITE

Haliastur indus (Boddaert)

Description.—Length 19 inches. Sexes alike. Head, neck and lower parts down to the middle of the abdomen white; remainder of the plumage chestnut, paler and duller under the wings and tail; outer flight-feathers black and the tip of the tail whitish. Most of the feathers of the body plumage have a dark shaft line.

FIG. 64—Brahminy Kite (1/7 nat. size)

Iris brown; bill bluish horn, cere yellowish; legs greenish-yellow.

The bill is rather large and compressed and sharply hooked; tail slightly rounded; upper portion of the tarsus feathered.

Field Identification. — Unmistakable; a bright chestnut bird of prey with black wing tips and a white head and breast, found near water.

Distribution.—The Brahminy Kite is a bird of wide distribution, almost throughout the Indian Empire and Ceylon, and extending eastward through Siam, China, and the Malay Peninsula to Australia. All Indian birds belong to the typical race. It is not found in the North-west Frontier Province or Baluchistan or in the Himalayas above 6000 feet, but it is otherwise fairly generally distributed, common on the sea coast and in the wetter districts, and avoiding semi-desert areas and thick forest. It is locally migratory, but is resident in the greater part of its range.

Habits, etc.—The Brahminy Kite, so called from its traditional association with Vishnu, resembles the ordinary Pariah Kite in its flight and habits, but differs from it in always frequenting the neighbourhood of water. Its habits are rather variable. At certain seaports, such as Bombay, it is a scavenger pure and simple, haunting the harbours and lifting refuse from the surface of the water with its claws, while it is bold enough to perch on the rigging of ships. Inland it is often a shy bird, beating backwards and forwards over the rice-fields like a Harrier, catching frogs on the ground and sweeping grasshoppers off the growing rice, or hunting the jheels and the neighbourhood of rivers. It sometimes robs Crows and Common Kites of their food. Termites and small fish are also eaten.

The ordinary cry is a peculiar squealing note.

The breeding season lasts from December to April, being rather earlier in the south than in the north.

The nest is a large loose structure of sticks on which the eggs lie on a deep hollow, which may be either unlined, sparsely lined with green leaves, or fairly thickly lined with rags, wool, hair and similar substances.

It is placed in the fork of a tree or the head of a palm, generally at a considerable height from the ground. The tree chosen is almost always in the vicinity of water.

The eggs are normally two in number, but three may occasionally be found. They are moderately broad ovals only slightly pointed towards one end; the texture is fine and hard with a slight gloss. The ground-colour is dingy greyish-white, sometimes unmarked, at other times feebly speckled, spotted and blotched, mostly towards the large end, with various shades of dull red and brown.

The eggs average about 2 by 1·65 inches.

THE COMMON PARIAH KITE

Milvus migrans (Boddaert)

Description.—Length 24 inches. Sexes alike. Upper plumage brown, the top of the head and hind neck rather paler and the sides of the wings rather darker; a dark patch behind the eye; the outer flight-feathers blackish and the quills more or less banded with dark cross-bars and mottled with whitish towards their bases; tail brown above, whity-brown below, with numerous darker cross-bars; lower parts a paler brown than the upper, whitish about the chin and rufous towards the tail. The whole body plumage is more or less marked with dark shaft-stripes, and the white bases of the feathers are conspicuous the moment the plumage is ruffled or worn.

Iris brown; bill black, cere and gape yellowish; legs yellow, claws black.

The bill is hooked but rather weak ; head flat ; legs short, feathered for about half the length of the tarsus ; wings long and pointed ; tail rather long and strongly forked.

Field Identification.—One of the most familiar birds of India : the large brown bird of magnificent easy flight which soars and scavenges about every bazaar and house. The forked tail at once identifies it.

Distribution.—The Common Pariah Kite, *Milvus migrans govinda*, a race of the Black Kite, which in various forms has a very wide distribution in the Old World, is found throughout India, Burma and Ceylon, extending still farther east to Hainan. Its abundance varies in accordance with that of the human population, but it avoids densely afforested tracts. It ascends the Himalayas up to about 12,000 feet but is not common over 8000 feet. Mainly a resident species, it is in places locally migratory.

FIG. 65—Common Pariah Kite (⅛ nat. size)

In the Kashmir Valley it is replaced by a larger race, *M. m. lineatus*, with the white wing-patch more pronounced.

Habits, etc.—There is very little need to introduce the Pariah Kite, which is one of the most noticeable and abundant birds of India, attracting the notice of the new arrival even before he has disembarked from the ship.

It is a fearless scavenger, and more or less spends its whole life in attendance upon man, either robbing him of food that he would fain keep or scavenging the offal that he has thrown away. Numbers frequent every bazaar and village, sitting on the buildings and trees awaiting something worthy of their attention, or patrolling with sweeping easy flight in wide circles and searching the ground for food. The flight is quite unmistakable with its lightness and buoyancy, a mixture of flapping with long leisurely strokes and short glides, while the direction is continuously changing with spirals and cants. The wings are frequently flexed from the first joint, and the primaries often appear to be below the level of the body. All food is taken in the same way, with a swift stoop and snatch ; and as the bird flies away it transfers the morsel from its foot to its beak, though with larger fragments which cannot be eaten in the air, it flies to some favourite perch to feed at leisure. If there are several Kites about, the capture of food by one of them is the signal for an immense amount of chivying and stooping, combined with much shrill screaming, in the course of which the desirable booty frequently changes owners many times.

When watching such a scene in the bazaar, it is interesting to remember that the allied Red Kite (*Milvus milvus*) was a similar scavenger in Mediæval England, and that in the fifteenth century strangers in London were taken to see the Kites round London Bridge as one of the sights of the town. It was from seeing the birds float all day over their heads that our ancestors named the child's paper toy.

At seaports this Kite joins the Gulls and Brahminy Kites in the harbour, perching on the rigging of ships and picking refuse off the water.

The call of the Kite, a shrill mewing squeal, long drawn and almost musical, is most frequently heard in the breeding season, though it is uttered at all times of the year. To it is due the vernacular name of "cheel" used for the bird.

The breeding season is rather variable according to locality from December to May, but the majority of eggs will be found in February.

The nest is a large clumsy mass of sticks and thorny twigs lined and intermingled with rags,* leaves, tow and other rubbish. It is generally placed in the fork of a tree, but often also on a horizontal bough, usually 20 feet from the ground. The tree chosen may be either in the middle of the most crowded bazaar or solitary in the fields. Nests on buildings are very rare.

One to four eggs are laid, but the usual clutch consists of two or three. They are a very perfect oval, sometimes slightly pointed at one end ; the texture is hard and fine, often with a slight glaze. In coloration they are exceedingly variable ; the ground-colour is pale greenish and greyish-white, blotched, clouded, speckled, streaked or spotted with various shades of brown and red from a pale buffy-brown to purple, and from blood-red to earth-brown.

In size they average about 2·20 by 1·75 inches.

* As Autolycus remarks (*Winter's Tale*, iv., sc. 3) "when the Kite builds, look to lesser linen."

THE MARSH HARRIER

CIRCUS ÆRUGINOSUS (Linnæus)

Description.—Length 22 inches. Male: Head, neck and breast buff or pale rufous with dark shaft-stripes; upper plumage dark brown; remainder of lower plumage ferruginous-brown, striped darker; the six outer flight-feathers black with their bases white; remaining flight-feathers and a patch on the coverts dark silvery-grey;

FIG. 66—Marsh Harrier Adult Male (⅛ nat. size)

tail grey above isabelline below, with the upper coverts a mixture of white, rufous and brown.

Female: Very similar to the male except that the entire lower plumage, save for the creamy-buff chin and throat, is dark chocolate-brown, the feathers of the breast with rufous and buff edges. The silver-grey of the wings and tail is replaced by dark brown.

Iris yellow or yellow-brown; bill black, cere and base greenish-yellow; legs yellow, claws black.

Build strong and slender; bill weak and sharply curved; a ruff of small crisp feathers extends across the throat and up the sides of the neck; wings long and pointed; tail long and even at the tip; long bare legs with sharp claws.

Field Identification.—A large brown Hawk with long wings and tail, which beats backwards and forwards over marshy ground, and robs the sportsman of wounded birds. The adult male is distinguished by the silvery wings and tail. Females and immature birds are dark

PLATE XVIII

1. Tawny Eagle. 2. Brown Fish-Owl. (Both about $\frac{1}{6}$ nat. size.)

[Face p. 374

chocolate-brown with a variable amount of creamy-buff on the head and shoulders, in the young forming a distinct cap on the head.

Distribution.—The Marsh Harrier is found throughout the greater part of Europe, Africa and Asia either as a breeding bird or a winter visitor, and it has been divided into two races. The typical race is a winter visitor to practically the whole of India, Ceylon and Burma, arriving about mid-September and leaving at the end of March or early in April.

Habits, etc.—The Marsh Harrier is a large, long-legged, long-winged and rather slender Hawk which is found very commonly in swampy plains and about the marshy ground of jheels and the edges of tanks and other similar places in which frogs congregate. It also visits irrigated cultivation. The major portion of its life is spent on the wing, beating backwards and forwards with great regularity over the ground, some 20 or 30 feet in the air, searching endlessly for food. The flight is light and graceful, though rather slow; first the wings beat with regularity, then for a few yards the bird sails along with stiff outspread wings banking at intervals and turning from side to side as if unable to decide on its ultimate direction. It chiefly feeds on frogs, but having a taste also for flesh it has learnt to wait on shooting parties in jheels; and all sportsmen in India know the chocolate-coloured bird with buff crown and buff shoulders which is prompt to make a meal of the wounded teal, duck or snipe, that fall some distance ahead of the line of guns, and which often by hunting in front of the line puts up numbers of snipe well out of shot. When not hunting it rests on the ground or on any post or dead tree that forms a suitable lookout. At times it rises into the sky and soars in wide circles, with the wings held well above the level of the back, apparently merely for pleasure.

In its northern breeding grounds the Marsh Harrier nests about April, building in reed-beds or rank marsh vegetation. The nest is a large heap of dead reeds and sedges, with the hollow lined with finer marsh grasses. The eggs number from four to six, and they are broad regular ovals, bluish-white in colour without markings.

They measure about 1·95 by 1·5 inches.

THE PALE HARRIER

CIRCUS MACROURUS (S. G. Gmelin)

Description.—Length: Male 18 inches, female 19 inches. Adult male: Forehead and a patch round the eye white; upper parts pale ashy-grey, more or less washed with brown; wing-quills ashy-grey, whitish at base, the outer quills largely black towards their tips;

upper tail-coverts barred grey and white; tail white, barred with grey, the central pair of feathers pale grey throughout; lower parts white, the throat and upper breast washed with grey.

Female: A line from the beak over each eye and a large patch under the eye buffy white; sides of the head dark brown, ruff feathers buffy white with broad brown shaft-streaks; upper plumage

FIG. 67—Pale Harrier (¼ nat. size)

dark brown, feathers of the head and hind neck and of the shoulder broadly margined with pale rufous; wing-quills dark brown above, whitish below, with blackish brown cross-bands, most of the quills and largest coverts lightly tipped with whitish; upper tail-coverts white, streaked with brown; central tail-feathers greyish-brown, outer tail-feathers buff, all with dark brown cross-bands; lower plumage creamy white, washed with buff and streaked with dark brown and buff, the streaks diminishing in number and growing more rufous towards the tail.

Immature birds of both sexes resemble the female but the upper parts have conspicuous buff fringes; there is a pale spot on the nape and the ruff is pale creamy buff outlining the dark face conspicuously. The under parts are bright uniform rufous-buff.

Iris yellow in adult, brown in immature birds; bill black, cere greenish; legs yellow, claws black.

Structure as in Marsh Harrier, but a more slightly-built bird.

Field Identification.—A slender Hawk with long narrow wings and tail which is almost always seen on the wing, hunting low over the ground with an easy gliding flight. Adult male grey and white with black wing tips. Adult females and immature birds are dark brown above with barred wings and tail and a white patch over the base of the tail. Adult females are streaked below, immature birds rich uniform rufous.

Distribution.—No sub-species. Breeds from the Baltic Sea provinces east to Tarbagatai and the Tian Shan, south to Rumania, Southern Russia and Ferghana. Winters in Africa, India, Ceylon, and Burma. It is generally distributed throughout India in winter.

Three other Harriers are fairly common winter visitors to India. Montagu's Harrier (*Circus pygargus*) is found throughout the country to Ceylon. The Hen Harrier (*Circus cyaneus*) is confined to the north. The Pied Harrier (*Circus melanoleucus*) keeps more to the south and east. Much practice is required to distinguish the females and young males of these species from each other and the Pale Harrier. The adult males are, however, fairly distinctive in the field. That of the Pied Harrier is conspicuously pied black and white. Both Montagu's Harrier and the Pale Harrier are grey and white with black wing tips. Montagu's Harrier may, however, be known by a black bar through the inner flight-feathers and marked rufous streaking on the flanks and abdomen. The Hen Harrier is very similar to the Pale Harrier but is slightly larger with heavier black wing tips, while the throat and breast are dark grey.

On account of its grey and white plumage with black on the wings the Black-winged Kite (*Elanus cæruleus*) may be mistaken for a Harrier. The very different flight, the habit of hovering like a Kestrel, the short tail, the crimson eye, and the fact that the black of the wings is on the shoulders, not at the tips, immediately separates it. Found throughout India and is resident.

Habits, etc.—The Pale Harrier and the other three species mentioned above are all very difficult birds to learn much about in their winter quarters in India. The Marsh Harrier, as already noted, obtrudes itself on the notice of the sportsmen, but these species are all very shy and elusive. One usually sees them in the distance as they hunt over a wide expanse of country and travel ceaselessly, doing a great deal of work to satisfy their voracious appetites. They chiefly frequent stony open country, cultivated fields, grassland or light scrub-jungle, and they travel but a few feet above the ground, ready to drop silently on mouse or bird, insect or reptile, surprised on the ground below them. When gorged they rest on the ground, sitting out in the open beyond possibility of sudden danger. They roost in reed-beds or similar cover, and the number of individuals which consort to a favourite roost is surprising, all the species in the neighbourhood coming to the same place. All Harriers soar high in the air at times, and all have the same type of flight as described under the Marsh Harrier.

In its more northern breeding range the Pale Harrier nests in April and May. The nest is placed on the ground in a natural hollow lined with grass and leaves, usually out on a dry open plain, but also in swamps.

The clutch consists of four or five eggs or occasionally six. These are broad obtuse ovals. The ground-colour is white sometimes unmarked, but more commonly spotted or blotched, sometimes quite heavily, with reddish-brown.

The egg measures about 1·75 by 1·35 inches.

THE LONG-LEGGED BUZZARD

Buteo rufinus (Cretzschmar)

Description.—Length: Male 22 inches, female 24 inches. Sexes alike. Colour very variable, with two main phases and innumerable intergradations between them.

Pale or rufous phase: Upper plumage brown, the feathers with white bases and broad light rufous edges, the sides of the head generally paler than the top; the flight-feathers are tipped with blackish-brown and mottled with white and grey and brown towards their bases; tail pale rufous, mottled towards the base with grey and white, and often with indistinct brown bands; throat and breast buffy-white with dark shaft-stripes; remainder of lower plumage white, rufous or brown, spotted or banded especially on the flanks with dark rufous-brown.

Dark phase: The entire plumage dark chocolate- or blackish-brown, with the base of the flight-feathers white, and with indistinct whitish bars in the tail.

Iris brownish-yellow; bill plumbeous, tip black; cere yellowish-green; legs dingy yellow.

The bill and legs are rather weak ; tarsus partly feathered at the top ; wings and tail ample and rather rounded.

Field Identification.—A heavy lumpish bird which sits dully on trees and on the ground ; varies in colour from pale buffy-brown and white to almost black, but most examples have the rounded tail rufous. In soaring the rounded tail is spread and the wings seen from far below are peculiarly moth-like in the arrangement of pattern, a crescent-shaped patch at the base of the outer flight-feathers being distinctive.

Distribution.—This Buzzard is divided into races which are widely spread throughout South-eastern Europe, North-eastern Africa and Asia. The typical form breeds from Greece through Southern Russia, Asia Minor and Palestine to West and Central Asia, including

FIG. 68—Long-legged Buzzard (⅛ nat. size)

the mountain ranges that border the North-western corner of India. In winter it is an abundant visitor to the plains of the north-west, including the North-west Frontier Province, Baluchistan, the Punjab, Sind, Rajputana, and the United Provinces. Its time of arrival varies from August to November, and it leaves in February and March. The Common Buzzard (*Buteo buteo*) is also found in India, and the two species are difficult to separate.

Habits, etc.—As a winter visitor to India this fine Buzzard is very common in the wide plains of the north-west, especially those which are semi-desert in character. It is most abundant in those tracts where desert gerbils and lizards afford it an easy sustenance, but it is also common enough in cultivation and in marshy ground. It is rather a sluggish bird, and is usually met with sitting lumpily on the ground or in a tree, and when travelling its flight is slow and heavy ; but it is gifted really with considerable powers of flight, and soars easily high above the ground for long periods, moving in great spirals with the broad rounded wings held stiffly outstretched and slightly raised, and the wide tail partly fanned. In this position it is easily recognised by the very moth-like pattern of the wings and in certain phases of plumage by the rufous tail.

The breeding season in the ranges of the North-west Frontier Province is believed to be from March to July. The nest is apparently placed on either a tree or the ledge of a cliff, and is a fairly large structure of sticks, lined with dry twigs. The eggs, two to four in number, are indistinguishable from those of the Common Pariah Kite, being broad regular ovals, greenish-white in ground-colour and richly blotched with reddish-brown.

They measure about 2·30 by 1·80 inches.

THE SHIKRA

Astur badius (Gmelin)

Description.—Length: Male 12 inches, female 14 inches. Male: Upper plumage ashy blue-grey, the sides of the head and neck paler and more rufescent and sometimes with a rufescent collar; flight-feathers blackish at the tips, the remainder of the inner webs whitish marked with blackish bars; tail marked with four or five broad dark brownish bars interrupted on the central and outer pairs of feathers; chin and throat buff or white with usually a median grey stripe; breast rusty red with numerous white bars, the red gradually fading away towards the tail.

The female is a browner grey on the upper plumage, and there are traces of barring on the central pair of tail-feathers.

In immature plumage both sexes are brown above, and the lower parts are marked with brown streaks and spots.

Iris orange-yellow; bill livid at base, blue-black at tip; cere greenish-yellow; legs yellow, claws black.

Bill short, stout and curved; wing short and rounded; feet rather long and stout.

Field Identification.—The common species of small Hawk in India; a small, stout Hawk grey above, rusty below with whitish bars, and a fierce orange eye; found sitting in trees or soaring over fairly open country. Distinguished from the true Sparrow-Hawk (*Accipiter nisus*), which also occurs, by the stouter feet and shorter toes, and by the paler coloration.

Distribution.—The Shikra has a wide distribution from Central Asia and Southern Persia throughout India, Burma and Ceylon, and eastwards to Southern China. It is divided into several races, distinguished by details of size and shade of coloration. *A. b.*

dussumieri is found throughout India, from the North-west Frontier Province and Kashmir to Northern Assam, extending in the Himalayas up to about 5000 feet. In Travancore and Ceylon it is replaced by the smaller and darker *A. b. badius*. These two races are resident, but in the winter the Central Asiatic race, *A. b. cenchroides*, a large

FIG. 69—Shikra (⅓ nat. size)

and pale bird, visits Baluchistan, Sind, North-west Frontier Province, and the Punjab.

Although it is seldom observed in a wild state the magnificent Goshawk (*Astur gentilis*) must be mentioned as the species most often observed in the hands of Indian falconers. The female is the " Baz " and the male the " Jura " of that fraternity.

Habits, etc.—The Shikra is one of the commonest and best-known Hawks in India. It avoids very heavy forest and desert but is found in every other type of country, preferring cultivated tracts with plenty of large trees. It spends most of its time sitting up in the leafy branches of large trees, but is also fond of soaring high in the air, circling for a time with wings outstretched and then flapping them vigorously. It is rather a noisy Hawk, and the shrill call of two notes *titu-titu* is a familiar sound in the breeding season.

The ordinary food consists of lizards, frogs, grasshoppers and small birds, but in the hands of the expert falconer it is very bold, taking quails, crows and partridges most successfully. It is a favourite bird with Indian falconers as it is easily trained and will take small birds within ten days of being caught; it is often used by them to catch food for their more valuable falcons and goshawks. On the fist it is carried unhooded; when flown at its quarry it is thrown from the hand, in which it is held tightly grasped round the wings, the belly resting on the palm of the hand, with the legs stretched backwards under the tail.

The breeding season lasts from April to June. The nest is a loosely-built cup of twigs and sticks, lined with fine grass roots; it is placed in a high fork of a tree fairly well screened by leaves. The time occupied in building the nest is usually out of all proportion to the result.

Three to five eggs are laid. They are moderately long ovals, slightly pointed at one end, smooth, fine and glossless in texture. In colour they are a delicate pale bluish-white, normally unmarked, but occasionally slightly speckled with grey.

In size they average about 1·55 by 1·22 inches.

THE LUGGER FALCON

Falco jugger J. E. Gray

(Plate xix, Fig. 3, opposite page 396)

Description.—Length: Male 16 inches, female 18 inches. Sexes alike. Forehead and a line over the eyes whitish with dark streaks; top of the head brown with rufous edges; a broad streak from the eye and a moustachial streak dark brown; remainder of upper plumage brown with an ashy tinge, the outer flight-feathers with broad white bars on their inner webs; tail brown tipped with white, all the feathers except the central pair with whitish bars on the inner webs; lower parts white marked with brown streaks on the breast and brown spots on the abdomen, and the flanks largely brown.

Iris dark brown; bill bluish-grey, the tip blackish; legs yellow, claws black.

The bill has a marked tooth behind the hooked tip; wing long and pointed; the tarsus is bare except on the upper part; claws curved and sharp.

Field Identification.—The ordinary resident true Falcon of India; ashy-brown above, white with brown markings below. Found in pairs in open plains; in flight the pointed wings and full tail are noticeable. Ashy-brown upper parts distinguish it from the Falcons of the Peregrine type, while the Saker Falcon may be separated from it by having white spots on the central tail-feathers.

Distribution.—This Falcon is fairly common throughout India from about 2500 feet in the foot-hills of the Himalayas down to about Southern Madras. On the west it occurs in Baluchistan and the North-west Frontier Province extending to Cachar in the east and it has once been obtained in Manipur. Outside these limits it has not been found and towards the south of its range it is not common. Wherever found it is a strictly resident species.

The well-known Peregrine Falcon (*Falco peregrinus*) of Europe, of which the adult has the upper parts bluish-grey with a black cheek stripe and the lower parts fulvous-white with dark barring, is a winter visitor to the whole of India and Ceylon. The Saker Falcon (*Falco cherrug*) with the upper parts brown and the lower parts white spotted with brown, is a winter visitor to the semi-desert areas of the north-west.

Habits, etc.—This Falcon avoids areas of heavy forest and is a bird of the open plains, wherever trees are found either in cultivation or in semi-desert country. It mates for life, and the birds of the pair keep very much together; it is a very pretty sight to watch a pair hunting as they deliberately work together, driving the quarry towards each other and stooping at it in turn. They often attend sportsmen out shooting and take birds that are wounded. The Lugger is a fine flier and on occasion can be courageous enough, but it belongs to the Saker or Desert Falcon group rather than to the Peregrine group, and has not quite the build and speed and courage of the latter. Its food, therefore, consists more frequently of lizards, gerbils, insects and small birds than of bigger game. It can be and often is trained by the falconer to kill crows, partridges, and similar quarry, but is naturally usually neglected in a country where nobler Falcons can be so easily obtained. The male, however, is frequently kept by the falconer as a decoy hawk with which to catch either Sakers or Peregrines. Silent as a rule, both sexes indulge in a harsh chattering scream when excited.

The eggs may be found from January to April, but the majority are probably laid in February.

The nest varies a good deal; the eggs may be laid in a hollow scraped on a rocky ledge of a cliff, or in a slight nest of sticks in a similar situation. A larger nest of sticks and twigs lined with grass, straw or leaves is also built on buildings or in trees, or old nests of other birds in similar situations are appropriated and repaired. Such appropriated nests always seem to be large ones, generally those of Eagles or Vultures.

Three to five eggs are laid. In shape they are a broad oval, slightly pointed at one end, of a dull, glossless, slightly chalky texture. In colour they are rather variable. The ground-colour is reddish, brownish or yellowish-brown, very thickly speckled and spotted all over with a darker and richer shade of the ground-colour; these markings sometimes collect in a cap at one end; some eggs are lightly and dully marked; others are richly coloured with large blotches and clouds.

The average size is about 2·00 by 1·55 inches.

THE TURUMTEE

FALCO CHICQUERA Daudin

(Plate xix, Fig. 1, opposite page 396)

Description.—Length: Male 12 inches, female 14 inches. Sexes alike. Top of the head, ear-coverts, and a narrow cheek-stripe chestnut; upper plumage ashy-grey, the shoulders and sides of the wings more or less barred with brown; outer flight-feathers blackish-brown, closely barred with white on the inner webs; tail grey with narrow black bars, a very broad black band close to the end, and a white tip; lower parts white, lightly streaked on the breast and barred on the flanks and abdomen with blackish.

Iris brown; bill greenish-yellow, blue-black at tip; cere and eyelids yellow; legs yellow, claws black.

The bill has a sharp tooth inside the hooked tip; wings long and pointed.

Field Identification.—A very pretty little ashy-grey Falcon with barred white under parts, easily recognised by the bright chestnut head. Found in pairs in open country.

Distribution.—The Turumtee or Red-headed Merlin is found almost throughout the plains of India from the foot-hills of the Himalayas right down to the south, and from the North-west Frontier Province and Sind across to Assam. It is a resident species.

Habits, etc.—This delightful little Falcon is usually found in wide cultivated plains, especially those where small groups of trees and long shady avenues are common. It avoids heavy forest. It pairs for life, and the birds of the pair usually go about together, and are very clever at hunting in company; for instance, I have seen one of a pair "waiting on" above a thorn tree in which some doves had taken refuge, while its mate made strenuous, though unsuccessful, endeavours to drive them out to it. For its size it is one of the most courageous of the Falcons, and is pugnacious to boot, a fact that is known to every crow and kite that lives anywhere in the vicinity of the tree where it elects to build its nest. The bird is well known to all Indian falconers, and it is occasionally trained and flown at rollers, crows, larks, and other similar small quarry. The flight is very swift and graceful with regular wing-beats, and the bird stoops at its quarry with wonderful skill and speed, a most finished performer. It has the same screaming cry as other Falcons, but is rather noisier than most of them.

The breeding season is from January to May, but most eggs will be found in March. All its nests are placed on trees, and never on cliffs or buildings.

Although this Falcon occasionally utilises the old nest of a Crow it usually builds its own nest afresh every year, placing it in one of the highest forks of a tree. It is a neat, well-built cup of sticks and fine twigs, the egg cavity being lined with fine roots and straw with a few feathers and shreds of cloth.

The normal clutch consists of four eggs, but three or five are occasionally found.

The egg is a regular rather long oval, and the texture is fine, but rather chalky, with very little gloss. The ground-colour is reddish-white, virtually concealed by frecklings and specklings of dull brownish-red, but many eggs are more dingy yellowish-brown in coloration.

In size the egg measures about 1·66 by 1·27 inches.

THE KESTREL

Falco tinnunculus Linnæus

Description.—Length 14 inches. Male: Top of the head and sides of the neck ashy-grey with fine black shaft lines; a dark grey cheek-stripe; sides of the face whitish with dark streaks; upper parts brick-red with a vinous tint and with scattered triangular black spots; a patch over the base of the tail ashy-grey; flight-feathers dark brown, their inner webs much indented with white; tail ashy-grey above, whitish below, with a broad black band near the end and white tips to the feathers; lower plumage rufous-fawn with the breast and flanks streaked and spotted with brown.

Female: Upper plumage bright rufous-brown, streaked on the head, and banded elsewhere with brownish-black; flight-feathers dark brown, their inner webs much indented with white; tail rufous-brown, barred with black, and with a broad black band near the end;

lower plumage rufous-fawn, the breast and flanks spotted with brown.

Iris dark brown ; bill bluish-black, paler at base ; gape, cere and eyelids yellow ; legs orange-yellow, claws black.

The bill is short and with a sharp tooth behind the hooked tip ; wings long and pointed ; tail long and slightly graduated.

Field Identification.—A small Falcon with pointed wings and rather long fan-shaped tail, easily recognised by a peculiar habit of hovering stationary in the air with flickering wings. The colour is reddish with a broad black band across the end of the tail ; the female has the back

FIG. 70—Kestrel Adult Male (¼ nat. size)

cross-barred with black, the male more lightly spotted, while the male has the upper surface of the head and tail bright blue-grey.

Distribution.—The Kestrel is a bird of wide distribution found throughout the Palæarctic area, and divided into a number of races which are often separated with difficulty ; of these we are concerned with two. The typical race of Europe and Northern Asia is the breeding form of the Himalayas at all altitudes and there it seems to be more or less a resident. This race is also a very abundant winter visitor to the whole of India. A darker form, *F. t. objurgatus*, is resident in the Nilgiris and, no doubt, also the Travancore ranges. The heavily-barred race of China and Japan (*F. t. interstinctus*) is a winter visitor to Eastern and Southern India and Ceylon in small numbers.

Habits, etc.—The Kestrel is necessarily a bird of open country as it feeds on lizards, grasshoppers and mice which it takes from the ground; small birds are also occasionally caught. It therefore spends most of its time hunting over cultivated tracts, bare hill-sides and open grassy plains; its flight is fast and strong, and it usually flies at a considerable height from the ground, travelling straight for a while and then moving in wide circles. Its course is constantly checked by the bird hanging stationary in mid-air, the head to wind, the wings fanning very rapidly, and the tail depressed and outspread. In this position it scans the ground intently, watching for some moving insect or mouse. If the chance is good, it drops perpendicularly to earth and makes its capture, or checks half-way and hovers again before the drop; or the quarry takes cover and the Kestrel flies on farther to undisturbed ground, to hover and search anew. This hovering is very characteristic, and to it are due the English country names of "Stannel" and "Windhover"; while the perpendicular drop to earth is very distinct from the stoop of most of the Falcons and Hawks.

It perches a good deal on rocks or trees, and thence watches for food, its head incessantly turning and bobbing. Then silently it leaves the perch and flies with half-bent wings towards the ground, putting on a desperate dash and spurt as it approaches the object of its stoop. All the movements of this little Falcon are graceful and a pleasure to watch.

The call is a shrill scream, *kee-kee-kee*, and when breeding the Kestrel is rather noisy and pugnacious, chasing and mobbing eagles, kites, and crows that approach the eyrie.

In Southern India the eggs are laid from February to April, and in the Himalayas from April to June.

The eyrie is, in our area, almost invariably in holes and rocky ledges of cliffs; though occasionally, as elsewhere, it is placed on ruined buildings and in trees. The nest, which is often a mere apology, is composed of twigs, roots, rags, strips of cloth, and other rubbish.

The clutch consists of two to six eggs, but four or five are the usual number.

The eggs are broad ovals, somewhat pointed towards one end; the texture is fine and rather chalky, and there is no gloss as a rule. The ground-colour is red, of various shades; it is blotched, mottled, freckled and spotted with darker tints of the same, the markings being thickly and evenly distributed. Some eggs are rather browner or yellower in general appearance.

In size they average about 1·55 by 1·20 inches.

THE COMMON GREEN PIGEON

CROCOPUS PHŒNICOPTERUS (Latham)

(Plate xxi, Fig. 1, opposite page 440)

Description.—Length 13 inches. Sexes alike. Head, neck and upper breast, save for a grey patch round the back of the head, greenish-yellow, deeper on the upper breast and hind back; an ashy-grey collar round the base of the neck; upper plumage yellowish olive-green; a lilac patch near the bend of the wing; quills and the larger coverts blackish, conspicuously edged with yellow; tail terminal half dove-grey, basal half yellowish-green above, black beneath; lower breast, abdomen, and whole inner surface of the wings light ashy-grey, in strong contrast with the yellow breast; lower flanks dark green with broad yellowish white edges; under tail-coverts dull chestnut with buff-tips.

Iris blue with an outer circle of pink; bill soft and swollen at base and greenish, the hard anterior portion bluish-white; legs orange-yellow, claws bluish.

A stout heavily-built bird with a rather swollen beak.

Field Identification.—Entirely arboreal, found in flocks in large fruit-bearing trees. A heavy stout pigeon, greenish-yellow and ashy-grey in colour, the wings blackish with very bright yellow edgings to the feathers; a small lilac patch on the shoulder.

Distribution.—The Green Pigeon is found almost throughout India, Burma and Ceylon, and farther east to Cochin-China and Siam. It is divided into races of which two concern us. The typical race has its main stronghold in Bengal and the strip of similar country that runs up under the Himalayas westward to the Jumna. *C. p. chlorogaster*, distinguished by having the lower breast and abdomen yellowish-green like the upper breast, instead of ashy-grey as in the typical form, is found throughout the Peninsula of India and Ceylon. No Green Pigeons of this species are found in Sind, Baluchistan, the North-west Frontier Province, the Himalayas, or in the desert regions of the North-west; but there is a large area of Northern India in which both races and intermediates between them are found on the same ground and in the same flocks.

Two smaller species of Green Pigeon are locally common in North-East and South-West India and Ceylon. These are the Orange-breasted Green Pigeon (*Dendrophassa bicincta*) with violet and orange patches on the breast and the Grey-fronted Green Pigeon (*Dendrophassa pompadora*) which has the back deep maroon, in both cases in the male.

Habits, etc.—These Green Pigeons are stoutly built, sluggish birds, usually rolling in fat, which are found in flocks and lead an entirely arboreal existence. Their feet are strong and adapted for climbing, and they move about the branches of a tree much like a parrot, in pursuit of the wild figs and fruits on which they feed; they are very fond of the figs of the banyan and peepul trees and frequent, therefore, in particular the large avenues of these trees which are common in Northern India. In colour they so closely resemble the leaves of the trees that they inhabit, and they are so sluggish in their movements, that the entire flock easily escapes notice in a tree; but when flushed the flight is strong and the birds travel well like other pigeons, though they are loath to desert their particular grove. At the nest the female sits close and will only leave on the near approach of the climber. The call is a peculiar, rather musical, whistle. They appear to drink very rarely, probably obtaining sufficient moisture from the fruits which form their food.

The breeding season is from March till June.

The nest is a slight platform of interlaced twigs, and is so sketchy in construction that the eggs are visible from below through the bottom: it is unlined and has only a slight depression on which the eggs rest. It is placed about 20 feet from the ground in a tree, often so as to be concealed by a bunch of foliage.

Two eggs are laid; they are similar to the eggs of all pigeons, a broad regular oval, pure unmarked white in colour, with a hard close texture and a good deal of gloss.

In size they average about 1·25 by 0·95 inches.

THE KOKLA GREEN PIGEON

SPHENOCERCUS SPHENURUS (Vigors)

Description.—Length 13 inches. Male: Head, neck and lower plumage yellowish-green, tinged with rufous on the crown, and with orange and pink on the upper breast; upper back greyish, passing into maroon-red on the middle of the back and at the bend of the wings; a patch above the base of the tail and the sides of the wings olive-green, quills blackish narrowly bordered with yellow; tail olive-green, the outer feathers and the under surface grey; lower flanks and thighs dark green with pale yellow edges; a patch of cinnamon buff under the tail.

Female: Similar to the male, but lacks the orange on the breast and the maroon-red on the wings and back which are olive-green; the patch under the tail is dark green with broad buff borders.

Iris bright blue with an outer ring of pink; bill and skin round the eyes blue; legs lake-red.

Bill swollen and soft at base; tail rather long and graduated, the under coverts being as long as the outer tail-feathers.

Field Identification.—Himalayan form; purely arboreal and comes to notice through the remarkable whistling call. Long graduated tail in combination with deep maroon on the back and wings, and orange and pink breast separate the male from other green pigeons.

Distribution.—The typical race of this Pigeon is found throughout the length of the Himalayas from Kashmir and Hazara to Bhutan, at elevations from 4000 to 8000 feet; to the east it extends through Assam, the Chin Hills and Shan States into Tenasserim. In the Western Himalayas it is purely a summer visitor, but in the eastern portion of its range it appears to be chiefly a resident species.

The Pin-tailed Green Pigeon *Sphenocercus apicicauda*, is very similar in colour but wants the maroon-red on back and has the two middle tail feathers greatly lengthened. It is found in the Himalayas from Kumaon, the Assam Hills and Burma.

Habits, etc.—The Kokla is a bird of shady wooded glens and hill-sides and is strictly arboreal in its habits, being only very occasionally seen on the ground and that only for drinking purposes. These pigeons feed entirely on fruits, and while in pursuit of them in the trees are very active, gliding about the branches almost like squirrels; with their strong short legs they are able to lean over and reach out to berries in the most wonderful manner. When not feeding they are rather sluggish and sit motionless in the trees, escaping notice from their colour; their presence, however, is betrayed by the beautiful call-note. This is a long melodious but slightly grating whistle, which from its length and tunefulness seems to be human rather than to proceed from the throat of a bird, much less a pigeon; it is roughly described by the words *Why, we what cheer; what are we waiting for?* The courting note is a low *coo-coo.* In summer this species is found only in pairs or small family parties, but in winter they collect into flocks like other green pigeons.

The flight is direct and swift in spite of the whole nature of the bird which is essentially dull and sluggish.

The breeding season is from April to June. The nest is a slight platform composed of coarse grass and small dry twigs placed in a branch of a tree at any height from 6 to 50 feet from the ground.

Two eggs are laid. These are in shape a very elongated oval, narrow and rounded at the ends; they are fine in texture with a fair gloss, and are pure spotless white.

They measure about 1·18 by 0·89 inches.

THE GREEN IMPERIAL PIGEON

MUSCADIVORA ÆNEA (Linnæus)

Description.—Length 17 inches. Sexes alike. Whole head, neck and lower parts ashy-grey with a pink tinge; back, rump and sides of the wings bright metallic green with a high gloss; wing quills blackish washed with ashy-grey; tail black washed above with metallic green, a dull liver-coloured patch under the tail.

Iris crimson; eye-rim purplish-red; bill horny grey, region of the nostrils dull purplish-red; legs purplish red, claws dusky horn.

Field Identification.—A large heavy Pigeon with ashy head, neck and underparts and bright metallic green saddle, wings and tail. A tree-haunting species with a peculiar resonant call.

Distribution.—A widely-spread species found in India, Ceylon, Burma, the Malay countries and islands to the Philippines, Borneo, Java and Flores. In India it is a resident with local movements based on food supply and is divided into two races merely on the question of size. *M. æ. pusilla* is the smaller race. It is found in Ceylon and in South India, extending up to about the 20th degree of latitude though on the Malabar coast it is rare above North Kanara. On the eastern side it intergrades through Orissa and Bengal into the larger *M. a. sylvatica* of Assam and the Himalayas from Nepal eastwards. It is found in the plains and the lower hills and valleys up to at least 3000 feet.

Jerdon's Imperial Pigeon (*Ducula badia*) is another large species—but dull black, brown and ashy-grey in plumage—found in South-west India with another race in the Eastern Himalayas and Assam.

Habits, etc.—The Green Imperial Pigeon is a forest-haunting bird found in many types of forest both heavy and light, evergreen and deciduous; it also visits low scrub. It goes about as a rule singly or in pairs or occasionally in small parties of three or four birds, but after the breeding season and in the neighbourhood of plentiful supplies of food it often collects into flocks comprising up to thirty individuals. These flocks have regular roosting places and may travel miles to their feeding grounds. The flight is rapid and powerful and is started with the loud fluttering put-put-put of the wings which is common to many of the family.

This pigeon apparently never descends to the ground even to drink. It feeds chiefly in the mornings and evenings, resting during the heat of the day in a shady tree. In disposition it is somewhat shy.

The food consists of wild fruits and berries which although often of large size are swallowed whole. The gape and gullet are remarkably capacious and elastic and can be extended to take in fruit a couple of inches in diameter. According to Jerdon the flocks visit the large salt swamps of the Malabar coast in order to eat the buds of *Aricennia* and other shrubs and plants that grow in brackish soil and tidal ground. This bird is not quarrelsome like many of the Green Pigeons and the members of the parties are always gentle and sociable together. If a bird is wounded by a sportsman, however, it erects its feathers so as to double its size in appearance and strikes out violently with the wings.

The call is remarkable and easily recognised. It is a deep resounding boom *wuh-wooh* or *gur-gur goom goom goom* astonishingly powerful for the size of the bird but only uttered at considerable intervals and that when the bird is at rest. It resounds through a yalley and has something almost weird and eerie about its tone.

The main breeding season is from February to April. The nest is built at a height of some 10 to 30 feet from the ground in trees and bamboos and is of the ordinary pigeon type, a flimsy platform of a few sticks and stiff straws and grasses.

One or two eggs are laid. The egg is of a broad oval, very obtuse at both ends, with a very fine compact shell and a slight gloss. It is pure white.

The egg measures about 1·6 by 1·25 inches.

THE BLUE ROCK-PIGEON

Columba livia Gmelin

(Plate xxi, Fig. 2, opposite page 440)

Description.—Length 13 inches. Sexes alike. Plumage slaty-grey almost throughout, the neck glossed all round with metallic green and purple ; the back and wings are rather darker in tint and there is sometimes a paler bar across the rump, in some specimens white ; two black bars across the wings ; tail with a broad black bar across the end and with a white patch at the base of the outer feathers ; under surface of the wings very pale grey or white.

Iris brownish-orange ; bill black, base swollen and mealy white ; legs reddish-pink.

The tail is rather short, and the wings rather long and pointed.

Field Identification.—The commonest Pigeon of India, slaty-grey in colour, with two dark wing-bars and metallic reflections round the neck ; abundant about cities and villages.

Distribution.—This Pigeon is very widely distributed around the shores of the Mediterranean, extending northwards to the British Isles and Faroes, and eastwards also into Africa, Asia Minor, Palestine, Turkestan, Transcaspia, and India, Ceylon and Upper Burma. It is divided into a number of local races, of which two are found in India. These birds are very variable in colour, partly no doubt owing to interbreeding with domestic stock, and there has been a good deal of confusion as to exactly what races are found in India. *C. l. intermedia* is the resident bird throughout the whole of India, except the north-west. It is a very dark bird with a dark grey rump. *C. l. neglecta*, the form found in Turkestan, North-eastern Persia, Afghanistan, and Kashmir, extends also in the North-west Frontier Province, Punjab, Baluchistan, and Sind. It is a paler bird, with the rump varying from pure white to pale blue-grey. This race is found up to 13,000 feet in the Western Himalayas, and is to some extent a local migrant.

The well-known Snow-Pigeon (*Columba leuconota*) of high altitudes in both the Eastern and Western Himalayas has a large proportion of the plumage white.

The Nilgiri Wood-Pigeon (*Columba elphinstonii*) is found in the higher parts of the Western Ghats, from Mahableshwar to Cape Comorin, being best known from the high sholas of the Nilgiris. The head is grey, with a spangled black and white neck patch; the upper parts are dark reddish-brown and blackish, while the lower plumage is ashy with a slight gloss.

Habits, etc.—The Blue Rock-Pigeon is one of the most familiar birds of India, being abundant wherever the buildings erected by man or the cliffs and rocks of nature afford it nesting places; its numbers respond to the amount of accommodation available, so that in places it becomes incredibly numerous even to the number of many thousands of pairs. This result is assisted by the fact that in most parts of India a certain measure of sanctity attaches to the birds and they are not molested; in some places food is distributed to them, with the result that they often become absurdly tame, feeding in crowded market places and nesting in the buildings around with complete disregard of their human neighbours. They have usually a morning and evening flight out to cultivation where they feed on corn and seeds in the fields, and they are undoubtedly responsible for a great deal of damage.

The flight is fast and straight and the birds generally collect into flocks, some twenty or thirty strong, so that, where there is no local prejudice against their being shot, excellent sport may be obtained by waiting in the line of flight in the mornings or evenings.

The love call is a rich *coo-roo, cooo-oo-oo*, similar to that of the domestic pigeon, and where the birds are very abundant the rise and fall of the cooing that goes on swells into a soft melodious rumbling that is very delightful.

Eggs may be found at any time of the year, but the breeding season proper is apparently from January to May; more than one brood is doubtless reared in the year. The nest is a fairly substantial platform of thin sticks, twigs and roots, with a slight depression in the centre. It is placed in or about houses, buildings and ruins in any situation that affords shelter from the elements, in the sides of wells, and in the crevices of rocks and cliffs.

The clutch consists of two eggs; these are broad or elongated ovals, rather variable in shape, fine and hard in texture, pure white, and rather glossy.

In size they average about 1·45 by 1·12 inches.

THE RUFOUS TURTLE-DOVE

Streptopelia orientalis (Latham)

Description.—Length 13 inches. Sexes alike. Head, neck and back brown tinged with vinous; on each side of the neck a patch of black feathers tipped with bluish-grey; sides of the wings blackish with broad ferruginous borders giving a scaled appearance; quills brown with pale edges; lower back and rump slaty-grey; upper tail-coverts brown; tail blackish-brown, all, except the central pair of feathers, tipped with slaty-grey; lower plumage vinous, paler on the chin and throat; wing lining and a patch under the tail dark slaty-grey.

Iris orange; eyelids pale blue with red edges; bill brown, vinous at base; legs vinous red, claws black.

The tail is rather long and graduated.

Field Identification.—A rather large vinous-brown Dove with conspicuous rufous scale markings on the wings, and a patch of black and blue-grey scale markings on the sides of the neck; dark graduated tail edged with white or slate-grey is conspicuous in flight. Shyer than most Indian Doves.

Distribution.—The Rufous Turtle-Dove is so closely allied to the Common Turtle-Dove (*S. turtur*) of Europe that its races are sometimes considered as races of the Western bird. Accepting, however, their distinctness, we may say that the Rufous Turtle-Dove extends in several races from Eastern Siberia, China, Japan and Tibet to the greater part of India, Ceylon and Burma; also Western Central Asia, Turkestan and Afghanistan. In India we are concerned with three forms, which differ chiefly in the tint of coloration. *S. o. meena* breeds in South-western Siberia and Turkestan, and the Himalayas from Afghanistan to Western Nepal at heights of from 4000 to 11,000 feet, migrating into the plains of India in winter. This form has the belly and tips of the tail-feathers white. *S. o. erythrocephala* is a more or less resident form breeding in the hilly portions of Southern and Central India. Finally, *S. o. agricola* is found in Eastern Bengal, Cachar and Assam, and along the base of the Himalayas under 4000 feet in the terais of Nepal and Sikkim; and again southwards into Burma.

Mention must just be made of the Emerald Dove (*Chalcophaps indica*) which is found along the Western Ghats, the Chota Nagpur area, Bengal and the Lower Himalayas as far west as the Jumna. The back- and wing-coverts are brilliant emerald green and the under parts deep vinaceous.

Habits, etc.—The Rufous Turtle-Dove when breeding is found usually in thick forest, but is otherwise mostly observed in the more open and cultivated areas where large trees, groves and gardens provide it with shelter in easy reach of the stubbles where it likes to feed on fallen grain and seeds. It is very active on the ground, running and walking freely, and when disturbed invariably takes refuge in trees. In winter and on migration numbers may be found in company,

FIG. 71—Rufous Turtle-Dove (¼ nat. size)

but they may hardly be said to gather into flocks, as the birds do not keep together, but fly off in all directions when disturbed. It drinks very frequently. The note is a dull sleepy drone, *cooo-cooo-kakour*, and the male has a breeding display which consists of flying into the air and volplaning down again with wings and tail stiffly outspread.

The breeding season is said to be practically throughout the year according to locality; in the Himalayas most nests are found in June, in North-eastern India in April and May, and in Central and Southern India from January to March.

The nest is the usual scanty platform of twigs and bents, through which the eggs and young can be seen; it is placed in a tree or bush at no great height from the ground and there is no particular effort at concealment.

The clutch consists of two eggs, which are regular ovals, pure white and very glossy.

They measure about 1·22 by 0·93 inches.

THE SPOTTED DOVE

STREPTOPELIA CHINENSIS (Scopoli)

Description.—Length 12 inches. Sexes alike. Top and sides of the head vinous-grey; back and sides of the neck black, each feather cloven at the tip and ending in two white spots; upper plumage brown, spotted on the upper back and wings with vinous pink, the spots in pairs on the feathers and on the wings divided by a wedge-shaped black shaft-stripe; an ashy band on the outer edge of the wing; wing-quills brown; the two middle pairs of tail-feathers brown, the others black with grey or white tips; lower plumage vinous, whitish on the throat and under the tail.

Iris hazel, surrounded by a reddish sclerotic membrane; skin round the eye reddish; bill dull leaden-black; legs dark purplish-red.

FIG. 72—Spotted Dove (⅓ nat. size)

Field Identification.—Easily recognised by the brown upper parts conspicuously spotted with vinous pink, by the white-spotted black patch on the neck, and by the vinous under plumage and grey band on the edge of the wing. Feeds much on the ground and is very tame.

Distribution.—The Spotted Dove is found throughout the greater part of India, Ceylon and Burma, extending eastwards to Siam, Cochin-China, the Malay Peninsula, Sumatra, and China. It is divided into several races which differ merely in small details of coloration. *S. c. suratensis* is found throughout most of India from the foot-hills of the Himalayas (up to about 5000 feet) down to Southern Travancore and is replaced in Ceylon by *S. c. ceylonensis*. On the west it is practically absent from the Punjab except in the foot-hills, and it is quite absent from Sind, Baluchistan and the North-west Frontier Province. On the east it extends through Assam, Cachar and Manipur. A resident species with slight local movements.

Habits, etc.—This Dove is a very familiar and widely-spread species, being found in almost every type of country, provided that water is easily accessible, as it is intolerant of thirst and drinks freely. It is, however, most common in fairly open cultivation, and it is much

PLATE XIX

1. Turumtee. 2. White-eyed Buzzard. 3. Lugger Falcon. 4. Spotted Owlet.
(All about $\frac{3}{8}$ nat. size.)

[*Face p.* 396

given to haunting roads and village paths where it walks about searching for grain and seeds; it is found also in the stubbles. It appears to pair for life, as the pairs keep very much together, feeding and flying in company and resting side by side in the trees. The call is a soft trisyllabic coo, represented by the syllables *ku-krroo-ku* or *oot-raow-oo*, and it is freely uttered.

When disturbed on the ground these Doves rise very straight into the air for a few feet, with a great fluster and clapping of wings, and then fly swiftly with quick distinct wing-beats and the tail partly spread so as to show the white edging. They seldom fly for any distance, and when settling slide downwards to the chosen perch with occasional wing-beats, the whole action and carriage appearing very stiff. The courting display consists of a flight straight up into the air with a volplane downwards, the wings and tail stiffly spread as in other Doves.

The breeding season is throughout the year, and probably several broods are reared annually. The nest is a slight and scanty platform of sticks, and it is placed usually at no great height from the ground, in and about buildings or on trees and bushes.

Two eggs are laid; they are the usual regular oval, pure white, fine and hard in texture with a good deal of gloss.

In size they average about 1·06 by 0·82 inches.

THE LITTLE BROWN DOVE

STREPTOPELIA SENEGALENSIS (Linnæus)

(Plate xx, Fig. 1, opposite page 418)

Description.—Length 10 inches. Sexes alike. Head, neck and breast lilac tinged with vinous; chin whitish; on the sides of the neck a gorget of black feathers forked at the ends which are broadly tipped with ferruginous; upper plumage light earthy-brown; an ashy-grey patch on the outer edge of the wings; quills dark brown; tail, central pair of feathers earthy-brown, the next two pairs chiefly grey, the outer pairs with the basal half blackish and the remainder white; the vinous breast passes into the white of the lower plumage; wing lining and flanks dark ashy-grey.

Iris dark brown with a whitish inner circle; bill black; legs lake-red, claws black.

The tail is rather long and graduated.

Field Identification.—A small rather slender Dove, very tame and confiding; brown in colour with a grey patch on the side of the wings and a black patch spotted squarely with ferruginous on the sides of the neck.

Distribution.—This dainty little Dove has a wide range through Africa, the Middle East and South-western Asia, and is divided into a number of races. *S. s. cambayensis* is found practically throughout the whole Peninsula of India westward of Bengal, but it is rare on the Malabar coast and does not extend to Bengal itself. In the Outer Himalayas it may occasionally be found up to 5000 feet. The Persian race, *S. s. ermanni*, apparently straggles into the north-western corner of India. In the main a strictly resident species, it is locally a partial migrant.

Habits, etc.—This is one of the most familiar and abundant of Indian Doves, and is well known from the fact that it frequents the neighbourhood of houses, walking about on the ground outside the verandahs and often coming into them for nesting purposes. It also rests and walks about on their roofs. It is quiet and gentle in its movements and far from shy, and in general acts up to the popular conception of a Dove, a conception which so many other species fall very short of.

It avoids heavy forest, but is abundant in cultivation and light bush-jungle, especially on low stony hills and in semi-desert areas. The flight is swift and strong, and when suddenly disturbed from the ground a curious effect is given to the flight by the extremely rapid wing-beats which seem almost in danger of upsetting the bird. The food consists of seeds and grain.

The call is a rather harsh coo, *cru-do-do-do-do.*

The breeding season is very irregular and extended, from January to October, and two or three broods are reared.

The nest is composed of thin twigs, mixed with grass stems and a few roots; it is in the shape of a very fragile platform, often nearly meriting Eha's familiar description of a dove's nest as composed of two short sticks and a long one. It is built in a variety of situations, though generally at no great height from the ground, in trees, bushes and plants, on rolled-up chicks in verandahs, on window-sills and beams, and even very occasionally on the ground.

The normal clutch consists of two eggs, but one and three are found, though rarely. The eggs are rather broad, nearly perfect ovals, pure white, of close texture and rather glossy.

They average about 1·00 by 0·85 inches in size.

THE INDIAN RING-DOVE

STREPTOPELIA RISORIA (Linnæus)

Description.—Length 12 inches. Sexes alike. Head and neck grey with a lilac tinge; a black collar narrowly bordered with white round the hind neck; upper plumage light brown passing into ashy-grey on the wings, the outer flight-feathers dark brown; central

FIG. 73—Indian Ring-Dove ($\frac{2}{5}$ nat. size)

tail-feathers light brown, remainder grey and blackish-brown with broad white tips; breast pale lilac passing through ashy-grey into slaty-grey under the tail; wing lining white.

Iris crimson, eyelids whitish; bill black; feet dark pink-red, claws horny.

The tail is rather long and graduated.

Field Identification.—A pale grey and brown Dove with a plain black collar round the base of the neck ; one of the commonest birds of India in open country.

Distribution.—This is by far the commonest Dove in India and is spread throughout India and Ceylon though it avoids forest areas. To the west it extends as far as the Balkan Peninsula, and in the Himalayas it is found at elevations up to 11,000 feet, extending also northwards to Turkestan. While mainly a resident species it is locally a migrant. From Burma to Cochin-China and Yunnan it is replaced by another race, *S. r. xanthocycla*, distinguished by the yellow skin round the eyes.

Habits, etc.—The Indian Ring-Dove avoids heavy forest and is found in great abundance in cultivation and open country wherever trees, large bushes and hedges provide cover for it. It comes freely into gardens, but is not so bold at entering verandahs or feeding on the paths as is the Little Brown Dove. These Doves collect freely into parties and flocks often of considerable size, and are very swift and strong fliers, leaving their perch with a sounding clatter of the hard-pointed wings. The call of this species is a dreamy *how-do-do*, well known by all residents in India as a sign of the hot weather. The food consists of the seeds of various grasses and weeds.

Most nests will be found in April and May ; but as the various pairs rear more than one brood and often nest at different times, the breeding season may be said to last throughout the year.

The nest is always placed on trees or bushes, in most cases at heights between 5 and 20 feet from the ground ; thorny bushes are usually preferred. Sites in buildings are not used after the manner of the Little Brown Dove.

The nest is the usual Dove platform of small sticks, dry grass stems and fine roots, sometimes fairly solid in construction with a saucer-like cavity for the eggs.

The clutch consists of two eggs. They are broad and perfect ovals, hard in texture and somewhat glossy. The colour is white but with a slight ivory tinge, approaching that of the eggs of the Red Turtle-Dove.

They average about 1·16 by 0·90 inches in size.

THE RED TURTLE-DOVE

ŒNOPOPELIA TRANQUEBARICA (Herman)

(Plate xx, Fig. 2, opposite page 418)

Description.—Length 9 inches. Male: Head dark ashy-grey down to a black collar round the hind neck; remainder of upper plumage vinous-red except for a dark slaty-grey patch on the base of the tail; wing-quills dark brown; central tail-feathers brown, next two pairs dark grey at base and paler at the ends, the three outer pairs black at the base and white at the ends; lower parts vinous-red, whitish under the chin and tail; wing lining grey.

Female: Brown above, greyish on head, rump, flanks and edge of wing; breast light brown; a black collar round the neck; tail as in the male.

Iris dark brown; eyelids plumbeous; bill black; legs vinaceous brown, claws black.

Field Identification.—The only Indian Dove in which the sexes are different; male warm vinous-red with grey head defined by a black neck-ring: female brown with a black neck-ring. Latter can be distinguished from the Indian Ring-Dove by the smaller size, compact shape and browner coloration.

Distribution.—Widely distributed in India, Ceylon and Burma, and extending through Siam, Cochin-China, and China to the Philippines, this beautiful bird is divided into three races. Two of these concern us. The typical race is found throughout India, occurring on the west in the North-west Frontier Province, but not in Baluchistan; and in the North-western Himalayas it is found only in the lowest of the foot-hills. In the Eastern Himalayas, however, it seems to ascend higher. Birds from Assam and Burma are more richly coloured and have been separated as *Œ. t. humilis*. In the main a resident species, but locally migratory.

Habits, etc.—The Red Turtle-Dove is a less familiar and confiding species than the other common Doves of India, and is usually found away from the immediate neighbourhood of villages and gardens. It is distributed in all types of country excepting extreme desert and heavy forest, and chiefly prefers cultivation with large and shady trees, but it is very local, common in some tracts and wanting in others without apparent reason. Water, however, is essential to it, as like other Doves it is a very thirsty bird.

Usually it is found in pairs, but occasionally large flocks collect, and these sometimes consist entirely of males.

It feeds entirely on the ground, collecting seeds and fallen grain, and when disturbed it usually flies straight away instead of getting into the nearest tree like the other common Doves. The flight is very swift, as might be guessed from the wing with its long first primary.

The call is very distinctive, a rather deep *cru-u-u-u-u* repeated four or five times quickly without pause, and with the emphasis on the first syllable.

The breeding season extends almost throughout the year in various parts of India, but most eggs are to be found about May; probably two broods are reared.

The nest is a very flimsy platform of twigs, bents and dry grass. It is always placed in trees and never on buildings. A large tree is generally preferred, and a favourite situation is towards the end of a lower bough at a height of 8 to 15 feet from the ground.

Two eggs are normally laid though clutches of three are sometimes found.

The egg is a slightly elongated oval, fine in texture and glossy; it is white in colour, but usually more tinged with the creamy tint of ivory than are most Dove's eggs.

The eggs measure about 1·02 by 0·08 inches.

BAR-TAILED CUCKOO-DOVE

MACROPYGIA UNCHALLA (Wagler)

Description.—Length 16 inches. Male: Forehead, sides of head and throat buff tinged vinous; crown and hind neck lilac-grey with a metallic gloss of green and reddish-lilac; back, rump and upper tail coverts black, barred with rufous chestnut; wings blackish-brown; middle tail feathers black with narrow rufous bars, less barring on next two pairs, and the remaining feathers slaty-grey with a black band near tip; breast greyish or brownish lilac with a metallic gloss; abdomen and under tail coverts buff; flanks ashy.

Female: Resembles the male above, but below the colour is buff barred with dark brown, and on chin, abdomen and under tail coverts these bars are obsolete.

Iris white, surrounded by a rim of lilac; bill blackish; legs purplish pink.

Field Identification.—This Dove is easily distinguished by the rufous colouring and very long graduated tail.

Distribution.—The Himalayas from Eastern Kashmir through Garhwal and Kumaon to Assam and the hills of Burma to Tenasserim.

Habits, etc.—The Bar-tailed Cuckoo-Dove is a bird of considerable elevations, in the breeding season from 2500 to 9000 feet, but normally it nests between 4000 and 7000 feet. At other seasons they are met with at a lower altitude, and some wander into the plains adjoining the foot-hills. In the hot weather and rains these Doves resort to thick evergreen or oak forest, while in the breeding season they frequent more open forests of chestnut and oak. The food consists of small fruits, acorns, berries, and they are very fond of the tender shoots of cultivated plants, especially mustard. They are usually found singly or in pairs and often congregate in large numbers in patches of cultivated crops. The male has a fine display; it perches on the highest branch of a tree where the female is sitting, then suddenly launches himself into the air with much clapping of wings. After reaching a considerable height the wings are spread straight out, the feathers of the body puffed up—especially those of the rump, and the bird returns in circles to his perch. Here he occasionally utters a booming note and, after a pause, starts his display again. This note is a deep *croo-um* audible at a great distance.

The breeding season is from April to June and the nest is of the usual pigeon type, but occasionally moss and grass are used for the lining. It is built in a stunted oak or sapling between 6 and 16 feet from the ground.

The eggs are one to two in number and pure white ovals.

They average about 1·4 by 1·0 inches.

THE IMPERIAL SANDGROUSE

PTEROCLES ORIENTALIS (Linnæus)

Description.—Length 14 inches. Male: Throat ferruginous-chestnut, extending round the sides of the neck to the back of the head; a triangular black patch on the throat; crown and sides of the head, the lower neck all round, and the upper breast pale earthy-brown; upper plumage blackish-grey, each feather fawn-coloured towards the base and tipped with ochraceous-yellow, the yellow becoming more pronounced towards the edge of the wing; quills slaty-grey, the shafts and concealed portions blackish; tail buff barred with black, the central pair of feathers tipped with greyish-black, the remainder with white; a black gorget across the breast, followed by a broad band of buff; abdomen and flanks black; wing lining white; legs and under tail-coverts buffy-white.

Female: Pale fawn colour, the head, neck and upper breast marked with black shaft streaks; chin and throat yellowish, bounded behind by a black line beyond which the fore-neck is ashy; back and upper plumage including the central tail-feathers with irregular curved black cross-bars; remainder of tail, the flight-feathers and the lower parts from the black gorget as in the male.

Iris brown; eye-rim pale lemon; bill bluish-grey; feet grey. Weight 17 to 18½ oz.

The wings are long and pointed; tail wedge-shaped (but without pin-tail feathers); tarsus feathered down the front, the toes short and bare.

Field Identification.—Sandgrouse occur in flocks in semi-desert country. They escape notice by their protective coloration while feeding on the ground, and are most often noticed in flight, travelling straight and fast, high in the air. Stout compact bodies, pointed wings and tails, close order, and fast regular wing-beats (the whole reminiscent of a flock of Parrakeets) are distinctive. This species may be easily recognised in flight by contrast between black bellies and white wing lining; on ground the larger size, combined with yellow markings of back and dark throat-patch of males, distinguish it from other Sandgrouse.

Distribution.—India is on the extreme eastern limit of the range of this fine Sandgrouse which is found from Spain and Portugal

FIG. 74—Imperial Sandgrouse ($\frac{1}{6}$ nat. size)

(I have seen it as far north as Navarre) through North Africa and South-western Asia. In India it is most abundant in the sandy semi-desert plains of the Lower Punjab and Rajputana; it is found on all sides of this area, in Sind and Baluchistan, the North-west Frontier Province and Upper Punjab, the United Provinces and towards the Runn of Cutch, but only locally and never in the same abundance. It is purely a winter visitor to India, arriving in October and leaving about the end of February.

The Painted Sandgrouse (*Pterocles indicus*) is resident in low rocky and scrub-covered hills throughout the greater part of India, but not in the Indo-Gangetic plain, the Chota Nagpur area or the Western Coast. It has no pin-tail feathers and is closely barred on the crown, body and wings; the chin and throat of the male are buff followed by a broad band each of chestnut, buff and black.

Habits, etc.—The Imperial Sandgrouse is found in great numbers in the sandy semi-desert plains of the north-west where it occurs in large flocks. Like the Common Sandgrouse, these birds are very regular in their habits; in the morning about 8 to 10 A.M. they flight to water to drink, all the flocks in the neighbourhood using the same place; after drinking they fly to the feeding ground which is bare open country with an occasional straggling bush or two, lying fallow after a rabi crop; here they find grains of that crop and the seeds of weeds. While feeding they keep close together and move with much deliberation, looking in the distance rather like a collection of mud-turtles. They remain, if not disturbed, on this ground till the evening, when a proportion again fly to drink and then they collect at their "jugging" places, which are usually in the young kharif crops and which may be recognised by the abundance of footmarks and droppings. The call is a clucking sound uttered on the wing, which is difficult to describe.

In favourable localities in the line of passage the migration of this species is almost as marked as that of the Cranes; innumerable flocks pass every morning following the same course.

Except at the drinking places this Sandgrouse is very difficult to shoot. At the approach of man it squats, and owing to its colour is very hard to distinguish on the sandy ground except that the dark throat-patch of the males often catches the eye. By circling round very carefully in an ever-decreasing circle it is often possible to get within shot before the birds rise, but they are, as a rule, very wary and suspicious, and do not allow a close approach. They are, in addition, one of the toughest game birds that I know, with their compact hard plumage and thick skin, and are very difficult to bring down unless shot properly in the head.

This species does not breed in India, but in its breeding range from Afghanistan and Baluchistan westwards the eggs are laid in May and June. The nest is a hollow scraped in open ground.

The clutch consists of two or three eggs. They are elliptical in shape, the texture is smooth and close with a marked gloss, and the shell is decidedly brittle.

In colour the ground is dull and pale, varying from cream to buff or greenish-grey; the markings consist of indefinite smudges, blotches and spots of brown of various shades, with secondary markings of lavender and purplish-grey.

In size they average about 1·86 by 1·27 inches.

THE COMMON SANDGROUSE

PTEROCLES EXUSTUS Temminck

(Plate xxiii, Fig. 1, opposite page 484)

Description.—Length 13 inches, including 2 inches for central tail-feathers. Male: Upper plumage isabelline-buff, feathers of the shoulders and wings tipped with paler buff or dark reddish-brown;

forehead, sides of the head, chin and throat dull ochraceous-buff; the longer flight-feathers blackish-brown, some of the inner ones obliquely tipped with white; central tail-feathers brown with long black tips, the remainder darker brown with white tips; breast buff with a slightly rufous tinge, crossed by a black gorget slightly edged in front with white; the buff shades into the dark brown flanks and abdomen; wing lining dark brown; legs and under tail-coverts very pale buff.

Female: Buff throughout, the crown and entire neck spotted with black; remainder of upper parts barred with black, except for a patch on the wing, some feathers having yellowish-buff ends tipped with brown; the longer flight-feathers dark brown, some of the inner ones obliquely tipped with white; chin and throat, sides of the head and a line over the eye unspotted yellowish-buff; upper breast spotted with dark brown, a rather broken blackish gorget followed by a broad band of pale buff; abdomen barred dark brown and rufous, darkest in the centre; wing lining brown; legs and under tail-coverts buff.

Iris dark brown; eyelids yellow; bill and feet slaty-plumbeous. Weight 8 to 9 oz.

The two central tail-feathers are elongated and pointed; tarsus feathered down the front, toes short and bare.

Field Identification.—The common small Sandgrouse of the plains with long pointed central tail-feathers. The male is sandy-buff with a black gorget and blackish-brown belly; the female buff barred with black, a gorget, and the belly barred with brown and rufous; distinguish on the wing by the dark under surface and dark wing lining.

Distribution.—The Common Sandgrouse is a widely-spread species, resident in portions of Africa, in Palestine, and Arabia, and in the Indian Peninsula. It is divided into several sub-species, but their distinctness is doubtful. The Indian race, *P. e. ellioti*, is found throughout the plains of India with the exception of the Bombay and Malabar coastland, the forest regions E. of 80 E. long. and Bengal. It is a resident species.

The very similar Spotted Sandgrouse (*Pterocles senegallus*), which, however, lacks the gorget markings in both sexes, is resident and fairly common in Sind and the neighbouring semi-desert areas. Another pin-tailed species, the large Pin-tailed Sandgrouse (*Pterocles alchata*), is found mostly in the Indus drainage. It is easily recognised by the handsome scale-marking of the wings and the white belly.

Habits, etc.—This familiar game-bird avoids rocks and hills, forests and swamps, and is found in the drier and barer portions of the plains on more or less sandy ground. Above all it prefers scattered cultivation, fallow stubble or fresh ploughed fields in the close neighbourhood of large barren plains. In such places it will be found in parties and small flocks feeding on seeds, squatting close to the ground on the approach of man and rising with a curious double clucking note. The flight is very swift and straight, though the flocks have a tendency to swing round in the air in a wide circle.

The most marked trait in these birds is their habit of flighting to water in the mornings. Their time and place of drinking are very constant, varying according to season from 8 to 10 A.M. Just before drinking time large flocks arrive from every quarter so that the sky is full of them. The first arrivals settle out on the open plain some half a mile from the drinking place, and all the other flocks settle near them; after about fifteen minutes the first batch get up and fly to the water and the rest follow. There is a similar but less marked drinking flight in the evenings, and in the hot weather they have regular places for dusting which are visited about an hour before sunset.

All Sandgrouse, of course, are incapable of settling anywhere but on the ground. The young of Sandgrouse are said to be watered by the male, who after drinking saturates his lower plumage with water to be sucked off the feathers by the chicks.

The majority of this species lay about April, but eggs may be found in almost every month of the year. The nest is a mere scrape or hollow on the ground, sometimes sheltered by low bushes, tufts of grass or large clods, and very occasionally lined sparsely with a little grass.

The normal clutch consists of three eggs. These are of a very curious shape, long and cylindrical like those of a Nightjar; the texture is fine and smooth and there is generally a fine gloss.

The ground-colour of the eggs is variable, pale stone-colour, greyish or dingy greenish, or light olive-brown. They are thickly spotted, streaked or irregularly blotched with olive-brown and pale inky-purple of various shades; different eggs vary greatly in the disposal, extent and thickness of their markings.

In size they average about 1·45 by 1·05 inches.

THE COMMON PEAFOWL

PAVO CRISTATUS Linnæus

Description.—Length, male, to end of tail 40 to 46 inches, to end of full train 78 to 90 inches; female 38 inches. Adult male: Feathers of the head short and curly, metallic-blue on the crown, changing to green elsewhere; crest with bare shafts and fan-shaped tips, black at the base, bluish-green at the end; neck all round rich blue; back covered with scale-like bronze-green feathers marked with black and copper; scapulars and most of the wing barred black and buff, primary quills and coverts pale chestnut, secondaries black;

train bronze-green shot in the centre with coppery-bronze, nearly all the feathers ending in an "eye," which consists of a purplish-black heart-shaped nucleus surrounded by blue within a coppery disk, with an outer rim of alternating green and bronze; tail dark brown; lower plumage dark glossy-green, becoming black under the tail; thighs buff.

Female: Head rufous-brown, crest shaped as in the male, the tips chestnut edged with green; upper plumage brown, faintly mottled with paler; wing-quills dark brown; tail dark brown the feathers with whitish tips; lower neck metallic-green; lower plumage buffy-white, inner portion of each breast-feather dark brown glossed with green; a patch under the tail dark brown.

FIG. 75—Common Peafowl (⅔ nat. size)

Iris dark brown; naked skin of face livid white; bill and legs horny-brown. Weight, male 9 to 11½ lb., female 6 to 9 lb.

A peculiar fan crest on the crown; enormously lengthened and modified upper tail-coverts form a lengthy train falling over the wedge-shaped tail; under tail-coverts disintegrated and downy; a spur in the male above the hind toe.

Field Identification.—Apart from the huge size and resplendent plumage of the male, the peculiar fan-shaped crest is sufficient to separate both sexes from any other species.

Distribution.—Confined as a wild bird to India and Ceylon. It is found almost throughout India from the Valley of the Indus eastwards except in the greater part of the Sunderbunds of Eastern Bengal. In Sind and the neighbouring desert areas it was apparently introduced by human agency. Along the Outer Himalayas it is found up to 2000 and locally up to 5000 feet, or even 6000 feet. In the southern ranges it occurs up to 6000 feet. A purely resident species.

Habits, etc.—In its truly wild state the Peafowl is a denizen of fairly thick jungle, especially when it is intersected by small rivers and streams and varied with low ranges of hills. In such jungles the birds live in small parties, resting and lazily feeding in the undergrowth by day, roosting on the trees at night, and, when surroundings permit, moving out into cultivation for the morning and evening feed. They are very wary and shy, running swiftly on foot amongst the bushes when approached, and being persuaded to fly with the utmost difficulty; though once on the wing they can travel fast with regular, comparatively slow flaps, sustained and without the gliding common to most game-birds.

Yet, for all its shyness, the Peafowl knows when to trust man. In the drier regions of the north-west where it has been introduced, or in those areas where sentiment and religion combined provide the indigenous bird with complete protection, as the emblem of the Lord Krishna, it becomes very numerous and trusting, living in regular droves on the outskirts of villages and feeding about the fields with an almost complete disregard of passers-by; while it sleeps by night on trees amongst the houses. In the vicinity of villages it is a foul feeder.

The food consists chiefly of vegetable matter and grain and seeds, and it often devours the cultivated kinds in quantities sufficient to render it a destructive nuisance; insects and larvæ of all kinds, molluscs, small reptiles, and even small mammals are also eaten. The call is a loud trumpet-like scream like the *miaou* of a gigantic cat; in Northern India this is said to form the syllables *minh-ao* "come rain," and the bird is credited with being especially noisy at the approach of rain.

The immature birds are good eating. The old birds, however, should be recommended to those who by choice pick out the oldest and toughest of their fowls for eating. As a general rule the Peafowl should be left alone by sportsmen; there is little interest in shooting them, and when killed they are only worth making into soup; to kill them is almost certain to offend local prejudice, even if it does not lead to serious trouble; while, to my mind at least, the cock is such a wonderful and beautiful creature that it is a pity to sacrifice him merely to the passing pleasure of the shot.

The domestication of the Peafowl is of very ancient date, as the gorgeous plumage of the males and their strutting, pompous pride have a very special appeal to Oriental minds. The introduction of the bird to Europe is usually attributed to the conquests of Alexander the Great. During the Middle Ages no formal banquet was considered complete without a Peacock served up in a lordly dish, garnished with its head and train. The first syllable of the bird's name comes through the Anglo-Saxon *Pawe*, from the Latin *Pavo*, and this in its turn comes through Greek and Persian onomatopœic words from the loud call.

The Peacock is polygamous, his harem consisting of from two to five hens, and he takes no share in family duties. The heraldic term of a "Peacock in its Pride" aptly expresses the male's display in which the train is expanded into a gorgeous fan round the posing bird.

The breeding season is prolonged, from January to October, the actual months varying locally and being dependent on the rains; the middle of June to the end of August may be considered the usual period.

The nest is a hollow scraped in the ground, more or less filled with leaves, small sticks, grass and other debris. Occasional nests may be found on buildings or in hollows amongst the branches of large trees, while exceptionally the eggs are laid in the old nests of Vultures.

The usual clutch consists of three to five eggs, but as many as eight may be found. The eggs are broad blunt ovals, with very thick and glossy shells closely pitted all over with minute pores. The colour varies from very pale fawn to warm buff, and some eggs are freckled with darker buff or pale reddish-brown.

The eggs vary from 2·45 to 3·0 inches in length, and 1·42 to 2·2 inches in breadth.

THE GREY JUNGLE-FOWL

GALLUS SONNERATI Temminck

Description.—Length, male 24 to 32 inches, including tail 12 to 18 inches; female 18 inches. Adult male: Crown and neck hackles blackish, each feather with a white shaft and ending in a white spot followed by a glossy brownish-yellow spot, these spots resembling sealing-wax and being formed by the soldering together of the webs; remainder of body plumage blackish, the feathers with white shafts and grey edges, the hackles at the sides of the rump and some of the upper tail-coverts ending in the yellow wax-like spots and edged with ferruginous; lower abdomen brownish-grey, the flanks tinged with ferruginous-brown; wings black, all the feathers with pale shafts and edges, the median coverts ending in long lanceolate brownish-orange wax-like spots fringed at the end with chestnut; tail and its coverts black, highly glossed with purple, green and bronze.

Female: Crown and neck speckled brown with pale shafts and edges to the feathers; upper plumage finely mottled blackish-brown and buff, the feathers over the shoulders with fine whitish shaft-lines; quills of the wings and tail dark brown, mottled on their exposed edges; chin and throat white; remainder of lower plumage white, the feathers with black borders which gradually disappear from the breast downwards.

Iris orange-red or yellowish-red; bill horny-brown; comb, face and wattles crimson; legs horny-yellow, claws black. Weight, male 1 lb. 10 oz. to 2 lb. 8 oz., female 1 lb. 9 oz. to 1 lb. 12 oz.

The male has the throat and sides of the face naked, the skin being produced into a pendulous wattle on each side of the throat, and a fleshy comb on the top of the head; the female has traces of a comb and a bare patch of skin round the eye. The tail of fourteen feathers is laterally compressed, and in the male consider-

FIG. 76—Grey Jungle-Fowl (⅓ nat. size)

ably graduated, lengthened and curled. The male has a long sharp spur above the hind toe.

Field Identification.—Easily recognised as a Jungle-Fowl by the strong resemblance of both sexes to domestic fowls. The grey-streaked plumage of the male, combined with the glossy black tail, and the curious waxen spots of the hackles of the neck and rump, and the black and white markings of the under surface of the female at once indicate the species.

Distribution.—A purely Indian species, occurring throughout Southern and Western India in hilly and jungly ground. A line from Baroda to Mount Aboo and through Jubbulpore to the mouth of the Godavari roughly indicates the northern boundary of its range and it extends almost to Cape Comorin. It is a resident species and occurs up to the summits of the hills.

Habits, etc. — The Grey Jungle-Fowl is by preference an inhabitant of the jungles that clothe the lower slopes and bases of the various hill ranges, particularly when these consist of moderately thin bamboo jungle. It is an exceedingly shy bird and remains during the day in cover, only coming out in the mornings and evenings to feed, and even then running back into cover at the least alarm. It is very punctual and regular in its habits, feeding daily at the same places and times. It roosts in trees and usually flies up into them when pursued by a dog. It is met with solitary or in pairs, and although numbers live in suitable jungles or collect to an abundant food-supply, they do not as a rule associate in parties. The food consists of grain and seeds, insects, grubs, small fruits, and berries and tender shoots.

The male usually carries the tail low, and when running it moves with a shame-faced crouching gait, the neck outstretched, the tail almost to the ground.

From October to May the males are in full plumage and then crow freely, mostly in the mornings and evenings. The crow is very peculiar, ***kuch-kaya-kya-kuck***, ending with a low double syllable ***kyukun, kyukun***, repeated slowly and softly, and only audible for a short distance. When disturbed by a dog they have a curious cackle, ***kuck-kuck-kuck***.

The breeding season is very irregular, depending on rain and food-supply. Most nests may be found from October to November or from February to May. The nest consists of a slight collection of sticks, leaves, bamboo spathes and other rubbish placed in a hollow on the ground, either natural or scraped out by the bird itself.

The normal clutch consists of four to seven eggs, though as many as thirteen have been recorded. The egg greatly resembles that of the domestic fowls, both in colour and shape ; the surface is fine, smooth and glossy. The colour varies from very pale cream to rich warm buff, generally unmarked but sometimes finely freckled, and occasionally even spotted and speckled with various shades of brown.

The average size is 1·80 by 1·40 inches.

THE RED JUNGLE-FOWL

Gallus gallus (Linnæus)

Description.—Length, male 26 to 28 inches, including tail 11 to 13 inches ; female 17 inches. Adult male : Crown and neck hackles golden-brown to orange-red, passing into golden-yellow, generally with lanceolate dark brown shaft - streaks ; upper back, smaller feathers of the wing, save for a central bar shiny chestnut-red, and inner edge of the wing black, glossed with green and purple; wing-quills blackish-brown, the inner feathers broadly edged with

FIG. 77—Red Jungle-Fowl (1/7 nat. size)

deep cinnamon; rump deep chestnut-red merging into golden-red and orange, all the feathers very shiny and with dark green bases; tail and its coverts black glossed with green and purple; lower parts black with a slight greenish gloss.

Female: Top of head and a collar round the throat dark rufous chestnut; back and sides of the neck brownish-black, mottled with brown, each feather elongated, pointed and edged with straw-yellow; upper parts finely vermiculated black and brown, with yellowish-white shafts; wing- and tail-quills dark brown, the exposed parts of all but the outermost wing-quills finely vermiculated with pale brown; lower parts light rufous brown, more rufous on the breast, more brown towards the tail, with paler shaft-stripes.

Iris light red to orange-red; comb and wattles crimson, sides of face paler; bill dark brown, reddish towards the base in males, horny-brown in females; legs slaty-plumbeous. Weight 1 lb. 2 oz. to 1 lb. 10 oz.

Characters as in the Grey Jungle-Fowl, with the addition of a second small white wattle by each ear.

Field Identification.—Indistinguishable in appearance, sex for sex, from those types of domestic fowls known as "Old English Game" or modern "Game-bantam." The orange-red and yellow hackles of the neck and rump and the uniform black under parts of the male, the uniform brown under parts and yellow neck markings of the female indicate the species.

Distribution.—Widely distributed in India, Burma, Yunnan, Siam, Indo-China and the Malay Peninsula to Sumatra. The Indian race, *G. g. murghi*, is found along the Outer Himalayas from the Jhelum River foot-hills to Assam, in Bengal, Orissa, the Northern Circars and the Eastern Central Provinces down to the Godavari; also near Pachmarhi. It is resident and occurs up to about 5000 feet in the Himalayas, though in greatest numbers below 3000 feet. The distribution of this Jungle-Fowl is practically the same as that of the Swamp-Deer and the Sal-Tree.

Habits, etc.—The Red Jungle-Fowl is essentially a forest bird, but it occurs in both tree forest and in the jungles of thick scrub and low trees and it certainly prefers the neighbourhood of cultivation and country round the base of hills. The birds feed in the cultivation in the early morning and late afternoon but retire by day to their forest haunts, where also they sleep in the trees at night. The calls of both sexes resemble those of domestic varieties but the cock's crow is shorter, especially the concluding note. The gait and carriage of the cock is as described under the last species.

The Red Jungle-Fowl is the species which is evidently to be regarded as the ancestor of all domesticated poultry. The full story of its domestication is lost in the mists of time, but it is commonly believed that this took place in the Indo-Burmese area and it is the tradition of the Chinese that they received their poultry from the West about 1400 B.C. On the other hand, from the evidence of seals, the fowl was evidently known to the civilisation that flourished in the Indus Valley about 2700-2500 B.C., and though it is commonly said not to have been figured in ancient Egyptian monuments, this is incorrect. There is a definite drawing of a cock's head in Rekhmara's tomb at Thebes (*circ.* 1500 B.C.) and Mr Howard Carter's discoveries at Tutankhamen's tomb (*circ.* 1400 B.C.) include a rough drawing of a cock on a flake of limestone in the talus slope below the tomb. It is also figured on Babylonian cylinders between the sixth and seventh centuries B.C., while the Greek tradition evidently was that it reached Greece by way of Persia as Aristophanes calls it the Persian bird. The cock is represented on the Lycian marbles (*circa* 600 B.C.) in the British Museum. Curiously enough the bird is not mentioned in the Old Testament nor directly by Homer, though one of his heroes is called Alektor, the Greek name for a cock.

The breeding season proper is from the end of March to May, but some nests may be found from January to October. The nest is made on the ground in any dense thicket and is composed of dry leaves, grass and stems, while there is a good deal of variation in the amount of care expended on its construction. The cocks appear to be monogamous.

The normal clutch consists of five or six eggs and probably never exceeds nine. Four eggs are sometimes found.

The eggs vary a good deal in size and shape, but typically are miniature hens' eggs. The shell is fine and smooth with a fair amount of gloss, though duller and coarser specimens with visible pores occur. They vary in colour from an almost pure white to a deep creamy-buff.

The egg measures about 1·78 by 1·36 inches.

THE COMMON KALIJ PHEASANT

Gennæus leucomelanus (Latham)

Description.—Length, male 23 to 26 inches, including tail 11 inches, female 20 inches. Adult male: A long loose crest, and the upper plumage black glossed with purplish steel-blue, the feathers with whitish edges, these edges growing more marked on the rump; wing- and tail-feathers blackish-brown largely glossed with green; lower plumage dark brown merging into sullied white on the breast where the feathers are lanceolated; many feathers have white shafts especially on the upper back and breast.

Female: Upper plumage, including crest, dark reddish-brown, the feathers very faintly vermiculated with black, and with their shafts and edges whitish; lower plumage similar but paler in tint, the chin, throat and centre of the abdomen becoming whitish; all but the central pair of tail-feathers black glossed with greenish.

Iris orange-brown, a bare fleshy patch round the eye scarlet; bill pale greenish-horn; legs livid fleshy with a purplish or brownish tinge. Weight, males 2 lb. to 2 lb. 12 oz., females 1 lb. 4 oz. to 2 lb. 4 oz.

A heavily-built, powerful bird, with short-rounded wings; the tail is a modification of that of the Jungle-Fowls, being long, compressed

FIG. 78—Common Kalij Pheasant (1/8 nat. size)

and graduated, the feathers pointed and slightly curved. The male has a heavy spur above the hind toe.

Field Identification.—Himalayan form. Distinguish from all other Indian Pheasants by the conjunction of the long hair-like crest with the compressed curved and pointed tail. The glossy black and white plumage of the males is also very distinctive.

Distribution.—The genus *Gennæus* includes the Kalij or Silver Pheasants which have a wide distribution in the Oriental region and afford, particularly in Burma, some perplexing problems in identification and distribution. In India, however, we are concerned merely with one species, which is found as a resident throughout the

Himalayas from Hazara to Bhutan at elevations from 1000 to 10,000 feet, being most common in a low zone from 2000 to 6000 feet. In this range there are three races, differing chiefly in the amount of white on the males. From Hazara to the western boundary of Nepal we have the whitest form, *G. l. hamiltonii*, in which the crest is white, and the white feather edges on the rump are very broad and conspicuous; in Nepal there is the typical race with the crest black and the white edges to the rump moderate in breadth; in Sikkim and Bhutan, *G. l. melanotus* has the crest black, and entirely lacks the white edges to the feathers of the upper plumage.

The well-known Koklas Pheasant (*Pucrasia macrolopha*), common in the Western Himalayas from Western Nepal into Afghanistan, is remarkable for its wedge-shaped tail and the unusual combination of a long crest with still longer side tufts. The male is rich chestnut below with the upper parts grey with black shaft-stripes, the head being largely black glossed with green.

Habits, etc.—This is the best-known and easiest to procure of all the Himalayan Pheasants, as it inhabits a lower zone than the others and is less shy and retiring in its habits. It is typically a bird of heavy undergrowth on the sides of ravines, though it is essential that this should be in or near forest and that there should be streams in the near vicinity. Whenever possible, it likes to move out to feed on open ground in the mornings and evenings, and it is therefore, when suitable conditions are present, often most numerous in the near vicinity of villages with their attendant cultivation. A few may always be found on the outskirts of the hill stations even during the crowded summer months. It lives and feeds on the ground, flying up into trees to roost and also often to avoid disturbance. The food consists of grain, seeds, berries and tender shoots, and of a variety of insects, worms, larvæ and similar objects.

Both sexes grunt and cluck in a soft undertone as they feed on the ground, and when flushed they give vent to a series of guinea-pig-like squeaks and chuckles that hardly seem to proceed from a bird. The males are very pugnacious and fight freely amongst themselves. There is a courting display in which the male standing on the ground draws himself up to his full height and makes a peculiar drumming whirring noise by rapidly vibrating his extended wings. Several birds are generally found together.

The breeding season is from the end of March to the end of June. The nest is a collection of leaves, grass and forest rubbish in a hollow scraped beneath the shelter of a stone or low bush or tuft of grass.

The number of eggs varies from four to fourteen, but the normal clutch consists of seven to nine eggs. They very closely resemble those of the domestic fowl, being smooth and rather glossy with a fine close grain. The colour varies from pale cream to rich reddish-buff, without markings. The surface is sometimes pitted with minute pores or covered with tiny white specks.

The average size is 1·95 by 1·42 inches.

THE MONAL

LOPHOPHORUS IMPEJANUS (Latham)

Description.—Length, male 28 inches, female 25 inches. Head and crest brilliant metallic-green; sides and back of the neck and wing-coverts metallic-purple, gradually becoming metallic-green towards the bend of the wing; wing-quills black; rump white; upper tail-coverts brilliant metallic-green; tail cinnamon-chestnut; lower parts black, washed on the chin and throat with metallic-green.

Female: Upper plumage dark brown, the feathers with narrow edges and broad central stripes of buff; wing-quills dark brown, mottled and lightly barred with rufous buff; rump pale buff-brown, the feathers with dark brown crescentic bars which on the tail-coverts almost cover the buff, the tail-coverts ending in a line of white; tail barred, with rufous-buff and dark brown, the tips white; chin and throat white; breast pale buffy-white the feathers pointed and lined with dark brown; remainder of lower parts pale buffy-white, the edges of the feathers freckled with dark brown, becoming stronger and gathered into lines on the flanks.

The young male resembles the female, but has a black patch on the throat.

Iris brown; naked eye-patch blue; bill dark horny-brown; legs yellowish or brownish-green, claws dark horny-brown. Weight, males 5 to 5½ lb., females 4 to 5 lb.

Bill stout and slightly curved; wings and tail slightly rounded; the male has a marked tuft of long spatulate feathers on the top of the head, the most brilliantly metalled plumage imaginable and heavy blunt spurs on the legs.

Field Identification.—Himalayas only, in steep hill-side forests. Male quite unlike any other bird of its size. Most brilliant metallic colouring, which in distance looks blackish with white rump and chestnut tail. Female variegated blackish-brown and buff. Peculiar whistle uttered in flight.

Distribution.—Safed Koh; Himalayas from Afghanistan and Chitral to Bhutan. Breeds in the Western Himalayas usually between 9000 and 11,000 feet and is found in winter at all elevations from tree-limit down to 6000 feet. In Sikkim the summer range is said to be from 10,000 to 15,000 feet. A resident species with no races.

PLATE XX

1. Little Brown Dove. 2. Red Turtle-Dove. 3. Rain-Quail. 4. Indian Courser. 5. White-breasted Waterhen. (All about $\frac{1}{3}$ nat. size.)

[*Face p.* 418

The Cheer Pheasant (*Catreus wallichii*) is another well-known game-bird of the Himalayas at moderate elevations from Khatmandu westwards. It is a plain-looking buff and grey and black barred bird with a bare red eye-patch and a long narrow pointed tail, broadly barred. Less well known but far more brilliant with their scarlet plumage and white spotting are the Crimson Horned Pheasant (*Tragopan satyra*) found from Garhwal to Assam and the Western Horned Pheasant (*Tragopan melanocephala*) found from Garhwal to Kashmir and Hazara. The male of the former has the lower parts chestnut-red, spotted with white. In the latter the lower parts are black spotted with white and there is a scarlet blaze on the throat.

Habits, etc.—This magnificent Pheasant is still common in the Himalayas where it is found in the higher forest-clad nullahs, preferably those where forests of oaks or firs or thickets of rhododendron are broken up by patches of grassy slope, and rocky crags and precipices discourage the intrusions of man. In such nullahs the Monal is often found in large numbers, not in flocks but in twos and threes, feeding and wandering under the trees and out on the sunlit slopes. Their favourite food is a hard knobby tuberous root which is common on the Alpine pastures, and for it they dig with the aid of the strong curved bill. Grass-seeds and flower-seeds, berries, fruits, beetles and insects are also eaten. The bird is very wary, launching itself with a series of wild ringing whistles down the khud-side at the slightest alarm, or flying straight out over the wide nullahs high out of shot till it looks like a Partridge in the sky. The ringing alarm whistle is very like that of a Curlew.

In the breeding season, which is in May and June, the male displays to the hens. On the ground he displays with the tail spread high over the back and slightly jerked, much after the fashion of the Peacock. He has also an aerial display in which he flies straight into the air from a steep hill-side, moving slowly with the wings held high above the line of the back, the tail being partly spread and the white rump very conspicuous.

The nest is a hollow scratched in the ground by the female under the shelter of a rock, the bole of a tree or some tuft of herbage. It is usually lined with dry leaves, moss and similar debris.

The clutch varies from two to six eggs, but is usually composed of four or five eggs.

The egg is a long oval, a good deal compressed towards the smaller end. The shell is fine and compact with a faint gloss. The ground-colour is buffy-white, spotted, freckled and occasionally blotched with deep reddish-brown. There is a good deal of variation in the amount of marking and it is usually most conspicuous about the middle of the egg.

The egg measures about 2·55 by 1·78 inches.

THE RED SPUR-FOWL

GALLOPERDIX SPADICEA (Gmelin)

Description.—Length 14 inches. Male: Top of the head dark brown shading paler and greyer on the forehead, sides of the head and all round the neck; upper plumage light chestnut, the feathers of the upper back margined with pale greyish-brown, the remainder finely vermiculated with black and buff; wing-quills dark brown; tail blackish-brown, the central pair of feathers and the outer margins of the next two or three pairs like the lower back; chin whitish; breast and upper abdomen chestnut, the feathers margined with pale greyish-brown; lower abdomen and thighs brown; a patch under the tail rufous-brown vermiculated with black.

Female: Forehead sandy-brown, becoming dark brown on the crown, nape and neck; upper plumage sandy or pale rufous-brown, each feather with two black bars, the black becoming less and the rufous more pronounced towards the tail; wing-quills dark brown; tail blackish, the central feathers with mottled buff bars that disappear on the outer feathers; chin and throat whitish; neck olive-brown, the feathers becoming rufous in the centre and tipped with black; breast and flanks bright ferruginous with narrow black tips; remainder of lower plumage brown, mottled with black and rufous under the tail. The amount of black on the lower plumage is very variable.

Iris dull yellow to brown; a bare patch round the eye red; bill horny-brown reddish at the base; legs brownish-red or red. Weight 8 to 13 oz.

Wings short and rounded; tail rather long and considerably rounded. There are spurs on the legs in both sexes, irregular in number and often different on both legs, up to four on one leg in the male and two in the female.

Field Identification.—Male uniform chestnut in appearance, the female light brown pencilled with black. Both sexes suggest a domestic hen-bantam with a longish tail held like a Partridge. A bird of thick jungle, remarkable for its spurs.

Distribution.—The Spur-Fowls are a small genus of three species confined solely to India and Ceylon. The Red Spur-Fowl is confined to India and is divided into three races. The typical race is found in the terai in Oudh, and again scattered about throughout the whole Peninsula of India south of the great Indo-Gangetic alluvial plain, wherever there are broken hills covered with forests or bamboo jungle. It extends as far south as the Palni Hills. Provided that the country is of the requisite type it is found at any elevation from sea-level up to 5000 feet and occasionally higher to 7500 feet. In Travancore it is replaced by the richly-coloured *G. s. stewarti*, which extends up to about 3000 feet. In the Aravalli Hills and Udaipur there is a pale race known as *G. s. caurina*. All races are strictly resident.

The Painted Spur-Fowl (*G. lunulata*), which is also found in Peninsular India, may easily be distinguished by the black and white spotting of the plumage of the male, while the female is a plain brown bird with a chestnut face.

Habits, etc.—The Red Spur-Fowls are birds of broken hilly country and dense cover, especially affecting bamboo jungle and well-wooded nullahs close to water. In such localities they live solitary or in pairs, though the young birds remain in company with their parents for some time. They live and feed on the ground in the thick cover that they affect, and are made to take wing with the utmost difficulty, preferring whenever possible to escape on foot, running at great speed and being adept at dodging from cover to cover. When forced to fly they rise with a great fluster and flapping of wings, but their speed is not great, for a glide follows every few beats of the wings and they soon drop back into cover. They rise with a loud cackling noise resembling that of a domestic hen and the crow of the cock is somewhat similar. At night they always roost on trees, and often take refuge in them by day when pursued by dogs. They visit cultivation and open ground more rarely than the Pheasants and Jungle-Fowl.

The food consists chiefly of grain and seeds of all kinds, and the different jungle fruits and berries; quantities of insects and larvæ are also eaten. The flesh is very good for the table.

The usual breeding season is in February and March in Travancore, and from February to June in the case of the other races. There is no real nest, the eggs being laid in a hollow or on the bare ground amongst dry grass and leaves. The site chosen is generally in fairly thick scrub or forest, and there is a decided preference for bamboo jungle with thick undergrowth.

The normal clutch consists of three eggs, but two to five may also be found.

The eggs are miniature fowl's eggs in appearance, rather narrow and pointed in shape; the shell is stout and the texture fine and smooth with a slight gloss. The colour varies from creamy white to warm pinkish-buff, without markings.

The eggs average 1·67 by 1·28 inches in size.

THE COMMON QUAIL

Coturnix coturnix (Linnæus)

Description.—Length 8 inches. Male: Top of the head black barred with brown, a pale buff line down the centre of the crown and a broader one above each eye; sides of the head white and brown, ear-coverts and a streak from the gape dark brown; upper plumage light brown with white shaft-streaks, blotched with black and barred with buff and rufous; wing-quills brown barred on the outer web with rufous except on the first primary which has the outer web unmarked whitish; tail-feathers blackish-brown with pale shaft-streaks and transverse bars; throat and fore-neck whitish, a broad central band and a narrow cross-stripe on each side curving up to the ear-coverts making a blackish anchor mark; a broken gorget of blackish-brown spots; breast rufous-buff with pale shaft-stripes, gradually passing into white from the lower breast downwards; flanks brown with blackish spots and broad whitish shaft-streaks.

The female wants the black anchor mark on the throat and has the breast usually spotted with black.

Iris yellow-brown; bill horny-brown; legs pale fleshy-brown or yellow. Weight 3½ to 4 oz.

The shape is plump and rounded and the legs lack the spurs usual among game-birds.

Field Identification.—A miniature Partridge in appearance with a striped head and rather sandy coloration streaked with white; in the male a distinctive black anchor mark on the throat. Found often in considerable numbers in cereal crops and grass. Very unobtrusive in habits and practically never seen except on the wing.

Distribution.—The Common Quail is a bird of very wide distribution in the Old World, being found almost throughout Europe and Africa and in the greater part of Asia. It is a highly migratory species, and the majority of the birds that visit India are winter visitors, though a number are undoubtedly resident in the country.

As a breeding species the Quail is found in some numbers from the extreme north-west, including Gilgit, Kashmir, the North-west Frontier Province and Baluchistan, to Purnea on the east and south to the Deccan, though the Punjab and United Provinces are the districts in which the bird breeds most commonly.

The migrant Quail first appear in the north-west early in August and the passage lasts, in the main, until the end of October; some birds come from due west, others by a more northerly route from over the Himalayas. They gradually spread over the whole country except for the extreme south and Ceylon. Soon after Christmas they commence to gather and move in a north-westerly direction again, passing through the extreme north-west in enormous numbers in March and April. The spring migration is always more noticeable than that in autumn, as the birds collect into larger flocks and the period of passage is shorter and more concentrated.

Habits, etc.—The Common or Grey Quail is extremely well known in India as a sporting bird for the gun, a favourite delicacy for the table, and amongst Indians as a cage-bird for fighting and betting purposes.

In the greater part of India, Quail are regarded by sportsmen merely in the light of an addition to a mixed bag. In the north-west, however, on the spring migration, they are so numerous as to

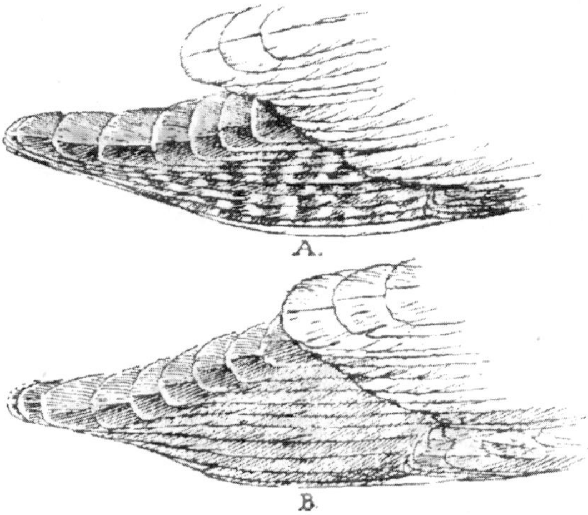

FIG. 79—Wings of (A) Common Quail; (B) Rain-Quail (Nat. size)

be the sole object of a day's sport. At this time they are chiefly found in the fields of growing corn, and it is the custom to collect the birds from far and wide into one particular area by means of call birds, set in cages on a long pole. The cornfields are then walked with a line of beaters. The Quail rise not in coveys but singly, though they are often so numerous that eight or ten birds may be on the wing at a given moment and very large bags are obtained; fifty to a hundred couple in a day's shooting is nothing unusual for two or three guns. The birds rise very suddenly and fly at a height of 5 to 15 feet from the ground, but although the flight is fast it is very straight and the birds are in consequence easy to hit.

Quail are netted alive in enormous numbers, and it is the practice in many establishments to buy up two or three hundred and fat them in underground pits to be killed and eaten as required. The food of the Israelites in the wilderness (Exod. xvi. 13) is believed to have been the Quail.

The food chiefly consists of grain and seeds, but insects and their larvæ are also eaten. All food is taken from the ground, and the bird never perches on trees.

The usual call of the Quail is a very liquid *wet-mi-lips*, even perhaps better represented by the Kashgari name of *Watwalak*, and it is uttered both by day and night. This is the call of the male, but there are other softer calls used by both sexes.

A Quail breeds, as it lives, in open country, in cultivation and standing crops, in hayfields and rough pastures. The nest is a hollow scraped in the ground and lined scantily with grass and a few leaves.

The breeding season in India is chiefly from March to May, but eggs have been found as late as September. The number of eggs is very variable, from three to ten or twelve. They are broad ovals, a good deal pointed towards the small end; the texture is hard and strong with a good deal of gloss. The ground-colour is a clear reddish or yellowish-buff, speckled, spotted and blotched in varying degrees with deep reddish-brown or bluish-black.

In size they average about 1·18 by 0·90 inches.

THE RAIN-QUAIL

Coturnix coromandelicus (Gmelin)

(Plate xx, Fig. 3, opposite page 418)

Description.—Length 7 inches. Very similar in plumage to the Common Quail, but easily recognised by having no rufous bars on the outer webs of the primary quills. The dark marks on the face and throat of the male are blacker, and in that sex there are broad black stripes on the feathers of the breast and flanks; in some examples almost the whole breast is black.

Iris brown; bill, male dusky blackish, female brownish-horn; legs pale fleshy. Weight 2¼ to 2½ oz.

Field Identification.—Very difficult to distinguish from the Common Quail in the field except by the call and smaller size, unless the black breast is visible. In the hand both sexes are at once distinguished by the primary flight-feathers which are plain on the outer webs, whereas the Common Quail has all the primaries except the first barred with rufous on the outer webs.

Distribution.—The Black-breasted or Rain Quail is peculiar to the Indian Empire. It is found throughout practically the whole of India from the extreme north-west and the extreme north-east down to Ceylon; in the three corners of this triangle, however, it is undoubtedly very scarce and recorded only from certain localities. In the Himalayas and other hill ranges it is found occasionally up to 6000 or 8000 feet.

The status of this Quail is not very clear; its name is due to the fact that in large areas, especially in the north-west, it merely appears during the rains and leaves after breeding; in other parts it appears to be largely a resident.

The tiny Blue-breasted Quail (*Excalfactoria chinensis*) is locally distributed in India east of a line from Bombay to Simla. The female in coloration recalls the Grey Quail. The male is a handsome bird with the lower parts slate-grey and chestnut with conspicuous black and white markings on the throat.

Habits, etc.—Like the Grey Quail, this species is purely a bird of open country, being found in cultivation and grass crops, and often in the close proximity of villages and houses. During the breeding season it is found in pairs, but otherwise is a solitary bird though suitable cover often attracts many individuals to the same ground. In the field it is difficult to distinguish from the Grey Quail, except from the fact that the call is different, a rapidly repeated and musical *whit-whit——whit-whit——*.

The breeding season is in the monsoon from the end of June until October, though the majority of eggs will be found in August or the beginning of September. The nest is a hollow scraped in the ground and lined sparsely with grass and leaves. It is placed amongst standing crops or in thin grass.

The normal clutch consists of about nine eggs, though the number is variable from four to ten or eleven.

The eggs are very variable, though the members of one clutch resemble each other closely. In shape they are broad ovals, rather pointed at the small end, fine and smooth in texture with a fair gloss. The ground-colour varies from faintly yellowish-white to rich brownish-buff; the markings are of three types, a finely and evenly speckled and spotted egg, a boldly blotched and freckled egg, and a marbled egg. These markings may be blackish, purplish, olive-brown or burnt-sienna, but all the markings on one egg are of one colour.

The eggs average about 1·10 by 0·84 inches in size.

THE JUNGLE BUSH-QUAIL

PERDICULA ASIATICA (Latham)

(Plate xxii, Fig. 2, opposite page 484)

Description.—Length 6 inches. Male: Forehead and a stripe over each eye chestnut bordered above with a buff stripe which runs from the beak to the sides of the neck; upper parts brown, the crown mottled with dull chestnut and blackish-brown, the remainder vermiculated with black and marked with buff which tends to be in streaks on the upper back and in bars on the rump; wings brown vermiculated with dark brown, the feathers barred with buff, lightly on the outermost flight-feathers, heavily on the coverts and innermost flight-feathers, the last being also broadly streaked with buff and blotched with black; tail pinkish-brown with black-edged buff cross-bars; ear-coverts dark brown; cheeks, chin, and throat chestnut, a broken buff stripe under the eye and ear; lower parts white finely banded with black, the white gradually becoming pinkish buff under the tail and the black bands growing wider apart and disappearing.

Female: Whole head and upper neck as in male. Upper parts greyish-brown vermiculated with blackish; wings as in male but more uniform, the buff barring and banding being largely eliminated; lower parts uniform dull rufous with a vinaceous tint.

Iris brown; bill blackish, base blue-grey; legs yellowish-red. Weight $2\frac{3}{4}$ oz.

The shape is plump and rounded. The males have a blunt tubercular spur on the leg.

Field Identification.—Miniature Quail found in large coveys which rise suddenly with the impression of a bursting firework, the birds flying in all directions and settling as suddenly as they rose. Brown and buff with chestnut faces and throats, the males with finely barred black and white under parts, the females with uniform vinaceous under parts.

Distribution.—Peculiar to India and Ceylon. Irregularly distributed throughout the Indian Peninsula from the foot-hills down to Cape Comorin. It is found in the Kashmir foot-hills, the Kuchamum Hills near Sambhar and Mount Aboo, but not west of those areas nor east of Midnapur and the Rajmahal Hills. A resident species found at all elevations up to about 4000 feet.

This species with its small size for a Galline bird and its habit of making exceedingly short flights when disturbed is sedentary beyond the average and has therefore developed into a number of races which are very distinct. Their distribution has not yet been fully worked out, but there is a pale race, *P. a. punjaubi*, in the North-west, a red race, *P. a. vidali*, in the Konkan, and a dark race, *P. a. ceylonensis*, in Ceylon. The typical race of the Deccan is very black-looking. The plumage stages and variations require much study and are hard to understand.

For the beginner the position is complicated by the existence of a second species, the Rock Bush-Quail (*Perdicula argoondah*), which occupies much of the same distribution as the Jungle Bush-Quail and in Mysore is represented by a brick-red race, *P. a. salimalii*. The male differs in having the upper parts more barred, the chestnut of the throat paler in colour and the buff streak above the eye wanting, whilst the female lacks the striking head markings and has the upper parts vinous-rufous, similar to but darker than the lower parts. There is a certain amount of variation in both forms.

The Painted Bush-Quail (*Cryptoplectron erythrorhynchum*) is a much more richly-coloured species with heavy black and white blotching on the flanks in both sexes. The male has a black face with a conspicuous white bar along the sides of the crown and a large white throat-patch. It is found in the Central Provinces and the ranges of Western and Southern India.

Habits, etc.—The Jungle Bush-Quail may be found in any kind of dry jungle from thin grass and bush scrub in the neighbourhood of cultivation to fairly dense deciduous forest. In such localities it is found in coveys of a dozen birds or more which lead a very united life, feeding very close together on the ground and rising in unison when disturbed. It is always rather a startling event to flush one of these coveys. They rise unexpectedly close to one's feet with a sudden chirp and whir, rather like a firework exploding, and scatter in all directions, flying fast for a short distance and then dropping into cover as suddenly as they rose. In a few minutes the scattered birds start to call *tiri-tiri-tiri* and running in the grass are soon reunited. The food consists of seeds and berries and small insects, grasshoppers, and the like.

The breeding season is rather extended, from about September till April. The nest is a pad of grass and grass roots placed in a hollow in the ground under cover of a small bush or tuft of grass.

The clutch varies from four to seven eggs, five or six being the usual number.

The egg is a regular oval, more or less pointed towards one end. The texture is stout and close with a fair gloss. The colour varies from pure white with a faint tinge of cream to light buff.

The egg measures about 1·0 by 0·83 inches.

THE CHUKOR

ALECTORIS GRÆCA (Meisner)

Description.—Length 15 inches. Upper parts brownish-olive to ashy, tinged across the shoulders and sometimes also the crown with vinous-red; sides of the crown grey bordered by a buff line over the eye; outer scapulars pure ashy with broad rufous edges; wing-quills brown partly edged with buff; tail ashy-drab, the terminal halves of the outer feathers pale chestnut; ear-coverts dull chestnut, a black band across the forehead through each eye and continued behind the eye and round the throat as a gorget; the enclosed area buffy-white with a small black spot on the chin and one each side by the gape; breast ashy slightly tinged with brown and washed on the sides with vinous; remainder of lower plumage buff, darkening towards the tail, the flanks heavily barred with black and chestnut.

Iris brown, yellowish or orange; bill and legs red, claws brown. Weight, male 1 lb. 3 oz. to 1 lb. 11 oz., female 13 to 19 oz.

The male has a short blunt spur above the hind toe.

Field Identification.—Hill ranges bordering North-western India. In parties on open hill-sides. An ashy and buff Partridge at once distinguished by the black loop on the face and throat and by the beautiful barring of the flanks.

Distribution.—Under the name of Greek Partridge this bird has a wide distribution in Europe and in Western and Central Asia, and it has been divided into a number of races. We are concerned only with the form *A. g. chukar*, so well known to sportsmen by its vernacular name of Chukor, and the paler Baluchistan race known as *A. g. koroviakovi.* The latter is found in Baluchistan and the Kirthar Range dividing it from Sind and also in the Salt Range. The former is found in the Himalayas as far east as Nepal. It is a resident bird, found from 1000 to 15,000 feet.

The Chukor chiefly differs from the well-known French Partridge (*Alectoris rufa*) of Europe in lacking the fringe of black spots outside the gorget band; and in having two black bands instead of one on the flank-feathers.

In the Salt Range and the lower hills west of the Indus the See-See (*Ammoperdix griseogularis*), a small sandy-coloured Partridge with striking head markings and flank-feathers in the male, is found on the same ground as the Chukor.

Sportsmen after big game in the Himalayas above tree-level soon make the acquaintance of the noisy Ram-Chukor or Snow Cock (*Tetraogallus himalayensis*), a big Partridge-like bird found in coveys on the alpine pastures. Weight 5 to 6 lbs.

Habits, etc.—The Chukor varies a good deal in its choice of ground, provided that it is on a hill-side and free from trees, other than juniper. On the frontier hills it is found on the hottest and most barren hill-sides, which fairly justify the native saying that the bird feeds on stones. In the Himalayas it is equally at home on open grassy hill-sides in the low hot valleys, on stony screes covered with a light growth of barberry bushes, and amongst the snows at 12,000 or 15,000 feet—a diversity of range unusual amongst birds. Incessant damp and heavy rainfall and forest, however, it cannot stand.

Except when actually breeding they are found in coveys; these in their origin are family parties consisting of a pair of old birds with their last brood; but as the winter progresses the coveys pack in

FIG. 80—Chukor (¼ nat. size)

suitable localities so that thirty to fifty birds may be found together until the spring breaks them up into pairs. They live and feed on the ground, and when approached usually run for some distance uphill before taking wing. The flight is very strong and fast, several wing-beats followed by a glide, and the coveys sweep round the contours of the hills or across small valleys for some distance before settling. They then generally scatter a little and squat and are found again with difficulty.

The call is a loud ringing *chuck-chuckor* uttered in various tones. This call and the pugnacious nature of the bird and the ease with which it is tamed render it a favourable cage-bird in North-western India.

The food consists largely of grain and seeds as well as roots, green shoots and leaves and a variety of insects and larvæ.

The breeding season is from April to August, early at low altitudes and late in the higher portions of the bird's range. The nest is a hollow scraped in the ground under the shelter of a stone or a tuft of herbage; it is lined with grass, dry leaves and other rubbish, usually somewhat sparsely.

The clutch varies from five to fourteen eggs, but the usual number of eggs is from eight to twelve. The egg is a rather pointed oval of a close and hard texture with a fair amount of gloss. The ground-colour is pale yellowish or greyish-stone, freckled sparsely all over with pale reddish-brown or pinkish-purple, a few of the freckles becoming small blotches.

In size the eggs average 1·68 by 1·25 inches.

THE BLACK PARTRIDGE

Francolinus francolinus (Linnæus)

Description.—Length 13 inches. Male: Top of the head and nape blackish-brown, the feathers broadly edged with pale brown and on the nape with white; sides of the head with the chin and throat black, enclosing a brilliant white patch behind the eye; a bright chestnut collar round the neck; upper back black, the feathers edged with rufous and spotted with white; the middle and lower back to the tail black with narrow white bars, the bars dying away on the outer tail-feathers; wings and their coverts dark brown with subterminal tawny-buff bands and pale edges, the quills also with tawny-buff transverse spots on each web forming imperfect bars; lower plumage from the chestnut collar deep black, the sides of the breast and flanks spotted with white; lower abdomen and thighs pale chestnut stippled with white, growing darker under the tail.

Female: Upper plumage, wings and tail as in the male, but the black is replaced by dark brown, the chestnut collar is only represented by a dull chestnut patch on the nape stippled with brown, and the bars of the lower back and tail are wider; sides of the head clear pale buff; ear-coverts dark brown; lower parts buff, the chin and throat whitish, the remainder irregularly barred with brown, the bars on the feathers waved or arrow-head shaped and broadest on the flanks; a chestnut patch under the tail.

Iris brown; bill black, in the female dusky brown; legs brownish-red, becoming almost orange in the breeding male. Weight, male 10 to 20 oz., female 8 to 17 oz.

The male has a blunt spur on the tarsus; this is sometimes faintly indicated in the female.

Field Identification.—A typical Partridge found in thick ground-cover, and attracting attention by its extraordinary creaking call. Both sexes have a peculiar scaled type of coloration on the top and sides of the body, while the male is conspicuous for its black under parts, white cheek and chestnut collar.

Description.—This Francolin was formerly found in Southern Europe, though it is now extinct there. At the present time it extends in various races from Asia Minor through Persia and Mesopotamia and Northern India to Manipur. *F. f. asiæ* is found throughout Northern India, excluding Sind and Baluchistan where a paler bird, *F. f. henrici*, occurs along the Himalayas to Western Nepal and in the plains to Behar. Southwards it extends to Deesa, Gwalior,

FIG. 81—Black Partridge (¼ nat. size)

Sambalpur, and the Chilka Lake in Orissa. In Central and Eastern Bengal, in Eastern Nepal and in Sikkim is found the much darker Assamese race *F. f. melanotus*. A resident species. In the Western Himalayas it is found up to 8000 feet, though not commonly above 5000 feet.

The Painted Partridge (*Francolinus pictus*) is found in the Peninsula south of the range of the Black Partridge and it extends down to about Coimbatore, though it is not found along the Malabar coast or apparently in Mysore. In plumage the Painted Partridge somewhat resembles the Black Partridge but lacks the black on the head, throat and under parts; there is no chestnut collar; the under parts are white with black bars and shaft-stripes giving a chequered appearance. The female has no chestnut patch on the nape.

Habits, etc.—The Black Partridge is one of the favourite game-birds of Northern India. In the plains it is most abundant in the high grass and tamarisk scrub alternating with patches of cultivation which are found about the rivers of the great alluvial plains. Away from the rivers it is found also in ordinary crops and bush jungle, while the tea gardens of the foot-hills are very suited to its needs. It is usually walked up with a few beaters, and rises well, flying hard and straight, affording pleasant shots. For although several birds may be found together in a patch of cover they do not rise in a covey but get up in twos and threes or singly. For the table the flesh is rather dry, being not so good as that of the Grey Partridge, though it is the fashion to despise this latter bird.

The call-note is well known, a peculiarly loud and grating cry of several syllables which once heard can never be forgotten, with its ring of pride and well-being. *Che-chirree, chick-chiree* expresses it well, but the Hindustani *subhán-teri-kudrat* (O Omnipotent, thy power) is the usual rendering. It is uttered from the ground but often for the purpose the bird perches on an ant-heap or mound, and I have heard of an instance when one was seen on a dead tree some 15 feet from the ground though this is unusual.

The food consists of grain, seeds, green shoots, ants, and various insects.

The breeding season is somewhat protracted, from April to October, and some pairs are probably double-brooded, though the majority of eggs will be found in June.

The nest is made in a hollow on the ground in tamarisk or grass jungle, or in crops growing in their vicinity. The hollow is lined with grass leaves and similar materials sometimes very sparsely, sometimes quite thickly.

The number of eggs is variable, from four to ten, but the normal clutch is probably from six to eight. The eggs may be described as miniatures of the eggs of the English Pheasant. In shape they are sphero-conoidal, stout and fine in texture, and rather glossy. The colour varies from pale stone-colour to deep olive-brown, sometimes with a greenish tinge. Many eggs are covered with specks of a white calcareous deposit.

In size they average about 1·55 by 1·28 inches.

THE GREY PARTRIDGE

Francolinus pondicerianus (Gmelin)

(Plate xxii, Fig. 5, opposite page 462)

Description.—Length 12 inches. Sexes alike. Top of the head and nape brown; forehead, cheeks and a long broad line over the eye rufous; ear-coverts brown; upper plumage light greyish-brown mixed with chestnut, each feather crossed with a whitish band bordered on both sides with dark brown, and many of the feathers with glistening white shaft-streaks; wing-quills brown mottled and towards the body banded with whitish; outer tail-feathers chestnut shading towards the ends into dark brown with pale tips; chin and throat rufous-buff defined by a thin blackish-brown gorget; remainder of lower plumage buff with narrow rather irregular blackish-brown bars which fade out towards the tail.

Iris brown; bill dusky plumbeous; legs dull red, claws blackish. Weight 11 to 12 oz.

The male has a short spur above the hind toe.

Field Identification. — A typical brown-looking Partridge with chestnut in the tail, and a distinct gorget line round the rufous throat. Found in pairs or coveys on fairly open dry ground, and remarkable for its readiness to perch in trees.

Distribution.—Found from the Persian Gulf through Southern Persia, Afghanistan and Baluchistan to India. It is divided into three races distinguished by depth of coloration. The Western race, *F. p. mecranensis*, reaches Baluchistan, but in Sind merges into *F. p. interpositus*, which extends throughout the whole of Northern India to a line in Bengal roughly through Midnapur and Rajmahal. Southward, about Ahmednagar and Belgaum, it is replaced by the typical race. There is a special race, *F. p. ceylonensis*, in Northern Ceylon. It is found up to about 1500 feet in the Himalayan foot-hills and other ranges, and is a strictly resident species.

The Common Hill-Partridge or "Peora" (*Arborophila torqueola*) found throughout the Himalayas is a tree-perching forest Partridge best known by its plaintive call—a low melancholy whistling note repeated at three second intervals and audible at a considerable distance. The colour is largely olive-brown variegated with chestnut and black with white spots on the flanks. The male has a chestnut crown and a black and white throat enclosed in a white gorget. The female has the throat rufous spotted with black.

Habits, etc.—The Grey Partridge is not found in heavy forest or on swampy ground. With these exceptions it is found in every type of country, being particularly partial to those tracts where patches of cultivation are surrounded by sandy waste ground and light scrub jungle. It is not so dependent on thick cover as the Black Partridge as it roosts commonly in trees, and also frequently takes refuge in them when disturbed; while many live in hedgerows and thickets on the outskirts of villages.

It associates in small coveys except when breeding. When disturbed the members of a covey do not rise together like the English Partridge, but scatter and run with great speed until they find thick cover in which to skulk, so that each bird has to be pursued separately while the remainder seize the opportunity to escape. When flushed the bird rises with a loud whir and flies rapidly with quick strong wing-beats, but it does not as a rule travel very far.

The males are very pugnacious, and therefore are easily captured with decoy birds; they are favourite cage-birds with Indians who esteem their loud calls and also keep them for fighting. The call is a peculiar loud shrill cry *tit-ee-roo, tit-ee-roo* or *pat-ee-la, pat-ee-la* preceded by two or three harsh notes, similar but each time uttered with a higher intonation as if the bird were seeking for the keynote of its call; morning and evening the wild ringing notes are amongst the familiar bird sounds of India.

The food consists of grain and seeds of all kinds, as well as of grasshoppers, white ants and other insects.

The ordinary breeding season is from February to June, but a few nests will also be found from September to October. The nest is a scrape in the ground under the shelter of a clod of earth, a tuft of vegetation or a bush. The scrape is sometimes left bare, but is more commonly lined with blades of grass and dry leaves.

The clutch consists of six to nine eggs. The eggs are moderately long ovals, a good deal pointed towards the small end, and the texture is fine, hard and glossy. The colour is unmarked white more or less tinged with pale brownish.

The average size is 1·3 by 1·05 inches.

THE LITTLE BUTTON-QUAIL

TURNIX SYLVATICA (Desfontaines)

Description.—Length 5 inches. Sexes alike. Crown mixed black and brown with a buffy-white line down the centre; sides of the head and a line over each eye buffy-white speckled with black; back of the neck rufous, the feathers edged with buff; upper plumage chestnut-brown, each feather finely barred with black and edged with yellowish-white, conspicuously on the shoulders and upper back, and on the wing-coverts so broadly as to appear entirely yellowish-white with chestnut black-edged spots; wing-quills brown, the outer feathers edged with buff; lower plumage whitish, the breast buff growing browner on the centre, the sides with black and chestnut spots.

Iris pale yellow; bill plumbeous; legs fleshy-white. Weight, 1·1 to 1·5 oz.

A plump rounded bird with a soft pointed tail. No hind toes.

Field Identification.—A tiny, plump, Quail-like bird with a pale stripe down the crown and a mixture of rufous-black and yellow in the upper plumage. The three toes distinguish the family from true Quails, and the pointed tail at once identifies this species.

FIG. 82—Little Button-Quail ($\frac{3}{5}$ nat. size)

Distribution.—The Little Button-Quail has been chosen to represent the Order of the Hemipodii, a group of small birds that greatly resemble the true Quails in appearance but differ markedly in anatomy and breeding characteristics. All Indian members of the family may at once be recognised as lacking the hind toe. This species has a very wide distribution from the Iberian Peninsula through Africa and Asia to Australia. All Indian birds belong to the same race *T. s. dussumier*. In the greater part of India it is a resident, but in the north-west its appearance is perhaps sporadic, depending on the rains. It has been found up to 8000 feet in the Outer Himalayas and other ranges, but not commonly.

The male of the Indian Button-Quail (*Turnix maculatus*) is very like the Little Button-Quail but has a yellow bill and lacks the long pointed tail-feathers. The female is easily distinguished by a broad rufous collar. It occurs throughout most of India. The Bustard-Quail (*Turnix suscitator*) is larger with the chin, throat and breast cream-coloured barred with black, the female having also a broad black band down the centre of those parts. The belly is brownish-buff. Throughout India and Ceylon except in dense forest and desert.

Habits, etc.—This, the most diminutive game-bird of India, avoids thick forest and hilly country, and lives by preference in cornfields and stretches of grassy plain though it may also be found in any type of low herbage and open scrub jungle. It is a most inveterate little skulker and is flushed with difficulty, rising often close by one's feet. When flushed it flies low over the ground and soon settles again, after which it is very difficult to put up a second time.

The food consists of seeds, tender shoots and insects.

This and the other species of *Turnix* are chiefly remarkable for their breeding habits. The females are larger than the males, and in most species the more brightly coloured, and they are the dominant factor in all domestic matters. The ordinary call-note is a soft booming sound ventriloquial in character, and usually described as a cross between a coo and a purr. This is uttered by the female and attracts the male, whom she courts, turning and twisting and posturing. The females are very pugnacious and fight amongst themselves fiercely for the possession of the male.

When the eggs are laid the male bird is left to brood them and to rear the chicks. The female deserts her mate and eggs and goes off in search of a fresh male, who in turn is left with a clutch of eggs to incubate. And it is believed that as many clutches of eggs are laid as the female can find husbands to court.

As a result of this system the breeding season is very prolonged and eggs may be found in almost every month of the year. The majority however are laid from June to September.

The nest is a slight pad of grass placed in a natural hollow in the ground where it is usually tucked away amongst the stems of a tuft of grass. Very occasionally the grass is bent over it in a sort of canopy.

The clutch consists of four eggs. The egg is a broad oval with the small end rather sharply pointed. The shell is very stout with a fine and close texture and a good deal of gloss. The ground-colour is greyish-white, sometimes with a yellowish or reddish tinge; the whole surface is closely stippled, speckled and spotted with yellowish- or greyish-brown, with secondary markings of pale purple or lavender; there are in addition generally some bold blotches of blackish- or dark reddish-brown, either generally distributed or gathered in a zone round the broad end. In some eggs these bolder markings are very numerous.

The egg averages about 0·84 by 0·66 inches.

THE WHITE-BREASTED WATERHEN

Amaurornis phœnicura (Pennant)

(Plate xx, Fig. 5, opposite page 418)

Description.—Length 12 inches. Sexes alike. A broad mask extending behind the eye to include the fore-neck and breast white; upper plumage generally and sides of the body dark slaty-grey washed with olive; a patch above the base of the tail olive-brown; quills blackish-brown, a fine white line down the edge of the wing; tail dark brown; abdomen buff in the centre darkening all round to pale dull chestnut.

Iris reddish-brown; bill green, the frontal portion red; legs olive-yellow.

The legs are long and stout with very long toes.

Field Identification.—A dark-coloured bird with chestnut under parts, and a conspicuous white mask and breast; with ungainly feet. Found in cover about water and often very noisy.

Distribution.—The White-breasted Waterhen is found almost throughout the Oriental region. Of the races into which it is divided only one, the typical race, is found throughout India, Burma and Ceylon. In India it is found on suitable waters throughout the country with the exception of the Upper Punjab and North-west Frontier Province and the hill ranges. It is mainly resident, but appears also to be locally migratory.

A smaller species, the Ruddy Crake (*Amaurornis fuscus*), with the upper parts dark olive-brown and the mask and lower parts vinous-chestnut, is common in Kashmir, Bengal and Assam, occurring also in other parts of Northern and South-west India. A still smaller bird (length 7 inches) is Baillon's Crake (*Porzana pusilla*) often found in great numbers on the northern jheels, flying over the water with the long legs hanging. The upper plumage is curiously marked as with smears of white paint.

Habits, etc.—This is one of the commonest water-birds of India, and is found wherever water is surrounded by a certain amount of thick cover, whether in marshes and tanks, or about village cultivation and in gardens. It usually feeds in the open on the land searching for grain, insects, mollusca and the like, and when disturbed is loath to take to flight but runs rapidly into cover. It is rather a quarrelsome species and is inclined to fight a good deal, the birds sparring together like chickens.

This species is probably most remarkable for its calls, being an exceedingly noisy bird. The ordinary note is a sharp metallic sound, much like the noise of pounding with pestle and mortar, and this is often kept up all night long. In the breeding season the call has thus been described by Eha : " It began with loud harsh roars which might have been elicited from a bear by roasting it slowly over a large fire, then suddenly changed to a clear note repeated like the coo of a dove."

The breeding season is in the rains from June to October. The nest is a saucer of sedges, dried grass, bamboo leaves and twigs. It is built on the water amongst rushes or bushes, or more usually in a raised situation in bushes, clumps of bamboo or trees at varying heights ; the vicinity of water is, however, essential, and the bird does not fly up to the nest but climbs up the surrounding vegetation.

The eggs are four to eight in number. They are moderately elongated ovals, rather obtuse at both ends ; the texture is hard and fine with a slight gloss. The ground is creamy stone-colour ; the markings consist of spots, speckles and blotches of brownish-red and pale purple, rather sparsely distributed on the body of the egg, but thick and confluent as a cap on the broad end.

In size they average about 1·57 by 1·18 inches.

THE WATERHEN

GALLINULA CHLOROPUS (Linnæus)

Description.—Length 12 inches. Sexes alike. Head and neck blackish-grey, passing into dark slaty-grey on the breast and flanks, the latter with a few broad white stripes ; upper plumage brownish-olive, the outer tail-feathers black and the wing-quills blackish-brown, the edge of the wing finely bordered with white ; middle of the abdomen whitish ; under tail-coverts white, a black patch in the centre.

Iris red ; frontal shield and base of bill red, tip greenish-yellow ; legs mixed greenish-yellow and slaty-green, with an orange-red ring above the joint.

The toes are fringed with a membrane and are exceedingly long.

Field Identification.—A water-bird found in the vicinity of thick cover. On land looks like a black chicken with large feet ; swims with a characteristic bobbing action. Easily identified by the red patch at the base of the beak, the red-gartered green legs, and by the habit of incessantly jerking up the tail and revealing the black-centred white patch below it.

Distribution. — The Moorhen or Waterhen is very generally distributed in Europe, Africa, Asia, America and the Hawaiian and other islands, and is divided into a number of sub-species, of which only one occurs in India. This, known as *G. c. indica,* differs from the typical European bird in its slightly smaller size. It is found virtually throughout India both in the plains and in the Himalayas and Nilgiris up to about 6000 feet. A resident species, it is also locally migratory.

The Blue-breasted Banded Rail (*Hypotænidia striata*) will be familiar to naturalists in Bengal. The dark brown upper parts with wavy white bars, the ashy-blue breast and the white bars on the flanks are distinctive.

Habits, etc.—In India the Moorhen is found in tanks and marshes, the two chief factors necessary to its presence being abundance of weeds, rushes and other cover, and a perennial supply of water. Jheels and marshes that dry up during portions of the year only shelter occasional stragglers. On rivers and streams it is seldom found in this country. It is essentially a water-bird, and spends practically all its time swimming about amongst the water-growth where it feeds largely on vegetable matter, but also on small mollusca and aquatic insects and their larvæ. It swims well, with a characteristic jerky bobbing movement of the head, and when necessary is a good diver, though this accomplishment does not appear to be used except to avoid danger. On land it walks well, with long strides, holding the tail erect so that the white under-coverts are very conspicuous, and when walking the head and tail are incessantly jerked as on the water. It feeds a good deal on land in the cover round water and often wanders right out into the open, running swiftly with head lowered back to the water on any alarm. The call is a loud harsh *prruk*, with something startling and sudden in the sound which is audible some distance away. The flight is rather heavy and laboured and usually low over the water though the bird is capable of rising into the air and going fairly fast. In flight the neck and legs are held extended. The Moorhen sometimes perches on trees climbing about the branches quite easily.

The breeding season in the plains is from July to September, but in the hills it starts earlier, in May; probably two broods are reared.

The nest is a mass of sedges and other vegetation heaped up to form a hollow for the eggs; it is placed either on the water amongst vegetation or in tufts of grass, or even sometimes a foot or two above the ground. According to situation it varies from a sketchy platform to a well-built nest.

Six to nine eggs are usually laid, but fourteen have been recorded.

The egg is a moderately broad oval, rather compressed towards the smaller end; the shell is compact and firm with little or no gloss. The ground is a pale stone-colour, tinged with pinkish when fresh; the markings consist of spots, speckles and blotches of deep red, reddish-brown and purple, the larger markings often being surrounded by a nimbus.

The eggs measure about 1·62 by 1·21 inches.

THE PURPLE COOT

PORPHYRIO POLIOCEPHALUS (Latham)

Description.—Length 17 inches. Sexes alike. Head pale brownish-grey, tinged with cobalt on the cheeks and throat and passing on the nape into the deep purplish-lilac of the upper plumage, flanks and abdomen; the sides of the wings and the breast light greenish-blue; wing- and tail-feathers black, the exposed portions blue; a white patch under the tail.

Iris deep red; bill and casque deep red mixed with brown; legs pale red, brown at the joints.

The bill is thick and compressed, rather short and high and terminates in a broad frontal shield or casque, square across the crown; legs and toes long and ungainly.

Field Identification.—A large blue and purple bird, with ungainly legs and feet, found in reed-beds in water; cannot be confused with any other species.

Distribution.—This species of Purple Coot is found from the Caspian Sea through Persia and Afghanistan to the whole of the Indian Empire; it extends eastwards to Siam. There are two races, of which we are concerned only with the typical form. This is found throughout the plains of India, east of a line through Gurdaspur and Jhang in the Punjab to Baluchistan and Sind; it has occurred in Kashmir but is not normally found in the Himalayas. A resident species.

The Water-Cock (*Gallicrex cinerea*) is found in the more swampy jheels of India, being particularly common in Bengal and Assam. The males are blackish and the females brown and the name comes from the pugnacious habits of the males and the posterior development of the frontal shield on the crown. In the breeding season this becomes a red fleshy horn-like peak in the male.

Habits, etc.—The Purple Coot is found wherever there are large swamps and jheels with plenty of rushes, bushes and weeds, and in such places it is usually abundant. It lives in small parties which spend their lives chiefly within the reed-beds, threading their way through the labyrinth of vegetation with remarkable ease, and clinging to the reeds and twigs with the huge feet like gigantic Reed-Warblers; they not infrequently sun themselves and preen their plumage on the broken-down reeds at the water's edge; but otherwise on the whole the bird is comparatively rarely seen unless beaten out of cover. The flight is very weak and laboured, and the bird seldom goes far on the wing, preferring to drop down again immediately into cover and escape on foot. Its food is mainly vegetable in character, and it does great damage amongst growing rice.

PLATE XXI

1. Common Green Pigeon. 2. Blue Rock-Pigeon. 3. Red-wattled Lapwing. (All about $\frac{1}{4}$ nat. size.)

[Face p. 440

The breeding season in India is in the rains from June to September, but most nests will be found in July and August. The birds in one particular jheel are all very regular in their dates of laying, but colonies in different jheels vary a good deal in this respect.

The nest is a massive heap of sedges and rushes firmly put together with a depression on the top for the eggs. Sometimes it is on the ground at the edge of water; at other times it is placed in or over water amongst rushes, tufts of grass, or in bushes at heights up to 3 feet above the surface of the water.

The number of eggs in the clutch is variable up to ten, and there is often a good deal of difference in the state of incubation of the eggs in one nest.

The egg is a broad and perfect oval, much the same shape as a hen's egg; the texture is firm and compact, but there is very little gloss.

When fresh the ground-colour varies from pale pinkish-stone to pure salmon-pink, but the rosy tint fades rapidly; the surface is fairly thickly spotted, blotched and occasionally streaked with red, and there are numerous secondary markings, pale purple blotches, clouds and spots. The markings are distributed evenly over the surface of the egg.

The average size is about 1·90 by 1·39 inches.

THE COMMON COOT

Fulica atra Linnæus

Description.—Length 16 inches. Sexes alike. Entire plumage blackish-grey, darker on the head, neck and lower tail-coverts, and paler below; edge of wing whitish.

Iris red; bill and frontal shield bluish-white; legs greenish, joints slaty.

The bill is compressed and rather deep, with a broad frontal shield on the forehead. The tarsus has a membranous fringe behind; the toes are long and fringed with a broad membrane divided into lobes.

Field Identification.—Found in flocks on open water; the white frontal shield shows up in contrast with the black plumage, and in flight the bird has an ungainly appearance with the heavy feet extending beyond the short tail.

Distribution.—The Coot is found throughout the greater part of Europe, Northern Africa and Asia, and is replaced by closely-allied forms in Australia and Tasmania. It is unknown in Ceylon, but in India it is found wherever suitable water occurs, and in the Himalayas breeds up to about 6000 or 8000 feet. It is a resident species in many parts of India, but in winter its numbers are greatly augmented by immigration, and at that season it is more generally distributed.

Habits, etc.—The Coot is more definitely aquatic than most of the Rail family, and frequents more open water, such as lakes, tanks and slowly-moving rivers. In ordinary jheels it will always be found out in the open water and not in the reed-beds except when breeding. Its food consists largely of vegetable matter which is taken both on the surface and by diving, but it also eats small fish, insects and mollusca, and is not above devouring the eggs and chicks of other aquatic birds.

In winter Coots collect in large herds; they do not, however, merge their own individuality in the herd or act entirely under mob

FIG. 83—Common Coot (¼ nat. size)

impulse, as will a flock of ducks. Disturb the Coots on the water and you will only affect those birds within the immediate range of your aggression; the remainder do not move automatically in response.

The size of the herds of Coot is often incredibly large, especially on the great lakes of Sind where the numbers of the birds may be estimated by the square mile. On the Munchur Lake, for instance, the water is covered with separate herds of Coot, each of which keeps more or less to a territory of its own separated by a gap of several hundred yards from the territory of the next herd. The noise of wings and paddling feet when one of these gatherings takes to flight is like the noise of great waves breaking on a shingle beach. For the Coot rises with difficulty, pattering at first along the surface of the water; though once on the wing it flies strongly with neck and legs outstretched, and rises well up into the air.

English sportsmen do not generally trouble to shoot the Coot as it is easy to hit, and the flesh is too fishy to be palatable ; but native fishermen regard it as a welcome article of diet, and it is netted in hundreds on the Sind lakes. Many are killed with bow and arrow or caught by hand. In the latter case they are grabbed from below by a man who wades up to his neck in water with his head concealed in a roughly-stuffed duck.

In Kashmir the Coot breeds in May and June, and in the plains in July and August.

The nest is a large mass of rushes and flags with a depression on top for the eggs ; it is built amongst reeds and other aquatic vegetation either on the water or on the ground at its edge. The clutch varies from six to ten eggs.

The egg is a somewhat broad oval, slightly compressed towards one end ; the texture is fine and hard with little gloss. The ground-colour is a pale buffy-stone, closely and evenly stippled all over, and also slightly spotted with black and dark brown.

In size the eggs average about 1·98 by 1·40 inches.

THE COMMON CRANE

GRUS GRUS (Linnæus)

Description.—Length 45 inches. Sexes alike. Crown and a patch in front of each eye sparsely covered with black hairs, the skin blackish in front and on the nape dingy red and warty ; on the lower nape, a slaty-blackish triangular patch, the point behind ; a white band down each side of the head from the eye joining behind the nape and covering the hind neck ; chin, cheeks, throat and foreneck slaty-blackish ; remainder of plumage above and below ashy-grey except the outer flight-feathers, the tips of the inner flight-feathers and the tips of the tail-feathers which are black.

Iris orange-red to reddish-brown ; bill dingy horny-green, yellowish towards the tip ; legs black, soles fleshy.

Bill pointed ; long neck and long legs ; the inner wing-feathers (tertiaries) are long, rather pointed, loose-textured and rather curly, hanging over and concealing the true flight-feathers and tail.

Field Identification.—A huge grey bird with long neck and legs, the head and upper neck blackish and white with a dull red patch on the nape. Tail concealed by a mass of drooping curly plumes. Found on open plains in large flocks which fly in regular formations with a creaking trumpeting note. The black markings on the head and neck and the black legs distinguish it from the Sarus Crane.

Distribution.—A migratory bird, breeding in Northern Europe and Northern Asia and wintering in Southern Europe, Northern Africa, South-western Asia, Northern India and China. In India it is found as a winter visitor through the plains of the north, extending as far south as the Bombay Deccan and Orissa. Indian birds are said to belong to the race *G. g. lilfordi* which breeds in Eastern Siberia and Turkestan.

The Demoiselle Crane (*Anthropoides virgo*) is also a common winter visitor in flocks to Northern India. It is rather a smaller grey bird and is easily recognised from all other Cranes by a white plume of soft feathers behind each eye and the black under surface of the whole neck, terminating in black plumes pendant over the breast.

Habits, etc.—The Common Crane and the Demoiselle Crane are not usually distinguished from each other in India and are well known collectively under the names of Kunj and Kulung. They have very similar habits and are often found together.

The Common Crane arrives in India in late September and in October and stays until March and the beginning of April. In North-west India the passage may be an impressive sight. Both species appear to travel together. The observer who is favourably situated will hear one morning a loud clanging call and looking towards the sound will see in the distant sky a vast tangled skein of birds. As it approaches it resolves itself into an immense concourse of Cranes flying at a tremendous height. The stream of birds travels across the sky like an army. Big flocks, small parties, single birds and chevrons extend as far as the eye can reach, all travelling the same line. Then perhaps the leading flock circles round in a vast swirl, feeling for its direction ; the next formations close up to it and again the army moves forward. As they go a single bird trumpets, answered by others.

The Crane's power of uttering these sonorous and trumpet-like notes is usually attributed to the peculiar formation of its trachea or windpipe which on quitting the lower end of the neck passes backward through the fork of the merrythought and is received in a hollow space formed by the bony walls of the breast bone. Here it makes three turns and then runs upwards and backwards into the lungs.

Whilst in India the Crane is found in parties or flocks which usually pass the middle of the day and the whole night in open river-beds or jheels where their vigilance protects them from surprise. Morning and evening they flight to feed in cultivation where they do much damage to young crops and grain. After such a diet their flesh is delicious eating. The Crane only perches on the ground.

The Common Crane breeds in the north about May and June. The nest is a large untidy heap of vegetable matter placed on the ground in open or thinly-wooded swamps and marshy clearings in forest. The clutch consists of two eggs. The egg is a long oval narrowing to the small end, greyish-olive to greenish-brown in colour, blotched and spotted with dark and light reddish-brown and ashy-grey.

The egg measures about 3·75 by 2·5 inches.

THE SARUS CRANE

ANTIGONE ANTIGONE (Linnæus)

Description.—Length 5 feet. Sexes alike. Head and upper neck bright red, ashy on the crown, bare except for black hairs, and a patch of grey feathers on the ears; neck white, passing at its base into the bluish ashy-grey of the whole body plumage; outer flight-feathers blackish-brown, the inner flight-feathers grey and whitish.

Iris orange; bill greenish-horny with a black tip; legs fleshy-red.

Bill pointed; the neck and legs are very long, the tibia being naked for some distance above the joint.

The inner wing-feathers (tertiaries) are elongated and pointed, and droop over the true flight-feathers.

Field Identification.—A huge grey bird with a reddish naked head and long legs, found in pairs about marshy spots; bold in demeanour and always frequents the same place.

Distribution.—The Sarus Crane is found throughout northern India, and Assam to Burma, Siam and Cochin-China. It is divided into two races, of which we are concerned only with the typical form. This is common over the whole of the United Provinces and Upper Bengal, and is found, though in smaller numbers, in the Punjab south of the Chenab, in eastern Rajputana and parts of the Central Provinces. It is a strictly resident species.

Habits, etc.—In the area which it inhabits the Sarus Crane is well known, as a pair may be found in every jheel and tank of importance and in suitable stretches of rice-fields. They never perch anywhere except on the ground. The birds pair for life, and are very devoted and close companions, feeding together a few yards apart, and always flying in close company one slightly behind the other. So obvious is their affection that the legend has arisen, that if one of the pair is killed the other dies of a broken heart. They are never molested by the people for fear of ill-luck, and are in consequence very tame and confiding. If caught young they become delightful pets, and kept loose in a garden make most efficient watch-dogs. The food consists of vegetable matter, insects, reptiles and molluscs.

Normally when feeding they are silent, but if disturbed in any way they give vent to a loud trumpet-like call which is also uttered freely on the wing. The flight is strong with regular rhythmic beats of the huge wings, but the birds seldom rise high above the ground, travelling as a rule within easy gun-shot.

FIG. 84—Sarus Crane ($\frac{1}{16}$ nat. size)

In the breeding season the pair frequently indulge in a striking dance, spreading their wings and lowering their heads and leaping into the air, trumpeting loudly the while. When disturbed at the nest the female lowers her head and walks away slowly in a crouching attitude.

The main breeding season is in the rains from July to September, though occasional nests may be found in other months.

The nest is a huge irregular mass of reeds, rushes and straw pulled up by the roots, and therefore much mixed with mud; it is built on the ground in the middle of a rice-field or patch of swamp, and is often surrounded by shallow water. There is usually no attempt at concealment, the sitting bird being visible some distance off.

One to three eggs are laid, but two are the normal number. The eggs are elongated ovals, a good deal pointed towards the small end. The shell is very hard and strong, pitted with small pores, and fairly glossy; flaws in the shell are common. The ground-colour varies from pure white to pinkish cream-colour or pale greenish. Some eggs are unmarked, but the majority are more or less spotted, blotched or clouded with pale yellowish-brown, purple, or purplish-pink, though the markings are seldom heavy.

The eggs measure between 3·5 and 4·5 inches in length, and 2·35 and 2·75 inches in breadth.

THE LIKH FLORIKEN

SYPHEOTIDES INDICA (Miller)

Description.—Length, male 18 inches; female 20 inches.

Male in breeding plumage: A tuft of narrow ribbon-like black feathers about 4 inches long, spatulate at the ends and curved upwards, behind each ear; head, neck and lower plumage black except for the chin and part of the throat which are white; a white band across the base of the hind neck; back and inner portion of the wings black with fine whitish mottling and arrow-marks, the black disappearing on the sides of the wings except for a bar; quills dark brown, all but the outmost banded with ochraceous-yellow, which is largely mottled with black; tail whitish, buff towards the base, mottled with black at the end and barred with black.

Male in winter plumage and female: Top of the head black, streaked with buff, and with a pale central band; head and neck finely vermiculated with black, the markings coarser on the sides; back black, mottled with sandy-buff and with buff arrow-markings; sides of the wings sandy-buff with irregular black bars; quills dark brown, all but the outermost banded with ochraceous-yellow, which is largely mottled with black; tail yellow-buff with black bars and mottled with black towards the tips, the central feathers mottled throughout; chin and throat white; fore-neck and upper breast buff with black streaks ; remainder of lower plumage buffy-white, the long feathers under the wings black.

Iris pale yellow, clouded with dusky in the male ; bill yellowish, dusky along the top ; legs dirty whitish-yellow.

Weight : male 14 oz. to 1 lb. 4 oz. ; female 1 lb. 2 oz. to 1 lb. 10 oz.

The bill, neck and legs are rather long.

Field Identification.—A small, long-legged Bustard, sandy-buff and blackish in colour, the male in the breeding season becoming black

FIG. 85—Likh Floriken (⅓ nat. size)

and white with graceful curved plumes behind the ears. Found chiefly in grassy plains, and has a curious habit of jumping into the air above the grass.

Distribution.—Confined to India. Its main stronghold is in the drier portions of the Peninsula lying east of the Western Ghats and south and east of the Godavari. It has not been recorded from the North-west Frontier Province or the Northern and Western Punjab or east of the Bay of Bengal, but within these limits it may be found in almost every part of India, even Lower Nepal and Baluchistan (where specimens have been obtained), though, as it is locally migratory and an irregular wanderer dependent on conditions of rainfall, its appearances are often erratic.

The larger Bengal Floriken (*Sypheotides bengalensis*) is very similarly coloured, but in place of the curious ear-plumes the male has a full crest and the feathers of the chin, throat and lower neck conspicuously elongated. This species is resident in the country between the base of the Himalayas and the Ganges and in the plain of Assam, being most common in the grasslands of the Terai. In the more desert country of North-west India the common Bustard is the Houbara (*Chlamydotis undulata*) which is a winter visitor from September to March. This species has a thick ruff of black and white feathers down each side of the neck. The lower parts are white. Beautiful bluish-grey bars run through the tail.

The Great Indian Bustard (*Choriotis nigriceps*), a huge bird with a black cap and whitish neck weighing up to 40 lb., is mostly found in North-west India.

Habits, etc.—This beautiful little Bustard is usually found singly in wide grassy plains or in crops of standing grain, and though numbers often occur in such localities they do not join into flocks. It may also be found in any other form of crop which is dry under foot, and neither too dense to make walking difficult nor too high to prevent it readily taking to flight. It of course never settles or feeds elsewhere than on the ground. In the cover that it frequents it is not shy, usually rising for the first time when disturbed, within easy shot; but after having been once flushed and allowed to settle again, it is difficult to find a second time, for it either runs some distance from the spot where it settled or else squats closely hidden on the ground.

On the wing it flies with a rather peculiar wheeling flight with quick wing-beats, but does not usually rise very high into the air.

The food consists chiefly of grasshoppers, but other insects, grain, seeds and tender shoots are also eaten.

The main breeding season is from August to October, but as the bird is essentially a " rains breeder," it is very irregular in its season and many nests are found earlier and later. It should, however, be clearly stated that wherever the bird appears as a rains visitor it is almost certainly breeding, and sportsmen who shoot this bird in the rains (as is unfortunately too common a custom) should understand that they are materially contributing to the extinction of a magnificent game-bird whose numbers are already seriously diminished.

The most marked characteristic of the species is its habit of suddenly jumping off the ground into the air above the grass, a habit that by revealing its often unsuspected presence, greatly adds to the ease with which its destruction is encompassed. This is done sometimes by the female, but the vast majority of the jumping birds are males, and as they jump they utter a guttural croak similar to that of a frog or to the noise of two sticks being hit together. The habit may be considered as a nuptial display. It is believed that the birds do not pair but that the males have each a particular territory, and that the females wander about until they succumb to the fascinations of a male and then lay and incubate their eggs and rear the young without his help. If this view is correct, the male would seem to jump to reveal his presence in the long grass and his readiness to court any female that has wandered into his territory.

No nest is made, the eggs being deposited on the ground in some thin patch in a field of grass. Two to five eggs are laid, but the normal clutch consists of four.

The egg is a very broad oval with only a slight difference between the two ends. The shell is stout and smooth, closely pitted with minute pores, and usually with a good deal of gloss.

The ground-colour varies from clear green to darkish olive-brown; the markings consist of cloudy streaks of brown of different shades, varying a good deal in intensity, but as a rule more marked towards the broad end.

In size they average about 1·88 by 1·59 inches.

THE STONE-CURLEW

BURHINUS ŒDICNEMUS (Linnæus)

Description.—Length 16 inches. Sexes alike. Upper parts ashy-brown to sandy-buff, the edges of the feathers rufescent, and the shafts with black stripes; a dark streak through the eye with a creamy streak above and another below it; a dark moustachial streak; sides of the wings brown marked with white and black, and with indistinct white and black bars across the wing; quills blackish-brown enclosing a white patch; tail ashy-brown, all the feathers except the middle pair with blackish tips, each crossed by a subterminal white bar; lower parts white, fore-neck and a patch under the tail pale rufous, the breast region streaked with dark brown.

Iris bright yellow; bill black, yellow about the base; legs yellow.

The head is large with a high forehead and very large eyes; the legs are long and bare, with only three toes, the nail of the middle toe dilated on the inner side; wings long and pointed; tail slightly rounded.

Field Identification.—A streaked-looking brown bird with long bare legs and a large head with huge yellow eyes; in flight a conspicuous white patch in the wings. Found running on sandy or stony ground.

Distribution.—The Stone-Curlew is widely distributed in Central and Southern Europe, in Northern and Eastern Africa, and in Asia.

It is divided into several races, of which two only appear in India. *B. œ. indicus* is the resident form which is found virtually throughout India, Ceylon and Burma. A pale desert race, *B. œ. sahariæ*, found in Africa, Transcaspia and Eastern Persia, partly replaces it in Baluchistan and Sind and the Punjab.

The Great Stone-Plover (*Esacus recurvirostris*) is resident in the wide sandy beds of the larger rivers of the plains of India, Burma and Ceylon. It is larger than the Stone-Curlew with a heavier beak and is greyer and more uniform in coloration, dark bands on the head and shoulder being conspicuous by contrast.

Habits, etc.—The Stone-Curlew, Norfolk-Plover or Thick-knee

FIG. 86—Stone-Curlew (¼ nat. size)

(as it is variously called) is somewhat locally distributed in India on account of its special requirements in the way of habitat. The country that it inhabits must be dry with patches of scrub and low jungle, or with large groves and dry jheels studded with tufts of grass ; in such localities it frequents the open wastes and ploughed fields, and it is also particularly partial to the huge old mango topes, which are characteristic of parts of India, surrounded with mud walls and thinly planted so as to be also reserves for grass.

This bird is strictly a ground species, and is largely nocturnal, as is suggested by the large eyes. Usually found singly or in pairs, it collects at times into parties. Owing to its shyness and protective coloration it generally escapes notice until it suddenly takes to wing in front of the observer ; it flies swiftly, low over the ground, with the long yellow legs outstretched behind, and in its manner of flight and with the conspicuous white patches in the wings it recalls the appearance of a Bustard. On the ground it runs rapidly in little bursts with short pattering steps, with the head lowered and the neck retracted in a thoroughly shame-faced manner. At times it squats, with the body pressed to the ground and the head and neck outstretched. The call is a loud *curlivee*, very eerie and plaintive in tone, which is usually uttered at dusk or during the hours of night.

The breeding season varies from February to August, but most eggs are laid about April.

The nest is a mere scrape on the ground, often amongst dry leaves or near the base of a bush or tuft of grass. Two or very rarely three eggs are laid. The egg is a broad oval, rather obtuse at both ends; the texture is fine and hard, but normally without gloss. The ground-colour is yellowish-white or buffy-brown; the markings are spots and specks, streaks and blotches of deep olive-brown or black, combined in an endless variety of designs over the surface of the egg; there are a few secondary markings of pale inky-purple.

In size the eggs average 1·9 by 1·39 inches.

In this species as in most of the Plovers and Waders the "incubation patches" are found in a lateral position instead of in the normal central position. These patches, which are physiological in origin, are produced by a local moult with a local increase of blood supply and serve to raise the temperature of the brooded eggs.

THE INDIAN COURSER

CURSORIUS COROMANDELICUS (Gmelin)

(Plate xx, Fig. 4, opposite page 418)

Description.—Length 9 inches. Sexes alike. Top of the head chestnut, darker behind where elongated feathers conceal a black spot; long white streaks over the eyes, meeting behind on the nape, and bordered throughout below by a black band; a rufous collar behind the black; upper plumage sandy-brown; wing-quills black, the innermost passing through grey and white into the colour of the back; a white patch on the base of the tail; central tail-feathers sandy-brown, the others grey-brown at the base, then black and tipped with white, the white increasing outwards till the outermost pair are quite white; chin white; neck and breast rufous passing into chestnut on the lower breast with a black patch on the upper abdomen; flanks and a patch under the tail white.

Iris dark brown; bill black; legs dead china-white.

The bill is slender, curved and pointed; wings pointed and tail short and square; legs long with three toes.

Field Identification.—A small Plover-like bird with long white legs which is found running rapidly on open sandy ground; the white eye-streaks bordered below with black and contrasting with the chestnut crown, and the chestnut breast and black belly are conspicuous.

Distribution.—This species is found in Africa and in India as well as in the extreme north of Ceylon. In India it is found in suitable areas from the base of the Himalayas right through the Peninsula, but it is rare on the Malabar coast and in Lower Bengal. Birds from India and Ceylon all belong to the typical race. On the West it extends to about the line of the Indus Valley though it is scarce in Northern Sind and the West and North-west Punjab, where it is replaced by the Cream-coloured Courser (*C. cursor*), which lacks the chestnut breast and black belly. A resident species.

Habits, etc.—The Indian Courser is a bird of dry open, more or less bare and moderately watered tracts, frequenting patches of barren stony land, or cultivation that is lying fallow. In such localities the Courser will be found, in pairs if breeding, in small parties at other seasons, running and feeding on the ground. When feeding this bird has curious and characteristic movements, as owing to the long legs, it has to dip down very suddenly and completely to reach the ground, with usually a quick run of several mincing steps between the dips. When disturbed the bird rises with a distinctive note and the wings look very pointed, the flight being strong and straight with marked beats of the wings. It does not as a rule fly very far before settling again, and then it runs swiftly in little spurts ; but when danger really threatens it can fly very high, fast and strongly, and no Falcon can take this little Plover on the wing.

The food largely consists of the small black beetles that are found on the dry ground that this species frequents. Weevils, ants, caterpillars and other larvæ and small molluscs are also eaten.

The breeding season lasts from March to July. The nest is a mere scrape on the ground, sometimes in the middle of a bare plain, at other times under a tuft of grass or low bush in stunted, straggling jungle on a dry plateau or faintly marked ridge.

The clutch consists of two or three eggs.

The eggs are almost spherical, of fine texture and without gloss. The ground-colour varies from cream to bright buff ; the markings consist of mottlings, clouds and spots of pale inky-grey, overlaid with lines, scratches, spots and streaks of blackish-brown, black, and rich olive.

The average size is 1·19 by 0·97 inches.

THE LITTLE INDIAN PRATINCOLE

GLAREOLA LACTEA Temminck

Description.—Length 7 inches. Sexes alike. Upper plumage pale sandy-grey; forehead brown, and a band from the eye to the beak black; outer quills blackish, gradually growing white inwards; tail and its coverts white, blackish towards the end, the black area longest on the central feathers, which lack the brown and white tips of the other feathers; lower plumage smoky-brown tinged with rufous, becoming white from the lower breast downwards; wing-lining black.

Iris dark brown; bill black, basal half red, yellowish-brown at gape; legs black.

The bill is short and curved with a wide gape; wings long and narrow; legs short, the hind toe raised above the level of the others, the middle and outer toes united by a small web.

Field Identification.—River bird, occasionally visiting jheels; found in big flocks; on the wing rather like a large brown Swallow, with black-tipped white tail and pointed dark wings, flying rapidly over the surface of water.

Distribution.—This Pratincole or Swallow-Plover is found in India, Ceylon, Burma, and Assam. It is practically confined in India to the beds of the various large rivers such as the Indus, Ganges, and Brahmaputra with their tributary rivers, so far as they continue to be broad streams with wide sand-banks, flowing peacefully when not in flood. It is locally migratory.

Habits, etc.—This quaint little bird is found about the sand-banks of the larger and more placid rivers, and only occasionally leaves them for an evening flight to open jheels in the vicinity. It is invariably found in large colonies, which are social in all the incidents of their life, breeding in large numbers together, and feeding in large flocks which skim about the surface of rivers and jheels, catching insects on the wing. In their flight, appearance and habits they well deserve the name of Swallow-Plover; to the uninitiated they might easily appear to be larger relatives of the flocks of Swallows that are often found under similar conditions. The flight is swift and graceful, and a curious low, rather harsh, note is freely uttered. In the evenings the flocks usually feed flying up stream, and on occasions they mount high up into the air and might easily be mistaken for a flock of Swifts.

The breeding season lasts from March to May. The birds nest in large colonies on island sand-banks or on the sandy margins of the rivers, and these colonies are frequently wiped out wholesale by temporary rises in the river-level. These inundations appear to be the only check on the undue increase of the birds, as they have no enemies to prey on them. Terns, Scissorsbills and various Plovers nest in close proximity to the Pratincoles.

The nests are mere hollows scraped in the sand, often through a hard crust that forms when alluvial mud has been deposited on top of the sand. They are placed either in the open or in the shade of the small tufts of tamarisk that grow on most of the sand-banks. To approach a colony is to provoke a scene of wholesale alarm. Some of the birds skim round about uttering their curious note, others flutter down on to the sand and there gasp and flutter, now lying

FIG. 87—Little Indian Pratincole (⅓ nat. size)

exhausted with outspread wings, now dragging themselves along in all the apparent throes of a mortal wound; more consummate acting to divert the intruder from the nests could hardly be imagined.

The eggs vary in number from two to four. They are broad ovals, pointed at one end; the texture is close but somewhat chalky and devoid of gloss. The ground-colour varies from pale greenish-white to pale fawn and stone-colour; the markings consist of spots, streaks, blotches, lines and clouds of olive, reddish-brown or purple, but the eggs are usually finely and lightly marked and blend fairly well with the sand on which they lie.

In size they average about 1·05 by 0·88 inches.

THE BRONZE-WINGED JACANA

METOPIDIUS INDICUS (Latham)

Description.—Length 11 inches. Sexes alike. Head, neck and lower parts to the abdomen black, glossed with dark green, the lower hind neck with a purple gloss; a white line over the eye and a white spot beneath it; back and wings olive-bronze, the flight-feathers black, glossed with dark green; lower back to the tail and its coverts chestnut, the tail-feathers darker; lower abdomen and thighs dull blackish-brown.

Iris brown; bill greenish-yellow, reddish at base, and a broad lappet at its base on the forehead livid; legs dull green.

The wing has a small tubercular spur at the bend; the toes are long with long straight claws, the claw of the hind toe being particularly exaggerated.

Field Identification.—A Rail-like bird with disproportionately long toes and claws which is found walking on weeds and plants on the surface of water. Blackish in colour with a bronze back and a short chestnut tail, easily distinguished from the Pheasant-tailed Jacana by this last feature.

Distribution.—This is a widely-spread bird found in India, Assam and Burma, extending through the Malay Peninsula to Siam, Sumatra, Java and Celebes. In India it is not found in the north-west at all, but is very common in the moister districts of Oudh, the Sub-Himalayan Terais of Rohilkhand and Gorakhpur and through most of Bengal, occurring also southwards through the Central Provinces and the Peninsula generally. It does not ascend any of the hill ranges, and it is a resident species.

Habits, etc.—The Bronze-winged Jacana is purely a water-bird, never frequenting rivers but living exclusively in jheels and swamps, especially those in which the surface of the water is paved and hidden from view by the leaves of the lotus and other water plants, with deep reed-beds along the sides. For life in such surroundings it is specially adapted, the toes being elongated and the claws straight and of great length, affording a snowshoe-like surface which allows the bird to move about on water, walking over the broad flat lotus leaves and the flimsiest of other weeds. It can swim and dive well when necessary, but in the choked waters that it frequents walking is a more valuable accomplishment for it. Although a well-known species, living often in ponds close to houses, it is rather shy, and when alarmed will conceal itself by lying close on the weeds with the head and neck well stretched out on a level with the body. It also, for more effectual concealment, will half submerge its body in the water. The food consists of vegetable matter, and also of insects, larvæ, molluscs and crustacea. It has a peculiar harsh cry.

The breeding season is in the rains from June to September. The nest is generally rather large, composed of rushes and water-weed twisted round and round to form a circular pad, with a depression for the eggs in the centre. It is placed in a well-sheltered spot, usually amongst thickly growing lotus leaves, either on the surface of the water or on the edge of an island.

The clutch normally consists of four eggs, but more are occasionally found.

The eggs are moderately broad ovals, a good deal pointed at one end, and of fine hard texture. They have the most brilliant gloss of all Indian eggs; so brilliant indeed that persons who are shown them for the first time will hardly credit the gloss with being natural in origin.

The ground-colour varies from pale stone-brown to deep rufous or olive-brown. The markings vary from reddish-brown to blackish-brown and black, and consist of the most inextricable network of lines, some fine, some coarse, evenly dispersed over the whole surface.

In size they average about 1·47 by 1·03 inches.

THE PHEASANT-TAILED JACANA

HYDROPHASIANUS CHIRURGUS (Scopoli)

Description.—Length: Male 12 inches, 6 inches longer in summer with the long tail plumes; female larger, total length with plumes in summer 21 inches. Sexes alike.

Winter plumage: Upper plumage brown, speckled with white on the forehead and hind neck; a white line over the eye, and from it a pale brownish-yellow band runs down the side of the neck, bordered below by a blackish band from the beak which expands into a broad gorget across the breast; remainder of lower plumage and outer tail-feathers white; central tail-feathers brown; wings whity-brown barred with dark brown, a white patch on the sides, the outer quills black, gradually becoming white inwards.

Summer plumage: Head and front of the neck white; a patch on the nape and a narrow line down each side of the neck black enclosing a patch of pale shining golden-yellow on the hind neck; the whole body chocolate brown, glossy on the upper parts; tail and a patch above it blackish; sides and underneath of the wings white, the quills as in winter.

Iris pale yellow; bill bluish in summer, in winter dark brown with the base yellow; legs pale plumbeous in summer, dull greenish in winter.

There is a strong sharp spur on the bend of the wing; the first flight-feather ends in a curious lanceolate appendage, and the fourth flight-feather in an attenuated point; the central tail-feathers are long and pointed in summer plumage. The toes are very long with long claws.

Field Identification.—A Rail-like bird with disproportionately long toes and claws which is found walking on weeds and plants on the surface of water. Distinguish from the Bronze-winged Jacana by the large amount of white in the wings in flight and in the breeding season by the long central tail-feathers.

Distribution.—This Jacana has a wider distribution than the last species, being found throughout India, Ceylon and Burma, and farther eastwards as far as South China, the Philippines, and Java. In India it is very generally distributed, occurring in the Himalayas

FIG. 88—Pheasant-tailed Jacana Summer plumage (1/3 nat. size)

commonly on the Kashmir lakes at 5000 feet and straggling up to 12,000 feet; to the west it reaches Baluchistan. While for the most part resident it is also partly migratory.

Habits, etc.—The Pheasant-tailed Jacana agrees with the Bronze-winged species in being adapted by its configuration to a purely aquatic life. It lives on tanks, marshes and lakes, where thickets of reeds and lotus and other floating plants occur, over which the long toes and claws allow it to walk at its ease; but it differs from the latter species in being less shy, more ready to frequent open water, and more accustomed to wander to flood water, streams, and similar spots free of weeds on which the Bronze-wing is never found. Although not strictly speaking a social species, many will be found on the same piece of water.

This bird rather resembles the Pond Heron in its capacity for startling the unobservant. Standing on submerged weeds in the water it easily escapes observation until it rises with a sudden startling flash of the white wings, flitting away over the water with a Wader-like flight until it settles again, and once more becomes invisible.

It has a very curious mewing call which might easily pass for that of an angry cat. It feeds on fresh-water molluscs and vegetable matter.

The breeding season is in the rains from June to August. The nest varies; sometimes it is a mass of weeds and rushes heaped together on a small island or in the water amongst thick grass or growing rice. At other times it is a floating structure of weed and grass barely able to contain the eggs which look almost as if they were floating in the water. In either case the eggs are half-immersed in the sun-warmed water, and its heat with that of the decaying vegetation must materially assist the process of incubation.

This species lays a clutch of four eggs which are arranged with the smaller ends fitting inwards like a clutch of Plover's eggs.

The eggs are markedly pyriform in shape with a compact and hard texture and a bright gloss. They are without markings, and when fresh are of a rich deep bronze colour, with either a rufous or greenish tinge; but as incubation progresses they bleach sadly under the combined influence of sun and water.

In size they average about 1·46 by 1·12 inches.

THE RED-WATTLED LAPWING

Lobivanellus indicus (Boddaert)

(Plate xxi, Fig. 3, opposite page 440)

Description.—Length 13 inches. Sexes alike. Head, neck and upper breast black, except for a broad white band from each eye which passes down the sides of the neck and joins the white lower parts; upper plumage and wings brown, glossed with greenish-bronze and slightly with red; a white wing-bar; the greater part of the flight-feathers black; sides of the lower back, rump and upper tail-coverts white; tail white with a broad black subterminal band, the central feathers having this band bordered on both sides with brown, the other feathers with white tips.

Iris red-brown, eyelids and a conspicuous wattle in front of the eye lake-red; bill red, tip black; legs bright yellow.

The wing has a tubercle at the bend which becomes a horny spur in the breeding season; legs long with small hind toe.

Field Identification.—A tame familiar Plover found in pairs, which rise with a loud *did-he-do-it*; brown above, white below with conspicuous black and white head and neck and long yellow legs; a marked red facial wattle.

It must not be confused with the Spur-wing Plover (*Hoplopterus duvaucelii*) which is confined to the beds of the larger rivers as far south as the Godavery but excluding the Indus drainage. This has no red-wattle, the black of the throat does not reach the breast and a black patch on the shoulder and a black horse-shoe on the belly are distinctive. The curious horny spur on the bend of the wing is not visible in the field.

Distribution.—The Red-wattled Lapwing has a wide distribution from Mesopotamia throughout India, Ceylon and Burma to Cochin-China, the Malay Peninsula and Sumatra. It is divided into races, of which two come into our area. The typical race is found throughout Southern India and in Ceylon, occurring in the Nilgiris up to about 6000 feet; *L. i. aigneri*, a slightly larger and paler bird with less bronze sheen, is found in Northern India generally, occurring in the Himalayas far into the inner valleys up to 6000 feet. It is a resident species.

The familiar Green Plover or Peewit (*Vanellus vanellus*) of Europe is a common winter visitor to North-west India in flocks, usually found on damp ground. The combination of peculiar long narrow pointed crest, black breast, greenish upper parts and patch of chestnut at the base of the tail are distinctive, as are the broad rounded wings and pied appearance in flight.

Habits, etc.—This long-legged Plover avoids both purely desert country and thick forest, but is otherwise a familiar bird throughout India, though it prefers open cultivation and the outskirts of tanks and jheels. It is found usually in pairs, and the birds seem conscious of the fact that their striking coloration is of the "obliterative" type, and by remaining motionless they frequently escape the notice of the passer-by. They, of course, never perch on trees, and when disturbed they do not fly far, but settle again quickly and then run a few steps; but the long wings are capable of a strong and sustained flight when required, and good sport may be obtained by flying trained falcons at this species. The call is a series of loud shrill notes well expressed by the words, *did-he-do-it pity-to-do-it* usually uttered on the wing when the bird is disturbed. Another common note sounds much like the syllable *ping*.

The breeding season is somewhat extended from March to August, but the majority of eggs are laid in May and June. The nest is placed on the ground in almost any open ground provided that water is reasonably near; a slightly elevated situation is often chosen, such as on a grave or small mound, and numbers of nests are placed on the ballast of railway lines; occasionally the nest is placed on the flat roof of a house.

The nest is a circular depression scraped in the soil, and it is sometimes encircled with small stones or pieces of hard clay.

The clutch consists of four eggs. They are pyriform, that is, broad and obtuse at one end and much pointed at the other. The ground-colour varies from pale olive-green to yellowish or reddish-buff. The texture is close and a little chalky with very little gloss. The markings of deep brown or black thickly cover the surface with blotches, streaks, spots and clouds, evenly distributed.

In size the eggs average about 1·65 by 1·2 inches.

THE YELLOW-WATTLED LAPWING

Lobipluvia malabarica (Boddaert)

Description.—Length 10 inches. Sexes alike. Top of the head and neck black, bordered behind the eyes with a white line; chin black; rest of the head, neck, upper breast, back, wing-coverts and inner flight-feathers light brown; wing-quills black, the bases of the outer feathers white on the inner webs, the white increasing on the inner flight-feathers and forming a white bar with the tips of the largest coverts; a patch above the tail white; tail white, lightly washed with brown, with a broad black band near the tip which gradually disappears on the outer feathers; lower parts from the breast white.

Iris silver, grey or pale yellow; bill black, yellow at base; wattle pale yellow; legs yellow, claws black.

A fleshy wattle in front of each eye, meeting above the beak and with a lappet descending on each side of the gape. Legs long and slender. No hind toe.

Field Identification.—Peninsular India. A quiet brown-looking Plover with black crown, white belly and wing-bar and long yellow legs; facial wattle yellow. Found in dry open country but not true desert. Smaller than Red-wattled Lapwing and easily distinguished from it by the colour of the wattle and by having the throat and breast light brown not glossy black.

Distribution.—Restricted to India and Ceylon. In India it is found in suitable country throughout the Peninsula up to the base of the Himalayas. On the east it extends to Calcutta and Dacca. On the west it ranges as far as the Sutlej in the Punjab and Karachi in Lower Sind, though it is absent from most of the desert country between those two areas. A resident species with some local migrations.

Mention should just be made of the Eastern Golden Plover (*Pluvialis dominica*), with its upper plumage brown spangled with golden-yellow, which is an abundant winter visitor to Assam and parts of Eastern India, occurring less commonly in other areas across the Peninsula: of the Sociable Plover (*Chettusia gregaria*), a nondescript brown and white bird in winter plumage which occurs commonly in flocks in open country: and of the White-tailed Lapwing (*Chettusia leucura*), a slender brown, black and white Plover which is a jheel-haunting species. Both of the latter are common in Northern India in winter, growing scarcer southwards.

Habits, etc.—The Yellow-wattled Lapwing is a bird of dry and open country where it is found on waste land and ploughed fields. In such areas it may be met in twos and threes or small parties feeding on the ground and searching for beetles, grubs, insects, white ants and similar food. Unlike the Red-wattled Lapwing it avoids the neighbourhood of water. The call is a plaintive *dee-wit dee-wit*, much less harsh and loud than that of the last species and the bird is altogether less demonstrative.

The breeding season lasts from March till the end of June, but most eggs are to be found in April and May.

The nest is usually made in the open without any attempt at concealment, and a ploughed field affords a favourite situation. The nest is a small circular depression in the ground, scooped out by the bird and entirely unlined. It is some 3 or 4 inches in diameter and an inch in depth and is often deepened by the addition of a little earth or tiny pieces of kunkur being scraped up against the margin all round.

The clutch consists of four eggs. They are pyriform, that is, broad and obtuse at one end and sharply pointed at the other, so that when they are arranged in the nest with the points inward to a common centre they take up the minimum of room—an admirable provision of nature which allows eggs large for the size of the bird to be satisfactorily brooded by it. This arrangement is common in the Plover family and is of course necessitated by the fact that the young Plover is hatched in an advanced stage of development and is able to run at birth.

The egg is of hard texture with no gloss. The ground-colour varies from buff to pale greenish or olive stone-colour, and it is fairly thickly studded with spots, streaks and blotches of deep brown, interspersed with spots and streaks of pale olive-brown and dingy inky-purple.

It measures about 1·45 by 1·07 inches.

THE LITTLE RING-PLOVER

CHARADRIUS DUBIUS Scopoli

(Plate xxii, Fig. 3, opposite page 462)

Description.—Length 6 inches. Sexes alike. A black band from the forehead through the eye to the ear-coverts, joined by a broader black band from the eyes over the top of the head, encloses a white band on the forehead; chin, throat and a broad collar round the neck

PLATE XXII

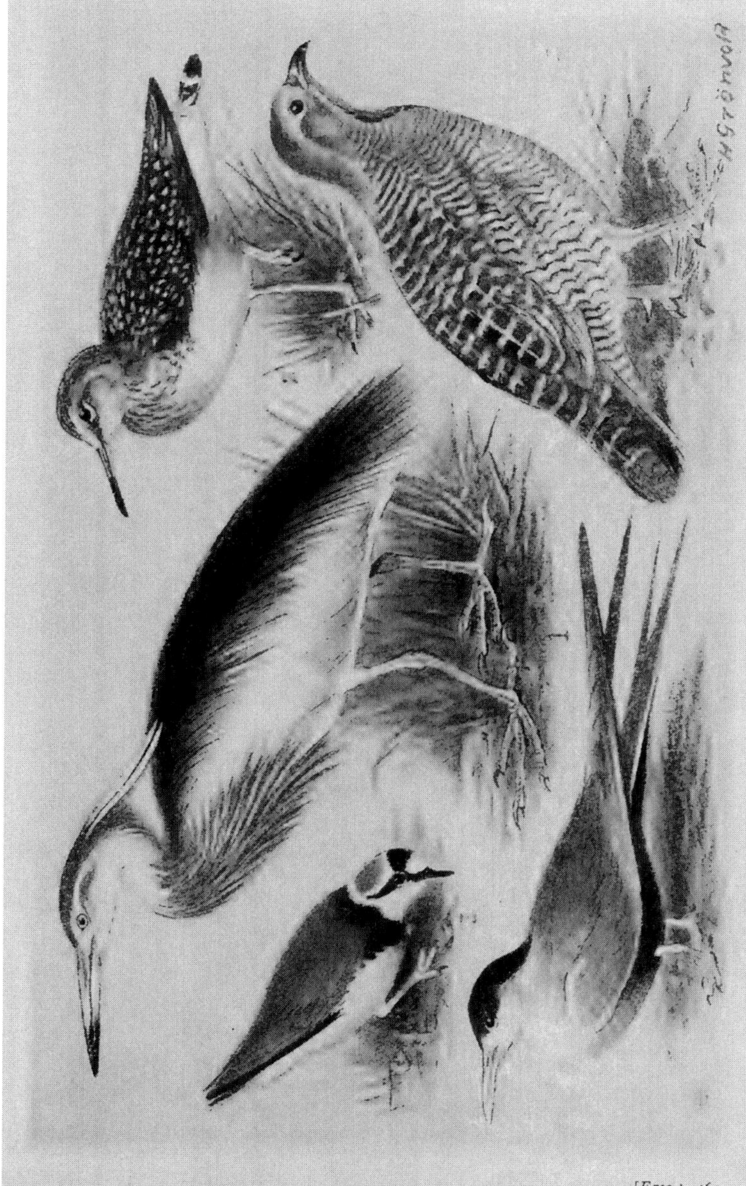

1. Paddy-bird. 2. Green Sandpiper. 3. Little Ring-Plover. 4. Black-bellied Tern. 5. Grey Partridge. (All about $\frac{1}{5}$ nat. size.)

[Face p. 462

white, the white running up behind the black bands; remainder of upper plumage brown; quills dark brown, the outermost blackish and the inner ones tipped with white; tail brown, darker towards the end, all except the central pair tipped with white, growing more extensive outwardly; lower plumage and wing-lining white.

Iris dark brown, eye-rim yellow; bill black, yellow at base; legs yellow, claws black.

The head and eyes are rather large; the wing is pointed and long; there is no hind toe.

Field Identification.—A very small Plover usually found on sandy or stony ground near water. Black bands on the head and breast divided by a white ring round the neck stand out in contrast with the brown upper parts. The swift flight is emphasised by sharply-pointed wings.

Distribution.—The Little Ring-Plover is distributed widely throughout Europe, Asia and Northern Africa. It is divided into three races, of which we are concerned with two. *Charadrius d. curonicus* breeds in Europe and North-western Africa, eastwards to Northern Asia and Kashmir. It winters in Africa, India, Ceylon and the Malayan Archipelago, arriving in India about August and leaving in April and May. *Charadrius d. jerdoni*, a smaller race, is the breeding bird throughout India up to the Himalayan foothills, found also in Borneo and New Guinea. It is probably a local migrant only.

The Kentish Plover (*Leucopolius alexandrinus*) is a winter visitor to the seashore and the sandy margins of rivers, jheels and tanks throughout India. It also breeds in Baluchistan, Sind, Cutch, and Ceylon. About the same size as the Little Ring-Plover, it lacks the black band on the breast and in breeding plumage has the crown rusty fulvous.

Habits, etc.—The Little Ring-Plover is essentially a bird of the sandy and stony margins of rivers and streams wherever they are fairly wide, and of the dried mud flats that form round the edges of drying jheels and swamps; it also wanders temporarily to various types of ground, where the presence of rubbish or the drying up of temporary ponds and inundations produces an abundant supply of flies and other insects that form its food. It perches nowhere except on the ground, and there it spends most of its time seeking for food and walking with dainty steps and little short runs, and bobbing down with a curious characteristic movement to pick up food. On the approach of an intruder it runs rapidly over the ground, largely escaping notice with its mixture of protective and obliterative plumage, the brown upper parts blending with the colour of the ground, and the black and yellow markings tending to break up the shape of the bird. Once compelled to take to wing it flies rapidly low over the ground with a wheeling motion, the pointed wings beating rapidly, and as it flies it utters a sharp plaintive pipe or whistle. This note is particularly marked in the breeding season, when it is uttered in the course of the fast flight round and about the female which forms part of the courting display, and which also is adopted as a relief to outraged nerves when the nest is in danger.

In the display proper the feathers on both sides of the breast are fluffed out and the tail is spread into a broad fan. At this period the male is very pugnacious and chases away other species of small birds from the vicinity of the nest.

Except when breeding, this Plover is usually found in small parties, of which the members run about independently on the ground, but at once unite when they take to wing.

In India the breeding season is from March to May. The nest is a slight depression scraped amongst sand or fine pebbles, generally in the bed of a small river or stream, or on the sand-banks of the large rivers.

The clutch consists of four eggs. They are broad ovals, very sharply pointed towards the small end. The shell is very fine and compact, but virtually without gloss. The ground-colour varies from buffish stone-colour to pale greenish-grey, and the markings consist of fine spots and speckles and fantastic little lines of brownish-purple or black, together with a few secondary markings of very pale inky-purple. The markings are generally and evenly distributed, except that they tend to be more numerous round the broad end.

The egg measures about 1·14 by 0·84 inches.

THE BLACK-WINGED STILT

HIMANTOPUS HIMANTOPUS (Linnæus)

Description.—Length 15 inches. Male in winter:—the plumage is white except as follows: Top of the head and the upper back sullied with brown bases to the feathers and a few dark tips; the wings and the back between them black, glossed with metallic green; the tail and its upper coverts sullied with drab grey.

In summer plumage the under parts are suffused with a rosy tint, and the top of the head becomes black and white in varying degrees.

The female has the black back and wings sullied with brown, and does not attain the rosy tint.

Iris red; bill black; legs lake-red, claws black.

The bill is long, straight and slender, the neck is long, the wings long and pointed; the legs are very long with the tibia bare for a great proportion of its length; there is no hind toe and the three front toes are partly joined with webs.

Field Identification.—A slender black and white bird with long straight beak and absurdly long red legs, always found wading in water. It can only be confused with the Avocet (*Recurvirostra avocetta*), which has the long beak curved sharply upwards.

Distribution.—A widely distributed species, the typical form occurring in Southern Europe, Africa and Central and Southern Asia, and being represented by other races in America, Australia, New Zealand and Ceylon. Some individuals are resident and breed in North-western India, in Kashmir, the Punjab, Sind, Sambhar Lake and Baluchistan. Others are winter immigrants from the north, so that the bird is widely distributed in India throughout the plains in

FIG. 89—Black-winged Stilt (⅛ nat. size)

winter. The resident race in Ceylon, *H. h. ceylonensis*, has less black on the head in breeding plumage.

Three other slightly larger waders, all brownish in coloration with white under parts, require mention as common winter visitors to India and Ceylon. The Curlew (*Numenius arquata*), remarkable for its long down-curved beak and loud plaintive calls, a shrill *cour-lie* or a musical *quoy-quoy*, is found both on the seashore and about inland waters throughout India. Its smaller counterpart the Whimbrel (*Numenius phœopus*) is more common on the coast. The Black-tailed Godwit (*Limosa limosa*) with a long straight bill is found in flocks on jheels in Northern India only.

Habits, etc.—The Stilt is purely a water-bird, and is found in small parties which feed about the shallower portions of lakes, jheels and marshes, even condescending to visit village ponds and flooded cultivation. Owing to its long legs and long bill, it is able to wade out into deeper water than most waders, and therefore tap supplies of food that are not available to them ; and when so wading its mode of progression appears somewhat awkward, as for each step the long legs have to be drawn out of the water backwards to avoid its resistance, brought forward in the air and again deliberately placed in the water. Stilts occasionally associate with Avocets and Godwits, similarly long-legged birds, but they do not as a rule mix with the other waders. The food consists of minute seeds of water-plants, insects and small molluscs and worms. In flight the long legs are extended straight beyond the tail. The ordinary call is very reminiscent of that of a Tern, and the alarm-note is a shrill pipe. At the nest colonies the birds are very noisy and demonstrative, flying towards any intruder, and passing backwards and forwards over his head with loud cries, though when the actual site of the nest is reached they retire and alight at a distance.

The breeding season is from April to June. The birds nest in colonies in shallow flooded salt-pans or about the margins of jheels, and the nests are built actually in the water or on mud and ground beside it. The nest is a hollow, natural or artificial, on the ground, sometimes bare, at other times lined with pieces of kunkur or the sticks and other debris from flood-wreck.

The clutch consists of three or four eggs which greatly resemble those of the Red-wattled Lapwing.

The egg is a moderately broad oval, elongated and sometimes pyriform ; the texture is fine and compact with a slight gloss. The ground-colour is olive-brown, greenish stone-colour or creamy-buff ; the markings consist of specks, spots, blotches and streaks of black and rich umber-brown, with a tendency to collect about the broad end.

In size the eggs average about 1·64 by 1·13 inches.

THE COMMON SANDPIPER

TRINGA HYPOLEUCUS Linnæus

Description.—Length 8 inches. Sexes alike. Winter plumage : Upper plumage olive-brown and rather glossy, the feathers dark shafted, and except on the head and neck with pale tips and a dark subterminal bar ; the outer quills dark brown, the inner quills white with a broad subterminal brown band ; central tail-feathers like the back, the outer banded dark brown and white ; an indistinct pale line above the eye ; sides of the head, neck and breast ashy-brown with darker streaks ; lower plumage white, a few dark streaks on the fore-neck.

In summer plumage the upper parts are darker and more heavily marked, and the fore-neck and breast are more streaked with brown.

Iris brown ; bill greyish-brown darker at tip and greenish at base ; legs pale green.

The bill is long, straight and slender ; the front toes are slightly webbed.

Field Identification.—A small wader with a slender bill, upper parts unbroken glossy brown, lower parts white, which is found solitary, feeding about the edges of open water ; incessantly wags the short tail up and down, has a chittering call, and in flight beats the wings in a curious stiff manner.

Distribution.—The distribution of this Sandpiper includes the greater part of the Old World. It breeds from the Arctic circle to the Mediterranean Basin in Europe, and in Asia north of the Himalayas eastwards to Japan. In winter it migrates southwards to Africa, India, the East Indies, Australia and Tasmania.

Within our limits the bird breeds in Kashmir and Lahul, and in the winter it is common throughout the whole of India, arriving about August, and leaving in early May.

Habits, etc.—In India this graceful little Sandpiper is usually found as a solitary bird feeding along the sides of ponds, rivers and streams, of canals, and even along the seashore. Although well able to swim, dive or wade if the necessity arises, it prefers to feed exactly along the edge of the water, tripping along the margin of sand or mud, just dipping its toes in the water and picking its food from the surface of the shore. Hence it is seldom found in marshy ground with other waders, but shares with the Green Sandpiper the edges of tanks and village ponds. It is very busy and active, incessantly nodding its head and jerking its tail up and down ; and when it takes to flight flies low and swiftly just above the surface of the water with curious stiff, downward wing-beats, the wings appearing hardly to rise above the level of the back. A shrill note *dee-dee-dee* is usually uttered on the wing. In the breeding season this is developed into a regular song, *kitty-needie, kitty-needie, kittie-needie,* uttered as the bird soars and then descends on quivering wings, while a whole series of chittering, piping whistles betray the bird's agitation when the nest or young are approached.

The food consists of insects and their larvæ, sand-hoppers, fresh-water shrimps and other similar small organisms.

In the Himalayas the breeding season is in May or June. The nest is placed on the banks and islands of mountain rivers at a short distance from the water, where low bushes grow amongst the sand and stones. It is a slight hollow on the ground, sparsely lined with fragments of sticks or dead leaves.

The clutch consists of four eggs. The eggs are pyriform or

elongated ovals, rather pointed towards the small end; the texture is fine and close, and there is a slight gloss.

The ground-colour is a creamy stone-colour or buff; the markings consist of specks and spots and small clouds of rich red-brown, reddish-purple, and inky-purple, and they are not very dense though sometimes tending to form a cap at the broad end.

In size they average about 1·45 by 1·05 inches.

THE GREEN SANDPIPER

TRINGA OCHROPUS Linnæus

(Plate xxii, Fig. 2, opposite page 462)

Description.—Length 9 inches. Sexes alike. Winter plumage: Top of the head and hind neck brown with an ashy tinge; upper plumage brown with an olive tinge, the feathers of the back and shoulders edged with alternating white and dark spots; rump brown; a patch on the base of the tail white, the remainder of the tail white barred with dark brown, the bars disappearing on the outer feathers; lower plumage white, the sides of the neck and breast with narrow brown streaks; wing-lining brown barred with white.

In summer the upper plumage is spotted with buff and white, and the brown streaking of the lower plumage is more marked.

Iris brown; bill dusky green, blackish at the tip; legs dingy green.

The bill is long and slender, and the front toes are partly joined with a web.

Field Identification.—A solitary Sandpiper found in similar places to the Common Sandpiper but distinguished from it by the larger size, much darker upper parts, and by the conspicuous white tail barred in the middle towards the end with dark brown. It rises with a distinctive loud whistle. In the hand it may be identified by its peculiar musky smell.

Distribution.—The Green Sandpiper breeds in Europe and Asia north of a line roughly through Germany, Bohemia, Galicia, and across Russia to Transcaspia and Turkestan. In winter it migrates south to Africa, India, China and the Malay Archipelago. At this season it is very common in the plains of Northern India, though less abundant in the South. In the Himalayas it is a passage migrant, halting at water at any elevation. It commences to arrive in India at the end of July, and leaves again by the beginning of May. A few non-breeding birds summer in India.

The Wood-Sandpiper (*Tringa glareola*) found throughout India in winter is very similar to the Green Sandpiper. It differs chiefly in its slighter build and in the paler coloration and larger spotting of the upper parts so that in the field it does not appear so conspicuously black and white. The fact that the Wood-Sandpiper collects freely into flocks and the sharp alarm-note *giff giff giff*, repeated by several birds till it becomes a chittering whistle, should enable the two species to be distinguished fairly readily.

Habits, etc.—Except when on migration it sometimes collects into parties of three or four individuals, the Green Sandpiper is a solitary bird, and is very familiar owing to the fact that it drops in to feed along the margins of any pond or tank however small, visiting also jheels, irrigation channels and casual flood water; salt tidal waters, however, it avoids. It feeds along the edge of the water in the same manner and often the same place with the Common Sandpiper, its tail incessantly wagging up and down. It is a curious mixture of confidence and shyness, feeding busily in the close neighbourhood of man until disturbed, and then becoming wild and difficult of approach. It rises with a clear loud whistle *ti-tiu*, zigzagging sharply in its flight at first and then mounting high and flying right away or circling in the sky like a Snipe. Individuals have marked predilections for particular patches of water, and may be found at them day after day.

The Wood-Sandpiper and the Green Sandpiper between them provide a large proportion of the small unidentified waders which the sportsman in India is apt to describe collectively as "Snippets."

As indicated above, the Green Sandpiper does not breed within our limits. In its northern summer haunts it nests in marshy forests from April to July, laying four eggs in the deserted nests of squirrels, thrushes and pigeons up in trees.

The eggs are pyriform, pale greenish or buff in ground-colour, spotted with purplish-brown and ashy-grey.

In size they average about 1·5 by 1·1 inches.

THE GREENSHANK

Tringa nebularia (Gunner)

Description.—Length 14 inches. Sexes alike. Winter plumage: Top of the head and the back and sides of the neck blackish-brown, the feathers broadly edged with white; back and wings ashy-brown edged with black and white and dark-shafted; outer flight-feathers blackish, inner flight-feathers ashy-brown, all edged with whitish; lower back, rump and tail white, the central tail-feathers irregularly banded with dark brown, the bands dying away on the outer feathers; a line over the eye and the area round the beak whitish; whole lower plumage white.

In summer plumage the head is streaked with brown, and the fore-neck and sides of the breast are spotted with brown; the feathers of the back have broad black centres.

Iris brown; bill dark olive-brown, blackish at the tip; legs yellowish-green.

The bill is long and slightly uptilted.

Field Identification.—A solitary wader found about all types of water; grey and brown above, white below, to be distinguished from the other common waders by the green legs, large size, greyer colour and the conspicuous whiteness of the lower back, rump and tail. The alarm whistle is also distinctive.

Distribution.—Breeds in the northern portions of Europe and Asia, passes on migration through temperate Europe and Asia, and winters in Africa, tropical Asia, Australia, Tasmania and New Zealand. In winter it is generally distributed in India, Ceylon and Burma, being most abundant in Northern India. In India it commences to arrive about August and departs in April and May, but non-breeding stragglers are met with throughout the summer.

The slightly smaller Redshank (*Tringa totanus*) and Dusky Redshank (*Tringa erythropus*), found throughout India—the latter mostly in the north—are easily distinguished by their orange-red legs. The Dusky Redshank is so called from its distinctive sooty-brown breeding plumage, assumed before it leaves India. In winter dress it shows less white in the expanded wing than the Common Redshank, owing to the secondaries being barred brown and white instead of pure white.

The well-known Ruff and Reeve (*Philomachus pugnax*) are common winter visitors to the plains, found in small flocks about shallow water, but they are usually in winter plumage though with sometimes slight traces of the remarkable ruff and lappets of the male breeding plumage.

Habits, etc.—The Greenshank is usually found in India, except on migration when small parties occur, as a solitary bird feeding on the edges of water of all kinds but preferably about the sandy margins of rivers or the edges of those tanks and jheels where no vegetation divides the water from the land. It is a frequent visitor to village ponds and the smallest patches of temporary water, such as flooded borrow-pits. Its greater size and hoary grey colour distinguish it from the Common Sandpiper and the Green Sandpiper which have similar habits. It is rather a shy bird, and when disturbed flies off with swift and erratic flight rising high into the air, and as it goes it utters a loud alarm whistle, a mellow but plaintive *thew-thew—tew-tew-theeuw*. The ordinary call in flight is *chee-wit*. It does not probe the mud for which its uptilted bill is not very suitable, but picks minute life from the surface of the mud or water.

In the north it breeds from May onwards. The nest is a depression in the ground lined with a few leaves and bents, and it is usually placed by some object such as a stone or piece of wood which serves to mark the site of the nest. It is placed on open moorland country, often close to forest.

The clutch normally consists of four eggs. These are broad ovals, sharply pointed towards the smaller end, fine in texture with a fair gloss. The ground-colour is a warm buffy-stone, spotted and blotched with reddish-brown or chocolate and ash colour.

The eggs measure about 2·0 by 1·35 inches.

THE LITTLE STINT

EROLIA MINUTA (Leisler)

Description.—Length 6 inches. Sexes alike. Winter plumage: A dark streak from the eye to the beak; area round base of bill, a streak above the eyes, and the entire lower plumage white, the sides of the breast usually brownish and striated; upper plumage brown, more or less tinged with grey, the feathers with broad blackish shaft-stripes; wing-coverts darker brown with pale edges, and a whitish wing-bar; quills blackish-brown, the innermost being largely white; the lower back to the upper tail-coverts dark brown down the centre and whitish at the sides; central tail-feathers dark brown, the outer feathers light smoky brown.

In summer the upper plumage is black with broad rufous edges; the fore-neck and upper breast are tinged with dull rufous and indistinctly spotted with dark brown.

Iris brown; bill black; legs dull lead colour.

The bill is fairly long and slender; the wing long and pointed, the tail slightly graduated.

Field Identification.—A tiny wader, about the size of a Sparrow, found in parties and flocks about water. Upper plumage dusky, under parts white.

Distribution.—The Little Stint breeds in Siberia and the North Russian tundras and in winter migrates to Africa and Southern Asia. At this season it is abundant in the well-watered parts of India and Ceylon; it commences to arrive about the beginning of August and departs again in April and early May.

The Dunlin (*Erolia alpina*), which winters in Northern India in some numbers, is larger with the beak longer and somewhat curved.

Habits, etc.—As we know it in India in winter, the Little Stint is an eminently social species, consorting not only in flocks composed only of its own species, but also in company with its near relation Temminck's Stint and with larger waders like the Dunlin and Curlew-Sandpiper. These flocks are sometimes of considerable size, and they are found both inland on rivers and jheels and also on the sea-coast. The chief requirement is a broad and flat foreshore of mud or sand on which the little birds feed at the water's edge, collecting minute insects, crustacea and worms, and the seeds of various aquatic plants. They are invariably very busy, pattering along with their tiny feet in and out of the water, their heads down busily collecting their minute food from the surface of the mud. They are usually tame and allow a near approach. When disturbed they rise with a soft *wick-wick-wick*.

Once on the wing the flight is very swift and strong; the birds dart along over the shore and water with a slightly erratic course, flashing dark and light by turns, as in unison they change their position, sometimes flying with one wing uppermost, sometimes the other, thus presenting the upper and lower surface alternately to the observer. Settling again they run rapidly for a few paces and then immediately start feeding as if there were no time to be lost.

Temminck's Stint (*Erolia temminckii*) may be distinguished from this bird in the field by the much darker upper parts, by the three pairs of white outer tail-feathers, and by the yellowish-olive legs. In Temminck's Stint the shafts of the primaries are brown except the first which is white; the Little Stint has the shafts of all the primaries largely white.

The Little Stint breeds at the end of June in grassy marshes in the Northern latitudes to which it retires. By way of nest it lines with willow leaves a cup-shaped depression in the swampy ground. The clutch consists of four eggs, pyriform in shape. The ground-colour varies from pale greenish to buffish-stone, blotched and spotted with rich reddish-brown.

The average size is 1·10 by 0·80 inches.

THE WOODCOCK

Scolopax rusticola Linnæus

Description.—Length 14 inches. Sexes alike. Upper plumage brownish-grey, irregularly barred, mottled and blotched with rufous, brown and black, a black line from the bill to the eye, an imperfect black line below the eye and two broad black bands across the back of the head; wings barred dark brown and rufous, the quills becoming dark brown with imperfect rufous bars; tail black, the feathers tipped with dark grey above and silvery white below and with rufous spots on their edges; lower parts brownish-white, the chin unmarked, the rest with narrow dark brown cross-bars which to some extent grow black and coalesce on the throat.

There is a good deal of variation in colour, some birds greyer and others browner, and in size, but this is individual and not connected with age, sex or locality.

Iris blackish-brown ; bill dusky-brown, livid at base of lower mandible ; legs fleshy-brown, claws blackish.

Weight 8 to 13½ ounces.

The bill is long and slender, grooved at the sides and pitted at the tip ; tail fan-shaped ; legs short with rather long toes.

Field Identification.—A dark-looking mottled bird, russet and black and grey, with rather rounded wings and a long bill pointing downwards, which is flushed suddenly from ground cover in open woodland and flies with a rapid twisting flight among the trees.

Distribution.—Found throughout Europe and Asia, breeding in the north and wintering in the south. In our area the Woodcock breeds in the Himalayas from 6000 feet upwards, no doubt to the limit of tree growth, from Chitral and Hazara as far east as Bhutan.

In winter between the beginning of October and the middle of March this species is to be found in the lower valleys and the foothills of the whole of the Himalayas, mostly at elevations from 4000 to 8000 feet, but here and there down to the level of the plains. On the west they are also found sparingly in the North-west Frontier Province and North Baluchistan. On the east they are rather commoner in the hills and neighbouring plains of Assam.

The Woodcock is also a winter visitor to both the Eastern and Western Ghats at all heights, being best known as a game bird in the Nilgiris. Stragglers reach the hills of Ceylon. There are virtually no records from the area between the winter quarters in north and south India.

Habits, etc.—Owing to its crepuscular habits the Woodcock is seldom seen except by the sportsman who regards it as a special prize and therefore concentrates on its pursuit. It rests by day in brambles, bracken and other vegetation both in open ground and more usually under tree growth and in woods and spinneys. It flights at dusk with great regularity to its feeding grounds. These are along the sides of ditches and in boggy hollows where it rummages amongst the debris of dead leaves and vegetation or probes with its beak in the soft ground. Most forms of small invertebrate life, adult or larval, are welcome to it, but its staple food is undoubtedly earthworms. For these it probes in the ground, driving the beak in often up to the base. In the breeding season this routine is diversified by the display flight known as " roding " which is familiar to those who camp in the Himalayas. In this the male flies at dusk along the hill-sides above the tree-tops and high in the open across the smaller nullahs following a regular circuit again and again. Whilst roding the actual flight is fast though the wings appear to have a slow Owl-like action, and as the bird goes it utters a low croaking sound or a thin *tsiwick*. When flushed by day the bird rises with a clatter of wings and dodges swiftly among the trees.

Few species can be more beautifully adapted to their mode of life. The long bill has its tip slightly swollen to accommodate a rich supply of sensory nerves. The ear has been shifted forward from the usual position to one close to the gape so that the bill must act as a telephone for it. Tactile sense and hearing thus help its random probings to discover the hidden earthworm, and when the worm is found its capture is assisted by the fact that the mandibles are very flexible at their tips. They can thus be opened sufficiently to capture the worm without the great effort involved if the whole of the beak had to be opened in the ground. The huge eyes, mark of a nocturnal creature —and the Woodcock may as well have the protection of darkness for daylight is unnecessary to its specialised feeding,—are set well towards the top of the skull. This gives a great range of vision in the normal feeding position to ensure the bird's safety, but to compensate for it the Woodcock has to hold its bill inclined downwards in flight and at rest. Finally, the beautifully marbled and barred plumage which ensures the invisibility of the bird as it rests on the ground by day amongst fallen leaves and dry stems also provides a perfect example of Protective Coloration. The minute first primary or outer flight-feather is the well-known "painting feather," a trophy beloved of sportsmen.

This species is also remarkable for the ability to transport its chicks from one place to another, flying with them held between the legs.

The breeding season in the Himalayas is from early May to late July. The nest may be found in any type of forest and is often placed in a damp ravine under or amongst fairly thick cover. It is merely a hollow scratched amongst dry leaves or bracken, enough of which is left to form a dry bed for the eggs.

The clutch consists of four eggs. Their shape is a broad blunt oval sometimes rather pointed at the smaller end. The texture is fine with a certain amount of gloss. The ground-colour varies from pale creamy-white to warm buff. The markings, which are generally numerous towards the larger end and scanty elsewhere, consist of large and small blotches of reddish-brown with secondary clouds and mottlings of lavender and grey.

The measurement is about 1·75 by 1·30 inches.

THE COMMON SNIPE

CAPELLA GALLINAGO (Linnæus)

Description.—Sexes alike. Length 11 inches. Top of the head black with a broad buffish-white band down the centre and a whitish stripe above each eye; chin and sides of the head whitish with a dark brown band from the beak through the eye; neck and upper breast buff streaked with dark brown; back black with a broad rufous-buff band down each shoulder, the feathers of the lower back fringed and barred with white; rump and upper tail-coverts rufous-buff marked with black; wings dark brown, the feathers more or less edged and tipped with whitish; tail black, the feathers tipped with buff and with rufous cross-bands near their ends; lower plumage white, the under wing-coverts and flanks barred with brown; lower tail-coverts banded buff and blackish.

Iris dark brown; bill blackish-brown, rufous-brown at base; legs olive-green.

Weight, 3½ to 5 oz.

Bill long and slender, thickening at the end, where it is honey-combed with nerve cells; eyes set far back in the head with the orifice of the ear below their hinder edge; twelve to eighteen tail-feathers, but usually fourteen.

Field Identification.—A small long-beaked bird which springs suddenly with a harsh call out of marshy herbage and mounts high in the air with rapid twisting flight; plumage dark brown streaked and variegated with black, rufous and buff, the lower parts white.

Distribution.—The Common or Full Snipe (also called Fantail Snipe in contra-distinction to the next species) is very widely distributed in Europe, Asia, Africa and America, and is divided into several races. Our Indian bird belongs to the typical race. This breeds over the greater part of Europe from Scandinavia to the Pyrenees and in Central and Northern Asia. In the Indian Empire it is known to breed in Kashmir and the Santhal Parganas. In winter numbers migrate southwards, and at that season they are found about the Mediterranean, in Northern and Eastern Africa, and throughout India, Ceylon and Burma to the Malay countries.

The Common Snipe commences to arrive in India in August, though not in numbers until October, and the great majority have gone again by the middle of May. This is the Snipe of the Upper Indo-Gangetic plain, of Sind and the Punjab, Rajputana, Guzerat, the United Provinces, and Northern Bengal. It is more numerous than the Pintail in the Peninsula north of the Godavari, but it is rare in Southern India.

Habits, etc.—The Snipe in India is found in a variety of situations where soft mud and water are found combined with cover. Its favourite haunts vary in different localities and probably depend on some food factor which is at present unknown. In one part it haunts rice-fields to the virtual exclusion of ordinary marshy ground, in other places the reverse. As the large eye indicates it is mainly nocturnal, but it also feeds a good deal in the early mornings and evenings. The rest of the day it drowses away in the shade of a tuft of grass or rushes, and when the sun is particularly hot even leaves the jheels to shelter in the cool depths of luxuriant crops or patches of scrub. It feeds on the seeds of marsh plants and small molluscs, but a great portion of the food consists of minute worms and larvæ obtained by boring

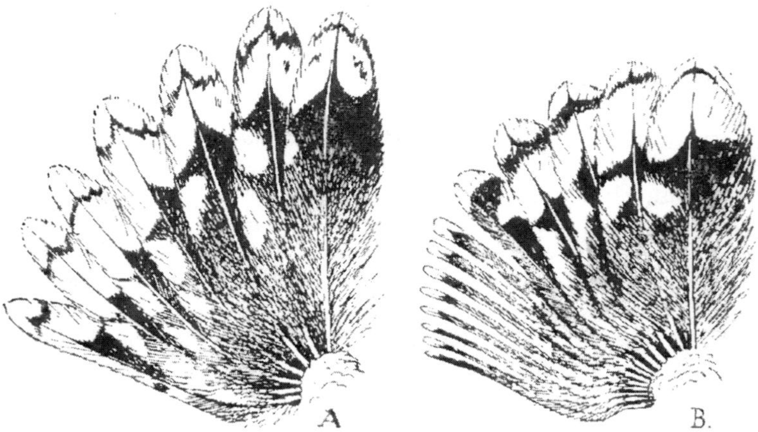

FIG. 90—Tails of (A) Common Snipe ; (B) Pintail Snipe (4/5 nat. size)

in soft mud. To this end the long beak is specially adapted, furnished with sensitive nerves at the end and muscles which allow the terminal half to open when the base is closed. Another curious feature in the bird is the position of the orifice of the ear, but the explanation of this is still unknown.

During the noontide siesta the Snipe is often very sluggish and unwilling to rise. At other times it is shy and active, rising off the ground very suddenly with an alarm-note of *scap-scap* (or *pénch* pronounced sharply with a nasal twang); it zigzags quickly over the ground, and if not minded to go far drops sharply again into cover with the wings high over its head as it drops. But if thoroughly alarmed it mounts into the sky at a great pace; though it is always reluctant to leave its chosen spot and often flies round at a great height in wide circles, calling occasionally, and then if the coast seems clear drops suddenly back into cover near the place where it originally rose. On the ground it is very jerky and nervous in its movements.

During the breeding season it develops two special characteristics, the habit of perching on dead trees and posts where it stands nodding its head, and a nuptial display. In this it flies in wide circles high over the nest place, uttering a call of *chip-per*, *chip-per*, and alternating this with sudden downward plunges in which a loud bleating sound is produced by the outermost pair of tail-feathers, which stand out separate to the others, and catch the air. This is known as "drumming."

In Kashmir the Snipe nests in May and June. The nest is a shallow cup of dried grass placed in the centre of a clump of thick grass in marshy ground.

The clutch consists of four eggs. In shape they are broad ovals, very compressed and pointed towards the smaller end. The texture is smooth and close with a fair gloss. The ground-colour varies from pale greenish or bluish to pale brown, blotched and spotted with various shades of sepia and ash colour. The markings tend to collect towards the broad end, but in many eggs they are disposed in lines with a distinct spiral twist owing to rotation of the egg in the oviduct. They are very large for the size of the bird and measure about 1·60 by 1·15 inches.

THE PINTAIL SNIPE

CAPELLA STENURA (Bonaparte)

Description.—So similar to the Common Snipe that no separate description is required. It is slightly duller in colour with less white in the wings. It may be identified at once by the tail which consists of twenty-six feathers, of which the outermost eight on each side are stiff, narrow and wire-like, and explain the name of Pintail.

Weight, $3\frac{3}{4}$ to 5 oz.

Field Identification.—Almost impossible to distinguish from the Common Snipe in the field except by a very slight difference in the call and by the slower heavier flight.

Distribution.—Breeds in Eastern Siberia as far west as the Yenesei Valley, and migrates in winter to South-eastern Asia and the Malay Archipelago. The Pintail enters India over the Eastern Himalayas, and is very common in Eastern and Southern India, growing scarcer towards the north and west. In Sind a few have been recorded, but it is unknown in the Punjab, North-west Frontier Province, Baluchistan and Kashmir. In Eastern India it arrives early in August and leaves again by the end of April.

The Wood-Snipe (*Capella nemoricola*), a slightly larger and darker species with barred under parts, is best known in India as a winter visitor in small numbers to the hill ranges of the south.

The Jack-Snipe (*Lymnocryptes minimus*) is a common winter visitor to India, and a scarce one in Ceylon and Burma. It is readily identified by its small size, wedged-shaped tail of twelve pointed feathers, and the patches of glossy green on the upper plumage.

Habits, etc.—The Pintail Snipe is found in India, like the Common Snipe and in many areas in company with it, in every type of marshy and flooded ground where soft mud combines with cover. It is, however, also occasionally found in dry grass, stubbles or low scrub, and this difference is due to the fact that the Pintail has not such a highly specialised bill as the Common Snipe, and therefore feeds less on worms and more on insects, larvæ and mollusca. On the wing the Pintail is a heavier and darker-looking bird, and there is a little difference in the alarm-call with which it rises; the flight also is not so swift. These differences are, however, very slight and only to be appreciated by the few.

In Eastern Siberia the Pintail breeds about June. The courting display appears to be very similar to that of the Common Snipe, while the nest and eggs also closely resemble those of the better-known species.

THE PAINTED SNIPE

Rostratula benghalensis (Linnæus)

Description.—Length, male 10 inches, female 11 inches. Male: Upper plumage olivaceous-brown indistinctly barred with blackish, the scapulars and inner wing-coverts with broad, dark green bars edged with white; a broad buff band down the middle of the crown from the beak, and another behind the eye and encircling it; a broad buff band down each side of the back; on the tertiaries and wing-coverts, buff black-edged bands come in and pass externally into spots; wing-quills bluish-grey finely barred with wavy black lines, oval buff spots on the outer webs which are black towards the base; rump and tail bluish-grey finely barred with black and conspicuously spotted and faintly tipped with buff; chin whitish; sides of the neck, throat and breast brown streaked with white, defined with a blackish gorget; lower plumage white extending in a narrow band on each side behind the gorget to join the buff shoulder lines; sides of the breast behind the white band olive-brown and black.

Female: A broad buff band down the middle of the crown; a white band behind the eye and encircling it; remainder of head and neck dull chestnut, becoming lighter towards the throat and darkening towards a blackish pectoral band; mantle grey washed with olive and narrowly barred with blackish; a broad buff band down each side of the back; a tuft of pure white lanceolate feathers underlying the scapulars; wing-coverts and inner flight-feathers bright olive-green closely barred with black; wing-quills, rump and tail and remainder of lower plumage as in the male.

Iris brown; bill pale fleshy-brown, darker towards the tip; legs greenish, claws brown.

Weight, male 3·5 to 4·9 oz., female 4·4 to 6·4 oz.

Bill long and slender, slightly swollen and bent downwards at the tip; legs with long toes, the tibia partly naked; wings short, broad and ample.

FIG. 91—Painted Snipe (⅓ nat. size)

Field Identification.—Heavy Rail-like flight, wonderfully painted plumage and clumsy build distinguish it from all other waders; the buff band along the crown and the heavy spectacle markings are distinctive.

Distribution.—The Painted Snipe is very widely distributed in Africa, Asia, Australia and Tasmania, the birds from the two latter places being separated from the typical form as another subspecies.

In India it is found practically throughout the country, occurring even in the Himalayas and other mountain ranges up to 5000 feet wherever suitable swamps occur. In the main a resident species, it is also a local migrant.

Habits, etc.—The Painted Snipe is found in swampy ground in jheels and along the edges of water channels where small patches of open water alternate with heavy cover. In such places they are found singly or in parties of ten to a dozen birds which lie closely and are flushed with difficulty. They rise from the ground heavily like a Rail, with trailing legs that are not tucked into place until the bird has flown several yards, and they fly with heavy laborious action till they drop back into cover a short distance away ; at the first opportunity they run back to the spot whence they were flushed. In habits they are largely crepuscular, feeding morning and evening and perhaps at night as well, and resting during the warmer hours. When feeding they often leave the swampy ground and work out into the open on to grassland or plough, running back to cover with lowered heads and shame-faced demeanour if disturbed. When necessary they can swim excellently.

The exact relationship of this species is not clear, but it is certainly not a true Snipe, and as a game-bird is neither worth shooting nor eating and should always be spared.

The call is a rather deep mellow note resembling the noise made by blowing into the mouth of a bottle, without blowing hard enough to produce a whistle.

As in the case of the Button-Quails, where also the females are larger and brighter than the males, the Painted Snipe is believed to be polyandrous. The point has not yet been settled beyond dispute, but it is apparently the case that the birds do not pair except very temporarily. As soon as the eggs are laid the male bird proceeds to incubate them and rear the chicks, while the female again pairs with another male who in turn is also provided with similar duties. To this state of affairs is attributed the fact that males are more numerous than females, and also the prolonged breeding season which extends virtually throughout the year, wherever conditions of food and water are suitable.

Another remarkable feature of the bird is its display, used both in courtship and as a protection against danger. In this the wings are spread and brought forward to beyond the top of the beak, while the tail is simultaneously expanded, until the bird becomes a patch of brightly-spotted markings. This is accompanied by a hissing, swearing note.

The nest is a compact flat pad, slightly depressed in the centre, of grass, straw, rushes and weeds, placed on the ground or in a tuft of herbage in any spot contiguous to water, usually in a wet situation but occasionally out in a dry field. The clutch consists of four eggs.

The egg is a moderately broad oval, with the small end rather compressed and lengthened. The shell is very hard and of a close compact texture with a slight gloss. The ground-colour is clear bright yellow, thickly and boldly blotched and streaked with an intensely deep and rich brown.

The egg measures about 1·40 by 0·99 inches.

THE BLACK-HEADED GULL

LARUS RIDIBUNDUS Linnæus

Description.—Length 16 inches. Sexes alike. Winter plumage: Head, neck, rump, tail and entire lower plumage white, a small brown mark in front of the eye and another behind the ear; back and wings pearl-grey, the outer flight-feathers with their coverts white and their tips conspicuously marked with black.

In summer plumage a deep brown hood is assumed covering the whole head and upper neck.

Iris dark brown; eye-rims, bill and legs deep red.

The bill is stout and compressed, the upper mandible curved and bent down over the tip of the lower mandible which has a conspicuous angle below near the end; wings long, exceeding the square tail; hind toe small; front toes fully webbed.

Field Identification.—A typical small Gull, easily recognised in winter plumage by the dark spot behind the ear and the white edge to the front of the end of the wing. It must, however, be distinguished from the Brown-headed Gull (*Larus brunneicephalus*), also common on the Indian coasts, a larger bird in which the point of the wing is black enclosing white patches called " mirrors." Breeds in Ladakh.

Distribution.—This Gull breeds in temperate Europe, southwards to the Mediterranean, and also in Western Asia. In winter it is also found in Northern Africa and Southern Asia as far south as India. In Eastern Siberia, China, Japan and the Philippines it is replaced by another race.

In India it commences to arrive in August and leaves towards the end of March, though some birds remain until early May. It is common in Kashmir and about the coasts and rivers of Northern India; on the west coast it is found as far south as Travancore.

Habits, etc.—This familiar European Gull is found in India both on the sea-coasts and inland, about tanks, jheels, and the larger rivers.

On the sea-coast it is most common in and around the harbours, where it is very much of a scavenger about the shipping, taking dead fish, crustacea and garbage of all kinds from the surface of the water or from where the tides have thrown it up along the shore. It cannot dive and, therefore, seldom catches live fish. Like all Gulls, it is a bird of very active habits and strong flight, flying and wheeling backwards and forwards over the water with an untiring buoyancy that is its essential characteristic. Numbers are found together and constitute large loosely-connected flocks which, when not feeding, rest either on the sea or sands and sometimes on level ground inland.

The cry is a querulous scream, *kree-ah*, and very little excites the birds to noisy vociferations of it.

Inland its distribution is somewhat difficult to understand. At some of the larger lakes it may be met with during the winter months, but it is probably safe to say that the bird is usually found inland while migrating; then also it is found in flocks which travel up the course of the larger rivers and break their stay for a short time on big tanks and lakes. In such places its food is largely of an animal nature, including all the smaller forms of invertebrate life that come within its ken.

In Europe the breeding season is from April onwards. The bird breeds in large colonies which are found in various situations on island-studded lakes, on sand-hills by the sea, in bogs and marshes often far inland. The nests are heaps of vegetable matter with a hollow for the eggs, and they are built on the ground or in reed-beds with no attempt at concealment. The eggs are frequently collected for human food and are freely sold under the name of Plover's eggs.

The normal clutch consists of three eggs, but two to four are found. The egg is a broad oval, rather pointed at one end. The ground-colour varies from light stone to dark brown, spotted and blotched with deep blackish-brown and purplish.

The egg measures about 2·05 by 1·5 inches.

THE WHISKERED TERN

CHLIDONIAS HYBRIDA (Pallas)

Description.—Length 10 inches. Sexes alike. The crown of the head greyish streaked with black, becoming more marked on the nape, and also forming an indefinite band through the eye; remainder of head, neck and lower parts white; remainder of upper plumage light ashy-grey, the flight-feathers being darker and with their concealed portions brown.

In summer plumage the top and sides of the head are black and the ashy-grey of the upper plumage becomes darker; fore-neck and breast dark grey passing into sooty black on the abdomen.

Iris brown; bill red; legs dull red.

The bill is short, slight and marginally compressed. The feet are weak with deeply-scalloped webs between the toes; the tail is short and very slightly forked, and the closed wings project beyond it.

Field Identification.—A graceful whitish bird, in summer with a black cap and belly, which feeds in companies over water or rice-fields, delicately capturing insects; distinguish in the field from the other common inland Terns by the short, scarcely forked tail, and in the hand by the very slight webs between the toes.

Distribution.—The Whiskered Tern is found in several races in the temperate parts of Europe, the whole of Africa, Southern Asia, the Malay Archipelago and Australia. The breeding race of India has been separated as smaller than the typical European bird under the name of *Ch. h. indica.* It breeds in Kashmir and in the United Provinces, and at other seasons may be found in suitable places throughout India, Ceylon and Burma. Another race, *Ch. h. javanica,* in which the lower parts are virtually black in breeding plumage, breeds in Assam and Burma and eastwards through the Malay States to Java, Borneo and Celebes. A migrant species, but its movements have not been worked out.

Habits, etc.—This species is one of the Marsh Terns as opposed to the River and Sea Terns. Except on migration, when it travels along the course of rivers, it lives and breeds on lakes and tanks, preferably those which are partly overgrown with lotus and other aquatic vegetation ; though it strays a good deal to rice-fields, small ponds and inundated areas in search of the insects which form the greater part of its food.

These birds feed on the wing in small companies in the most methodical manner, starting at one end of the jheel and working up against wind to the far end ; as they go each bird dips down incessantly to pick food off the water or weeds. Dragon-flies and their larvæ appear to be their staple food, but water-beetles and other aquatic insects are freely taken. Arrived at the end of the jheel the flock flies back to the start again ; those that are satisfied rest on a rocky islet or the bough of some water-logged fallen tree and preen their plumage ; the unsatisfied commence another beat in search of further food.

The breeding season lasts from June to August. The nest is a slight platform of rushes and long trailers of weed wound round and round in circular form and placed on the broad leaves of lotus plants with which they are firmly intertwined. It is placed out in deep water in the centre of the chosen lake or jheel, free of the reeds and rushes.

The number of eggs varies from two to four, but the normal clutch probably consists of three eggs.

The egg is a moderately broad oval, a good deal pointed at one end ; the texture is fine and close but there is little gloss. The ground-colour is generally a pale, clear olive-green, but it varies also from pale olive stone-colour to rich blue-green. The markings consist of streaks, spots and blotches of deep blackish-brown or reddish-brown, with secondary markings of pale purplish-brown. There is a good deal of variation in the character and extent of these markings.

The egg measures about 1·51 by 1·09 inches.

THE COMMON RIVER TERN

STERNA AURANTIA Gray

Description.—Length 16 inches. Sexes alike. Winter plumage: Crown dull grey; upper plumage french-grey, paling to pearl-grey on the rump and tail; lower plumage very delicate greyish-white.

In summer plumage the top and sides of the head are black glossed with green, with a whitish spot under each eye.

Iris brown; bill deep yellow; legs red.

FIG. 92—Common River Tern ($\frac{1}{8}$ nat. size)

Bill long, slender and compressed; feet small with the front toes webbed; wings and tail long, the latter deeply forked.

Field Identification.—A very graceful grey and white bird with long pointed wings and a long deeply-forked tail and usually a black cap, which is invariably found by water. For differences from other Terns see under the next species.

Distribution.—This Tern is found throughout India and Burma and in the Malay Peninsula. It is not found in Baluchistan or in the mountain areas, but is otherwise fairly generally distributed throughout India. It is a resident species, though individuals wander about a good deal according to the water-supply.

PLATE XXIII

1. Common Sandgrouse. 2. Jungle Bush-Quail (male and female). 3. Cotton-Teal (male and female). 4. Gadwall.
(Gadwall $\frac{1}{4}$ nat. size ; remainder $\frac{1}{3}$ nat. size.)

[Face p. 484

Habits, etc.—This Tern is essentially a river bird occurring singly or in small parties about all the rivers of India where they flow through the plains, and leaving them only for temporary visits to jheels and tanks. Only stragglers ever visit tidal waters. These Terns spend the greater portion of their time fishing. They fly along some 20 to 30 feet above the surface of the water, the strong, deep, regular beats of the long pointed wings producing a distinctive but slightly jerky flight, and as they fly their keen eyes watch the water below for shoals of the small fishes on which they feed. The actual capture of a fish is effected by a perpendicular drop into the water and it is eaten on the wing, swallowed invariably head foremost. Once a suitable fishing ground is discovered the direct purposeful flight is abandoned for graceful wheeling curves which show to the full the powers of flight that have earned the marine Terns their name of Sea-Swallows. After their appetites are satisfied they sit in parties on the sand-banks near the water's edge, often in company with other species. They never perch on trees, nor do they settle on the water or swim.

The River Tern breeds from March till May on the bare, glittering sand-banks of the rivers, generally on islands, but also along the shore. Several pairs generally breed near one another, and the same sand-banks are usually tenanted by colonies of Skimmers, Little Indian Pratincoles, Black-bellied Terns, Little Terns, and pairs of the Great Stone-Plover, the Spurwing-Plover, and the Little Ring-Plover.

The nest is a small depression scraped in the sand which is at this season almost too hot to touch with the naked hand. During the daytime therefore the Terns are very casual about brooding their eggs and spend much of their time fishing in the vicinity. A human being has, however, only to set foot on the sand-bank for a scene of great excitement to ensue. Sitting birds rise from the nests, others arrive from the river, and while the sand is covered with Pratincoles fluttering and staggering in simulated death throes, the air is filled with Terns flashing backwards and forwards and wheeling round and round overhead, their shrill plaintive cries indicating only too surely the presence of the eggs and offspring they seek to protect.

The clutch consists of two or three eggs. They are broad ovals in shape, very smooth and fine in texture with little gloss. The ground is a delicate greenish-grey or buffy stone-colour. This is covered with small blotches, lines and streaks of dark brown, and with secondary markings underlying them of clouds and streaks of pale inky-purple.

In size they average about 1·65 by 1·25 inches.

THE BLACK-BELLIED TERN

STERNA MELANOGASTER Temminck

(Plate xxii, Fig. 4, opposite page 462)

Description.—Length 13 inches. Sexes alike. Top and sides of the head black; upper plumage ashy-grey slightly tinged with brown on the innermost flight-feathers, the outer flight-feathers frosted and whitish with their inner webs brownish; tail paler grey than the back, the long outer feathers white; lower plumage white on the chin gradually passing through grey on the neck into chocolate and then into black from the breast to the tail; wing-lining white.

For a short period after breeding the black cap and dark under parts become white.

Iris dark brown; bill orange-yellow; legs orange-red.

Structure as in the Common River Tern.

Field Identification.—Five species of Tern are found commonly inland in winter in India. All may have the cap black according to age and season. The Whiskered Tern may at once be separated from the other four by the short almost square tail and the deeply-scalloped webs of the feet. It shares with the Black-bellied Tern the further distinction of a black belly in full plumage.

The other four species have long deeply-forked tails and fully-webbed feet. The black bill and legs distinguish the Gull-billed Tern (*Gelochelidon nilotica*) at all seasons, while the Little Tern (*Sterna albifrons*) may always be known by its small size. The others being thus eliminated, it should always be possible to separate the River Tern and Black-bellied Tern by size and build alone, the former being a heavier and more clumsy bird, while the latter generally has the black belly or some traces of it.

Distribution.—This Tern is peculiar to India, Burma and Ceylon. In India its western boundary appears to be the Indus Valley, and it is not found in the Himalayas above 2500 feet. It is very abundant in Northern India but less common in the South. A resident species, though individuals wander a good deal.

Habits, etc.—The habits of the Black-bellied Tern are very similar to those of the Common River Tern, in company with which it is generally found. Its main habitat is in the beds of the big rivers of the plains, where it fishes in the channels and nests upon the sand-banks, but it also freely visits jheels and tanks; it flies and fishes singly and in parties. It has much the same flight and methods of fishing as the River Tern, but it is more of an adept at catching insects, lifting them from the surface of water with a gentle glide or chasing them over land in the evenings. The flight is swift enough for the capture of tiger-beetles, and grasshoppers and termites are eaten in quantities. Fish are swallowed head first, so that the sharp fins fold against the body and do not harm the gullet. Prawns for the same reason are swallowed tail first, as their sharp points are the legs and mandibles which project forwards.

As indicated under the last species it breeds on the sand-banks of the larger rivers from March to May, sometimes solitary, but usually in the mixed colonies with other species.

The nest is a mere scrape in the sand, and the clutch in this species varies from two to four eggs. The eggs may generally be distinguished from those of the River Tern by their smaller size and more elongated shape. They are broad ovals, and generally without gloss. The ground-colour is cream or buffy-brown of various shades, speckled, streaked and spotted, and with a few blotches of reddish or purplish brown; there are also faint secondary markings of spots, clouds and streaks of pale purple.

In size they average about 1·25 by 0·95 inches.

THE INDIAN SKIMMER

RHYNCHOPS ALBICOLLIS Swainson

Description.—Length 17 inches. Sexes alike. The top of the head blackish-brown; back and wings blackish-brown, the inner flight-feathers broadly tipped with white; a line down the centre of the rump to the inner webs of the central tail-feathers blackish-brown; remainder of plumage white.

Iris brown; bill deep orange, the tips of the mandibles yellow; legs bright vermilion.

The curious bill is described below; wings very long and pointed, tail short and slightly forked; feet small and webbed.

Field Identification.—A white Tern-like bird, with a black cap and back and immensely large black wings, which can be mistaken for nothing else, as the curious beak and the feeding habits correlated with it are unique. It occurs only by water.

Distribution.—Found on the larger rivers of India and Burma, extending to the west as far as Persian Baluchistan. A local migrant.

Habits, etc.—The Skimmer or Scissorbill is purely a water-bird, found almost entirely on the larger, broader rivers where their course is placid, flowing smoothly between sand-banks. Occasionally it visits jheels and tanks in the neighbourhood of such rivers, but only when there is a clear expanse of water free of weeds. For of all the curious and specialised birds of India the Skimmer is one of the most curious and highly specialised. In appearance at a distance it would pass for a very clumsy black and white Tern, remarkable for the expanse of wing and the deep deliberate flapping of its flight; but at a short distance attention is attracted by the curious bill. Of this both mandibles are deep and greatly compressed, much as if two knife-blades had been set edge to edge; the upper mandible is considerably shorter than the lower which projects beyond it. The reason for the shape of this curious organ is soon apparent, as one cannot watch a party of Skimmers on the wing for long without seeing it in use. Singly or in parties of ten to twenty birds they fly slowly backwards and forwards along the surface of the water as if they were ploughing it, the elongated portion of the lower mandible cutting through the surface, leaving scarcely a ripple. The older writers attributed this habit to a meaningless fascination in disturbing the placid surface of the waters; but the more prosaic habit of mind of the modern naturalist has ascertained by observation that the bird is

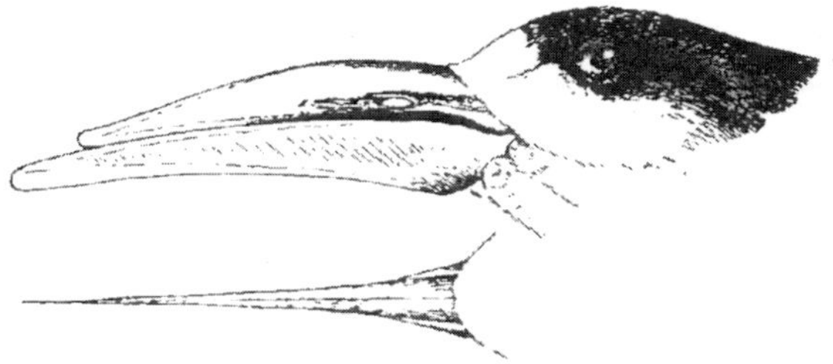

FIG. 93—Indian Skimmer (½ nat. size)

catching fish. It skims with the beak wide open in shallow water, the lower mandible below the water, the upper mandible clear of the surface; a small fish strikes the razor edge and runs up the incline, and the jaws close swiftly across the fish, held crossways firmly in three cutting edges; for an examination of the beak shows that the two mandibles close together in the same fashion as a curling-iron. The nestling Scissorsbill has the perfectly normal bill of a young Tern.

The breeding season lasts from March to May. The nest is a mere scrape on the bare sand-banks of the rivers that this species frequents, and the colonies are always shared by Terns and Pratincoles. When disturbed the birds flap lazily round in the neighbourhood uttering all the while a ceaseless twittering cry.

The full clutch consists of four eggs.

The egg is a moderately broad oval, more or less pointed towards the smaller end; the texture is fine and compact and there is a slight gloss.

The ground-colour is variable, delicate greenish or greyish-white, pale salmon-colour or pale buff. The markings consist of bold blotches and streaks, chiefly the latter, of rich umber-chocolate or reddish-brown, underlaid by similar streaks and blotches of more or less pale inky-purple; there is as a rule a considerable twist apparent in the markings of the eggs as if they had been deposited while the egg was rotating.

The average size is about 1·60 by 1·18 inches.

THE SPOTTED-BILLED PELICAN

Pelecanus roseus Gmelin

Description.—Length 5 feet. Sexes alike. Full adult breeding plumage: White almost throughout, crown and neck feathers short and curly with their bases dark brown; lower back, rump, flanks, and a patch below the tail vinaceous-pink; a slight crest and a mane of larger feathers down the back of the neck brownish; the flight-feathers blackish-brown, growing white inwardly, the larger wing and upper tail-coverts with black shafts; tail light ashy-brown.

In other plumages the vinaceous-pink tinge is lacking and the plumage is much sullied with brown.

Iris white or yellowish, bare skin round the eye yellow and livid; bill pinkish-yellow, the sides of the upper mandible with large bluish-black spots, tip of the mandibles orange-yellow; pouch dull purple, blotched and spotted with bluish-black; legs dark brown.

The upper mandible is long, flat and boat-shaped, terminating in a hooked nail; the lower mandible consists of two flexible arches which support a huge elastic pouch; body large and squat with short legs and webbed feet.

Field Identification.—The huge squat Pelican with its enormous beak and elastic pouch is familiar to every one through picture, story and Zoo, though the identification of the various species in the field is a matter of difficulty. In flight the birds appear white with the points of the wings black.

Distribution.—Throughout the better watered tracts of India, Ceylon, and Burma and the whole Oriental region. A migratory bird.

Two other species of very similar appearance, the Rosy Pelican (*Pelecanus onocrocotalus*) and the Dalmatian Pelican (*Pelecanus crispus*), are found in North-western and Northern India respectively.

Habits, etc.—This Pelican is purely a water-bird, being found wherever there are large expanses of water suitable for it to fish in. It is found singly or in small parties, but also often in large flocks. It is seldom seen on land, as it is a bad and clumsy walker, but in the water it swims well and buoyantly. The food consists of fish which are caught not by diving, of which the bird is incapable, but by scoops of the great lower mandible with its pendant and elastic pouch of naked membrane which acts as an ideal landing-net. When in flocks Pelicans capture their prey by forming a line or lines across

FIG. 94—Spotted-billed Pelican (1/8 nat. size)

the water and driving the fish before them into shallow water by beating the water with their wings.

On the wing the Pelican flies well, with the neck bent and the head close to the shoulders, the great wings beating in rhythmic unison. The flocks fly in regular lines or wedges like Geese and often ascend to a great height in the air.

In India the Pelican is only known to breed in the Madras Presidency, where a few small colonies may be found in the first half of the year. Other colonies breed in Ceylon, but the majority of this species nest in Burma where they collect for the purpose in November. Oates has described a vast breeding colony in the forests of the Sittang in Burma, which he calculated to be twenty miles long and five miles broad. Here this Pelican was nesting in company with Adjutants, and the total number of birds was estimated in millions. The huge nests were composed entirely of sticks without lining, and three to fifteen nests would be placed in a single tree at the height of 100 feet from the ground. The most striking point about this Pelicanry was the complete silence that prevailed, save for the whistle of the wings of birds flying far overhead which sounded like the music of an æolian harp.

The clutch consists of three eggs. The egg is long and narrow, equally pointed at both ends. The true shell is smooth and white but it is covered with an outer coating of chalky texture. This, when the egg is fresh, is pure white, but it gradually becomes stained, and is dark brown or black by the time that the chick hatches.

The egg measures from 2·65 to 3·3 inches in length by about 2·10 inches in breadth.

THE LITTLE CORMORANT

PHALACROCORAX NIGER (Vieillot)

Description.—Length 20 inches. Sexes alike. Black throughout with a slight green gloss; a white patch bordering the throat pouch; the scapulars and wing-coverts are dark silvery-grey with broad black borders to the feathers.

In the breeding season the white throat is lost, but scattered white feathers grow on the head and a few white hair-like plumes on the sides of the neck.

Iris greenish-brown; bill brown, livid purple while breeding; eyelids and the gular pouch and legs blackish, livid while breeding.

Bill rather slender and compressed, rounded and sharply hooked at the end; a gular pouch under the bill; tail wedge-shaped; toes flattened and webbed.

Field Identification.—A water-bird, dark glossy black, with an upright carriage and a habit of sitting on stumps and trees with the wings outspread. Swims and dives excellently and flies well. Distinguish by small size from other Cormorants.

Distribution.—Found throughout India, Ceylon, Burma, the Malay Peninsula, Sumatra, and Borneo. In India it is not found in the Himalayas or other hill ranges, in Baluchistan, or in the extreme north-west of the Punjab or in the North-west Frontier Province, but it is otherwise found wherever suitable water exists. It is a resident species.

The Common Cormorant (*Phalacrocorax carbo*), in addition to being much larger, is distinguished in the breeding season by more white on the head and neck and a large white patch on each flank. Immature birds are browner with white under parts. It is found throughout India.

Habits, etc.—This is the commonest species of Cormorant in India and is often very abundant. Although occasionally found on

FIG. 95—Little Cormorant (⅛ nat. size)

the sea-coast it is a bird of fresh water, preferring marshes and tanks even to rivers. It is found singly and in parties, and in suitable localities large numbers collect though not as one flock; they roost in company in trees.

The Little Cormorant lives on small crabs, tadpoles, frogs and fish which it catches under water, swimming and diving with the utmost ease; compared with a duck it swims very low in the water, and at a hint of danger it can submerge leaving only the head and neck above the surface like a periscope. It rises with difficulty from the water with a long flapping struggle, but once on the wing flies strongly and swiftly with the head and neck outstretched in front and the feet stretched straight behind. Out of the water it perches both on the ground and on rocks and on trees, but its favourite perch is a low stump sticking out of water; it stands very upright and has the family habit of sitting for long periods with the wings outstretched to catch the sun.

The breeding season in India is from July to September, and the birds breed in colonies often of great size. The nest is a flattish cup of sticks which is comparatively small for the size of the bird, and sometimes, indeed, was originally the property of a crow or egret; old nests are repaired from year to year. They are occasionally placed in reed-beds, but the majority of colonies are built in trees standing in water or in its immediate vicinity by jheels and tanks. A number of nests may be found in one tree, and the trees are often of small size.

The clutch consists of three to five eggs.

The eggs are long ovals, pointed towards the small end; the shell is firm and hard; greenish-blue in colour, but covered with an exterior chalky coating, which, when laid, is white or bluish-white, but is soon stained to yellow or brown. Portions of this chalky coat flake off in the nest, revealing the greenish-blue shell beneath.

In size the eggs average about 1·75 by 1·15 inches.

THE INDIAN DARTER

ANHINGA MELANOGASTER Pennant

Description.—Length 3 feet. Sexes alike. Crown and neck brown, all the feathers with pale edges, the back of the neck blackish; a fine line over the eye, chin, throat and a separate line half-way down the sides of the neck white; upper back black with brown edges; remainder of the plumage glossy black, the wing-feathers nearest the body and the coverts with silvery-white shaft-streaks.

Iris yellow; bill blackish-brown, lower mandible yellowish; legs black.

Bill straight, slender and sharply pointed; neck long and slender; scapulars long and lanceolate; tail long and wedge-shaped; feet webbed.

Field Identification.—A large black water-bird with long snaky neck and spear-like beak, and white on the throat and neck; swims, dives and flies well and perches on trees.

Distribution.—Throughout the Oriental region. This bird is found throughout India in suitable localities from the valley of the Indus eastward, but it does not ascend the hills. A resident species.

Habits, etc.—The Darter frequents fresh water, whether rivers, lakes or jheels, the only requisite being that the water should be deep enough for it to swim and dive in. It does not visit the sea, though it may be found in tidal estuaries and creeks. It is a social bird, found in parties at all seasons and it has a predilection for the society of the Little Cormorant, both species breeding, fishing and resting in company.

This bird is a highly specialised form whose whole structure and habits are adapted to one end, the capture of fish. It is a most wonderful swimmer and diver. It swims very low in the water, with, as a rule, only its head and neck uncovered ; and as it moves along the head turns from side to side and the long neck twists and bends with

FIG. 96—Indian Darter (1/8 nat. size)

snake-like movements that at once suggest the name of Snake-bird, so often applied to the species. As a fish rises or swims past the beak darts forward with the velocity of a spring impaling it or seizing it between the mandibles ; the sudden rapier-like thrust is explained by a bend in the neck at the 8th and 9th vertebræ which straightens for the thrust and acts as a spring. It follows fish and captures them under water, diving whilst swimming or with a plunge from its perch. It emerges with the captured fish in its beak, throws it up into the air and catches it in position to swallow head foremost.

When sated these birds emerge from the water and settle on trees and stumps in company with Cormorants, and, like them, hang out their wings to dry. When approached they crane their long necks and tiny snake-like heads at the intruder in a most ridiculous manner, till too near an approach sends the whole lot off into the water with mighty flappings and splashings. Close to the ground or water they are very ungainly on the wing, but once high in the air they can fly strongly like a Cormorant. The voice is a hoarse dissyllabic croak.

The breeding season is in January and February or from June to August according to the influence of the monsoon in different parts of India. The birds build in colonies in company with Cormorants and Herons, constructing rough unlined stick nests in clumps of trees; the same sites and nests are used year after year.

The clutch consists of three or four eggs.

The egg is a much elongated oval, more or less pointed towards one end; the true shell is of a somewhat pale greenish-blue tint, only visible in places after the flaking off of a superimposed chalky greenish-white coating which is gradually stained brown as incubation proceeds.

The egg measures about 2·15 by 1·37 inches.

THE WHITE IBIS

THRESKIORNIS MELANOCEPHALUS (Latham)

Description.—Length 30 inches. Sexes alike. Head and neck naked, dark bluish-black in colour; the plumage is white throughout, the tips of the primaries mottled with brown and the ends of the tertiaries slaty-grey.

In breeding plumage these grey tertiaries are longer and looser in texture, and the feathers round the base of the neck and on the upper breast become more plume-like.

Iris red-brown; bill black; legs glossy black.

The bill is long, slender and curved; the long toes are edged with a membrane which makes them slightly webbed at the base.

Field Identification.—A large white bird with a long curved black beak, long black legs and a naked black head and neck. Found about water.

Distribution.—Throughout India, Ceylon and Burma, and also in China and Southern Japan. It is found everywhere in India, in suitable localities as far westwards as the Jhelum River in the Punjab and the Indus in Sind, and in Las Belas, but it does not ascend any of the hill ranges. A resident species, wandering locally in different years.

Habits, etc.—The White Ibis is a bird of inland waters, chiefly preferring the larger marshes and jheels where wide areas of water are covered with bushes and trees; it is also found about rivers, tanks and inundated cultivation, and near such places also wanders on to the neighbouring grasslands. It is found in small parties

FIG. 97—Black Ibis and White Ibis (⅛ nat. size)

which associate freely with other forms of Ibis and Storks. These birds wade about in the water or stalk along the edges of it collecting the molluscs, crustaceans and similar organisms on which they feed; when sated they rest in little groups standing on the sand-banks or in shallow water or perched on favoured groups of trees. This species is said to have a peculiar booming call, but it is as a rule silent.

The breeding season lasts from June to August. The nests are built in small colonies of less than a dozen pairs which breed either by themselves or in company with Herons, Egrets and Cormorants; it is immaterial whether the locality chosen is in wild secluded jheels or on the outskirts of villages.

The nest is composed of sticks, unlined, but with a fairly deep hollow for the eggs; it is placed on small trees in jheels or on large trees near villages.

The clutch varies from two to four eggs.

The egg is very variable in size and shape; typically it is a long oval, much pointed at the smaller end and rather chalky in texture. When freshly laid it is of a delicate bluish or greenish-white, but this soon stains to a dull and dirty brown. Occasional eggs are delicately spotted with yellowish-brown.

The average measurement is 2·50 by 1·70 inches.

THE BLACK IBIS

PSEUDIBIS PAPILLOSUS (Temminck)

Description.—Length 27 inches. Sexes alike. Head naked, covered with black skin except for an area on the crown which is covered with red papillæ (hence the name Warty-headed Ibis sometimes used); wings black, glossed with purplish and green, and with a large white patch on the coverts; remainder of the plumage dark olive-brown, with a slight greenish gloss on the back.

Iris dull orange-red; bill greenish-leaden; legs brick-red.

Bill long, slender and curved; the toes are bordered by a membrane which makes them slightly webbed at the base.

Field Identification.—A large black bird easily identified by the bare head, long curved beak and conspicuous white wing-patch; perches on trees and feeds on the ground.

Distribution.—The Black Ibis is found from Continental India through Assam to parts of Burma, Siam and Cochin-China. It is divided into two races, of which we are concerned only with the typical form. This is found throughout the plains of India from roughly the valley of the Indus on the west to as far south as Mysore and east to Assam and Arrakan. It avoids the west coast of India and also Lower Burma. It is a resident species.

The Glossy Ibis (*Plegadis falcinellus*) is also common locally throughout India as a breeding species. This is a smaller species, blackish and chestnut in colour with metallic reflections and may be known by the feathered head.

Habits, etc.—The Black Ibis is less of a marsh bird than the White Ibis, and is generally found in open country or in cultivation, feeding on the ground in pairs or parties. They appear to be less inclined to rest and meditate than the other large birds to which they are related, such as the White Ibis, Storks and Herons, and always are busily engaged in searching the ground for fallen grain, insects, worms, crustacea and similar food. They roost, as they breed, in trees, and they have regular lines of flight to and from the roosting places, flying in wedge-shaped formation like Geese and Cranes. The call is similar to that of a bird of prey, a screaming cry of two or three notes.

The breeding season is rather irregular from March to November, varying in different localities and also perhaps in different years.

The nest is a large structure of sticks, with the egg cavity lined with straw, grass, feathers and rags. It is built high on the top of a large tree, and though, as a rule, the nest is solitary, occasionally two or three may be found together. It is not unusual for old nests of the larger Raptorial birds to be adopted by this species.

The clutch consists of three or four eggs.

The egg is a moderately long oval, more or less pointed towards one end. The texture is rather coarse, and the colour is a beautiful sea-green; most eggs are unmarked, but a few are spotted, speckled or streaked with brown or yellowish-brown.

In size the egg averages 2·43 by 1·7 inches.

THE SPOONBILL

PLATALEA LEUCORODIA Linnæus

Description.—Length 33 inches. Sexes alike. Pure white throughout, a patch of cinnamon-buff on the lower fore-neck in adults. A crest of pointed and drooping plumes is assumed in the breeding season.

Iris red; bill black, yellowish towards the tip; a patch of bare yellow skin between the eye and the beak; bare skin on the throat reddish-yellow; legs black.

The bill is broad, long and flattened, expanding into a flat spoon at the tip; neck and legs long, the toes bordered by a membrane and webbed at the base.

Field Identification.—Found in parties about water; a tall white long-legged bird immediately identified by the black spoon-shaped bill.

Distribution.—Widely spread through Central and Southern Europe, in Africa and in Asia, the Spoonbill is divided into two races. The larger Eastern race, *P. l. major*, is found from Egypt through

Central Asia to India, Ceylon, Burma, China and Japan. It is found throughout India, except in the drier and the more hilly regions, and is a resident bird. The typical race is said to appear in India as a winter migrant.

Habits, etc.—The Spoonbill in India is found in flocks which rest by day on the bare margins of the larger more open jheels, the shores of tidal creeks, and the sand-banks of the rivers. They occasionally feed by day in company with the numbers of other water-

FIG. 98—Spoonbill (⅛ nat. size)

birds that frequent similar situations; but more usually the flocks are to be seen standing at the edge of the water idly dozing in the sunlight, though not bereft of caution, and as evening falls they flight to the feeding grounds in shallow water. They travel in single file in long white gleaming lines at a considerable height above the ground; they fly with the long necks and legs extended, and move in a very regular and stately manner.

The food consists largely of vegetable substances, but all sorts of aquatic insects and their larvæ, frogs, molluscs and small fish are also eaten. The feeding action is most remarkable; the bird wades quickly through the water with its neck stretched out and the beak half-immersed, turning from side to side with a regular sweeping action like a man scything grass, so that the beak is passed sideways open through the water to close on anything palatable.

The only call is a low grunting note, inaudible save at close quarters.

The breeding season varies a good deal according to locality, but it appears to last mainly from August to November.

The Spoonbill nests in colonies which are often of considerable size and usually close to, but separate from, colonies of Ibises, Storks and other similar birds. These colonies build in large trees close to a lake or jheel, and it seems a matter of no moment to them whether the spot is lonely and secluded or in the middle of a village site.

The nest is a large massive platform of sticks, used and repaired year after year.

The usual clutch consists of four eggs, but five are sometimes laid. The egg is an elongated oval, much pointed towards the smaller end. The texture is somewhat coarse, slightly chalky and entirely without gloss. The ground-colour is white, not quite pure in tint, and the markings consist of smudged and ill-defined blotches and spots of brown of various shades sometimes dark and clear in tint, at other times feeble and half-washed out; these markings are mostly confined to the broad end, and are generally all of the same character on one egg.

The egg measures about 2·70 by 1·80 inches.

THE WHITE-NECKED STORK

DISSOURA EPISCOPUS (Boddaert)

Description.—Length 36 inches. Sexes alike. Crown black glossed with green; remainder of head and neck and the lower abdomen to and including the tail, white; the rest of the plumage black glossed with purple and green.

Iris crimson; facial skin plumbeous; bill black, tinged in places with red; legs red.

Bill long, stout and pointed; neck and legs long, wings and tail short; the three front toes are united by a web at the base; much bare skin about the base of the beak.

Field Identification.—This large Stork can be confused with no other species owing to the distinctive plumage, the white neck contrasting with the glossy black crown, back, breast and wings.

Distribution.—The White-necked Stork has a wide distribution through Africa, India, Ceylon and Burma, Siam, and the Malay States to the Philippines. It is divided into two races, of which only the typical form is found in our area. This is found from the Salt Range in the north-west (though there is only one record for Sind, at Sukkur) practically throughout India. It is a resident species.

Habits, etc.—This solemn-looking Stork is found singly, in pairs or in small parties in open well-watered country, frequenting flooded or irrigated land, small patches of marsh, and rice-fields, and in such situations it ascends the foot-hills of the Himalayas up to about 4000 feet. It is very quiet and sedentary in its habits, for the most part standing about in meditation on the ground or feeding in company with other Storks and Ibises. Out of the breeding season it seldom

FIG. 99—White-necked Stork ($\frac{1}{10}$ nat. size)

settles on trees, and I have only once seen a pair sitting on a building. It is, however, a good flier, and at times may be seen soaring like other Storks and Vultures at a great height from the ground.

The diet is very mixed, consisting of reptiles, frogs, fish and a variety of other living creatures that it finds in the vicinity of water.

The breeding season is rather extended; the majority of nests will be found from June to August, but some birds breed in practically every month of the year. The nest is a large rudely-constructed cup of twigs and small branches, sometimes thinly lined with down and feathers, and at other times densely lined with these materials and straw and dry grass.

The nests are built in large trees, sometimes at some distance from water or in a village site, and they are placed at a height of 20 or 30 feet from the ground.

The clutch consists of three or four eggs. They are rather variable in shape, and have a fine but chalky texture without gloss. In colour they are a faintly bluish-white, unmarked, but in the nest they gradually become stained to a dirty earthy-brown colour.

In size they average about 2·5 by 1·83 inches.

THE BLACK-NECKED STORK

XENORHYNCHUS ASIATICUS (Latham)

Description.—Length 52 inches. Sexes alike. Head and neck black, richly glossed with bluish-green except for a patch on the nape coppery-brown, passing into purple on the edges; a broad patch down each side of the upper surface including the innermost flight-feathers and the largest wing-coverts, a line of coverts under the wing and the whole tail black, richly glossed with metallic green; rest of plumage white.

Iris bluish-brown; bill black, gular skin and eyelids dusky purple; legs coral-red.

Bill very long and massive, slightly uptilted; neck long; legs very long. Four toes, moderate in length, the front three united by a small web at the base.

Field Identification.—A gigantic Stork with a very massive beak and long legs which is found solitary or in pairs. In flight appears pied black and white, the wings from beneath showing white with a black line along the arm and another along the body edge. The combination of black beak, black feathered head and neck and red legs effectually establishes the identity. The Black Stork (*Ciconia nigra*), a winter visitor to Northern India, is the only other species with a black feathered head and neck but the bill and the legs are red and in flight the whole wing appears black from below.

Distribution.—Widely distributed from Ceylon and India to Australia. The typical race is found in Ceylon, India, Burma, Siam, Cochin-China and the Malay States. In India it is very generally distributed in suitable areas as a resident species.

The famous Adjutant Bird (*Leptoptilos dubius*) of old Calcutta stories, a winter visitor to Bengal and Assam, is the largest and most impressive of the Indian Storks. The Smaller Adjutant (*Leptoptilos javanicus*) is resident in parts of Southern and Eastern India. Both these species are distinguished from all other Indian Storks by the naked head and neck, the larger bird being essentially a scavenger.

Habits, etc.—This fine Stork is not a gregarious species and it is usually to be met with solitary or in pairs resting on the top of trees or feeding along the edges of rivers, tanks and marshes. It is also partial to salt-water lagoons with shallow foreshores in which it wades out far from the edge of the water, its length of leg giving it great powers of exploration and enabling it to keep so far out in the open that it is with difficulty approached. When disturbed it flies off with slow and heavy flaps of the wings and after acquiring sufficient impetus sails quietly along on outstretched wings. It feeds on fish, reptiles, frogs, crabs, molluscs and similar forms of life.

The Black-necked Stork has a singular habit of dancing. A pair will gravely stalk up to each other and when about a yard apart will stand face to face, extend their long wings and while they flutter these very rapidly, so that the points of the wings of the one flap against the points of the other's wings, advance their heads till they nearly meet; both simultaneously clatter their bills like a couple of watchman's rattles. This display lasts for nearly a minute, after which one walks a little apart, to be followed after a moment by the other, when they repeat the performance, and so on perhaps for a dozen times.

The breeding season extends from October to January. The nest is built at the top of a tree, usually a very large one, and it is always solitary, never in the colonies of other Storks, Ibises and Herons. It is always a large structure and is sometimes enormous, measuring as much as 6 feet by 3 feet and deep in proportion. Externally it is composed of sticks and small branches. Internally it is carefully lined with rushes, grass, water-weeds and similar material, whilst very occasionally there is a regular parapet of mud. In some cases the nest is used year after year.

The clutch usually consists of four eggs, three to five being sometimes laid. The egg is normally a broad oval, compressed at one end so as to be slightly pyriform. The texture is rather coarse with the surface smooth though dull and mostly glossless. When fresh the egg is nearly pure white, with a very faint tinge of bluish-grey but it soon becomes dirty and stained.

In size the egg measures about 2·90 by 2·10 inches.

THE PAINTED STORK

IBIS LEUCOCEPHALUS (Pennant)

Description.—Length 40 inches. Sexes alike. The whole head, neck and body white with a broad black band glossed with green across the breast; wings black glossed with green, the smaller coverts above and below with broad white edges and the greater coverts rosy pink; feathers at the junction of the wings and body pink with white edges; tail black.

Iris pale yellow; bill and bare facial skin orange-yellow, plumbeous at the base of the bill; legs brown.

Bill long, broad at the base and curved at the tip with both mandibles partly cylindrical; front of head naked; legs long with long toes and the tibia half-naked.

Field Identification.—A large long-legged Stork with a bill curving down towards the tip. Plumage white with a black band across the breast, the wing- and tail-quills black, but most easily identified by the conspicuous pink patch on the side of the wing. Common in parties on rivers and jheels.

Distribution.—Found throughout India south of the Himalayas as well as in Ceylon, Burma, Southern China and Cochin-China. A resident with local seasonal movements.

Habits, etc.—The Painted Stork (or, as it is sometimes called, the Pelican Ibis) is a common bird in well-watered parts of India, frequenting rivers, tanks, ponds and marshes usually in parties but occasionally solitary. It stalks about the shallows with its bill in the water partially open and ready to seize any fish, eel, frog or crab that comes its way. If the fish be a spiny one it crushes the spines between its strong mandibles and then swallows it head foremost. During the heat of the day it stands motionless in water digesting the morning meal. Like other Storks these birds have a habit of clattering the mandibles and shaking the head from side to side. Except for the ability to make a harsh croaking noise they are said to be voiceless. If brought up from the nest this species makes an excellent pet, becoming very docile and tame, answering to its name like a dog.

The breeding season follows immediately on the monsoon and is somewhat irregular and extended, lasting from September till April.

The birds nest in colonies, seventy to a hundred nests being found together on trees, so closely packed that half a dozen trees may suffice for the whole colony. Some colonies are in remote swamps on the large trees that rise among the water-logged grass and scrub. Others are to be found in the middle of villages or over village tanks where the birds pay no attention to the busy activities below them. Tamarind, peepul and banyan trees are usually chosen, and the nests are built on the tops of the upper boughs often 60 or 70 feet from the ground so that the birds can arrive or leave without brushing their wings. The Painted Storks are of course usually only part of still larger colonies of a number of other species of water-birds, the Storks' nests being surrounded by those of Spoonbills, Cormorants, Darters, Herons and Egrets, the whole forming a picture of bird-life hard to surpass.

The actual nests are loose ragged platforms composed of thin sticks and twigs with a hollow for the eggs. They strike one as rather small for the size of the bird.

The usual clutch consists of two to four eggs. These vary a good deal in size and shape but are typically elongated ovals, a good deal compressed towards one end. The shell is rather fine and compact but it is entirely devoid of gloss. In colour it is dull white, occasionally with a few dingy brown spots and streaks but it soon becomes stained and soiled as incubation progresses.

In size the egg averages about 2·77 by 1·88 inches.

THE OPEN-BILL

Anastomus oscitans (Boddaert)

Description.—Length 32 inches. Sexes alike. Entire plumage white except for the wing-quills, their neighbouring line of coverts and the tail which are black, glossed with dark green and purple.

In many birds the white is sullied with smoky grey, darkest on the nape and upper back. There has been some dispute about the identity of this grey phase, but it may represent the breeding plumage.

Iris pale brown; bill dull greenish, tinged with reddish beneath; bare facial skin blackish; legs pale fleshy.

Bill long and stout with both mandibles slightly curved so as to meet along the base and at the tip, leaving a wide gap just beyond the centre, the upper edge of this gap provided with lamellæ. Neck and legs long and the toes proportionately longer than in most Storks.

Field Identification.—A small white Stork with the tail and the flight-feathers black. Identified at once by the curious beak of which the mandibles do not meet properly, leaving a gap between them which is visible even in flight at a distance. In coloration it can only be confused with the slightly larger white Stork (*Ciconia ciconia*) of Europe, which is at once identified by the bright red normal shaped bill and the red legs.

This occurs in winter throughout India and in Ceylon, but is rare south of the Deccan. It is a common species in the plains of the north-west.

Distribution.—India, Ceylon, Assam, Burma, Siam and Cochin-China. No sub-species. It is found throughout India in suitable areas and is resident, though it moves about locally in accordance with water conditions.

Habits, etc.—The Open-Bill is probably the commonest and most widely distributed Stork in India, being found in all well-watered districts in the vicinity of rivers, lakes and marshes. It also visits irrigated land. It is a social bird and often gathers into considerable flocks. There is little to remark about the ordinary habits of the Open-Bill beyond the fact that it indulges in the dances common to most members of the family, that it makes the usual clattering noise with the beak and that it is a strong flier, accustomed to soar for long periods high in the air. Interest must be chiefly centred in the meaning of the curious beak and this is still a point which needs investigation. The chief food of the Open-Bill is undoubtedly fresh-water mollusca, though it occasionally eats fish, crabs and similar food. It has been suggested, therefore, that the gap in the beak is caused by wear, due to the constant crushing of the shells of mollusca. This explanation seems hardly adequate as it neither accounts for the unusual shape of the beak as a whole, the presence of the lamellæ on the upper mandible or the fact that similar wear does not take place

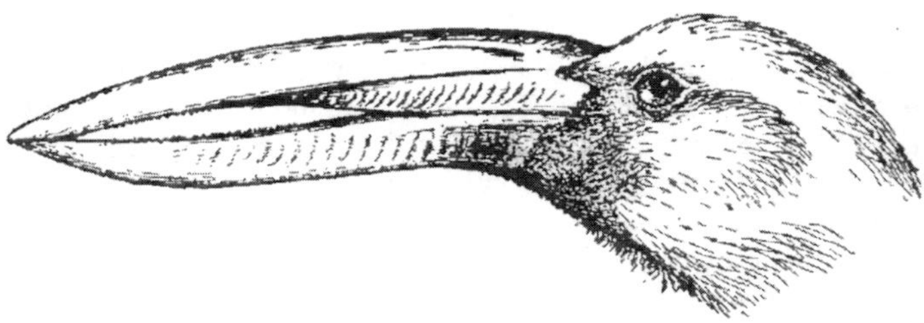

FIG. 100—Open-Bill ($\frac{2}{5}$ nat. size)

in other Storks which also to some extent feed on mollusca. The problem may be commended to field observers in India.

The breeding season in Northern India is in July and August. In Ceylon it is in January, February and March, and in Southern Madras eggs are said to have been taken in December.

The species is colonial in its breeding habits, and as many as 400 or 500 pairs have been found in a single colony. As a rule the colony only consists of the one species. At other times it includes other Herons and Ibises. The nest is a circular platform of sticks with a slight depression in the centre, scantily lined with grass and leaves. It is built on large trees and a single tree may contain as many as 60 nests. The condition of the branches and the ground under such trees may easily be imagined, and the fact that the lining of the nests is usually wet adds to the decay and fermentation characteristic of such a colony.

The clutch consists of four or five eggs.

The egg is usually a typical oval in shape, with a texture close and satiny. When fresh the colour is a kind of creamy-white without

PLATE XXIV

1. Pochard (male and female). 2. Night Heron. 3. Ruddy Sheldrake. (All about $\frac{1}{5}$ nat. size.)

[Face p. 506

markings, but this soon becomes soiled, and the egg then appears the dirty yellowish-brown common to incubated eggs of many water-birds.

The egg measures about 2·25 by 1·6 inches.

THE COMMON HERON

ARDEA CINEREA Linnæus

Description.—Length 40 inches. Sexes alike. Top of the head and crest and a band behind the eye purplish-black, the rest of the head white; neck white, tinged with greyish-lilac and streaked on the lower fore-neck with black; upper plumage ashy-grey, paler on the outer wing-coverts and with elongated whitish tips to the feathers of the shoulders; flight-feathers bluish-black; long breast plumes white; a black patch of long plumes on each side of the breast continued as a black band down each side of the body; sides of body and wing-lining grey; remainder of lower plumage white.

Iris golden-yellow; a bare patch of greenish skin in front of the eye; bill dusky yellow, culmen brownish; legs greenish-brown and greenish-yellow.

Bill long, compressed and pointed; neck and legs long; wings ample and rounded; tail short; toes long and slender with a slight web between the outer and middle toes; middle claw pectinated.

There are concealed patches of powder-down on each side of the rump and breast.

These patches, found in most members of the family, are believed to be connected with the cleaning of the plumage of the sticky slime inherent in a fish diet.

Field Identification.—A tall grey bird marked with black and white and with a sharp long bill, which broods almost motionless by the side of water. In flight recognisable at all distances by the slow flapping of the heavy rounded wings and by the long legs projecting behind.

Distribution.—The Common Heron is one of the widely spread and familiar birds of the Old World, being found through the greater part of Europe, Asia and Africa. It is divided into races, and birds found in India, Ceylon and Burma are said to belong to the Eastern race, *A. c. rectirostris*, though the typical race of Europe may occur in North-western India as a migrant. In India it appears to be mainly a resident species; it is generally distributed in the plains and in the hills up to about 5000 feet.

The Purple Heron (*Ardea purpurea*) found in suitable places throughout India is far more retiring and is usually flushed out of reed-beds. The rufous-buff neck, darker upper parts and chestnut under parts distinguish it from the Common Heron.

Habits, etc.—Although gregarious in the nesting season, and occasionally met in small parties or flocks at other times, the Heron is essentially a solitary bird ; and in that character it is familiar to the mass of mankind, who in the gaunt, motionless, silent figure see a suitable foil to the majesty of the scenery in which it is usually found. Mountain lake and purling mountain stream, the sand-banks and broad waters of the mighty rivers of the plains, tropical jheel, and dirty village pond, all alike afford the spectacle of a Heron at its fishing. Sometimes it wades in shallow water with slow deliberate paces, the neck outstretched ; more often it stands motionless at the edge of the water, the head sunk between the shoulders, and nothing but the cold keen eye to show that it is not asleep ; but woe betide the luckless frog or fish that trades on this immobility and ventures within reach. A thrust of the long neck and spear-point beak and the Heron has fed. Small mammals and birds, mollusca, insects and crustacea are also eaten, but the diet mainly consists of fish, whose scales are ejected in the form of castings.

The flight of the Heron is very majestic and characteristic, and when travelling the bird mounts high in the air and is recognisable a long way off. The head is drawn back within the shoulders and the long legs trail behind, while the large rounded wings beat with a slow methodical laboured rhythm. The call is a loud harsh *frarnk*, usually uttered in flight. The bird is partly nocturnal in its habits.

In India the breeding season extends from March to August.

The nest is a large, flat, loosely-built structure of twigs and sticks, scantily lined as a rule with straw and leaves. It is placed in trees at a considerable height from the ground. Many pairs breed in company, sometimes in a colony by themselves, at other times in company with different species of Egret. Occasionally they breed in reed-beds and then the nests are made of rushes and reeds.

The clutch in India normally consists of three eggs.

The egg is a moderately broad oval with a firm and rather coarse shell studded with minute pores, slightly chalky in texture and entirely without gloss. The colour is a delicate sea-green which soon fades.

In size the eggs average about 2·27 by 1·66 inches.

THE LITTLE EGRET

EGRETTA GARZETTA (Linnæus)

Description.—Length 25 inches. Sexes alike. Entire plumage pure white. In the breeding season the feathers of the breast are lengthened and lanceolate in shape and there is a crest of two long attenuated feathers. The feathers of the back are also greatly elongated and turn upwards at their ends, the rami being widely spaced, long and drooping; these are the "Egret" or "Osprey" plumes of the millinery trade.

Iris yellow; bill black, the base of the lower mandible and a bare patch round the eye greenish-yellow; legs black, toes and extreme base of tarsus yellow.

A miniature Heron in structure.

Field Identification.—A long-legged, long-necked, white bird, found generally in parties, about the neighbourhood of water. The pointed beak and small size at once separate it from the Spoonbill. Difficulty is sometimes found in identifying it in the field from the Large Egret (*Egretta alba*), the Smaller Egret (*Egretta intermedia*), the Reef Heron (*Demiegretta asha*) and the Cattle Egret, all white Herons, locally common. The points to remark for the Little Egret are its small size, the black beak at all seasons, and the two long crest plumes in breeding plumage. The Cattle Egret has the beak always yellow. The Reef Heron, a dimorphic bird, white or grey in colour, found along the west coast of India and in the Andaman Islands, has the beak and legs variable in colour but never black. The Large Egret and the Smaller Egret have the beak black whilst breeding, but yellow at other seasons. The former is generally solitary, and may be at once known by its size equal to that of the Common (Grey) Heron. In breeding plumage it has neither crest nor breast plumes. The Smaller Egret has no crest plumes in breeding plumage, but both breast and dorsal plumes, the latter being very long and exaggerated.

Distribution.—The typical race is widely distributed in Southern Europe, Africa and Southern Asia to Africa and Japan. It is common throughout the plains of India, Ceylon and Burma. There is a closely allied race in the Malayan Archipelago and Australia.

Habits, etc.—The Little Egret is found very generally throughout India wherever water is plentiful. Paddy-fields, marshes and tanks, rivers and creeks, and even irrigated fields and the neighbourhood of canals are all frequented by the birds. They live in parties and feed on the ground, wading about in the shallow margins of the water or stalking over the neighbouring grassland. Their food consists very largely of fish and frogs, but lizards, worms, grasshoppers, locusts, aquatic insects, freshwater mollusca and crustacea are all eaten. They rest either on the ground or on trees. The flight is rather slow and laboured with regular beats of the broad rounded wings, and in flight the head is retracted to the shoulders, and the legs outstretched beyond the tail.

The outstanding characteristic of the bird is, of course, the wonderful nuptial plumes from which the name is derived. These plumes have long been used amongst Eastern nations as an ornament to the

FIG. 101—Little Egret ($\frac{3}{10}$ nat. size)

head-dress, and the gift of a jewelled aigrette was one of the most distinguished compliments that an Oriental ruler could pay. Such a compliment was paid to Nelson by the Sultan after the Battle of the Nile. These aigrettes have an ungraceful copy in the stiff plumes mounted on the front of the Hussar busby and other military head-dresses.

In the last century the Little Egret with others of the family suffered greatly from the depredations of the plume-trade, since the aigrettes were in great demand for ladies' fashions. As the birds nest in large colonies and the aigrettes are only donned in the breeding season, much harm was done and great cruelty inflicted, whole colonies being wiped out by the adults being shot and the young left to starve in the nests. It was discovered in Sind, however, that the birds would breed in confinement and that the plumes could easily and more profitably be harvested from the captive birds. Egret-farming has since rapidly spread, and under present conditions it is permissible to hope that the Egrets may not be exterminated in India as they almost were in Egypt.

The breeding season in Northern India is in July and August, and in December in the south. This Egret invariably breeds in colonies in trees, generally in company with other species of Herons and Ibises, the various nests all jumbled up indiscriminately. The colonies are often placed in the centre of towns and villages. The nest is a rough shallow cup of sticks, occasionally lined with a little sedge or coarse grass.

The clutch consists of four or five eggs. They are moderately broad ovals, with a firm and rather coarse glossless shell fitted with minute pores. The colour is a delicate sea-green or bluish-green which soon fades.

The egg measures about 1·73 by 1·32 inches.

THE CATTLE EGRET

Bubulcus ibis (Linnæus)

Description.—Length 20 inches. Sexes alike. Entire plumage pure white.

When breeding hair-like plumes appear on head and neck, except on the forehead and the chin, and long " egret " plumes are developed on the back ; all these are orange-buff.

Iris pale golden-yellow ; a patch of bare skin from the eye to the beak greenish-yellow ; bill yellow ; legs black, in places mottled with yellowish.

A miniature Heron in structure.

Field Identification.—A slender white bird with long neck and legs usually found in attendance on herds of cattle. In the breeding season the buff egret plumes distinguish it from all other species, though it still looks white at a distance ; but when these are shed it is difficult to distinguish from the other species of Egret, which are also pure white in colour. The yellow bill separates it from the Little Egret, the black legs from the Reef Heron (*Demiegretta asha*), and size alone from the Large Egret (*E. alba*) and the Smaller Egret (*E. intermedia*).

Distribution.—The Cattle Egret is a widely spread species inhabiting the warmer parts of Europe and Asia and the whole of Africa.

It is divided into two races: the typical form is found in Europe and Africa, while *B. i. coromandus*, the race which is found in India, Ceylon and Burma, extends also to Southern Japan. In India it is generally spread throughout the plains except in the drier portions of the north-west. It is not found in the hills. A resident species.

Habits, etc.—The Cattle Egret or Buff-backed Heron is common enough in the well-watered parts of India where jheels, rivers, and inundations occur and cause the formation of grazing grounds for cattle, with lush green grass. This species, however, is not nearly so much a bird of the water as most of the Herons and Egrets, but it has specialised in the direction of attendance on cattle. Where herds of cattle commonly graze, there will this Egret be found, in parties large or small, attending the cattle closely, sometimes perching on their backs but more generally stalking round their legs. For though it feeds sometimes on small fish, tadpoles, and aquatic insects, its chief food consists of grasshoppers and flies, and these it obtains in plenty while attending the cattle, pecking them off the grass, and off the animals themselves. It also performs a definite service by ridding their skins of leeches, ticks and other parasites. It is a tame, confiding bird and is not molested by the cattle-herds, nor are its nuptial plumes sought after by plume-hunters, who confine their attention to the White Egrets.

The breeding season is dependent on the monsoons, in Northern India from June to August, and in the south in November and December. It breeds in colonies, usually in company with other similar species.

The nest is a rough unlined structure of sticks placed in trees, often at a considerable height from the ground.

The clutch consists of four or five eggs. The egg is a rather broad oval, somewhat pointed towards one end; the texture is compact and fine without gloss. The egg of this species is nearly always distinguishable from those of the other small Herons by its colour, white with a faint blue or green tinge, as opposed to the usual delicate sea-green tint.

The average measurement is 1·71 by 1·32 inches.

THE PADDY-BIRD

Ardeola grayi (Sykes)

(Plate xxii, Fig. 1, opposite page 462)

Description.—Length 18 inches. Sexes alike. Winter plumage: Head and neck dark brown streaked with pale yellowish-buff, darker on the crown and paler on the fore-neck; chin and throat white; the back and the shoulders ashy-brown with pale yellowish stripes on the latter; remainder of the plumage white, the upper breast streaked with brown.

In breeding plumage the head and neck are light yellowish-brown, the crown brown, and the chin and throat white; a white crest of long pointed feathers; back deep maroon, the feathers long and hair-like with dark slaty ends, and a line of brownish-buff feathers as a border; upper breast ashy-brown with narrow whitish streaks, the feathers long and rather disintegrated.

Iris bright yellow; eyelids greenish-yellow; bill bluish at the base, yellowish about the middle, and black at the tip; legs dull green.

The neck and legs are shorter than in the true Egrets.

Field Identification.—A very small Heron, the commonest of its family in India, found by every piece of water; it escapes notice by its dingy coloration until it springs to life with a flash of white wings.

Distribution.—The Paddy-bird or Pond-Heron is found in the west as far as the Persian Gulf, and from there extends throughout India, Ceylon and Burma to the Malay Peninsula. Within our area it is found practically everywhere in the plains, extending also in the hills up to 4000 feet. In the main a resident species it is locally migratory.

Habits, etc.—This must be one of the commonest and most familiar birds in India, being found wherever there is water. It feeds chiefly on frogs, crabs, small fishes, insects, and the other miscellaneous life that has its being in or near water; in pursuit of this mixed dietary the Paddy-bird spends its life on the edge of water, fresh or salt, in mangrove swamp, jheel and river, on lake and village pond, in road-side ditch or borrow-pit. No puddle is too small, no water too dirty for its attention. It sits there motionless on the mud, or ankle-deep in water, hunched up with the head and long neck drawn back within the shoulders, or stalks slowly along moving each foot with slow meticulous caution. But the quick stab of the pointed beak with all the length of the neck behind it is too quick for fish or grasshopper, and the little Heron never goes hungry in its hunting, for all its sluggard aspect. Its dull colours assimilate with the mud and herbage, and the bird is tame and confiding, with the result that it is seldom noticed until it rises close to the passer-by, springing into life with a sudden flash of the white wings, and a harsh croak which expresses its annoyance at the disturbance. To this invisibility is due the name of "blind heron" that it bears in several dialects. Though seemingly a misanthrope by nature, the Paddy-bird is found in great numbers in suitable places, and the birds collect to roost or to rest in shady branches in the daytime. They breed also more or less in company though hardly in defined colonies, and numbers of their nests will be found wherever Night Herons and Egrets collect to breed.

The breeding season lasts from May to September, and locally apparently to December, but most nests will be found in July and August.

The nest is a rough shallow cup of sticks, often small and very loosely put together; it is placed in the smaller forks of trees or large bushes, at heights varying from 10 to 30 feet from the ground, and the little Herons scramble and clamber along the branches with great facility, an accomplishment shared by the chicks when they are two-thirds grown.

The clutch varies from four to six eggs. The eggs are slightly elongated ovals, often perceptibly pointed at both ends; the texture is compact and fine, somewhat chalky and without any gloss. In colour they are a deep sea-green or greenish-blue, which is very liable to fade.

In size they average about 1·48 by 1·17 inches.

THE NIGHT HERON

Nycticorax nycticorax (Linnæus)

(Plate xxiv, Fig. 2, opposite page 506)

Description.—Length 23 inches. Sexes alike. Top of the head with a drooping crest and the back black glossed with metallic green; a few long narrow white feathers of great length spring from the crest; forehead, a streak over the eye, cheeks and the lower plumage white; sides and back of the neck, flanks, wings, rump and tail light ashy with a faint pinkish tinge.

Iris blood-red; bare skin from the eyes to the beak yellowish-green, dull livid in the breeding season; bill black, yellowish at the base except when breeding; feet yellowish-green.

The bill is stouter and deeper than in the other Herons, and the neck is short and thick.

Field Identification.—A small heavy Heron largely nocturnal in its habits, and sleeping by day in thick trees. The grey colour with white on the face and under surface, and the greenish-black crown and back are distinctive.

Distribution.—The typical race is found through South and Central Europe as well as nearly the whole of Africa and the greater part of Asia; other races are found in North America and the West Indies. In India it is very general, being found throughout the plains and in the North-western Himalayas up to 5000 or 6000 feet. In the main a resident species, it is also locally migratory.

Another heavy looking species of similar size is the Bittern (*Botaurus stellaris*) which may be flushed from reed-beds in winter in Northern

India. The colour is buffy-brown, streaked, barred and mottled with dark brown and black.

Habits, etc.—The Night Heron is very common and abundant, though like many species that are colonial in their habits and dependent on water, its distribution is rather irregular. It is definitely a nocturnal species and is very shy and secretive.

The members of a colony spend their day sleeping and brooding in the thick foliage of a clump of trees, waiting till the fall of dusk. Then the whole colony moves off to the feeding grounds, in a continuous stream, each bird flying separately and each at intervals uttering the harsh raucous *wock*, which is almost a quack rather than a croak. The flight is dignified and moderately fast, the bird looking very short and heavy with its head tucked into its shoulders and the regularly flapping broad round wings. The roosting place once left behind, the birds spread far afield for the night's fishing in every little pond and jheel and stretch of water. The food is varied, like that of all the Herons, and consists of small fish, amphibia, crustacea, and aquatic insects.

The breeding season is in July and August in the plains, but early in April and May in Kashmir. The nest is a rough and slight structure of sticks, unlined, and placed in a tree, usually at a good height from the ground. A few nests are solitary, but usually the birds build in colonies, and generally these colonies are in association with those of other species of Herons and Egrets.

The clutch consists of four or five eggs.

The egg is a moderately broad oval, as a rule rather obtuse at both ends. The texture is fine and hard, without gloss. The colour is a delicate pale sea-green, without markings.

The eggs measure about 1·92 by 1·35 inches.

THE CHESTNUT BITTERN

IXOBRYCHUS CINNAMOMEUS (Gmelin)

Description.—Length 15 inches. Male: whole upper plumage including the wings and tail rich chestnut, somewhat variable in tint; the whole lower plumage rich tawny ochraceous, the concealed bases of the feathers white, and a white stripe on each side of the throat; traces of a brown stripe down the middle of the fore-neck; a patch of black, buff-edged feathers on each side of the breast, largely concealed by the breast feathers.

Female: Upper parts dull chestnut-brown, washed with sooty on the crown; wings paler, the coverts mottled with buff and dark brown, the quills dark brown towards their bases; lower parts yellowish tawny streaked with dark brown, a darker broken band down the centre of the throat and neck.

Iris yellow to pale red; bill yellow, blackish along the top; facial skin reddish-purple in males, yellow in females; legs yellowish-green, soles yellow.

Bill stout, straight and pointed. Head narrow continuing the long neck; wings rounded; tail short. The feathers of the upper breast are elongated.

Field Identification.—A miniature Heron which lives by day in dense patches of reeds from which it is flushed with great difficulty. The rich tawny-chestnut colour, which includes the wings, separates it from all other forms. In flight the head is drawn back to the body, the rounded wings flap slowly and the legs are held out straight behind.

Distribution.—No sub-species. Widely distributed in India, Ceylon, Burma, China and the Malay States to the Philippines and Celebes. Very generally distributed throughout India, but dependent on suitable reed-beds for its distribution. A local migrant, but its movements are not properly known.

The Little Bittern (*Ixobrychus minutus*) and the Yellow Bittern (*Ixobrychus sinensis*) are two other species of similar size and habits, but immediately separated by having the wing-quills black. The Little Bittern breeds very commonly on the Kashmir Lakes and less commonly in Sind. The male is easily recognised in flight by the black crown and black back. The female is not ordinarily distinguishable in the field from both sexes of the Yellow Bittern, though these latter may be known in the hand by the vinaceous red sides to the neck, this part being yellowish-brown in the female Little Bittern. The Yellow Bittern is found more or less throughout India in large reed-beds. Another miniature Heron found by suitable water throughout India, but not in reed-beds, is the Little Green Heron (*Butorides striatus*) which may be recognised by the amount of green in its plumage.

Habits, etc.—The Chestnut Bittern has been chosen to illustrate the habits of the three species mentioned above which individually are seldom found in any numbers and yet collectively are very characteristic birds of the jheels of India. They are largely nocturnal in their habits. By day they hide in dense cover in reed-beds, swamps or rice-fields and can only be driven out by careful beating. By night they fly out to fish in more open places where they catch a miscellaneous diet of fish, frogs, worms and various water-insects and larvæ. Like the larger Herons they have the gift of patience and sit solitary waiting for their prey; but they can also be very active, climbing about the reeds and stems on foot. All three species probably have the habit, known in the Little Bittern when danger threatens, of standing with the head and neck extended skywards, the feathers closely pressed against the skin, the whole attitude and coloration being protective amongst the varied lights and shades of a reed-bed. To this the streaking on the lower plumage greatly contributes. The ordinary call is a slight croak.

The breeding season is in the rains from June to September.

The nest is a slight shallow pad composed of short lengths of sedge, lined with rather finer grass. It is built, of course, in a dense reed-bed, and may be placed near the surface of the water on the roots of the reeds or at any height in the reed-bed, either on a bush or more usually on a number of reeds bent down for the purpose.

The clutch consists of four or five eggs.

The egg is a broad regular oval, very fine and compact in texture but without gloss. The colour is dull white, sometimes with a very faint bluish tinge, but the egg very quickly becomes dirty and stained. Both sexes incubate, and incubation in this genus usually starts with the laying of the first egg so that the young found in a nest are of different sizes.

The egg measures about 1·30 by 1·05 inches.

THE NUKTA

SARKIDIORNIS MELANOTOS (Pennant)

Description.—Length, male 30 inches; female 26 inches. Male: Head and neck white, spotted with glossy black, the black prevailing along the top of the head and back of the neck; a collar round the lower neck, and the lower plumage pure white, washed with pale ashy-grey on the sides of the breast and flanks; the whole upper plumage, wings and tail, except the brownish-grey lower back, black glossed with green, purple and blue, a black bar extending on to each side of the upper breast and another on to the lower flanks.

The female is similar but smaller, with more black on the head and neck and less gloss elsewhere.

Iris brown; bill black; legs greenish-plumbeous.

The male has a black fleshy knob (the comb) on the top of the beak which becomes greatly developed in the breeding season.

Field Identification.—A large Goose-like duck, glossy black above white below, with a spotted head and neck. The size and coloration is distinctive apart from the curious comb of the drake.

Distribution.—Found in India, Ceylon and Burma in suitable localities; also in Africa south of the Sahara and in Madagascar.

The typical race is found virtually throughout India except in the North-west Frontier Province and Baluchistan, the Northern and Western Punjab, and the north-western portions of Sind; it is confined to the plains and appears to be a local migrant.

The Flamingo (*Phœnicopterus ruber*) is usually placed near the geese and ducks. The rosy-pink and white plumage with black flight-quills, the long legs and neck and the unique bill bent downwards and adapted for feeding in an inverted position render identification easy. It is found on lagoons throughout India, but is most numerous as a non-breeding visitor to North-west India. It breeds in Cutch.

Habits, etc.—The Nukta or Comb-duck is common in well-watered and well-wooded parts of India, and is generally found in large marshy tanks and jheels with reedy margins and plenty of trees in the vicinity. In such places it is found in pairs and family parties, and not being semi-nocturnal in its habits like most of the ducks and geese, is to

FIG. 102—Nukta (½ nat. size)

be seen moving about freely on the wing at all times of day. It roosts, as it nests, in trees.

The flight is powerful and fairly rapid, and when a pair are on the wing together the male usually leads. The voice is more like that of a goose than a duck, and in the vicinity of the nest the bird tends to be rather noisy, heralding the approach of an intruder with loud trumpet-calls; the ordinary note of the male is a low grating noise. It is not a particularly wary species, but as the flesh is very indifferent for the table it is a pity to shoot so handsome a bird.

The food consists largely of the grains of wild and cultivated rice, but the roots, seeds and shoots of various water-plants are also eaten, as well as a certain amount of worms and spawn and larvæ of aquatic insects.

The breeding season is from June to September, depending a good deal on the commencement of the rains.

The nest is normally built in trees and is a rough structure of sticks and grass lined with a few dead leaves and feathers ; it is placed either in a hole in a trunk, or in the depression so often found where several large branches join the trunk of a tree ; mango trees are usually favoured.

The normal clutch consists of seven to twelve eggs, but the number frequently exceeds this, and forty eggs have been recorded in a single nest, though these may have been the product of two females.

The eggs are very regular ovals, slightly pointed at one end. The texture is wonderfully close and compact, and when fresh, the eggs both in colour and appearance seem made of polished ivory ; with the progress of incubation some of the gloss departs and the shells become stained and dirty.

In size the eggs average about 2·40 by 1·70 inches.

THE COTTON-TEAL

NETTAPUS COROMANDELIANUS (Gmelin)

(Plate xxiii, Fig. 3, opposite page 484)

Description.—Length 13 inches. Male in summer plumage: Top of the head dark brown ; a black collar glossed behind with green round the lower neck ; remainder of the head and neck white ; upper plumage dark brown glossed with metallic-green or purple ; primaries dark brown on their basal halves, then white with the tips black ; secondaries dark brown glossed with metallic-green or purple and tipped with white ; upper tail-coverts dark brown mottled and finely barred with white ; lower plumage white, the sides finely vermiculated with brown ; wing-lining and a patch under the tail dark chocolate-brown.

In winter the male loses its collar and resembles the female except for the white wing-bar and some of the green gloss on the upper plumage and wings.

Female : Top of the head and a line through the eye brown ; remainder of head and neck and lower parts sullied white, the head and neck being speckled with brown marks that become defined wavy lines on the breast ; upper parts, wings and tail brown, the inner wing-quills tipped with white and the upper tail-coverts mixed with it.

Iris red in males, brown in females ; bill brown above yellowish below, in breeding males black ; legs greenish-yellow, in breeding males black and dusky yellow.

The beak is short and Goose-like, that is, very high at the base and narrowing gradually in front.

Field Identification.—The smallest of the Indian Ducks, being easily recognised by its size and the predominance of white in the plumage. The drake in full plumage is dark glossy brown above with a white wing-bar and a black collar; the female is brown above and lacks the wing-bar and collar.

Distribution.—The Cotton-Teal is found in India, Ceylon and Burma, and it extends eastwards through the Malay countries to China and southwards to the Philippines and Celebes. In India it is generally distributed in the plains except along the western border from Malabar to the Northern Punjab, where it is scarce or wanting. A resident species, it is also locally migratory.

Habits, etc.—This curious little Duck finds its usual habitat in those overgrown ponds and broad dykes and channels where much of the water is choked with a growth of grass and weeds. It may also be found on open sheets of water, but even then it keeps to the weediest stretches and the near neighbourhood of cover. It lives in parties and small flocks, and by nature, when undisturbed, is familiar and unwary. It spends all its time in the water and dives well, but being a poor walker it seldom ventures out on to land though it perches at times on trees. The flight is fast, and as a rule it flies low over the water, twisting and turning skilfully to avoid stumps and clumps of vegetation. On the wing it is very noisy, uttering a peculiar cackling note which has been likened to the words *fixed bayonets*.

The breeding season is from June to August.

This Duck nests in the holes and hollows of trees in the near vicinity of water; the site may be at any height from the ground, from near water-level to about 30 feet up; though the majority of nests are placed at a height of about 10 or 15 feet. The hole is thickly lined with twigs, grass and feathers, all the work being done apparently by the female alone.

The normal clutch varies from eight to fourteen eggs, but as many as twenty-two have been recorded.

The egg is a very regular oval, almost indeed spherical in shape. The shell is very fine and smooth in texture, ivory-white in colour with a high gloss.

In size it averages about 1·7 by 1·29 inches.

THE BAR-HEADED GOOSE

ANSER INDICUS (Latham)

Description.—Length 30 inches. Sexes alike. Head white, with two short black bars on the nape; a white band down each side of the neck; hind-neck dark brown, passing into the pale ashy-grey of the upper plumage; on the upper back and shoulders the feathers have paler tips and the greater coverts are broadly edged with white; flight-feathers black, the outer ones with much of the base grey; tail pale grey with white edges; fore-neck brownish-ashy, passing gradually into whity-brown on the breast; sides of the breast browner, darkest on the flanks, barred with the pale tips of the feathers; remainder of lower plumage white.

Iris brown; bill yellow, with the nail blackish; legs orange.

A heavily-built bird, with a long neck and short rounded tail. Bill short and high at the base, almost conical in shape; legs short and stout with webbed toes.

FIG. 103—Bar-headed Goose (½ nat. size)

Field Identification.—A typical Goose, grey-brown and white in colour and easily identified from all other species by the two dark bars on the back of the head.

Distribution.—In summer the Bar-headed Goose breeds in Central Asia and Western China southwards as far as Ladakh and Tibet. In winter it moves south to India and Burma, arriving in October and leaving in March.

In Northern India it is abundant in winter from the Indus Valley eastwards across to Assam, most numerous on the west and less so to the east. About the Central Provinces it grows less common and south of that it is scarce, though stragglers are found right down into Southern India.

The Greylag Goose (*Anser anser*) is also a common winter visitor to Northern India, where it is abundant in Kashmir, the Punjab,

Sind and the United Provinces. The white nail to the bill and the grey rump assist its identification. Considerable doubt attaches to the identity of other species found in India, but the White-fronted Goose (*Anser albifrons*) with a white nail and a dark greyish-brown rump occurs in small numbers in the North-west. In this species a white band about the base of the beak is most distinct.

Habits, etc.—This typically Indian Goose is found on the larger lakes and jheels of Northern India but it is chiefly a riverain species, spending the hours of rest and daylight on the sand-banks of the great rivers of the north and feeding by night in the cultivation that extends about their banks. These, like other species of geese, graze on green vegetable food, and they do a lot of damage to the young shoots of wheat, barley and rice, and also in the grain-fields, which are visited night after night. There is a well-marked morning and evening flight to and from the feeding grounds, and where the birds are not much disturbed they start feeding early in the evenings and also continue after dawn.

At all times they are very wary and difficult to approach, and the flocks are usually credited with posting definite sentinels.

This Goose is found normally in large flocks of 20 to 100 birds, but occasionally small parties and pairs separate off by themselves. They fly high in the air with a very measured beat of the wings and keep in regular formations of lines and wedges. The call is a deep sonorous note, uttered by several birds in unison and usually described as "gaggling."

In Ladakh and Tibet the eggs are laid in May and June. The nests are placed on islands of the salt lakes at 13,000 and 14,000 feet elevation, and are mere hollows in the soil lined with the bird's own down. Where suitable islands do not exist, nests are placed on the ledges of cliffs.

The full clutch usually consists of five or six eggs. The egg is a long-pointed oval, strong in texture with a rather coarse grain and little gloss. The colour is a very pale creamy-white which soon becomes soiled.

The egg measures about 3·20 by 2·23 inches.

THE WHISTLING TEAL

Dendrocygna javanica (Horsfield)

Description.—Length 17 inches. Sexes alike. Top of the head brown, darkening behind; remainder of head and neck light brown, darkening behind and paling to almost white on the chin and throat; back and shoulders dark brown, with broad pale rufous tips to the feathers; wings black with a chestnut patch on the shoulder; rump blackish; upper tail-coverts chestnut; tail dark brown; lower parts light ferruginous, becoming pale yellowish-brown on the upper breast and whitish below the tail; flanks light brown, with broad whitish shaft-streaks.

Iris brown, eyelids bright yellow; bill brownish-blue, the nail nearly black; legs brownish-blue.

The nail at the tip of the bill is prominent and sharply bent downwards; wings broad and rounded; legs long and stout.

Field Identification.—A heavy dark brown Duck with rounded wings which frequents overgrown swamps and settles in trees; the whistling call is distinctive. The chestnut upper tail-coverts distinguish it from the Larger Whistling Teal, in which they are whitish.

Distribution.—Found in India, Ceylon and Burma, extending also eastwards to the Malay Peninsula, Siam, Cochin-China, Southern China, Sumatra, Borneo and Java. In India it is found almost throughout the plains except in the North-west Frontier Province and in the Northern and Western Punjab. A local migrant, its movements depending on the water-supply.

The Larger Whistling Teal (*Dendrocygna fulva*) has a remarkable distribution in India, Burma and Ceylon, Africa and Central and South America. In our area it seems to be common only in Lower Bengal and Assam.

Habits, etc.—This Duck avoids rivers and open weedless stretches of water and prefers tanks, backwaters, swamps, and lakes where there is an abundant growth of weeds and vegetation. Trees also are essential to its comfort, as it not only breeds in them but roosts and rests on the branches often in preference to water. It is usually found in flocks of fifty individuals and more, and in specially favoured localities it collects in vast numbers, surpassing those of all other Duck. Its dietary is very varied, but a vegetable diet seems to be preferred, and large quantities of mollusca are devoured. It is not suitable for the table.

The Whistling Teal is a strong quick swimmer and it dives well; the flight is not very fast, though the wings are beaten very rapidly and with great effort. As the name denotes, the call is a regular whistle, not very clear, rather sibilant, and by no means harsh or shrill. It is constantly uttered on the wing, especially when the bird first takes to flight. There is also a low chuckling call, almost a quack.

The breeding season is from late June until September. A certain number of nests are to be found on the ground or a few feet above it in masses of dense herbage. But the ordinary nest is in a tree, either in the deserted nests of crows and kites, or in hollows in the trunks and branches or between the boughs. The trees chosen are usually in the vicinity of water; and the nest is seldom more than 20 feet from the ground.

In the more open situations in trees the nest is a well-made structure of twigs and sticks lined with grass and a few feathers, but in deeper holes in trees the eggs are sometimes merely laid on the natural debris in the bottom of the hole.

The average clutch consists of eight to ten eggs, though more or less are often laid.

The egg is a spherical oval, very smooth and fine in texture, neither close-grained nor glossy, but rather chalky. The colour is ivory white, which soon becomes stained.

It measures about 1·85 by 1·50 inches.

THE RUDDY SHELDRAKE

Casarca ferruginea (Pallas)

(Plate xxiv, Fig. 3, opposite page 506)

Description.—Length 26 inches. Male: Head and neck buff, passing on the neck into the orange-brown of the body plumage; lower back and rump vermiculated with black; wings whitish-buff, quills black, the inner quills with the outer webs metallic-green and bronze; tail and its upper coverts black; lower abdomen chestnut; wing-lining white. There is sometimes a black ring round the neck.

The female is sometimes duller in tint with the head paler, almost whitish; she lacks the black neck ring.

Iris dark brown; bill and legs black.

Very similar to a goose in structure, but the bill is flatter and more duck-like.

Field Identification.—Easily distinguished from all other ducks by its bright orange-brown coloration and paler head and neck, contrasting in flight with the black quills and white wing-lining. Chiefly found on the sand-banks of rivers, and usually in pairs.

Distribution.—Breeds from South Russia and the Balkan Peninsula eastwards through Middle Asia to China and Japan. In winter it moves southwards to North Africa, India, Ceylon and Burma, and Southern China to Formosa. In India it arrives about October and stays until April, and is found throughout the length and breadth of the country in suitable places.

The Sheldrake (*Tadorna tadorna*) can be confused with no other Indian duck, with its white plumage banded with black and chestnut, the greenish black head and bright green speculum. It is an uncommon winter visitor to Northern India.

Habits, etc.—The Ruddy Sheldrake or Brahminy Duck in India is essentially a bird of the larger rivers where the water is clean and free of vegetation and there are extensive sand-banks and sandy islets left by the falling floods of the summer. In such localities it is found in pairs which spend the greater portion of their time on the sandy margins of the water, comparatively seldom entering it; but when they do so they swim well, with the head erect, the front half of the body low and the stern held high; on land they walk with ease. During the day they generally rest, sitting and standing about together, and at night they feed, often separating in the process. This has given rise to the native legend that in the pairs of Brahminies are enshrined the souls of erring lovers doomed as punishment to remain in sight and hearing but separated by the flowing stream; the ordinary call which is freely uttered is a loud rather melodious *a-onk*, which for the purposes of the legend is considered to form the names of Chakwa and Chakwi, and the lovers are credited with the eternal query in hope *Chakwa aunga* (Chakwa, shall I come?) answered sadly in the terms of the punishment *Chakwi na ao* (No, Chakwi). A warning note—a rolling *k-r-r-r-rew*—seems to be uttered only by the male.

In the absence of rivers and sand-banks the Brahminy visits lakes and large tanks, but only those of the most open character. On the wing they rise high into the air and fly strongly with rather slow wing-beats, and through this and their bright coloration which catches the sun they are easily recognisable at a great distance. On migration numbers of pairs collect into loose flocks. Calm and confiding in its demeanour when danger does not threaten, it is one of the wariest of the family, and to bring it to bag is always a triumph for the sportsman. In the main it is a vegetable feeder, and is therefore, as a rule, quite good eating; though there is a prejudice against it for the table as it is supposed to feed on carrion.

The breeding season in Ladakh is in May and June. Here it nests in holes and crevices of the high cliffs that overhang the rivers and lakes, building a nest of down and feathers. Six to ten eggs are laid. The egg is a moderately broad oval, slightly pointed at one end. The texture is fine and smooth with a slight gloss and the colour is creamy-white.

The egg measures about 2·5 by 1·8 inches.

THE MALLARD

ANAS PLATYRHYNCHA Linnæus

Description.—Length 24 inches. Male: Head and upper neck glossy emerald-green divided by a white ring from the deep chestnut breast; upper back finely vermiculated with brown and white washed on the shoulders with chestnut; middle back dark brown; rump and a patch above and below the tail black, partly glossed with purple or green; wings brown, the speculum * metallic violet-purple between two white bars edged interiorly with black; tail greyish-white, the four central feathers black glossed with blue-green and curled over backwards; lower plumage finely vermiculated grey and white; under surface of wings white.

Female: Brown above, the feathers edged with buff, and on the upper back and shoulders with concentric buff bands; sides of the head paler than the crown, with a darker streak through the eye; chin and throat brownish-buff; wings as in the male; under parts buff with brown centres to the feathers, the upper breast browner; tail brown with whitish-buff edges.

Iris brown; bill greenish-yellow, blackish towards the tip, duller and yellower in the female; legs orange-red.

After breeding, the drake moults about June into a plumage resembling that of the female, and reassumes his own distinctive dress by another moult in September. This is known as the " eclipse," and as the wing-quills are shed simultaneously and not in pairs in the usual manner, the bird is, for a time, virtually flightless. The female undergoes similar moults, and these are found in most of those species of duck in which the males are brilliantly coloured and do not assist in rearing the young. With the exception of the Spotbill all the following species have an " eclipse " plumage.

Field Identification.—The most generally known of all wild duck. The mottled brown and buff duck and the greyish-white-looking drake, with his dark green head and chestnut breast separated by a white ring, are easily identified by the violet-purple speculum bordered above and below by black and white bands.

Distribution.—The Mallard breeds throughout the Northern Hemisphere, and in winter is found southwards to Northern Africa, Madeira, the Canaries and Northern India. It is found also in North America (though the Greenland and Iceland birds have been separated as sub-species), wintering south to Mexico, the West Indies and Panama. Within our limits it breeds in very great numbers in Kashmir

* Speculum is the name applied to the rectangular patch of metallic colour found on the wing of many freshwater ducks.

and great numbers winter there. It is abundant also in winter in the North-west Frontier Province, Baluchistan, the Punjab, Sind, and in lesser numbers in the United Provinces. A few wander to Rajputana, the Central Provinces, Bombay, Bengal and Assam, but it is unknown in Southern India. It is most numerous from December to February.

Habits, etc.—The Mallard in India is found in pairs, small parties, and in flocks numbering up to forty or fifty birds, which may be found in all places where wild duck congregate, jheels, rivers, lakes and tanks, small reedy channels and irrigated cultivation. They swim and walk well, and when feeding do not dive, though they frequently depress the head and neck so far below water that their bodies are vertically inclined, the tail sticking straight into the air, while their feet paddle to maintain the balance. They rise quickly into the air straight off the surface of the water, and once on the wing the flight is very fast, the strong regular beat of the wings producing a whistling sound audible some distance away. They feed both by day and night, and have a regular flight to and from favoured feeding grounds at dusk and dawn; though this habit is not quite so marked in India as in the west, owing to the greater abundance of safe feeding places. The ordinary note of the male is a low and soft sound between a croak and a murmur, while the female has a louder and clearer jabber. But when flushed both sexes quack, that of the female being also louder.

The breeding season in Kashmir is in May and June. The nest is built of coarse flags and grasses, more or less lined with feathers and down from the bird's own breast; it is placed in clumps of rushes along the edges of jheels and water-courses.

The clutch consists of six to twelve eggs.

The egg is a moderately broad regular oval, of a fine and smooth texture with a slight gloss. Freshly laid it is of a dull pale greenish tint, but this soon fades and stains into a dingy brown colour.

In size the eggs average about 2·20 by 1·60 inches.

THE SPOTBILL

ANAS PŒCILORHYNCHA Forster

Description.—Length 24 inches. Sexes alike. Head and neck whitish with brown streaks except on the chin and throat, the marking being heaviest on the top of the head and in a band through the eye; upper back brown with pale edges to the feathers; wings brown, the speculum bright metallic-green, between two white bars edged interiorly with black, above the speculum a broad white streak; lower back, tail and a patch above and below black; breast and lower abdomen fulvous-white spotted with brown; lower abdomen dark brown; under surface of wings white.

Iris brown; bill black with a yellow tip and a red spot on each side of the base; legs orange-red.

Field Identification.—A large duck in which both sexes wear a grey version of the plumage of the female Mallard. They are readily distinguished from her by the green (as opposed to purple) speculum, the bright red spots at the base of the beak, and the clumsier build.

Distribution.—The Spotbill is found almost throughout the Indian Empire, Siam, Cochin-China, China and Eastern Siberia. It is divided into three races, but we are only concerned with the typical form which occurs in India, Ceylon and Assam north of the Brahmaputra. In India it is very generally distributed south of the Himalayas from the Indus Valley eastwards, being most common in North-western and Central India. It is only locally migratory.

Habits, etc.—Apart from the fact that it is a resident species, the Spotbill differs from most of our Indian migratory ducks in its lack of sociability; it rarely associates closely with other species, and is usually found only in pairs or small parties of ten to a dozen birds of its own species. These avoid large open waters, and prefer small weedy jheels with plenty of cover or straggling creeks well screened by trees. Fresh water is essential to them, even brackish water, like the Sunderbunds, not being to their taste.

The Spotbill is a good bird for the table, as it is largely a vegetable feeder, and indeed often does a good deal of damage to the rice crops, trampling down and spoiling as much as it eats; water-molluscs, frogs, worms, and insects are also eaten. From the sporting point of view it is less interesting than most of our other ducks. It is not shy, and resting amongst cover often gets up practically at the feet of the sportsman, rising slowly and with a good deal of fuss, but once well on the wing it is a most deceptive bird to shoot, its size making the flight appear slower than it really is.

When wounded it dives well and conceals itself skilfully in the weeds or under water, holding itself submerged with only its bill exposed for air.

The ordinary note is a quack, very similar to that of the Mallard.

The breeding season is rather variable, from March to December, according to locality and the state of the rainfall, and at times the bird appears to be double-brooded.

The nest is a compact well-made structure of grasses, rushes and weeds, lined with the down of the parent bird. It is well concealed in herbage on the ground on small islands or bunds at the edge of streams and ponds, or even in grass some distance away from water.

The clutch consists of eight to ten eggs, and fourteen have been recorded. The egg is a broad regular oval, rather pointed at the small end and the texture is smooth and fine with a slight gloss. The colour is a pale buffy-drab, which grows stained with incubation.

The eggs measure about 2·15 by 1·70 inches.

THE GADWALL

CHAULELASMUS STREPERUS (Linnæus)

(Plate xxiii, Fig. 4, opposite page 484)

Description.—Length 20 inches. Male: Head and neck greyish-white speckled with brown, the crown and a band through the eye chiefly brown; lower neck and upper back dark brown with concentric whitish bars; back brown, the feathers edged and vermiculated with fulvous white; rump and a patch above and below the tail black; wings greyish-brown, the speculum white, edged exteriorly with black and divided by a broad shaded black bar from a patch of chestnut on the wing-coverts; tail greyish-brown; lower plumage whitish with heavy brown crescents on the breast and narrow wavy brown bars on the sides and flanks.

Female: Head and neck streaked brown and white, browner above and whiter beneath; upper plumage dark brown, the feathers edged with rufous buff; rump blackish-brown; wings and tail as in the male except that the chestnut patch is very indistinct; breast pale rufous spotted with brown; abdomen white.

Iris brown; bill leaden-grey, in female dusky with orange sides; legs dull orange-yellow, webs dusky.

Field Identification.—A large, rather dully-coloured duck which may be recognised at once by the white speculum divided by a black bar from a patch of chestnut on the wing-coverts. The drake has the tail set in a patch of velvet black, with the breast boldly marked in brown and white crescents.

Distribution.—The Gadwall is found throughout the Northern Hemisphere, breeding in the temperate portions of Europe, North-western Asia and America. In winter it migrates southwards to Abyssinia, India, Burma, China, Mexico, and Florida. In India it is a most abundant winter visitor from about October to April, found in great numbers through Northern India down to Northern Bombay. South of that it grows less common until Mysore is its southern limit.

The Wigeon (*Mareca penelope*) is also a common winter visitor to India, being most numerous in the North-west. The drake is unmistakable. His creamy-golden forehead and crown stand out in contrast with the chestnut head and neck; the back and flanks are vermiculated grey, whilst sharply-defined black under tail-coverts and a large white shoulder-patch are points to observe. The female is slighter in build than the Gadwall and more rufous and has the tail slightly pointed. The Marbled Duck (*Marmaronetta angustirostris*) is far scarcer and more irregular in appearance in Northern India. It is remarkable for the curiously mottled grey and brown plumage of both sexes and the absence of a speculum.

Habits, etc.—Except that it avoids the sea-coast the Gadwall is found in India wherever other ducks are found, in all types of river, marsh and tank, and it is certainly one of the most abundant species throughout the whole of Continental India. It is usually found in flocks of ten to thirty individuals and is not particularly shy though it is a fine sporting bird, rising quickly and cleanly from the water and flying after the fashion of a Teal, fast and high with noisy wings, which appear more pointed than those of the Mallard. On the water it sits higher than the Mallard, with the stern more elevated. Normally it does not dive, but can do so strongly when wounded.

The call may be described as a chuckling croak. The flesh is very good eating, as the bird is chiefly a vegetarian, and feeds largely on rice, becoming very fat, and in the varied bags of duck that are obtainable in India the Gadwall holds a high place.

In the north the breeding season is about May.

The nest is placed in a hollow of the ground amongst thick vegetation on the edge of water and is made of reeds and grass with a mixture of down and feathers.

The normal clutch consists of six to ten eggs, but as many as sixteen have been found. The egg is a regular blunt oval, fine and smooth in texture with a slight gloss; in colour it is a warm yellowish cream.

It measures about 2·26 by 1·51 inches.

THE COMMON TEAL

NETTION CRECCA (Linnæus)

Description.—Length 15 inches. Male: Head and upper neck chestnut, with a broad metallic-green band edged with a buff line running back from the eye and enclosing it, a buff line also connects it with the side of the chin; chin blackish-brown; lower neck all round, back and sides of the body narrowly barred black and white; a broad buff line edged exteriorly with black along each shoulder; rump brown; upper tail-coverts black edged with fulvous; wings brown, the speculum bright emerald-green edged with velvet-black more broadly towards the edge of the wing, and divided by a pale cinnamon and white bar from the lesser wing-coverts; tail brown; breast whitish spotted with black; abdomen white; under the tail a black patch with buff sides.

Female: Upper parts, wings and tail dark brown, the edges of the feathers paler; wings as in the male; lower parts whitish, the sides and lower surface of the head and neck marked with brown, and the breast spotted with brown.

Iris brown; bill dark slaty-grey; legs brownish or greenish-grey.

Field Identification.—A very small duck, distinguished from other Indian species by the conspicuous emerald green and black speculum and the pale cinnamon bar on the coverts. The chestnut head and buff-edged green eye-patch, the fine black and white barring of the body and the black and white line down the shoulders of the drake in full plumage are very distinctive.

Distribution.—The Teal is very generally distributed in Europe, Northern Africa and Asia, breeding in the northern and more temperate parts of this area and moving southwards in winter. Another race occurs in North America. The typical race does not breed anywhere within the confines of the Indian Empire, but in winter it is very generally distributed in India, Burma and Ceylon from about October to March, a few being met with from August to May.

The Garganey (*Querquedula querquedula*) is found throughout India and is one of the earliest ducks to arrive, at the end of August. The broad white eye-stripe, the pale blue shoulder to the wing and the elongated scapulars of the male are distinctive. The female resembles the duck Teal but is paler. The Baikal Teal (*Nettion formosum*), with its green and creamy-white head markings, and the Falcated Teal (*Eunetta falcata*), with bushy green crest and long sickle-shaped tertiaries, are both rare stragglers to India and Burma.

Habits, etc.—The Teal is one of the most abundant and favoured by the sportsman of the many species of wild-fowl which congregate in India in winter. It is found in any type of water or marshy ground, on rivers and lakes, in jheels and irrigation, in the muddy village pond or the roadside ditch; its numbers vary with the accommodation from single birds and pairs to flocks many hundreds strong, though probably the most usual formation in which to find it is a flock numbering some thirty or forty birds; these associate with other species of duck on the water and when disturbed often fly with them, but the alliance is only temporary, the association of the hour.

The Teal is very largely a night feeder, and is, therefore, one of the species most frequently observed at the flight, and though it feeds a good deal by day numbers will be flushed from thick cover about the edges of water, where they idly doze away the hours of sunshine in the shade. The bird is chiefly a vegetable feeder, and obtains much of its food on foot, for it is a good walker, dredging and sifting the mud in shallow water with its beak. It also feeds while swimming, and though not a diver, except when wounded, is able to "stand on its head" in the water, tail in air, after the fashion of the domestic duck and its wild progenitor, the Mallard.

The flight is exceedingly swift and strong, and on the wing the bird is a master of the art of twisting and wheeling. It is not a noisy duck; the note of the male is a low far-sounding *krit-krit*, while the female has a short sharp *quack*.

In the North, about April or May, the Teal breeds in boggy patches on moorland, in the glades of woods or in marshes. The nest is placed on the ground and is a mass of leaves, grasses, bracken and other vegetable matter, lined with down and a few feathers. It is well concealed under tufts of grass or bushes.

The clutch varies from eight to twelve eggs, but as many as twenty have been found. The egg is a broad regular oval, compressed towards one end; the texture is fine, close and smooth and there is a slight gloss. The colour is a pale uniform buff, sometimes tinged with green.

The egg measures about 1·60 by 1·20 inches.

THE PINTAIL

DAFILA ACUTA (Linnæus)

Description.—Length 22 to 29 inches, of which 5 to 8 inches belongs to the tail. Male: Head and fore-neck umber-brown; hind-neck black; a white band down each side of the neck from the nape to join the white of the lower parts; upper plumage and sides of the body finely barred and vermiculated with black and white; longer scapulars lanceolate in shape, velvet-black, edged with light brown; wings greyish-brown, the speculum metallic-green edged on three sides with black, the black being deepest and widest interiorly, a buff bar above the speculum and a white bar below it; upper tail-coverts black and grey; tail brown, the long central feathers black; breast and abdomen white, speckled with grey towards the tail; lower flanks buff; a black patch below the tail.

Female: Greyish-brown above, streaked paler, with concentric pale bars on the back; wing greyish-brown, the speculum dull and ill-defined with little trace of green or black, and set between two white bars; chin and throat white; lower plumage whitish marked with dusky brown.

Iris dark brown; bill bluish-plumbeous, black along the top; legs greyish-plumbeous.

The neck is long and the central tail-feathers long and pointed.

Field Identification.—A very slender and graceful duck with long neck and sharply-pointed tail. The drake is easily distinguished by the brown head, the white line running down the sides of the neck to the white breast, and the buff spot before the black patch under the tail. In the absence of a distinctive speculum and marking, the female is difficult to recognise except by her shape, but she is only likely to be confused with female Gadwall and Wigeon. In both of these, however, the speculum has a white inner border formed by the outer web of the next secondary.

Distribution.—The typical race of Pintail breeds in the Northern Hemisphere across Northern Europe, Northern and Central Russia and Northern Asia, migrating south in winter to Central and Southern Europe, Northern Africa and Southern Asia, including India, Ceylon and Burma. American birds have been separated sub-specifically.

In India it is purely a winter visitor, arriving at the end of October and leaving in March, and it is found practically throughout the country, though it is by no means universally distributed.

Similarity of name must not lead to confusion with the Stiff-tailed Duck (*Erismatura leucocephala*) which is a scarce visitor to North West India. This is a curious brown bird with a white face, and it is remarkable for its diving powers and the habit of swimming with the tail erect.

Habits, etc.—The Pintail easily holds the first place amongst the ducks of India as a sporting bird, as a good bird for the table, and for grace of shape and carriage. It is always found in flocks, seldom in number less than twenty birds, and often numbering several hundreds; and as by day these flocks keep to fairly open water well in the middle of jheels where a light growth of weeds and lilies gives them a measure of concealment without obstructing their view they are difficult to approach. They rise from the water with some difficulty, but once on the wing they fly very swiftly, their whole build being for speed, and soon rise out of shot. It is a peculiarity of this species that the adult males usually gather into separate flocks, apart from the ducks and immature males, and it is usually the latter which do not fly so high that come into the shooter's bag.

As divers the Pintails are of no account but they swim well, sitting very lightly on the water, and with their long necks and pointed tails attain an unmistakable grace and beauty of carriage. They walk well, but are seldom seen on land except when feeding on irrigated or flooded land where they are sometimes found in the early mornings; for they feed at night and then leave the safety of the waters, where they spent the day, to visit secluded creeks and channels and canal irrigation.

They are easily recognised on the wing by their long necks and tails, and by the low hissing swish of their wings. Usually a silent species, they occasionally utter a soft quack, generally as an alarm-note.

The breeding season in the North is from April to August. The nest is built on islands in the middle of lakes or in swampy marshes with little open water. It is the usual duck nest of flags and grasses, with an inner lining of feathers and down, placed on the ground and well concealed amongst herbage.

The clutch consists of six to eight eggs. These are very fine and close in texture with a fair amount of gloss; the shells are thinner than those of most ducks. The colour is a pale dull greenish-stone.

In size the egg averages 2·15 by 1·5 inches.

THE SHOVELLER

Spatula clypeata (Linnæus)

Description.—Length 20 inches. Male: Head and upper neck glossy green; hind neck and back dark brown, the feathers pale edged; rump and upper tail-coverts black glossed with green; tail dark brown, the outer feathers broadly edged with white; sides of the wings bluish-grey divided by a broad white bar from the green speculum; scapulars long and pointed, bluish-grey and black, with white shaft-streaks; wing-quills dark brown; lower neck and breast with a line to the scapulars pure white; lower breast and abdomen chestnut, with a white patch on the lower flanks; under the tail a patch of black glossed with green.

Female: Upper plumage brown, each feather with a pale reddish border, and most of the feathers, except of the head and neck, with concentric rufous bands; sides of the wings dull bluish-grey divided by a broad white bar from the green speculum; wing- and tail-quills brown; lower plumage brownish-buff more rufous on the abdomen, the fore-neck speckled with dark brown, and the breast and flanks marked with crescentic brown bars which fade away towards the tail.

Iris yellow, brown in the female; bill black in adult male, dark brown with the lower mandible dull orange in females and young males; legs orange-red.

The bill is long and flat, twice as broad at the tip as at the base, and the sides of the upper mandible are much turned down near the tip; the sides are set with fine exposed plates (lamellæ) like the teeth of a comb.

Field Identification.—Heavy spatulate beak, conspicuous in flight and at rest, separates this duck from all other Indian species. The full-plumaged male is also easy to recognise, with the green head, white breast and scapular line and the chestnut under parts, but it must be remembered that this plumage is not usually fully developed in India till February. In both sexes the green speculum divided by a white bar from the blue-grey shoulder are distinctive.

Distribution.—Breeds throughout the greater part of Europe, Northern Asia and North America, migrating in winter to the Mediterranean Basin, Egypt, Tropical Africa, and most of Southern Asia to China and Japan; also in America southwards to the West Indies and Central America. In winter it is found throughout India, arriving about the end of October and staying later than most ducks until the end of April. Common in the North, it grows scarcer towards the South.

Habits, etc.—The Shoveller is usually found singly, in pairs or in parties of ten or a dozen individuals, and therefore, though common,

FIG. 104—Shoveller (⅛ nat. size)

it is never so abundant numerically as the other species of ducks which collect into large flocks. It is a specialised form, its bill being developed for the purpose of sieving mud and muddy water for the minute living organisms and aquatic seeds that they contain; for this reason it is less seldom found on the open clearer waters than in the shallower, more dirty and weedy jheels and ponds where, as a rule, it feeds about the margins. It is more likely than other ducks to be found about small and filthy village ponds, and at such places if undisturbed it becomes very tame and bold, living in them for weeks and feeding on all sorts of miscellaneous foods. Small wonder is it then that the flesh of the Shoveller is rank and unpleasant to eat and that experienced sportsmen neglect the bird. Nor is it interesting to shoot: it is easily approached when on the water and rises heavily and awkwardly, taking some time to get under way, though once in the air it flies well and strongly. It is a poor swimmer and diver, as is only to be expected of a bird that spends most of its time with its head and neck under water straining mud; it is, therefore, easy to retrieve when wounded.

As a rule a silent bird, it occasionally utters a creaking *quack* or a low *took-took* in flight.

In the North the breeding season is from April onwards. The nest is built in meadows near water or in marshy ground, and is well concealed in herbage on the ground. It is rather a bulky structure made of soft reeds and rushes with a lining of down.

Eight or nine eggs are usually laid, but sixteen have been recorded. They are rather long ovals, pointed at the smaller end, fine and close in texture with a fair gloss. The colour is yellowish-grey with either a green or cream tinge.

The average size is 2·1 by 1·45 inches.

THE POCHARD

NYROCA FERINA (Linnæus)

(Plate xxiv, Fig. 1, opposite page 506)

Description.—Length 18 inches. Male: Head and neck rufous-chestnut; base of neck all round with upper back and breast glossy-black; lower back and a patch above and below the tail black; remainder of plumage pale grey finely vermiculated with black except the quill-feathers which are brown, greyer in the wings and darker in the tail.

Female: Head, neck and breast rufous-brown, blackish on the crown and mixed with greyish-white on the cheeks and throat; back, shoulders and wing-coverts grey, more or less vermiculated with black; rump and upper tail-coverts blackish; wing- and tail-feathers brown; lower parts sullied white turning brown on the flanks and under the tail.

Iris reddish-yellow; bill bluish-grey, the tip and base black; legs bluish-grey, the webs blackish.

The hind toe is broadly lobed, as in all diving ducks.

Field Identification.—A squat, heavily-built duck. The drake is easily distinguished by the vermiculated grey plumage ending sharply in black on the breast and tail, and the bright chestnut head. The duck is a dull grey and brown bird with whitish throat and abdomen, which lacks the white wing-bar of the White-eye and Tufted Duck.

Distribution.—The Pochard breeds throughout a large area of Northern and Central Europe and across Siberia. It is largely migratory, and in winter occurs throughout temperate Europe, Egypt,

North-western Africa and Southern Asia to China and Japan. Another sub-species is found in North America.

In India the Pochard arrives about the end of October, but is not common till November, and it leaves again about March, a few staying into April. It is found throughout Northern India in large numbers, growing scarcer towards the south, being very rare in Mysore.

The Red-crested Pochard (*Netta rufina*) is a winter visitor to Northern and Central India. The male may be known by the combination of red head and crimson bill, glossy black under parts, white wing-bar and white shoulder-patch. The female is much duller and lacks the black under parts, but the dull red bill and the contrast between the dusky crown and whitish cheeks and throat are marked.

Habits, etc.—With the Pochard we have the first of the diving ducks which obtain the greater part of their food, consisting of the roots and buds of aquatic plants, by diving deep under water. This explains, therefore, the fact that this species in India is mainly met with in the larger jheels and tanks out in the open deeper water free from surface vegetation. It mostly feeds by night, and by day rests in flocks on the water, riding with the body low in the water very much down by the stern, and the head and neck drawn in on the body. It swims well, but seldom visits the land, where it walks but poorly.

In rising from the water the Pochard is slow and awkward, but once on the wing it is a straight and strong flier with quick beats of the short wings which make a peculiar rustling sound. The flocks travel in a mass and not in formation, and mount high into the air. The note is a harsh croak *kurr-kurr*.

The breeding season in the north is in May.

The nest is built in rough grass or reed-beds either on the land at the edge of the water or actually on the water. On land it consists of a hollow in the ground roughly lined with grass and reeds together with feathers and down; but out amongst the reeds on the water it is a most solid structure like the nest of a Coot.

The clutch consists of eight or ten eggs, but fourteen have been recorded. The eggs are very regular broad ovals, smooth in texture but dull and glossless. In colour they are a dull greenish-grey.

They measure about 2·30 by 1·70 inches.

THE WHITE-EYE

NYROCA NYROCA (Güldenstädt)

Description.—Length 16 inches. Male: Head, neck and breast dull chestnut, a white spot on the chin and a blackish-brown collar round the lower neck joining the upper back; upper plumage blackish-brown; wings dark brown, a broad white band running through the flight-feathers; tail dark brown; lower plumage white, sullied with brown on the lower abdomen, the sides of the body reddish-brown growing darker towards the tail.

Female: Similar but duller; head and neck reddish-brown; upper plumage brown; the reddish-brown of the breast is mixed with white and is not sharply divided from the white of the lower plumage as in the male.

Iris white in male, brown in female; bill bluish-black; legs plumbeous-grey, webs blackish.

Field Identification.—A small dark duck with white under parts and a white bar through the wing; the white eye of the drake contrasting with the reddish-brown head is distinctive. Females and young males must not be confused with those of the Tufted Duck, a heavier bird with less white in the wing and less rufous in colour.

Distribution.—The typical race breeds in the Basin of the Mediterranean in Central and Eastern Europe and in Western Asia as far as Kashmir. In winter it extends into Africa as far south as the Canaries and Abyssinia, and in Asia to India and Arrakan.

In India proper the typical race arrives about the end of October and leaves again in March. It is very abundant in Continental India, but gradually grows rarer southwards, and is not found at all in Southern India.

The Eastern race, *N. n. baeri*, which breeds in Eastern Siberia and winters in China and Japan occurs as far west as Bengal. In this the head is black or blackish-brown glossed with green.

The Tufted Duck (*Nyroca fuligula*) is a common winter visitor to all except the extreme south of India. The drake is glossy black with a long pendant crest and white under parts, appearing on the water as coal-black with an oval white flank. His yellow eye leads to confusion with the Golden-eye (*Bucephala clanga*), a rare winter visitor to northern India, whose male also looks vivid black and white but may be known by a circular white patch below the eye. Another black and white bird is the drake of the Smew (*Mergellus albellus*) in which the head is white with a broken black line through the eye. This also winters in northern India but is commoner.

Habits, etc.—The White-eye may be found on every type of water, fresh or salt, either in the hills or plains or along the sea-coast. It is by preference, however, a bird of the more secluded and weedy jheels, where the whole shores are overgrown with herbage and occasional patches of open water are surrounded by water-lilies and rushes.

In such places this duck is very abundant in small flocks, though the members of a flock scatter amongst the cover to rest and rise only two or three at a time.

Although retiring in its habits the White-eye is neither shy nor difficult to approach; it rises rather badly for a duck and at first flies low over the water, though once on the wing it travels fast and high. It is a most expert swimmer and diver, and one dropped wounded into the weedy water that it frequents is seldom brought to bag.

The food is very varied, consisting of vegetable matter and aquatic seeds, of insects and their larvæ, small fish and especially molluscs. The flesh in consequence varies, and is sometimes excellent for the table, sometimes almost uneatable.

The harsh call rather resembles that of the Pochard, and is variously expressed by the syllables *kek-kek-kek* or *koor-kirr-kirr*.

In Kashmir the breeding season commences in April, and the majority of eggs are laid about June. It was at one time customary for the fishermen to collect large cargoes of ducks' eggs, both of the White-eye and Mallard, for sale in the markets of Srinagar, but this has now been stopped.

The nest is built either on the ground or in the water amongst rushes and other vegetation; it is a moderate-sized structure of dry rushes and sedges with an inner lining of finer grasses and weeds; feathers and down are padded round the eggs. The egg is a regular perfect oval, smooth and fine in texture with very little gloss. The colour is a delicate tint of *café-au-lait*.

The average size is 2·1 by 1·5 inches.

THE LITTLE GREBE

Podiceps ruficollis (Pallas)

Description.—Length 9 inches. Sexes alike. Summer plumage: Top of the head and hind-neck blackish-brown; face round the bill and chin blackish; sides of the head and of the neck, throat and fore-neck chestnut; upper parts dark brown, the outer flight-feathers paler brown with their bases white and the inner flight-feathers almost entirely white; breast, flanks and under the tail dark brown mixed with white; abdomen silky white.

In winter plumage the crown and hind-neck are brown, the chin white, and the chestnut of the neck is replaced by rufous.

Iris red-brown; bill black with a white tip, the base greenish-yellow; legs blackish-green, inside of the tarsus pale olive-green.

Bill compressed and sharply pointed; tail quite rudimentary, consisting of short downy feathers; legs compressed, with broad lateral lobes coalescing at the base and not contracted at the joints as in the Coot. The plumage is very silky and waterproof.

Field Identification.—The smallest of the true water-birds of India, swimming low in the water and disappearing under it at the least provocation. Its size at once distinguishes it.

Distribution.—The Little Grebe has a very wide distribution, being found in various races throughout the greater part of Europe, Africa, Asia, Australia and New Zealand. *P. r. capensis*, the form

FIG. 105—Little Grebe (⅓ nat. size)

found in India, Burma and Ceylon, distinguished from the typical race by the white bases to the primaries and the greater amount of white in the secondaries, is also found in Persia, Turkestan and portions of Africa. Within our limits it is found everywhere on suitable water both in the plains and in the hills up to 5000 feet, and in the Nilgiris up to 8000 feet. It is partly resident and partly migratory.

The Great Crested Grebe (*Podiceps cristatus*) is found in Northern India as a fairly common winter visitor to the larger jheels and in some areas it undoubtedly breeds. It is much larger than the Little Grebe, and in the water appears as a slender long-necked sharp-beaked bird, dark above and white below. In the breeding season conspicuous black "ear-tufts" on the crown, chestnut tippet and flanks make it a most handsome species.

Habits, etc.—The Little Grebe or Dabchick is an example of a family which is highly specialised for a purely aquatic life. It is found in tanks and the deeper jheels. It may be said virtually never to land on terra firma; except when travelling it spends its whole life in the water swimming like a Cormorant, very low in the beam and ready to dive at the least sign of danger. Much of its food in the way of small fishes is captured under water, for it dives well and can swim far beneath the surface; though it also feeds on the surface and there procures vegetable matter, small mollusca and water insects. Quantities of their own feathers are found in the gizzards of Grebes, either with or without pebbles, and they are apparently swallowed for the same digestive purposes for which the latter are swallowed by most birds.

It rises from the water with some difficulty owing to the comparatively small size of its wings, but once in the air travels well and fast. On settling it strikes the water with the breast, which is well cushioned with fat, down and feathers, instead of thrusting forward its feet as a brake after the fashion of ducks and geese.

The wing-feathers in autumn are shed simultaneously as in the ducks, so that for a short period the bird is quite flightless.

Ordinarily it is found singly or in small parties, but on the Manchar Lake in Sind it gathers in winter into enormous flocks, hundreds strong. Numbers breed on the same water, but their nesting habits can hardly be called colonial.

The breeding season extends from May to September.

The nest is a mere mass of water-weed, based on a tuft of grass or aquatic plants, but practically floating in water as a rule. On this three to seven eggs are laid, and they are covered over with a pad of weed by the parent bird when she leaves the nest, however hurriedly. The combined heat of the sun and the fermentation of this decaying vegetable matter in the water is largely responsible for the incubation of the eggs which commences as soon as the first one is laid, with the result that there is always a slight difference between the ages of the young Grebes. The young are remarkable for their striped coloration; they leave the nest as soon as hatched and swim instinctively, keeping up all the time a low monotonous chirrup.

The egg is a moderately elongated oval, much pointed at both ends; the texture is fairly close and chalky with little or no gloss. When first laid the eggs are unmarked white, faintly tinged with blue or green, but they rapidly become discoloured to dark earthy-brown.

In size they measure about 1·40 by 1 inch.

INDEX

[The scientific names are in italics, and the names of genera are indicated by capitals.]

M

Q

R

S

T